GORE-TEX ® *fabrics*

*G*UIDE TO GOLF COURSES IN BRITAIN 1991

GORE

Creative Technology
Worldwide

Produced by the Publishing Division of The Automobile Association

Gazetteer compiled by the AA's Information Research Unit, Information Control.

Maps prepared by the Cartographic Department of The Automobile Association

© The Automobile Association 1991

Cover design The Paul Hampson Partnership

Illustrations Steven Knight

Head of Advertisement Sales
Christopher Heard, Tel 0256 20123 (ex 21544)

Advertisement Production
Karen Weeks, Tel 0256 20123 (ext 21545)

Typeset, printed and bound in Great Britain by William Clowes Limited, Beccles and London

Colour section typeset by Microset Graphics Limited, Basingstoke

Colour section printed by J.B. Shears & Sons Ltd, Basingstoke

A CIP catalogue record for this book is available from the British Library.

Published by The Automobile Association, Fanum House, Basingstoke, Hampshire RG21 2EA

ISBN 0 7495 0206 1

Contents

Choosing the best
says a lot about you

Two of the Best

...two brand~new courses that definitely shouldn't be avoided like the yips

In the pages that follow we take a look at two recently opened, top-of-the-range golf complexes. Both have ties with the other side of the Atlantic; one being owned by a Canadian company, the other designed by a famous American professional — Johnny Miller.

The pair are essentially US-style facilities. Both are vast, multi-million pound ventures, both illustrate how big business is gripping golf as the sport's popularity mushrooms, and both plan to offer an amazing array of facilities. They are shining examples of the new breed of super club, where sophisticated golf is intertwined with today's demands for corporate hospitality; where hotels, leisure villages, fairway housing and golf courses are combined on one integrated site.

They have International-class golf courses with superb playing conditions, which seemingly defy the very myths surrounding young greens and playing surfaces; their designs are quite stunning too.

So turn the page and read all about these new heavyweights of the fairway, see how they differ from a traditional-style British club, run by the members, for the members. Then why not go out and play them for yourself.

Collingtree Park

For years, champion golfer Johnny Miller dreamed of designing a British course, and at Collingtree Park that dream has finally come true.

Officially opened in June 1990, this 18-hole resort golf course and Academy, is the first UK course to carry Johnny Miller's famous name. Though Collingtree is his first UK creation, he has designed 11 other courses around the world, from Florida and California to Japan.

Collingtree is set in 273 acres in the heart of Northamptonshire, close to junction 15 on the M1. The complex is situated in wooded parkland on the site of an old mansion. Although the house has long since gone, its former grounds now bask in an oasis of manicured lakes and lush green turf.

Johnny Miller, who won both US and British Opens, has combined his natural artistic flair and game skill to create this lovely course, one which he feels will be both enjoyable and challenging, even to the most critical of golfers. And, without doubt, he has certainly brought an American flavour to it, the centrepiece of which is the stunning island green at the 18th hole.

... the American's

At 6,871 yards, with a par of 72, the course has plenty of trees and open spaces combined with lakes – 11 acres of them in all, another obvious Americanism. But it's the 18th hole at Collingtree that's Miller's special touch, and it has to go down as his signature here. It's a little different and a little special for an English course, and visually it looks awfully daunting to play. No doubt a few balls will be lost in the lake encircling the green over the next few years. The island green is believed to be the first of its kind in Great Britain and does indeed mark Collingtree as a course of some style, and as a course with a difference.

In its construction some 400,000 cubic metres of earth were moved, 5 miles of paths were laid out for golf buggies, in excess of 35,000 trees and shrubs have been planted, and there is a full electronic irrigation system for tees, fairways and greens.

The project is a flagship development for Collingtree's owners, International Resort Holdings, and is seen as their prototype leisure complex of the future. Their theme here is entertainment, so whether it's a relaxing round of golf with friends or business colleagues, or enjoying one of the special tuition programmes within the Golf Academy, they've truly thought of every detail.

dream

Collingtree Park Golf Course

While the course and Academy are indeed at Collingtree's heart, when complete, the complex will also boast 185 executive houses, 65 apartments, 28 retirement homes, 12 sheltered houses for the old, a 60-bed nursing home, and a £6.5million, 65-bedroomed country-house style hotel with full leisure and conference facilities, situated alongside the 18th hole and due to open during 1992.

Included as part of the membership fee is the free use of buggy carts for each round of golf and free driving-range balls. Cart paths have been laid around the entire course to assist all-year round play, and green fee paying visitors, at around £40, also get a buggy.

The impressive Golf Academy contains a unique facility under one roof and comprises: a 16-bay floodlit driving range, with featured bunkers and trees; two par 4 and one par 3 practice holes; indoor video teaching room; golf club custom – fit centre with computerised swing analyser; and a comprehensively-equipped sports shop. It

also boasts a vast array of teaching schemes and schools to suit all levels, both for the individual as well as catering for business entertainment needs.

Complex Director at Collingtree, Geoffrey Hillman, has extensive experience of corporate entertaining, and combines the talents of Savoy trained, Head Chef Richard Saddington, and Director of Golf, John Cook, former English Amateur Champion and PGA tournament winner, to ensure success. Course Superintendent is Peter Jones, whose green keeping skills are evident for all to see who visit Collingtree. His previous work includes the remodelling of nine of the holes on the Dukes Course at Woburn.

So, why not go along to Collingtree, pay the value-for-money green fee of around £40, warm up by hitting a few free range balls, pick up your golf buggy and go out and play Miller's stimulating 18 holes, which are guaranteed to delight. And just see if you can't keep your ball out of the water on the island 18th.

Johnny Miller

9

Collingtree Park Golf Course

For gazetteer entry see under Collingtree, Northamptonshire.

The course that
Jenti built

BODMIN GOLF & COUNTRY CLUB
BODMIN, CORNWALL, U.K.
Tel: 0208 73600   0208 74689

Proprietors: Jenti & Sue Madhvani

Limited number of Country
Memberships available

Unique and Prestigious Residential Development

The East Sussex

... planned to be the most

Officially opened in May 1990, the East Sussex National has been created with a £30 million budget. No expense has been spared in developing the club into today's highly prestigious golfing complex, arguably to emerge as the most luxurious in Britain, possibly Europe, and, as the developers intend, evolving into one of the world's finest private clubs.

Its courses have been built with tournaments in mind, and the 18th green on the East Course will accommodate no-less-than 50,000 spectators. They are cared for and maintained by a 40 strong green staff. As would be expected, membership is exclusive indeed, limited to just 1,000 members; 250 British, 250 overseas and 500 expatriates. Currently you will need to take out a £20,000 debenture and find a further £1,280 for your annual subscription.

Aimed at the 21st century, quite obviously the ESN is destined to become internationally top flight, and its Golf Village is intended to offer one of the most complete golfing facilities anywhere in the world. Already it boasts two championship courses, which are designed and maintained to American standards — one is reserved daily for members; a teaching academy with three holes, a par 3, 4 and 5; two driving ranges and two putting greens; at least six professionals in attendance, headed by Paul Dellanzo; a 7,000 square foot golf shop offering the finest range of golf products and services; plus the delights of the elegant Horsted Place Hotel, an intimate country house rated highly by the AA with three red stars, and sited on the West Course.

But catch your breath before you read on, because future plans here (scheduled for completion by 1993) are equally vast and include; a 35,000 square foot Member's clubhouse with meeting facilities, casual and formal dining, lounges and locker rooms; a luxury 211-room hotel, also including casual and formal dining, lounges, locker rooms and retail shops; expansive meeting and conference facilities with telecommunication equipment; an indoor driving range, teaching academy classrooms and the latest in audio-visual teaching aids; health spa with two squash courts, saunas, a pool, massage room, exercise areas and recovery rooms; tennis, lawn bowling and croquet . . . impressed? The man behind this huge golfing venture is Brian Turner, Canadian head of Thornbrook Properties, the Canadian Company which owns the club.

The ESN is based at Little Horsted, near Uckfield, and is set in 1,100 acres of rolling Sussex hills, with an abundance of centuries-old oaks and colourful flora. Rising behind the picturesque landacape loom the South Downs, guarding the southern coastline and providing the golfer with wonderful vistas.

This exciting project has brought together some of the game's most experienced and highly regarded experts in course design. Bob Cupp, former Senior Designer for Jack Nicklaus, has designed the first two courses here. And, to ensure the best use of the natural terrain, he was given the opportunity to design both courses before an acres of land was allocated to the Village Complex.

luxurious club in the world

The East Sussex National Golf Club

It took months of research and the utilization of several hybrid Bent grasses for the world's top agronomists and turf technicians to produce ESN's superior playing conditions. In fact, the hallowed turf here is based on the exclusive use of three strains of Bent grass — PennCross for the tees, PennEagle for fairways and PennLinks for greens. Supervision is by the leading experts on turf management, with everyday maintenance carried out by a 40 strong green staff.

The East Course's most obvious feature is the 18th green, with its capacity to hold 50,000 spectators, and, as a gallery course, it will be the primary tournament one. Measuring 7,081 yards from championship gold tees, with a Par 72 and nine water holes, it provides a true test. Arguably equal, is the West Course, measuring 7,154 yards, also with a Par of 72. Its design is again skillfully blended into the Sussex Countryside and encompasses the imposing 140-year-old Horsted Place Hotel, which overlooks the 9th green, and the timeless beauty of a Norman church, reflected in the pond at the 3rd.

. . planned to be the most luxurious club

Walking the fairways here is much like strolling across an expensive Persian carpet, and the greens and tees are equally wonderful. They are so good that our Walker Cup team, which triumphed in the States, practiced here before their victorious trip to Atlanta. Its no surprise though, as the greens here are much closer to the speed of Augusta National than most British Courses. But maybe that's because the Course Superintendent is Ken Siems, who used to work at the Augusta National. Consultant agronomist is Dr Duich, Professor at Penn State University, and William Fuller is the turf management consultant.

in the world

The East Sussex National Golf Club

There will be no club captain, no committee at ESN. The courses, clubhouse, hotel and golf village, as with everything here, will be handled by professionals.

So that's what you get if you visit ESN, quality! But at a price, so do save up for the pleasure of playing a days golf in paradise; it will cost you £100, but I'm sure you'll agree, this treat is worth every penny.

For gazetteer entry see under Uckfield, East Sussex.

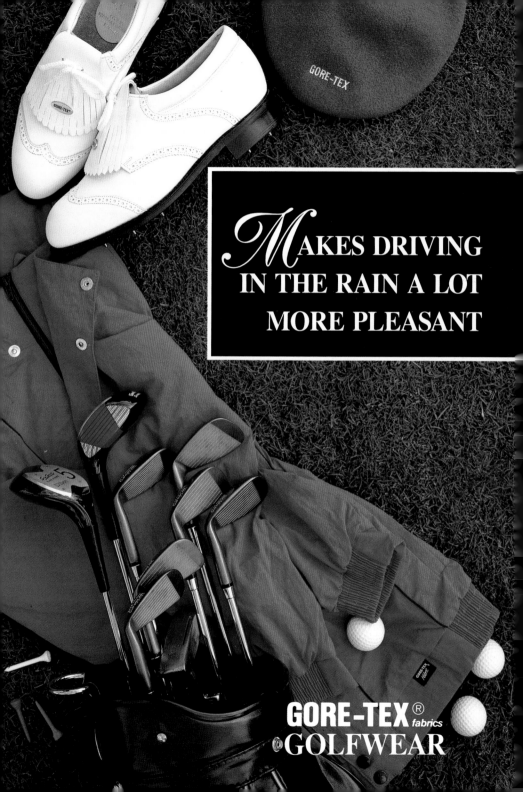

*M*AKES DRIVING
IN THE RAIN A LOT
MORE PLEASANT

GORE-TEX ® *fabrics*
GOLFWEAR

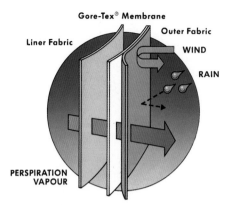

Gore-Tex® Membrane
Outer Fabric
Liner Fabric
WIND
RAIN
PERSPIRATION
VAPOUR

YOU'LL BREATHE EASY IN GORE-TEX FABRIC

GORE-TEX fabric consists of three layers. Between the outer fabric and the lining is a membrane of PTFE, engineered to contain 9 billion pores per square inch. Each one is 20,000 times smaller than a water droplet, forming an impenetrable barrier to wind, rain and snow. Yet every pore is 700 times larger than a vapour molecule, allowing perspiration to escape easily from the body. So perspiration gets out, while wind and rain stay out. Keeping the wearer dry and comfortable in all weathers.

From the warm rains of Augusta to the icy squalls of St. Andrews, GORE-TEX fabric gives remarkable protection to the world's leading professional golfers. And all year round, it gives comfort in bad weather to an ever-increasing number of enthusiastic club players.

ENJOY THE FAIRWAY ON THE FOULEST DAYS

We all know that golf isn't just a fair weather sport. Yet playing in adverse conditions needn't mean suffering unnecessary discomfort. Just ask any professional golfer. GORE-TEX fabric lets them stay dry and comfortable. Because unlike ordinary waterproofs, GORE-TEX fabric is highly breathable. So keeping the elements outside, doesn't mean trapping sweat inside. More importantly, it won't interfere with your game. Specialist tailoring by top manufacturers means that staying dry won't cramp your swing. And if you wear a golf suit and hat made from GORE-TEX fabric, you can leave your umbrella in the lockeroom.

Look for the GORE-TEX label in your club professional's shop and all good sports shop. Better all-weather clothing means a longer playing season for you, and that can't hurt your handicap either.

AFTER THE ROUGH THE TUMBLE

Unlike ordinary weatherproof materials, GORE-TEX fabric is easily washable. Follow the instructions carefully and your GORE-TEX fabric clothing will remain just as waterproof, and breathable after washing and even tumble drying as it was before. Full washing instructions included in the Guarantee booklet attached to every garment.

AN UNMATCHED GUARANTEE

Used with care, your GORE-TEX performance clothing should last for many years. That's why we can now offer a new garment guarantee which is

GORE-TEX®
Guaranteed To Keep You Dry™

GORE
Creative Technologies
Worldwide

Its basis is a licensing agreement between W.L.Gore and the manufacturer whereby a binding contract is signed by both parties agreeing the quality standards, requirements and specifications for the construction and testing of all GORE-TEX garments.

Our partnership with the manufacturer means that all garments sold to our customer will be of the highest standards. So much so, that we have extended our original warranty on the fabric to a full three year guarantee on the whole garment. Further endorsing our commitment to you, the end user.

THE COMPLETE
WEATHER PROTECTION

PRO-QUIP – suits, hat and mitts TECNIC – shoe

PRO-QUIP – ladies suits TECNIC – ladies shoe

ALL SQUARE – suits
KANGOL – hats

SHOES – ETONIC, STYLO, TECNIC

SHOE
AND
SOCK
AWARDS
1990

TECNIC GTX 102 MENS GOODYEAR WELTED GOLF SHOE

"It is very important for me to feel comfortable on the golf course that's why I choose Sunderland."

GORE-TEX fabric sock

TECNIC – ladies shoe

SUNDERLAND –
Classic suits and hats

SUNDERLAND – ladies Classic suits

BELSTAFF – suits

PGA
EUROPEAN TOUR

WINDSTOPPER SWEATERS

BRUCE CLARK – suits

KANGOL – hat

Should you require details about your nearest stockist of the GORE-TEX fabric golf clothing and accessories, then please ring or write to the addresses below. For further details on any other type of sportswear please contact W. L. GORE & ASSOCIATES at their Livingston plant. Freephone **0800 833357.**

SUITS

R. C. Redman (Pro Quip) Ltd*
Wisloe Road
Cambridge
Gloucestershire GL2 7AF
Tel: 0453 890707 Fax: 0453 890826
Telex: 437127 RCRPQ G

Sunderland Sportswear*
PO Box 14
Glasgow G2 1ER
Tel: 041 552 3261/4
Fax: (G3) 041 552 8518
Telex: 779553 (Sunspo)

Bruce Clark (Scotland) Ltd*
Unit 3
Primrose Industrial Estate
Primrose Lane
Rosyth
Dunfermline

(* also hats)

All Square Golf Company
Globe Mills
City Road
Bradford
Yorkshire BD8 8JL
Tel: 0274 731375

Belstaff International Ltd
Caroline Street
Longton
Stoke-on-Trent
Tel: 0782 599261 Fax: 0782 599065
Telex: 36500

SHOES

Tecnic Shoes
Bramic Golf Ltd
Hatch Lane
Liss
Hampshire GU33 7NJ
Tel: 0730 893451

Etonic Shoes
Abu Garcia Ltd
Unit 5
Aston Way
Middlewich Motorway Estate
Middlewich
Cheshire CW10 0HS
Tel: 0836 585881

Stylo Shoes
Matchmakers House
Clayton Wood Bank
Leeds LS16 6RJ
Tel: 0532 783501
Fax: 0532 557369
Telex: 0532 557369

HATS

Kangol
David Allan & Company Ltd
Unit 8
2 North Avenue
Clydebank Business Park
Glasgow G81 2DR
Tel: 041 941 3133 Fax: 041 951 1827

GORE-TEX ® fabrics

GORE
Creative Technologies
Worldwide

W. L. Gore & Associates (UK) Limited, Kirkton Campus, Livingston EH54 7BH
Telephone: 0506 412525 Telex: 727236 Fax: 0506 420004

Fairway Hotels

Where to play and stay on the spot

Last year we offered our readers a list of recommended hotels that have their own golf course, where guests could stay in comfort within a nine-iron shot of the first tee.

However, with the continuing growth and popularity of the game in the UK, helped on by big business, recent Ryder Cup victories and our professional's successes in the 'majors', many more hotels have expanded their leisure facilities to include golf.

So, to keep you up-to-date with this trend, this edition of the Guide provides a full list of *AA hotels that offer golf* to guests. Secondly, we also include a useful list of those appointed hotels that have indicated they offer *golfing breaks*.

So if you are a travelling or holiday golfer who wishes to stay in sight of the course in comfortable accommodation, then these two lists should prove invaluable.

Full details of the Association's appointed hotels can be found in the 'AA Hotels and Restaurants in Britain' guide, 1991 edition, available from good bookshops and AA shops priced £11.95.

AA Hotels offering Golf

Listed below by country and county, are a selection of hotels appointed by the AA that offer golf to their guests. Many have their own courses, others have arrangements with adjacent clubs and will book rounds for guests. Courses could be 36, 18 or 9 hole, and range from stern championship tests to, in a few instances, humble par 3 approaches.

Therefore, it is advisable to check with the hotel before booking to ascertain the exact golfing facility offered.

ENGLAND

Avon
- **Midsomer Norton**
Centurion Hotel
★★★63% ☎ (0761) 417711

Berkshire
- **Windsor**
Oakley Court Hotel
★★★★73% ☎ (0628) 74141

Buckinghamshire
- **Taplow**
Cliveden Hotel
★★★★★ (Red)♨ ☎ (0628) 668561

Cambridgeshire
- **Bar Hill**
Cambridgeshire Moat House
★★★61% ☎ (0954) 780555
- **St Neots**
Abbotsley Golf Hotel
★★64% ☎ (0480) 74000

Cheshire
- **Disley**
Moorside Hotel
★★★62% ☎ (0663) 64151
- **Pott Shrigley
(nr Macclesfield)**
Shrigley Hall Golf
& Country Club
★★★★58% ☎ (0625) 575757

Cornwall & Isles of Scilly
- **Mawnan Smith**
Budock Vean Hotel
★★★69% ☎ (0326) 250288
- **St Austell**
Carlyon Bay Hotel
★★★★61% ☎ (072681) 2304
- **St Mellion**
St Mellion Hotel
★★★68% ☎ (0579) 50101
- **Torpoint**
Whitsand Bay Hotel
★67% ☎ (0503) 30276

Cumbria
- **Broughton in Furness**
Eccle Ring Hotel
★★61% ☎ (0229) 716398

Devon
- **Chittlehamholt**
Highbullen Hotel
★★★♨74% ☎ (07694) 561
- **Plymouth**
Elfordleigh Hotel
& Country Club
★★★64% (0752) 336428
- **Sidmouth**
Mount Pleasant Hotel
★★68% ☎ (0395) 514694
- **Thurlestone**
Thurlestone Hotel
★★★★68% ☎ (0548) 560382
- **Torquay**
Palace Hotel
★★★★53% ☎ (0803) 200200
- **Woolacombe**
Woolacombe Bay Hotel
★★★59% ☎ (0271) 870388

Dorset
- **Ferndown**
Dormy Hotel
★★★★65% ☎ (0202) 872121
- **Studland**
Knoll House Hotel
★★★67% ☎ (092944) 251

Co Durham
- **Darlington**
Blackwell Grange Moat House
★★★★61% ☎ (0325) 380888

East Sussex
- **Hastings & St Leonards**
Beauport Park Hotel
★★★73% ☎ (0424) 851222
- **Rottingdean**
White Horse Hotel
★★61% ☎ (0273) 300301
- **Uckfield**
Horsted Place Hotel
★★★(Red)♨ ☎ (082575) 581

Gloucestershire
- **Gloucester**
Gloucester Hotel
& Country Club
★★★68% ☎ (0452) 25653

- **Tewkesbury**
Tewkesbury Park Hotel
Golf & Country Club
★★★65% ☎ (0684) 295405

Greater London
- **Croydon**
Selsdon Park Hotel
★★★★62% ☎ 081-657 8811
- **West Drayton**
Holiday Inn
★★★★59% ☎ (0895) 445555

Hampshire
- **Brook**
Bell Inn
★★★69% ☎ (0703) 812214
- **New Milton**
Chewton Glen Hotel
★★★★(Red) ♨ ☎ (0425) 275341

Hereford & Worcester
- **Stourport-on-Severn**
Stourport Moat House
★★★63% ☎ (0299) 827733

Kent
- **Hythe**
Hythe Imperial Hotel
★★★★64% ☎ (0303) 267441
Stade Court Hotel
★★★65% ☎ (0303) 268263
- **Maidstone**
Tudor Park Hotel
★★★67% ☎ (0622) 34334

Lancashire
- **Chorley**
Shaw Hill Hotel,
Golf & Country Club
★★★61% ☎ (02572) 69221

Lincolnshire
- **Sutton on Sea**
Grange & Links Hotel
★★60% ☎ (0507) 441334

Norfolk
- **Barnham Broom**
Barnham Broom Hotel,
Conference & Leisure Centre
★★★65% ☎ (060545) 393

- **West Runton**
  Links Country Park Hotel
  & Golf Club
  ★★★65% ☎ (026375) 691

North Yorkshire
- **Aldwark**
  Aldwark Manor Hotel
  ★★★⚑78% ☎ (03473) 8146
- **Hackness**
  Hackness Grange Country Hotel
  ★★★⚑68% ☎ (0723) 82345
- **Harrogate**
  Grafton Hotel
  ★69% ☎ (0423) 508491

Northamptonshire
- **Staverton**
  Staverton Park Hotel
  & Golfing Complex
  ★★★72% ☎ (0327) 705911

Shropshire
- **Telford**
  Telford Hotel, Golf
  & Country Club
  ★★★65% ☎ (0952) 585642
- **Weston**
  Hawkstone Park Hotel
  ★★★53% ☎ (093924) 611
- **Whitchurch**
  Terrick Hall Country Hotel
  ★★★62% ☎ (0948) 3031

Staffordshire
- **Onneley**
  Wheatsheaf Inn at Onneley
  ★★67% ☎ (0782) 751581

Suffolk
- **Hintlesham**
  Hintlesham Hall Hotel
  ★★★(Red) ⚑ ☎ (047387) 334

Surrey
- **Bagshot**
  Pennyhill Park Hotel
  ★★★★⚑70% ☎ (0276) 71774
- **Ockley**
  Gatton Manor Hotel & Golf Club
  ★★67% ☎ (030679) 555

Tyne & Wear
- **Newcastle upon Tyne**
  Swallow Gosforth Park Hotel
  ★★★★65% ☎ 091-236 4111
- **Washington**
  Washington Moat House
  ★★★68% ☎ 091-417 2626

Warwickshire
- **Stratford-upon-Avon**
  Welcombe Hotel & Golf Course
  ★★★★62% ☎ (0789) 295252
- **Wishaw**
  The Belfry
  ★★★★68% ☎ (0675) 70301

West Midlands
- **Meriden**
  Forest of Arden Hotel,
  Golf & Country Club
  ★★★72% ☎ (0676) 22335

West Sussex
- **Copthorne**
  Copthorne Effingham Park Hotel
  ★★★★65% ☎ (0342) 714994
- **Goodwood**
  Goodwood Park Hotel,
  Golf & Country Club
  ★★★65% ☎ (0243) 775537
- **Thakeham**
  Abingworth Hall
  ★★★⚑74% ☎ (0798) 813636

CHANNEL ISLANDS
Guernsey
- **Catel**
  Hotel Hougue du Pommier
  ★★65% ☎ (0481) 56531
- **St Peter Port**
  St Pierre Park Hotel
  ★★★★67% ☎ (0481) 28282

Jersey
- **St Peter**
  Mermaid Hotel
  ★★★63% ☎ (0543) 41255

ISLE OF MAN
- **Castletown**
  Castletown Golf Links Hotel
  ★★★66% ☎ (0624) 822201

ISLE OF WIGHT
- **Ventnor**
  Ventnor Towers Hotel
  ★★★64% ☎ (0983) 852277

WALES
Dyfed
- **Ammanford**
  Mill at Glynhir
  ★★67% ☎ (0269) 850672
- **Gwbert-on-Sea**
  Cliff Hotel
  ★★★55% ☎ (0239) 613241

Gwent
- **Chepstow**
  St Pierre Hotel,
  Golf & Country Club
  ★★★69% ☎ (0291) 625261
- **Newport**
  Priory Hotel
  ★★61% ☎ (0633) 421241

Gwynedd
- **Bala**
  Bala Lake Hotel
  ★★63% ☎ (0678) 520344
- **Harlech**
  The Castle Hotel
  ★★63% ☎ (0766) 780529

South Glamorgan
- **Porthkerry**
  Egerton Grey Country House Hotel
  ★★★76% ☎ (0446) 711666

SCOTLAND
Dumfries & Galloway
- **Portpatrick**
  ★★56% Portpatrick Hotel
  ☎ (077681) 333
- **Powfoot**
  Golf Hotel
  ★★61% ☎ (04617) 254

Grampian
- **Banchory**
  Raemoir Hotel
  ★★★⚑75% ☎ (03302) 4884
- **Maryculter**
  Maryculter House Hotel
  ★★★68% ☎ (0224) 732124

Highland
- **Brora**
  The Links Hotel
  ★★★59% ☎ (0408) 21225
  Royal Marine Hotel
  ★★62% ☎ (0408) 21252
- **Kyle of Lochalsh**
  Kyle Hotel
  ★★65% ☎ (0599) 4204
- **Lybster**
  Portland Arms
  ★★58% ☎ (05932) 208
- **Skeabost Bridge**
  Skeabost House Hotel
  ★★★⚑66% ☎ (047032) 202
- **Spean Bridge**
  Spean Bridge Hotel
  ★★58% ☎ (039781) 250

Strathclyde
- **Barrhill**
  Kildonan Hotel
  ★★★⚑77% ☎ (046582) 360
- **Gigha Island**
  Gigha Hotel
  ★★64% ☎ (05835) 254
- **Kilwinning**
  Montgreenan Mansion House
  Hotel
  ★★★⚑67% ☎ (0294) 57733
- **Langbank**
  Gleddoch House Hotel
  ★★★⚑70% ☎ (047554) 711
- **Turnberry**
  Turnberry Hotel
  ★★★★★63% ☎ (0655) 31000

Tayside
- **Arbroath**
  Letham Grange Hotel
  ★★★66% ☎ (024189) 373
- **Auchterarder**
  The Gleneagles Hotel
  ★★★★★(Red) ☎ (0764) 62231
- **Kinross**
  Green Hotel
  ★★★62% ☎ (0577) 63467
- **Perth**
  Murrayshall Country House Hotel
  ★★★⚑78% ☎ (0738) 51171
- **Spittal of Glenshee**
  Dalmunzie House Hotel
  ★★⚑64% ☎ (025085) 224

AA Hotels offering Golfing Breaks

Taking a short break is a marvellous way to restore the spirits during the long months between annual holidays, and, for the golfer, it offers the added bonus of playing a new course with a new challenge, whilst staying in comfortable, relaxed accommodation.

Listed below, again in country and county order, are a selection of AA-appointed hotels that offer golfing breaks. These may range from packages offering unlimited golf to tutorials for the beginner, or perhaps with the option of professional coaching for the seasoned club player.

It may be that the hotel has its own golf course, a resident professional, or that, as in many cases, it arranges golf at a nearby club. The package may well include half-board terms and inclusive golf or professional coaching, but equally, any of these items could well be optional extras.

For full details of breaks, their exact content, minimum duration, seasonal availability, prices etc, contact the hotel direct on the number provided.

Note: It may well be the case that some of the hotels on our previous list, **AA Hotels offering golf**, also provide some kind of golfing holiday. However, the list of hotels that follows has been specially selected from the '**AA Short Breaks in Britain 1991**' guide (available from good bookshops and AA shops, priced £5.99), for which hotels confirmed they offer bargain breaks, and that their short-break package also includes golf.

ENGLAND
Avon
- **Bristol**
Redwood Lodge Hotel & Country Club
★★★69% ☎ (0272) 393901
- **Weston-Super-Mare**
Beachlands Hotel
★★64% ☎ (0934) 621401

Cambridgeshire
- **Bar Hill**
Cambridge Moat House
★★★61% ☎ (0954) 780555

Cheshire
- **Mottram St Andrew**
Mottram Hall
★★★70% ☎ (0625) 828135
- **Pott Shrigley**
Shrigley Hall Golf & Country Club
★★★★58% ☎ (0625) 575757

Cornwall & Isles of Scilly
- **Bude**
Camelot Hotel
★★64% ☎ (0288) 352361
Hotel Penarvor
★★61% ☎ (0288) 352036
- **St Austell**
Carlyon Bay Hotel
★★★★61% ☎ (072681) 2304
- **St Ives**
Boskerris Hotel
★★58% ☎ (0736) 795295
- **Talland Bay**
Talland Bay Hotel
★★★71% ☎ (0503) 72667
- **Torpoint**
Whitsand Bay
★67% ☎ (0503) 30276

Cumbria
- **Keswick**
Chaucer House Hotel
★★66% ☎ (07687) 72318 & 73223
- **Silloth**
Golf Hotel
★★66% ☎ (06973) 31438
- **Windermere**
Wild Boar Hotel
★★★70% ☎ (09662) 5225

Derbyshire
- **Chesterfield**
Chesterfield Hotel
★★★64% ☎ (0246) 271141

Devon
- **Bideford**
Yeoldon House Hotel
★★58% ☎ (0237) 474400
- **Clawton**
Court Barn Country House Hotel
★★68% ☎ (040927) 219
- **Croyde**
Kittiwell House Hotel
★★66% ☎ (0271) 890247
- **Exmouth**
Royal Beacon Hotel
★★★59% ☎ (0395) 264886
- **Ottery St Mary**
Salston Hotel
★★★58% ☎ (0404) 815581
- **Saunton**
Saunton Sands Hotel
★★★★59% ☎ (0271) 890212

Dorset
- **Bournemouth**
Winterbourne Hotel
★★62% ☎ (0202) 296366
- **Ferndown**
Dormy Hotel
★★★★65% ☎ (0202) 872121

Co Durham
- **Neasham**
Newbus Arms Hotel & Restaurant
★★★63% ☎ (0325) 721071

East Sussex
- **Alfriston**
  The Star
  ★★★65% ☎ (0323) 870495
- **Eastbourne**
  Lansdowne Hotel
  ★★★71% ☎ (0323) 25174
- **Lewes**
  White Hart Hotel
  ★★60% ☎ (0273) 474676 & 476694

Gloucestershire
- **Amberley**
  Amberley Inn
  ★★68% ☎ (0453) 872565
- **Cheltenham**
  Prestbury House Hotel
  ★★69% ☎ (0242) 529533
- **Gloucester**
  Gloucester Hotel & Country Club
  ★★★68% ☎ (0452) 25653
- **Tetbury**
  Hare & Hounds
  ★★★62% ☎ (066688) 233
- **Tewkesbury**
  Tewkesbury Park Hotel & Country Club
  ★★★65% ☎ (0684) 295405

Hereford & Worcester
- **Hereford**
  Netherwood Country House
  ★★⚑64% ☎ (0432) 272388

Kent
- **Larkfield**
  Larkfield Hotel
  ★★★60% ☎ (0732) 846858

Lincolnshire
- **Lincoln**
  Eastgate Post House Hotel
  ★★★58% ☎ (0522) 520341

Merseyside
- **Southport**
  Prince of Wales Hotel
  ★★★★54% ☎ (0704) 536688
  Scarisbrick Hotel
  ★★★61% ☎ (0704) 43000

Norfolk
- **Titchwell**
  Titchwell Manor Hotel
  ★★71% ☎ (0485) 210221
- **Yarmouth (Great)**
  Imperial Hotel
  ★★69% ☎ (0493) 851113

North Yorkshire
- **Bolton Abbey**
  Devonshire Arms Country House Hotel
  ★★★75% ☎ (075671) 441
- **Harrogate**
  Grants
  ★★★68% ☎ (0423) 502550
- **Leyburn**
  Golden Lion Hotel
  ★57% ☎ (0969) 22161

Oxfordshire
- **Bloxham**
  Olde School Hotel
  ★★64% ☎ (0295) 720369
- **Deddington**
  Holcombe House Hotel & Restaurant
  ★★66% ☎ (0869) 38274

Somerset
- **Wells**
  Swan Hotel
  ★★★62% ☎ (0749) 78877

Suffolk
- **Hintlesham**
  Hintlesham Hall Hotel
  ★★★(Red)⚑ ☎ (047387) 334

Tyne & Wear
- **Washington**
  Washington Moat House
  ★★★68% ☎ 091-417 2626

Warwickshire
- **Stratford-upon-Avon**
  Welcombe Hotel
  ★★★★62% ☎ (0789) 295252

West Midlands
- **Sutton Coldfield**
  Sutton Court Hotel
  ★★★60% ☎ 021-355 6071

West Sussex
- **Crawley**
  The George
  ★★★62% ☎ (0293) 24215
- **Goodwood**
  Goodwood Park Hotel
  ★★★65% ☎ (0243) 775537

Wiltshire
- **Bradford-on-Avon**
  Woolley Grange
  ★★★⚑77% ☎ (02216) 4705

Isle of Man
- **Castletown**
  Castletown Golf Links Hotel
  ★★★66% ☎ (0624) 822201
- **Douglas**
  Sefton Hotel
  ★★★64% ☎ (0624) 26011

WALES
Clwyd
- **Colwyn Bay**
  Hotel 70 Degrees
  ★★★58% ☎ (0492) 516555
  Stanton House Hotel
  ★★54% ☎ (0492) 44363

Dyfed
- **Lamphey**
  Court Hotel
  ★★★⚑64% ☎ (0646) 672273

- **Saundersfoot**
  St Brides Hotel
  ★★★65% ☎ (0834) 812304

Gwent
- **Monmouth**
  Kings Head Hotel
  ★★★63% ☎ (0600) 2177
  Riverside Hotel
  ★★62% ☎ (0600) 5577 & 3236

Gwynedd
- **Aberdovey**
  Maybank Hotel & Restaurant
  ★68% ☎ (065472) 500 due to change to (0654) 767500
- **Abersoch**
  Neigwl Hotel
  ★★76% ☎ (075881) 2363
- **Bala**
  Plas Coch Hotel
  ★★57% ☎ (0678) 520309
- **Conwy**
  The Castle
  ★★★63% ☎ (0492) 592324
- **Deganwy**
  Bryn Cregin Garden Hotel
  ★★66% ☎ (0492) 585266
- **Llandudno**
  Risboro Hotel
  ★★★61% ☎ (0492) 76343
  Royal Hotel
  ★★61% ☎ (0492) 76476
  Quinton Hotel
  ★63% ☎ (0492) 76879 & 75086
- **Nefyn**
  The Nanhoron Arms
  ★★★68% ☎ (0758) 720203

Powys
- **Brecon**
  Lansdowne Hotel
  ★65% ☎ (0874) 3321
- **Builth Wells**
  Lion Hotel
  ★★59% ☎ (0982) 553670

SCOTLAND
Borders
- **Peebles**
  Park Hotel
  ★★★58% ☎ (0721) 20451
- **St Boswells**
  Buccleuch Arms Hotel
  ★★65% ☎ (0835) 22243
- **Walkerburn**
  Tweed Valley Hotel & Restaurant
  ★★⚑66% ☎ (089687) 636

Central
- **Strathblane**
  Kirkhouse Inn
  ★★66% ☎ (0360) 70621

Dumfries & Galloway
- **Portpatrick**
  Portpatrick Hotel
  ★★56% ☎ (077681) 333

Fife
- **St Andrews**
  Rusack's Hotel
  ★★★★60% ☎ (0334) 74321
  St Andrews Golf Hotel
  ★★★67% ☎ (0334) 72611

Grampian
- **Banchory**
  Raemoir Hotel
  ★★★✦75% ☎ (03302) 4884
- **Elgin**
  Eight Acres Hotel
  ★★★57% ☎ (0343) 543077
- **Macduff**
  The Highland Haven
  ★★58% ☎ (0261) 32408
- **Maryculter**
  Maryculter House Hotel
  ★★★68% ☎ (0224) 732124
- **Tynet**
  Mill House Hotel
  ★★56% ☎ (05427) 233

Highland
- **Beauly**
  Priory Hotel
  ★★63% ☎ (0463) 782309

- **Brora**
  Links Hotel
  ★★★59% ☎ (0408) 21225
  Royal Marine Hotel
  ★★62% ☎ (0408) 21252
- **Dornoch**
  Dornoch Castle Hotel
  ★★65% ☎ (0862) 810261
- **Inverness**
  Craigmonie Hotel
  ★★★73% ☎ (0463) 231649
- **Kingussie**
  Columba House Hotel
  ★★67% ☎ (0540) 661402

Lothian
- **Aberlady**
  Kilspindie House Hotel
  ★★64% ☎ (08757) 682
- **North Berwick**
  Marine Hotel
  ★★★64% ☎ (0620) 2406

Strathclyde
- **Ayr**
  Caledonian Hotel
  ★★★64% ☎ (0292) 269331

- **Langbank**
  Gleddoch House Hotel
  ★★★✦70% ☎ (047554) 711
- **Troon**
  Marine Highland Hotel
  ★★★★65% ☎ (0292) 314444

Tayside
- **Auchterarder**
  The Gleneagles Hotel
  ★★★★★(Red) ☎ (0764) 62231
- **Blairgowrie**
  Angus Hotel
  ★★60% ☎ (0250) 2838
- **Dundee**
  Stakis Earl Grey
  ★★★66% ☎ (0382) 29271
- **Kinross**
  Green Hotel
  ★★★62% ☎ (0577) 63467
- **Montrose**
  Park Hotel
  ★★★58% ☎ (0674) 73415
- **Pitlochry**
  Birchwood Hotel
  ★★64% ☎ (0796) 2477

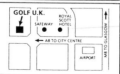

About This Book

The gazetteer contains around 1,600 of Britain's golf course, concentrating on those which welcome visiting golfers, and we have endeavoured to include all the information you would need to know before your visit. However, it is always a good idea to check in advance as details can change after we go to print. Some courses will always want advance notice, possibly also a letter of introduction from your own club, and, if this is the case, the gazetteer entry will include this information. We also tell you how to get there, what kind of course you can expect, club facilities, including catering and accommodation, any other leisure facilities and an indication of what green fees you can expect to pay. It is particularly important to check on fees as they are liable to change during the currency of the guide.

For each course listed, we recommend a near-by AA appointed hotel, giving its classification, full name and address, telephone number and total number of bedrooms, including the number with private bath or shower. In some cases the hotel will be within the grounds of the golf course itself.

HOW TO USE THE GAZETTEER

The gazetteer is arranged in county order and covers England, the Channel Islands and Isle of Man, Scotland and Wales. Within each county, the courses are in alphabetical order of the towns under which they are listed. If you are not sure where your chosen course may be, there is an alphabetical index of courses at the end of the book. Should you be travelling in an unfamiliar part of the country and want to know the choice of courses available to you, consult the atlas at the end of the book where the locations of all courses listed in the guide are pin-pointed.

Those courses which are considered to be of particular merit or interest are printed in green within the gazetteer, a copy of their score card has been included in many cases and they have been further enhanced by the inclusion of a more detailed description. They may be very historic clubs or they may have been chosen because

their courses are particularly testing or enjoyable to play; some have been included because they are in holiday areas and have proved popular with visiting golfers. Such a selection cannot be either exhaustive or totally objective and the courses included are not intended to represent any formal category on quality or other grounds. Championship courses have a full-page entry and include a selection of places to eat as well as stay.

A number of golf clubs have chosen not to have an entry in our gazetteer, usually because they do not have facilities for visitors or because they are private. if you know of any courses which do welcome visitors and which are not yet in our guide, we would be pleased to hear from you.

NB Although we make every effort to obtain up to date information from golf clubs, in some cases we have been unable to verify details with the club's management. Where this is the case, the course name is shown in **_bold italics_** and you would be strongly advised to check with the club in advance of your visit.

It should also be noted that where included score card and gazetteer entry yardages vary, this represents the yardage difference between tee marker positions.

Map References

To help you find the golf courses, each town heading is located on the atlas at the back of the book. After the town name there is a map reference, the first figure being the map page number and the second being the grid reference - read the letter across the map and the number vertically. Within that square on the map you should find the town you are looking for.

KEY TO HOTEL CLASSIFICATION

The AA System of star rating is the market leader in hotel classifications and has long been universally recognised as an accurate, objective indication of the facilities one can expect to find at any hotel in the AA scheme.

★ Hotels generally of a small scale with good facilities and furnishings. Adequate bath and lavatory arrangements. Meals provided for residents, but availability to no-residents may be limited. The AA now accepts private hotels at one and two star level, where the requirements for ready public access and full lunch service may be relaxed.

★★ Hotels offering a higher standard of accommodation and some bedrooms with private facilities. The AA now accepts private hotels at one and two star level where the requirements for ready public access and full lunch service may be relaxed.

★★★ Well-appointed hotels with more spacious accommodation, the majority of bedrooms having a private bath or shower room with lavatory. Fuller meal facilities are provided.

★★★★ Exceptionally well-appointed hotels offering a high standard of comfort and service, and all bedrooms providing a private bath or shower room with lavatory.

★★★★★ Luxury hotels offering the highest international standards.

This denotes a AA Country House hotel where a relaxed, informal atmosphere and personal welcome prevail. Some of the facilities may differ, however, from those found in urban hotels of the same classification. Country House hotels are often secluded and, though not always rurally situated, are quiet. Hotels attracting frequent conferences or functions are not normally granted this symbol.

Red Star Hotels

Red stars are the AA's highest accolade and are awarded, on an annual basis, only to hotels that AA inspectors consider to be of outstanding merit within their classification. You will find a warm welcome and a high standard of hospitality. They are indicated by the word 'Red' after the star classification.

Percentage Ratings For Quality

The AA has recently introduced a new assessment scheme whereby hotels are awarded a percentage score, within their particular star classification, based on quality. The percentage scores, printed immediately after the stars, are an indication of where each hotel stands in comparison to others within the same star classification. Hotels have been assessed for quality under a number of broad headings: hospitality, cleanliness, services, food, bedrooms, overall impression and the inspector's personal view. All hotels recognised by the AA may be expected to score at least 50%, and a score of around 61% is considered to be the average benchmark. Hotels with a higher percentage rating will have many extra touches, above what is normally required of an AA hotel of that particular star rating.

Club Accommodation

Some courses offer accommodation at their club. Where this facility exists, the word 'accommodation' appears in the entry. This has been listed as a further facility for those who might wish to stay at the club. However, the only accommodation appointed by the AA is the star-rated hotel which appears at the foot of each entry.

Symbols and Abbreviations

In order to maximise the space available, we have used certain symbols and abbreviations within the gazetteer entries and these are explained in the panel below:

(4 A2)	atlas grid reference
☎	telephone number
(☎)	advance telephone call required
✉	introduction from own club secretary
⊗	lunch
🍴	dinner
🍺	bar snacks
☕	tea/coffee
♀	bar open mid-day and evenings
👔	changing rooms
🏪	well-stocked shop
⛳	clubs for hire
(	professional at club
M	member
WE	weekend
BH	bank holiday

ENGLAND

AVON

BATH   Map 1 J3

Bath ☎ (0225) 463834
Sham Castle, North Rd (1.5m SE city centre off A36)
Considered to be one of the finest courses in the west, this is the site of Bath's oldest golf club. An interesting course situated on high ground overlooking the city and with splendid views over the surrounding countryside. The rocky ground supports good quality turf and there are many good holes. The 17th is a dog-leg right past, or over the corner of an out-of-bounds wall, and thence on to an undulating green.
18 holes, 6369yds, Par 71, SSS 70, Course record 65. Membership 650.

Visitors welcome must contact in advance ✉ Societies welcome (☎)
Green fees £18 per day (£22 WE & BH)
Facilities ⊗ ⅲ ᴸ ⬛ ♀ ⌂ 🏠 ⌐ ꞁ Peter J Hancox
Hotel ★★★61% Francis Hotel, Queen Square, BATH ☎(0225) 424257 94⇉

Lansdown ☎ (0225) 425007
Lansdown (3m SW of exit 18 off M4)
A flat parkland course in open situation.
18 holes, 6299yds, Par 71, SSS 70. Membership 725.

Visitors welcome (must have current handicap certificate) must contact in advance Societies welcome (☎)
Green fees £18 per day; £14 per round (£22/£18 WE)
Facilities ⊗ ⅲ ⬛ ♀ ⌂ 🏠 ⌐ ꞁ Terry Mercer
Hotel ★★★67% Lansdown Grove Hotel, Lansdown Rd, BATH ☎(0225) 315891 45⇉🕅

BRISTOL   Map 1 H3

Bristol and Clifton ☎ (0272) 393474
Beggar Bush Ln, Failand (4m W on B3129 off A369)
A downland course with splendid turf and fine tree-lined fairways. The 222-yard (par 3) 13th with the green well below, and the par 4 16th, with its second shot across an old quarry, are outstanding. There are splendid views over the Bristol Channel towards Wales. The Coca Cola Professional Tournament has been held here. Course record holder Peter Oosterhuis. Snooker.
18 holes, 6270yds, Par 70, SSS 70, Course record 64. Membership 800.

Visitors welcome (handicap certificate required) must contact in advance Societies welcome (☎)
Green fees £20 per day/round (£25 WE & BH)
Facilities ⊗ ⅲ ᴸ ⬛ ♀ ⌂ 🏠 ⌐ ꞁ Peter Mawson

Hotel ★★★69% Redwood Lodge Hotel & Country Club, Beggar Bush Ln, Failand, BRISTOL ☎(0272) 393901 112⇉

Filton ☎ (0272) 694169
Golf Course Ln, Filton (5m NW off A38)
Parkland course with a par 4 testing hole; 'dog-leg' 383 yds.
18 holes, 6042yds, Par 69, SSS 69, Course record 64. Membership 700.

Visitors welcome (ex WE) ✉ Societies welcome (☎)
Green fees £14 per round
Facilities ⊗ by prior arrangement ⅲ by prior arrangement ᴸ ⬛ ♀ (ex Sun) ⌂ 🏠 ⌐ ꞁ Nicholas Lumb
Hotel ★★★68% Crest Hotel, Filton Rd, Hambrook, BRISTOL ☎(0272) 564242 197⇉🕅

Henbury ☎ (0272) 500044
Henbury Hill, Westbury-on-Trym (3m NW of city centre on B4055 off A4018)
A parkland course, tree-lined and on two levels. The River Trym comes into play on the 7th drop-hole with its green set just over the stream. The last nine holes have the beautiful Blaise Castle woods for company.
18 holes, 5850yds, Par 70, SSS 69, Course record 63. Membership 725.

SCORE CARD: White Tees					
Hole	Yds	Par	Hole	Yds	Par
1	476	5	10	273	4
2	373	4	11	230	3
3	374	4	12	362	4
4	134	3	13	152	3
5	476	5	14	530	5
6	461	4	15	403	4
7	158	3	16	330	4
8	389	4	17	166	3
9	328	4	18	424	4
Out	3169	36	In	2870	34
			Totals	6039	70

Visitors welcome (WE/BH with M only) must contact in advance ✉ Societies welcome (Tue & Fri only)
Green fees £18
Facilities ⊗ ⅲ by prior arrangement ᴸ ⬛ ♀ ⌂ 🏠 ꞁ Nick Riley
Hotel ★★★50% St Vincent Rocks Hotel, Sion Hill, Clifton, BRISTOL ☎(0272) 739251 46⇉🕅

Knowle ☎ (0272) 770660
Brislington (3m SE of city centre off A379)
A parkland course with nice turf but now somewhat naked after the loss of its fine elm trees. The first five holes climb up and down hill but the remainder are on a more even plane.
18 holes, 6016yds, Par 69, SSS 69. Membership 800.

SCORE CARD: Medal Tees					
Hole	Yds	Par	Hole	Yds	Par
1	322	4	10	136	3
2	471	4	11	388	4
3	350	4	12	154	3
4	383	4	13	491	5
5	307	4	14	423	4
6	184	3	15	180	3
7	317	4	16	426	4
8	156	3	17	403	4
9	374	4	18	551	5
Out	2864	34	In	3152	35
			Totals	6016	69

Visitors welcome (h'cap cert required, WE must play with M) must contact in advance ✉ Societies welcome (Thu only ☎)
Green fees £20 per day (£25 WE)

Facilities ⊗ ⅲ by prior arrangement ⅃ ⬛ ♀ ⌂ ⌂ 𝄢 Gordon Brand
Hotel ★★★(red)⚑Hunstrete House Hotel, CHELWOOD ☎(0761) 490490 13⇔♙ Annexe:11⇔♙

Mangotsfield ☎ (0272) 565501
Carsons Rd, Mangotsfield (6m NE of city centre off B4465)
An easy, hilly parkland course. Caravan site.
18 holes, 5337yds, Par 68, SSS 66, Course record 65.
Membership 500.

Visitors welcome (ex competition days) must contact in advance Societies welcome (Wkdays only.☎ 2 wks adv)
Green fees Not confirmed
Facilities ⊗ ⅃ ⬛ ♀ ⌂ ⌂ 𝄢 Craig Trewin
Hotel ★★★68% Crest Hotel, Filton Rd, Hambrook, BRISTOL ☎(0272) 564242 197⇔♙

Shirehampton Park ☎ (0272) 822083
Park Hill, Shirehampton (4m W of city centre on A4)
A lovely course in undulating parkland comprising two loops. There are views over the Portway beside the River Avon, where sliced balls at the opening hole are irretrievable.
18 holes, 5493yds, Par 68, SSS 67, Course record 61.
Membership 600.

Visitors welcome (WE only with M) Societies welcome (Mon (if booked))
Green fees £15 per day (£12 WE with M)
Facilities ⊗ ⅃ ⬛ ♀ ⌂ ⌂ Brent Ellis
Hotel ★★★69% Redwood Lodge Hotel & Country Club, Beggar Bush Ln, Failand, BRISTOL ☎(0272) 393901 112⇔

CHIPPING SODBURY   Map 1 J2

Chipping Sodbury
☎ (0454) 319042
(.5m N)
A parkland course of Championship proportions. The whole course may be seen from the large opening tee by the clubhouse at the top of the hill. Two huge drainage dykes cut through the course and form a distinctive hazard on eleven holes.

SCORE CARD: White Tees					
Hole	Yds	Par	Hole	Yds	Par
1	423	4	10	334	4
2	533	5	11	527	5
3	450	4	12	437	4
4	352	4	13	402	4
5	525	5	14	152	3
6	166	3	15	381	4
7	407	4	16	517	5
8	158	3	17	400	4
9	368	4	18	380	4
Out	3382	36	In	3530	37
			Totals	6912	73

New Course 18 holes,
6912yds, Par 73, SSS 73, Course record 68. Old
Course 9 holes, 6194yds, Par 70, SSS 69. Membership
750.

Visitors welcome (WE pm with handicap certificate) Societies welcome (by letter)
Green fees £16 per day (£20 WE)
Facilities ⊗ ⅲ by prior arrangement ⅃ ⬛ ♀ ⌂ ⌂ 𝄢 S C Harris
Hotel ★★67% Cross Hands Hotel, OLD SODBURY ☎(0454) 313000 24rm(3⇔17♙)

CLEVEDON   Map 1 H3

Clevedon ☎ Bristol (0272) 874057
Castle Rd, Walton St Mary (1m NE of town centre)
Situated on the cliff-top overlooking the Severn estuary and with distant views of the Welsh coast. Excellent parkland course in first-class condition. Magnificent scenery and some tremendous 'drop' holes.
18 holes, 5887yds, Par 69, SSS 69, Course record 65.
Membership 700.

Visitors welcome (handicap certificate required) must contact in advance Societies welcome (Mon only)
Green fees £16 per day (£24 WE & BH)
Facilities ⊗ (ex Tue) ⅲ (ex Tue) ⅃ (ex Tue) ⬛ ♀ ⌂ ⌂ 𝄢 Christine Langford
Hotel ★★★60% Commodore Hotel, Beach Rd, Sand Bay, Kewstoke, WESTON-SUPER-MARE ☎(0934) 415778 12⇔♙ Annexe:7rm(4♙)

LONG ASHTON   Map 1 H3

Long Ashton ☎ (0272) 392316
The Clubhouse (.5m N on B3128)
A high downland course with nice turf, some wooded areas and a spacious practice area. Good drainage ensures pleasant winter golf. Additional facilities are a large putting-green and a billiard-room.
18 holes, 6051yds, Par 70, SSS 70, Course record 64.
Membership 600.

Visitors welcome must contact in advance ✉ Societies welcome (☎)
Green fees Not confirmed
Facilities ⊗ ⅲ by prior arrangement ⅃ ⬛ ♀ ⌂ ⌂ 𝄢 Denis Scanlan
Hotel ★★★69% Redwood Lodge Hotel & Country Club, Beggar Bush Ln, Failand, BRISTOL ☎(0272) 393901 112⇔

MIDSOMER NORTON   Map 1 J3

Fosseway Country Club ☎ (0761) 412214
Charlton Ln (SE of town centre off A367)
Very attractive parkland course, not demanding but with lovely views. Club has indoor-heated swimming pool, sauna baths, squash courts, bowling green and snooker. Accommodation.
9 holes, 4012yds, Par 62, SSS 61. Membership 260.

Visitors welcome (ex Wed eve, Sun am & competitions) Societies welcome (☎)
Green fees £10 per day (£15 WE & BH)
Facilities ⊗ ⅲ ⅃ ⬛ ♀ ⌂
Hotel ★★60% Court Hotel, EMBOROUGH ☎(0761) 232237 10⇔♙

Each golf course entry has a recommended hotel. For a wider choice of places to stay, consult *AA Hotels and Restaurants in Britain* or *AA-inspected Bed and Breakfast in Britain*.

SALTFORD

Map 1 J3

Saltford ☎ (0225) 32207
Golf Club Ln (S side of village)
Parkland course with easy walking and panoramic
views over the Avon Valley. The par 4, 2nd and 13th are
notable.
18 holes, 6081yds, Par 69, SSS 69. Membership 800.

Visitors welcome (handicap cert required) ⊠ Societies
welcome (Mon & Thu only ☎)
Green fees £14 per day (£16 WE)
Facilities ⊗ ⅢⅢ ⬓ ⬛ ♀ ⚐ ⬔ ☗ (
Hotel ★★★(red)⚕Hunstrete House Hotel, CHELWOOD
☎(0761) 490490 13⊏⬔ Annexe:11⊏⬔

WESTON-SUPER-MARE

Map 1 G3

Weston-Super-Mare ☎ (0934) 626968
Uphill Rd North (S side of town centre off A370)
A compact and interesting layout with the opening
hole adjacent to the beach. A sandy links-type
course, it is slightly undulating and has beautifully
maintained turf and greens. The 15th is a testing
455-yard, par 4.
*18 holes, 6251yds, Par 70, SSS 70, Course record 66.
Membership 700.*

Visitors welcome (ex competition days) must
contact in advance Societies welcome (by letter)
Green fees £12 (£22 WE)
Facilities Catering available ♀ ⬔ ⚐ (Terry
Murray
Hotel ★★64% Beachlands Hotel, 17 Uphill Rd
North, WESTON-SUPER-MARE ☎(0934) 621401
18⊏⬔

Worlebury ☎ (0934) 625789
Monks Hill (5m NE off A370)
Fairly easy walking on this seaside course situated on
the ridge of Worlebury Hill. Snooker.
18 holes, 5936yds, Par 70, SSS 70. Membership 600.

Visitors welcome Societies welcome (by letter)
Green fees £15 per day (£25 WE)
Facilities ⊗ ⅢⅢ by prior arrangement ⬓ ⬛ ♀ ⬔ ⚐
⬔ (Gary Marks
Hotel ★★★56% Royal Pier Hotel, Birnbeck Rd,
WESTON-SUPER-MARE ☎(0934) 626644 40rm(33⊏3⬔)

For a full list of the golf courses
included in this book, check
with the index on page 284

WICK

Map 1 J3

Tracy Park ☎ Abson (027 582) 2251
Tracy Park (S side of village off A420)
A new club at Wick, near Bristol. The course,
situated on the south-western escarpment of the
Cotswolds, is undulating with fine views. The
clubhouse dates back to 1600 and is a building of
great beauty and elegance, set in the 220 acre estate
of this golf and country club. Natural water hazards
affect a number of holes. Facilities include tennis
(hardcourt), outdoor heated swimming pool, squash
and snooker.
*27 holes, 6850yds, Par 72, SSS 73, Course record 66.
Membership 1050.*

Visitors welcome must contact in advance ☎
Societies welcome (by letter)
Green fees Not confirmed
Facilities ⊗ ⅢⅢ by prior arrangement ⬓ ⬛ ♀ ⬔
⚐ ⬔ (Grant Aitken
Hotel ★★★67% Lansdown Grove Hotel,
Lansdown Rd, BATH ☎(0225) 315891 45⊏⬔

BEDFORDSHIRE

ASPLEY GUISE

Map 4 C8

Aspley Guise & Woburn
Sands ☎ Milton Keynes
(0908) 583596
West Hill (2m W of M1
junc 13)
A fine undulating course in
expansive heathland
interspersed with many
attractive clumps of gorse,
broom and bracken. Some
well-established silver birch
are a feature. The 7th, 8th
and 9th are really tough
holes to complete the first
half.
*18 holes, 6248yds, Par 71, SSS 70, Course record 67.
Membership 580.*

SCORE CARD: White Tees					
Hole	Yds	Par	Hole	Yds	Par
1	294	4	10	182	3
2	505	5	11	349	4
3	304	4	12	399	4
4	164	3	13	147	3
5	429	4	14	503	5
6	347	4	15	195	3
7	223	3	16	358	4
8	526	5	17	386	4
9	424	4	18	513	5
Out	3216	36	In	3032	35
			Totals	6248	71

Visitors welcome (with M at WE) ⊠ Societies
welcome (normally booked 12 mths ahead)
Green fees £19 per day ; £15 per round
Facilities ⊗ ⅢⅢ ⬓ ⬛ (Full catering daily ex Mon)
♀ ⬔ ⚐ ⬔ (Glyn McCarthy
Hotel ★★61% Swan Revived Hotel, High St,
NEWPORT PAGNELL ☎(0908) 610565 42⊏⬔

BEDFORD

Map 4 C7

Bedford & County ☎ (0234) 52617
Green Ln, Clapham (2m N off A6)
Pleasant parkland course with views over Bedford and
surrounding countryside. The 15th is a testing par 4.
18 holes, 6347yds, Par 70, SSS 70. Membership 600.

Visitors welcome (h'cap cert required, WE only with
M) Societies welcome (Mon, Tue, Thu Fri ☎)

Green fees £20 (£8 with M); (WE £12 with M)
Facilities ⊗ ⅏ ㇿ ♨ ♀ ⛰ 🏠 (E Bullock
Hotel ★★★78% Woodlands Manor Hotel, Green Ln,
Clapham, BEDFORD ☎(0234) 63281 26⇨🏠 Annexe:3⇨

Bedfordshire ☎ (0234) 261669
Bromham Rd, Biddenham (1m W on A428)
Parkland course, tree hazards, easy walking.
18 holes, 6196yds, Par 70, SSS 69. Membership 600.

Visitors welcome (ex WE) must contact in advance
Societies welcome (☎)
Green fees £20
Facilities ⊗ ⅏ by prior arrangement ㇿ ♨ ♀ ⛰ 🏠
(Gary Buckle
Hotel ★★★78% Woodlands Manor Hotel, Green Ln,
Clapham, BEDFORD ☎(0234) 63281 26⇨🏠 Annexe:3⇨

Mowsbury ☎ (0234) 771042
Cleat Hill, Kimbolton Rd (2m N of town centre on B660)
Parkland municipal course. 14-bay driving range and
squash facilities.
18 holes, 6514yds, Par 72, SSS 71. Membership 370.

Visitors welcome Societies welcome
Green fees Not confirmed
Facilities ♀ ⛰ 🏠 ⛳ (
Hotel ★★★78% Woodlands Manor Hotel, Green Ln,
Clapham, BEDFORD ☎(0234) 63281 26⇨🏠 Annexe:3⇨

DUNSTABLE   Map 2 D1

Dunstable Downs
☎ (0582) 604472
Whipsnade Rd (2m S off
B4541)
A fine downland course set
on two levels with far-
reaching views and
frequent sightings of
graceful gliders. The 9th
hole is one of the best short
holes in the country. There
is a modernised clubhouse.
*18 holes, 6184yds, Par 70,
SSS 70, Course record 65.
Membership 695.*

SCORE CARD					
Hole	Yds	Par	Hole	Yds	Par
1	484	5	10	411	4
2	167	3	11	454	4
3	531	5	12	458	4
4	343	4	13	328	4
5	161	3	14	308	4
6	355	4	15	340	4
7	352	4	16	440	4
8	448	4	17	317	4
9	123	3	18	164	3
Out	2964	35	In	3220	35
			Totals	6184	70

Visitors welcome (WE with M) ✉ Societies
welcome (☎)
Green fees £22 per day; £22 per round
Facilities ⊗ (Tue-Fri) ⅏ (Tue-Fri) ㇿ ♨ ♀ ⛰ 🏠
(Michael Weldon
Hotel ★★★69% Old Palace Lodge Hotel, Church
St, DUNSTABLE ☎(0582) 662201 49⇨

LEIGHTON BUZZARD   Map 4 C8

Leighton Buzzard ☎ (0525) 373811
Plantation Rd (1.5N of town centre off A418)
Parkland course with easy walking.
18 holes, 5464yds, Par 69, SSS 68. Membership 610.

Visitors welcome (ex Tue pm & with M only WE & BH)
✉ Societies welcome (☎)
Green fees Not confirmed
Facilities ⊗ ⅏ ㇿ ♨ ♀ ⛰ 🏠 ⛳ (Lee J Munkey
Hotel ★★★72% Swan Hotel, High St, LEIGHTON
BUZZARD ☎(0525) 372148 38⇨🏠

LUTON   Map 2 D1

South Beds ☎ (0582) 591500
Warden Hill (3m N off A6)
27-hole downland course, slightly undulating. Snooker.
*Galley Course 18 holes, 6362yds, Par 71, SSS 70. Warden
Course 9 holes, 2424yds, Par 32. Membership 940.*

Visitors welcome (restricted Tue) must contact in
advance ✉ Societies welcome (Wed-Fri only ☎)
Green fees Galley Course £20 per day; Warden Course
£9 per 18 holes
Facilities ⊗ by prior arrangement ⅏ by prior
arrangement ㇿ ♨ ♀ ⛰ 🏠 (Eddie Cogle
Hotel ★★★67% Strathmore Thistle Hotel, Arndale
Centre, LUTON ☎(0582) 34199 150⇨🏠

Stockwood Park ☎ (0582) 413704
London Rd (1m S on A6)
Municpal parkland course.
18 holes, 5964yds, Par 69, SSS 69. Membership 550.

Visitors welcome Societies welcome (Mon-Thu only)
Green fees Not confirmed

Facilities ♀ (1030–2200) ⌂ 🏠 ⊤ (
Hotel ★★★63% Chiltern Crest Hotel, Waller Av,
Dunstable Rd, LUTON ☎(0582) 575911 93⇦🏠

MILLBROOK

Map 4 C7

Mill Brook ☎ (0525) 840252
(E side of village off A507)
Parkland course, on rolling countryside high above the
Bedfordshire plains, with several water hazards. Laid
out on well-drained sandy soil with many fairways lined
with silver birch, pine and larch.
18 holes, 6806yds, Par 73, SSS 73. Membership 550.

Visitors welcome (wkdays only & with M at WE)
Societies welcome (wkdays ex Thu ☎)
Green fees £20 per day; £10 per round am, £16 pm
Facilities ⊗ ⫼ 🔛 ⬛ ♀ ⌂ 🏠 (Terry Devine
Hotel ★★★♨71% Flitwick Manor Hotel, Church Rd,
FLITWICK ☎(0525) 712242 15⇦🏠

SANDY

Map 4 D7

John O'Gaunt ☎ Potton (0767) 260360
Sutton Park (3m NE of Biggleswade on B1040)
Two tree-lined parkland courses.
*18 holes, 6513yds, Par 71, SSS 71. Carthagena Course 18
holes, 5869yds, Par 69, SSS 68. Membership 1250.*

Visitors welcome must contact in advance Societies
welcome (by letter)
Green fees £25 per day (£40 WE)
Facilities ⊗ ⫼ 🔛 ⬛ ♀ ⌂ 🏠 (Peter Round
Hotel ★★★78% Woodlands Manor Hotel, Green Ln,
Clapham, BEDFORD ☎(0234) 63281 26⇦🏠 Annexe:3⇦

SHEFFORD

Map 4 D7

Beadlow Manor Hotel & Golf & Country Club
☎ (0525) 60800
(2m W on A507)
27 hole golf and leisure complex. Golf courses of
undulating nature with water hazards on numerous
holes. Two courses.
18 holes, 6231yds, Par 71, SSS 70. Membership 750.

Visitors welcome ✉
Green fees Not confirmed
Facilities ♀ ⌂ 🏠 ⊤ (
Hotel ★★★♨71% Flitwick Manor Hotel, Church Rd,
FLITWICK ☎(0525) 712242 15⇦🏠

TILSWORTH

Map 4 C8

Tilsworth ☎ Leighton Buzzard (0525) 210721
Dunstable Rd (.5m NE off A5)
A 9-hole parkland course. 30-bay floodlit driving range.
*9 holes, 2768yds, Par 70, SSS 67, Course record 67.
Membership 200.*

Visitors welcome (Sun am) must contact in advance
Societies welcome (by letter)
Green fees £4.25 per day (£5.25 WE) for 18 holes

Facilities ⊗ (ex Sun) ⫼ (Thu-Sat) 🔛 (Thu-Sat) ⬛ ♀
⌂ 🏠 ⊤ (Nick Webb
Hotel ★★★69% Old Palace Lodge Hotel, Church St,
DUNSTABLE ☎(0582) 662201 49⇦

WYBOSTON

Map 4 D7

Wyboston Lakes ☎ Huntingdon (0480) 219200
(NE side of village off A1)
Parkland course, with narrow fairways and small
greens, set around four lakes and a river.
Accommodation. Fishing.
18 holes, 5721yds, Par 69, SSS 69. Membership 300.

Visitors welcome must contact in advance for WE
Societies welcome (☎)
Green fees Not confirmed
Facilities ♀ ⌂ 🏠 ⊤ (Paul Ashwell
Hotel ★★★78% Woodlands Manor Hotel, Green Ln,
Clapham, BEDFORD ☎(0234) 63281 26⇦🏠 Annexe:3⇦

BERKSHIRE

ASCOT

Map 2 D4

Berkshire ☎ (0990) 21496
Swinley Rd (2.5m NW of M3 jct 3 on A332)
Heathland course.
*Red Course 18 holes, 6356yds, Par 72, SSS 70. Blue
Course 18 holes, 6258yds, Par 71, SSS 70.
Membership 900.*

Visitors welcome must contact in advance ✉
Societies welcome
Green fees Not confirmed
Facilities ⊗ ⬛ ♀ ⌂ 🏠 (K A MacDonald
Hotel ★★★★60% The Berystede, Bagshot Rd,
Sunninghill, ASCOT ☎(0990) 23311 due to change to
(0344) 23311 91⇦🏠

Lavender Park ☎ (0344) 884074
Swinley Rd (3.5m SW on A332)
Public parkland course. Driving range with 9-hole par 3
course, floodlit until 2200 hrs. Driving range, ten
snooker tables.
9 holes, 1104yds, Par 28.

Visitors welcome Societies welcome
Green fees £2.30 (£2.50 WE & BH)
Facilities ⊗ 🔛 ⬛ ♀ 🏠 ⊤ (G Casey
Hotel ★★★★60% The Berystede, Bagshot Rd,
Sunninghill, ASCOT ☎(0990) 23311 due to change to
(0344) 23311 91⇦🏠

Royal Ascot ☎ (0990) 25175
Winkfield Rd (.5 N on A330)
Heathland course exposed to weather.
18 holes, 5653yds, Par 68, SSS 67. Membership 575.

Visitors welcome (restricted WE & BH) Societies
welcome (☎)
Green fees Not confirmed
Facilities ⊗ by prior arrangement ⫼ by prior
arrangement 🔛 ⬛ ♀ ⌂ 🏠 (C Dell

Hotel ★★★★60% The Berystede, Bagshot Rd, Sunninghill, ASCOT ☎(0990) 23311 due to change to (0344) 23311 91⇗👣

Swinley Forest
☎ (0344) 20197
(1.5m S, off A330)
An attractive and immaculate course of heather and pine situated in the heart of Swinley Forest. The 17th is as good a short hole as will be found, with a bunkered plateau green. Course record holder is P. Alliss.
18 holes, 6001yds, Par 68, SSS 69, Course record 64. Membership 350.

	SCORE CARD				
Hole	Yds	Par	Hole	Yds	Par
1	370	4	10	210	3
2	350	4	11	286	4
3	305	4	12	480	5
4	165	3	13	160	3
5	465	5	14	375	4
6	437	5	15	433	5
7	410	5	16	430	5
8	155	3	17	180	3
9	430	5	18	360	4
Out	3087	38	In	2914	36
			Totals	6001	74

Visitors welcome (Invitation only) must contact in advance Societies welcome (☎)
Green fees £35 per day
Facilities ⊗ ⛳ 🍺 ♀ ⛷ 🏠 ⛵ ⸨ R C Parker
Hotel ★★★★60% The Berystede, Bagshot Rd, Sunninghill, ASCOT ☎(0990) 23311 due to change to (0344) 23311 91⇗👣

CHADDLEWORTH   Map 2 A3

West Berkshire ☎ (04882) 574
(1m S of village off A338)
Challenging and interesting downland course with testing 635 yds (par 5) 5th hole.
18 holes, 7069yds, Par 73, SSS 74. Membership 900.

Visitors welcome (restricted WE) must contact in advance Societies welcome (☎)
Green fees £20 per wkday
Facilities ⊗ ⛳ 🍺 ♀ ⛷ 🏠 ⛵ ⸨ David Sheppard
Hotel ★★★56% The Chequers, Oxford St, NEWBURY ☎(0635) 38000 56⇗👣

COOKHAM   Map 2 D3

Winter Hill ☎ (06285) 27613
Grange Ln (1m NW off B4447)
Parkland course set in a curve of the Thames with wonderful views across the river to Cliveden.
18 holes, 6408yds, Par 72, SSS 71, Course record 70. Membership 800.

Visitors welcome (restricted WE) must contact in advance Societies welcome
Green fees £19 per day
Facilities ⊗ ⛳ 🍺 ♀ ⛷ 🏠 ⸨
Hotel ★★★★73% Compleat Angler Hotel, Marlow Bridge, MARLOW ☎(06284) 4444 due to change to (0628) 484444 46⇗

This guide is updated annually – make sure you use an up-to-date edition.

CROWTHORNE   Map 2 C4

East Berkshire ☎ (0344) 772041
Ravenswood Ave (W side of town centre off B3348)
An attractive heathland course with an abundance of heather and pine trees. Walking is easy and the greens are exceptionally good. Some fairways become tight where the heather encroaches on the line of play. The course is testing and demands great accuracy.
18 holes, 6345yds, Par 69, SSS 70, Course record 65. Membership 500.

Visitors welcome (h'cap cert required, with M at WE & BH) must contact in advance ✉ Societies welcome (Thu & Fri only ☎)
Green fees £28 (WE with M £12)
Facilities ⊗ ⋔ by prior arrangement ⛳ 🍺 (11am-4pm) ♀ ⛷ 🏠 ⛵ ⸨ Arthur Roe
Hotel ★★★★⚑70% Pennyhill Park Hotel, London Rd, BAGSHOT ☎(0276) 71774 22⇗👣
Annexe:41⇗👣 **See advertisement on page 41**

DATCHET   Map 2 D3

Datchet ☎ (0753) 43887
Buccleuch Rd (NW side of Datchet off B470)
Meadowland course, easy walking.
9 holes, 5978yds, Par 70, SSS 69, Course record 63. Membership 385.

Visitors welcome (wkdays before 1500) Societies welcome (Tue only)
Green fees £20 per day; £15 per round
Facilities ⛳ 🍺 ♀ ⛷ 🏠 ⸨ Andy Grieg
Hotel ★★52% The Manor Hotel, The Village Green, DATCHET ☎(0753) 43442 30⇗👣

HURLEY   Map 2 C3

Temple ☎ Littlewick Green (0628) 824248
Henley Rd (1m SE on A432)
An open, parkland course with many excellent greens relying on natural slopes rather than heavy bunkering. On one 'blind' punchbowl hole there is actually a bunker on the green. Good drainage assures play when many other courses are closed. Squash.
18 holes, 5824yds, Par 69, SSS 68. Membership 600.

Visitors welcome must contact in advance Societies welcome (book one year in advance)
Green fees £30 per day (£40 WE)
Facilities ⊗ ⋔ ⛳ 🍺 ♀ ⛷ 🏠 ⛵ ⸨ Alan Dobbins
Hotel ★★★★73% Compleat Angler Hotel, Marlow Bridge, MARLOW ☎(06284) 4444 due to change to (0628) 484444 46⇗

Each golf course entry has a recommended hotel. For a wider choice of places to stay, consult *AA Hotels and Restaurants in Britain* or *AA-inspected Bed and Breakfast in Britain*.

MAIDENHEAD   Map 2 D3

Maidenhead ☎ (0628) 24693
Shoppenhangers Rd (S side of town centre off A308)
A pleasant parkland course on level ground with
easy walking to good greens. Perhaps a little short
but there are many natural features and some first-
rate short holes.
18 holes, 6344yds, Par 70, SSS 70, Course record 66.
Membership 730.

Visitors welcome (up to 12 noon Fri) must contact
in advance ⊠ Societies welcome (by letter)
Green fees Not confirmed
Facilities ⊗ ⅃ ᗣ ♀ ㅿ 🖻 ☂ (Lee Elstone
Hotel ★★★★71% Fredrick's Hotel,
Shoppenhangers Rd, MAIDENHEAD ☎(0628) 35934
37⇨🏌

NEWBURY   Map 2 B4

Newbury & Crookham ☎ (0635) 40035
Bury's Bank Rd, Greenham (2m SE off A34)
A well-laid out, attractive course running mostly
through woodland, and giving more of a challenge than
its length suggests.
18 holes, 5880yds, Par 68, SSS 68, Course record 63.
Membership 800.

Visitors welcome (WE & BH with M) ⊠ Societies
welcome (☎)
Green fees £20 per round/day
Facilities ⊗ ⅢⅢ by prior arrangement ⅃ ᗣ ♀ ㅿ 🖻
(David Harris
Hotel ★★★56% The Chequers, Oxford St, NEWBURY
☎(0635) 38000 56⇨🏌

READING   Map 2 C4

Calcot Park ☎ (0734) 427124
Bath Rd, Calcot (2.5m W on A4)
A delightfully sporting parkland course just outside
the town. Hazards include a lake and many trees.
The 6th is the longest, a 497 yard par 5, with the teeshot hit downhill over cross-bunkers to a well-
guarded green. The 13th (188 yards) requires a big
carry over a gully to a plateau green.
18 holes, 6283yds, Par 70, SSS 70. Membership 700.

Visitors welcome (ex WE & BH)
Green fees Not confirmed
Facilities ㅿ 🖻 (
Hotel ★★★70% The Copper Inn, Church Rd,
PANGBOURNE ☎(0734) 842244 22⇨🏌

Reading ☎ (0734) 472909
17 Kidmore End Rd, Emmer Green (2m N off B481)
Tree-lined parkland course part hilly and part flat.
18 holes, 6204yds, Par 70, SSS 70. Membership 700.

Visitors welcome (with M Fri & WE, club M/h'cap cert
reqd) Societies welcome (book one year in advance)
Green fees £25 per wkday

Facilities ⊗ ⅢⅢ by prior arrangement ⅃ ᗣ ♀ ㅿ 🖻
(Tim Morrison
Hotel ★★★★60% Ramada Hotel, Oxford Rd, READING
☎(0734) 586222 196⇨🏌

SINDLESHAM   Map 2 C4

Bearwood ☎ Arborfield Cross (0734) 760060
Mole Rd (1m SW on B3030)
Parkland course.
9 holes, 5628yds, Par 70, SSS 67, Course record 70.
Membership 570.

Visitors welcome (h'cap cert required, WE & BH with
M) ⊠
Green fees £20 per day (18 holes)
Facilities ⊗ by prior arrangement ⅢⅢ by prior
arrangement ⅃ ᗣ ♀ ㅿ 🖻 (B F Tustin
Hotel ★★60% Cantley House Hotel, Milton Rd,
WOKINGHAM ☎(0734) 789912 29⇨🏌

SONNING   Map 2 C3

Sonning ☎ (0734) 693332
Duffield Rd (1m S off A4)
A quality parkland course and the scene of many
county championships. Wide fairways, not
overbunkered, and very good greens. Holes of
changing character through wooded belts.
18 holes, 6360yds, Par 70, SSS 70. Membership 600.

Visitors welcome (weekdays only) ⊠ Societies
welcome (by letter)
Green fees Not confirmed
Facilities ⊗ ⅢⅢ by prior arrangement ⅃ ᗣ ♀ ㅿ
🖻 (Richard McDougall
Hotel ★★★★60% Ramada Hotel, Oxford Rd,
READING ☎(0734) 586222 196⇨🏌

STREATLEY   Map 2 B3

Goring & Streatley
☎ Goring (0491) 873229
Rectory Rd (N of village off
A417)
A parkland/moorland
course that requires
'negotiating'. Four well-
known first holes lead up to
the heights of the 5th tee, to
which there is a 300ft climb.
Wide fairways, not
overbunkered, with nice
rewards on the way home
down the last few holes.
Snooker.
18 holes, 6275yds, Par 71, SSS 70, Course record 65.
Membership 750.

SCORE CARD: White Tees					
Hole	Yds	Par	Hole	Yds	Par
1	369	4	10	382	4
2	425	4	11	324	4
3	344	4	12	152	3
4	139	3	13	363	4
5	485	5	14	300	4
6	392	4	15	511	5
7	452	4	16	206	3
8	377	4	17	496	5
9	149	3	18	420	4
Out	3121	35	In	3154	36
			Totals	6275	71

Visitors welcome (with M only WE) Societies
welcome (☎)
Green fees £20 per day

Facilities ⊗ ⅏ by prior arrangement ⚐ ⬛ ♀ ⚲
🏠 ⛳ ⚑ Roy Mason
Hotel ★★★73% Swan Diplomat Hotel, High St,
STREATLEY ☎(0491) 873737 46⇒🏠

SUNNINGDALE   Map 2 D4

Sunningdale See page 42

Sunningdale Ladies ☎ Ascot (0344) 20507
Cross Rd (1m S off A30)
A short 18-hole heathland course designed for Ladies
golf.
18 holes, 3616yds, Par 60, SSS 60. Membership 350.

Visitors welcome (☎ in advance) Societies welcome
(Ladies societies only)
Green fees Not confirmed
Facilities ⊗ (ex Sun and Mon) ⚐ ⬛ ♀ ⚲
Hotel ★★★★60% The Berystede, Bagshot Rd,
Sunninghill, ASCOT ☎(0990) 23311 due to change to
(0344) 23311 91⇒🏠

WOKINGHAM   Map 2 C4

Downshire ☎ Bracknell (0344) 424066
Easthampstead Park (3m SW of Bracknell)
Municipal parkland course with many water hazards,
easy walking. Testing holes: 7th (par 4), 15th (par 4),
16th (par 3).
18 holes, 6382yds, Par 73, SSS 70.

Visitors welcome must contact in advance Societies
welcome (☎)
Green fees £8.50 per round
Facilities ⊗ ⚐ ⬛ ♀ ⚲ 🏠 ⛳ ⚑ Geoffrey Legouix
Hotel ★★★★60% The Berystede, Bagshot Rd,
Sunninghill, ASCOT ☎(0990) 23311 due to change to
(0344) 23311 91⇒🏠

BUCKINGHAMSHIRE

AYLESBURY   Map 2 C2

Ellesborough
☎ Wendover (0296) 622114
Butlers Cross (1m E of
Ellesborough on B4010)
Used to be part of the
property of Chequers, and
under the shadow of the
famous monument at the
Wendover end of the
Chilterns. A downland
course, it is rather hilly
with most holes enhanced
by far-ranging views over
the Aylesbury countryside.
*18 holes, 6271yds, Par 71, SSS 70, Course record 66.
Membership 780.*

SCORE CARD: White Tees					
Hole	Yds	Par	Hole	Yds	Par
1	353	4	10	141	3
2	515	5	11	310	4
3	414	4	12	331	4
4	378	4	13	393	4
5	189	3	14	559	5
6	405	4	15	128	3
7	395	4	16	262	4
8	180	3	17	441	4
9	391	4	18	486	5
Out	3220	35	In	3051	36
			Totals	6271	71

▶

SCORE CARD: Old Course (White Tees)					
Hole	Yds	Par	Hole	Yds	Par
1	494	5	10	463	4
2	456	4	11	299	4
3	296	4	12	423	4
4	161	3	13	178	3
5	400	4	14	477	5
6	388	4	15	226	3
7	383	4	16	423	4
8	172	3	17	421	4
9	267	4	18	414	4
Out	3017	35	In	3324	35
			Totals	6341	70

SUNNINGDALE   Map2 D4

Sunningdale Ascot ☎ (0990) 21681 Ridgemount Rd (1m S, off A30)

Many famous golfers maintain that Sunningdale, on the borders of Berkshire, is the most attractive inland course in Britain. The great Bobby Jones once played the 'perfect' round of 66 made up of threes and fours on the Old Course. Later, Norman von Nida of Australia shot a 63 while the then professional at the club, Arthur Lees, scored a 62 to win a huge wager.

While the Old Course, with silver birch, heather and perfect turf, is lovely to behold, the New Course alongside is considered by many to be its equal. But just as golfers want to play the Old Course at St Andrews, and miss the redesigned Jubilee, so visitors to Sunningdale opt for the Old, and fail to realise what they are overlooking by not playing the New.

To become a member of this club takes years of waiting. Maybe it is the quality of the courses, maybe the clubhouse atmosphere and perhaps the excellence of the professionals shop has something to do with it; but added up it has to be the most desirable place to spend a day.

The classic Old Course is not long, measuring just 6341 yards, and because the greens are normally in excellent condition, anyone with a 'hot' putter can have an exciting day, providing they keep teeshots on the fairway and don't stray into the gorse and pine trees which lie in wait.

Founded just ninety years ago, the Old Course was designed by Willie Park, while H.S. Colt created the New Course in 1922. Most golfers will agree that there isn't one indifferent hole on either course and, on a sunny day, if you had to be anywhere in the world playing well, then we opt for the elevated tenth tee on the Old. What bliss.

36 holes. Old Course 18 holes, Par 70, SSS 70. New Course 6676 yds, Par 70, SSS 72

Visitors   welcome weekdays only. Must contact in advance. Handicap cert required ✉. Societies welcome (one years notice)

Green fees   £69 per day

Facilities   ⊗ ⼚ ⬤ ♀ ⛺ 🝔 ⼧ ᚠ

WHERE TO STAY AND EAT NEARBY

HOTELS:

ASCOT   ★★★★ 56% The Royal Berkshire, London Rd, Sunninghill ☎ (0990) 23322. 64⟨⁵ ᚠ Annexe 18⟨⁵

              ★★★★ 50% Berystede, Bagshot Rd, Sunninghill ☎ (0990) 23311. 91⟨⁵ᚠ.♀English & French cuisine.

              (Note: During the currency of this publication Ascot telephone numbers are liable to change).

MAIDENHEAD ★★★★ 71% Fredrick's, Shoppenhangers Rd ☎ (0628) 35934. 37⟨⁵ᚠ. ♀ English & French cuisine.

RESTAURANTS:

BRAY   ✗✗✗✗ The Waterside, River Cottage, Ferry Road ☎ Maidenhead (0628) 20691 & 22941. ♀ French cuisine.

EGHAM   ✗✗ La Bonne Franquette, 5 High Street ☎ (0784) 439494. ♀ French cuisine.

Visitors welcome (ex Tue am, & WE with M only) must contact in advance ✉ Societies welcome (Wed & Thu only)
Green fees £25 per day; £20 per round (£10 WE with M)
Facilities ⊗))Ⅲ by prior arrangement ⛾ ☕ 🍷 ⛶ 🏠 ⛳ ⚐ Paul Warner
Hotel ★★★(red)Bell Inn, ASTON CLINTON ☎(0296) 630252 21⇨ ⚑

BEACONSFIELD

Map 2 D3

Beaconsfield ☎ (0494) 676545
Seer Green (2m E, S of Seer Green)
An interesting and, at times, testing course which frequently plays longer than appears on the card. Each hole differs to a considerable degree and here lies the charm. Walking is easy, except perhaps to the 8th.
18 holes, 6487yds, Par 72, SSS 71. Membership 862.

Visitors welcome (WE & BH with member) must contact in advance ✉ Societies welcome (☎)
Green fees £25 per day; £20 per round
Facilities ⊗))Ⅲ ⛾ ☕ 🍷 ⛶ 🏠 ⛳ ⚐ Mike Brothers
Hotel ★★★56% Bellhouse Hotel, Oxford Rd, BEACONSFIELD ☎(0753) 887211 136⇨

BLETCHLEY

Map 4 B8

Windmill Hill ☎ Milton Keynes (0908) 648149
Tattenhoe Ln (W side of town centre on A421)
Long, open-parkland course designed by Henry Cotton and opened in 1972.
18 holes, 6773yds, Par 73, SSS 73. Membership 600.

Visitors welcome Societies welcome (☎)
Green fees £4.50 per round (£6.30 WE & BH)
Facilities ⊗ by prior arrangement))Ⅲ by prior arrangement ☕ 🍷 ⛶ 🏠 ⛳ ⚐ C Clingan
Hotel ★★★72% Swan Hotel, High St, LEIGHTON BUZZARD ☎(0525) 372148 38⇨ ⚑

BOW BRICKHILL

Map 4 C8

Woburn ☎ Milton Keynes (0908) 370756
(.5m E)
These two 18-hole golf courses are set amid the beautiful surroundings of the Duke of Bedford's estate near Woburn, and are suitably named the Duke's and the Duchess. Tennis and outdoor swimming pool (members only).
Duke's Course 18 holes, 6940yds, Par 72, SSS 74.
Duchess Course 18 holes, 6641yds, Par 72, SSS 72.
Membership 900.

SCORE CARD: Duke's Course (White Tees)

Hole	Yds	Par	Hole	Yds	Par
1	514	5	10	404	4
2	385	4	11	502	5
3	134	3	12	193	3
4	395	4	13	419	4
5	510	5	14	565	5
6	207	3	15	432	4
7	464	4	16	449	4
8	409	4	17	425	4
9	177	3	18	356	4
Out	3195	35	In	3745	37
			Totals	6940	72

Visitors welcome (with M at WE) must contact in advance ✉ Societies welcome (☎)
Green fees Not confirmed
Facilities ⊗))Ⅲ by prior arrangement (groups only) ☕ 🍷 ⛶ 🏠 ⚐ A Hay
Hotel ★★★♛71% Flitwick Manor Hotel, Church Rd, FLITWICK ☎(0525) 712242 15⇨ ⚑

BUCKINGHAM

Map 4 B8

Buckingham ☎ (0280) 815566
Tingewick Rd (1.5m W on A421)
Undulating parkland course cut by a stream. Snooker.
18 holes, 6082yds, Par 70, SSS 69, Course record 67. Membership 680.

Visitors welcome (with M only WE) must contact in advance Societies welcome (☎)
Green fees Not confirmed
Facilities ⊗))Ⅲ (ex Mon) ⛾ ☕ 🍷 ⛶ 🏠 ⚐ Tom Gates
Hotel ★★50% The White Hart Hotel, Market Square, BUCKINGHAM ☎(0280) 815151 19⇨ ⚑

BURNHAM

Map 2 D3

Burnham Beeches ☎ (06286) 61448
Green Ln (.5m NE)
Set in the centre of the lovely Burnham Beeches countryside. Wide fairways, carefully maintained greens, some hills, and some devious routes to a few holes. A good finish.
18 holes, 6415yds, Par 71, SSS 71. Membership 670.

Visitors welcome (weekdays only) Societies welcome
Green fees Not confirmed
Facilities ⛶ 🏠 ⛳ ⚐
Hotel ★★★65% Burnham Beeches Moat House, Grove Rd, BURNHAM ☎(0628) 603333 75⇨

CHALFONT ST GILES

Map 2 D3

Harewood Downs ☎ Little Chalfont (0494) 762184
Cokes Ln (2m N off A413)
A testing, undulating parkland course. Snooker.
18 holes, 5958yds, Par 69, SSS 69, Course record 65. Membership 550.

Visitors welcome (h'cap cert required) must contact in advance ✉ Societies welcome (by letter)
Green fees £20 per day
Facilities ⊗))Ⅲ ⛾ ☕ (catering by prior arrangement) 🍷 (by prior arrangement) ⛶ 🏠 ⚐ G C Morris
Hotel ★★★56% Bellhouse Hotel, Oxford Rd, BEACONSFIELD ☎(0753) 887211 136⇨

This guide is updated annually – make sure you use an up-to-date edition.

CHESHAM
Map 2 D2

Chesham & Ley Hill ☎ (0494) 784541
Ley Hill Common (2m E)
Heathland course on hilltop with easy walking. Subject to wind.
9 holes, 5296yds, Par 67, SSS 66, Course record 64. Membership 430.

Visitors welcome (Mon & Thu, Wed after 1200, Fri before 1300) Societies welcome (subject to approval, Thu only)
Green fees £17 per day; £12 per round
Facilities ⊗ by prior arrangement ⋙ by prior arrangement ⅃ ⅃ ⅄ ⅃
Hotel ★★62% The Crown Hotel, High St, AMERSHAM ☎(0494) 721541 23rm(13⇔1♠)

DAGNALL
Map 2 D2

Whipsnade Park ☎ (044284) 2330
Studham Ln (1m E off B4506)
Parkland course situated on downs overlooking the Chilterns and adjoining Whipsnade Zoo. Easy walking, good views.
18 holes, 6800yds, Par 72, SSS 72, Course record 70. Membership 500.

Visitors welcome (WE with M) must contact in advance Societies welcome (☎)
Green fees £25 per day; £17 per round
Facilities ⊗ ⋙ ⅃ ⅃ ⅄ ⅃ ⅃ ⅃ ⅃ Mike Lewendon
Hotel ★★★69% Old Palace Lodge Hotel, Church St, DUNSTABLE ☎(0582) 662201 49⇔

DENHAM
Map 2 D3

Denham ☎ Uxbridge (0895) 832022
Tilehouse Ln (2m NW)
A beautifully maintained parkland/heathland course, home of many county champions. Slightly hilly and calling for good judgement of distance in the wooded areas.
18 holes, 6451yds, Par 70, SSS 71, Course record 66. Membership 550.

Visitors welcome (Fri-Sun M guests only) must contact in advance ⊠ Societies welcome (☎ bookings 1yr in advance)
Green fees £36.50 per day; £24 per round
Facilities ⊗ ⅃ ⅃ ⅃ ⅄ ⅃ ⅃ ⅃ John Sheridan
Hotel ★★64% Ethorpe Hotel, Packhorse Rd, GERRARDS CROSS ☎(0753) 882039 29⇔♠

FLACKWELL HEATH
Map 2 D3

Flackwell Heath ☎ Bourne End (06285) 20027
Treadaway Rd, High Wycombe (NE side of town centre)
Open heath and tree-lined course on hills overlooking Loudwater and the M40. Quick drying.
18 holes, 6150yds, Par 71, SSS 69, Course record 65. Membership 800.

Visitors welcome (WE with M) ⊠ Societies welcome (Wed & Thu,)

Green fees £22 per day
Facilities ⊗ ⅃ ⅃ ⅄ ⅃ ⅃ ⅃ ⅃ Brian Plucknett
Hotel ★★★56% Bellhouse Hotel, Oxford Rd, BEACONSFIELD ☎(0753) 887211 136⇔

GERRARDS CROSS
Map 2 D3

Gerrards Cross ☎ (0753) 883263
Chalfont Park (NE side of town centre off A413)
A wooded, parkland course which has been modernised in recent years and is now a very pleasant circuit with infinite variety. The best part lies on the plateau above the clubhouse where there are some testing holes.
18 holes, 6295yds, Par 69, SSS 70. Membership 780.

Visitors welcome must contact in advance ⊠ Societies welcome (Book one year ahead)
Green fees £27 per day/round (after 1400 £20)
Facilities ⅃ ⅄ ⅃ ⅃
Hotel ★★★56% Bellhouse Hotel, Oxford Rd, BEACONSFIELD ☎(0753) 887211 136⇔

HALTON
Map 2 C2

Chiltern Forest ☎ Aylesbury (0296) 631267
Aston Hill (1m NE off A4011)
Hilly, wooded parkland course on two levels. 12-holes at present, 14-holes by April 1991.
14 holes, 6173yds, Par 72, SSS 70, Course record 67. Membership 570.

Visitors welcome (WE with M) Societies welcome (☎ or letter)
Green fees £15 per day
Facilities ⊗ ⋙ ⅃ ⅃ (no catering Tue and Thu) ⅄ ⅃ ⅃ ⅃ C Skeet
Hotel ★★62% Rose & Crown Hotel, High St, TRING ☎(044282) 4071 27⇔♠

IVER
Map 2 D3

Iver ☎ (0753) 655615
Hollow Hill Ln, Langley Park Rd (1.5m SW off B470)
Parkland course.
9 holes, 2953yds, Par 72, SSS 69 or 3107yds, Par 74, SSS 69. Membership 500.

Visitors welcome Societies welcome (☎)
Green fees Not confirmed
Facilities ⊗ ⅃ ⅃ ⅄ ⅃ ⅃ ⅃ ⅃ Terry Notley
Hotel ★★★★64% Holiday Inn Slough/Windsor, Ditton Road, Langley, SLOUGH ☎(0753) 44244 302⇔♠

IVINGHOE
Map 2 D2

Ivinghoe ☎ Cheddington (0296) 668696
Wellcroft (N side of village)
A 9-hole, testing parkland course with water on three holes. Easy walking.
9 holes, 4508yds, Par 62, SSS 62, Course record 61. Membership 250.

Visitors welcome (after 0800) Societies welcome (☎)
Green fees £5 per round (£6.50 WE)

Facilities ⊗ 🕳 🍺 ⚲ 🏌 🏠 ⛳ ☏ Bill Garrad
Hotel ★★★(red)Bell Inn, ASTON CLINTON ☏(0296)
630252 21⇔🚶

LITTLE CHALFONT   Map 2 D2

Little Chalfont ☏ (0494) 764877
Lodge Ln (Between Little Chalfont & Chorleywood)
Flat course surrounded by woods.
9 holes, 5800yds, Par 68, SSS 68, Course record 66.
Membership 300.

Visitors welcome Societies welcome (☏)
Green fees £7 per round (£9 WE)
Facilities ⊗ 🍴 🕳 🍺 ⚲ 🏌 🏠 ⛳ ☏ J Dunne
Hotel ★★62% The Crown Hotel, High St, AMERSHAM
☏(0494) 721541 23rm(13⇔1🚶)

MILTON KEYNES   Map 4 B7

Abbey Hill ☏ (0908) 563845
Two Mile Ash (2m W of new town centre off A5)
Undulating municipal course within the new city.
Tight fairways and well-placed bunkers. Stream comes
into play on five holes. Also Par 3 course.
18 holes, 6177yds, Par 68, SSS 69, Course record 67.
Membership 600.

Visitors welcome Societies welcome (☏ 562408)
Green fees £5 (£7 WE)
Facilities ⊗ 🍴 🕳 🍺 ⚲ 🏌 🏠 ⛳ ☏ S Harlock
Hotel ★★61% Swan Revived Hotel, High St, NEWPORT
PAGNELL ☏(0908) 610565 42⇔🚶

PRINCES RISBOROUGH   Map 2 C2

Whiteleaf ☏ (0844) 274058
Whiteleaf (1m NE off A4010)
Short 9-hole parkland course requiring great accuracy.
Fine views.
9 holes, 5391yds, Par 66, SSS 66, Course record 64.
Membership 350.

Visitors welcome (with M at WE) must contact in
advance Societies welcome (contact secretary)
Green fees £25 per day ; £15 per round
Facilities ⊗ 🍴 🕳 🍺 (no catering or bar Mon) ⚲ 🏌
🏠 ☏ K Ward
Hotel ★★★(red)Bell Inn, ASTON CLINTON ☏(0296)
630252 21⇔🚶

STOKE POGES   Map 2 D3

Farnham Park ☏ (028814) 3332
Park Rd (W side of village off B416)
Public parkland course in pleasing setting.
18 holes, 5787yds, Par 69, SSS 68, Course record 65.
Membership 600.

Visitors welcome Societies welcome
Green fees £6 (£8 WE)
Facilities ⊗ 🍴 🕳 🍺 ⚲ 🏌 🏠 ⛳ ☏ Paul Harrison
Hotel ★★★★64% Holiday Inn Slough/Windsor,
Ditton Road, Langley, SLOUGH ☏(0753) 44244 302⇔🚶

Stoke Poges
☏ Slough (0753) 26385
Park Rd (1.5m W off B416)
Judgement of the distance
from the tee is all important
on this first-class parkland
course. There are many
outstanding par 4's of
around 440 yds, several
calling for much thought.
Fairways are wide and the
challenge seemingly
innocuous. Snooker and
sauna.

SCORE CARD					
Hole	Yds	Par	Hole	Yds	Par
1	502	5	10	390	4
2	411	4	11	156	3
3	198	3	12	435	4
4	425	4	13	502	5
5	496	5	14	429	4
6	412	4	15	326	4
7	150	3	16	187	3
8	354	4	17	421	4
9	454	4	18	406	4
Out	3402	36	In	3252	35
			Totals	6654	71

18 holes, 6654yds, Par 71, SSS 72, Course record 65.
Membership 720.

Visitors welcome (ex WE) must contact in advance
✉ Societies welcome (☏)
Green fees £32 per day ; £22 per round
Facilities ⊗ 🍴 🕳 🍺 ⚲ 🏌 🏠 ⛳ ☏
Hotel ★★★★64% Holiday Inn Slough/Windsor,
Ditton Road, Langley, SLOUGH ☏(0753) 44244
302⇔🚶

WESTON TURVILLE   Map 2 C2

Weston Turville ☏ Aylesbury (0296) 24084
New Rd (.5m N off B4544)
Parkland course, with views of the Chiltern Hills. Flat,
easy walking with water hazards. Squash.
18 holes, 6002yds, Par 69, SSS 69. Membership 550.

Visitors welcome (except Sun a.m.) Societies welcome
Green fees £11 per round (£15 WE)
Facilities ⊗ 🍴 🕳 🍺 ⚲ 🏌 🏠 ⛳ ☏ Gary George
Hotel ★★★(red)Bell Inn, ASTON CLINTON ☏(0296)
630252 21⇔🚶

WEXHAM STREET   Map 2 D3

Wexham Park ☏ (0753) 663271
(.5m S)
Gently undulating parkland course. Two courses.
*18 holes, 5836yds, Par 69, SSS 68 or 9 holes, 2283yds, Par
32, SSS 32. Membership 500.*

Visitors welcome Societies welcome (ex WE ☏)
Green fees Not confirmed
Facilities ⊗ 🍴 by prior arrangement 🕳 🍺 ⚲ 🏌 🏠
⛳ ☏ David Morgan
Hotel ★★★★64% Holiday Inn Slough/Windsor,
Ditton Road, Langley, SLOUGH ☏(0753) 44244 302⇔🚶

Each golf course entry has a recommended
hotel. For a wider choice of places to stay,
consult *AA Hotels and Restaurants in Britain* or
AA-inspected Bed and Breakfast in Britain.

CAMBRIDGESHIRE

CAMBRIDGE   Map 4 E6

Cambridgeshire Moat House ☎ (0954) 780555
Moat House Hotel, Bar Hill (5m NW on A604).
Undulating parkland course with lake and water
hazards, easy walking. Accommodation. Tennis
(hardcourt), indoor-heated swimming pool, squash,
sauna, solarium and gymnasium. Course record
holders, Paul Way and Peter Townsend.
*18 holes, 6734yds, Par 72, SSS 72, Course record 68.
Membership 500.*

Visitors welcome must contact in advance ✉
Societies welcome (☎)
Green fees £18.50 per day (£25 WE & BH)
Facilities ⊗ ⊪ ⊾ ⬤ ♀ ⚖ 🖿 ⍲ ⫯ Geoff Huggett
Hotel ★★★61% Cambridgeshire Moat House, BAR
HILL ☎(0954) 780555 100⇨🐾

Gog Magog ☎ (0223) 247626
Shelford Bottom (3m SE on A1307)
Situated just outside the centre of the university
town, Gog Magog, established in 1901, is known as
the nursery of Cambridge under-graduate golf. The
course is on high ground and it is said that if you
stand on the highest point and could see far enough
to the east the next highest ground would be the
Ural Mountains. The courses (there are two of
them) are open but there are enough trees and other
hazards to provide plenty of problems. Views from
the high parts are superb. The nature of the ground
ensures good winter golf.
*Old Course 18 holes, 6354yds, Par 70, SSS 70, Course
record 64. New Course 9 holes, 5833yds, Par 69, SSS
68. Membership 1100.*

Visitors welcome (☎ WE with M) ✉ Societies
welcome (by reservation)
Green fees Not confirmed
Facilities ⊗ ⊪ by prior arrangement ⊾ ⬤ ♀ ⚖
🖿 ⫯ Ian Bamborough
Hotel ★★★64% Gonville Hotel, Gonville Place,
CAMBRIDGE ☎(0223) 66611 62⇨

ELY   Map 4 F5

Ely City ☎ (0353) 662751
Cambridge Rd (SW side of city centre on A10)
Parkland course slightly undulating with water
hazards formed of lakes and natural dykes. Magnificent
views of Cathedral. Course record holder Lee Trevino.
*18 holes, 6602yds, Par 72, SSS 72, Course record 66.
Membership 1000.*

Visitors welcome (h'cap cert must be produced) must
contact in advance ✉ Societies welcome (Tue-Fri ☎)
Green fees £20 per day (£30 WE & BH)
Facilities ⊗ ⊪ ⊾ ⬤ ♀ ⚖ 🖿 ⍲ ⫯ Fred Rowden
Hotel ★★★62% Fenlands Lodge Hotel, Soham Rd,
Stuntney, ELY ☎(0353) 667047 Annexe:9⇨🐾

GIRTON   Map 4 E6

Girton ☎ Cambridge (0223) 276169
Dodford Ln (NW side of village)
Flat, open parkland course with easy walking.
*18 holes, 6085yds, Par 69, SSS 69, Course record 68.
Membership 700.*

Visitors welcome (with M only WE) must contact in
advance Societies welcome (☎)
Green fees £21 per wkday (£16 with h'cap cert)
Facilities ⊗ ⊪ ⊾ ⬤ (catering during bar hours)
♀ ⚖ 🖿 ⍲ ⫯ John Sharkey
Hotel ★★★★55% Post House Hotel, Lakeview,
Bridge Rd, Impington, CAMBRIDGE ☎(0223) 237000
120⇨🐾

PETERBOROUGH   Map 4 D5

Orton Meadows ☎ (0733) 237478
Ham Ln, Oundle Rd (3m W of town on A605)
Municipal, parkland course on either side of the Nene
Valley Railway, with lakes and water hazards. Also 12-
hole pitch and putt course.
18 holes, 5800yds, Par 68, SSS 68. Membership 750.

Visitors welcome must contact in advance Societies
welcome (☎)
Green fees £5 per day (£7.50 WE & BH)
Facilities ⚖ 🖿 ⍲ ⫯
Hotel ★★76% The Haycock Hotel, WANSFORD
☎(0780) 782223 51⇨🐾

Peterborough Milton ☎ (0733) 380489
Milton Ferry (3m W on A47)
Well-bunkered parkland course set in the grounds of the
Earl Fitzwilliam's estate. Easy walking.
18 holes, 6221yds, Par 70, SSS 70. Membership 800.

Visitors welcome ✉ Societies welcome (weekdays only
☎)
Green fees £20 per day (£25 WE)
Facilities ⊗ ⊪ ⊾ ⬤ ♀ ⚖ 🖿 ⫯ Nigel Bundy
Hotel ★★76% The Haycock Hotel, WANSFORD
☎(0780) 782223 51⇨🐾

Thorpe Wood ☎ (0733) 267701
Thorpe Wood (3m W of city centre on A47)
Gently undulating, municipal parkland course designed
by Peter Alliss and Dave Thomas.
*18 holes, 7086yds, Par 71, SSS 74, Course record 74.
Membership 850.*

Visitors welcome must contact in advance Societies
welcome (☎)
Green fees £5 (£7.50 WE & BH)
Facilities ⊗ by prior arrangement ⊪ by prior
arrangement ⊾ by prior arrangement ⬤ by prior
arrangement ♀ ⚖ 🖿 ⍲ ⫯
Hotel ★★★60% Bull Hotel, Westgate, PETERBOROUGH
☎(0733) 61364 112⇨

RAMSEY   Map 4 D5

Ramsey ☎ (0487) 812600
4 Abbey Ter (S side of town)
Flat, parkland course with water hazards.
18 holes, 6145yds, Par 71, SSS 70, Course record 66.
Membership 750.

Visitors welcome (h'cap cert required, with M at WE &
BH) must contact in advance Societies welcome
(contact secretary)
Green fees £20 per day/round
Facilities ⊗ ⅏ by prior arrangement ⣿ ⬛ ♀ ⚐ 🗄
⟊ ⟊ Barney Puttick
Hotel ★★★71% The Old Bridge Hotel, HUNTINGDON
☎(0480) 52681 26⇥♠

ST IVES   Map 4 E6

St Ives ☎ (0480) 68392
Westwood Rd (W side of town centre off A1123)
Picturesque parkland course.
9 holes, 3302yds, Par 68, SSS 69. Membership 305.

Visitors welcome (☎ for details)
Green fees Not confirmed
Facilities ♀ ⚐ 🗄
Hotel ★★★62% Slepe Hall Hotel, Ramsey Rd, ST IVES
☎(0480) 63122 16rm(15⇥)

ST NEOTS   Map 4 D6

Abbotsley Golf & Squash Club
☎ Huntingdon (0480) 215153
(2m SE off B1046)
Attractive, parkland course surrounding moated
country house and hotel. Pleasant views. Floodlit
driving range. Accommodation. Squash, snooker, sauna
and solarium.
18 holes, 5780yds, Par 70, SSS 68. Membership 700.

Visitors welcome (not before 1000 at WE) Societies
welcome (by telephone)
Green fees £12 per day (£18 WE & BH)
Facilities ⊗ ⅏ ⣿ ⬛ ♀ ⚐ 🗄 ⟊ ⟊ Vivien Saunders
Hotel ★★59% Grange Hotel, 115 High St, BRAMPTON
☎(0480) 459516 9rm(1⇥7♠)

St Neots ☎ (0480) 72363
Crosshall Rd (W side of town centre on A45)
Parkland course close to the Kym and Great Ouse rivers
with easy level walking.
18 holes, 6027yds, Par 69, SSS 69, Course record 65.
Membership 600.

Visitors welcome (☎ h'cap cert required, with M at
WE) Societies welcome (☎)
Green fees £25 per day; £15 per round
Facilities ⊗ ⅏ ⣿ ⬛ ♀ ⚐ 🗄 ⟊ Graham Bithrey
Hotel ★★59% Grange Hotel, 115 High St, BRAMPTON
☎(0480) 459516 9rm(1⇥7♠)

For an explanation of the symbols and
abbreviations used, see page 33.

CHESHIRE

ALDERLEY EDGE   Map 3 H2

Alderley Edge ☎ (0625) 585583
Brook Ln (1m NW on B5085)
Well-wooded undulating pastureland course. A stream
crosses 7 of the 9 holes. Snooker.
9 holes, 5828yds, Par 68, SSS 68, Course record 65.
Membership 350.

Visitors welcome ✉ Societies welcome (Thu only)
Green fees £15 per day ; (£20 WE & BH)
Facilities ⊗ by prior arrangement ⅏ by prior
arrangement ⣿ ⬛ (no catering Mon) ♀ (ex Mon) ⚐
🗄 ⟊ ⟊ M Stewart
Hotel ★★★72% Alderley Edge Hotel, Macclesfield Rd,
ALDERLEY EDGE ☎(0625) 583033 32⇥♠

ALSAGER   Map 3 H2

Alsager Golf & Country Club ☎ (0270) 875700
Audley Rd (2m NE M6 junct 10)
An 18-hole parkland course situated in rolling Cheshire
countryside. Clubhouse is well appointed with good
facilities and a friendly atmosphere. Rapidly improving
course. Snooker and bowling green.
18 holes, 6206yds, Par 70, SSS 70, Course record 69.
Membership 600.

Visitors welcome (with M only wknds) must contact in
advance advisable Societies welcome (Mon, Wed & Thu
only by letter)
Green fees £12 (£16 WE)
Facilities ⊗ ⅏ ⣿ ⬛ ♀ ⚐ 🗄 ⟊ ⟊ Nick Rothe
Hotel ★★★64% Manor House Hotel, Audley Rd,
ALSAGER ☎(0270) 884000 27⇥♠

CHESTER   Map 3 G2

Chester ☎ (0244) 677760
Curzon Park (1m SW of city centre)
Meadowland course on two levels contained within a
loop of the River Dee. The car park overlooks the
racecourse across the river and the clubhouse stands
just 1 mile SW of the city centre. Snooker.
18 holes, 6487yds, Par 72, SSS 71, Course record 66.
Membership 700.

Visitors welcome must contact in advance Societies
welcome (☎)
Green fees £16 (£20 WE & BH)
Facilities ⊗ ⅏ ⣿ ⬛ (no catering Mon) ♀ ⚐ 🗄 ⟊
⟊ G Parton
Hotel ★★★★71% Chester International Hotel,
Trinity St, CHESTER ☎(0244) 322330 150⇥

Upton-by-Chester ☎ (0244) 381183
Upton Ln, Upton-by-Chester (N side off A5116)
Pleasant tree-lined, parkland course. Not easy for low-
handicap players to score well. Testing holes are 2nd
(par 4), 14th (par 4) and 15th (par 3). Snooker.
18 holes, 5808yds, Par 69, SSS 68, Course record 62.
Membership 700.

▶

Visitors welcome must contact in advance Societies welcome (except Mon & Fri (am))
Green fees £20 per day; £15 per round (£20 per round WE)
Facilities ⊗ (ex Mon) 〴 (Wed-Fri) ⬟ ◫ ♀ ⌂ 🕮 ʃ
Hotel ★★★★65% Mollington Banastre Hotel, Parkgate Rd, CHESTER ☎(0244) 851471 64⇨

Vicars Cross ☎ (0244) 335174
Littleton (3m E on A51)
Parkland course, with undulating terrain. Snooker.
18 holes, 6238yds, Par 71, SSS 70. Membership 650.

Visitors welcome (no casual visitors Fri-Sun & BH)
Societies welcome (☎ confirm in writing)
Green fees Not confirmed
Facilities ⊗ 〴 ⬟ ◫ ♀ ⌂ 🕮 ʃ John Forsythe
Hotel ★★★★65% Mollington Banastre Hotel, Parkgate Rd, CHESTER ☎(0244) 851471 64⇨

CONGLETON
Map 3 H2

Astbury ☎ (0260) 272772
Peel Ln, Astbury (1.5m S between A34 and A527)
Parkland course in open countryside, bisected by a canal. Snooker.
18 holes, 6269yds, Par 71, SSS 70, Course record 65. Membership 700.

Visitors welcome (with M only WE) ✉ Societies welcome (Thu by written request)
Green fees £15 per day
Facilities ⊗ 〴 by prior arrangement ⬟ ◫ by prior arrangement ♀ ⌂ 🕮 ⫟ ʃ S R Bassil
Hotel ★★★62% Saxon Cross Motor Hotel, Holmes Chapel Rd, SANDBACH ☎(0270) 763281 52⇨❧

Congleton ☎ (0260) 273540
Biddulph Rd (1.5m SE on A527)
Superbly-manicured parkland course with views over three counties from the balcony of the clubhouse. Snooker.
9 holes, 5055yds, Par 68, SSS 65. Membership 400.

Visitors welcome (ex during competitions)
Green fees £12 (£20 WE & BH)
Facilities ⊗ (ex Thu-Mon) 〴 by prior arrangement ⬟ ◫ ♀ ⌂ 🕮 ʃ John Colclough
Hotel ★★★65% Chimney House Hotel, Congleton Rd, SANDBACH ☎(0270) 764141 50⇨

CREWE
Map 3 H2

Crewe ☎ (0270) 584099
Fields Rd, Haslington (2.25m NE off A534)
Undulating parkland course. Snooker.
18 holes, 6202yds, Par 70, SSS 70, Course record 67. Membership 600.

Visitors welcome (with M only WE & BH) Societies welcome (Tue only ☎)
Green fees £20 per day; £15 per round

Facilities ⊗ 〴 ⬟ ◫ ♀ ⌂ 🕮 ʃ Ron E Rimmer
Hotel ★★★58% Crewe Arms Hotel, Nantwich Rd, CREWE ☎(0270) 213204 53⇨❧

DELAMERE
Map 3 G2

Delamere Forest ☎ Sandiway (0606) 882807
Station Rd (1.5m N off B5152)
Played mostly on open heath, there is great charm in the way this course drops down into the occasional pine sheltered valley.
18 holes, 6305yds, Par 72, SSS 70, Course record 63. Membership 600.

Visitors welcome (restricted WE & BH) must contact in advance Societies welcome (☎)
Green fees £15 per day (£20 WE & BH)
Facilities ⊗ 〴 (societies only) ⬟ ◫ ♀ ⌂ 🕮 ʃ Ellis B Jones
Hotel ★★★65% Hartford Hall Hotel, School Ln, Hartford, NORTHWICH ☎(0606) 75711 21⇨

DISLEY
Map 5 E8

Disley ☎ (0663) 62071
Stanley Hall Ln, Jacksons Edge (NW side of village off A6)
Parkland/moorland course with trees. Often breezy. Good views. Testing hole: 5th (par 5). Snooker.
18 holes, 6015yds, Par 70, SSS 69, Course record 63. Membership 400.

Visitors welcome (Thu Fri WE & BH) ✉ Societies welcome
Green fees Not confirmed
Facilities 〴 ⬟ ◫ ♀ ⌂ 🕮 ⫟ ʃ A G Esplin
Hotel ★★★62% Alma Lodge Hotel, 149 Buxton Rd, STOCKPORT ☎061-483 4431 58rm(52⇨)

ECCLESTON
Map 3 G2

Eaton ☎ (0244) 680474
Eaton Park (1m S)
A very testing, well-wooded parkland course.
18 holes, 6446yds, Par 72, SSS 71. Membership 530.

Visitors welcome must contact in advance ✉ Societies welcome (☎)
Green fees Not confirmed
Facilities ⊗ by prior arrangement 〴 by prior arrangement ⬟ ◫ ♀ ⌂ 🕮 ʃ A Mitchell
Hotel ★★★★(red)The Chester Grosvenor Hotel, Eastgate St, CHESTER ☎(0244) 324024 86⇨❧

ELLESMERE PORT
Map 3 G2

Ellesmere Port ☎ 051-339 7689
Chester Rd, Hooton (NW side of town centre on A41)
Municipal parkland course with natural hazards of woods, brook and ponds. Squash.
18 holes, 6384yds, Par 70, SSS 72, Course record 66. Membership 300.

Visitors welcome must contact in advance Societies welcome (contact professional)

Green fees £3.20 (£4 WE & BH)
Facilities ⊗ ⫿ by prior arrangement ⤷ ⬛ ♀ △ 🏠
⫟ ⦅ David John Yates
Hotel ★★62%, Berni Royal, Childer Thornton,
ELLESMERE PORT ☏051-339 8101 47⇨🐾

HELSBY   Map 3 G2

Helsby ☏ (0928) 722021
Towers Ln (1m S off A56)
Quiet parkland course with natural hazards. Snooker.
18 holes, 5906yds, Par 70, SSS 68, Course record 68.
Membership 575.

Visitors welcome (except WE & BH with M only) must
contact in advance Societies welcome (Tue & Thu)
Green fees £15 per round
Facilities ⊗ ⫿ ⤷ ⬛ ♀ △ 🏠 ⦅ Ian Wright
Hotel ★★★★(red)The Chester Grosvenor Hotel,
Eastgate St, CHESTER ☏(0244) 324024 86⇨🐾

KNUTSFORD   Map 5 D8

Knutsford ☏ (0565) 3355
Mereheath Ln (N side of town centre off A50)
A good 9-hole parkland course set in beautiful old deer
park. It demands some precise iron play.
9 holes, 6328yds, Par 70, SSS 70. Membership 135.

Visitors welcome (restricted Wed pm) must contact in
advance ✉

Green fees Not confirmed

▶

Facilities ♀ 🏌 📷
Hotel ★★★61% The Swan Hotel, BUCKLOW HILL
☎(0565) 830295 70🛏🐾

> **Mere Golf & County Club**
> ☎ Bucklow Hill (0565) 830155
> Chester Rd, Mere (1m E of junc 19 of M6)
> A gracious parkland championship course designed
> by James Braid and set in the Cheshire sand belt,
> with several holes close to a lake. The round has a
> tight finish with four testing holes.
> *18 holes, 6849yds, Par 71, SSS 73. Membership 600.*
>
> **Visitors** welcome must contact in advance Societies
> welcome (Mon Tue & Thu only)
> **Green fees** Not confirmed
> **Facilities** ♀ 🏌 📷 🐾 ✆
> **Hotel** ★★★61% The Swan Hotel, BUCKLOW HILL
> ☎(0565) 830295 70🛏🐾

LYMM

Map 5 D8

Lymm ☎ (092575) 5020
Whitbarrow Rd (.5m N off A6144)
First ten holes are gently undulating with the
Manchester Ship Canal running alongside the 9th hole.
The remaining holes are comparatively flat. Snooker.
18 holes, 6304yds, Par 71, SSS 70, Course record 68.
Membership 625.

Visitors welcome (ex Thu am, WE & BH, h'cap cert
required) must contact in advance Societies welcome
(☎)
Green fees £18
Facilities ⊗ ⅲ ┗ ♣ ♀ 🏌 📷 🐾 ✆ G J Williams
Hotel ★★★59% Lymm Hotel, Whitbarrow Rd, LYMM
☎(092575) 2233 22🛏🐾 Annexe:47🛏🐾

MACCLESFIELD

Map 3 H2

Macclesfield ☎ (0625) 23227
The Hollins (SE side of town centre off A523)
Very hilly 9-hole heathland course situated on the edge
of the Pennines. Excellent views. Currently being
extended to 18-holes. Snooker.
9 holes, 5974yds, Par 69, SSS 69, Course record 63.
Membership 600.

Visitors welcome Societies welcome (☎)
Green fees £15 per day (£17 WE)
Facilities ⊗ ⅲ by prior arrangement ┗ ♣ (no
catering Tue) ♀ (ex Tue) 🏌 📷 ✆
Hotel ★★63% Crofton Hotel, 22 Crompton Rd,
MACCLESFIELD ☎(0625) 34113 8rm(2🛏5🐾)

This guide is updated annually – make sure you
use an up-to-date edition.

POTT SHRIGLEY

Map 5 E8

Shrigley Hall Hotel ☎ Bollington (0625) 575757
Shrigley Park
Parkland course with breathtaking views over the Peak
District and Cheshire Plain. Designed by Donald Steel,
this championship course provides a real sporting
challenge, while the magnificent hotel provides a wealth
of sporting, conference and banqueting facilities as well
as accommodation and food.
18 holes, 6305yds, Par 71, SSS 71, Course record 68.

Visitors welcome must contact in advance Societies
welcome (☎)
Green fees £20 per day; £15 per round (£25 per round
WE)
Facilities ⊗ ⅲ ┗ ♣ ♀ 🏌 📷 🐾 ✆ Granville Ogden
Hotel ★★★★58% Shrigley Hall Golf & Country Club,
Shrigley Park, POTT SHRIGLEY ☎(0625) 575757 58🛏

POYNTON

Map 5 E8

Davenport ☎ (0625) 876951
Worth Hall, Middlewood Rd (1m E off A523)
Undulating parkland course. Extensive view over
Cheshire Plain from elevated 5th tee. Testing 17th hole,
par 4. Snooker.
18 holes, 6006yds, Par 69, SSS 69. Membership 600.

Visitors welcome Societies welcome (by letter)
Green fees Not confirmed
Facilities 🏌 📷 🐾 ✆ Wyn Harris
Hotel ★★★62% Alma Lodge Hotel, 149 Buxton Rd,
STOCKPORT ☎061-483 4431 58rm(52🛏)

PRESTBURY

Map 3 H2

Prestbury ☎ (0625) 829388
Macclesfield Rd (S side of village off A538)
Rather strenuous parkland course, undulating, with
many plateau greens. Good views. Snooker.
18 holes, 6359yds, Par 71, SSS 71, Course record 66.
Membership 725.

Visitors welcome (with M only WE) must contact in
advance ✉ Societies welcome (Thu only)
Green fees £22 per day
Facilities ⊗ ⅲ by prior arrangement ┗ ♣ ♀ 🏌 📷
🐾 ✆ Tim Rastall
Hotel ★★★70% Mottram Hall Hotel, Prestbury,
MOTTRAM ST ANDREW ☎(0625) 828135 95🛏🐾

RUNCORN

Map 5 C8

Runcorn ☎ (0928) 572093
Clifton Rd (1.25m S of Runcorn Station)
Parkland course with tree-lined fairways and easy
walking. Fine views over Mersey and Weaver valleys.
Testing holes: 7th par 5; 14th par 5; 17th par 4.
Snooker.
18 holes, 6035yds, Par 69, SSS 69, Course record 66.
Membership 575.

Visitors welcome (wkdays ex 0900-1000, 1200-1330 &
Tue am) ✉ Societies welcome (by letter)

Green fees £14 per wkday (WE only with M)
Facilities ⊗ (ex Thu) ⅲ by prior arrangement 🏌 ⬛ ♀ 🏖 🍴 ⚑ Geof Berry
Hotel ★★★64% Crest Hotel, Wood Ln, Beechwood, RUNCORN ☎(0928) 714000 134⇌🛏

SANDBACH

Map 3 H2

Malkins Bank ☎ Crewe (0270) 765931
Betchton Rd, Malkins Bank (1.5m SE off A533)
Parkland course. Tight 13th hole with stream running through.
18 holes, 6071yds, Par 70, SSS 69. Membership 500.

Visitors welcome Societies welcome (apply for booking form)
Green fees £3.65 per round (£4.40 WE & BH)
Facilities 🏌 ⬛ ♀ 🏖 🍴 ⚑ David Wheeler
Hotel ★★★62% Saxon Cross Motor Hotel, Holmes Chapel Rd, SANDBACH ☎(0270) 763281 52⇌🛏

Sandbach ☎ Crewe (0270) 21177
Middlewich Rd (.5m W on A533)
Meadowland, undulating course with easy walking. Limited facilities.
9 holes, 5533yds, Par 67, SSS 67. Membership 450.

Visitors welcome (ex Tue & with M only WE & BH) must contact in advance Societies welcome (by letter)
Green fees Not confirmed
Facilities ⊗ ⅲ 🏌 ⬛ ♀ 🏖
Hotel ★★★62% Saxon Cross Motor Hotel, Holmes Chapel Rd, SANDBACH ☎(0270) 763281 52⇌🛏

SANDIWAY

Map 3 G2

Sandiway ☎ (0606) 883247
(1m E on A556)
Delightful, undulating woodland and heath golf with long hills up to the 8th, 16th and 17th holes. Many dog-legged and tree-lined holes give opportunities for the deliberate fade or draw.
18 holes, 6435yds, Par 70, SSS 72. Membership 750.

SCORE CARD					
Hole	Yds	Par	Hole	Yds	Par
1	405	4	10	467	4
2	523	5	11	219	3
3	193	3	12	446	4
4	502	5	13	138	3
5	416	4	14	441	4
6	151	3	15	362	4
7	413	4	16	519	5
8	357	4	17	305	4
9	396	4	18	182	3
Out	3356	36	In	3079	34
			Totals	6435	70

Visitors welcome must contact in advance ✉
Societies welcome (by letter)
Green fees £25 per day (£30 WE)
Facilities ⊗ ⅲ 🏌 ⬛ ♀ 🏖 🍴 ⚑ W Laird
Hotel ★★★65% Hartford Hall Hotel, School Ln, Hartford, NORTHWICH ☎(0606) 75711 21⇌

For an explanation of the symbols and abbreviations used, see page 33.

WARRINGTON

Map 5 D8

Birchwood ☎ (0925) 818819
Kelvin Close, Birchwood (4m NE on A574)
Very testing course with natural water hazards. The 11th hole is particularly challenging. Snooker and sauna.
18 holes, 6808yds, Par 71, SSS 73, Course record 64. Membership 1150.

Visitors welcome (except Sun) Societies welcome (Mon-Thu only)
Green fees £18 per day (£25 WE & BH)
Facilities ⊗ ⅲ 🏌 ⬛ ♀ 🏖 🍴 ⚑ Derrick Cooper
Hotel ★★★66% Post House Hotel, Lodge Ln, Newton-Le-Willows, HAYDOCK ☎(0942) 717878 142⇌

Leigh ☎ Culcheth (092576) 2943
Kenyon Hall, Kenyon (5m NE off A579)
A pleasant parkland course with a fair number of trees. Any discrepancy in length is compensated by the wide variety of golf offered here. The course is well maintained and there is a comfortable clubhouse. Snooker.
18 holes, 5374yds, Par 69, SSS 68, Course record 64. Membership 750.

Visitors welcome (ex during competitions) ✉
Societies welcome (by letter)
Green fees Not confirmed

▶

Facilities ⊗ by prior arrangement ⅷ by prior arrangement 🏌 (ex Mon) 🍴 ♀ △ 🏠 ♟ Andrew Baguley
Hotel ★★58% Patten Arms, Parker St, WARRINGTON ☎(0925) 36602 43⇨🐾

Poulton Park ☎ Padgate (0925) 812034
Dig Ln, Cinnamon Brow, Padgate (3m from Warrington on A574)
Tight meadowland course with good greens.
9 holes, 2648yds, Par 68, SSS 66, Course record 67. Membership 350.

Visitors welcome (ex 1700-1800 wkdays; 1200-1330 Sat) Societies welcome (by letter)
Green fees £12 per day (£14 WE & BH)
Facilities ⊗ ⅷ 🏌 🍴 ♀ △ 🏠 ♟ Steven McCarthy
Hotel ★★★62% Fir Grove Hotel, Knutsford Old Rd, WARRINGTON ☎(0925) 67471 40⇨🐾

Walton Hall ☎ (0925) 630619
Warrington Rd, Higher Walton (2.5m S off A56)
Municipal parkland course on Walton Hall estate.
18 holes, 6843yds, Par 72, SSS 73, Course record 70. Membership 200.

Visitors welcome Societies welcome (by letter)
Green fees £4.50 wkdays (£5.50 WE)
Facilities 🏌 🍴 ♀ △ 🏠 ♟ ♟
Hotel ★★58% Patten Arms, Parker St, WARRINGTON ☎(0925) 36602 43⇨🐾

Warrington ☎ (0925) 65431
The Hill Warren, London Rd, Appleton (2.5m S on A49)
Meadowland, with varied terrain and natural hazards.
18 holes, 6305yds, Par 72, SSS 70. Membership 400.

Visitors welcome Societies welcome (by letter)
Green fees Not confirmed
Facilities ♀ △ 🏠 ♟
Hotel ★★70% Rockfield Hotel, 3 Alexandra Rd, Grappenhall, WARRINGTON ☎(0925) 62898 & 63343 6⇨🐾 Annexe:7rm(5⇨🐾)

WIDNES

Map 5 C8

St Michael Jubilee ☎ 051-424 6230
Dunalk Rd (W side of town centre off A562)
Recently extended, municipal parkland course, dominated by the 'Stewards Brook'. The old and the new sections are split by the main road and joined by an underpass.
18 holes, 2648yds, Par 69, SSS 68.

Visitors welcome Member must accompany must contact in advance ✉ Societies welcome (by letter)
Green fees Not confirmed
Facilities ♀ △ 🏠 ♟
Hotel ★58% Rockland Hotel, View Rd, RAINHILL ☎051-426 4603 10⇨ Annexe:3⇨🐾

Widnes ☎ 051-424 2440
Highfield Rd
Parkland course, easy walking. Snooker.
18 holes, 5719yds, Par 69, SSS 68, Course record 65. Membership 300.

Visitors welcome (after 0900, competition days after 1630) ✉ Societies welcome (by letter)
Green fees £12 per day (£15 WE & BH)
Facilities △ 🏠 ♟ Frank Robinson
Hotel ★58% Rockland Hotel, View Rd, RAINHILL ☎051-426 4603 10⇨ Annexe:3⇨🐾

WILMSLOW

Map 5 D8

Wilmslow ☎ (0565) 872148
Great Warford, Mobberley (2m SW off B5058)
A fine parkland championship course, of middle length, fair to all classes of player and almost in perfect condition.
18 holes, 6500yds, Par 71, SSS 71, Course record 64. Membership 660.

Visitors welcome must contact in advance Societies welcome (☎)
Green fees £30 per day; £20 per round (£40/£30 WE & BH)
Facilities ⊗ ⅷ by prior arrangement 🏌 🍴 ♀ △ 🏠 ♟ John Nowicki
Hotel ★★★★60% Belfry Hotel, Stanley Rd, HANDFORTH ☎061-437 0511 82⇨

WINSFORD

Map 3 G2

Knights Grange ☎ (0606) 552780
Sports Complex (N side of town off A54)
Municipal course.
9 holes, 3105yds, SSS 70. Membership 100.

Visitors welcome
Green fees Not confirmed
Facilities ♀ △ ♟
Hotel ★★64% Woodpecker Hotel, London Rd, NORTHWICH ☎(0606) 45524 33⇨🐾

CLEVELAND

BILLINGHAM

Map 5 G3

Billingham ☎ Stockton (0642) 554494
Sandy Ln (1m W of town centre E of A19)
Parkland course on edge of urban-rural district, with hard walking and water hazards; testing 15th hole.
18 holes, 6946yds, Par 73, SSS 71, Course record 65. Membership 750.

Visitors welcome (WE & BH with M) ✉ Societies welcome (by letter)
Green fees £15 per day (£20 WE & BH)
Facilities ⊗ ⅷ by prior arrangement 🏌 ♀ △ 🏠 ♟ ♟
Hotel ★★★52% Billingham Arms Hotel, The Causeway, Billingham, STOCKTON-ON-TEES ☎(0642) 553661 69⇨🐾

EAGLESCLIFFE

Map 5 F3

Eaglescliffe and District
☎ (0642) 780098
Yarm Rd (E side of village off A135)
This hilly course offers both pleasant and interesting golf to all classes of player. It lies in a delightful setting on a rolling plateau, shelving to the River Tees. There are fine views to the Cleveland Hills. Snooker.
18 holes, 6275yds, Par 72, SSS 70, Course record 67. Membership 470.

SCORE CARD: White Tees					
Hole	Yds	Par	Hole	Yds	Par
1	333	4	10	478	5
2	383	4	11	200	3
3	467	4	12	534	5
4	182	3	13	482	5
5	281	4	14	449	4
6	352	4	15	162	3
7	498	5	16	349	4
8	348	4	17	160	3
9	318	4	18	299	4
Out	3162	36	In	3113	36
			Totals	6275	72

Visitors welcome (restricted Tue, Thu & WE) Societies welcome (☎ not WE)
Green fees £14 per day (£20 WE & BH)
Facilities ⊗ (ex Mon and Sat) ⅶ (ex Sun-Mon) ⅃ (ex Sun-Mon) ⬤ ♀ △ 🖻 ✆ James Munro
Hotel ★★★★55% Swallow Hotel, 10 John Walker Square, STOCKTON-ON-TEES ☎(0642) 679721 124⇩🏾

HARTLEPOOL

Map 5 G2

Castle Eden & Peterlee ☎ Wellfield (0429) 836510
Castle Eden (2m S of Peterlee on B1281 off A19)
Beautiful parkland course alongside a nature reserve. Hard walking, trees provide wind shelter. Snooker.
18 holes, 6107yds, Par 70, SSS 69, Course record 66. Membership 750.

Visitors welcome (M only 1200-1330 & 1600-1830) must contact in advance Societies welcome (☎ (0429) 836689)
Green fees £15 per day, (£20 WE & BH)
Facilities ⊗ ⅶ by prior arrangement ⅃ ⬤ ♀ △ 🖻 ✆ ✆ Tim Jenkins
Hotel ★★★65% Hardwick Hall Hotel, SEDGEFIELD ☎(0740) 20253 17⇩

Hartlepool ☎ (0429) 274398
Hart Warren (N side off King Oswy Drive)
A seaside course, half links, overlooking the North Sea. A good test and equally enjoyable to all handicap players. The 10th, par 4, demands a precise second shot over a ridge and between sand dunes to a green down near the edge of the beach, alongside which several holes are played. Snooker.
18 holes, 6005yds, Par 70, SSS 70, Course record 63. Membership 600.

Visitors welcome (with M Sun) Societies welcome (by letter)
Green fees £14 per day (£20 WE)
Facilities ⊗ ⅶ ⅃ ⬤ ♀ △ 🖻 ✆ Malcolm Cole
Hotel ★★★65% Hardwick Hall Hotel, SEDGEFIELD ☎(0740) 20253 17⇩

To see a full range of AA guides and maps, visit your local AA Shop or any good bookshop.

MIDDLESBROUGH

Map 5 G3

Middlesbrough ☎ (0642) 311515
Brass Castle Ln, Marton (5m S off A172)
Undulating parkland course, prevailing winds. Testing 9th, 16th and 17th holes. Snooker.
18 holes, 6136yds, Par 70, SSS 69. Membership 900.

Visitors welcome (restricted Tue & Sat) Societies welcome (Wed, Thu & Fri only ☎)
Green fees £16 per day (£20 WE & BH)
Facilities ⊗ ⅶ ⅃ ⬤ ♀ △ 🖻 ✆ D J Jones
Hotel ★★★50% Marton Way Toby Hotel, Marton Rd, MIDDLESBROUGH ☎(0642) 817651 53⇩

Middlesbrough Municipal ☎ (0642) 315533
Ladgate Ln (2.5m S of town centre on B1380 off A172)
Parkland course with stream running through and good views.
18 holes, 6314yds, Par 71, SSS 70. Membership 400.

Visitors welcome
Green fees Not confirmed
Facilities ♀ △ 🖻 ☍
Hotel ★★★50% Marton Way Toby Hotel, Marton Rd, MIDDLESBROUGH ☎(0642) 817651 53⇩

REDCAR

Map 5 G3

Cleveland ☎ (0642) 471798
Queen St (8m E of Middlesborough on A19/A172)
Links championship course. Snooker.
18 holes, 6707yds, Par 72, SSS 72, Course record 68. Membership 800.

Visitors welcome (ex WE) must contact in advance Societies welcome (by letter)
Green fees £12 per day (£18 WE & BH)
Facilities ⊗ ⅶ ⅃ ⬤ ♀ △ 🖻 ✆ D Masey
Hotel ★★★67% Park Hotel, Granville Ter, REDCAR ☎(0642) 490888 25⇩🏾

Wilton ☎ (0642) 465265
Wilton Castle (3m W on A174)
Parkland course with some fine views.
18 holes, 6104yds, Par 70, SSS 69. Membership 750.

Visitors welcome (restricted Sat) Societies welcome (☎)
Green fees £10 per day/round
Facilities ⊗ ⅶ by prior arrangement ⅃ ⬤ ♀ △ 🖻 ✆ R Smith
Hotel ★★★67% Park Hotel, Granville Ter, REDCAR ☎(0642) 490888 25⇩🏾

SALTBURN-BY-THE-SEA

Map 5 G3

Saltburn by the Sea ☎ (0287) 22812
Hob Hill, Guisborough Rd (S side of town centre on B1268)
Undulating meadowland course surrounded by woodland. Particularly attractive in autumn. There are fine views of the Cleveland Hills and of Tees Bay.
18 holes, 5803yds, Par 70, SSS 68. Membership 850.

Visitors welcome ⊠ Societies welcome (by letter)

▶

Green fees Not confirmed
Facilities ♀ ⚲ 🏠 ⛳
Hotel ★★★50% Marton Way Toby Hotel, Marton Rd, MIDDLESBROUGH ☎(0642) 817651 53⇨

SEATON CAREW
Map 5 G3

Seaton Carew	SCORE CARD: Brabazon Course				
☎ Hartlepool (0429) 266249	(White Tees)				
Tees Rd (SE side of village	Hole	Yds	Par	Hole	Yds	Par
off A178)	1	363	4	10	394	4
A championship links	2	555	5	11	477	5
course taking full	3	172	3	12	390	4
advantage of its dunes,	4	399	4	13	537	5
bents, whins and gorse.	5	385	4	14	512	5
Renowed for its par 4	6	165	3	15	208	3
(17th); just enough fairway	7	358	4	16	434	4
for an accurate drive	8	349	4	17	413	4
followed by another precise	9	363	4	18	375	4
shot to a pear-shaped,	Out	3109	35	In	3740	38
sloping green that is				Totals	6849	73

Seaton Carew
☎ Hartlepool (0429) 266249
Tees Rd (SE side of village off A178)
A championship links course taking full advantage of its dunes, bents, whins and gorse. Renowed for its par 4 (17th); just enough fairway for an accurate drive followed by another precise shot to a pear-shaped, sloping green that is severely trapped. Snooker.
The Old Course 18 holes, 6604yds, Par 72. Brabazon Course 18 holes, 6849yds, Par 73. Membership 650.

Visitors welcome Societies welcome (by letter)
Green fees £18 per day (£25 WE & BH)
Facilities ⊗ ⍢ 🍴 ⚲ ♀ ⚲ 🏠 ⛳ ⌊ W Hector
Hotel ★★★52% Billingham Arms Hotel, The Causeway, Billingham, STOCKTON-ON-TEES ☎(0642) 553661 69⇨🏠

STOCKTON-ON-TEES
Map 5 F3

Teesside ☎ (0642) 676249
Acklam Rd, Thornaby (1.5m SE on A1130)
Flat parkland course, easy walking.
18 holes, 6472yds, Par 72, SSS 71, Course record 65. Membership 500.

Visitors welcome (with M only weekdays after 1630, WE 1100) Societies welcome (☎)
Green fees £10 per day (£14 WE)
Facilities ⊗ ⍢ 🍴 ⚲ (no catering Mon) ♀ ⚲ 🏠 ⌊ Ken Hall
Hotel ★★★55% Post House Hotel, Low Ln, Thornaby-on-Tees, STOCKTON-ON-TEES ☎(0642) 591213 135⇨🏠

CORNWALL & ISLES OF SCILLY

BODMIN
Map 1 C6

Bodmin Golf & Country Club ☎ (0208) 73600 or 77325
Lanhydrock (2m SE)
New championship standard parkland/moorland course opening Spring 1991. Accommodation, changing-rooms and main catering facilities (lunch and dinner) under construction at time of going to press.
18 holes, 6142yds, Par 71.

Visitors welcome must contact in advance Societies welcome (☎)
Green fees Not confirmed

Facilities 🍴 ⚲ ♀ ⚲ 🏠 ⛳
Hotel ★★55% Westberry Hotel, Rhind St, BODMIN ☎(0208) 72772 15rm(5⇨4🏠) Annexe:8⇨🏠

BUDE
Map 1 D5

Bude & North Cornwall ☎ (0288) 352006
Burn View (N side of town)
Seaside links course with natural sand bunkers, superb greens and breathtaking views. Club established in 1891. Snooker.
18 holes, 6202yds, Par 71, SSS 70, Course record 70. Membership 850.

Visitors welcome Member must accompany must contact in advance Societies welcome (wkdays only)
Green fees £17 per day; (WE £25 per day)
Facilities ⊗ ⍢ 🍴 ⚲ ♀ (all day) ⚲ 🏠 ⌊ P J Yeo
Hotel ★★64% Camelot Hotel, Downs View, BUDE ☎(0288) 352361 21⇨🏠

CAMBORNE
Map 1 B7

Tehidy Park ☎ Portreath (0209) 842208
(2m NE off A30)
A well-maintained parkland course providing good holiday golf. Snooker.
18 holes, 6241yds, Par 72, SSS 70. Membership 1000.

Visitors welcome (handicap certificate required) must contact in advance ✉ Societies welcome (by letter h'cap cert mandatory)
Green fees £20 daily (£25 WE & BH); £15 per round (£20 WE & BH)
Facilities ⊗ ⍢ 🍴 ⚲ ♀ ⚲ 🏠 ⛳ ⌊ James Dumbreck
Hotel ★★★58% Penventon Hotel, REDRUTH ☎(0209) 214141 50⇨🏠

CARLYON BAY
Map 1 C7

Carlyon Bay Hotel ☎ (072681) 4228
(2.5m E of St Austell off A3082)
Championship-length cliff-top course moving into parkland. Magnificent views surpassed only by the quality of the course. The 230-yard (par 3) 18th, with railway and road out-of-bounds, holds the player's interest to the end. Accommodation.
18 holes, 6501yds, Par 72, SSS 71. Membership 550.

Visitors welcome must contact in advance Societies welcome
Green fees Not confirmed
Facilities ♀ ⚲ 🏠 ⛳ ⌊
Hotel ★★★61% Carlyon Bay Hotel, Sea Rd, Carlyon Bay, ST AUSTELL ☎(072681) 2304 70⇨

To see a full range of AA guides and maps, visit your local AA Shop or any good bookshop.

CONSTANTINE   Map 1 B6

Trevose
☎ Padstow (0841) 520208
(N side of village off B3276)
A pleasant holiday seaside
course with early holes
close to the sea on excellent
springy turf. It is a good
and enjoyable test. Self-
catering accommodation is
available at the club as well
as tennis, outdoor heated
swimming pool (May-Sept)
and snooker.
*18 holes, 6608yds, Par 71,
SSS 71. Short Course 9 holes, 1350yds, Par 29, SSS
29. Membership 650.*

SCORE CARD: Championship Tees					
Hole	Yds	Par	Hole	Yds	Par
1	443	4	10	467	4
2	386	4	11	199	3
3	166	3	12	448	4
4	500	5	13	507	5
5	461	4	14	317	4
6	323	4	15	327	4
7	428	4	16	225	3
8	156	3	17	388	4
9	451	5	18	416	4
Out	3314	36	In	3294	35
			Totals	6608	71

Visitors welcome (h'cap cert required for main
course) Member must accompany must contact in
advance ✉ Societies welcome (ex Jul-Sep)
Green fees £10-£25
Facilities ⊗ ﹒ ⅃ ⅃ ⅃ ⅃ ⅃ ⅃ ⅃ Gary Alliss
Hotel ★★★76% Treglos Hotel, CONSTANTINE BAY
☎(0841) 520727 44⊸⅃

We make every effort to provide accurate information, but some details may change after we
go to print.

FALMOUTH
Map 1 B8

Falmouth ☎ (0326) 311262
Swanpool Rd (SW side of town centre)
Seaside/parkland course with outstanding coastal
views. Sufficiently bunkered to punish any inaccurate
shots. Five acres of practice grounds with putting
green.
18 holes, 5581yds, Par 69, SSS 67, Course record 65.
Membership 600.

Visitors welcome must contact in advance Societies
welcome (by letter)
Green fees £20 per day; £15 per round
Facilities ⊗ ℳ by prior arrangement ⌶ ♨ ♀ ♨ ▥
⛳ ℭ David J Short
Hotel ★★★★76% Penmere Manor Hotel, Mongleath
Rd, FALMOUTH ☎(0326) 211411 39⇨↟

LAUNCESTON
Map 1 D6

Launceston ☎ (0566) 3442
St Stephens (NW side of town centre on B3254)
Undulating parkland course with views over the Tamar
Valley to Dartmoor and Bodmin Moor.
18 holes, 6055yds, Par 69, SSS 69, Course record 64.
Membership 800.

Visitors welcome must contact in advance ✉ Societies
welcome (by letter)
Green fees £17 per day (£15 WE)
Facilities ⊗ ℳ by prior arrangement ⌶ ♨ ♀ ♨ ▥
⛳ ℭ John Tozer
Hotel ★★★71% Arundell Arms, LIFTON ☎(0566)
84666 24⇨↟

LELANT
Map 1 A8

West Cornwall
☎ Penzance (0736) 753401
(N side of village off A3074)
A seaside links with
sandhills and lovely turf
adjacent to the Hayle
estuary and St Ives Bay. A
real test of the player's skill,
especially 'Calamity
Corner' starting at the 5th
on the lower land by the
River Hayle. A small (3
hole) course is available for
practice. Snooker.
18 holes, 5854yds, Par 69, SSS 68, Course record 65.
Membership 900.

SCORE CARD: White Tees					
Hole	Yds	Par	Hole	Yds	Par
1	229	3	10	305	4
2	382	4	11	362	4
3	342	4	12	494	5
4	352	4	13	264	4
5	179	3	14	446	4
6	333	4	15	135	3
7	191	3	16	521	5
8	325	4	17	194	3
9	406	4	18	394	4
Out	2739	33	In	3115	36
			Totals	5854	69

Visitors welcome
Green fees £14 daily (£18 WE); £12 round (£18 WE)
Facilities ⊗ ℳ ⌶ ♨ ♀ ♨ ▥ ⛳ ℭ Paul
Atherton
Hotel ★★58% Boskerris Hotel, Boskerris Rd,
Carbis Bay, ST IVES ☎(0736) 795295 18rm(16⇨↟)

LOOE
Map 1 D7

Looe ☎ Widegates (05034) 239
Widegates (3.5m NE off B3253)
Exposed and somewhat windy course on high moorland,
designed by Harry Vardon in 1934. Easy walking. Fine
views over Looe coastline.
18 holes, 5940yds, Par 70, SSS 68. Membership 550.

Visitors welcome Societies welcome (☎ 2 wks advance)
Green fees £22 per day; £15 per round (£25/18 WE &
BH)
Facilities ⊗ ℳ ⌶ ♨ ♀ ♨ ▥ ⛳
Hotel ★★★63% Hannafore Point Hotel, Marine Dr,
Hannafore, LOOE ☎(05036) 3273 38⇨↟

LOSTWITHIEL
Map 1 C7

Lostwithiel Golf & Country Club
☎ Bodmin (0208) 873550
Lower Polscoe (1m outside Lostwithiel off A390)
An 18-hole undulating, parkland course with water
hazards. Overlooked by Restormel Castle, and the River
Fowey flows alongside the course. Accommodation,
driving range and numerous sports and leisure
facilities.
18 holes, 6098yds, Par 72.

Visitors welcome (handicap cert required) must contact
in advance Societies welcome (☎)
Green fees Not confirmed
Facilities ⊗ (Sun only) ℳ ⌶ ♨ ♀ ♨ ▥ ℭ
Hotel ★★67% Restormel Lodge Hotel, Hillside
Gardens, LOSTWITHIEL ☎(0208) 872223 21⇨↟
Annexe:12⇨

MAWNAN SMITH
Map 1 B8

Budock Vean Hotel ☎ Falmouth (0326) 250288
(1.5m SW)
Undulating parkland course. Accommodation (see
below). Tennis, indoor heated swimming pool and
snooker.
9 holes, 5007yds, Par 68, SSS 65. Membership 250.

Visitors welcome (ex BHs) must contact in advance ✉
Societies welcome (hotel residents only)
Green fees Not confirmed
Facilities ♀ ♨ ▥ ⛳ ℭ David Short
Hotel ★★★69% Budock Vean Hotel, MAWNAN SMITH
☎(0326) 250288 59⇨↟

MULLION
Map 1 B8

Mullion ☎ (0326) 240685
Cury Cross Lanes (1.5m NW off A3083)
Links course with panoramic views of sea edge.
Well-known ravine hole (7th).
18 holes, 5616yds, Par 69, SSS 67, Course record 66.
Membership 860.

Visitors welcome (must have handicap certificate)
Societies welcome (☎)
Green fees Not confirmed

Facilities ⊗ ⫙ ᴸᴮ ᴸᴾ ♀ ⟰ ☖ ⌐ ⟮ M F Singleton
Hotel ★★★73% Polurrian Hotel, MULLION
☎(0326) 240421 39⟿⟰

NEWQUAY   Map 1 B7

Newquay ☎ (0637) 872091
Tower Rd (W side of town)
Seaside course close to the beach and open to wind.
Tennis, snooker and gymnasium.
18 holes, 6140yds, Par 69, SSS 69, Course record 63.
Membership 500.

Visitors welcome ✉ Societies welcome (☎)
Green fees £14 per day (£17 WE & BH)
Facilities ⊗ ⫙ (Tue-Sat) ᴸᴮ ᴸᴾ ♀ ⟰ ☖ ⟮ Paul
Muscroft
Hotel ★★★60% Hotel Mordros, 4 Pentire Av,
NEWQUAY ☎(0637) 876700 30⟿⟰

Treloy ☎ (0637) 872063
Treloy Tourist Park
A new 9-hole play-as-you-pay course (opening Spring
1991) constructed to American specifications with tees
and greens available all year round. Large contoured
and mounded greens. Offers an interesting round for all
categories of player.
9 holes, 2500yds, Par 32.

Visitors welcome must contact in advance Societies
welcome (☎ or letter)

Green fees Not confirmed
Facilities 🖭 ⛴ 🏠 ⛳ ⟨ Robert Sandon
Hotel ★★★60% Euro Hotel, Esplanade Rd, Pentire,
NEWQUAY ☎(0637) 873333 78rm(66⇔10♥)

PERRANPORTH   Map 1 B7

Perranporth ☎ Truro (0872) 572454
Budnick Hill (.75m NE on B3285)
There are three testing par 5 holes on this links course
(2nd, 5th, 11th) and a fine view over Perranporth Beach
from all holes. Snooker.
18 holes, 6286yds, Par 72, SSS 70. Membership 600.

Visitors welcome (restricted Sun am & competition
days) must contact in advance ✉ Societies welcome
(☎)
Green fees £15 per day (£18 WE & BH)
Facilities ⊗ 🍽 🖳 🖭 (no catering Mon) ⚲ ⛴ 🏠 ⛳
⟨ D Michell
Hotel ★67% Beach Dunes Hotel, Ramoth Way, Reen
Sands, PERRANPORTH ☎(0872) 572263 7rm(3⇔♥)
Annexe :3⇔♥

PORTWRINKLE   Map 1 D7

Whitsand Bay Hotel ☎ St Germans (0503) 30276
(E side of village off B3247)
Seaside course laid-out on cliffs overlooking Whitsand
Bay. Easy walking after 1st hole. The par 3 (3rd) hole is
well-known. Accommodation. Indoor heated swimming
pool, fishing, sauna, solarium and gymnasium.
*18 holes, 5512yds, Par 68, SSS 67, Course record 62.
Membership 450.*

Visitors welcome ✉ Societies welcome (☎)
Green fees Not confirmed
Facilities ⊗ by prior arrangement 🍽 by prior
arrangement ⚲ ⛴ 🏠 ⛳ ⟨ D S Poole
Hotel ★67% Whitsand Bay Hotel, Portwrinkle,
TORPOINT ☎(0503) 30276 30rm(28⇔)

PRAA SANDS   Map 1 A8

Praa Sands ☎ Penzance (0736) 763445
Germoe Cross Roads (N side of village on A394)
A parkland course with beautiful sea views from every
green and clubhouse.
*9 holes, 4036yds, Par 62, SSS 60, Course record 59.
Membership 300.*

Visitors welcome (restricted Fri pm & Sun am May-Sep)
Societies welcome (☎)
Green fees £10 per round
Facilities ⊗ 🍽 🖳 🖭 ⚲ ⛴ 🏠 ⛳ ⟨ Paul Atherton
Hotel ★★🏌70% Nansloe Manor Hotel, Meneage Rd,
HELSTON ☎(0326) 574691 7⇔♥

For a full list of the golf courses
included in this book, check
with the index on page 284

ROCK   Map 1 C6

St Enodoc ☎ Trebetherick (020886) 3216
(W side of village)
Seaside course with natural hazards.
*18 holes, 6207yds, Par 69, SSS 70, Course record 65.
Holywell Course 18 holes, 4165yds, Par 62, SSS 61.
Membership 1100.*

Visitors welcome ✉ Societies welcome (by letter)
Green fees Not confirmed
Facilities ⊗ 🍺 🖭 ⚲ ⛴ 🏠 ⛳ ⟨ Nick Williams
Hotel ★★67% St Enodoc Hotel, ROCK ☎(020886) 3394
13⇔♥

ST AUSTELL   Map 1 C7

St Austell ☎ (0726) 72649
Tregongeeves Ln (1m SW off A390)
Very interesting, inland parkland course designed by
James Braid. Undulating, well-covered with tree
plantations and well-bunkered. Notable holes are 8th
(par 4) and 16th (par 3).
*18 holes, 5981yds, Par 69, SSS 69, Course record 67.
Membership 800.*

Visitors welcome (h'cap cert required) Societies
welcome (by letter)
Green fees Not confirmed
Facilities ⊗ 🍽 🍺 🖭 ⚲ ⛴ 🏠 ⛳ ⟨
Hotel ★★★60% Porth Avallen Hotel, Sea Rd, Carlyon
Bay, ST AUSTELL ☎(072681) 2802 & 2183 23rm(18⇔1♥)

ST MARY'S

Isle of Scilly ☎ (0720) 22692
(1m N of Hugh Town)
Links course, glorious views.
9 holes, 2987yds, Par 36, SSS 69. Membership 300.

Visitors welcome
Green fees Not confirmed
Facilities ⚲ ⛴ ⛳
Hotel ★★Godolphin Hotel, Church St, Hugh Town,
ST MARY'S ☎(0720) 22316 31rm(25⇔2♥)

For reference:

Each golf course entry has a recommended
hotel. For a wider choice of places to stay,
consult *AA Hotels and Restaurants in Britain* or
AA-inspected Bed and Breakfast in Britain.

ST MELLION

Map 1 D6

St Mellion Golf & Country Club
☎ Liskeard (0579) 50101 (.5m NW off A388)
St Mellion is one of those fairly new, and delightful, resort courses which offers more than two 18 hole courses. Its Jack Nicklaus designed course has been featured on television - venue of the Benson and Hedges International Open. Accommodation. Tennis, indoor heated swimming pool, squash, snooker, sauna, solarium and gymnasium.
Nicklaus Course 18 holes, 6626yds, Par 72, SSS 72, Course record 65. The Old Course 18 holes, 5927yds, Par 70, SSS 68, Course record 62. Membership 4500.

SCORE CARD: Nicklaus Course					
Hole	Yds	Par	Hole	Yds	Par
1	400	4	10	410	4
2	518	5	11	181	3
3	356	4	12	525	5
4	175	3	13	361	4
5	315	4	14	158	3
6	420	4	15	411	4
7	480	5	16	520	5
8	135	3	17	426	4
9	375	4	18	460	4
Out	3174	36	In	3452	36
			Totals	6626	72

Visitors welcome (handicap certificate required) must contact in advance ✉ Societies welcome (by letter)
Green fees £50 per round (Nicklaus course) £17 (Old course)
Facilities ⊗ ⅲ ㏇ 📖 ♀ ⌂ 🏠 🍴 ⸙ Tony Moore
Hotel ★★★68% **St Mellion**, ST MELLION ☎Liskeard (0579) 50101 Annexe: 24⇨🛏

TRURO

Map 1 B7

Truro ☎ (0872) 72640
Treliske (1.5m W on A390)
Parkland course. Snooker.
18 holes, 5347yds, Par 66, SSS 66, Course record 61. Membership 900.

Visitors welcome (handicap certificate required) must contact in advance Societies welcome (by letter)
Green fees £15 per day (£20 WE & BH)
Facilities ⊗ ⅲ ㏇ 📖 ♀ (ex Sun) ⌂ 🏠 ⸙ ⸙ Nigel Bicknell
Hotel ★★★63% **Brookdale Hotel**, Tregolls Rd, TRURO ☎(0872) 73513 & 79305 21⇨🛏

CUMBRIA

ALSTON

Map 6 H7

Alston Moor ☎ (0434) 381675
The Hermitage (1.75m NE on B6277)
Meadowland course.
9 holes, 5380yds, Par 66, SSS 66. Membership 150.

Visitors welcome Societies welcome (☎)
Green fees Not confirmed
Facilities 📖 ♀ ⌂ ⸙
Hotel ★63% **Hillcrest Hotel**, Townfoot, ALSTON ☎(0434) 381251 & 381444 11rm

APPLEBY-IN-WESTMORLAND

Map 5 D3

Appleby ☎ Appleby-in-Westmoreland (07683) 51432
Brackenber Moor (1m E of Appleby .5m off A66)
This remotely situated, heather and moorland course offers interesting holiday golf with the rewarding bonus of several long par-4 holes that will be remembered. There are superb views. Snooker.
18 holes, 5755yds, Par 68, SSS 67. Membership 740.

Visitors welcome (restricted WE & BH) Societies welcome (by letter)
Green fees £10 per day (£14 WE & BH)
Facilities ⊗ ⅲ ㏇ 📖 ♀ ⌂ 🏠
Hotel ★★★♨68% **Appleby Manor Country House Hotel**, Roman Rd, APPLEBY-IN-WESTMORLAND ☎(07683) 51571 23⇨🛏 Annexe:7⇨🛏

ASKAM-IN-FURNESS

Map 5 B4

Dunnerholme ☎ Dalton-in-Furness (0229) 62675
Duddon Rd (1m N on A595)
Unique 10-hole (18 tee) links course with view of Lakeland hills, and a stream running through.
10 holes, 6181, Par 71, SSS 69. Membership 425.

Visitors welcome Societies welcome (☎)
Green fees £8 (£10 WE & BH)
Facilities ㏇ 📖 ♀ ⌂ 🏠
Hotel ★★61% **Eccle Riggs Hotel**, Foxfield Rd, BROUGHTON IN FURNESS ☎(0229) 716398 & 716780 12⇨🛏

BARROW-IN-FURNESS

Map 5 B5

Barrow ☎ (0229) 25444
Rakesmoor Ln, Hawcoat (2m N off A590)
Pleasant course laid out on meadowland with extensive views of the nearby Lakeland fells. Snooker.
18 holes, 6209yds, Par 71, SSS 70, Course record 66. Membership 560.

Visitors welcome must contact in advance Societies welcome (☎)
Green fees £10 per day
Facilities ⊗ ⅲ ㏇ 📖 ♀ ⌂ 🏠 ⸙ ⸙ Mark Booth
Hotel ★★66% **Lisdoonie Hotel**, 307/309 Abbey Rd, BARROW-IN-FURNESS ☎(0229) 27312 12⇨🛏

Furness ☎ (0229) 41232
Central Dr, Walney Island (1.75 E of town centre off A590)
Links golf with a fairly flat first half but a much sterner second nine played across subtle sloping ground. There are good views of the Lakes, North Wales and the Isle of Man. Snooker.
18 holes, 6363metres, Par 71, SSS 71, Course record 67. Membership 800.

Visitors welcome Societies welcome (by letter)
Green fees £10 per day
Facilities ⊗ by prior arrangement ⅲ ㏇ 📖 ♀ ⌂ 🏠 ⸙
Hotel ★★66% **Lisdoonie Hotel**, 307/309 Abbey Rd, BARROW-IN-FURNESS ☎(0229) 27312 12⇨🛏

BOWNESS-ON-WINDERMERE   Map 5 C4

Windermere ☎ Windermere (09662) 3123
Cleabarrow (1m E on B5284)
Enjoyable holiday golf on a short, slightly hilly but
sporting course in this delightful area of the Lake
District National Park. Superb views of the
mountains as the backcloth to the lake and the
course. Fishing. Snooker.
*18 holes, 5006yds, Par 67, SSS 65, Course record 58.
Membership 870.*

Visitors welcome (if M of recognised club with
h'cap cert) must contact in advance Societies
welcome (by letter)
Green fees £17 per day (£22 WE & BH)
Facilities ⊗ (ex Mon) ⊞ (ex Mon) ⅃ ⬛ ♀ ⤳ ⌷
⊤ ⸀ W S M Rooke
Hotel ★★★70% Wild Boar Hotel, Crook,
WINDERMERE ☎(09662) 5225 36⇥⋔

BRAMPTON   Map 6 H6

Brampton ☎ (06977) 2255
Talkin Tarn (1.5m SE of Brampton on B6413)
Challenging golf across glorious rolling fell country,
demanding solid driving and many long second
shots. A number of particularly fine holes, the pick
of which may arguably be, the 3rd and 11th. The
course offers unrivalled panoramic views from its
hilly position. Snooker.
*18 holes, 6420yds, Par 72, SSS 71, Course record 67.
Membership 750.*

Visitors welcome Societies welcome (by letter)
Green fees £12 wkdays (£16 WE)
Facilities ⊗ ⊞ ⅃ ⬛ ♀ ⤳ ⌷ ⊤ ⸀ Stephen
Harrison
Hotel ★★69% Tarn End Hotel, Talkin Tarn,
BRAMPTON ☎(06977) 2340 6⇥⋔

CARLISLE   Map 5 C2

Carlisle ☎ (0228) 513303
Aglionby (On A69 1m E of M6 junc 43)
Majestic looking parkland course with great appeal.
A complete but not too severe test of golf, with fine
turf, natural hazards, a stream and many beautiful
trees.
*18 holes, 6270yds, Par 71, SSS 70, Course record 65.
Membership 1000.*

Visitors welcome (with M on Sat, restricted Tue
pm/comps) must contact in advance ✉ Societies
welcome (Mon, Wed & Fri only ☎)
Green fees Summer £20, winter £10 (Sun £25)
Facilities ⊗ ⊞ ⅃ ⬛ ♀ ⤳ ⌷ ⊤ ⸀ John Smith
More
Hotel ★★★68% Cumbrian Hotel, Court Square,
CARLISLE ☎(0228) 31951 70⇥⋔

To see a full range of AA guides and maps, visit
your local AA Shop or any good bookshop.

Stony Holme Municipal ☎ (0228) 34856
St Aidans Rd (3m E off A69)
Municipal parkland course, bounded on three sides by
the River Eden.
*18 holes, 5783yds, Par 69, SSS 68, Course record 68.
Membership 350.*

Visitors welcome must contact in advance Societies
welcome (☎)
Green fees Not confirmed
Facilities ⊗ ⊞ ⅃ ⬛ ♀ ⤳ ⌷ ⊤ ⸀ S Ling
Hotel ★★★61% Crest Hotel, Parkhouse Rd,
Kingstown, CARLISLE ☎(0228) 31201 94⇥⋔

COCKERMOUTH   Map 5 B3

Cockermouth ☎ (07687) 76223
Embleton (3m E off A66)
Fell-land course, fenced, with exceptional views and a
hard climb on the 3rd and 11th holes. Testing holes:
10th and 11th (rearranged by James Braid). Snooker.
*18 holes, 5496yds, Par 69, SSS 67, Course record 65.
Membership 539.*

Visitors welcome (restricted Wed, Sat & Sun) Societies
welcome (☎ or letter)
Green fees £8 per round (£10 WE)
Facilities ⅃ ⬛ ♀ ⤳
Hotel ★★★61% The Trout Hotel, Crown St,
COCKERMOUTH ☎(0900) 823591 22⇥⋔

GRANGE-OVER-SANDS
Map 5 C4

Grange-over-Sands ☎ (05395) 33180
Meathop Rd (NW of town centre off B5277)
Parkland course with trees, ditches and easy walking.
18 holes, 5670yds, Par 69, SSS 68, Course record 64.
Membership 500.

Visitors welcome Societies welcome (by letter)
Green fees £15 per day (£20 WE & BH)
Facilities ⊗ by prior arrangement ⅏ by prior
arrangement ▙ by prior arrangement ☞ ♀ ⌂ ⛳
Hotel ★★★65% Grange Hotel, Lindale Rd, Station
Square, GRANGE-OVER-SANDS ☎(05395) 33666 41⇨�

Grange Fell ☎ (05395) 32536
Fell Rd (1m W)
Hillside course with magnificent views over
Morecambe Bay and the surrounding Lakeland
mountains.
9 holes, 2413mtrs, Par 70, SSS 66, Course record 68.
Membership 300.

Visitors welcome (closed most Sun)
Green fees £10 per day (£15 WE & BH)
Facilities ♀ ⌂
Hotel ★★69% Netherwood Hotel, Lindale Rd,
GRANGE-OVER-SANDS ☎(05395) 32552 33rm(27⇨🌮)

KENDAL
Map 5 C4

Kendal ☎ (0539) 724079
The Heights (W side of town centre)
Elevated moorland course affording breathtaking views
of Lakeland fells and surrounding district.
18 holes, 5534yds, Par 66, SSS 67, Course record 63.
Membership 700.

Visitors welcome (h'cap cert required) Societies
welcome (☎)
Green fees £12 per day (£16 WE & BH)
Facilities ⊗ (ex Mon) ⅏ (Tue-Sat) ☞ (ex Mon) ♀ ⌂
⌂ ⛳ ⌁ D J Turner
Hotel ★★★57% Woolpack Hotel, Stricklandgate,
KENDAL ☎(0539) 723852 53⇨🌮

KESWICK
Map 5 B3

Keswick ☎ Threlkeld (07687) 79324
Threlkeld Hall (4m E off A66)
Varied fell and tree-lined course with commanding
views of Lakeland scenery. Fishing.
18 holes, 6175yds, Par 71, SSS 72, Course record 69.
Membership 670.

Visitors welcome (restricted competition days) must
contact in advance Societies welcome (☎)
Green fees £10 per day (£15 WE)
Facilities ⊗ ⅏ by prior arrangement ▙ ☞ ♀ (Apr-
Oct) ⌂ ⌂ ⛳ ⌁ Harry Waller
Hotel ★★★67% Borrowdale Hotel, BORROWDALE
☎(07687) 77224 34⇨🌮

MARYPORT
Map 5 B2

Maryport ☎ (0900) 812605
Bank End (1m N on B5300)
A tight seaside links course exposed to Solway breezes.
Fine views across Solway Firth.
18 holes, 6272yds, Par 71, SSS 71, Course record 70.
Membership 380.

Visitors welcome Societies welcome (☎)
Green fees £10 per day (£12 WE & BH)
Facilities ⊗ (by prior arrangement Mon-Fri) ▙ ☞ ♀
⌂
Hotel ★★64% Ellenbank Hotel, Birkby, MARYPORT
☎(0900) 815233 26⇨🌮

PENRITH
Map 5 C3

Penrith ☎ (0768) 62217
Salkeld Rd (.75m N off A6)
A beautiful and well-balanced course, always
changing direction, and demanding good length
from the tee. It is set on rolling moorland with
occasional pine trees and some fine views. Snooker.
18 holes, 6026yds, Par 69, SSS 69, Course record 64.
Membership 870.

Visitors welcome (restricted WE) must contact in
advance ✉ Societies welcome (restricted WE)
Green fees £15 per day (£20 WE & BH)
Facilities ⌂ ⌂ ⛳ ⌁
Hotel ★★64% George Hotel, Devonshire St,
PENRITH ☎(0768) 62696 31⇨🌮

ST BEES
Map 5 A3

St Bees ☎ (0946) 823987
(.5m W of village off B5345)
Links course, down hill and dale, with sea views.
9 holes, 5082yds, Par 64, SSS 65. Membership 275.

Visitors welcome
Green fees Not confirmed
Hotel ★★★56% Blackbeck Bridge Inn, EGREMONT
☎(094684) 661 22⇨🌮

SEASCALE
Map 5 B4

Seascale ☎ (09467) 28202
The Banks (NW side of village off B5344)
A tough links requiring length and control. The
natural terrain is used to give a variety of holes and
considerable character. Undulating greens add to
the challenge.
18 holes, 6419yds, Par 71, SSS 71, Course record 69.
Membership 700.

Visitors welcome must contact in advance Societies
welcome (☎)
Green fees £15 per day (£18 WE & BH)

This guide is updated annually – make sure you
use an up-to-date edition.

Facilities ⊗ ⨌ ▙ ▆ (all catering by prior arrangement Mon-Tue) ♀ △ 🏠 ⛳
Hotel ★★★56% Blackbeck Bridge Inn, EGREMONT ☎(094684) 661 22⇥🏌

SEDBERGH

Map 5 D4

Sedbergh ☎ (05396) 20993
The Riggs (1m S off A683)
Open fell course, very hilly. Rough, with natural hazards, and hard walking. Four short, par 3's.
9 holes, 2167yds, Par 64, SSS 61, Course record 64. Membership 80.

Visitors welcome (ex Sun am) Societies welcome
Green fees £3 per day
Facilities △
Hotel ★★69% Garden House Hotel, Fowl-ing Ln, KENDAL ☎(0539) 731131 10⇥🏌

SILECROFT

Map 5 B4

Silecroft ☎ Millom (0229) 774250
(1m SW)
Seaside links course parallel to the coast of the Irish Sea. Often windy. Easy walking. Spectacular views inland of Lakeland hills.
9 holes, 5712yds, Par 68, SSS 68. Membership 400.

Visitors welcome (restricted WE) Societies welcome (14 days notice ☎)
Green fees £8 per day
Facilities △
Hotel ★★61% Eccle Riggs Hotel, Foxfield Rd, BROUGHTON IN FURNESS ☎(0229) 716398 & 716780 12⇥🏌

SILLOTH

Map 6 F6

Silloth on Solway
☎ (06973) 31304
(S side of village off B5300)
Billowing dunes, narrow fairways and constant subtle problems of tactics and judgement, make these superb links on the Solway an exhilarating and searching test. The 13th is a good long hole. Snooker.
18 holes, 6343yds, Par 72, SSS 71, Course record 68. Membership 600.

SCORE CARD					
Hole	Yds	Par	Hole	Yds	Par
1	380	4	10	308	4
2	325	4	11	389	4
3	362	4	12	192	3
4	377	4	13	482	5
5	486	5	14	484	5
6	184	3	15	417	4
7	408	4	16	179	3
8	183	4	17	486	5
9	127	3	18	387	4
Out	3019	35	In	3324	37
			Totals	6343	72

Visitors welcome (ex pre 0930, 0930-1130 Sat, 1100-1300 Sun) must contact in advance ✉ Societies welcome (☎)
Green fees £14 (£20, one round only WE & BH)
Facilities ⊗ ⨌ by prior arrangement ▙ ▆ ♀ △ 🏠 ⛳ ✦ John Burns
Hotel ★★66% Golf Hotel, Criffel St, SILLOTH ☎(06973) 31438 22⇥🏌

ULVERSTON

Map 5 B4

Ulverston ☎ (0229) 52824
Bardsea Park (2m S off A5087)
Inland golf of a comparatively quiet nature with many medium length holes on undulating parkland. The two-shot 3rd will stand comparison anywhere and the 17th is a testing par 4.
18 holes, 6142yds, Par 71, SSS 69, Course record 66. Membership 700.

Visitors welcome (ex competition days) must contact in advance ✉ Societies welcome (☎)
Green fees £16 per day (£20 WE & BH)
Facilities ⊗ ⨌ ▙ ▆ (catering limited on Mon) ♀ (ex Mon) △ 🏠 ⛳ ✦ M R Smith
Hotel ★★58% Sefton House Hotel, Queen St, ULVERSTON ☎(0229) 52190 14rm(4⇥6🏌)

WORKINGTON

Map 5 A3

Workington ☎ (0900) 603460
Branthwaite Rd (1.75m off A596)
Meadowland course, undulating, with natural hazards created by stream and trees. Good views of Solway Firth and Lakeland Hills. Snooker.
18 holes, 6202yds, Par 72, Course record 65. Membership 700.

Visitors welcome (h'cap cert required) ✉ Societies welcome (☎)
Green fees £12-£20
Facilities ⊗ (ex Mon) ⨌ (ex Mon-Thu) ▙ (ex Mon) ♀ △ 🏠 ⛳ ✦ N Summerfield
Hotel ★★★67% Washington Central Hotel, Washington St, WORKINGTON ☎(0900) 65772 40⇥🏌

DERBYSHIRE

ALFRETON

Map 3 K2

Alfreton ☎ (O773) 832070
Wingfield Rd, Oakerthorpe (1m W on A615)
A small parkland course with tight fairways and many natural hazards.
9 holes, 5074yds, Par 66, SSS 65. Membership 280.

Visitors welcome (with M only Mon & WE) Societies welcome (☎)
Green fees £12 per day; £10 per round
Facilities ⊗ (ex Mon) ⨌ by prior arrangement ▙ ▆ ♀ △ 🏠
Hotel ★★★62% Swallow Hotel, Carter Ln East, SOUTH NORMANTON ☎(0773) 812000 123⇥🏌

ASHBOURNE

Map 3 J3

Ashbourne ☎ (0335) 42078
Clifton (1.5m SW on A515)
Undulating parkland course. Snooker.
9 holes, 5359yds, Par 66, SSS 66. Membership 350.

Visitors welcome (ex competition days) Societies welcome (☎)
Green fees £6 per day (£10 WE & BH)

▶

Facilities ⊗ ⑈ ⓛ ⬛ (no catering Tue and Thu am) ⚑ ⌂

Hotel ★★63% Meynell Arms Hotel, Ashbourne Rd, KIRK LANGLEY ☎(033124) 515 10rm(5⇆2♠)

BAKEWELL   Map 3 J2

Bakewell ☎ (0629) 812307
Station Rd (E side of town off A6)
Parkland course, hilly, with plenty of natural hazards to test the golfer. Magnificent views across the Wye Valley.
9 holes, 5240yds, Par 68, SSS 66. Membership 400.

Visitors welcome Societies welcome
Green fees Not confirmed
Facilities ⚑ ⌂ 🖻 ⌇
Hotel ★★66% Milford House Hotel, Mill St, BAKEWELL ☎(0629) 812130 12⇆♠

BAMFORD   Map 5 F8

Sickleholme ☎ Hope Valley (0443) 51306
Saltergate Ln (.75m S on A6013)
Downland type course in the lovely Peak District. Fine views.
18 holes, 6064yds, Par 69, SSS 69. Membership 600.

Visitors welcome (restricted Wed am) must contact in advance Societies welcome (☎)
Green fees Not confirmed
Facilities ⊗ by prior arrangement ⑈ by prior arrangement ⓛ by prior arrangement ⬛ by prior arrangement ⚑ ⌂ 🖻 ⌇ P H Taylor
Hotel ★★★64% George Hotel, Main Rd, HATHERSAGE ☎(0433) 50436 18⇆♠

BUXTON   Map 3 J2

Buxton & High Peak ☎ (0298) 23453
Town End (1m NE off A6)
Meadowland course in the Peak District.
18 holes, 5701yds, Par 69, SSS 68. Membership 500.

Visitors welcome must contact in advance ☎ Societies welcome
Green fees Not confirmed
Facilities ⚑ ⌂ 🖻 ⌐
Hotel ★★★60% Palace Hotel, Palace Rd, BUXTON ☎(0298) 22001 122⇆

Each golf course entry has a recommended hotel. For a wider choice of places to stay, consult *AA Hotels and Restaurants in Britain* or *AA-inspected Bed and Breakfast in Britain.*

Cavendish ☎ (0298) 23494
Gadley Ln (.75m W of town centre off A53)
This parkland/downland course with its comfortable clubhouse nestles below the rising hills. Generally open to the prevailing west wind, it is noted for its excellent surfaced greens which contain many deceptive subtleties. Good holes include the 8th, 9th and 18th. Snooker.
18 holes, 5833yds, Par 68, SSS 68. Membership 600.

SCORE CARD: White Tees					
Hole	Yds	Par	Hole	Yds	Par
1	365	4	10	443	4
2	321	4	11	411	4
3	284	4	12	357	4
4	123	3	13	184	3
5	428	4	14	509	5
6	410	4	15	127	3
7	314	4	16	408	4
8	388	4	17	168	3
9	143	3	18	450	4
Out	2776	34	In	3057	34
			Totals	5833	68

Visitors welcome must contact in advance Societies welcome (☎ (0298) 25052)
Green fees £20 per day (£30 WE & BH)
Facilities ⊗ by prior arrangement ⑈ (by prior arrangement 24 hrs) ⓛ ⬛ ⚑ ⌂ 🖻 ⌐ ⌇ John Nolan
Hotel ★★★66% Lee Wood Hotel, 13 Manchester Rd, BUXTON ☎(0298) 23002 & 70421 38⇆♠

CHAPEL-EN-LE-FRITH   Map 5 E8

Chapel-en-le-Frith ☎ (0298) 812118
The Cockyard, Manchester Rd (1m W on A6)
Fairly easy parkland course, with testing holes at the 15th (par 4) and 17th (517 yds), par 5. Good views.
18 holes, 6089yds, Par 70, SSS 69. Membership 643.

Visitors welcome must contact in advance Societies welcome (by letter)
Green fees £12 per day (£20 WE & BH)
Facilities ⊗ ⑈ by prior arrangement ⓛ ⬛ ⚑ ⌂ 🖻 ⌐ ⌇ D J Cullen
Hotel ★★★66% Lee Wood Hotel, 13 Manchester Rd, BUXTON ☎(0298) 23002 & 70421 38⇆♠

CHESTERFIELD   Map 3 K2

Chesterfield ☎ (0246) 279256
Walton (2m SW off A632)
A varied and interesting, undulating parkland course with trees picturesquely adding to the holes and the outlook alike. Stream hazard on back nine. Snooker.
18 holes, 6326yds, Par 71, SSS 70, Course record 65. Membership 850.

Visitors welcome (except WE) must contact in advance Societies welcome (☎ or by letter)
Green fees £20 per day
Facilities ⌂ 🖻 ⌇ M McLean
Hotel ★★★64% Chesterfield Hotel, Malkin St, CHESTERFIELD ☎(0246) 271141 72⇆♠

We make every effort to provide accurate information, but some details may change after we go to print.

Stanedge ☎ (0246) 566156
Walton Hay Farm, Walton (5m SW off B5057)
Moorland course in hilly situation open to strong
winds. Some fairways are narrow. Accuracy is
paramount.
18 holes, 4867yds, Par 64, SSS 64, Course record 64.
Membership 300.

Visitors welcome (wkdays to 1400, Sat & Sun with M)
Societies welcome (by letter)
Green fees £8 per round
Facilities � symbols
Hotel ★★★64% Chesterfield Hotel, Malkin St,
CHESTERFIELD ☎(0246) 271141 72⇨🛏

Tapton Park ☎ (0246) 273887
Murray House, Tapton (.5m E of Chesterfield Station)
Parkland course with some fairly hard walking. The 626
yd (par 5) 5th is a testing hole. Pitch-and-putt course.
18 holes, 5242yds, Par 70, SSS 69. Membership 486.

Visitors welcome (no caddies) must contact in advance
Societies welcome (☎)
Green fees Not confirmed
Facilities ♀ ⛳ 🏠 🔧 🍴
Hotel ★★★64% Chesterfield Hotel, Malkin St,
CHESTERFIELD ☎(0246) 271141 72⇨🛏

CODNOR   Map 3 K3

Ormonde Fields ☎ Ripley (0773) 742987
Nottingham Rd (1m SE on A610)
Parkland course with undulating fairways and natural
hazards. The par 4 (4th) and the par 3 (11th) are notable.
There is a practice area.
18 holes, 6011yds, Par 69, SSS 69, Course record 70.
Membership 500.

Visitors welcome (restricted WE) must contact in
advance Societies welcome (☎)
Green fees £10 (£15 WE & BH)
Facilities ⊗ 🏵 ⛳ 🏠 ♀ ⛳ 🏠 🔧 🍴 Stuart Betteridge
Hotel ★★★52% Post House Hotel, Bostocks Ln,
SANDIACRE ☎(0602) 397800 107⇨🛏

DERBY   Map 3 K3

Allestree Park ☎ (0332) 550616
Allestree Hall (3m N on A6)
Municipal parkland course in rather hilly country.
18 holes, 5749yds, Par 68, SSS 68, Course record 64.
Membership 250.

Visitors welcome (restricted WE & BH) Societies
welcome (restricted WE & BH)
Green fees £3.80 (£4.80 WE)
Facilities ⛳ 🏠 (lunchtime) ♀ ⛳ 🏠 🔧 🍴 Robert
Brown
Hotel ★★70% Kedleston Hotel, Kedleston Rd,
Quarndon, DERBY ☎(0332) 559202 & 556507 14⇨🛏

For an explanation of the symbols and
abbreviations used, see page 33.

Derby ☎ (0332) 766323
Shakespeare St, Sinfin (3.5m S of city centre)
Parkland course.
18 holes, 6144yds, Par 70, SSS 69, Course record 66.
Membership 450.

Visitors welcome (starting time must be booked at
weekend) must contact in advance Societies welcome
(☎)
Green fees Not confirmed
Facilities ⊗ ⛳ 🏠 ♀ ⛳ 🏠 🔧 🍴 Robert Brown PGA
Hotel ★★★61% International Hotel, Burton Rd
(A5250), DERBY ☎(0332) 369321 41⇨🛏 Annexe:10⇨🛏

Mickleover ☎ (0332) 513339
Uttoxeter Rd, Mickleover (3m W off A516/B5020)
Undulating parkland course in pleasant setting.
18 holes, 5702yds, Par 69, SSS 67, Course record 64.
Membership 650.

Visitors welcome must contact in advance Societies
welcome (☎)
Green fees £15 per day (£20 WE)
Facilities ⊗ 🏵 ⛳ 🏠 ♀ ⛳ 🏠 🔧 🍴 Paul Wilson
Hotel ★★★68% Crest Hotel, Pasture Hill, Littleover,
DERBY ☎(0332) 514933 66⇨🛏 Annexe:2⇨🛏

DRONFIELD   Map 3 K2

Hallowes ☎ (0246) 413734
Hallowes Ln (S side of town)
Attractive moorland course set in the Derbyshire hills.
Several testing Par 4's and splendid views.
18 holes, 6330yds, Par 71, SSS 70, Course record 66.
Membership 600.

Visitors welcome (WE with M, restricted Wed) must
contact in advance ✉ Societies welcome (pre booked)
Green fees £22 per day; £18 per round
Facilities ⊗ 🏵 ⛳ 🏠 ♀ ⛳ 🏠 🍴 Martin Heggie
Hotel ★★53% Manor Hotel, 10 High St, DRONFIELD
☎(0246) 413971 10⇨🛏

DUFFIELD   Map 3 K3

Chevin ☎ (0332) 841864
Golf Ln (N side of town off A6)
A mixture of parkland and moorland, this course is
rather hilly which makes for some hard walking. The
8th calls for a very hard drive. Snooker.
18 holes, 6057yds, Par 69, SSS 69, Course record 65.
Membership 500.

Visitors welcome (with member only WE & BH) must
contact in advance ✉
Green fees £22
Facilities ⊗ ⛳ 🏠 ♀ ⛳ 🏠 🍴 Willie Bird
Hotel ★★70% Kedleston Hotel, Kedleston Rd,
Quarndon, DERBY ☎(0332) 559202 & 556507 14⇨🛏

To see a full range of AA guides and maps, visit
your local AA Shop or any good bookshop.

GLOSSOP
Map 5 E7

Glossop and District ☎ (04574) 3117
Hurst Ln, off Sheffield Rd (1m E off A57)
Moorland course in good position, excellent natural hazards.
11 holes, 5723yds, Par 68, SSS 68. Membership 250.

Visitors welcome (ex BH)
Green fees Not confirmed
Facilities ♀ (ex Thu in winter) 🏌 📷
Hotel ★★70% York House Hotel, York Place, Richmond St, ASHTON-UNDER-LYNE ☎061-330 5899 24rm(18⇨5🏠) Annexe:10⇨

KEDLESTON
Map 3 K3

Kedleston Park
☎ Derby (0332) 840035
Kedleston Quarndon (2m SE)
The course is laid out in mature parkland with fine trees and background views of historic Kedleston Hall. Many testing holes are included in each nine and there is an excellent modern clubhouse. Snooker and sauna.
18 holes, 6289yds, Par 70, SSS 70. Membership 850.

			SCORE CARD		
Hole	Yds	Par	Hole	Yds	Par
1	491	5	10	358	4
2	415	4	11	184	3
3	413	4	12	414	4
4	163	3	13	369	4
5	551	5	14	332	4
6	506	5	15	408	4
7	163	3	16	184	3
8	312	4	17	519	5
9	404	4	18	425	4
Out	3418	37	In	3198	35
			Totals	6611	72

Visitors welcome (ex WE) must contact in advance ✉ Societies welcome (☎)
Green fees £20 per day; £15 per round
Facilities ⊗ 🍴 ⅃ 💪 ♀ 🏌 📷 ⛳ ⌊ Jim Hetherington
Hotel ★★70% Kedleston Hotel, Kedleston Rd, Quarndon, DERBY ☎(0332) 559202 & 556507 14⇨🏠

MATLOCK
Map 3 K2

Matlock ☎ (0629) 582191
Chesterfield Rd (1m NE of Matlock on A632)
Moorland course with fine views of the beautiful Peak District. Snooker.
18 holes, 5756yds, Par 70, SSS 68. Membership 620.

Visitors welcome (with M only WE & BH) Societies welcome (☎: not WE & BH)
Green fees £18 per day/round
Facilities ⊗ by prior arrangement 🍴 by prior arrangement ⅃ 💪 (ex Mon) ♀ 🏌 📷 ⌊ M Deeley
Hotel ★★★58% New Bath Hotel, New Bath Rd, MATLOCK ☎(0629) 583275 55⇨

This guide is updated annually – make sure you use an up-to-date edition.

MICKLEOVER
Map 3 K3

Pastures ☎ Derby (0332) 513921 (ext 348)
Pastures Hospital (1m SW off A516)
Small course laid-out on undulating meadowland in the grounds of a psychiatric hospital, with good views across the Trent valley. Fishing and snooker.
9 holes, 5005yds, Par 64, SSS 64, Course record 62. Membership 320.

Visitors welcome (ex Sun) Member must accompany must contact in advance Societies welcome (☎)
Green fees £7 per day
Facilities ♀ 🏌
Hotel ★★★61% International Hotel, Burton Rd (A5250), DERBY ☎(0332) 369321 41⇨🏠 Annexe:10⇨

MORLEY
Map 3 K3

Breadsall Priory ☎ Derby (0332) 832235
Moor Rd (.75m W)
Wooded parkland course set in 200 acres of beautiful countryside, the site of a 13th century priory. The hotel provides a host of sports and leisure facilities.
18 holes, 5844yds, Par 72, SSS 70, Course record 66. Membership 750.

Visitors welcome must contact in advance Societies welcome (☎ & by letter)
Green fees £20 per day; (£22 WE & BH)
Facilities ⊗ 🍴 ⅃ 💪 ♀ 🏌 📷 ⌊ Andrew Smith
Hotel Breadsall Priory Hotel, Golf & Country Club, Moor Rd, MORLEY ☎(0332) 832235 94⇨🏠

NEW MILLS
Map 5 E8

New Mills ☎ (0663) 743485
Shaw Marsh (.5m N off B6101)
Moorland course with panoramic views and first-class greens.
9 holes, 5633yds, Par 68, SSS 67, Course record 67. Membership 350.

Visitors welcome (with M only WE & special days) must contact in advance Societies welcome (☎)
Green fees £8 (£10 WE)
Facilities ⊗ by prior arrangement 🍴 by prior arrangement ⅃ 💪 ♀ 🏌 📷 ⛳ ⌊ Andrew Hoyles
Hotel ★★★62% Alma Lodge Hotel, 149 Buxton Rd, STOCKPORT ☎061-483 4431 58rm(52⇨)

RENISHAW
Map 3 K2

Renishaw Park ☎ Eckington (0246) 432044
Golf House (.5m NW on A616)
Part parkland and part meadowland with easy walking. Snooker.
18 holes, 5949yds, Par 71, SSS 68. Membership 500.

Visitors welcome Societies welcome (by letter)
Green fees Not confirmed
Facilities ⊗ 🍴 by prior arrangement ⅃ 💪 ♀ 🏌 📷 ⛳ ⌊ Simon Elliot
Hotel ★★★64% Sitwell Arms Osprey Hotel, RENISHAW ☎(0246) 435226 30⇨🏠

SHIRLAND

Map 3 K2

Shirlands Golf & Squash Club ☎ (0773) 834935
Lower Delves (S side of village off A61)
Rolling parkland and tree-lined course with extensive
views of Derbyshire countryside.
18 holes, 6072yds, Par 71, SSS 69, Course record 67.
Membership 350.

Visitors welcome (WE by appointment) must contact in
advance Societies welcome (contact Professional)
Green fees Not confirmed
Facilities ⌂ 🏠 ⛳ (Neville Hallam
Hotel ★★★62% Swallow Hotel, Carter Ln East,
SOUTH NORMANTON ☎(0773) 812000 123⇨🏌

STANTON-BY-DALE

Map 3 K3

Erewash Valley ☎ Sandiacre (0602) 323258
(1m W)
Parkland/meadowland course overlooking valley and
M1. Unique 4th and 5th in Victorian quarry bottom:
5th-testing par 3. Snooker.
18 holes, 6487yds, Par 72, SSS 71, Course record 67.
Membership 860.

Visitors welcome (ex before 1200 WE & BH) must
contact in advance preferably with introduction
Societies welcome (by letter)
Green fees £20 per day (£20 per round WE & BH)
Facilities ⊗ by prior arrangement 🏵 by prior
arrangement 🖼 ☕ ♀ ⌂ 🏠 (M J Ronan
Hotel ★★★52% Post House Hotel, Bostocks Ln,
SANDIACRE ☎(0602) 397800 107⇨🏌

DEVON

AXMOUTH

Map 1 G6

Axe Cliff ☎ Seaton (0297) 24371
(.75m S on B3172)
Undulating links course with coastal views.
18 holes, 5056yds, Par 67, SSS 65. Membership 400.

Visitors welcome (Sun only after 1300) must contact in
advance Societies welcome
Green fees Not confirmed
Facilities ⊗ 🏵 by prior arrangement 🖼 ☕ ♀ ⌂ 🏠
⛳
Hotel ★★60% Anchor Inn, BEER ☎(0297) 20386
9rm(2⇨2🏌)

BIGBURY-ON-SEA

Map 1 E7

Bigbury ☎ (0548) 810557
Kingsbridge (1m S on B3392)
Downland course with easy walking. Exposed to winds.
18 holes, 5862yds, Par 69, SSS 68. Membership 850.

Visitors welcome (handicap certificate required) must
contact in advance Societies welcome (☎)
Green fees Not confirmed

Facilities ⊗ 🏵 by prior arrangement 🖼 ☕ ♀ ⌂ 🏠
⛳ (Simon Lloyd
Hotel ★69%, Henley Hotel, BIGBURY-ON-SEA ☎(0548)
810240 8rm(6⇨🏌)

BUDLEIGH SALTERTON

Map 1 F6

East Devon ☎ (03954) 3370
North View Rd (W side of
town centre off A376)
An interesting course with
downland turf, much
heather and gorse, and
superb views over the bay.
The early holes climb to the
cliff edge. The downhill
17th, has a heather section
in the fairway leaving a
good second to the green.
18 holes, 6214yds, Par 70,
SSS 70. Membership 850.

SCORE CARD: White Tees					
Hole	Yds	Par	Hole	Yds	Par
1	343	4	10	155	3
2	341	4	11	337	4
3	414	4	12	483	5
4	151	3	13	143	3
5	361	4	14	404	4
6	524	5	15	301	4
7	392	4	16	402	4
8	206	3	17	453	4
9	464	4	18	340	4
Out	3196	35	In	3018	35
			Totals	6214	70

Visitors welcome must contact in advance ✉
Societies welcome (by letter)
Green fees Not confirmed
Facilities ⊗ 🏵 🖼 ☕ ♀ ⌂ 🏠 ⛳ (Trevor
Underwood
Hotel ★★★58% The Imperial, The Esplanade,
EXMOUTH ☎(0395) 274761 57⇨🏌

CHITTLEHAMHOLT

Map 1 E5

Highbullen Hotel
☎ (07694) 561 due to change to (0769) 540561
A 9-hole, par 31, parkland course with water hazards
and outstanding scenic views to Exmoor and Dartmoor.
Excellent sports, leisure and accommodation facilities
are offered by the hotel.
9 holes, 2024yds, Par 31, SSS 30, Course record 29.

Visitors welcome (dress restrictions)
Green fees £8 per day, £6 after 5pm (free to hotel
residents)
Facilities ⊗ 🏵 🖼 ☕ ♀ ⌂ 🏠 ⛳ (Paul Weston
Hotel ★★★🏌74%, Highbullen Hotel,
CHITTLEHAMHOLT ☎(07694) 561 12⇨ Annexe:23⇨

CHULMLEIGH

Map 1 E5

Chulmleigh ☎ (0769) 80519
Leigh Rd (SW side of village)
Challenging par 3 courses on undulating meadowland.
Tennis.
Summer Course 18 holes, 1450yds, Par 54, SSS 54, Course
record 52. Winter Course 9 holes, 2360yds, Par 58, SSS 58,
Course record 62. Membership 150.

Visitors welcome Societies welcome (☎)
Green fees £8 per day; £4 per round
Facilities ⊗ 🖼 ☕ ♀ ⌂ 🏠 ⛳ (Michael Blackwell
Hotel ★★🏌73% Marsh Hall Hotel, SOUTH MOLTON
☎(07695) 2666 7⇨🏌

CHURSTON FERRERS
Map 1 F7

Churston
☏ Churston (0803) 842751
(NW side of village on A379)
A cliff-top, downland course with splendid views over Brixham harbour and Tor Bay. There is some gorse with a wooded area inland. A variety of shot is called for, with particularly testing holes at the 3rd, 9th and 15th - all par 4.
18 holes, 6219yds, Par 70, SSS 70, Course record 64. Membership 600.

SCORE CARD: White Tees					
Hole	Yds	Par	Hole	Yds	Par
1	242	3	10	296	4
2	378	4	11	354	4
3	437	4	12	412	4
4	173	3	13	296	4
5	558	5	14	519	5
6	473	4	15	345	4
7	341	4	16	326	4
8	168	3	17	175	3
9	387	4	18	339	4
Out	3157	34	In	3062	36
			Totals	6219	70

Visitors welcome (ex before 0900) must contact in advance ✉ Societies welcome (☏)
Green fees £20 (£25 WE)
Facilities ⊗ ⅢI by prior arrangement ⅃ ■ ♀ ⅃
🏠 ⎰ R Penfold
Hotel ★★60% Dainton Hotel, 95 Dartmouth Rd, Three Beaches, Goodrington, PAIGNTON ☏(0803) 550067 & 525901 11⇦🐾

CREDITON
Map 1 F5

Downes Crediton ☏ (03632) 3991 & 3025
Hookway (1.5m SE off A377)
Converted farmhouse course with lovely views. Parkland with hilly back nine.
18 holes, 5868yds, Par 69, SSS 68. Membership 700.

Visitors welcome (restricted WE) must contact in advance Societies welcome (☏)
Green fees £15 per day (£20 WE & BH)
Facilities ⊗ ⅢI ⅃ ■ ♀ ⅃ 🏠 ⎰ ⎰ H Finch
Hotel ★★★73% Barton Cross Hotel & Restaurant, Huxham, STOKE CANON ☏(0392) 841245 & 841584 6⇦🐾

DAWLISH WARREN
Map 1 F6

Warren ☏ (0626) 862255
(W side of village)
Typical flat, genuine links course lying on spit between sea and Exe estuary. Picturesque scenery, a few trees but much gorse. Testing in windy conditions. The 7th hole provides the opportunity to go for the green across a bay on the estuary.
18 holes, 5968yds, Par 69, SSS 69, Course record 65. Membership 600.

Visitors welcome (handicap certificate required) must contact in advance Societies welcome (☏)
Green fees £17 per day (£20 WE)
Facilities ⊗ ⅢI ⅃ ■ ♀ ⅃ 🏠 ⎰ ⎰ Geoff Wicks
Hotel ★★★59% Langstone Cliff Hotel, Dawlish Warren, DAWLISH ☏(0626) 865155 64⇦🐾

For an explanation of the symbols and abbreviations used, see page 33.

EXETER
Map 1 F5

Exeter ☏ Topsham (039287) 4139
Topsham Rd, Countess Wear (SE side of city centre off A379)
A sheltered parkland course known as the flattest course in Devon. 15th & 17th are testing par 4 holes. Tennis, outdoor and indoor swimming pools (heated), squash, snooker, sauna, solarium and gymnasium.
18 holes, 5993yds, Par 69, SSS 69, Course record 62. Membership 850.

Visitors welcome must contact in advance ✉ Societies welcome (Thu only ☏)
Green fees £20 per day
Facilities ⊗ ⅢI ⅃ ■ ♀ ⅃ 🏠 ⎰
Hotel ★★★61% Countess Wear Lodge Hotel, Topsham Rd, Exeter Bypass, EXETER ☏(0392) 875441 44⇦🐾

HOLSWORTHY
Map 1 D5

Holsworthy ☏ (0409) 253177
Killatree (1.5m W on A3072)
Pleasant parkland course.
18 holes, 6012yds, Par 70, SSS 69, Course record 66. Membership 530.

Visitors welcome (ex WE & competition days) Societies welcome (by letter)
Green fees £10 per day ; £40 per week
Facilities ⊗ ⅢI ⅃ ■ ♀ ⅃ 🏠 ⎰ ⎰ Tim McSherry
Hotel ★★★68% Court Barn Country House Hotel, CLAWTON ☏(040927) 219 8rm(4⇦3🐾)

HONITON
Map 1 G5

Honiton ☏ (0404) 44422
Middlehills (1.25m SE)
Level parkland course with easy walking and good views. 4th hole is a testing par 3.
18 holes, 5931yds, Par 68, SSS 68. Membership 800.

Visitors welcome must contact in advance ✉ Societies welcome (by letter)
Green fees £14 per day (£17 WE & BH)
Facilities ⊗ ⅢI (summer only) ⅃ ■ ♀ ⅃ 🏠 ⎰
Adrian Cave
Hotel ★★66% Home Farm Hotel, Wilmington, HONITON ☏(040483) 278 7rm(3⇦) Annexe:6⇦🐾

ILFRACOMBE
Map 1 E4

Ilfracombe ☏ (0271) 862176
Hele Bay (1.5m E off A399)
A sporting, clifftop, downland course with views over the Bristol Channel from every tee.
18 holes, 5872yds, Par 70, SSS 68, Course record 66. Membership 637.

Visitors welcome (h'cap cert required, restricted times) Societies welcome (☏)
Green fees £14 per day/round
Facilities ⊗ ⅢI ⅃ ■ ♀ ⅃ 🏠 ⎰ ⎰ David Hoare
Hotel ★★65% Elmfield Hotel, Torrs Park, ILFRACOMBE ☏(0271) 863377 12rm(11🐾)

MORETONHAMPSTEAD   Map 1 E6

Manor House Hotel ☎ (0647) 40355
(3m W off B3212)
This enjoyable parkland course is a sporting circuit
with just enough hazards (most of them natural) to
make any golfer think. Accommodation. Tennis
(hardcourt), squash, fishing and snooker.
18 holes, 6016yds, Par 69, SSS 69, Course record 65.
Membership 250.

Visitors welcome (starting times by arrangement)
must contact in advance Societies welcome (☎)
Green fees £25 per day ; £18 per round (£30/20 WE)
Facilities ⊗ ⅲ ᴸ ⬛ ♀ ⚲ 🏠 ⚑ ⴊ Richard
Lewis
Hotel ★★★⚑73% The Bel Alp House, HAYTOR
☎(03646) 217 due to change to (0364) 661217 9⇨⁵🐾

NEWTON ABBOT   Map 1 F6

Newton Abbot (Stover)☎ (0626) 52460
Bovey Rd (3m N on A382)
Parkland/heathland course with river meandering
through. Fairly flat.
18 holes, 5886yds, Par 69, SSS 68, Course record 63.
Membership 875.

Visitors welcome (proof of membership of recognised
club) must contact in advance ✉ Societies welcome
(Thu only)
Green fees £17 per day/round
Facilities ⊗ ⅲ by prior arrangement ᴸ ⬛ ♀ (ex Sun)
⚲ 🏠 ⴊ Malcolm Craig
Hotel ★★61% Queens Hotel, Queen St, NEWTON
ABBOT ☎(0626) 63133 & 54106 24rm(17⇨1🐾)

OKEHAMPTON   Map 1 E5

Okehampton ☎ (0837) 52113
Tors Rd (1m S off A30)
Interesting parkland/moorland course with true
Dartmoor turf.
18 holes, 5191yds, Par 68, SSS 67, Course record 62.
Membership 500.

Visitors welcome (must have registered h'cap) must
contact in advance Societies welcome (by letter)
Green fees £12.50 per day (£16.50 WE & BH)
Facilities ⊗ ⅲ ᴸ ⬛ ♀ ⚲ 🏠 ⚑ ⴊ Phillip Blundell
Hotel ★★64% Oxenham Arms, SOUTH ZEAL ☎(0837)
840244 & 840577 8rm(7⇨🐾)

PLYMOUTH   Map 1 D7

Elfordleigh ☎ (0752) 336428
Plympton (8m NE off B3416)
Charming, saucer-shaped parkland course with
alternate tees for 18 holes. Fairly hard walking.
Accommodation, tennis (hardcourt), indoor heated
swimming pool, squash, snooker, solarium, gymnasium.
9 holes, 5773yds, Par 68, SSS 68, Course record 63.
Membership 300.

▶

Visitors welcome (ex summer WE, h'cap cert required) must contact in advance Societies welcome (☎)
Green fees £15
Facilities ⊗ ⑂ ⓑ ▆ ♀ ⚙ 🛍 ⚑ ⚒ Ross Troake
Hotel ★★★58% Novotel Plymouth, Marsh Mills Roundabout, 270 Plymouth Rd, PLYMOUTH ☎(0752) 221422 101⇴⚑

Staddon Heights ☎ (0752) 402475
Plymstock (5m SW)
Seaside course that can be windy. Walking easy. Snooker.
18 holes, 5945yds, Par 68, SSS 68, Course record 59. Membership 600.

Visitors welcome (ex Sun) ⊠ Societies welcome (apply to secretary)
Green fees £12 day (£15 WE/BH)
Facilities ⊗ ⑂ ⓑ ▆ ♀ ⚙ 🛍 ⚒ John Cox
Hotel ★★★57% Astor Hotel, Elliot Street, The Hoe, PLYMOUTH ☎(0752) 225511 56rm(49⇴4⚑)

SAUNTON Map 1 D4

Saunton ☎ Braunton (0271) 812436
(S side of village off B3231)
Two traditional links courses (one a championship). Windy, with natural hazards.
East Course 18 holes, 6705yds, Par 71, SSS 73, Course record 67. West Course 18 holes, 6356yds, Par 71, SSS 71, Course record 67. Membership 1180.

Visitors welcome (h'cap cert required) ⊠ Societies welcome (by letter)
Green fees Not confirmed
Facilities ⊗ ⑂ ⓑ ▆ ♀ ⚙ 🛍 ⚒ J McGhee
Hotel ★★★★59% Saunton Sands Hotel, SAUNTON ☎(0271) 890212 90⇴

SIDMOUTH Map 1 G6

Sidmouth ☎ (0395) 513451
Cotmaton Rd, Peak Hill (W side of town centre)
Situated on the side of Peak Hill, offering good views.
18 holes, 5109yds, Par 66, SSS 65. Membership 700.

Visitors welcome must contact in advance Societies welcome
Green fees Not confirmed
Facilities ♀ ⚙ 🛍 ⚑ ⚒
Hotel ★★★65% Victoria Hotel, Esplanade, SIDMOUTH ☎(0395) 512651 61⇴

SOUTH BRENT Map 1 E7

Wrangaton (S Devon)☎ (0364) 73229
Golf Links Rd, Wrangaton (2.25 m SW off A38)
Moorland/parkland course within Dartmoor National Park. Spectacular views towards sea and rugged terrain. Natural fairways and hazards include bracken, sheep and ponies.
18 holes, 5918yds, Par 69, SSS 70, Course record 66. Membership 600.

Visitors welcome (restricted competition days) must contact in advance ⊠ Societies welcome (one months notice by letter)
Green fees £15 per day (£20 WE & BH)
Facilities ⊗ ⓑ ▆ ♀ ⚙ 🛍 ⚑ ⚒ Martin Keitch
Hotel ★★❦74% Glazebrook House Hotel & Restaurant, SOUTH BRENT ☎(03647) 3322 11⇴⚑

TAVISTOCK Map 1 D6

Hurdwick ☎ (0822) 612746
Tavistock Hamlets (1m N)
A new 18-hole Executive course (second 9 holes to open June 1991) and designed by Hawtree of Oxford. The idea originated in America and the concept of Executive Golf is that a round should take no longer than 2 1/2 to 3 hours whilst offering a solid challenge, thus suiting the busy business person.
18 holes, 4558yds, Par 67. Membership 100.

Visitors welcome Societies welcome (☎)
Green fees £15-£25 per day ; £6-£14 per round
Facilities ⓑ ▆ ♀ ⚙
Hotel ★★★57% Bedford Hotel, Plymouth Rd, TAVISTOCK ☎(0822) 613221 30⇴

Tavistock ☎ (0822) 612049
Down Rd (1m SE)
Set on Whitchurch Down in south-west Dartmoor with easy walking and magnificent views over rolling countryside into Cornwall. Downland turf with some heather, and interesting holes on undulating ground. Snooker.
18 holes, 6250yds, Par 70, SSS 70, Course record 66. Membership 700.

Visitors welcome (ex competion days) must contact in advance ⊠ Societies welcome (☎)
Green fees £15 per day (£18 WE & BH)
Facilities ⊗ ⑂ ⓑ ▆ ♀ ⚙ 🛍 ⚑ ⚒ Richard Hall
Hotel ★★★57% Bedford Hotel, Plymouth Rd, TAVISTOCK ☎(0822) 613221 30⇴

TEDBURN ST MARY Map 1 F5

Fingle Glen ☎ (0647) 61818
(5m from city centre on A30)
9-hole course containing six par 4's and three par 3's, set in 52 acres of rolling countryside. Testing 4th, 5th and 9th holes. 12-bay floodlit driving range.
9 holes, 2326yds, Par 66, SSS 63, Course record 66. Membership 350.

Visitors welcome Societies welcome (2 wks advance ☎)
Green fees £4.40-£5.50, 9 hole ; (£6-£7.50 WE)
Facilities ⊗ ⑂ ⓑ ▆ ♀ ⚙ 🛍 ⚑ ⚒ Stephen Gould
Hotel ★★★61% Countess Wear Lodge Hotel, Topsham Rd, Exeter Bypass, EXETER ☎(0392) 875441 44⇴⚑

We make every effort to provide accurate information, but some details may change after we go to print.

TEIGNMOUTH   Map 1 F6

Teignmouth ☎ (0626) 774194
Exeter Rd (2m NW off B3192)
This fairly flat heathland course is high up, offering a fine seascape from the clubhouse. Good springy turf with some heather and an interesting layout makes for very enjoyable holiday golf.
18 holes, 5880yds, Par 70, SSS 68. Membership 900.

Visitors welcome (Yellow tees only) must contact in advance ✉ Societies welcome (Contact Sec for details)
Green fees £19-£22
Facilities ⊗ ⅏ by prior arrangement ⅂ ☛ ♀ ⅄ 🏠 ⌁ ⎰ Peter Ward
Hotel ★★58% Cockhaven Manor Hotel, Cockhaven Rd, BISHOPSTEIGNTON ☎(0626) 775252 12rm(4⇨7🐾)

THURLESTONE   Map 1 E7

Thurlestone
☎ Kingsbridge (0548) 560405
(S side of village)
Situated on the edge of the cliffs with typical downland turf and good greens. The course, after an interesting opening hole, rises to higher land with fine seaviews, and finishes with an excellent 502-yard downhill hole to the clubhouse. Tennis.

SCORE CARD: White Tees					
Hole	Yds	Par	Hole	Yds	Par
1	271	4	10	434	4
2	379	4	11	366	4
3	170	3	12	459	4
4	366	4	13	209	3
5	221	3	14	518	5
6	148	3	15	505	5
7	344	4	16	417	4
8	429	4	17	152	3
9	413	4	18	502	5
Out	2741	33	In	3562	37
			Totals	6303	70

18 holes, 6303yds, Par 70, SSS 70, Course record 67. Membership 750.

Visitors welcome (h'cap cert is mandatory) must contact in advance ✉
Green fees £18 per day; £70 weekly
Facilities ⊗ ⅂ ☛ ♀ ⅄ 🏠 ⌁ ⎰ Neville Whitley
Hotel ★★★★68% Thurlestone Hotel, THURLESTONE ☎(0548) 560382 68⇨🐾

TIVERTON   Map 1 F5

Tiverton ☎ (0884) 252187
Post Hill
A parkland course where the many different species of tree are a feature and where the lush pastures ensure some of the finest fairways in the south-west. There are a number of interesting holes which visitors will find a real challenge.
18 holes, 6263yds, Par 71, SSS 71. Membership 930.

Visitors welcome (must be member of a club with h'cap cert) must contact in advance ✉ Societies welcome (☎)
Green fees £18 per day (£25 WE & BH)
Facilities ⊗ ⅂ ☛ ♀ ⅄ 🏠 ⌁ ⎰ Robert Freeman
Hotel ★★61% Hartnoll Hotel, Bolham, TIVERTON ☎(0884) 252777 11⇨ Annexe:5🐾

TORQUAY   Map 1 F6

Torquay ☎ (0803) 314591
30 Petitor Rd, St Marychurch (1.25m N)
Unusual combination of cliff and parkland golf, with wonderful views over the sea and Dartmoor.
18 holes, 6198yds, Par 69, SSS 69, Course record 66. Membership 1060.

Visitors welcome (h'cap cert required) must contact in advance ✉ Societies welcome (☎)
Green fees £18 per day (£22 WE & BH)
Facilities ⊗ ⅏ ⅂ ☛ ♀ ⅄ 🏠 ⌁ ⎰ Martin Ruth
Hotel ★★55%, Norcliffe Hotel, 7 Babbacombe Downs Rd, Babbacombe, TORQUAY ☎(0803) 328456 20⇨🐾

TORRINGTON   Map 1 D5

Torrington ☎ Great Torrington (0805) 22229
Weare Trees, Great Torrington (1.25m NW)
Hard walking on hilly commonland course. Outstanding views. 2nd hole is a testing 241-yd, par 3.
9 holes, 4418yds, Par 64, SSS 62, Course record 65. Membership 405.

Visitors welcome (ex Sun am) must contact in advance Societies welcome (apply to secretary)
Green fees £8 (£10 WE & BH)
Facilities ⊗ ⅏ ⅂ ☛ ♀ ⅄ 🏠
Hotel ★★50% Beaconside Hotel, LANDCROSS ☎(02372) 77205 9rm(4⇨2🐾)

WESTWARD HO
Map 1 D4

Royal North Devon ☎ (0237) 473817
(N side of village off B3236)
Links course with sea views.
18 holes, 6644yds, Par 71, SSS 72. Membership 550.

Visitors welcome
Green fees Not confirmed
Facilities ♀ ⚲ 🏠 🛒 ⎰
Hotel See advertisement on page 71

YELVERTON
Map 1 E6

Yelverton ☎ (0822) 852824
Golf Links Rd (1m S off A386)
An excellent course on the moors with virtually no
trees. It is exposed to high winds. The fairways are
tight but there is plenty of room. The longest hole is
the 8th, a 573-yard, par 5. Snooker.
18 holes, 6293yds, Par 70, SSS 70. Membership 840.

Visitors welcome (must be a M of a club with h'cap
cert) must contact in advance ✉ Societies welcome
(h'cap cert required)
Green fees £14 per day (£18 WE & BH)
Facilities ⊗ ⅲ by prior arrangement ⌱ ⚲ ♀ ⚲
🏠 ⎰ Iain Parker
Hotel ★★★70% Moorland Links Hotel,
YELVERTON ☎(0822) 852245 30⇨🐾

DORSET

BLANDFORD FORUM
Map 1 J5

Ashley Wood ☎ (0258) 452253
Wimborne Rd (2m E on B3082)
Undulating downland course with superb views and
excellent drainage. Snooker.
*9 holes, 6274yds, Par 70, SSS 70, Course record 67.
Membership 520.*

Visitors welcome (ex before 1200 WE & Tue am) must
contact in advance ✉ Societies welcome (by letter)
Green fees £12 per round (£14 WE)
Facilities ⊗ ⅲ by prior arrangement ⌱ ⚲ ♀ ⚲ 🏠
⎰ Spencer Taylor
Hotel ★★★64% Crown Hotel, 1 West St, BLANDFORD
FORUM ☎(0258) 456626 29⇨🐾

BOURNEMOUTH
Map 1 K6

Knighton Heath ☎ (0202) 572633
Francis Av, West Howe (N side of town centre off A348)
Undulating heathland course on high ground inland
from Bournemouth.
*18 holes, 6206yds, Par 70, SSS 70, Course record 66.
Membership 700.*

Visitors welcome (handicap cert required) must contact
in advance Societies welcome (☎)
Green fees £22 per day (£25 WE)

Facilities ⊗ ⅲ by prior arrangement ⌱ ⚲ ♀ ⚲ 🏠
⎰ Michael Torrens
Hotel ★★★61% Bournemouth Heathlands Hotel, 12
Grove Rd, East Cliff, BOURNEMOUTH ☎(0202) 23336
116⇨🐾

Queen's Park ☎ (0202) 36198
Queens Park Dr West (2m NE of town centre off A338)
Undulating parkland course of pine and heather, with
narrow, tree-lined fairways. Public course played over
by 'Boscombe Golf Club' and 'Bournemouth Artisans
Golf Club'.
18 holes, 6505yds, Par 72, SSS 72.

Visitors welcome must contact in advance Societies
welcome
Green fees Not confirmed
Facilities ⊗ ⅲ ⌱ ⚲ ♀ ⚲ 🏠 ⎰ John Sharkey
Hotel ★★60% Hotel Riviera, West Cliff Gardens,
BOURNEMOUTH ☎(0202) 552845 34⇨🐾

BRIDPORT
Map 1 H6

Bridport & West Dorset ☎ (0308) 421095
East Cliff, West Bay (2m S)
Seaside course on the top of the east cliff, with fine
views over Lyme Bay and surrounding countryside. At
the 13th hole (par 3), the green is 70 ft below the tee.
*18 holes, 5246yds, Par 67, SSS 66, Course record 61.
Membership 700.*

Visitors welcome (ex competition days etc) Societies
welcome (☎ or letter)
Green fees £15 per day/round (£20 WE & BH)
Facilities ⊗ ⅲ by prior arrangement ⌱ ⚲ (no
catering Mon) ♀ (restricted Sun) ⚲ 🏠 ⎰ John Parish
Hotel ★★★62% Haddon House Hotel, West Bay,
BRIDPORT ☎(0308) 23626 & 25323 13⇨🐾

BROADSTONE
Map 1 K5

Broadstone (Dorset) ☎ (0202) 692595
Wentworth Dr (N side of village off B3074)
Typical heathland course.
18 holes, 6183yds, Par 69, SSS 69. Membership 800.

Visitors welcome (ex WE & BH) must contact in
advance ✉ Societies welcome (☎ or letter)
Green fees £25 per day ; £22 per round
Facilities ⊗ by prior arrangement ⅲ by prior
arrangement ⌱ by prior arrangement ⚲ by prior
arrangement ♀ ⚲ 🏠 🛒 ⎰ Nigel Tokely
Hotel ★★★57% King's Head Hotel, The Square,
WIMBORNE ☎(0202) 880101 27⇨

CHRISTCHURCH
Map 1 K5

Iford Bridge ☎ (0202) 473817
Barrack Rd (W side of town centre on A5)
Parkland course with the River Stour running through.
5th hole is a par 4 over the river. A driving range and
tennis courts are also available.
9 holes, 4754yds, Par 68, SSS 66, Course record 62.

Visitors welcome Societies welcome (☎ or letter)
Green fees £3.80 (£4.30 WE & BH)-18 holes
Facilities ㋐ ⛳ ♀ 🏠 🏌 ⚑ Peter L Trith
Hotel ★★★72% Waterford Lodge Hotel, 87 Bure Ln,
Friars Cliff, Mudeford, CHRISTCHURCH ☎(0425) 272948
& 278801 20⇄

DORCHESTER   Map 1 J6

Came Down ☎ (0305) 813494
Came Down
Scene of the West of England Championships on
several occasions, this fine course lies on a high
plateau commanding glorious views over Portland.
Three par 5 holes add interest to a round. The turf is
of the springy, downland type.
18 holes, 6244yds, Par 70, SSS 71, Course record 67.
Membership 700.

Visitors welcome (handicap certificate required)
must contact in advance ✉ Societies welcome (☎
Wed only)
Green fees £16 per day (£20 WE & BH)
Facilities ㋐ ⛾ (ex Sun-Tue) ㋐ ⛳ ♀ △ 🏠 🏌
⚑ Robert Preston
Hotel ★★★71% King's Arms Hotel, DORCHESTER
☎(0305) 65353 31⇄

FERNDOWN   Map 1 K5

Ferndown ☎ (0202) 872022
119 Golf Links Rd (S side of
town centre off A347)
Fairways are gently
undulating amongst
heather, gorse and pine
trees giving the course a
most attractive appearance.
There are a number of dog-
leg holes and, on a clear
day, there are views across
to the Isle of Wight.
Old Course 18 holes,
6442yds, Par 71, SSS 71.
New Course 9 holes, 5604yds, Par 70, SSS 68.
Membership 700.

SCORE CARD: Old Course (White Tees)					
Hole	Yds	Par	Hole	Yds	Par
1	396	4	10	485	5
2	175	3	11	438	4
3	398	4	12	186	3
4	398	4	13	488	5
5	206	3	14	152	3
6	409	4	15	398	4
7	480	5	16	305	4
8	304	4	17	397	4
9	427	4	18	403	4
Out	3190	35	In	3252	36
			Totals	6442	71

Visitors welcome (ex prior 0930 at WE) must
contact in advance ✉ Societies welcome (Tue & Fri
only apply by letter)
Green fees Old Course £25 per day/round, New
Course £15 per day/round (£30/£20 WE)
Facilities ㋐ ㋐ ⛳ ♀ △ 🏠 🏌 ⚑ D N Sewell
Hotel ★★★★65% Dormy Hotel, New Rd,
FERNDOWN ☎(0202) 872121 130⇄⚑

Each golf course entry has a recommended
hotel. For a wider choice of places to stay,
consult *AA Hotels and Restaurants in Britain* or
AA-inspected Bed and Breakfast in Britain.

HIGHCLIFFE   Map 1 K5

Highcliffe Castle ☎ (0425) 272210
107 Lymington Rd (SW side of town on A337)
Picturesque parkland course with easy walking.
18 holes, 4686yds, Par 64, SSS 63. Membership 450.

Visitors welcome (must be M of recognised club) ✉
Societies welcome (Tue only)
Green fees £14 per day; (£20 am & £16 pm WE)
Facilities ㋐ ⛾ by prior arrangement ㋐ ⛳ ♀ △ 🏠
🏌 ⚑ Ronald E Crockford
Hotel ★★★72% Waterford Lodge Hotel, 87 Bure Ln,
Friars Cliff, Mudeford, CHRISTCHURCH ☎(0425) 272948
& 278801 20⇄

LYME REGIS   Map 1 G6

Lyme Regis ☎ (02974) 2963
Timber Hill (1.5m N on A3052)
Undulating meadowland course with cliff-top views of
Golden Cap and Lyme Bay.
18 holes, 6262yds, Par 71, SSS 70, Course record 68.
Membership 535.

Visitors welcome (ex Thu am & Sun am) must contact
in advance ✉ Societies welcome (Tue, Wed & Fri by
letter)
Green fees £18 per day (£20 WE)
Facilities ㋐ ⛾ by prior arrangement ㋐ ⛳ ♀ △ 🏠
⚑ Andrew Black
Hotel ★★★58% Mariners Hotel, Silver St, LYME
REGIS ☎(02974) 2753 17⇄⚑

LYTCHETT MATRAVERS   Map 1 J5

Bulbury Woods ☎ Morden (092945) 574
Halls Rd (2m W of Lytchett Minster)
Parkland course.
18 holes, 5970yds, Par 69, SSS 68. Membership 600.

Visitors welcome must contact in advance Societies
welcome (by letter)
Green fees £25 per day; £15 per round
Facilities ⛾ (Fri & Sat evenings) ㋐ ⛳ ♀ △ 🏠
⚑ John Sharkey
Hotel ★★★77% Priory Hotel, Church Green,
WAREHAM ☎(0929) 552772 & 551666 15⇄⚑ Annexe:4⇄

POOLE   Map 1 K6

Parkstone ☎ Canford Cliffs (0202) 707138
Links Rd, Parkstone (E side of town centre off A35)
Heathland course.
18 holes, 6250yds, Par 72, SSS 70. Membership 800.

Visitors welcome (handicap certificate required)
must contact in advance ✉ Societies welcome (☎)
Green fees £30 per day; £24 per round (£36/£30 WE
& BH)
Facilities ㋐ ⛾ ㋐ ⛳ ♀ △ 🏠 🏌 ⚑ Nigel
Blenkarne
Hotel ★★★★51% Hospitality Inn, The Quay,
POOLE ☎(0202) 666800 68⇄⚑

SHERBORNE

Map 1 H5

Sherborne ☎ (0935) 814431
Higher Clatcombe (2m N off B3145)
A sporting course of first-class fairways with far-reaching views over the lovely Blackmore Vale and the Vale of Sparkford. Parkland in character, the course has many well-placed bunkers. The dog-leg 2nd calls for an accurately placed tee shot, and another testing hole is the 7th, a 194-yard, par 3. There is a practice area.
18 holes, 5949yds, Par 70, SSS 68. Membership 700.

Visitors welcome (☎) must contact in advance ✉
Societies welcome (☎ well in advance)
Green fees Not confirmed
Facilities ⊗ ⊞ ⊫ ⬛ ♀ ⟂ 🏠 ℂ Stewart Wright
Hotel ★★★62% Post House Hotel, Horsecastles Ln, SHERBORNE ☎(0935) 813191 60⊸🐾

SWANAGE

Map 1 K6

Isle of Purbeck ☎ (09244) 21044
(2.5m N on B3351)
A heathland course sited on the Purbeck Hills with grand views across Swanage, the Channel and Poole Harbour. Holes of note include the 5th, 8th, 14th, 15, and 16th where trees, gorse and heather assert themselves. The very attractive clubhouse is built of the local stone.
18 holes, 6283yds, Par 70, SSS 71. Membership 650.

Visitors welcome Societies welcome (by letter)
Green fees Not confirmed
Facilities ♀ ⟂ 🏠 ⊤ ℂ
Hotel ★★★60% The Pines Hotel, Burlington Rd, SWANAGE ☎(0929) 425211 51rm(49⊸🐾)

WAREHAM

Map 1 J6

East Dorset ☎ Bere Regis (0929) 472244
Hyde (5m NW on unclass Puddletown Rd, off A352)
Attractive heathland course with many holes cut out of a forest of rhododendrons. An additional 9 holes under construction and due to open in 1992. Floodlit 22-bay driving range, club fitting centre, indoor putting area and extensive golf shop.
18 holes, 6146yds, Par 69, SSS 69. Membership 840.

Visitors welcome (0900-1200 & 1300-1600) must contact in advance ✉ Societies welcome (by letter)
Green fees £12 per round; £15 per day (£14/£16 WE)
Facilities ⊗ ⊞ by prior arrangement ⊫ ⬛ ♀ ⟂ 🏠 ⊤ ℂ Graham Packer
Hotel ★★68% Kemps Country House Hotel, East Stoke, WAREHAM ☎(0929) 462563 5rm(1⊸3🐾)
Annexe:4⊸

Each golf course entry has a recommended hotel. For a wider choice of places to stay, consult *AA Hotels and Restaurants in Britain* or *AA-inspected Bed and Breakfast in Britain*.

WEYMOUTH

Map 1 J6

Weymouth ☎ (0305) 773981
Links Rd, Westham (N side of town centre off B3157)
Seaside parkland course. The 5th is played off an elevated green over copse.
18 holes, 5979yds, Par 70, SSS 69, Course record 63. Membership 700.

Visitors welcome (some wknd restrictions) must contact in advance ✉ Societies welcome (☎)
Green fees £15 (£20 WE & BH)
Facilities ⊗ ⊞ ⊫ ⬛ ♀ ⟂ 🏠 ℂ D Lochrie
Hotel ★★63% Hotel Rex, 29 The Esplanade, WEYMOUTH ☎(0305) 760400 31⊸🐾

CO DURHAM

BARNARD CASTLE

Map 5 E3

Barnard Castle
☎ Teesdale (0833) 38355
Harmire Rd (.75m N on B6278)
Flat moorland course high above the River Tees and presenting fine views. A small stream runs in front of, or alongside, many of the holes adding challenge and enjoyment to the game.
18 holes, 5838yds, Par 71, SSS 68, Course record 63. Membership 600.

			SCORE CARD		
Hole	Yds	Par	Hole	Yds	Par
1	295	4	10	183	3
2	480	5	11	480	5
3	159	3	12	365	4
4	488	5	13	363	4
5	521	5	14	356	4
6	311	4	15	129	3
7	308	4	16	160	3
8	142	3	17	349	4
9	535	5	18	214	3
Out	3239	38	In	2599	33
			Totals	5838	71

Visitors welcome (must be M of recognised club)
Societies welcome (on completion of booking form)
Green fees £12 per day (£16 WE & BH)
Facilities ⊗ ⊞ ⊫ ⬛ (catering by prior arrangement) ♀ ⟂ 🏠 ⊤ ℂ J Harrison
Hotel ★★70% Rose & Crown Hotel, ROMALDKIRK ☎(0833) 50213 6⊸🐾 Annexe:5⊸🐾

BEAMISH

Map 6 K6

Beamish Park ☎ 091-370 1133
(1m NW off A693)
Parkland course. Designed by Henry Cotton and W Woodend.
18 holes, 6205yds, Par 71, SSS 70, Course record 67. Membership 520.

Visitors welcome (ex before 0900) Societies welcome
Green fees Not confirmed
Facilities ⟂ 🏠 ℂ Chris Cole
Hotel ★★★66% Beamish Park Hotel, Beamish Burn Rd, MARLEY HILL ☎(0207) 230666 47⊸🐾

For an explanation of the symbols and abbreviations used, see page 33.

BISHOP AUCKLAND
Map 6 K6

Bishop Auckland
☎ (0388) 602198
Durham Rd (1m NE on
A689)
A rather hilly parkland
course with many well-
established trees offering a
challenging round. A small
ravine adds interest to
several holes including the
short 7th, from a raised tee
to a green surrounded by a
stream, gorse and bushes.
Snooker.

SCORE CARD: Medal Tees					
Hole	Yds	Par	Hole	Yds	Par
1	286	4	10	193	3
2	559	5	11	493	5
3	529	5	12	221	3
4	521	5	13	438	4
5	214	3	14	386	4
6	341	4	15	400	4
7	143	3	16	370	4
8	182	3	17	370	4
9	494	5	18	280	4
Out	3269	37	In	3151	35
			Totals	6420	72

*18 holes, 6420yds, Par 72, SSS 71, Course record 65.
Membership 750.*

Visitors welcome (wkdays only) must contact in
advance ✉ Societies welcome (wkdays only ☎ or by
letter)
Green fees £15 per day; £12 per round (£15 WE)
Facilities ⊗ Ⅲ ଐ ॑॓ ♀ ☖ ⋒ ⌇ David
Skiffington
Hotel ★★68% Park Head Hotel, New Coundon,
BISHOP AUCKLAND ☎(0388) 661727 8⤳⋔
Annexe:7⤳

BURNOPFIELD
Map 6 K6

Hobson Municipal ☎ (0207) 70941
Hobson (.75m S on A692)
Five-year-old meadowland course.
*18 holes, 6582yds, Par 71, SSS 71, Course record 69.
Membership 500.*

Visitors welcome Societies welcome (☎ professional)
Green fees £5.50 per day (£6.50 WE & BH)
Facilities ⊗ Ⅲ ଐ ॑॓ ♀ ☖ ⋒ ⚑ ⌇ J W Ord
Hotel ★★★66% Swallow Hotel-Gateshead, High West
St, GATESHEAD ☎091-477 1105 103⤳⋔

CHESTER-LE-STREET
Map 6 K6

Chester-le-Street ☎ Durham (091) 3883218
Lumley Park (.5m E off B1284)
Parkland course in castle grounds, good views, easy
walking. Snooker.
*18 holes, 6054yds, Par 70, SSS 69, Course record 67.
Membership 650.*

Visitors welcome (restricted WE & BH) must contact in
advance ✉ Societies welcome (by letter)
Green fees £12 per day/round (£18 WE & BH)
Facilities ⊗ Ⅲ ଐ ॑॓ ♀ ☖ ⋒ ⚑ ⌇ A Hartley
Hotel ★★★69% Ramside Hall Hotel, Belmont,
DURHAM ☎091-386 5282 82⤳⋔

For a full list of the golf courses
included in this book, check
with the index on page 284

CONSETT
Map 6 K6

Consett & District ☎ (0207) 502108
Elmfield Rd (N side of town on A691)
Undulating parkland/moorland course.
18 holes, 6000yds, Par 71, SSS 69. Membership 650.

Visitors welcome must contact in advance Societies
welcome
Green fees £10 per day (£15 WE & BH)
Facilities ⊗ Ⅲ ଐ ॑॓ (no catering Thu) ♀ (ex Thu)
☖ ⋒ ⌇ S Corbally
Hotel ★★67% Lord Crewe Arms Hotel, BLANCHLAND
☎(0434675) 251 8⤳⋔ Annexe:10⤳⋔

CROOK
Map 5 E2

Crook ☎ Bishop Auckland (0388) 762429
Low Jobs Hill (.5m E off A690)
Meadowland/parkland course in elevated position with
natural hazards, varied holes and terrain. Panoramic
views over Durham and Cleveland Hills.
*18 holes, 6075yds, Par 68, SSS 69, Course record 64.
Membership 430.*

Visitors welcome (dress restrictions) Societies welcome
(☎)
Green fees £8 per day (£12 WE)
Facilities ⊗ Ⅲ ଐ ॑॓ ♀ ☖
Hotel ★★68% Park Head Hotel, New Coundon, BISHOP
AUCKLAND ☎(0388) 661727 8⤳⋔ Annexe:7⤳

DARLINGTON
Map 5 F3

Blackwell Grange ☎ (0325) 464464
Briar Close (1m SW off A66)
Pleasant parkland course with good views, easy
walking.
18 holes, 5621yds, Par 68, SSS 67. Membership 625.

Visitors welcome (restricted Wed & Sun) Societies
welcome (☎)
Green fees Not confirmed
Facilities ⊗ (Tue-Sat) Ⅲ (Tue-Sat) ଐ (Tue-Sat) ॑॓
(Tue-Sat) ⋒ ⚑ ⌇ Ralph Givens
Hotel ★★★★61% Blackwell Grange Moat House,
Blackwell Grange, DARLINGTON ☎(0325) 380888 99⤳⋔

Darlington ☎ (0325) 463936
Haughton Grange (N side of town centre off A1150)
Fairly flat parkland course with tree-lined fairways,
and large first-class greens. Championship standard.
Snooker.
18 holes, 6271yds, Par 70, SSS 70. Membership 750.

Visitors welcome (restricted WE, BH & competition
days) must contact in advance ✉ Societies welcome (☎
or by letter)
Green fees £20 per day; £15 per round (WE & BH only
with M)
Facilities ⊗ (ex Mon) Ⅲ (ex Mon) ଐ ॑॓ ♀ ☖ ⋒ ⚑
⌇ Ian Todd
Hotel ★★★61% Swallow King's Head Hotel,
Priestgate, DARLINGTON ☎(0325) 380222 60⤳⋔

Stressholme ☎ (0325) 461002
Snipe Ln (SW side of town centre on A67)
Picturesque municipal course.
18 holes, 6511yds, Par 71, SSS 71. Membership 650.

Visitors welcome
Green fees Not confirmed
Facilities 🍸 🧥 🛒 ⛳
Hotel ★★★★61% Blackwell Grange Moat House, Blackwell Grange, DARLINGTON ☎(0325) 380888 99🛁🚿

DURHAM
Map 6 K7

Brancepeth Castle ☎ 091-378 0075
Brancepeth Village (4.5m SW on A690)
Parkland course overlooked at the 9th hole by beautiful Brancepeth Castle.
18 holes, 6300yds, Par 70, SSS 70, Course record 64. Membership 780.

Visitors welcome (parties restricted WE) Societies welcome (☎)
Green fees £22 (£28 WE & BH)
Facilities ⊗ by prior arrangement 🍽 by prior arrangement 🍳 ☕ 🍸 🧥 🛒 ⛳ 🏌 D C Howdon
Hotel ★★★★68% Royal County Hotel, Old Elvet, DURHAM ☎091-386 6821 152🛁🚿

Durham City ☎ 091-378 0806
Littleburn, Langley Moor (1.5m S off A1050)
Parkland course bordered on several holes by the River Browney.
18 holes, 6211yds, Par 71, SSS 70, Course record 66. Membership 700.

Visitors welcome (ex WE & BH) Societies welcome (☎ or by letter)
Green fees £12 per day (£16 WE & BH)
Facilities ⊗ 🍽 🍳 ☕ 🍸 🧥 🛒 🏌 Stephen Corbally
Hotel ★★★66% Three Tuns Hotel, New Elvet, DURHAM ☎091-386 4326 48🛁🚿

Mount Oswald ☎ 091-386 7527
Mount Oswald Manor, South Rd (1m S off A1050)
Flat, wooded parkland course with Georgian clubhouse.
18 holes, 6009yds, Par 71, SSS 69, Course record 66. Membership 150.

Visitors welcome Societies welcome (☎)
Green fees £12 per day; £7 per round (£14/£8 WE)
Facilities ⊗ 🍽 🍳 ☕ 🍸 🧥 ⛳
Hotel ★★★57% Bridge Toby Hotel, Croxdale, DURHAM ☎091-378 0524 46🛁🚿

MIDDLETON ST GEORGE
Map 5 F3

Dinsdale Spa ☎ Dinsdale (0325) 332297
(1.5m SW)
A mainly flat, parkland course on high land above the River Tees with views of the Cleveland Hills. Water hazards front the 8th, 9th and 18th tees and the prevailing west wind affects the later holes. There is a practice area by the clubhouse.
18 holes, 6094yds, Par 70, SSS 69. Membership 850.

Visitors welcome (ex Tue & WE) must contact in advance ✉ Societies welcome (☎)
Green fees £15 per day; £12.50 per round
Facilities ⊗ 🍽 🍳 ☕ (all catering by prior arrangement) 🍸 (by prior arrangement) 🧥 🛒 ⛳ 🏌 D N Dodds
Hotel ★★★64% St George Hotel, Middleton St George, TEES-SIDE AIRPORT ☎(0325) 332631 59🛁🚿

SEAHAM
Map 5 F2

Seaham ☎ (0783) 812354
Dawdon (S side of town centre)
Undulating heathland course.
18 holes, 5972yds, Par 70, SSS 69. Membership 600.

Visitors welcome (with M only WE)
Green fees Not confirmed
Facilities 🍸 🧥 🛒
Hotel ★★★63% Swallow Hotel, Queen's Pde, Seaburn, SUNDERLAND ☎091-529 2041 65🛁

STANLEY
Map 6 K6

South Moor ☎ (0207) 232848
The Middles, Craghead (1.5m SE on B6313)
Moorland course with natural hazards. Snooker.
18 holes, 6445yds, Par 72, SSS 71. Membership 525.

Visitors welcome must contact in advance Societies welcome
Green fees Not confirmed
Facilities ⊗ 🍽 🍳 ☕ 🍸 🧥 🛒 ⛳ 🏌 Allan Hartley
Hotel ★★★66% Beamish Park Hotel, Beamish Burn Rd, MARLEY HILL ☎(0207) 230666 47🛁🚿

EAST SUSSEX

BEXHILL
Map 2 G7

Cooden Beach ☎ Cooden (04243) 2040
Cooden (2m W on A259)
The course is close by the sea, but is not real links in character. Despite that, it is dry and plays well throughout the year. There are some excellent holes such as the 4th, played to a built-up green, the short 12th, and three good holes to finish. Snooker.
18 holes, 6450yds, Par 72, SSS 71, Course record 65. Membership 700.

Visitors welcome (restricted WE) must contact in advance ✉ Societies welcome (☎)
Green fees £20 per day (£25 WE & BH)
Facilities ⊗ 🍽 🍳 ☕ 🍸 🧥 🛒 ⛳ 🏌 K R Robson
Hotel ★★★62% Cooden Resort Hotel, COODEN BEACH ☎(04243) 2281 34🛁🚿

Highwoods ☎ Bexhill-on-Sea (0424) 212625
Ellerslie Ln (1.5m NW)
Undulating course. Snooker.
18 holes, 6218yds, Par 70, SSS 70, Course record 66. Membership 820.

Visitors welcome (with M only Sun) must contact in advance ✉ Societies welcome (6 mths prior notice)
Green fees Not confirmed
Facilities ⊗ (Sun only) ㊉ (Mon-Sat 10am-2pm) ♨ ♀ ⚐ 🏠 (R McLean & M Andrews
Hotel ★★★64% Granville Hotel, Sea Rd, BEXHILL-ON-SEA ☎(0424) 215437 50⇨

BRIGHTON & HOVE   Map 2 E7

Brighton & Hove ☎ Brighton (0273) 556482
Dyke Rd (4m NW)
Downland course with sea views. Snooker.
18 holes, 5722, Par 68, SSS 68. Membership 320.

Visitors welcome (ex Sun am) must contact in advance Societies welcome (☎)
Green fees Not confirmed
Facilities ♀ ⚐
Hotel ★★★58% Courtlands Hotel, 19-27 The Drive, HOVE ☎(0273) 731055 53⇨🏠 Annexe:5⇨

Dyke
☎ Poynings (079156) 296
Dyke Rd (4m N between A23 & A27)
The course has some glorious views both towards the sea and inland. The best hole on the course is probably the 17th; it is one of those teasing short holes of just over 200 yards, and is played across a gully to a high green. Snooker.
18 holes, 6577yds, Par 72, SSS 71. Membership 700.

SCORE CARD: White Tees					
Hole	Yds	Par	Hole	Yds	Par
1	502	5	10	412	4
2	503	5	11	539	5
3	334	4	12	364	4
4	499	5	13	388	4
5	191	3	14	161	3
6	446	4	15	365	4
7	325	4	16	457	4
8	163	3	17	202	3
9	403	4	18	323	4
Out	3366	37	In	3211	35
			Totals	6577	72

Visitors welcome (After 1400 Sun) Societies welcome (☎)
Green fees Not confirmed
Facilities ⊗ ⦀ by prior arrangement ㊉ ♨ ♀ ⚐ 🏠 ⚐ (Paul Longmore
Hotel ★★★58% Courtlands Hotel, 19-27 The Drive, HOVE ☎(0273) 731055 53⇨🏠 Annexe:5⇨

East Brighton ☎ Brighton (0273) 604838
Roedean Rd (E side of town centre on B2118)
Undulating downland course, overlooking the sea. Windy.
18 holes, 6337yds, Par 72, SSS 70, Course record 63. Membership 700.

Visitors welcome (Not before 0900 wkdays; ☎ at WE) ✉ Societies welcome (☎ at least 1 month prior)
Green fees £19 (£27 WE)
Facilities ⊗ ⦀ ㊉ ♨ (no catering Mon) ♀ ⚐ 🏠 (W Street
Hotel ★★★58% Courtlands Hotel, 19-27 The Drive, HOVE ☎(0273) 731055 53⇨🏠 Annexe:5⇨

Hollingbury Park ☎ Brighton (0273) 552010
Ditchling Rd (2m N of town centre)
Municipal course in hilly situation on the Downs, overlooking the sea.
18 holes, 6500yds, Par 72, SSS 71, Course record 65. Membership 330.

Visitors welcome Societies welcome (1 month advance booking)
Green fees £15 per day; £10 per round (£12 WE)
Facilities ⊗ ♨ ♀ ⚐ 🏠 ⚐ (P Brown
Hotel ★★★58% Courtlands Hotel, 19-27 The Drive, HOVE ☎(0273) 731055 53⇨🏠 Annexe:5⇨

Waterhall ☎ Brighton (0273) 508658
Seddlescombe Rd (3m N off A27)
Hilly downland course with hard walking and open to the wind. Private club playing over municipal course.
18 holes, 5773yds, Par 69, SSS 68. Membership 400.

Visitors welcome (ex WE competition days & prior 1030 WE) Societies welcome (by letter)
Green fees £13.80 per day; £9.20 per round (£11.50 WE & BH)
Facilities ㊉ ♨ ♀ ⚐ 🏠 ⚐ (Paul Chapman-Mitchell
Hotel ★★★58% Courtlands Hotel, 19-27 The Drive, HOVE ☎(0273) 731055 53⇨🏠 Annexe:5⇨

CROWBOROUGH   Map 2 F6

Crowborough Beacon
☎ (0892) 661511
Beacon Rd (1m SW on A26)
A picturesque course in pleasant heathland. Though most fairways are wide and open, one or two are distinctly tight where a wayward shot results in a lost ball. By no means an easy course, with testing holes at the 2nd, 6th and 16th.
18 holes, 6318yds, Par 71, SSS 70. Membership 700.

SCORE CARD: Medal Tees					
Hole	Yds	Par	Hole	Yds	Par
1	409	4	10	492	5
2	457	4	11	335	4
3	144	3	12	415	4
4	360	4	13	136	3
5	358	4	14	504	5
6	193	3	15	365	4
7	497	5	16	350	4
8	325	4	17	145	3
9	396	4	18	437	4
Out	3139	35	In	3179	36
			Totals	6318	71

Visitors welcome (ex WE) must contact in advance ✉ Societies welcome (Mon Tues & Wed only ☎)
Green fees £33 per day; £22 per round
Facilities ⊗ ⦀ ㊉ ♨ ♀ ⚐ 🏠 ⚐ (Dennis Newnham
Hotel ★★★76% Spa Hotel, Mount Ephraim, TUNBRIDGE WELLS ☎(0892) 20331 76⇨🏠

EASTBOURNE   Map 2 G7

Eastbourne Downs ☎ (0323) 20827
East Dean Rd (1m W of town centre on A259)
Downland/seaside course.
18 holes, 6635yds, Par 72, SSS 72, Course record 67. Membership 705.

Visitors welcome (after 1300 Sat & Sun) Societies welcome (☎)

▶

Green fees £18 per round (£20 WE)
Facilities ⊗ (Wed-Sun) ▥ (Tue-Sat by prior
arrangement) ▙ ▦ ♀ ⚲ 🏠 ⛳ 🥂 T Marshall
Hotel ★★★★61% Cavendish Hotel, Grand Pde,
EASTBOURNE ☎(0323) 410222 114⊶🛏

Royal Eastbourne ☎ (0323) 29738
Paradise Dr (.5m W of town
centre)
A famous club which
celebrated its centenary in
1987. The course plays
longer than it measures.
Testing holes are the 8th, a
par 3 played to a high green
and the 16th, a par 5 right-
hand dog-leg.
Accommodation, snooker.
*18 holes, 6109yds, Par 70,
SSS 69, Course record 62. Membership 920.*

SCORE CARD: White Tees					
Hole	Yds	Par	Hole	Yds	Par
1	439	4	10	436	4
2	265	4	11	388	4
3	333	4	12	349	4
4	508	5	13	173	3
5	499	5	14	358	4
6	380	4	15	183	3
7	429	4	16	489	5
8	168	3	17	221	3
9	330	4	18	161	3
Out	3351	37	In	2758	33
			Totals	6109	70

Visitors welcome (handicap certificate required)
must contact in advance Societies welcome (☎)
Green fees £10-£24 WE
Facilities ⊗ ▥ by prior arrangement ▙ ▦ ♀ ⚲
🏠 ⛳ 🥂 Richard Wooller
Hotel ★★★71% Lansdowne Hotel, King Edward's
Pde, EASTBOURNE ☎(0323) 25174 130⊶🛏

Willingdon ☎ (0323) 410981
Southdown Rd (.5m N of town centre off A22)
Unique, hilly downland course set in oyster-shaped
amphitheatre.
*18 holes, 6049yds, Par 69, SSS 69, Course record 63.
Membership 550.*

Visitors welcome (with M only Sun) must contact in
advance ✉ Societies welcome (☎ Mon-Fri only)
Green fees £17 per day/round (£20 WE & BH)
Facilities ⊗ ▥ by prior arrangement ▙ ▦ ♀ ⚲ 🏠
⛳ 🥂 C J Patey
Hotel ★★★63% The Wish Tower, King Edward's Pde,
EASTBOURNE ☎(0323) 22676 67rm(59⊶)

FOREST ROW — Map 2 F5

Royal Ashdown Forest ☎ (034282) 2018
Chapel Ln (SE side of village)
Undulating heathland course. Long carries off the
tees and magnificent views over the Forest. Not a
course for beginners. (Also shorter course through
woods and moorland).
*Old Course 18 holes, 6439yds, Par 72, SSS 71, Course
record 67. New Course 18 holes, 5549yds, Par 68, SSS
67. Membership 450.*

Visitors welcome (restricted WE & Tue) must
contact in advance ✉ Societies welcome (by letter)
Green fees £25 per day (£27.50 WE)

Facilities ⊗ ▙ ▦ ♀ ⚲ 🏠 ⛳ 🥂 Martin
Landsborough
Hotel ★★★58% Roebuck Hotel, Wych Cross,
FOREST ROW ☎(034282) 3811 28⊶🛏

HASTINGS & ST LEONARDS — Map 2 H7

Beauport Park ☎ Hastings (0424) 52977
St Leonards-on-Sea (3m N of Hastings on A2100)
Played over Hastings Public Course. Undulating
parkland with stream and fine views.
18 holes, 6033yds, Par 70, SSS 70. Membership 290.

Visitors welcome Societies welcome (by letter)
Green fees Not confirmed
Facilities ♀ ⚲ 🏠 ⛳ 🥂
Hotel ★★★73% Beauport Park Hotel, Battle Rd,
HASTINGS ☎(0424) 851222 23⊶🛏

LEWES — Map 2 F7

Lewes ☎ (0293) 473245
Chapel Hill (E side of town centre off A26)
Downland course. Fine views.
*18 holes, 5951yds, Par 71, SSS 69, Course record 67.
Membership 720.*

Visitors welcome (ex WE after 1400) must contact in
advance Societies welcome (☎)
Green fees £14 per day (£25 WE & BH)
Facilities ⊗ ▥ ▙ ▦ ♀ ⚲ 🏠 🥂 Paul Dobson
Hotel ★★60% White Hart 55 High St, LEWES ☎(0273)
474676 & 476694. 19rm(14⊶🛏) Annexe: 21⊶🛏

NEWHAVEN — Map 2 F7

Peacehaven ☎ (02739) 514049
Brighton Rd (.75m W on A259)
Downland course, sometimes windy. Testing holes: 1st
(par 3), 4th (par 4), 9th (par 3).
9 holes, 5235yds, Par 69, SSS 65. Membership 200.

Visitors welcome Societies welcome (by letter)
Green fees Not confirmed
Facilities ♀ ⚲ 🏠 ⛳
Hotel ★★★65% The Star, ALFRISTON ☎(0323) 870495
34⊶🛏

RYE — Map 2 H6

Rye ☎ (0797) 225241
Camber (2.75m SE off A259)
Links course with superb views.
*Old Course 18 holes, 6310yds, Par 68, SSS 71, Course
record 64. Jubilee Course 9 holes, 6141yds, Par 71,
SSS 70. Membership 1000.*

Visitors welcome Member must accompany must
contact in advance
Green fees £22 per round (£25 WE)
Facilities ⊗ ▦ (4pm-6pm) ♀ ⚲ 🏠 🥂 Peter
Marsh
Hotel ★★68% George Hotel, High St, RYE ☎(0797)
222114 22⊶

SEAFORD   Map 2 F7

Seaford ☎ (0323) 892442
Firle Rd, East Blatchington
(1m N)
The great H. Taylor did not
perhaps design as many
courses as his friend and
rival, James Braid, but
Seaford's original design
was Taylor's. It is a splendid
downland course with
magnificent views and some
fine holes. Accommodation.
Snooker.
18 holes, 6233yds, Par 69,
SSS 70, Course record 66. Membership 800.

SCORE CARD					
Hole	Yds	Par	Hole	Yds	Par
1	354	4	10	315	4
2	426	4	11	361	4
3	169	3	12	148	3
4	366	4	13	434	4
5	384	4	14	405	4
6	390	4	15	206	3
7	145	3	16	533	5
8	441	4	17	388	4
9	395	4	18	373	4
Out	3070	34	In	3163	35
			Totals	6233	69

Visitors welcome (wkdays only after 1200 (ex Tue))
must contact in advance Societies welcome (☎)
Green fees £20 day; (£15 1200-1500, £10 after 1500)
Facilities ⊗ ⅢⅢ ⅃ ⅃ ♀ ⌂ ⌂ ⟨
Hotel ★★★65% The Star, ALFRISTON ☎(0323)
870495 34⟵⁣⁣↪

TICEHURST   Map 2 G6

Dale Hill ☎ (0580) 200112
(N side of town off B2087)
Undulating parkland/woodland course.
18 holes, 6021yds, Par 69, SSS 69, Course record 71.
Membership 650.

Visitors welcome (restricted WE am) Societies welcome
(by letter)
Green fees £15 day/round (£20 WE)
Facilities ⊗ ⅢⅢ by prior arrangement ⅃ ⅃ ♀ ⌂ ⌂
⟨
Hotel ★★64% Tudor Court Hotel, Rye Rd,
HAWKHURST ☎(0580) 752312 18⟵⁣⁣↪

UCKFIELD   Map 2 F6

East Sussex National
☎ (0825) 75577
Little Horsted (S on A22)
Created with a £30 million
budget, the East Sussex
National, which runs round
the elegant Horsted Place
Hotel, is a wonderful
creation for golfers and is
planned to be the most
luxurious golf club in the
world. Its two courses have
been created with
tournaments in mind and

SCORE CARD: East Course					
(Gold Tees)					
Hole	Yds	Par	Hole	Yds	Par
1	357	4	10	507	5
2	525	5	11	400	4
3	459	4	12	401	4
4	219	3	13	196	3
5	469	4	14	544	5
6	276	4	15	469	4
7	581	5	16	186	3
8	144	3	17	452	4
9	471	4	18	456	4
Out	3501	36	In	3611	36
			Totals	7112	72

the 18th green has been designed so that 50, 000
spectators can see. Accommodation. **See colour**
feature.
East Course 18 holes, 7082yds, Par 72, SSS 71.
West Course 18 holes, 7120yds, Par 72, SSS 71.
Membership 1000.

Visitors welcome (handicap certificate required)
must contact in advance Societies welcome (☎)
Green fees £100 includes golf cart
Facilities ⅃ ⅃ ♀ ⌂ ⌂ ⌂ ⟨ Paul Dellanzo
Hotel ★★★(red)⚑Horsted Place Hotel, Little
Horsted, UCKFIELD ☎(082575) 581 17⟵⁣⁣↪

Piltdown ☎ Newick (082572) 2033
(3m NW off A272)
Natural heathland course with much heather and gorse.
No bunkers, easy walking, fine views.
18 holes, 6059yds, Par 69, SSS 68, Course record 67.
Membership 380.

Visitors welcome (phone for details of restricted times)
must contact in advance ✉ Societies welcome (by
letter)
Green fees £30 per day or round
Facilities ⊗ ⅢⅢ by prior arrangement ⅃ ⅃ ♀ ⌂ ⌂
⌂ ⟨ John Amos
Hotel ★★66% Halland Forge Hotel, HALLAND
☎(082584) 456 Annexe:20⟵⁣⁣↪

To see a full range of AA guides and maps, visit
your local AA Shop or any good bookshop.

ESSEX

ABRIDGE
Map 2 F3

Abridge Golf and Country Club
☎ Stapleford (04028) 396
Epping Ln, Stapleford Tawney (1.75m NE)
A parkland course with easy walking. The quick drying course is by no means easy to play. This has been the venue of several professional tournaments. Abridge is a Golf and Country Club and has all the attendant facilities including indoor-heated pool, snooker and sauna.
18 holes, 6703yds, Par 72, SSS 72. Membership 600.

Visitors welcome (with M only WE) must contact in advance ⊠ Societies welcome (Mon & Wed only ☎)
Green fees £30 per day
Facilities ⊗ (ex Fri) ᴸ (ex Fri) 🍺 ♀ ⚐ 🏠 ⎰
Hotel ★★★57% Post House Hotel, High Rd, Bell Common, EPPING ☎(0378) 73137 Annexe :82⇨🐾

BASILDON
Map 2 G3

Basildon ☎ (0268) 533297
Clay Hill Ln, Kingswood (1m S off A176)
Undulating municipal parkland course. Testing 13th hole (par 4).
18 holes, 6122yds, Par 70, SSS 69, Course record 63. Membership 300.

Visitors welcome Societies welcome (☎)
Green fees £5.25 per day (£10 WE)
Facilities ⊗ (ex Sun) ∭ (Sun only) ᴸ 🍺 ♀ ⚐ 🏠 ⎠ ⎰
Hotel ★★★66% Crest Hotel, Cranes Farm Rd, BASILDON ☎(0268) 533955 110⇨🐾

Pipps Hill Country Club ☎ (0268) 27278
Cranes Farm Rd (N side of town centre off A127)
Flat course with ditches and pond.
9 holes, 2829yds, Par 34, SSS 34. Membership 400.

Visitors welcome Societies welcome
Green fees Not confirmed
Facilities ♀ ⚐
Hotel ★★★66% Crest Hotel, Cranes Farm Rd, BASILDON ☎(0268) 533955 110⇨🐾

BENFLEET
Map 2 H3

Boyce Hill ☎ (0268) 793625
Vicarage Hill, South Benfleet (.75m NE of Benfleet Station)
Hilly parkland course with good views.
18 holes, 5287yds, Par 68, SSS 68. Membership 600.

Visitors welcome (with M only WE) Societies welcome (Thu only)
Green fees £18 per day/round
Facilities ⊗ ᴸ 🍺 ♀ ⚐ 🏠 ⎰ ⎠
Hotel ★★★66% Crest Hotel, Cranes Farm Rd, BASILDON ☎(0268) 533955 110⇨🐾

BRAINTREE
Map 4 G8

Braintree ☎ (0376) 46079
Kings Ln, Stisted (1m W off A120)
Parkland course with many rare trees.
18 holes, 6153yds, Par 70, SSS 69, Course record 65. Membership 750.

Visitors welcome (with M Sun & BH) must contact in advance ⊠ Societies welcome (☎)
Green fees £20 per day (£35 WE & BH)
Facilities ⊗ ∭ ᴸ 🍺 ♀ ⚐ 🏠 ⎰ Tony Parcell
Hotel ★★55% The Saracen's Head, High St, GREAT DUNMOW ☎(0371) 873901 24⇨

Towerlands ☎ (0376) 26802
Panfield Rd (On B1053)
Undulating, grassland course. Sports hall, squash, indoor bowls, driving range, equestrian centre.
9 holes, 2703yds, Par 34, SSS 66. Membership 300.

Visitors welcome Societies welcome
Green fees £6 (9 holes) ; £7.50 (18 holes) (WE 18 holes only £10)
Facilities ⊗ ∭ by prior arrangement ᴸ 🍺 ♀ ⚐ 🏠
Hotel ★★66% White Hart Hotel, Bocking End, BRAINTREE ☎(0376) 21401 35⇨🐾

BRENTWOOD
Map 2 G3

Bentley ☎ Coxtie Green (0277) 373179
Ongar Rd (3m NW on A128)
Parkland course with water hazards.
18 holes, 6709yds, Par 72, SSS 70, Course record 68. Membership 550.

Visitors welcome (BH after 1100 only) must contact in advance ⊠ Societies welcome (☎)
Green fees £20 per day ; £15 per round
Facilities ∭ by prior arrangement ᴸ 🍺 ♀ ⚐ 🏠 ⎰ Keith Bridges
Hotel ★★★58% Post House Hotel, Brook St, BRENTWOOD ☎(0277) 260260 120⇨

Hartswood ☎ (0277) 218850
King George's Playing Fields, Ingrave Rd (.75m SE on A128)
Municipal parkland course, easy walking.
18 holes, 6238yds, Par 70, SSS 70. Membership 500.

Visitors welcome Societies welcome
Green fees Not confirmed
Facilities ♀ ⚐ 🏠 ⎠
Hotel ★★★58% Post House Hotel, Brook St, BRENTWOOD ☎(0277) 260260 120⇨

Warley Park ☎ (0277) 224891
Magpie Ln, Little Warley (2.5m S off B186)
Parkland course with reasonable walking. Numerous water hazards. There is also a golf-practice ground. Snooker.
27 holes, 3240yds, Par 36, SSS 71. Membership 650.

Visitors welcome must contact in advance ⊠ Societies welcome

Green fees Not confirmed
Facilities ⊗ ⍫ ⅃ ⬛ ♀ ⌂ 📷 ⌐ ⌐ P O'Connor
Hotel ★★★58% Post House Hotel, Brook St,
BRENTWOOD ☎(0277) 260260 120⇥

BURNHAM-ON-CROUCH   Map 2 H3

Burnham-on-Crouch ☎ (0621) 782282
Ferry Rd, Creeksea (1.25m W off B1010)
Undulating meadowland course, easy walking, windy.
9 holes, 5918yds, Par 68, SSS 68, Course record 66.
Membership 400.

Visitors welcome (Mon-Wed & Fri 0930-1400 Thu 1200-
1400) Societies welcome (twice per month)
Green fees £18 per day/round
Facilities ⍫ by prior arrangement (Wed and Fri) ⅃
(Tue-Fri) ⬛ (Tue-Fri) ♀ (Tue-Fri) ⌂
Hotel ★56% Ye Olde White Harte Hotel, The Quay,
BURNHAM-ON-CROUCH ☎(0621) 782106 11⇥♦

CHELMSFORD   Map 2 G2

Channels ☎ (0245) 440005
Belstead Farm Ln, Little Waltham (3.5m NE off A130)
Built on land from reclaimed gravel pits, 18 very
exciting holes and an excellent test of golf. Fishing.
18 holes, 6325yds, Par 70, SSS 69. Membership 750.

Visitors welcome (with M only WE) must contact in
advance Societies welcome (by letter)
Green fees Not confirmed
Facilities ♀ ⌂ 📷 ⌐
Hotel ★★★59% South Lodge Hotel, 196 New London
Rd, CHELMSFORD ☎(0245) 264564 24⇥♦ Annexe:17⇥

Chelmsford ☎ (0245) 256483
Widford (1.5m S of town centre off A12)
An undulating parkland course, hilly in parts, with
3 holes in woods and 4 difficult par 4's. From the
reconstructed clubhouse there are fine views over
the course and the wooded hills beyond.
18 holes, 5912yds, Par 68, SSS 68. Membership 650.

Visitors welcome (WE with M) must contact in
advance ✉ Societies welcome (☎ 9 mths notice)
Green fees On application
Facilities ⊗ (ex Mon) ⍫ (Fri and Sat only) ⅃ ⬛
♀ ⌂ 📷 ⌐ D Bailey
Hotel ★★★59% South Lodge Hotel, 196 New
London Rd, CHELMSFORD ☎(0245) 264564 24⇥♦
Annexe:17⇥

Each golf course entry has a recommended
hotel. For a wider choice of places to stay,
consult *AA Hotels and Restaurants in Britain* or
AA-inspected Bed and Breakfast in Britain. •

CHIGWELL   Map 2 F3

Chigwell ☎ 081-500 2059
High Rd (.5m S on A113)
A course of high quality,
mixing meadowland with
parkland. For those who
believe 'all Essex is flat' the
undulating nature of
Chigwell will be a
refreshing surprise. The
greens are excellent and the
fairways are wide.
18 holes, 5897yds, Par 69,
SSS 68. Membership 667.

SCORE CARD: White Tees					
Hole	Yds	Par	Hole	Yds	Par
1	466	4	10	163	3
2	187	3	11	387	4
3	476	5	12	383	4
4	379	4	13	364	4
5	478	5	14	191	3
6	137	3	15	460	4
7	363	4	16	312	4
8	309	4	17	332	4
9	354	4	18	538	5
Out	3149	36	In	3130	35
			Totals	6279	71

Visitors welcome (mid-week only, (with M WE))
must contact in advance ✉ Societies welcome (by
letter)
Green fees £25 per day; £20 per round
Facilities ⊗ ⅃ ⬛ ♀ ⌂ 📷 ⌐ R Beard
Hotel ★★57% Roebuck Hotel, North End,
BUCKHURST HILL ☎081-505 4636 29⇥

CHIGWELL ROW   Map 2 F3

Hainault Forest ☎ 081-500 0385
Romford Rd (.5m S on A113)
Club playing over Borough of Redbridge public courses;
hilly parkland subject to wind. Two courses, driving
range.
No 1 Course 18 holes, 5900yds, Par 71, SSS 71, Course
record 65. No 2 Course 18 holes, 6600yds, Par 70, Course
record 68. Membership 600.

Visitors welcome Societies welcome (by letter)
Green fees £6 per day (£8 WE)
Facilities ⊗ by prior arrangement ⍫ by prior
arrangement ⅃ ⬛ ♀ (M only) ⌂ 📷 ⌐ ⌐ E A Frost
Hotel ★★★59% Hilton National, Southend Arterial
Rd, HORNCHURCH ☎(04023) 46789 137⇥♦

CLACTON-ON-SEA   Map 2 J2

Clacton ☎ (0255) 421919
West Rd (1.25m SW of town centre)
Windy, seaside course.
18 holes, 6244yds, Par 70, SSS 68, Course record 65.
Membership 630.

Visitors welcome must contact in advance Societies
welcome (by letter)
Green fees £15 per round (£25 WE)
Facilities ⊗ ⅃ ⬛ ♀ ⌂ 📷 ⌐ S Levermore
Hotel ★★65% Maplin Hotel, Esplanade, FRINTON-ON-
SEA ☎(0255) 673832 12rm(9⇥1♦)

COLCHESTER   Map 4 H8

Birch Grove ☎ Layer de la Haye (020634) 276
Layer Rd, Kingsford (2.5m S on B1026)
A pretty, undulating course surrounded by woodland -
small but challenging.
9 holes, 2054yds, Par 62, SSS 60, Course record 61.
Membership 250.

▶

Visitors welcome (restricted Sun am) Societies welcome
(☎)
Green fees £10 per day (£12 WE & BH)
Facilities ⊗ ⅲ by prior arrangement ᕋ ☕ ♀ △ 🏠
Hotel ★★65% Kings Ford Park Hotel, Layer Rd, Layer
De La Haye, COLCHESTER ☎(0206) 34301 13↰🐾

Colchester ☎ (0206) 853396
Braiswick (1.5m NW of town centre on B1508)
A fairly flat parkland course.
18 holes, 6319yds, Par 70, SSS 70, Course record 63.
Membership 650.

Visitors welcome (WE with M) must contact in advance
✉ Societies welcome (☎)
Green fees £20 per day
Facilities ⊗ ⅲ by prior arrangement ᕋ ☕ ♀ △ 🏠
⛏ Paul Hodgson
Hotel ★★★60% George Hotel, 116 High St,
COLCHESTER ☎(0206) 578494 47↰🐾

Stoke-by-Nayland ☎ Nayland (0206) 262836
Keepers Ln, Leavenheath (1.5m NW of Stoke-by-
Nayland on B1068)
Two undulating courses (Gainsborough and Constable)
situated in Dedham Vale. Some water hazards and
hedges. On Gainsborough the 10th (par 4) takes 2 shots
over a lake; very testing par 3 at 11th. Squash and
sauna.
Gainsborough Course 18 holes, 6250yds, Par 72, SSS 71.
Constable Course 18 holes, 6276yds, Par 72, SSS 71.
Membership 1450.

Visitors welcome (restricted WE) must contact in
advance ✉ Societies welcome (weekdays only ☎)
Green fees £18 per day (£20 WE)
Facilities ⊗ ⅲ ᕋ ☕ ♀ △ 🏠 ⛏ Kevin Lovelock
Hotel ★★★(red)🍴Maison Talbooth, Stratford Rd,
DEDHAM ☎(0206) 322367 10↰🐾

FRINTON-ON-SEA   Map 2 K1

Frinton-on-Sea ☎ (0255) 674618
1 The Esplanade (SW side of town centre)
Flat seaside course, easy walking, windy. Also a 9-hole
course. Snooker.
18 holes, 6259yds, Par 71, SSS 70, Course record 66.
Membership 700.

Visitors welcome (handicap certificate required) must
contact in advance ✉ Societies welcome (by letter)
Green fees £20 per day
Facilities ⊗ ⅲ by prior arrangement ᕋ ☕ ♀ △ 🏠
⛏ Peter Taggart
Hotel ★★65% Maplin Hotel, Esplanade, FRINTON-ON-
SEA ☎(0255) 673832 12rm(9↰1🐾)

For a full list of the golf courses
included in this book, check
with the index on page 284

HARLOW   Map 2 F2

Canons Brook ☎ (0279) 421482
Elizabeth Way (3m S of M11)
Parkland course designed by Henry Cotton.
18 holes, 6745yds, Par 73, SSS 73. Membership 850.

Visitors welcome (ex WE) Member must accompany
must contact in advance Societies welcome (☎)
Green fees £20 per day/per round
Facilities ⊗ (Tue-Sat) ⅲ (Tue-Sat) ☕ (Tue-Sat) ♀
△ 🏠 ⛏
Hotel ★★★70% Churchgate Manor Hotel, Churchgate
St, Old Harlow, HARLOW ☎(0279) 420246 85↰

HARWICH   Map 4 J8

Harwich & Dovercourt ☎ (0255) 3616
Station Rd, Parkeston, Dovercourt (W side .25m from
docks on A120)
Flat moorland course with easy walking.
9 holes, 5692yds, Par 68, SSS 70. Membership 350.

Visitors welcome (with M only WE) must contact in
advance ✉ Societies welcome (by letter)
Green fees Not confirmed
Facilities ⊗ ⅲ ᕋ ☕ ♀ △ 🏠
Hotel ★★55% Cliff Hotel, Marine Pde, Dovercourt,
HARWICH ☎(0255) 503345 28↰🐾

INGRAVE   Map 2 G3

Thorndon Park ☎ Brentwood (0277) 811666
Ingrave Rd (W side of village on A128)
Among the best of the Essex courses with a fine new
purpose-built clubhouse and a lake. The springy turf
is easy on the feet. Many newly planted young trees
now replace the famous old oaks that were such a
feature of this course.
18 holes, 6455yds, Par 71, SSS 71. Membership 650.

Visitors welcome (ex WE) must contact in advance
Societies welcome (☎)
Green fees Not confirmed
Facilities ᕋ ☕ ♀ △ 🏠 ⛏ Brian White
Hotel ★★★58% Post House Hotel, Brook St,
BRENTWOOD ☎(0277) 260260 120↰

MALDON   Map 2 H2

Forrester Park ☎ (0621) 891406
Beckingham Rd, Great Totham (3m SE of Witham on
A12)
Tight, undulating parkland course with tree-lined
fairways and good views over the Blackwater estuary.
Easy walking. Attractive 16th-century clubhouse.
Other facilities include tennis courts and a children's
room.
18 holes, 6073yds, Par 71, SSS 69, Course record 73.
Membership 850.

Visitors welcome (ex WE, Tue am & Wed) must contact
in advance Societies welcome (☎)
Green fees £15 per day; £12 per round (£15 WE & BH)

Facilities ⊗ 🛉 🍺 ⛾ ⛺
Hotel ★★55% Blue Boar Hotel, Silver St, MALDON
☎(0621) 852681 23⇱🏃 Annexe:5⇱

Maldon ☎ (0621) 853212
Beeleigh, Langford (1m NW off B1018)
Flat, parkland course in a triangle of land by the River
Chelmer, the Blackwater Canal and an old railway
embankment. Alternate tees on 2nd 9 holes.
9 holes, 6197yds, Par 71, SSS 69. Membership 480.

Visitors welcome (after 1400 & at WE with M only) ⊠
Societies welcome (Mon & Thu)
Green fees £12 per day ; £10 per round
Facilities ⊗ � 🛉 🍺 (all catering by prior
arrangement) ⛾ ⛺ 🏠
Hotel ★★55% Blue Boar Hotel, Silver St, MALDON
☎(0621) 852681 23⇱🏃 Annexe:5⇱

ORSETT   Map 2 G3

Orsett ☎ Grays Thurrock (0375) 891352
Brentwood Rd (1.5m SE off A128)
A very good test of golf - this heathland course with
its sandy soil is quick drying and provides easy
walking. Close to the Thames estuary it is seldom
calm and the main hazards are the prevailing wind
and thick gorse. Any slight deviation can be
exaggerated by the wind and a lost ball in the gorse
results. The clubhouse has been modernised.
Snooker.
18 holes, 6614yds, Par 72, SSS 72, Course record 68.
Membership 900.

Visitors welcome (restricted WE & BH) must
contact in advance ⊠ Societies welcome (☎)
Green fees £25 per day
Facilities ⊗ � by prior arrangement 🛉 🍺 ⛾ ⛺
🏠 ⭐ ⅃ Robert Newberry
Hotel ★★★66% Crest Hotel, Cranes Farm Rd,
BASILDON ☎(0268) 533955 110⇱🏃

PURLEIGH   Map 2 H2

Three Rivers ☎ Maldon (0621) 828631
Stow Rd (1m from Purleigh on B1012)
Parkland course. Accommodation. Tennis, outdoor
heated swimming pool, squash, snooker, sauna, solarium
and gymnasium.
Kings Course 18 holes, 6348yds, Par 73, SSS 70, Course
record 61. Queens Course 9 holes, 1071yds, Par 27.

Visitors welcome (ex WE & BH) must contact in
advance ⊠ Societies welcome (Tue & Thu only ☎)
Green fees £16.50 per day
Facilities ⊗ � 🛉 🍺 ⛾ ⛺ 🏠 ⭐ ⅃ Lionel Platts
Hotel ★★55% Blue Boar Hotel, Silver St, MALDON
☎(0621) 852681 23⇱🏃 Annexe:5⇱

Each golf course entry has a recommended
hotel. For a wider choice of places to stay,
consult *AA Hotels and Restaurants in Britain* or
AA-inspected Bed and Breakfast in Britain.

ROCHFORD   Map 2 H3

Rochford Hundred ☎ (0702) 544302
Hall Rd (W on B1013)
Parkland course with ponds and ditches as natural
hazards.
18 holes, 6292yds, Par 72, SSS 70, Course record 65.
Membership 800.

Visitors welcome (☎ for details) ⊠ Societies welcome
(by letter)
Green fees Not confirmed
Facilities ⊗ by prior arrangement � by prior
arrangement 🛉 ⛾ ⛺ 🏠 ⅃ Gary Shipley
Hotel ★66% Balmoral Hotel, 34 Valkyrie Rd,
Westcliffe-on-Sea, SOUTHEND-ON-SEA ☎(0702) 342947
22⇱🏃

SAFFRON WALDEN   Map 4 F7

Saffron Walden ☎ (0799) 22786
Windmill Hill (NW side of town centre off B184)
Undulating parkland course, beautiful views.
18 holes, 6617yds, Par 72, SSS 72, Course record 67.
Membership 800.

Visitors welcome (with M only WE) must contact in
advance ⊠ Societies welcome (by letter)
Green fees Not confirmed
Facilities ⊗ 🛉 🍺 ⛾ ⛺ 🏠 ⅃ Philip Davis
Hotel ★★65% Saffron Hotel, 10-18 High St, SAFFRON
WALDEN ☎(0799) 22676 21rm(8⇱8🏃)

SOUTHEND-ON-SEA   Map 2 H3

Belfairs ☎ (0702) 525345
Eastwood Rd North, Leigh on Sea (3m W N of A13)
Municipal parkland course run by Southend-on-Sea
Borough Council. Tight second half through thick
woods, easy walking. Tennis (hardcourt).
18 holes, 5795yds, Par 70, SSS 68. Membership 300.

Visitors welcome (restricted WE & BH)
Green fees £8 per day (£12 WE & BH)
Facilities 🏠 ⭐ ⅃ Roger Foreman
Hotel ★66% Balmoral Hotel, 34 Valkyrie Rd,
Westcliffe-on-Sea, SOUTHEND-ON-SEA ☎(0702) 342947
22⇱🏃

Thorpe Hall ☎ (0702) 582205
Thorpe Hall Av, Thorpe Bay (2m E off A13)
Parkland course. Squash, snooker and sauna.
18 holes, 6286yds, Par 71, SSS 71, Course record 67.
Membership 1000.

Visitors welcome (with M only WE & BH) must contact
in advance ⊠ Societies welcome (one years notice)
Green fees £25 per day/round
Facilities ⊗ � 🛉 🍺 (no catering Mon) ⛾ ⛺ 🏠
⅃ Garry Harvey
Hotel ★66% Balmoral Hotel, 34 Valkyrie Rd,
Westcliffe-on-Sea, SOUTHEND-ON-SEA ☎(0702) 342947
22⇱🏃

SOUTH OCKENDON

Map 2 G3

Belhus Park Municipal ☎ (0708) 854260
Belhus Park (.5m N of M25 (junc 30) on B1335)
Flat parkland, easy going. Indoor heated swimming
pool, squash, sauna, solarium, gymnasium and driving
range.
18 holes, 5501yds, Par 68, SSS 68.

Visitors welcome
Green fees Not confirmed
Facilities ♀ ⌂ 🏠 ⛳ ℓ
Hotel ★★★59% Hilton National, Southend Arterial
Rd, HORNCHURCH ☎(04023) 46789 137⌁🛏

Thurrock Belhus Park ☎ (0708) 354260
Belhus Park (2m SW off B1335)
Municipal parkland type course with easy walking.
Swimming pool.
18 holes, 5450yds, Par 67. Membership 250.

Visitors welcome Societies welcome (by letter)
Green fees Not confirmed
Facilities ⅃ ⌷ ♀ ⌂ 🏠 ⛳ ℓ Steve Wimbleton
Hotel ★★★59% Hilton National, Southend Arterial
Rd, HORNCHURCH ☎(04023) 46789 137⌁🛏

STAPLEFORD ABBOTTS

Map 2 F3

Stapleford Abbotts ☎ (04023) 81108
Horsemanside, Tysea Hill (1m E off B175)
Currently an 18-hole championship course and 9-hole
par 3. In September 1991 there will be a new clubhouse
and an additional 18-hole championship course. Many
lakes on each course. Accommodation.
*Abbotts Course 18 holes, 6487yds, Par 72, SSS 71. Friars
Course 9 holes, 1140yds, Par 27. Membership 500.*

Visitors welcome (not before 1200 WE) must contact in
advance ✉ Societies welcome (☎)
Green fees £35 per day (£25 WE)
Facilities ⊗ ⅃ ⌷ ♀ ⌂ 🏠 ⛳ ℓ Scott Cranfield
Hotel ★★57% Roebuck Hotel, North End, BUCKHURST
HILL ☎081-505 4636 29⌁

THEYDON BOIS

Map 2 F2

Theydon Bois ☎ (037881) 3054
Theydon Rd (1m N)
A new nine holes have been added to the old nine
built into Epping Forest. They are well-planned and
well-bunkered but are situated out in the open on
the hillside. The old nine in the Forest are short and
have three bunkers among them, but even so a
wayward shot can be among the trees. The autumn
colours here are truly magnificent.
*18 holes, 5472yds, Par 68, SSS 68, Course record 64.
Membership 625.*

Visitors welcome (with M only WE am) must
contact in advance ✉ Societies welcome (Mon &
Tue only ☎)
Green fees £20 per day (£13 after 1600); £30 WE &
BH (£18 after 1700)

Facilities ⊗ ⅃ by prior arrangement ⅃ by prior
arrangement ⌷ ♀ ⌂ 🏠 ⛳ ℓ Robert Joyce
Hotel ★★★57% Post House Hotel, High Rd, Bell
Common, EPPING ☎(0378) 73137 Annexe:82⌁🛏

TOLLESHUNT D'ARCY

Map 2 H2

Quietwaters ☎ Maldon (0621) 860410
Colchester Rd (1.75m NE on B1026)
Two 18-hole courses. The Links is a seaside course with
a number of greenside ponds and strategically placed
bunkers, while the Lakes is a championship course with
large water features and mounding between fairways.
Hotel and extensive sports facilities under construction
and due to open September 1990.
*Links Course 18 holes, 6100yds, Par 71, SSS 70, Course
record 67. Lakes Course 18 holes, 6000yds, Par 72, SSS
72. Membership 585.*

Visitors welcome (restricted WE) must contact in
advance Societies welcome (☎)
Green fees £18 per day; £14 per round (£23/£18 WE)
Facilities ⊗ ⅃ ⌷ ♀ ⌂ 🏠 ℓ
Hotel ★★65% Kings Ford Park Hotel, Layer Rd, Layer
De La Haye, COLCHESTER ☎(0206) 34301 13⌁🛏

WOODHAM WALTER

Map 2 H2

Bunsay Downs ☎ Danbury (024541) 2648
Little Baddow Rd
Attractive 9-hole public course. Also 9-hole par 3 course.
18 holes, 5826yds, Par 68, SSS 68. Membership 520.

Visitors welcome Societies welcome
Green fees £8 per round
Facilities ⊗ ⅃ ⅃ ⌷ ♀ ⌂ 🏠 ⛳ ℓ
Hotel ★★55% Blue Boar Hotel, Silver St, MALDON
☎(0621) 852681 23⌁🛏 Annexe:5⌁

Warren ☎ Danbury (024541) 3258
(.5m SW)
Parkland course with natural hazards and good views.
Snooker.
18 holes, 6211yds, Par 70, SSS 70. Membership 820.

Visitors welcome (WE-before 3pm with M only) ✉
Societies welcome
Green fees £26 per day; £22 per round
Facilities ⊗ ⅃ ⅃ ⌷ ♀ ⌂ 🏠 ⛳ ℓ Mickey Walker
Hotel ★★55% Blue Boar Hotel, Silver St, MALDON
☎(0621) 852681 23⌁🛏 Annexe:5⌁

GLOUCESTERSHIRE

CHELTENHAM

Map 3 H7

Cotswold Hills ☎ (0242) 515264
Ullenwood (3m S off A436)
A gently undulating course with open aspects and views
of the Cotswolds.
18 holes, 6345yds, Par 70, SSS 72. Membership 750.

Visitors welcome ✉ Societies welcome (☎)
Green fees Not confirmed

Facilities ⊗ 🛍 🍺 ♀ ⌂ 🏠 🍴 (Noel Boland
Hotel ★★★66% Crest Hotel, Crest Way, Barnwood,
GLOUCESTER ☎(0452) 613311 123⇔

Lilley Brook ☎ (0242) 526785
Cirencester Rd, Charlton Kings (3m S on A435)
Undulating parkland course. Magnificent views over
Cheltenham and surrounding coutryside.
18 holes, 6226yds, Par 69, SSS 70, Course record 63.
Membership 700.

Visitors welcome (handicap certificates required) must
contact in advance ✉ Societies welcome (Wed & Thu
☎)
Green fees £18 per day (£25 WE & BH)
Facilities ⊗ (ex Mon) 🍽 (ex Mon) 🛍 🍺 ♀ ⌂ 🏠 🍴
(F E Hadden
Hotel ★★★★50% The Queen's, Promenade,
CHELTENHAM ☎(0242) 514724 77⇔

CIRENCESTER   Map 3 J8

Cirencester ☎ (0285) 652465
Cheltenham Rd, Bagendon (1.5m N on A435)
Undulating Cotswold course.
18 holes, 6001yds, Par 70, SSS 69, Course record 64.
Membership 700.

Visitors welcome (ex competition days) must contact in
advance ✉ Societies welcome (by letter)
Green fees £20 per day (£25 WE & BH)
Facilities ⊗ 🍽 by prior arrangement 🛍 🍺 ♀ ⌂ 🏠
🍴 (Geoff Robbins
Hotel ★★★52% Stratton House Hotel, Gloucester Rd,
CIRENCESTER ☎(0285) 651761 25⇔

CLEEVE HILL   Map 3 J7

Cleeve Hill ☎ (024267) 2592
nr Prestbury (1m NE on A46)
Hilly commonland course.
18 holes, 6800yds, Par 72, SSS 71, Course record 68.
Membership 350.

Visitors welcome must contact in advance Societies
welcome (☎)
Green fees £6.50 (WE £7.50)
Facilities ⊗ 🍽 🛍 🍺 ♀ ⌂ 🏠 🍴 (David Finch
Hotel ★★★65% Hotel De La Bere, Southam,
CHELTENHAM ☎(0242) 237771 32⇔🐾 Annexe:25⇔

COLEFORD   Map 3 G8

Royal Forest of Dean ☎ Dean (0594) 32583
Lords Hill (Off M5/M50 4m from Monmouth)
Parkland course. Accommodation - hotel in grounds.
Tennis (hardcourt), outdoor swimming pool and
bowling green.
18 holes, 5535yds, Par 69, SSS 67. Membership 500.

Visitors welcome must contact in advance Societies
welcome (☎)
Green fees £14 (£16 WE & BH)

Facilities ⊗ 🍽 🛍 🍺 ♀ ⌂ 🏠 🍴 (John Nicol
Hotel ★★63% The Speech House, Forest of Dean,
COLEFORD ☎(0594) 822607 14rm(3⇔)

DURSLEY   Map 1 J2

Stinchcombe Hill
☎ (0453) 542015
Stinchcombe Hill (1m W off
A4135)
High on the hill with
splendid views of the
Cotswolds, the River
Severn and the Welsh hills.
A downland course with
good turf, some trees and an
interesting variety of
greens.
*18 holes, 5723yds, Par 68,
SSS 68, Course record 64.*
Membership 500.

SCORE CARD					
Hole	Yds	Par	Hole	Yds	Par
1	275	4	10	405	4
2	419	4	11	142	3
3	434	4	12	331	4
4	197	3	13	437	4
5	374	4	14	355	4
6	139	3	15	145	3
7	435	4	16	309	4
8	367	4	17	321	4
9	162	3	18	476	5
Out	2802	33	In	2921	35
			Totals	5723	68

Visitors welcome (ex WE) must contact in advance
Societies welcome (by letter)
Green fees £13 per day (£15 WE)
Facilities ⊗ 🍽 🛍 🍺 ♀ ⌂ 🏠 (Tony Valentine
Hotel ★★63% The Old Schoolhouse Hotel,
Canonbury St, BERKELEY ☎(0453) 811711 7⇔🐾

GLOUCESTER

Map 3 H7

Gloucester Hotel & Country Club ☎ (0452) 411331
Matson Ln, Robinswood Hill (2m SW off M5)
Undulating, wooded course, built around a hill with
superb views over Gloucester and the Cotswolds.
The 12th is a drive straight up a hill, nicknamed
'Coronary Hill'. Accommodation. Tennis, indoor-
heated swimming pool, squash, snooker, sauna,
solarium and gymnasium.
18 holes, 5900yds, Par 70, SSS 69, Course record 65.
Membership 500.

Visitors welcome (Must book at WE, handicap cert
required) Societies welcome (at WE only)
Green fees £14 per day (£18 per round WE)
Facilities ⊗ Ⅲ by prior arrangement ⅃ ☕ ♀ ᄼ
🏠 ⊓ ⌀ R Jewell/P Darnell
Hotel ★★★68% Gloucester Hotel & Country Club,
Robinswood Hill, GLOUCESTER ☎(0452) 25653
97↺🏵 Annexe:10↺🏵

LYDNEY

Map 3 G8

Lydney ☎ Dean (0594) 842614
Lakeside Av (SE side of town centre)
Flat parkland/meadowland course with prevailing wind
along fairways.
9 holes, 5329yds, Par 66, SSS 66, Course record 63.
Membership 350.

Visitors welcome (with M only WE & BH) Societies
welcome (☎)
Green fees £12 per day
Facilities ⅃ (summer only) ☕ ♀ (summer only) ᄼ
Hotel ★★63% The Speech House, Forest of Dean,
COLEFORD ☎(0594) 822607 14rm(3↺)

MINCHINHAMPTON

Map 3 H8

Minchinhampton ☎ Nailsworth (045383) 3866
New Course (1.5m)
Cotswold upland courses in rural surroundings.
*Old Course 18 holes, 6295yds, Par 72, SSS 70, Course
record 67. New Course 18 holes, 6675yds, Par 72, SSS 72,
Course record 67. Membership 1600.*

Visitors welcome (handicap certificate required) must
contact in advance Societies welcome (☎)
Green fees Old Course £9 per day (£12 WE & BH) New
Course £20 per day (£25 WE & BH)
Facilities ⊗ Ⅲ (ex Sun and Mon) ⅃ ☕ ♀ ᄼ 🏠 ⊓
⌀ Chris Steele
Hotel ★★★⚑65% Burleigh Court, Brimscombe,
STROUD ☎(0453) 883804 11↺🏵 Annexe:6↺🏵

PAINSWICK

Map 3 H8

Painswick ☎ (0452) 812180
(1m N on A46)
Downland course set on Cotswold Hills at Painswick
Beacon, with fine views. Short course more than
compensated by natural hazards and tight fairways.
18 holes, 4895yds, Par 67, SSS 64, Course record 62.
Membership 350.

Visitors welcome (with M on Sun) Societies welcome
(by letter)
Green fees £12 per day; £7.50 per round (£15/£10 Sat)
Facilities ⅃ ☕ ♀ ᄼ
Hotel ★★★64% Painswick Hotel, Kemps Ln,
PAINSWICK ☎(0452) 812160 15↺🏵

TEWKESBURY

Map 3 H7

***Tewkesbury Park Hotel
Golf & Country Club***
☎ (0684) 295405
Lincoln Green Ln (1m SW
off A38)
A parkland course in a
sheltered situation beside
the River Severn. The par 3,
5th is an exacting hole
calling for accurate
distance judgment. The
hotel and country club also
offers tennis, indoor-heated
swimming pool, squash,
snooker, sauna, solarium, gymnasium.
18 holes, 6197yds, Par 73, SSS 70, Course record 68.
Membership 553.

SCORE CARD: White Tees					
Hole	Yds	Par	Hole	Yds	Par
1	519	5	10	200	3
2	321	4	11	422	4
3	503	5	12	517	5
4	431	4	13	416	4
5	146	3	14	339	4
6	575	5	15	501	5
7	128	3	16	178	3
8	349	4	17	371	4
9	352	4	18	265	4
Out	3324	37	In	3209	36
			Totals	6533	73

Visitors welcome must contact in advance ✉
Societies welcome (by letter)
Green fees Not confirmed
Facilities ⊗ Ⅲ ⅃ ☕ ♀ ᄼ 🏠 ⊓ ⌀ Peter Cane
Hotel ★★★65% Tewkesbury Park Hotel Golf &
Country Club, Lincoln Green Ln, TEWKESBURY
☎(0684) 295405 78↺🏵

WESTONBIRT

Map 1 J2

Westonbirt ☎ (066688) 242
Westonbirt School (E side of village off A433)
A parkland course with good views.
9 holes, 4504yds, Par 64, SSS 64, Course record 62.
Membership 200.

Visitors welcome Societies welcome (☎)
Green fees £5 per day (£5 per round WE & BH)
Facilities ᄼ
Hotel ★★★62% Hare & Hounds Hotel, Westonbirt,
TETBURY ☎(066688) 233 22↺🏵 Annexe:8↺🏵

GREATER LONDON

Those courses which fall within the confines of the
London Postal District area (ie have London postcodes -
W1, SW1 etc) are listed under the county heading of
London in the gazetteer (see page 140).

ADDINGTON

Map 2 F4

Addington Court ☎ 081-657 0281
Featherbed Ln (1m S off A2022)
Challenging, well-drained courses designed by F.
Hawtree. Two 18-hole courses, 9-hole course and a pitch-
and-putt course.
Old 18 holes, 5604yds, Par 68, SSS 67. Membership 350.

Visitors welcome Societies welcome
Green fees Not confirmed
Facilities ⊗ ⮂ ⬛ ♀ ⛳ 🏠 ⛾ ⌁
Hotel ★★★★62% Selsdon Park Hotel, Sanderstead, CROYDON ☎081-657 8811 170⇨🛏️🐾

Addington Palace ☎ 081-654 3061
Gravel Hill (.5m SW on A212)
Hard-walking parkland course, with two (par 4) testing holes (2nd and 10th).
18 holes, 6262yds, Par 71, SSS 71. Membership 600.

Visitors welcome (with M only WE & BH) Societies welcome (Tue, Wed & Fri only)
Green fees Not confirmed
Facilities ⊗ (Tue-Fri and Sun) ⵆ by prior arrangement ⮂ ⬛ ♀ ⛳ 🏠 ⌁ M Pilkington
Hotel ★★★★62% Selsdon Park Hotel, Sanderstead, CROYDON ☎081-657 8811 170⇨🐾

BARNEHURST   Map 2 F3

Barnehurst Golf Club ☎ (0322) 51205
Mayplace Rd East (.75m NW of Crayford off A2000)
Parkland course, easy walking.
9 holes, 5320yds, Par 66, SSS 66. Membership 300.

Visitors welcome (restricted Tue, Thu, Sat (pm) & Sun) Societies welcome
Green fees £4.45 (£7 WE)
Facilities ⊗ ⮂ ⬛ ♀ ⛳ 🏠 ⛾ ⌁
Hotel ★★★70% Crest Hotel, Black Prince Interchange, Southwold Rd, BEXLEY ☎(0322) 526900 106⇨🐾

BARNET   Map 2 E3

Arkley ☎ 081-449 0394
Rowley Green Rd (2m W off A411)
Wooded parkland course situated on high ground, with fine views.
9 holes, 6045yds, Par 69, SSS 69, Course record 63. Membership 350.

Visitors welcome (WE with M) Societies welcome (☎ Wed-Fri only)
Green fees £20 per day ; £15 per round
Facilities ⊗ ⵆ ⮂ ⬛ ♀ ⛳ 🏠 ⌁
Hotel ★★★58% Hilton National Hotel, Elton Way, Watford Bypass, BUSHEY ☎(0923) 35881 196⇨🐾

Dyrham Park Country Club ☎ 081-440 3361
Galley Ln (3m NW off A1081)
Parkland course. Also offers tennis, outdoor-heated swimming pool, fishing and snooker facilities.
18 holes, 6369yds, Par 71, SSS 70, Course record 65. Membership 1200.

Visitors welcome Member must accompany Societies welcome (Wed only)
Green fees Not confirmed
Facilities ⊗ ⵆ (Thu evening Club night) ⮂ ⬛ ♀ (all day) ⛳ 🏠 ⛾ ⌁ Bill Large

Hotel ★★★65% Crest Hotel, Bignells Corner, SOUTH MIMMS ☎(0707) 43311 123⇨🐾

Old Fold Manor ☎ 081-440 9185
Old Fold Ln, Hadley Green (N side of town centre on A1000)
Heathland course, good test of golf. Snooker.
18 holes, 6449yds, Par 71, SSS 71, Course record 66. Membership 529.

Visitors welcome (with M only WE & BH) ✉ Societies welcome (by letter)
Green fees £25 per day ; £20 per round
Facilities ⊗ ⵆ ⮂ ⬛ (all catering by prior arrangement) ♀ (by prior arrangement) ⛳ 🏠 ⛾ ⌁ Peter Jones
Hotel ★★54% Holtwhites Hotel, 92 Chase Side, ENFIELD ☎081-363 0124 30rm(28⇨🐾)

BECKENHAM   Map 2 F4

Beckenham Place ☎ 081-658 5374
The Mansion (.5m N on B2015)
Picturesque course in the grounds of a public park. The course is played over by the Braeside Golf Club.
18 holes, 5722yds, Par 68, SSS 68. Membership 200.

Visitors welcome Societies welcome
Green fees Not confirmed
Facilities ♀ ⛳ 🏠 ⛾ ⌁
Hotel ★★★58% Bromley Court Hotel, Bromley Hill, BROMLEY ☎081-464 5011 122⇨🐾

Langley Park ☎ 081-658 6849
Barnfield Wood Rd (.5 N on B2015)
This is a pleasant, well-wooded, parkland course with natural hazards including a lake at the 18th hole.
18 holes, 6588yds, Par 69, SSS 71, Course record 65. Membership 650.

Visitors welcome (ex WE) must contact in advance ✉ Societies welcome (Wed only)
Green fees £25 per day/round
Facilities ⊗ ⮂ ⬛ ♀ ⛳ 🏠 ⛾ ⌁ George Ritchie
Hotel ★★★58% Bromley Court Hotel, Bromley Hill, BROMLEY ☎081-464 5011 122⇨🐾

BEXLEYHEATH   Map 2 F4

Bexleyheath ☎ 081-303-6951
Mount Dr, Mount Rd (1m SW)
Undulating course.
9 holes, 5239yds, Par 66, SSS 66, Course record 64. Membership 350.

Visitors welcome (weekdays only ex BH) Societies welcome (☎)
Green fees £12
Facilities ⊗ (Tue-Fri) ⵆ (Tue, Wed and Fri) ⮂ ⬛ ♀ ⛳
Hotel ★★★70% Crest Hotel, Black Prince Interchange, Southwold Rd, BEXLEY ☎(0322) 526900 106⇨🐾

BIGGIN HILL   Map 2 F4

Cherry Lodge ☎ (0959) 72250
Jail Ln (1m E)
Undulating parkland course with good views. Sauna.
18 holes, 6652yds, Par 72, SSS 72. Membership 800.

Visitors welcome (ex WE) must contact in advance
Societies welcome (☎)
Green fees £30 per day; £20 per round
Facilities ⊗ ⅢⅢ ⅬⅬ 🍺 ♀ 🛆 🏠 (Nigel Child
Hotel ★★★63% Kings Arms Hotel, Market Square,
WESTERHAM ☎(0959) 62990 18⇨

BROMLEY   Map 2 F4

Magpie Hall Lane ☎ 081-462 7014
Magpie Hall Ln (2m SE off A21)
Flat course, ideal for beginners.
9 holes, 2745yds, Par 70, SSS 67. Membership 100.

Visitors welcome Societies welcome
Green fees Not confirmed
Facilities ♀ 🏠 🍹 (
Hotel ★★★58% Bromley Court Hotel, Bromley Hill,
BROMLEY ☎081-464 5011 122⇨

Shortlands ☎ 081-460 2471
Meadow Rd, Shortlands (.75m W off A222)
Easy-walking parkland course with a brook as a natural
hazard.
9 holes, 5261yds, Par 65, SSS 66. Membership 410.

Visitors welcome (non competition days only) Member
must accompany ✉
Green fees Not confirmed
Facilities 🛆 🏠 (J Bates
Hotel ★★★58% Bromley Court Hotel, Bromley Hill,
BROMLEY ☎081-464 5011 122⇨

Sundridge Park ☎ 081-460 0278
Garden Rd (N side of town centre off A2212)
The East course is longer than the West but many
think the shorter of the two courses is the more
difficult. The East is surrounded by trees while the
West is more hilly, with good views. Both are
certainly a good test of golf.
*East Course 18 holes, 6410yds, Par 70, SSS 71. West
Course 18 holes, 6027yds, Par 68, SSS 69.
Membership 1200.*

Visitors welcome must contact in advance ✉
Societies welcome (☎)
Green fees £30 per day
Facilities ⊗ by prior arrangement ⅢⅢ by prior
arrangement Ⅼ 🍺 ♀ 🛆 🏠 (
Hotel ★★★58% Bromley Court Hotel, Bromley
Hill, BROMLEY ☎081-464 5011 122⇨

Each golf course entry has a recommended
hotel. For a wider choice of places to stay,
consult *AA Hotels and Restaurants in Britain* or
AA-inspected Bed and Breakfast in Britain.

CARSHALTON   Map 2 E4

Oaks Park Sports Centre ☎ 081-643 8363
Woodmansterne Rd (.5m S on B278)
Public parkland course with floodlit, covered driving
range.
*18 holes, 5873yds, Par 70, SSS 70 or 9 holes, 1590yds, Par
29, SSS 29. Membership 500.*

Visitors welcome must contact in advance Societies
welcome
Green fees Not confirmed
Facilities ♀ 🛆 🏠 🍹 (
Hotel ★★★63% Post House Hotel, Purley Way,
CROYDON ☎081-688 5185 86⇨

CHESSINGTON   Map 2 E4

Chessington ☎ 081-391-0948
Garrison Ln (Opp Chessington South Station nr Zoo)
Parkland course designed by Patrick Tallack.
9 holes, 1400yds, Par 27, SSS 28. Membership 200.

Visitors welcome (must book 0730-1200 weekends only)
Societies welcome (☎ 1 mths notice)
Green fees Not confirmed
Facilities ⊗ ⅢⅢ 🍺 ♀ 🛆 🏠 🍹 (B Cliff
Hotel ★★59% Heathside Hotel, Brighton Rd, BURGH
HEATH ☎(0737) 353355 47⇨

CHISLEHURST   Map 2 F4

Chislehurst ☎ 081-467 2782
Camden, Park Rd
Pleasantly wooded, undulating parkland/heathland
course. Magnificent clubhouse with historical
associations. Snooker.
18 holes, 5128yds, Par 66, SSS 65. Membership 800.

Visitors welcome (with M WE) must contact in advance
✉ Societies welcome (by letter)
Green fees £20 per day (Mon-Fri)
Facilities ⊗ ⅢⅢ by prior arrangement Ⅼ 🍺 ♀ 🛆 🏠
🍹 (Stuart Cortorphine
Hotel ★★★58% Bromley Court Hotel, Bromley Hill,
BROMLEY ☎081-464 5011 122⇨

COULSDON   Map 2 E4

Coulsdon Court ☎ 081-660 0468
Coulsdon Rd (.75m E off A23 on B2030)
A public parkland course with good views. Clubhouse
formerly owned by the Byron family. Tennis
(hardcourts), squash, solarium and gymnasium.
18 holes, 6030yds, Par 70, SSS 68. Membership 450.

Visitors welcome (Mid-week booking for WE) Societies
welcome
Green fees Not confirmed
Facilities ⊗ ⅢⅢ Ⅼ 🍺 ♀ 🛆 🏠 🍹 (
Hotel ★★★★62% Selsdon Park Hotel, Sanderstead,
CROYDON ☎081-657 8811 170⇨

Woodcote Park ☎ 081-668 2788
Meadow Hill, Bridle Way (1m N of town centre off A237)
Slightly undulating parkland course. Snooker.
18 holes, 6600yds, Par 71, SSS 71. Membership 700.

Visitors welcome (ex WE) must contact in advance ✉
Societies welcome (☎)
Green fees Not confirmed
Facilities ⊗ by prior arrangement ⫙ by prior
arrangement ⮕ ⯑ ♀ ⌂ ☎ ⦔ Ian Martin
Hotel ★★★63% Post House Hotel, Purley Way,
CROYDON ☎081-688 5185 86⇆🏌

CROYDON
Map 2 F4

Croham Hurst ☎ 081-657 5581
Croham Rd (1.5m SE)
Parkland course with tree-lined fairways and bounded
by wooded hills. Easy walking.
*18 holes, 6274yds, Par 70, SSS 70, Course record 64.
Membership 800.*

Visitors welcome (WE & BH with M) must contact in
advance ✉ Societies welcome (Book 1 year in advance)
Green fees £27 per day
Facilities ⊗ ⫙ by prior arrangement ⮕ ⯑ ♀ ⌂ ☎
⦔ Eric Stillwell
Hotel ★★★★62% Selsdon Park Hotel, Sanderstead,
CROYDON ☎081-657 8811 170⇆🏌

Selsdon Park ☎ 081-657 8811
Sanderstead (3m S on A2022)
Surrey parkland course. Accommodation, with full use
of hotel's sporting facilities by residents.
18 holes, 6402yds, Par 71, SSS 69.

Visitors welcome (restricted WE for non-residents)
must contact in advance Societies welcome (☎)
Green fees £20-£30 (18-36 holes)
Facilities ⊗ ⫙ ⮕ ⯑ ♀ ⌂ ☎ ⊶ ⦔ Tom O'Keefe &
Iain Naylor
Hotel ★★★★62% Selsdon Park Hotel, Sanderstead,
CROYDON ☎081-657 8811 170⇆🏌

Shirley Park ☎ 081-654 1143
Addiscombe Rd (E side of town centre on A232)
This parkland course lies amid fine woodland with good views of Shirley Hills. The more testing holes come in the middle section of the course. The remarkable 7th hole calls for a 187-yard iron or wood shot diagonally across a narrow valley to a shelved green set right-handed into a ridge.
18 holes, 6210yds, Par 71, SSS 70. Membership 950.

SCORE CARD: White Tees					
Hole	Yds	Par	Hole	Yds	Par
1	409	4	10	365	4
2	304	4	11	435	4
3	165	3	12	327	4
4	537	5	13	151	3
5	367	4	14	391	4
6	381	4	15	339	4
7	187	3	16	282	4
8	356	4	17	222	3
9	516	5	18	476	5
Out	3222	36	In	2988	35
			Totals	6210	71

▶

Visitors welcome (WE with M) must contact in advance ⊠ Societies welcome (☎)
Green fees £17.50 per day
Facilities ⊗ by prior arrangement Ⅲ by prior arrangement ⅃ ⚏ ♀ △ 🖼 ⋲ Hogan Stott
Hotel ★★★59% Holiday Inn, 7 Altyre Rd, CROYDON ☎081-680 9200 214⇔🏕

DOWNE
Map 2 F4

High Elms ☎ (0689) 58175
High Elms Rd (1.5m NE)
Municipal parkland course. Very tight 13th, 230 yds (par 3).
18 holes, 6340yds, Par 71, SSS 70.

Visitors welcome
Green fees Not confirmed
Facilities △ ⚐
Hotel ★★★58% Bromley Court Hotel, Bromley Hill, BROMLEY ☎081-464 5011 122⇔🏕

West Kent ☎ Orpington (0689) 51323
West Hill Downe (.75m SW)
Partly hilly downland course.
18 holes, 6392yds, Par 70, SSS 70, Course record 62. Membership 750.

Visitors welcome (with M only WE, Handicap cert required) must contact in advance ⊠ Societies welcome (☎)
Green fees £30 per day ; £20 per round
Facilities ⊗ by prior arrangement ⅢM by prior arrangement ⅃ ⚏ ♀ (all day) △ 🖼 ⋲ Roger Fidler
Hotel ★★★58% Bromley Court Hotel, Bromley Hill, BROMLEY ☎081-464 5011 122⇔🏕

ENFIELD
Map 2 F2

Crews Hill ☎ 081-363 6674
Cattlegate Rd, Crews Hill, Crews Hill (3m NW off A1005)
Parkland course in country surroundings.
18 holes, 6230yds, Par 70, SSS 70. Membership 529.

Visitors welcome must contact in advance 24hrs ⊠ Societies welcome (by letter)
Green fees Not confirmed
Facilities ⊗ by prior arrangement ⅢM by prior arrangement ⅃ (ex Mon) ⚏ ♀ △ 🖼 ⋲ J Reynolds
Hotel ★★54% Holtwhites Hotel, 92 Chase Side, ENFIELD ☎081-363 0124 30rm(28⇔🏕)

Enfield ☎ 081-363 3970
Old Park Rd South (W side of town centre off A110)
Parkland course. Salmons Brook crosses 7 holes. Saxon Moat ancient monument.
18 holes, 6137yds, Par 72, SSS 70, Course record 66. Membership 625.

Visitors welcome (with M only WE) must contact in advance ⊠ Societies welcome (☎ or letter)
Green fees Not confirmed

Facilities ⊗ ⚏ ♀ △ 🖼 ⋲ Ian Martin
Hotel ★★54% Holtwhites Hotel, 92 Chase Side, ENFIELD ☎081-363 0124 30rm(28⇔🏕)

Enfield Municipal ☎ 01-363 4454
Beggars Hollow, Clay Hill (N side of town centre)
Municipal, flat, wooded parkland course. 9th hole is a left-hand dog-leg with second shot over a brook.
18 holes, 5881yds, Par 68, SSS 68.

Visitors welcome (Club facilities only with member) Member must accompany
Green fees Not confirmed
Hotel ★★54% Holtwhites Hotel, 92 Chase Side, ENFIELD ☎081-363 0124 30rm(28⇔🏕)

GREENFORD
Map 2 E3

Ealing ☎ 081-997 0937
Perivale Ln
Flat, parkland course relying on natural hazards; trees, tight fairways, and the River Brent which affects 9 holes. Snooker.
18 holes, 6216yds, Par 70, SSS 70, Course record 65. Membership 650.

Visitors welcome (Mon-Fri only on application to pro shop) must contact in advance Societies welcome (Mon, Wed & Thu only ☎)
Green fees £30 per day or round
Facilities ⊗ (Mon-Fri) ⅢM by prior arrangement ⅃ (Mon-Sat) ⚏ ♀ △ 🖼 ⋲ Arnold Stickley
Hotel ★★56% Osterley Hotel, 764 Great West Rd, OSTERLEY ☎081-568 9981 57⇔🏕 Annexe:5rm

Horsenden Hill ☎ 081-902 4555
Woodland Rise (3m NE on A4090)
A well-kept, tree-lined short course.
9 holes, 1618yds, Par 28, SSS 28. Membership 135.

Visitors welcome
Green fees Not confirmed
Facilities △ 🖼 ⚐
Hotel ★★★62% Master Brewer Motel, Western Av, HILLINGDON ☎(0895) 51199 106⇔

Perivale Park ☎ 081-578 1693
Ruislip Rd East (E side of town centre, off A40)
Parkland course.
9 holes, 2600yds, Par 68, SSS 65. Membership 180.

Visitors welcome
Green fees Not confirmed
Facilities △ 🖼 ⚐
Hotel ★★★70% Carnarvon Hotel, Ealing Common, LONDON ☎081-992 5399 145⇔🏕

This guide is updated annually – make sure you use an up-to-date edition.

HADLEY WOOD   Map 2 E2

Hadley Wood ☎ 081-449 4328
Beech Hill (E side of village)
A parkland course on the north-west edge of London at Barnet. Easily accessible. The gently undulating fairways have a friendly width inviting the player to open his shoulders, though the thick rough can be very punishing to the unwary. The course is pleasantly wooded and there are some admirable views. Snooker.
18 holes, 6473yds, Par 72, SSS 71, Course record 67. Membership 600.

Visitors welcome (WE with M) ✉ Societies welcome (☎)
Green fees £27.50 per day; £22 per round
Facilities ⊗ ⑂ 🏌 🍺 (☎ for details) ♀ ⛳ 🏠 ⚑
⚐ Alan McGinn
Hotel ★★★★62% West Lodge Park Hotel, Cockfosters Rd, HADLEY WOOD ☎081-440 8311 48⇔⚐ Annexe:2⇔⚐

HAMPTON WICK   Map 2 E4

Home Park ☎ 081-977 2658
(Off A308 on W side of Kingston Bridge)
Flat, parkland course with easy walking.
18 holes, 6218yds, Par 71, SSS 71. Membership 500.

Visitors welcome Societies welcome (☎)
Green fees Not confirmed
Facilities ⊗ ⑂ 🏌 🍺 ♀ ⛳ 🏠 ⚐ Len Roberts
Hotel ★★★64% Richmond Hill, 146-150 Richmond Hill, RICHMOND ☎081-940 2247 & 081-940 5466 123⇔⚐

HILLINGDON   Map 2 D3

Hillingdon ☎ (0895) 33956
Dorset Way, Vine Ln (W side of town off A4020)
Parkland course.
9 holes, 5459yds, Par 68, SSS 67, Course record 65. Membership 400.

Visitors welcome (ex WE, BH & Thu) ✉ Societies welcome (by letter)
Green fees £15 per round
Facilities ⊗ ⑂ by prior arrangement 🏌 🍺 ♀ ⛳ 🏠
⚐ D J McFadden
Hotel ★★★62% Master Brewer Motel, Western Av, HILLINGDON ☎(0895) 51199 106⇔

HOUNSLOW   Map 2 E3

Airlinks ☎ 081-561 1418
Southall Ln (W of Hounslow off M4 junc 3)
Meadowland/parkland course designed by P. Alliss and D. Thomas.
18 holes, 5883yds, Par 71, SSS 69, Course record 60. Membership 500.

Visitors welcome (ex before 1200 Sat & Sun) Societies welcome (by letter)
Green fees £6.50 per round (£8.50 WE)

Facilities 🏌 🍺 ♀ ⛳ 🏠 ⚑ ⚐
Hotel ★★★60% Master Robert Hotel, Great West Rd, HOUNSLOW ☎081-570 6261 100⇔

Hounslow Heath Municipal ☎ 081-570 5271
Staines Rd
Parkland course in a conservation area, planted with an attractive variety of trees. The 15th hole lies between the fork of two rivers.
18 holes, 5820yds, Par 69, SSS 68. Membership 300.

Visitors welcome (ex WE) Societies welcome (☎)
Green fees Not confirmed
Facilities ⛳ 🏠 ⚑ ⚐
Hotel ★★★65% Post House Hotel, Sipson Road, West Drayton, WEST DRAYTON ☎081-759 2323 569⇔⚐

ILFORD   Map 2 F3

Ilford ☎ 081-554 2930
Wanstead Park Rd (NW side of town centre off A12)
Fairly flat parkland course intersected five times by a river. Snooker.
18 holes, 5702yds, Par 68, SSS 68. Membership 592.

Visitors welcome (restricted BH) must contact in advance Societies welcome (by letter)
Green fees £20 per day; £10 per round (£24/£12 WE)
Facilities ⊗ ⑂ 🏌 🍺 ♀ ⛳ 🏠
Hotel ★★★68% Woodford Moat House, Oak Hill, WOODFORD GREEN ☎081-505 4511 99⇔⚐

ISLEWORTH   Map 2 E3

Wyke Green ☎ 081-560 8777
Syon Ln (1.5m N on B454 off A4)
Fairly flat parkland course.
18 holes, 6242yds, Par 69, SSS 70, Course record 65. Membership 700.

Visitors welcome (restricted WE & BH) must contact in advance Societies welcome (☎)
Green fees £22 per day (£33 WE & BH)
Facilities ⊗ ⑂ (no catering Mon) 🏌 🍺 ♀ ⛳ 🏠
⚐ Tony Fisher
Hotel ★★★60% Master Robert Hotel, Great West Rd, HOUNSLOW ☎081-570 6261 100⇔

KINGSTON UPON THAMES   Map 2 E4

Coombe Hill ☎ 081-942 2284
Golf Club Dr, Coombe Ln West (1.75m E on A238)
A splendid course in wooded terrain. The undulations and trees make it an especially interesting course of great charm. And there is a lovely display of rhododendrons in May and June. Snooker and sauna.
18 holes, 6303yds, Par 71, SSS 71. Membership 550.

SCORE CARD: Medal Tees					
Hole	Yds	Par	Hole	Yds	Par
1	320	4	10	440	4
2	368	4	11	408	4
3	407	4	12	186	3
4	510	5	13	314	4
5	452	5	14	494	5
6	180	3	15	494	5
7	346	4	16	400	4
8	418	4	17	145	3
9	184	3	18	390	4
Out	3185	36	In	3118	35
			Totals	6303	71

▶

Visitors welcome (WE with M) must contact in advance ✉ Societies welcome (Bookings previous year)
Green fees £45 per day
Facilities ⊗ ⅃ ♨ ♟ ♟ ⚲ ☖ ✆ Craig Defoy
Hotel ★★★★63% **Cannizaro House** West Side, Wimbledon Common, LONDON SW19 ☎081-879 1464 48➪♪

Coombe Wood ☎ 081-942 0388
George Rd (1.25m NE on A308)
Parkland course.
18 holes, 5210yds, Par 66, SSS 66, Course record 62. Membership 650.

Visitors welcome (WE with M) must contact in advance Societies welcome (Wed, Thu & Fri)
Green fees £25-£30 per day
Facilities ⊗ ⅢⅬ ♨ (catering by prior arrangement)
♟ ⚲ ☖ ✆ David Butler
Hotel ★★★63% **Kingston Lodge** Kingston Hill, KINGSTON UPON THAMES ☎081-541 4481 61➪♪

MITCHAM   Map 2 E4

Mitcham ☎ 081-648 4197
Carshalton Rd (1m S)
Heathland course (gravel base), wooded.
18 holes, 5935yds, Par 69, SSS 68, Course record 65. Membership 500.

Visitors welcome must contact in advance Societies welcome (☎)
Green fees £8
Facilities ⊗ Ⅼ ♨ ♟ ⚲ ☖ ✆ J Godfrey
Hotel ★★★63% Post House Hotel, Purley Way, CROYDON ☎081-688 5185 86➪♪

NEW MALDEN   Map 2 E4

Malden ☎ 081-942 0654
Traps Ln (N side of town centre off B283)
Parkland course with the hazard of the Beverley Brook which affects 4 holes (3rd, 7th, 8th and 12th). Snooker.
18 holes, 6201yds, Par 71, SSS 70, Course record 65. Membership 800.

Visitors welcome (WE pm only, not competition days) must contact in advance Societies welcome (by letter)
Green fees Not confirmed
Facilities ⊗ ⅢⅬ ♨ ♟ ⚲ ☖ ✆ Robert Hunter
Hotel ★★★63% Kingston Lodge Hotel, Kingston Hill, KINGSTON UPON THAMES ☎081-541 4481 61➪♪

NORTHWOOD   Map 2 D3

Haste Hill ☎ (09274) 22877
The Drive (.5m S off A404)
Parkland course with stream running through. Excellent views.
18 holes, 5787yds, Par 68, SSS 68. Membership 350.

Visitors welcome
Green fees Not confirmed

Facilities ♟ ⚲ ☖ ✆
Hotel ★★66% Harrow Hotel, Roxborough Bridge, 12-22 Pinner Rd, HARROW ☎081-427 3435 76➪♪

Northwood ☎ (09274) 25329
Rickmansworth Rd (SW side of village off A404)
A very old club to which we are told golfers used to drive from London by horse-carriage. They would find their golf interesting as present-day players do. The course is relatively flat although there are some undulations, and trees and whins add not only to the beauty of the course but also to the test of golf.
18 holes, 6493yds, Par 71, SSS 71, Course record 65. Membership 800.

Visitors welcome (WE with M) Societies welcome (Mon, Thu & Fri only ☎)
Green fees £19 per round
Facilities ⊗ Ⅲ by prior arrangement Ⅼ ♨ ♟ ⚲ ☖ ✆
Hotel ★★66% Harrow Hotel, Roxborough Bridge, 12-22 Pinner Rd, HARROW ☎081-427 3435 76➪♪

Sandy Lodge ☎ (09274) 25429
Sandy Lodge Ln (N side of town centre off A4125)
Heathland course; links-type, very sandy.
18 holes, 6081yds, Par 70, SSS 69, Course record 64. Membership 700.

Visitors welcome (restricted WE & BH) must contact in advance ✉ Societies welcome (by letter)
Green fees not confirmed
Facilities ⊗ Ⅲ Ⅼ ♨ (catering by prior arrangement)
♟ (1100-2300) ⚲ ☖ ✆ Alex Fox
Hotel ★★★62% Bedford Arms Thistle Hotel, CHENIES ☎(09278) 3301 10➪♪

ORPINGTON   Map 2 F4

Cray Valley ☎ (0689) 39677 & 31927
Sandy Ln (1m off A20)
An open parkland course with two man-made lakes and open ditches.
18 holes, 5624yds, Par 69, SSS 67. Membership 640.

Visitors welcome Societies welcome (☎)
Green fees £9 per round (£13 WE)
Facilities ⚲ ☖
Hotel ★★★58% Bromley Court Hotel, Bromley Hill, BROMLEY ☎081-464 5011 122➪♪

Lullingstone Park ☎ (0959) 34542
Parkgate, Chelsfield (Leave M25 junct 4 and take Well Hill turn)
Popular 27-hole public course set in 690 acres of undulating parkland. Championship length 18-holes, plus 9-hole course and a further 9-hole pitch and putt.
18 holes, 6759yds, Par 72, Course record 69 or 9 holes, 2432yds, Par 33. Membership 400.

Visitors welcome Societies welcome (☎)
Green fees On application

Facilities ⛳ 🏨 ⛳ (David Cornford
Hotel ★★★58% Bromley Court Hotel, Bromley Hill,
BROMLEY ☎081-464 5011 122⇔🐾

Ruxley ☎ (0689) 71490
Sandy Ln, St Paul's Cray (2m NE on A223)
Parkland course with public driving range. Difficult 6th
hole, par 4. Easy walking and good views.
18 holes, 4885yds, Par 65, SSS 65, Course record 66.
Membership 250.

Visitors welcome (not WE & BH am) Societies welcome
(2 weeks notice ☎)
Green fees £9 per day (£12 WE)
Facilities ⊗ (ex WE) 🍴 ♀ ⛳ 🏨 (Roger Cornwell
Hotel ★★★58% Bromley Court Hotel, Bromley Hill,
BROMLEY ☎081-464 5011 122⇔🐾

PINNER   Map 2 E3

Grims Dyke ☎ 081-428 4539
Oxhey Ln, Hatch End (3m N on A4008)
Parkland course.
18 holes, 5600yds, Par 69, SSS 67, Course record 65.
Membership 590.

Visitors welcome (Sun with M) ✉ Societies welcome
(☎)
Green fees £30 per day
Facilities 🍴 🍴 ♀ ⛳ 🏨 (Carl Williams
Hotel ★★66% Harrow Hotel, Roxborough Bridge, 12-
22 Pinner Rd, HARROW ☎081-427 3435 76⇔🐾

Pinner Hill ☎ 081-866 0963
Southview Rd, Pinner Hill (2m NW off A404)
Parkland course.
18 holes, 6280yds, Par 72, SSS 70, Course record 63.
Membership 750.

Visitors welcome (Mon-Fri, h'cap cert required ex Wed
& Thu) must contact in advance for Sat play ✉
Societies welcome (☎)
Green fees £22 (Wed & Thu £9.50) (£30 WE)
Facilities ⊗ 🍴 🍴 🍴 (catering by prior arrangement)
♀ ⛳ 🏨 ⛳ (Mark Grieve PGA
Hotel ★★66% Harrow Hotel, Roxborough Bridge, 12-
22 Pinner Rd, HARROW ☎081-427 3435 76⇔🐾

PURLEY   Map 2 F4

Purley Downs ☎ 081-657 8347
106 Purley Downs Rd (E side of town centre off A235)
Hilly downland course. Notable holes are 6th and 12th.
Snooker.
18 holes, 6237yds, Par 70, SSS 70.

Visitors welcome (with M only WE) Societies welcome
Green fees Not confirmed
Facilities ♀ ⛳ 🏨 (
Hotel ★★★63% Post House Hotel, Purley Way,
CROYDON ☎081-688 5185 86⇔🐾

Richmond ☎ 081-940-4351
Sudbrook Park, Petersham (1.5m S off A307)
A beautiful and historic wooded, parkland course on
the edge of Richmond Park, with six par-3 holes. The
4th is often described as the best short hole in the
south of England. Low scores are uncommon
because cunningly sited trees call for great
accuracy. The clubhouse is one of the most
distinguished small Georgian mansions in England.
18 holes, 5965yds, Par 70, SSS 69. Membership 700.

Visitors welcome Societies welcome (by letter)
Green fees £16 per day (£20 WE)
Facilities ⊗ 🍴 by prior arrangement 🍴 🍴 ♀ ⛳
🏨 ⛳ (
Hotel ★★★64% Richmond Hill, 146-150 Richmond
Hill, RICHMOND ☎081-940 2247 & 081-940 5466
123⇔🐾

Royal Mid-Surrey ☎ 081-940 1894
Old Deer Park (.5m N of Richmond upon Thames off
A316)
A long playing parkland course. The flat fairways
are cleverly bunkered. The 18th provides an
exceptionally good par 4 finish with a huge bunker
before the green to catch the not quite perfect long
second. Snooker.
Outer Course 18 holes, 6337yds, Par 69, SSS 70,
Course record 64. Inner Course 18 holes, 5544yds, Par
68, SSS 67. Membership 1200.

Visitors welcome (ex WE) must contact in advance
Societies welcome (☎)
Green fees £40 per day (£30 after 1630)
Facilities ⊗ 🍴 🍴 ♀ ⛳ 🏨 ⛳ (David Talbot
Hotel ★★★64% Richmond Hill, 146-150 Richmond
Hill, RICHMOND ☎081-940 2247 & 081-940 5466
123⇔🐾

ROMFORD   Map 2 F3

Maylands Golf Club & Country Park
☎ Ingrebourne (04023) 42055
Colchester Rd, Harold Park
Picturesque, undulating parkland course.
18 holes, 6351yds, Par 70, SSS 69, Course record 66.
Membership 700.

Visitors welcome (WE with M) ✉ Societies welcome
(Mon, Wed & Fri only ☎)
Green fees £20 (£30 WE & BH) for 18 holes
Facilities ⊗ 🍴 🍴 🍴 ♀ ⛳ 🏨 (John Hopkin
Hotel ★★★58% Post House Hotel, Brook St,
BRENTWOOD ☎(0277) 260260 120⇔

For an explanation of the symbols and
abbreviations used, see page 33.

Romford ☎ (0708) 40986
Heath Dr, Gidea Park (1m
NE on A118)
A many-bunkered parkland
course with easy walking.
It is said there are as many
bunkers as there are days in
the year. The ground is
quick drying making a good
course for winter play when
other courses might be too
wet.
*18 holes, 6374yds, Par 72,
SSS 70. Membership 693.*

SCORE CARD					
Hole	Yds	Par	Hole	Yds	Par
1	359	4	10	448	4
2	306	4	11	485	5
3	190	3	12	391	4
4	480	5	13	208	3
5	503	5	14	448	4
6	141	3	15	327	4
7	336	4	16	335	4
8	361	4	17	172	3
9	386	4	18	498	5
Out	3062	36	In	3312	36
			Totals	6374	72

Visitors welcome (with M only WE & BH) must
contact in advance ✉ Societies welcome (☎)
Green fees Not confirmed
Facilities ⊗ �🍽 🛒 ☎ ♀ ⛳ 🏠 (Harry Flatman
Hotel ★★★58% Post House Hotel, Brook St,
BRENTWOOD ☎(0277) 260260 120⇨

RUISLIP   Map 2 D3

Ruislip ☎ (08956) 32004
Ickenham Rd (.5m SW on B466)
Municipal parkland course. Many trees.
18 holes, 5346yds, Par 67, SSS 66. Membership 300.

Visitors welcome
Green fees Not confirmed
Facilities ♀ ⛳ 🏠 ⛳
Hotel ★★★62% Master Brewer Motel, Western Av,
HILLINGDON ☎(0895) 51199 106⇨

SIDCUP   Map 2 F4

Sidcup ☎ 081-300 2864
7 Hurst Rd (N side of town centre off A222)
Easy walking parkland course with natural water
hazards.
9 holes, 5692yds, Par 68, SSS 67. Membership 450.

Visitors welcome (with M only WE & BH ☎ for details)
Green fees Not confirmed
Facilities ♀ (ex Mon) ⛳ 🏠
Hotel ★★★58% Bromley Court Hotel, Bromley Hill,
BROMLEY ☎081-464 5011 122⇨🏠

SOUTHALL   Map 2 E3

West Middlesex ☎ 081-574-3450
Greenford Rd (W side of town centre on A4127 off
A4020)
Gently undulating parkland course. Clubhouse includes
3 squash courts.
18 holes, 6242yds, Par 69, SSS 70. Membership 500.

Visitors welcome (restricted WE & BH) Societies
welcome (by letter)
Green fees Not confirmed
Facilities ♀ ⛳ 🏠 (
Hotel ★★★60% Master Robert Hotel, Great West Rd,
HOUNSLOW ☎081-570 6261 100⇨

STANMORE   Map 2 E3

Stanmore ☎ 081-954 2599
Gordon Av (S side of town centre)
Parkland course.
*18 holes, 5884yds, Par 68, SSS 68, Course record 66.
Membership 528.*

Visitors welcome (WE & BH with M) must contact in
advance Tue-Thu play ✉ Societies welcome (Wed &
Thu only ☎)
Green fees £7.50 per round Mon & Fri, other weekdays
on application
Facilities ⛳ 🏠 ⛳ (V R Law
Hotel ★★66% Harrow Hotel, Roxborough Bridge, 12-
22 Pinner Rd, HARROW ☎081-427 3435 76⇨🏠

SURBITON   Map 2 E4

Surbiton ☎ 081-398 3101
Woodstock Ln (2m S off A3)
Parkland course with easy walking.
*18 holes, 6211yds, Par 70, SSS 70, Course record 64.
Membership 750.*

Visitors welcome (WE & BH with M) must contact in
advance ✉ Societies welcome (by letter)
Green fees £24 per round ; £36 per day
Facilities ⊗ 🍽 by prior arrangement 🛒 ♀ ⛳
⛳ (P Milton
Hotel ★★62% Haven, Portsmouth Rd, ESHER ☎081-
398 0023 16⇨🏠 Annexe: 4⇨🏠

TWICKENHAM   Map 2 E4

Fulwell ☎ 081-977-1833
Wellington Rd, Hampton Hill (1.5m S on A311)
Championship-length parkland course with easy
walking. The 575-yd, 17th, is notable.
*18 holes, 6490yds, Par 71, SSS 71, Course record 68.
Membership 650.*

Visitors welcome (ex WE) must contact in advance ✉
Societies welcome (by letter)
Green fees £22 per day
Facilities ⊗ 🍽 by prior arrangement 🛒 ♀ ⛳ 🏠
⛳ (
Hotel ★★★64% Richmond Hill, 146-150 Richmond
Hill, RICHMOND ☎081-940 2247 & 081-940 5466 123⇨🏠

Strawberry Hill ☎ 081-894 0165
Wellesley Rd (S side of town centre off A311)
Parkland course with easy walking.
*9 holes, 2381yds, Par 64, SSS 62, Course record 59.
Membership 350.*

Visitors welcome (WE with M only) Societies welcome
(by letter)
Green fees £12 per day ; £10 per round
Facilities ⊗ (Wed-Fri) 🍽 by prior arrangement 🛒 🛒
♀ ⛳ 🏠 (Peter Buchan
Hotel ★★★64% Richmond Hill, 146-150 Richmond
Hill, RICHMOND ☎081-940 2247 & 081-940 5466 123⇨🏠

Twickenham ☎ 081-941 0032
Staines Rd (2m W on A305)
Municipal commonland course.
9 holes, 3180yds, Par 72, SSS 71. Membership 250.

Visitors welcome
Green fees Not confirmed
Facilities ♀ ⛳ 🏠 ⛳ ⛷
Hotel ★★★64% Richmond Hill, 146-150 Richmond
Hill, RICHMOND ☎081-940 2247 & 081-940 5466 123⇌🏌

UPMINSTER   Map 2 G3

Upminster ☎ (04022) 22788
114 Hall Ln (N side of town centre)
Parkland course adjacent to river.
18 holes, 5951yds, Par 68, SSS 69. Membership 800.

Visitors welcome (with M only WE) ⌧ Societies
welcome (by letter)
Green fees Not confirmed
Facilities ♀ ⛳ 🏠 ⛷
Hotel ★★★59% Hilton National, Southend Arterial
Rd, HORNCHURCH ☎(04023) 46789 137⇌🏌

UXBRIDGE   Map 2 D3

Harefield Place ☎ (0895) 37287
The Drive, Harefield Place (2m N off B467)
Municipal parkland course, undulating and tricky.
Snooker.
18 holes, 5737yds, Par 68, SSS 68. Membership 700.

Visitors welcome Societies welcome (Thu only ☎)
Green fees Not confirmed
Facilities ⊗ � ⛳ ⛳ ♀ ⛳ 🏠 ⛷ ⛷ Phil Howard
Hotel ★★★62% Master Brewer Motel, Western Av,
HILLINGDON ☎(0895) 51199 106⇌

WEMBLEY   Map 2 E3

Sudbury ☎ 081-902 3713
Bridgewater Rd (SW side of town centre on A4090)
Parkland course. Snooker.
*18 holes, 6282yds, Par 69, SSS 70, Course record 63.
Membership 650.*

Visitors welcome (WE with M only) must contact in
advance ⌧ Societies welcome (by letter)
Green fees £30 per day ; £20 per round
Facilities ⊗ � ⛳ ⛳ ♀ ⛳ 🏠 ⛷ Neil Jordan
Hotel ★★66% Harrow Hotel, Roxborough Bridge, 12-
22 Pinner Rd, HARROW ☎081-427 3435 76⇌🏌

WEST DRAYTON   Map 2 D3

Holiday ☎ (0895) 444232
Stockley Rd (1m SE off A408)
Fairly large, testing, hilly par 3 course suitable both for
beginners and scratch players. Accommodation, food
and sports facilities at hotel.
9 holes, 3900yds, Par 30, SSS 32. Membership 280.

Visitors welcome Societies welcome (☎ or letter)
Green fees Not confirmed

Facilities catering available at hotel ♀ ⛳ 🏠 ⛷
Hotel ★★★★59% Holiday Inn, Stockley Rd, West
Drayton, WEST DRAYTON ☎(0895) 445555 396⇌🏌

WOODFORD GREEN   Map 2 F3

Woodford ☎ 081-504-0553
Sunset Av (NW side of town centre off A104)
Forest land course where grazing cattle create natural
hazards.
*9 holes, 5806yds, Par 70, SSS 70, Course record 68.
Membership 400.*

Visitors welcome (WE, BH & Tue am with M only) must
contact in advance Societies welcome (☎ or by letter)
Green fees Not confirmed
Facilities ⊗ by prior arrangement ⊯ by prior
arrangement ⛳ ⛳ ♀ ⛳ 🏠 ⛷ Ashley Johns
Hotel ★★★68% Woodford Moat House, Oak Hill,
WOODFORD GREEN ☎081-505 4511 99⇌🏌

GREATER MANCHESTER

ALTRINCHAM   Map 5 D8

Altrincham ☎ 061-928 0671
Stockport Rd (.75 E of Altrincham on A560)
Parkland course with easy walking, and some natural
hazards.
18 holes, 6200yds, Par 71, SSS 69. Membership 300.

Visitors welcome must contact in advance Societies
welcome
Green fees Not confirmed
Facilities ⛳ 🏠 ⛷ ⛷
Hotel ★★★65% Cresta Court Hotel, Church St,
ALTRINCHAM ☎061-927 7272 139⇌🏌

Dunham Forest ☎ 061-928 2605
Oldfield Ln (1.5m W off A56)
Attractive parkland course cut through magnificent
beech woods. Tennis, squash and snooker.
18 holes, 6636yds, Par 72, SSS 72. Membership 600.

Visitors welcome (ex WE & BH) Societies welcome
(Mon, Thu & Fri only)
Green fees £20 per day (£25 WE)
Facilities ⊗ � ⛳ ⛳ ♀ ⛳ 🏠 ⛷ ⛷ Ian Wrigley
Hotel ★★★66% Bowdon Hotel, Langham Rd, Bowdon,
ALTRINCHAM ☎061-928 7121 82⇌

Ringway ☎ 061-980 2630
Hale Mount, Hale Barns (2.5m SE on A538)
Parkland course, with interesting natural hazards. Easy
walking, good views. Snooker.
*18 holes, 6494yds, Par 71, SSS 71, Course record 67.
Membership 720.*

Visitors welcome ⌧ Societies welcome (Thu only May-
Sep)
Green fees £20 per day (£25 WE & BH)

▶

Facilities ⊗ ⅏ (Wed-Sat) 🏌 (ex Sun) 🍺 ♀ ⛳ 🏠 ⛳
⛳ Nick Ryan
Hotel ★★★65% Cresta Court Hotel, Church St,
ALTRINCHAM ☎061-927 7272 139⇦🛏

ASHTON-IN-MAKERFIELD
Map 5 C7

Ashton-in-Makerfield ☎ (0942) 727267
Garswood Park, Liverpool Rd (.5m W of M6 (Junc 24) on
A58)
Well-wooded parkland course.
18 holes, 6180yds, Par 70, SSS 69, Course record 66.
Membership 750.

Visitors welcome (restricted Sat & BH; with M only
Sun) Societies welcome (by letter)
Green fees £18 per day
Facilities ⊗ ⅏ 🏌 🍺 ♀ ⛳ 🏠 ⛳ ⛳ Peter Allan
Hotel ★★★66% Post House Hotel, Lodge Ln, Newton-
Le-Willows, HAYDOCK ☎(0942) 717878 142⇦

ASHTON-UNDER-LYNE
Map 5 E7

Ashton-under-Lyne ☎ 061-330 1537
Gorsey Way, Higher Hurst (1.5m NE)
A testing, varied moorland course, with large greens.
Easy walking. Three new holes have improved the
course. Snooker.
18 holes, 6209yds, Par 70, SSS 70, Course record 68.
Membership 650.

Visitors welcome (with M only WE & BH) Societies
welcome (☎)
Green fees £15 per day
Facilities ⊗ ⅏ by prior arrangement 🏌 🍺 ♀ ⛳ 🏠
⛳
Hotel ★★70% York House Hotel, York Place,
Richmond St, ASHTON-UNDER-LYNE ☎061-330 5899
24rm(18⇦5🛏) Annexe:10⇦

Dukinfield ☎ 061-338 2340
Lyne Edge, Yew Tree Ln (S off B6175)
Small but tricky moorland course with several difficult
par-3 holes.
18 holes, 5586yds, Par 68, SSS 67, Course record 67.
Membership 400.

Visitors welcome (ex Wed pm, WE with M) Societies
welcome (☎)
Green fees £10.50
Facilities ⊗ ⅏ 🏌 🍺 ♀ ⛳ 🏠
Hotel ★★70% York House Hotel, York Place,
Richmond St, ASHTON-UNDER-LYNE ☎061-330 5899
24rm(18⇦5🛏) Annexe:10⇦

We make every effort to provide accurate information, but some details may change after we
go to print.

Bolton ☎ (0204) 43067
Lostock Park, Chorley New Rd (3m W on A673)
This well-maintained parkland course is always a
pleasure to visit. The 12th hole should be treated
with respect and so too should the final four holes
which have ruined many a card. Snooker.
18 holes, 6233yds, Par 70, SSS 70, Course record 66.
Membership 600.

Visitors welcome (restricted WE) Societies welcome
(☎ Thu only)
Green fees £22 per day (£26 WE & BH)
Facilities ⊗ ⅏ by prior arrangement 🏌 🍺 ♀ ⛳
🏠 ⛳ ⛳ Bob Longworth
Hotel ★★★61% Pack Horse Hotel, Bradshawgate,
Nelson Square, BOLTON ☎(0204) 27261
74rm(68⇦3🛏)

Bolton Municipal ☎ (0204) 42336
Links Rd (3m W on A673)
A parkland course.
18 holes, 6336yds, Par 71, SSS 70, Course record 68.

Visitors welcome Societies welcome (☎)
Green fees £3.50 (£4.50 WE)
Facilities ⊗ ⅏ 🏌 🍺 ♀ ⛳ 🏠 ⛳ ⛳ A K Holland
Hotel ★★★62% Crest Hotel, Beaumont Rd, BOLTON
☎(0204) 651511 100⇦🛏

Breightmet ☎ (0204) 27381
Red Bridge, Ainsworth (E side of town centre off A58)
Long parkland course. Snooker.
9 holes, 6203yds, Par 71, SSS 69. Membership 300.

Visitors welcome (ex WE) must contact in advance
Societies welcome (Tue & Thu only ☎)
Green fees £8 per day (£10 WE & BH)
Facilities ⊗ by prior arrangement ⅏ by prior
arrangement 🏌 🍺 ♀ ⛳
Hotel ★★★61% Pack Horse Hotel, Bradshawgate,
Nelson Square, BOLTON ☎(0204) 27261 74rm(68⇦3🛏)

Dunscar ☎ (0204) 53321
Longworth Ln, Bromley Cross (3m N off A666)
A scenic moorland course with panoramic views. A
warm friendly club. Snooker.
18 holes, 5968yds, Par 71, SSS 69, Course record 64.
Membership 600.

Visitors welcome (after 0930, limited WE) must contact
in advance ✉ Societies welcome (☎)
Green fees £15 per day (£20 WE)
Facilities ⊗ ⅏ 🏌 🍺 ♀ ⛳ 🏠 ⛳ ⛳ Gary Treadgold
Hotel ★★★64% Egerton House Hotel, Blackburn Rd,
Egerton, BOLTON ☎(0204) 57171 33⇦🛏

Great Lever & Farnworth ☎ (0204) 656137
Lever Edge Ln (SW side of town centre off A575)
Downland course with easy walking. Snooker.
18 holes, 5859yds, Par 70, SSS 69. Membership 450.

Visitors welcome (ex WE) must contact in advance
Societies welcome (ex WE)

Green fees Not confirmed
Facilities ⊗ ⊞ ⤊ ⬤ ♀ ⚞ 🛍
Hotel ★★★61% Pack Horse Hotel, Bradshawgate, Nelson Square, BOLTON ☎(0204) 27261 74rm(68⇨3🏾)

Harwood ☎ (0204) 22878
Springfield, Reading Brook Rd, Harwood (2.5m NE off B6196)
Parkland course. Snooker.
9 holes, 5960yds, Par 71, SSS 69. Membership 378.

Visitors welcome (ex WE unless with M) Societies welcome (by letter)
Green fees Not confirmed
Facilities ⤊ (WE only) ⬤ ♀ ⚞ 🛍 ⛟ ⚞ Maxwell Evans
Hotel ★★★64% Egerton House Hotel, Blackburn Rd, Egerton, BOLTON ☎(0204) 57171 33⇨🏾

Old Links ☎ (0204) 42307
Chorley Old Rd (NW of town centre on B6226)
Moorland course. Snooker.
18 holes, 6406yds, Par 72, SSS 72, Course record 64. Membership 750.

Visitors welcome (ex championship days) must contact in advance Societies welcome (by letter)
Green fees £20 per day (£25 WE)
Facilities ⊗ ⊞ by prior arrangement ⤊ (no catering Mon) ⬤ ♀ ⚞ 🛍 ⚞ Paul Horridge
Hotel ★★★61% Pack Horse Hotel, Bradshawgate, Nelson Square, BOLTON ☎(0204) 27261 74rm(68⇨3🏾)

Regent Park ☎ (0204) 44170
Links Rd, Chorley New Rd (3.5m W off A673)
Parkland course.
18 holes, 6069yds, Par 70, SSS 69. Membership 230.

Visitors welcome Societies welcome (☎)
Green fees £4 per day (£4.50 WE & BH)
Facilities ⊗ ⊞ by prior arrangement ⤊ ⬤ ♀ ⚞ 🛍 ⛟ ⚞ Keith Holland
Hotel ★★★62% Crest Hotel, Beaumont Rd, BOLTON ☎(0204) 651511 100⇨🏾

BRAMHALL   Map 5 E8

Bramall Park ☎ 061-485 3199
20 Manor Rd (NW side of town centre off B5149)
Well-wooded parkland course with splendid views of the Pennines. Snooker.
18 holes, 6043yds, Par 70, SSS 70. Membership 600.

Visitors welcome must contact in advance Societies welcome (by letter)
Green fees Not confirmed
Facilities ⊗ by prior arrangement ⊞ by prior arrangement ⤊ ⬤ ♀ ⚞ 🛍 ⚞ M Proffitt
Hotel ★★★67% Bramhall Moat House, Bramhall Ln South, BRAMHALL ☎061-439 8116 65⇨🏾

This guide is updated annually – make sure you use an up-to-date edition.

Bramhall ☎ 061-439 4057
Ladythorn Rd (E side of town centre off A5102)
Undulating parkland course, easy walking. Snooker.
18 holes, 6300yds, Par 70, SSS 70, Course record 64. Membership 720.

Visitors welcome (except Thu) must contact in advance Societies welcome (Wed only)
Green fees £20 per day (£30 WE & BH)
Facilities ⊗ ⊞ ⤊ ⬤ ♀ ⚞ 🛍 ⚞ Brian Nield
Hotel ★★★67% Bramhall Moat House, Bramhall Ln South, BRAMHALL ☎061-439 8116 65⇨🏾

BROMLEY CROSS   Map 5 D7

Turton ☎ Bolton (0204) 852235
Wood End Farm, Chapeltown Rd (3m N on A676)
Moorland course.
9 holes, 5805yds, Par 69, SSS 68, Course record 67. Membership 325.

Visitors welcome (ex WE & BH) Societies welcome (by letter)
Green fees £10 per day
Facilities ⊗ ⊞ ⤊ ⬤ (no catering Mon) ♀ ⚞
Hotel ★★★64% Egerton House Hotel, Blackburn Rd, Egerton, BOLTON ☎(0204) 57171 33⇨🏾

BURY   Map 5 D7

Bury ☎ 061-766 4897
Unsworth Hall, Blackford Bridge (2m S on A56)
Hard walking on hilly course. Snooker.
18 holes, 5961yds, Par 69, SSS 69, Course record 66. Membership 650.

Visitors welcome (ex WE) Societies welcome (☎ or by letter)
Green fees £15 per day (£20 WE & BH)
Facilities ⊗ ⊞ ⤊ ⬤ ♀ ⚞ 🛍 ⛟ ⚞ M Peel
Hotel ★60% Woolfield House Hotel, Wash Ln, BURY ☎061-797 9775 16rm(3⇨7🏾)

Lowes Park ☎ 061-764 1231
Hill Top, Walmersley (N side of town centre off A56)
Moorland course, with easy walking. Usually windy.
9 holes, 6009yds, Par 70, SSS 69. Membership 250.

Visitors welcome (ex Wed & WE) must contact in advance Societies welcome (☎ or by letter)
Green fees £7 per day (£10 WE & BH)
Facilities ⊗ ⊞ ⤊ ⬤ (no catering Mon) ♀ (ex Mon) ⚞
Hotel ★60% Woolfield House Hotel, Wash Ln, BURY ☎061-797 9775 16rm(3⇨7🏾)

Walmersley ☎ 061-764 0018
Garretts Close, Walmersley (3m N off A56)
Moorland hillside course, with wide fairways and large greens. Testing holes: 2nd (442 yds) par 5; 4th (444 yds) par 4.
9 holes, 3057yds, Par 72, SSS 70, Course record 66. Membership 350.

►

Visitors welcome (restricted WE) must contact in advance ✉ Societies welcome (☎ at least 1 mth prior)
Green fees £10
Facilities ⊗ by prior arrangement ⅢⅢ by prior arrangement 🍴 ♨ ♀ △
Hotel ★★★62% Old Mill Hotel, Springwood, RAMSBOTTOM ☎(070682) 2991 36⇆

CHEADLE Map 5 E8

Cheadle ☎ 061-491 4452
Cheadle Rd (S side of village off A5149)
Parkland course. Snooker.
9 holes, 5006yds, Par 64, SSS 65. Membership 300.

Visitors welcome (ex Tue & Sat) must contact in advance ✉ Societies welcome (by letter)
Green fees £10 per day (£12 WE & BH)
Facilities ⊗ ⅢⅢ by prior arrangement 🍴 ♨ ♀ △ 🏠
ℓ Martin Redrup
Hotel ★★59% Wycliffe Villa, 74 Edgeley Rd, Edgeley, STOCKPORT ☎061-477 5395 12⇆🏌

DENTON Map 5 E7

Denton ☎ 061-336 3218
Manchester Rd (1.5m W on A57)
Easy, flat parkland course with brook running through. Notable hole is one called 'Death and Glory'.
18 holes, 6290yds, Par 72, SSS 70. Membership 600.

Visitors welcome (ex WE) must contact in advance
Green fees Not confirmed
Facilities ♀ △ 🏠 ℓ
Hotel ★★70% York House Hotel, York Place, Richmond St, ASHTON-UNDER-LYNE ☎061-330 5899 24rm(18⇆5🏌) Annexe:10⇆

FAILSWORTH Map 5 E7

Brookdale ☎ 061-681 4534
Ashbridge, Woodhouses (N side of Manchester)
Undulating parkland course, with river crossed 5 times in play. Hard walking. Snooker.
18 holes, 6040yds, Par 68, SSS 68. Membership 500.

Visitors welcome (restricted Sun) must contact in advance ✉ Societies welcome (by letter)
Green fees Not confirmed
Facilities ⊗ by prior arrangement ⅢⅢ by prior arrangement 🍴 by prior arrangement ♨ by prior arrangement ♀ △ 🏠 🍴 ℓ Phillip Devalle
Hotel ★★60% Midway Hotel, Manchester Rd, Castleton, ROCHDALE ☎(0706) 32881 25⇆🏌

FLIXTON Map 5 D7

William Wroe Municipal ☎ 061-748 8680
Pennybridge Ln (E side of village off B5158)
Parkland course, with easy walking.
18 holes, 4395yds, Par 64, SSS 61, Course record 60. Membership 225.

Visitors welcome (restricted WE) must contact in advance 24hrs
Green fees Not confirmed
Facilities △ 🏠 🍴 ℓ Roland West
Hotel ★62%, Beaucliffe Hotel, 254 Eccles Old Rd, Pendleton, SALFORD ☎061-789 5092 21rm(2⇆15🏌)

GATLEY Map 5 D7

Gatley ☎ 061-437 2091
Waterfall Farm, Styal Rd, Heald Green (S side of village off B5166)
Parkland course. Moderately testing. Squash, snooker.
9 holes, 5934yds, Par 69, SSS 68, Course record 67. Membership 375.

Visitors welcome (ex Tue & Sat) Societies welcome (☎)
Green fees £10 per day
Facilities △ 🏠 ℓ
Hotel ★★★60% Belfry Hotel, Stanley Rd, HANDFORTH ☎061-437 0511 82⇆

HALE Map 5 D8

Hale ☎ 061-980 4225
Rappax Rd (1.25m SE)
Beautiful, undulating parkland course, with the River Bollin winding round fairways.
9 holes, 5780yds, Par 70, SSS 68. Membership 300.

Visitors welcome (ex before 1630 Thu ; WE with M only) Societies welcome (contact by letter)
Green fees £14 per day
Facilities △ 🏠 ℓ J Jackson
Hotel ★★★66% Bowdon Hotel, Langham Rd, Bowdon, ALTRINCHAM ☎061-928 7121 82⇆

HAZEL GROVE Map 5 E8

Hazel Grove ☎ 061-483 3978
Buxton Rd (1m E off A6)
Moorland course. Snooker.
18 holes, 6300yds, Par 71, SSS 70, Course record 65. Membership 640.

Visitors welcome must contact in advance Societies welcome (☎ must book Thu & Fri)
Green fees £15 per day (£20 WE & BH)
Facilities ⊗ ⅢⅢ 🍴 ♨ (no catering Mon) ♀ (ex Mon) △ 🏠 🍴 ℓ
Hotel ★58% Acton Court Hotel, Buxton Rd, STOCKPORT ☎061-483 6172 37rm(13⇆15🏌)

HINDLEY Map 5 D7

Hindley Hall ☎ (0942) 55131
Hall Ln (1m N off A58)
Parkland course with mostly easy walking. Snooker.
18 holes, 5875yds, Par 69, SSS 68, Course record 63. Membership 500.

Visitors welcome (restricted Wed and WE) must contact in advance ✉ Societies welcome (☎)
Green fees £18 per day (£20 WE & BH)

Facilities ⊗ 〉||| (no catering Mon) 🄻 ◤ ♀ 🛆 🖼
〖 Steve Yates
Hotel ★★61% Brocket Arms Hotel, Mesnes Rd, WIGAN
☎(0942) 46283 27⇆🐾

HORWICH   Map 5 D7

Horwich ☎ (0204) 696980
Victoria Rd (SE side of village A673)
Moorland course with natural hazards and generally
windy. Hard walking.
9 holes, 5404yds, Par 66, SSS 67, Course record 65.
Membership 200.

Visitors welcome Member must accompany Societies
welcome (apply by letter)
Green fees Not confirmed
Facilities ♀ 🛆
Hotel ★★★62% Crest Hotel, Beaumont Rd, BOLTON
☎(0204) 651511 100⇆🐾

HYDE   Map 5 E7

Werneth Low ☎ 061-368 2503
Werneth Low (2m S of town centre)
Hard walking but good views from this moorland
course. Exposed to wind.
9 holes, 5734yds, Par 70, SSS 68. Membership 350.

Visitors welcome (ex WE & BH, Tue mornings)
Societies welcome
Green fees £9.50 per day (£14.50 WE)
Facilities ⊗ 〉||| by prior arrangement 🄻 ◤ ♀ 🛆 🖼
〖 Tony Bacchus
Hotel ★★★62% Alma Lodge Hotel, 149 Buxton Rd,
STOCKPORT ☎061-483 4431 58rm(52⇆)

LEIGH   Map 5 D7

Pennington ☎ (0942) 607278
St Helen's Rd (SW side of town centre off A572)
Municipal parkland course, with natural hazards of
brooks, ponds and trees, and easy walking.
9 holes, 2919yds, Par 35, SSS 34. Membership 150.

Visitors welcome Societies welcome
Green fees Not confirmed
Facilities ◤ 🖼 ⋔ 〖
Hotel ★★60% Kirkfield Hotel, 2/4 Church St, NEWTON
LE WILLOWS ☎(09252) 28196 & 20489 16⇆🐾

MANCHESTER   Map 5 D7

Davyhulme Park ☎ 061-748 2260
Gleneagles Rd, Davyhulme (8m S adj to Park Hospital)
Parkland course. Snooker.
18 holes, 6237yds, Par 72, SSS 70, Course record 67.
Membership 500.

Visitors welcome (ex Wed & Sat (with M only Sun)) ✉
Societies welcome (☎)
Green fees £16 (£20 WE & BH)

Facilities ⊗ 〉||| by prior arrangement 🄻 ◤ ♀ 🛆 🖼
⋔ 〖 Hugh Lewis
Hotel ★62% Beaucliffe Hotel, 254 Eccles Old Rd,
Pendleton, SALFORD ☎061-789 5092 21rm(2⇆15🐾)

Didsbury ☎ 061-998 9278
Ford Ln, Northenden (6m S of city centre off A5145)
Parkland course. Snooker.
18 holes, 6273yds, Par 70, SSS 70. Membership 700.

Visitors welcome (restricted Tue, Wed & WE) Societies
welcome (☎)
Green fees Not confirmed
Facilities 🛆 🖼 ⋔ 〖
Hotel ★★★53% Post House Hotel, Palatine Rd,
Northenden, MANCHESTER ☎061-998 7090 200⇆🐾

Fairfield ☎ 061-336 3950
Booth Rd, Audenshaw (1.5m W of Audenshaw off A635)
Parkland course with reservoir (sailing available).
Course demands particularly accurate placing of shots.
Snooker.
18 holes, 5664yds, Par 70, SSS 68, Course record 65.
Membership 400.

Visitors welcome (not am at WE) Societies welcome (☎
or by letter)
Green fees £11 per day (£15 WE & BH)
Facilities ⊗ 〉||| 🄻 ◤ (catering by prior arrangement)
♀ 🛆 🖼 〖 Dean Butler
Hotel ★★70% York House Hotel, York Place,
Richmond St, ASHTON-UNDER-LYNE ☎061-330 5899
24rm(18⇆5🐾) Annexe:10⇆

Houldsworth ☎ 061-224 5055
Wingate House, Higher Levenshulme (4m SE of city
centre off A6)
Flat meadowland course, tree-lined and with water
hazards. Testing holes 9th (par 5) and 13th (par 5).
18 holes, 6083yds, Par 70, SSS 68, Course record 63.
Membership 500.

Visitors welcome (ex WE & BH) must contact in
advance Societies welcome (☎)
Green fees £12 per day ; £9 per round
Facilities 🛆 🖼 ⋔ 〖 David Naylor
Hotel ★★★58% Willow Bank Hotel, 340-342 Wilmslow
Rd, Fallowfield, MANCHESTER ☎061-224 0461
124rm(110⇆12🐾)

Northenden ☎ 061-998 4738
Palatine Rd (6.5m S of city centre on B1567 off A5103)
Parkland course. Snooker.
18 holes, 6469yds, Par 72, SSS 71, Course record 63.
Membership 600.

Visitors welcome must contact in advance Societies
welcome (Tue & Fri only ☎)
Green fees £15 per day (£20 WE)
Facilities ⊗ 〉||| 🄻 ◤ ♀ 🛆 🖼 〖 W McColl
Hotel ★★★53% Post House Hotel, Palatine Rd,
Northenden, MANCHESTER ☎061-998 7090 200⇆🐾

Pike Fold ☎ 061-740-1136
Cooper Ln, Victoria Av, Blackley (4m N of city centre off Rochdale Rd)
Undulating meadowland course.
9 holes, 5789yds, Par 70, SSS 68, Course record 66.
Membership 200.

Visitors welcome (with M only WE & BH) ✉ Societies welcome (☎)
Green fees £6 round/day (£8 WE)
Facilities ⊗ ⅢⅢ ⅃ 💻 ♀ ⚘
Hotel ★★★58% The Bower Hotel, Hollinwood Av, Chadderton, OLDHAM ☎061-682 7254 66⇔🏃

Withington ☎ 061-445 9544
243 Palatine Rd, West Didsbury (4m SW of city centre off B5167)
Parkland course. Snooker.
18 holes, 6410yds, Par 71, SSS 71, Course record 68.
Membership 550.

Visitors welcome (ex Thu, restricted WE) must contact in advance Societies welcome (ex Thu)
Green fees £17 per day (£20 WE)
Facilities ⊗ ⅢⅢ by prior arrangement ⅃ 💻 ♀ ⚘ 🏠
ⓕ R J Ling
Hotel ★★★53% Post House Hotel, Palatine Rd, Northenden, MANCHESTER ☎061-998 7090 200⇔🏃

Worsley ☎ 061-789 4202
Stableford Av, Monton Green, Eccles (6.5m NW of city centre off A572)
Well-wooded parkland course. Snooker.
18 holes, 6200yds, Par 72, SSS 70. Membership 700.

Visitors welcome ✉ Societies welcome (Mon, Wed & Thu only)
Green fees Not confirmed
Facilities ⊗ ⅢⅢ ⅃ 💻 ♀ ⚘ 🏠 ⵁ ⓕ Ceri Cousins
Hotel ★★★★66% Hotel Piccadilly, Piccadilly, MANCHESTER ☎061-236 8414 271⇔🏃

MELLOR   Map 5 E8

Mellor & Townscliffe ☎ 061-427 2208
Gibb Ln, Tarden (.5m S)
Parkland and moorland course, undulating with some hard walking. Good views. Testing 200 yd, 9th, par 3.
18 holes, 5925yds, Par 70, SSS 69. Membership 550.

Visitors welcome (restricted Sat) Societies welcome (by letter)
Green fees £12 per day; £10 per round (£15 WE & BH)
Facilities ⊗ ⅢⅢ ⅃ 💻 (no catering Tue) ♀ (ex Tue) ⚘ 🏠 ⓕ Michael J Williams
Hotel ★69% Springfield Hotel, Station Rd, MARPLE ☎061-449 0721 6⇔🏃

Each golf course entry has a recommended hotel. For a wider choice of places to stay, consult *AA Hotels and Restaurants in Britain* or *AA-inspected Bed and Breakfast in Britain*.

MIDDLETON   Map 5 D7

Manchester ☎ 061-643 2718
Hopwood Cottage, Manchester (2.5m N off A664)
Moorland golf of unique character over a spaciously laid out course with generous fairways sweeping along to large greens. A wide variety of holes will challenge the golfer's technique, particularly the testing last three holes.
Driving range, snooker.
18 holes, 6454yds, Par 72, SSS 72, Course record 66.
Membership 650.

SCORE CARD: White Tees					
Hole	Yds	Par	Hole	Yds	Par
1	332	4	10	331	4
2	491	5	11	352	4
3	515	5	12	427	4
4	190	3	13	150	3
5	314	4	14	478	5
6	451	4	15	429	4
7	285	4	16	222	3
8	155	3	17	445	4
9	511	5	18	386	4
Out	3234	37	In	3220	35
			Totals	6454	72

Visitors welcome (restricted WE) must contact in advance ✉ Societies welcome (☎ or by letter)
Green fees £20 per day/round (£25 WE & BH)
Facilities ⊗ by prior arrangement ⅢⅢ by prior arrangement ⅃ 💻 ♀ ⚘ 🏠 ⓕ Brian Connor
Hotel ★★60% Midway Hotel, Manchester Rd, Castleton, ROCHDALE ☎(0706) 32881 25⇔🏃

North Manchester ☎ 061-643 9033
Rhodes House, Manchester Old Rd (W side of town centre off A576)
A long, tight course with natural water hazards. Snooker.
18 holes, 6527yds, Par 72, SSS 72, Course record 66.
Membership 800.

Visitors welcome Societies welcome (☎)
Green fees £20 per day; £16 per round
Facilities ⊗ 💻 ♀ ⚘ 🏠 ⵁ ⓕ Peter Lunt
Hotel ★★★58% The Bower Hotel, Hollinwood Av, Chadderton, OLDHAM ☎061-682 7254 66⇔🏃

MILNROW   Map 5 E7

Tunshill ☎ (0706) 342095
Kiln Ln (1m NE M62 exit junc 21 off B6225)
Testing moorland course, particularly 6th and 15th (par 5's). Snooker.
9 holes, 5804yds, Par 70, SSS 68, Course record 66.
Membership 265.

Visitors welcome (restricted WE & eves) must contact in advance Societies welcome (by letter)
Green fees £7 per day (£8 WE)
Facilities ⊗ (by prior arrangement wkdays) ⅢⅢ ⅃ 💻 ♀ (by prior arrangement wkdays lunchtime) ⚘
Hotel ★★★68% Norton Grange Hotel, Manchester Rd, Castleton, ROCHDALE ☎(0706) 30788 50⇔🏃

For a full list of the golf courses included in this book, check with the index on page 284

OLDHAM Map 5 E7

Crompton & Royton ☎ 061-624 2154
Highbarn (.5m NE of Royton)
Moorland course. Snooker.
*18 holes, 6187yds, Par 70, SSS 69, Course record 65.
Membership 600.*

Visitors welcome must contact in advance Societies
welcome (ex WE ☎)
Green fees Not confirmed
Facilities ⊗ Ⅷ ⅃ ➡ ♀ ♨ 📷 ℓ D A Melling
Hotel ★★★58% The Bower Hotel, Hollinwood Av,
Chadderton, OLDHAM ☎061-682 7254 66⇨🐾

Oldham ☎ 061-624 4986
Lees New Rd (2.5m E off A669)
Moorland course, with hard walking.
18 holes, 5045yds, Par 66, SSS 65. Membership 300.

Visitors welcome must contact in advance WE
Societies welcome
Green fees Not confirmed
Facilities ⊗ (ex Mon) Ⅷ (ex Mon) ⅃ (ex Mon) ➡ (ex
Mon) ♀ ♨ 📷 🐾 ℓ Andrew Laverty
Hotel ★★70% York House Hotel, York Place,
Richmond St, ASHTON-UNDER-LYNE ☎061-330 5899
24rm(18⇨5🐾) Annexe:10⇨

Werneth ☎ 061-624 1190
Green Ln, Garden Suburb (S side of town centre off
A627)
Semi-moorland course, with a deep gulley and stream
crossing eight fairways. Testing hole: 3rd (par 3).
Snooker.
*18 holes, 5363yds, Par 68, SSS 66, Course record 62.
Membership 460.*

Visitors welcome (ex Tue & WE) must contact in
advance Societies welcome (☎)
Green fees Not confirmed
Facilities ⊗ Ⅷ ⅃ ➡ ♀ ♨ 📷 ℓ Terry Morley
Hotel ★★70% York House Hotel, York Place,
Richmond St, ASHTON-UNDER-LYNE ☎061-330 5899
24rm(18⇨5🐾) Annexe:10⇨

PRESTWICH Map 5 D7

Prestwich ☎ 061-773 2544
Hilton Ln (N side of town centre on A6044)
Parkland course, near to Manchester city centre.
Snooker.
18 holes, 4712yds, Par 64, SSS 63. Membership 450.

Visitors welcome (restricted WE) ✉ Societies welcome
(by letter)
Green fees Not confirmed
Facilities ⊗ Ⅷ ⅃ ➡ (no catering Mon) ♀ (ex Mon)
♨ 📷 ℓ G P Coope
Hotel ★62% Beaucliffe Hotel, 254 Eccles Old Rd,
Pendleton, SALFORD ☎061-789 5092 21rm(2⇨15🐾)

ROCHDALE Map 5 E7

Rochdale ☎ (0706) 43818
Edenfield Rd, Bagslate (1.75m W on A680)
Parkland course with enjoyable golf. Snooker.
18 holes, 5780yds, Par 71, SSS 68. Membership 700.

Visitors welcome (booking required Wed & Fri only)
must contact in advance Societies welcome (by letter)
Green fees £16 per day (£20 WE)
Facilities ⊗ by prior arrangement Ⅷ by prior
arrangement ⅃ ➡ ♀ ♨ 📷 🐾 ℓ Andrew Laverty
Hotel ★★60% Midway Hotel, Manchester Rd,
Castleton, ROCHDALE ☎(0706) 32881 25⇨🐾

Springfield Park ☎ (0706) 56401 (WE only)
Springfield Park, Bolton Rd (1.5m SW off A58)
Parkland-moorland course situated in a valley. The
River Roch adds an extra hazard to the course.
*18 holes, 5233yds, Par 67, SSS 66, Course record 67.
Membership 270.*

Visitors welcome (booking at WE) Societies welcome
Green fees £3.50 (£4.50 WE)
Facilities 📷 🐾 ℓ David Wills
Hotel ★★60% Midway Hotel, Manchester Rd,
Castleton, ROCHDALE ☎(0706) 32881 25⇨🐾

ROMILEY Map 5 E8

Romiley ☎ 061-430 2392
Goose House Green (E side of town centre off B6104)
Parkland course, well-wooded. Snooker.
18 holes, 6335yds, Par 70, SSS 70. Membership 700.

Visitors welcome must contact in advance Societies
welcome (by letter)
Green fees Not confirmed
Facilities ⊗ by prior arrangement Ⅷ by prior
arrangement ⅃ ➡ ♀ ♨ 📷 ℓ Garry Butler
Hotel ★★★62% Alma Lodge Hotel, 149 Buxton Rd,
STOCKPORT ☎061-483 4431 58rm(52⇨)

SALE Map 5 D7

Ashton on Mersey ☎ 061-973 3220
Church Ln (1m W of M63 junc 7)
Parkland course with easy walking. Clubhouse recently
destroyed by fire, services being restored.
9 holes, 6146yds, Par 72, SSS 69. Membership 360.

Visitors welcome (with M only Sun & BH, not Sat)
Green fees Not confirmed
Facilities ⊗ Ⅷ ⅃ ➡ ♀ ♨ 📷 ℓ Paul Wagstaff
Hotel ★★★65% Cresta Court Hotel, Church St,
ALTRINCHAM ☎061-927 7272 139⇨🐾

Sale ☎ 061-973 1638
Golf Rd (NW side of town centre off A6144)
Parkland course. Snooker.
*18 holes, 6346yds, Par 71, SSS 70, Course record 67.
Membership 686.*

Visitors welcome (dress regulations in club house)
Societies welcome (by letter)

▶

Green fees £15 per day (£22 WE & BH)
Facilities ⊗ ⅏ 🗑 💺 ♀ 🛆 🛖 ⟨ A M Lake
Hotel ★★★65% Cresta Court Hotel, Church St,
ALTRINCHAM ☎061-927 7272 139⇌🅑

SHEVINGTON
Map 5 C7

Gathurst ☎ Appley Bridge (02575) 2861
62 Miles Ln (W side of village B5375 off junc 27 of M6)
Testing parkland course, with easy walking. Snooker.
9 holes, 6282yds, Par 72, SSS 70, Course record 67.
Membership 350.

Visitors welcome (after 1700, with M Wed, WE & BH)
⊠ Societies welcome (by letter)
Green fees £10
Facilities ⊗ 🗑 💺 ♀ 🛆 🛖 ⟨ David Clarke
Hotel ★★66% Bellingham Hotel, 149 Wigan Ln,
WIGAN ☎(0942) 43893 30⇌🅑

STALYBRIDGE
Map 5 E7

Stamford ☎ (04575) 2126
Huddersfield Rd (2m NE off A635)
Moorland course. Snooker.
18 holes, 5619yds, Par 70, SSS 67, Course record 66.
Membership 400.

Visitors welcome (☎ for details) Societies welcome (one
months notice by letter)
Green fees Not confirmed
Facilities ⊗ (ex Mon) ⅏ (ex Mon) 🗑 💺 ♀ 🛆 🛖 🏌
Hotel ★★70% York House Hotel, York Place,
Richmond St, ASHTON-UNDER-LYNE ☎061-330 5899
24rm(18⇌5🅑) Annexe:10⇌

STOCKPORT
Map 5 E8

Heaton Moor ☎ 061-432 2134
Heaton Mersey (N of town centre off B5169)
Parkland course, easy walking.
18 holes, 5907yds, Par 70, SSS 69, Course record 66.
Membership 400.

Visitors welcome (restricted Tue & BH) Societies
welcome (by letter)
Green fees Not confirmed
Facilities ⊗ ⅏ by prior arrangement 🗑 💺 ♀ 🛆 🛖
🏌 ⟨ C Loydall
Hotel ★★★62% Alma Lodge Hotel, 149 Buxton Rd,
STOCKPORT ☎061-483 4431 58rm(52⇌)

Marple ☎ 061-427 2311
Barnsfold Rd, Hawk Green, Marple (S side of town
centre)
Parkland course.
18 holes, 5475yds, Par 68, SSS 67, Course record 66.
Membership 500.

Visitors welcome ⊠ Societies welcome (☎)
Green fees Not confirmed
Facilities ⊗ ⅏ 🗑 💺 ♀ 🛆 🛖 ⟨ I Scott
Hotel ★★★62% Alma Lodge Hotel, 149 Buxton Rd,
STOCKPORT ☎061-483 4431 58rm(52⇌)

Reddish Vale ☎ 061-480 2359
Southcliffe Rd, Reddish (1.5m N off Reddish road)
Undulating course in valley. Course designed by Dr. A
Mackenzie. Snooker.
18 holes, 6086yds, Par 69, SSS 69, Course record 64.
Membership 500.

Visitors welcome (with M only WE) Societies welcome
(☎)
Green fees Not confirmed
Facilities ⊗ ⅏ by prior arrangement 🗑 💺 ♀ 🛆 🛖
⟨ R A Brown
Hotel ★★★62% Alma Lodge Hotel, 149 Buxton Rd,
STOCKPORT ☎061-483 4431 58rm(52⇌)

Stockport ☎ 061-427 2001
Offerton Rd (4m SE on A627)
A beautifully situated course in wide open countryside.
It is not too long but requires that the player plays all
the shots, to excellent greens.
18 holes, 6290yds, Par 71, SSS 71. Membership 500.

Visitors welcome Societies welcome (Wed & Thu only
by letter)
Green fees Not confirmed
Facilities ⊗ (ex Sun-Mon) ⅏ (ex Sun-Mon) 🗑 (ex Sun-
Mon) 💺 ♀ 🛆 🛖 ⟨ R G Tattersall
Hotel ★★★62% Alma Lodge Hotel, 149 Buxton Rd,
STOCKPORT ☎061-483 4431 58rm(52⇌)

SWINTON
Map 5 D7

Swinton Park ☎ 061-794 1785
East Lancashire Rd (1m W off A580)
One of Lancashire's longest inland courses.
Clubhouse extensions have greatly improved the
facilities at this club. Snooker.
18 holes, 6712yds, Par 73, SSS 72. Membership 600.

Visitors welcome (restricted WE) must contact in
advance ⊠ Societies welcome (by letter)
Green fees £20 per day (£16 per round)
Facilities ⊗ ⅏ 🗑 💺 ♀ 🛆 🛖 ⟨ J Wilson
Hotel ★62% Beaucliffe Hotel, 254 Eccles Old Rd,
Pendleton, SALFORD ☎061-789 5092 21rm(2⇌15🅑)

UPPERMILL
Map 5 E7

Saddleworth ☎ Saddleworth (0457) 873653
Mountain Ash, Ladcastle Rd, Oldham (E side of town
centre off A670)
Moorland course, with superb views of Pennines.
Snooker.
18 holes, 5976yds, Par 71, SSS 69, Course record 64.
Membership 660.

Visitors welcome (restricted WE) must contact in
advance Societies welcome (by letter)
Green fees £12.50 (£16 WE)
Facilities ⊗ by prior arrangement ⅏ by prior
arrangement 🗑 💺 ♀ 🛆 🛖 ⟨ T Shard
Hotel ★★70% York House Hotel, York Place,
Richmond St, ASHTON-UNDER-LYNE ☎061-330 5899
24rm(18⇌5🅑) Annexe:10⇌

URMSTON   Map 5 D7

Flixton ☎ 061-748 2116
Church Rd, Flixton (S side of town centre on B5213)
Parkland course bounded by River Mersey. Snooker.
9 holes, 6410yds, Par 71, SSS 71, Course record 63. Membership 400.

Visitors welcome (WE & BH with M only) Societies welcome (by letter to Steward)
Green fees £15 per day
Facilities ⊗ by prior arrangement ⫿⫿ by prior arrangement ⅃ ♀ 🏠 ᒥ Bob Ling
Hotel ★★★55% Ashley Hotel, Ashley Rd, Hale, ALTRINCHAM ☎061-928 3794 49⇨ᑭ

WALKDEN   Map 5 D7

Brackley Municipal ☎ 061-790 6076
(2m NW on A6)
Mostly flat course.
9 holes, 3003yds, Par 35, SSS 69.

Visitors welcome
Green fees Not confirmed
Facilities 🏠 ᒥ
Hotel ★62% Beaucliffe Hotel, 254 Eccles Old Rd, Pendleton, SALFORD ☎061-789 5092 21rm(2⇨15ᑭ)

WESTHOUGHTON   Map 5 D7

Westhoughton ☎ (0942) 811085
Long Island (.5m NW off A58)
Compact downland course. Snooker.
9 holes, 5772yds, Par 70, SSS 68, Course record 64. Membership 300.

Visitors welcome (with M only WE) Societies welcome (☎)
Green fees £10 per day
Facilities ⊗ by prior arrangement ⫿⫿ by prior arrangement ⅃ 🍺 ♀ (2000-2300) 🏠 ᒥ Stephen Yates
Hotel ★★★62% Crest Hotel, Beaumont Rd, BOLTON ☎(0204) 651511 100⇨ᑭ

WHITEFIELD   Map 5 D7

Stand ☎ 061-766 2388
The Dales, Ashbourne Grove (1m W off A667)
A fine test of golf; accuracy from the tee is the key to success here. A very demanding finish. Fishing and snooker.
18 holes, 6255yds, Par 72, SSS 70. Membership 600.

Visitors welcome must contact in advance ✉ Societies welcome (by letter)
Green fees Not confirmed
Facilities ⊗ ⫿⫿ ⅃ 🍺 ♀ 🏠 ᒥ Mark Dance
Hotel ★60% Woolfield House Hotel, Wash Ln, BURY ☎061-797 9775 16rm(3⇨7ᑭ)

For an explanation of the symbols and abbreviations used, see page 33.

Whitefield ☎ 061-766 3096
Higher Ln (N side of town centre on A665)
Fine sporting parkland course with well-watered greens. Tennis and snooker.
18 holes, 6041yds, Par 69. Membership 500.

Visitors welcome must contact in advance ✉ Societies welcome (by letter)
Green fees £18 (£25 WE &BH)
Facilities Catering on request ♀ 🏠 🏠 ᒥ ᒥ Paul Reeves
Hotel ★★★★55% Portland Thistle Hotel, 3/5 Portland St, Piccadilly Gdns, MANCHESTER ☎061-228 3400 205⇨ᑭ

WIGAN   Map 5 C7

Haigh Hall ☎ (0942) 831107
Haigh Country Park, Haigh (2m NE off B5238)
Municipal parkland course, with hard walking, and a canal forms the west boundary. Adjacent to 'Haigh Country Park' with many facilities.
18 holes, 6423yds, Par 70, SSS 71, Course record 66. Membership 150.

Visitors welcome
Green fees Not confirmed
Facilities ⊗ ⫿⫿ 🍺 ♀ (WE afternoons only) 🏠 🏠 ᒥ ᒥ Ian Lee
Hotel ★★61% Brocket Arms Hotel, Mesnes Rd, WIGAN ☎(0942) 46283 27⇨ᑭ

Wigan ☎ Standish (0257) 421360
Arley Hall, Haigh (3m NE off B5238)
Among the best of the county's 9-hole courses. The fine old clubhouse is the original Arley Hall and is surrounded by a moat. Snooker.
9 holes, 6058yds, Par 70, SSS 69. Membership 370.

Visitors welcome (ex WE & BH) must contact in advance Societies welcome (by letter)
Green fees £13 per day (£18 WE & BH)
Facilities ⊗ by prior arrangement ⫿⫿ by prior arrangement ⅃ 🍺 ♀ 🏠
Hotel ★★66% Bellingham Hotel, 149 Wigan Ln, WIGAN ☎(0942) 43893 30⇨ᑭ

WOODFORD   Map 5 D8

Avro ☎ 061-439 2709
Old Hall Ln (W side of village on A5102)
An attractive, tight and challenging 9-hole course.
9 holes, 5735yds, Par 69, SSS 68. Membership 370.

Visitors welcome Member must accompany
Green fees Not confirmed
Facilities 🍺 🏠
Hotel ★★★67% Bramhall Moat House, Bramhall Ln South, BRAMHALL ☎061-439 8116 65⇨ᑭ

Opening times of bar and catering facilities vary from place to place – it is wise to check in advance of your visit.

WORSLEY   Map 5 D7

Ellesmere ☎ 061-790 2122
Old Clough Ln (N side of village off A580)
Parkland course with natural hazards. Testing holes:
3rd (par 5), 9th (par 3), 13th (par 4). Hard walking.
Snooker.
18 holes, 5954yds, Par 69, SSS 69, Course record 66.
Membership 550.

Visitors welcome (ex club competition days) must
contact in advance ✉ Societies welcome (Mon-Wed
only ☎ or by letter)
Green fees £14 per day (£18 WE & BH)
Facilities ⊗ ⊞ by prior arrangement ⤷ ⬛ ♀ ⌂ 🗄
👕 (Ewan McDonald
Hotel ★62% Beaucliffe Hotel, 254 Eccles Old Rd,
Pendleton, SALFORD ☎061-789 5092 21rm(2⇨15🔥)

HAMPSHIRE

ALDERSHOT   Map 2 C5

Army ☎ (0252) 540638
Laffans Rd (1.5m N of town centre off A323/A325)
Picturesque heathland course with 3, par 3's, over 200
yds.
18 holes, 6550yds, Par 71, SSS 71. Membership 800.

Visitors welcome Member must accompany Societies
welcome (Mon & Thu only)
Green fees With M only £8 per day/round
Facilities ⊗ ⤷ ⬛ ♀ ⌂ 🗄(
Hotel ★★★60% Queens Hotel, Lynchford Rd,
FARNBOROUGH ☎(0252) 545051 110⇨

ALRESFORD   Map 2 B6

Alresford ☎ (0962) 733746
Cheriton Rd, Tichborne Down (1m S on B3046)
Undulating parkland course with testing 4th and 10th
holes (par 4).
12 holes, 6038yds, Par 70, SSS 69, Course record 63.
Membership 490.

Visitors welcome (not before 1200 WE & BH) must
contact in advance Societies welcome (☎ followed by
letter)
Green fees £18.50 per day; £12.50 per round (£24 WE &
BH)
Facilities ⊗ ⊞ ⤷ ⬛ ♀ ⌂ 🗄👕(Malcolm Scott
Hotel ★★63% Grange Hotel, 17 London Rd,
Holybourne, ALTON ☎(0420) 86565 27rm(23⇨🔥)
Annexe:6⇨🔥

ALTON   Map 2 C5

Alton ☎ (0420) 82042
Old Odiham Rd (2m N off A32)
Undulating meadowland course.
9 holes, 5744yds, Par 68, SSS 68, Course record 65.
Membership 340.

Visitors welcome (h'cap 18 or less required WE, or with
M) Societies welcome (weekdays only)
Green fees £15 per day; £10 per round (£20/£15 WE &
BH)
Facilities ⬛ ♀ ⌂ 🗄(Andrew Lamb
Hotel ★★★59% Alton House Hotel, Normandy St,
ALTON ☎(0420) 80033 38⇨🔥

AMPFIELD   Map 2 A6

Ampfield Par Three ☎ Braishfield (0794) 68480
Winchester Rd (4m NE of Romsey on A31)
Pretty parkland course designed by Henry Cotton, easy
walking.
18 holes, 2478yds, Par 54, SSS 53, Course record 49.
Membership 520.

Visitors welcome (h'cap cert required WE & BH) must
contact in advance Societies welcome (apply by letter)
Green fees £14 per day (£15 per round WE)
Facilities ⊗ ⤷ ⬛ ♀ ⌂ 🗄👕(Richard Benfield
Hotel ★★★62% Potters Heron Hotel, AMPFIELD
☎(0703) 266611 60⇨🔥

ANDOVER   Map 2 A5

Andover ☎ (0264) 358040
51 Winchester Rd (1m S on A3057)
Hilly downland course, fine views.
18 holes, 5933yds, Par 69, SSS 68, Course record 66.
Membership 500.

Visitors welcome (restricted WE (am)) Societies
welcome
Green fees £10 per round £15 per day (£20 WE & BH)
Facilities ⊗ ⊞ (ex Sun evening and during Club
matches) ⤷ ⬛ ♀ ⌂ 🗄👕(Andrea Timms
Hotel ★★61% Danebury Hotel, High St, ANDOVER
☎(0264) 23332 24⇨

BARTON-ON-SEA   Map 2 A7

Barton-on-Sea
☎ New Milton
(0425) 615308
Marine Dr East (E side of
town)
Though not strictly a links
course, it is right on a cliff
edge with views over the
Isle of Wight and
Christchurch Bay. On a
still day there is nothing
much to it - but when it
blows the course undergoes
a complete change in
character.
18 holes, 5565yds, Par 67, SSS 67, Course record 62.
Membership 700.

SCORE CARD: Medal Tees					
Hole	Yds	Par	Hole	Yds	Par
1	363	4	10	367	4
2	372	4	11	311	4
3	167	3	12	580	5
4	343	4	13	122	3
5	137	3	14	376	4
6	469	4	15	163	3
7	366	4	16	387	4
8	164	3	17	157	3
9	349	4	18	352	4
Out	2730	33	In	2835	34
			Totals	5565	67

Visitors welcome (after 0830 Mon-Fri & 1115 WE &
BH) must contact in advance ✉ Societies welcome
(Wed & Fri, book well in advance)

Green fees £21 per day (£24 WE & BH)
Facilities ⊗ ⅏ (by prior arrangement for parties)
🏌 🍴 ♀ 🏌 ⌂ ⚑ ⛳ ⛳ P Coombs
Hotel ★★★★(red)⚑Chewton Glen Hotel,
Christchurch Rd, NEW MILTON ☎(0425) 275341
58⇥♉

BASINGSTOKE
Map 2 B5

Basingstoke
☎ (0256) 465990
Kempshott Park (3.5m SW
on A30 M3 exit 7)
A well-maintained
parkland course with wide
and inviting fairways. You
are inclined to expect
longer drives than are
actually achieved - partly
on account of the trees.
There are many two-
hundred-year-old beech
trees, since the course was
built on an old deer park.
18 holes, 6309yds, Par 70, SSS 69, Course record 65.
Membership 725.

SCORE CARD: White Tees					
Hole	Yds	Par	Hole	Yds	Par
1	499	5	10	415	4
2	368	4	11	433	4
3	157	3	12	209	3
4	466	4	13	402	4
5	177	3	14	431	4
6	362	4	15	343	4
7	422	4	16	364	4
8	251	4	17	166	3
9	334	4	18	510	5
Out	3036	35	In	3273	35
			Totals	6309	70

Visitors welcome (with M only WE) ✉ Societies
welcome (Wed & Thu only)
Green fees Not confirmed
Facilities ⊗ ⅏ 🏌 🍴 ♀ ⌂ ⚑ ⛳
Hotel ★★★61% Crest Hotel, Grove Rd,
BASINGSTOKE ☎(0256) 468181 85⇥♉

BORDON
Map 2 C5

Blackmoor ☎ (0420) 472775
Whitehill
A first-class moorland course with a great variety of
holes. Fine greens and wide pine tree-lined fairways
are a distinguishing feature. The ground is mainly
flat and walking easy.
18 holes, 6232yds, Par 69, SSS 70, Course record 65.
Membership 680.

Visitors welcome (ex WE) must contact in advance
✉ Societies welcome (☎)
Green fees £25 per day
Facilities ⊗ ⅏ 🏌 🍴 ♀ ⌂ ⚑ ⛳ Andrew Hall
Hotel ★★★56% Bush Hotel, The Borough,
FARNHAM ☎(0252) 715237 68⇥♉

Each golf course entry has a recommended
hotel. For a wider choice of places to stay,
consult *AA Hotels and Restaurants in Britain* or
AA-inspected Bed and Breakfast in Britain.

BROCKENHURST
Map 2 A7

Brokenhurst Manor
☎ Lymington (0590) 23332
Sway Rd (1m S on B3055)
An attractive woodland
course set at the edge of the
New Forest, with the
unusual feature of three
loops of six holes each to
complete the round.
Fascinating holes include
the short 5th and 12th, and
the 4th and 17th, both dog-
legged.
18 holes, 6222yds, Par 70, SSS 70, Course record 64. Membership 750.

SCORE CARD: White Tees					
Hole	Yds	Par	Hole	Yds	Par
1	316	4	10	208	3
2	495	5	11	404	4
3	174	3	12	168	3
4	374	4	13	412	4
5	167	3	14	297	4
6	327	4	15	322	4
7	384	4	16	520	5
8	449	4	17	414	4
9	459	4	18	332	4
Out	3145	35	In	3077	35
			Totals	6222	70

Visitors welcome (handicap certificate required)
must contact in advance ✉ Societies welcome (Thu
only ☎)
Green fees £27.50 per day (£32.50 WE & BH)
Facilities ⊗ ⅏ by prior arrangement (no catering
Mon and Tue) 🏌 🍴 ♀ ⌂ ⚑ ⛳ C Bonner
Hotel ★★★62% Balmer Lawn Hotel, Lyndhurst
Rd, BROCKENHURST ☎(0590) 23116 58⇥♉

If you know of a golf course, not in this guide
already, which welcomes visitors, we would be
pleased to hear about it.

BROOK

Map 2 A6

Bramshaw ☎ Southampton (0703) 813433
(On B3079 1m W of M27 junc 1)
Two 18-hole courses. The Manor course is parkland
with excellent greens; the Forest course is set
amidst the beautiful New Forest. Easy walking, well
wooded with streams. The Bell Inn Hotel provides
fine accommodation just a wedge shot from the first
tee.
Manor Course 18 holes, 6233yds, Par 71, SSS 70,
Course record 66. Forest Course 18 holes, 5774yds,
Par 69, SSS 68, Course record 66. Membership 1400.

Visitors welcome (WE with M) Member must
accompany must contact in advance Societies
welcome (ex WE ☎)
Green fees £25 per day
Facilities ⊗ ⅏ ᒻ ◗ ♀ △ 🏠 ⌇ Alan Egford
Hotel ★★★69% Bell Inn, BROOK ☎(0703) 812214
22⊸⅃◖

BURLEY

Map 1 K5

Burley ☎ (04253) 2431
(E side of village)
Undulating heather and gorseland. The 7th requires an
accurately placed tee shot to obtain par 4.
9 holes, 6149yds, Par 71, SSS 69, Course record 70.
Membership 520.

Visitors welcome (h'cap cert required, restricted times)
must contact in advance
Green fees £10 per day (£12.50 WE & BH)
Facilities △
Hotel ★★69% Struan Hotel & Restaurant, Horton Rd,
ASHLEY HEATH ☎(0425) 473553 & 473029 10rm(2◖)

CORHAMPTON

Map 2 B6

Corhampton ☎ Droxford (0489) 877279
Sheep's Pond Ln (1m W off B3055)
Downland course.
18 holes, 6088yds, Par 69, SSS 69. Membership 600.

Visitors welcome (WE & BH with M) must contact in
advance Societies welcome (Mon & Thu only ☎)
Green fees £28 per day; £18 per round
Facilities ⊗ ⅏ ᒻ ◗ (no catering Tue) ♀ △ 🏠 ᵞ
⌇ John Harris
Hotel ★★73% Old House Hotel, The Square, WICKHAM
☎(0329) 833049 9⊸◖ Annexe:3⊸◖

CRONDALL

Map 2 C5

Crondall ☎ Aldershot (0252) 850880
Heath Ln (.5m E of village off A287)
Gently undulating course overlooking pretty village.
16-bay floodlit driving range, practice green and
practice bunker.
18 holes, 6278yds, Par 71, SSS 70. Membership 400.

Visitors welcome must contact in advance WE & BH
Societies welcome (☎)
Green fees £14 per round (£18 WE & BH)

Facilities ⊗ (ex Sat) ⅏ (ex Sun-Mon) ᒻ ◗ ♀ △ 🏠
ᵞ ⌇ Peter Rees
Hotel ★★★56% Bush Hotel, The Borough, FARNHAM
☎(0252) 715237 68⊸◖

DIBDEN

Map 2 A7

Dibden ☎ Southampton (0703) 845596
Main Rd (2m NW of Dibden Purlieu)
Municipal parkland course with views over
Southampton Water. A pond guards the green at the par
5, 3rd hole.
18 holes, 6206yds, Par 71, SSS 70. Membership 550.

Visitors welcome Societies welcome (☎)
Green fees Not confirmed
Facilities ⊗ ⅏ by prior arrangement ᒻ ◗ ♀ △ 🏠
ᵞ ⌇ Alan Bridge
Hotel ★★★62% Forest Lodge Hotel, Pikes Hill,
Romsey Rd, LYNDHURST ☎(0703) 283677 19⊸◖

EASTLEIGH

Map 2 A6

Fleming Park ☎ (0703) 612797
Magpie Ln (E side of town centre)
Parkland course with stream-'Monks Brook'-running
through.
18 holes, 4436yds, Par 65, SSS 62. Membership 300.

Visitors welcome
Green fees Not confirmed
Facilities ♀ △ 🏠 ᵞ ⌇
Hotel ★★★62% Southampton Park Hotel,
Cumberland Place, SOUTHAMPTON ☎(0703) 223467
72⊸◖

FARNBOROUGH

Map 2 C5

Southwood ☎ (0252) 548700
Ively Rd (.5m W)
Municipal parkland course with stream running
through.
18 holes, 5553yds, Par 69, SSS 67, Course record 64.
Membership 560.

Visitors welcome must contact in advance Societies
welcome (☎ or by letter)
Green fees £8 per round
Facilities ⊗ ⅏ by prior arrangement ᒻ ◗ ♀ △ 🏠
ᵞ ⌇ Bob Hammond
Hotel ★★★60% Queens Hotel, Lynchford Rd,
FARNBOROUGH ☎(0252) 545051 110⊸

Each golf course entry has a recommended
hotel. For a wider choice of places to stay,
consult *AA Hotels and Restaurants in Britain* or
AA-inspected Bed and Breakfast in Britain.

FLEET

Map 2 C5

North Hants ☎ (0252) 616443
Minley Rd (.25m N of Fleet station on B3013)
Picturesque tree-lined course with much heather
and gorse close to the fairways. A comparatively
easy par-4 first hole may lull the golfer into a false
sense of security, only to be rudely awakened at the
testing holes which follow. The ground is rather
undulating and, though not tiring, does offer some
excellent 'blind' shots, and more than a few
surprises in judging distance.
18 holes, 6090yds, Par 69, SSS 69. Membership 650.

Visitors welcome (with M only WE) must contact in
advance ✉ Societies welcome (Tue & Wed only)
Green fees £25 per day; £18 per round
Facilities ⊗ ⤵ ♨ ♀ ♨ ☖ ♐
Hotel ★★★56% Lismoyne Hotel, Church Rd,
FLEET ☎(0252) 628555 44⇥♠

GOSPORT

Map 2 B7

Gosport & Stokes Bay ☎ (07017) 581625
Military Rd, Haslar (S side of town centre)
A testing seaside course with plenty of gorse and short
rough. Changing winds.
9 holes, 5668yds, Par 72, SSS 69. Membership 370.

Visitors welcome (ex WE & BH)
Green fees Not confirmed
Facilities ♀ ♨
Hotel ★★57% Anglesey Hotel, Crescent Rd,
Alverstoke, GOSPORT ☎(0705) 582157 & 523932 18⇥♠

HARTLEY WINTNEY

Map 2 C4

Hartley Wintney ☎ (025126) 4211
London Rd (NE side of village on A30)
Easy walking, parkland course in countryside. Testing
par 4 at 4th and 13th.
*9 holes, 6096yds, Par 70, SSS 69, Course record 63.
Membership 420.*

Visitors welcome (ex Wed, WE & BH) must contact in
advance Societies welcome (Tue & Thu only)
Green fees £18 per day (£22 WE & BH)
Facilities ⊗ ♨ by prior arrangement ⤵ ♨ ♀ ♨ ☖
♐ Martin Smith
Hotel ★★★56% Lismoyne Hotel, Church Rd, FLEET
☎(0252) 628555 44⇥♠

This guide is updated annually – make sure you
use an up-to-date edition.

HAYLING ISLAND

Map 2 C7

Hayling ☎ (0705) 464446
Ferry Rd (SW side of island at West Town)
A delightful links course among the dunes offering
fine sea-scapes and views across to the Isle of Wight.
Varying sea breezes and sometimes strong winds
ensure that the course seldom plays the same two
days running. Testing holes at the 12th and 13th,
both par 4. Club selection is important.
*18 holes, 6489yds, Par 71, SSS 71, Course record 66.
Membership 950.*

Visitors welcome (handicap cert required) must
contact in advance ✉ Societies welcome (by letter)
Green fees on application
Facilities ⊗ by prior arrangement ♨ by prior
arrangement ⤵ ♨ ♀ ♨ ☖ ♐ ♐ R C A Gadd
Hotel ★★★64% Post House Hotel, Northney Rd,
HAYLING ISLAND ☎(0705) 465011 96⇥

For a full list of the golf courses
included in this book, check
with the index on page 284

KINGSCLERE   Map 2 B4

Sandford Springs ☎ (0635) 297881
Wolverton (on A339)
The course has unique variety in beautiful
surroundings. There are water hazards, woodlands
and gradients to negotiate, providing a challenge for
all playing categories. From its highest point there
are extensive views. There will be 27 holes in
operation by the summer of 1991.
18 holes, 6064yds, Par 70, SSS 69. Membership 500.

Visitors welcome (with M only WE) must contact in
advance Societies welcome (☎)
Green fees £30 per day ; £20 per round
Facilities ⊗ ⓛ ⚏ ♀ ♨ 🖻 ⫟ ℓ Kim Brake/
Anthony Dillon
Hotel ★★★62% Hilton National Hotel, Popley
Way, Aldermaston Roundabout, Ringway North
(A339), BASINGSTOKE ☎(0256) 20212 138⇨🐾

KINGSLEY   Map 2 C5

Dean Farm ☎ Bordon (0420) 2313
(W side of village off B3004)
Undulating downland course. Tennis.
9 holes, 1350yds, Par 27.

Visitors welcome
Green fees Not confirmed
Facilities ⓛ ⚏
Hotel ★★63% Grange Hotel, 17 London Rd,
Holybourne, ALTON ☎(0420) 86565 27rm(23⇨🐾)
Annexe :6⇨🐾

LECKFORD   Map 2 A5

Leckford ☎ (0264) 810710
(1m SW off A3057)
A testing downland course with good views.
9 holes, 6444yds, Par 70, SSS 71. Membership 200.

Visitors welcome (☎ WE) Member must accompany
must contact in advance
Green fees Not confirmed
Facilities ♨
Hotel ★★★56% Grosvenor Hotel, High St,
STOCKBRIDGE ☎(0264) 810606 25⇨🐾

LEE-ON-SOLENT   Map 2 B7

Lee-on-Solent ☎ (0705) 551170
Brune Ln (1m N off B3385)
A modest parkland/heathland course, yet a testing one.
The five short holes always demand a high standard of
play and the 13th is rated one of the best in the country.
*18 holes, 5959yds, Par 69, SSS 69, Course record 66.
Membership 700.*

Visitors welcome (only with M at WE) must contact in
advance Societies welcome (☎)
Green fees £18 per day
Facilities ⊗ ⫟ ⓛ ⚏ ♀ ♨ 🖻 ℓ
Hotel ★★66% Red Lion Hotel, East St, FAREHAM
☎(0329) 822640 44⇨🐾

LIPHOOK   Map 2 C6

Liphook ☎ (0428) 723271
Wheatsheaf Enclosure (1.5m SW off A3)
Heathland course with easy walking and fine views.
18 holes, 6250yds, Par 70, SSS 70. Membership 800.

Visitors welcome (ex Sun am) must contact in
advance ✉ Societies welcome (☎)
Green fees £30 day (£40 WE/BH) ;£20 round £30
WE/BH
Facilities ⊗ ⫟ by prior arrangement ⓛ ⚏ ♀ ♨
🖻 ⫟ ℓ Ian Large
Hotel ★★★69% Lythe Hill Hotel, Petworth Rd,
HASLEMERE ☎(0428) 51251 due to change to 651251
40⇨

Old Thorns London Kosaido ☎ (0428) 724555
Longmoor Rd (1m W on B2131)
A challenging 18-hole championship course designed
around magnificent oaks, beeches and Scots pine.
Accommodation, tennis, indoor heated swimming pool,
sauna and solarium.
18 holes, 6041yds, Par 72, SSS 70.

Visitors welcome must contact in advance Societies
welcome (☎)
Green fees Not confirmed
Facilities ⊗ ⫟ ⓛ ⚏ ♀ ♨ 🖻 ⫟ ℓ Philip Loxley
Hotel ★★★69% Lythe Hill Hotel, Petworth Rd,
HASLEMERE ☎(0428) 51251 due to change to 651251
40⇨

LYNDHURST   Map 2 A7

New Forest ☎ (0703) 282450
Southampton Rd (0.5m NE off A35)
This picturesque heathland course is laid out in a
typical stretch of the New Forest on high ground a
little above the village of Lynhurst. Natural hazards
include the inevitable forest ponies. The first two
holes are somewhat teasing, as is the 485-yard (par 5)
9th. Walking is easy and there are 10 starting
points.
18 holes, 5742yds, Par 69, SSS 68. Membership 900.

Visitors welcome (after 1000 Sat, 1330 Sun & 0900
wkdays) Societies welcome (☎ & confirm by letter)
Green fees £12 per day (£15 WE & BH)
Facilities ⊗ ⓛ ⚏ ♀ ♨ 🖻 ℓ Ken Gilhespy
Hotel ★★★68% Crown Hotel, High St,
LYNDHURST ☎(0703) 282922 41⇨

PETERSFIELD   Map 2 C6

Petersfield ☎ (0730) 63725
Heath Rd (E side of town centre off A3)
Part-heath, parkland course with a lake, and good
views.
*18 holes, 5710yds, Par 69, SSS 68, Course record 66.
Membership 650.*

Visitors welcome (restricted WE & BH) Societies
welcome (by letter)

Green fees £18 day (£24 WE); £12 per round (£18 WE)
Facilities ⊗ by prior arrangement ⅏ by prior
arrangement ⌸ ⚌ ♀ ⌂ 🖻 (Stephen Clay
Hotel ★★★66% Spread Eagle Hotel, South St,
MIDHURST ☎(0730) 816911 37⇨ Annexe:4❧

PORTSMOUTH & SOUTHSEA Map 2 B7

Great Salterns Public Course
☎ Portsmouth (0705) 664549 & 699519
Eastern Rd (NE of town centre on A2030)
Flat seaside course known as Great Salterns. Easy
walking. Testing 13th hole approx 130 yds across lake
(no alternative).
18 holes, 5855yds, Par 71, SSS 68. Membership 700.

Visitors welcome Societies welcome (☎)
Green fees Not confirmed
Facilities ♀ 🖻 ᵀ (Terry Healy
Hotel ★★★55% Hospitality Inn, St Helens Pde,
SOUTHSEA ☎(0705) 731281 115⇨❧

Southsea ☎ Portsmouth (0705) 660945
The Mansion, Great Salterns, Eastern Rd (.5m off M27)
Municipal, meadowland course.
*18 holes, 5900yds, Par 72, SSS 68, Course record 64.
Membership 650.*

Visitors welcome Societies welcome
Green fees Not confirmed
Facilities 🖻 ᵀ (Terry Healy
Hotel ★★★55% Hospitality Inn, St Helens Pde,
SOUTHSEA ☎(0705) 731281 115⇨❧

ROMSEY   Map 2 A6

Dunwood Manor Country Club
☎ Lockerley (0794) 40549
Shootash Hill (4m W off A27)
Parkland course, fine views. Testing hole: Reynolds
Leap (par 4). Snooker.
*18 holes, 5865yds, Par 69, SSS 67, Course record 61.
Membership 700.*

Visitors welcome (restricted WE) must contact in
advance ✉ Societies welcome (☎)
Green fees £20 per day; £15 per round (£25 WE)
Facilities ⊗ ⅏ ⌸ ⚌ ♀ ⌂ 🖻 ᵀ (Gary Stubbington
Hotel ★★★62% Potters Heron Hotel, AMPFIELD
☎(0703) 266611 60⇨❧

Romsey ☎ Southampton (0703) 734637
Romsey Rd, Nursling (3m S on A3057)
Parkland/woodland course with narrow tree-lined
fairways. 6 holes are undulating, rest are sloping. There
are superb views over the Test valley.
18 holes, 5740yds, Par 69, SSS 68. Membership 750.

Visitors welcome (with M only WE) ✉
Green fees Not confirmed
Facilities ⊗ ⅏ ⌸ ⚌ ♀ ⌂ 🖻 (Mark Desmond
Hotel ★★★55% Hospitality Inn, St Helens Pde,
SOUTHSEA ☎(0705) 731281 115⇨❧

ROTHERWICK   Map 2 C5

Tylney Park ☎ Hook (0256) 762079
(.5m SW)
Parkland course. Practice area.
*18 holes, 6109yds, Par 70, SSS 69, Course record 65.
Membership 700.*

Visitors welcome (with M or handicap certificate WE)
Societies welcome (☎)
Green fees £14 per day (£25 WE)
Facilities ⊗ by prior arrangement ⅏ by prior
arrangement ⌸ ⚌ ♀ ⌂ 🖻 ᵀ (C De Bruin/M
Kimberley
Hotel ★★★★♨79% Tylney Hall Hotel, ROTHERWICK
☎(0256) 764881 35⇨ Annexe :56⇨

ROWLANDS CASTLE   Map 2 C7

Rowlands Castle
☎ Portsmouth
(07051) 412784
Links Ln (W side of village
off B2149)
Exceptionally dry in
winter, the course is a
testing one with a number
of tricky dog-legs and
bunkers much in evidence.
The 7th is the longest hole
on the course and leads to a
well-guarded armchair
green.

SCORE CARD: White Tees					
Hole	Yds	Par	Hole	Yds	Par
1	326	4	10	441	4
2	182	3	11	181	3
3	370	4	12	490	5
4	356	4	13	380	4
5	351	4	14	161	3
6	397	4	15	430	4
7	522	5	16	337	4
8	366	4	17	509	5
9	368	4	18	460	4
Out	3238	36	In	3389	36
			Totals	6627	72

*18 holes, 6381yds, Par 72, SSS 70, Course record 66.
Membership 850.*

Visitors welcome (only with M Sat, restricted Sun)
must contact in advance Societies welcome (Tue &
Thu only, by letter)
Green fees £20 per day (£25 WE & BH)
Facilities ⊗ ⌸ ⚌ ♀ ⌂ 🖻 (Peter Klepacz
Hotel ★★★65% Brookfield, Havant Rd,
EMSWORTH ☎(0243) 373363 41⇨

SHEDFIELD   Map 2 B7

Meon Valley Hotel Golf & Country Club
☎ Wickham (0329) 833455
Sandy Ln (off A334 between
Botley and Wickham)
It has been said that a golf
course architect is as good
as the ground on which he
has to work. Here Hamilton
Stutt had magnificent
terrain at his disposal and a
very good and lovely course
is the result. The hotel
provides many sports
facilities.

SCORE CARD: White Tees					
Hole	Yds	Par	Hole	Yds	Par
1	484	5	10	544	5
2	458	4	11	362	4
3	403	4	12	153	3
4	168	3	13	330	4
5	444	4	14	233	3
6	369	4	15	315	4
7	155	3	16	474	4
8	552	5	17	386	4
9	393	4	18	296	4
Out	3426	36	In	3093	35
			Totals	6519	71

18 holes, 6519yds, Par 71, SSS 71. Membership 500.

▶

Visitors welcome must contact in advance Societies welcome (by letter)
Green fees Not confirmed
Facilities ⊗ 𝔐 🦶 💪 ♀ ⛄ 🧥 🍴 John Stirling
Hotel ★★73% Old House Hotel, The Square, WICKHAM ☎(0329) 833049 9⊸🛏 Annexe:3⊸🛏

SOUTHAMPTON   Map 2 A6

Southampton ☎ (0703) 760472
Golf Course Rd, Bassett (4m N of city centre off A33)
This beautiful, municipal, parkland course always ensures a good game, fast in summer, slow in winter. Three par 4's over 450 yds.
18 holes, 6213yds, Par 69, SSS 70. Membership 500.

Visitors welcome Societies welcome
Green fees Not confirmed
Facilities ♀ ⛄ 🍴 🍴
Hotel ★★57% Star Hotel, High St, SOUTHAMPTON ☎(0703) 339939 45rm(14⊸21🛏)

Stoneham ☎ (0703) 769272
Bassett Green Rd, Bassett
(4m N of city centre off A27)
A hilly, heather course with sand or peat sub-soil, the fairways are separated by belts of woodland and gorse. The interesting 4th is a difficult par 4 and the fine 11th has cross-bunkers about 150 yards from the tee.
18 holes, 6310yds, Par 72, SSS 70, Course record 65. Membership 800.

SCORE CARD					
Hole	Yds	Par	Hole	Yds	Par
1	507	5	10	185	3
2	191	3	11	389	4
3	356	4	12	516	5
4	462	4	13	255	4
5	304	4	14	476	5
6	501	5	15	419	4
7	233	3	16	120	3
8	168	3	17	377	4
9	374	4	18	477	5
Out	3096	35	In	3214	37
			Totals	6310	72

Visitors welcome (ex WE) must contact in advance Societies welcome (apply to secretary)
Green fees £25 per day/round
Facilities ⊗ 𝔐 by prior arrangement 🦶 💪 ♀ (all day) ⛄ 🍴 Ian Young
Hotel ★★★52% Polygon Hotel, Cumberland Place, SOUTHAMPTON ☎(0703) 330055 119⊸

SOUTHWICK   Map 2 B7

Southwick Park Naval Recreation Centre
☎ Cosham (0705) 370683
Pinsley Dr (.5m SE off B2177)
Set in 100 acres of parkland.
18 holes, 5855yds, Par 69, SSS 68, Course record 64. Membership 700.

Visitors welcome (wkdays am only) must contact in advance Societies welcome (Tue only ☎)
Green fees £12 per round
Facilities ⊗ by prior arrangement 𝔐 by prior arrangement 🦶 ♀ ⛄ 🍴 John Green
Hotel ★★73% Old House Hotel, The Square, WICKHAM ☎(0329) 833049 9⊸🛏 Annexe:3⊸🛏

TADLEY   Map 2 B4

Bishopswood ☎ (0734) 815213
Bishopswood Ln (1m W off A340)
Wooded course, fairly tight, with stream and natural water hazards. Floodlit driving range.
9 holes, 6474yds, Par 72, SSS 71, Course record 68. Membership 400.

Visitors welcome (Tue, Thu & Fri only.Mon & Wed with M) must contact in advance Societies welcome (☎)
Green fees 9 holes £7; 18 holes £12
Facilities ⊗ 𝔐 🦶 💪 ♀ ⛄ 🍴 Steve Ward
Hotel ★★★62% Hilton National Hotel, Popley Way, Aldermaston Roundabout, Ringway North (A339), BASINGSTOKE ☎(0256) 20212 138⊸🛏

TIDWORTH   Map 1 K3

Tidworth Garrison
☎ Stonehenge (0980) 42301
Bulford Rd (W side of village off A338)
A breezy, dry downland course with lovely turf, fine trees and views over Salisbury Plain. The 3rd and 12th holes are notable. The 564-yard 13th, going down towards the clubhouse, gives the big hitter a chance to let fly.
18 holes, 5990yds, Par 69, SSS 69, Course record 65. Membership 650.

SCORE CARD: Medal Tees					
Hole	Yds	Par	Hole	Yds	Par
1	324	4	10	135	3
2	163	3	11	416	4
3	393	4	12	173	3
4	451	4	13	564	5
5	160	3	14	156	3
6	480	5	15	383	4
7	293	4	16	343	4
8	429	4	17	336	3
9	375	4	18	416	4
Out	3068	35	In	2922	34
			Totals	5990	69

Visitors welcome (after 1530 summer WE & BH) must contact in advance Societies welcome (by letter)
Green fees Not confirmed
Facilities ⊗ 𝔐 🦶 💪 ♀ ⛄ 🍴 Terry Gosden
Hotel ★★★63% Ashley Court, Micheldever Rd, ANDOVER ☎(0264) 57344 35⊸🛏

WATERLOOVILLE   Map 2 B7

Waterlooville ☎ Portsmouth (0705) 263388
Cherry Tree Av, Cowplain (NE side of town centre off A3)
Parkland course, easy walking.
18 holes, 6647yds, Par 72, SSS 72, Course record 66. Membership 800.

Visitors welcome (wkdays only) must contact in advance Societies welcome (Thu only apply by letter)
Green fees £24 per day ; £20 per round
Facilities ⊗ 𝔐 by prior arrangement 🦶 💪 ♀ ⛄ 🍴 John Hay
Hotel ★★★60% The Bear, East St, HAVANT ☎(0705) 486501 42⊸

We make every effort to provide accurate information, but some details may change after we go to print.

WINCHESTER   Map 2 B6

Hockley ☎ Twyford (0962) 713165
Twyford (2m S on A333)
High downland course with good views.
18 holes, 6279yds, Par 71, SSS 70. Membership 775.

Visitors welcome (with M only at WE) Societies
welcome (by letter)
Green fees £22 per day (£24 WE)
Facilities ⊗ (ex Mon) ⊮ (ex Mon) 🏌 ⚏ ♀ ⌂ 🏠 ⛳
⛴ Terry Lane
Hotel ★★★★50% Wessex Hotel, Paternoster Row,
WINCHESTER ☎(0962) 61611 94⇌🐾

Royal Winchester
☎ (0962) 852462
Sarum Rd (1.5m W off
A3090)
The Royal Winchester Club
must be included in any list
of notable clubs, because of
its age (it dates from 1888)
and also because the Club
was involved in one of the
very first professional
matches. Today it still
flourishes on its present
sporting, downland course.

SCORE CARD: White Tees					
Hole	Yds	Par	Hole	Yds	Par
1	284	4	10	490	5
2	348	4	11	188	3
3	204	3	12	382	4
4	374	4	13	456	4
5	357	4	14	263	4
6	465	4	15	414	4
7	158	3	16	501	5
8	360	4	17	148	3
9	482	5	18	338	4
Out	3032	35	In	3180	36
			Totals	6212	71

*18 holes, 6212yds, Par 71, SSS 70, Course record 67.
Membership 700.*

Visitors welcome (WE with M) must contact in
advance ✉ Societies welcome (by letter)
Green fees £20 per day weekdays
Facilities ⊗ ⊮ 🏌 ⚏ ♀ ⌂ 🏠 ⛳ ⛴ D P Williams
Hotel ★★★⚑78% Lainston House Hotel,
Sparsholt, WINCHESTER ☎(0962) 63588
32rm(30⇌1🐾)

HEREFORD & WORCESTER

ALVECHURCH   Map 3 J5

Kings Norton ☎ Wythall (0564) 826706
Brockhill Ln, Weatheroak (3m NE)
An old club with 3, 9-hole courses, the Blue, Red and
Yellow. A parkland course, with some exacting
water hazards, it has housed important events.
There is also a 12-hole, par 3 course available for
play. Snooker.
*18 holes, 7064yds, Par 72, SSS 74, Course record 65.
Membership 950.*

Visitors welcome (ex WE) Societies welcome (☎)
Green fees £20 per day/round
Facilities ⊗ ⊮ 🏌 ⚏ ♀ ⌂ 🏠 ⛳ ⛴ Clive Haycock
Hotel ★★★69% Post House Hotel, Otley Rd,
BRAMHOPE ☎(0532) 842911 129⇌

Opening times of bar and catering facilities vary
from place to place – it is wise to check in
advance of your visit.

BEWDLEY   Map 3 H5

Little Lakes Golf and Country Club ☎ (0299) 266385
Lye Head (2.25m W off A456)
This testing 9-hole course offers alternative tees for the
second 9 with some pleasing views. Swimming pool,
tennis, fishing and riding available.
*9 holes, 6247yds, Par 73, SSS 72, Course record 70.
Membership 500.*

Visitors welcome (ex WE) must contact in advance
Societies welcome (☎)
Green fees Not confirmed
Facilities ⊗ ⊮ (Mon-Sat) 🏌 ⚏ ♀ ⌂ 🏠 ⛴ Mark
Laing
Hotel ★★53% Black Boy Hotel, Kidderminster Rd,
BEWDLEY ☎(0299) 402119 17rm(5⇌) Annexe:8rm(2⇌)

BLAKEDOWN   Map 3 H5

Churchill and Blakedown ☎ (0562) 700200
Churchill Ln (W side of village off A456)
Pleasant course on hilltop with extensive views.
9 holes, 6472yds, Par 72, SSS 71. Membership 400.

Visitors welcome (with M only WE & BH) Societies
welcome (ex WE)
Green fees £15 per day/round
Facilities ⊗ ⊮ 🏌 ⚏ (no catering Mon) ♀ ⌂ 🏠 ⛳
Hotel ★★68% Gainsborough House Hotel, Bewdley
Hill, KIDDERMINSTER ☎(0562) 820041 42⇌🐾

BROADWAY   Map 3 J7

Broadway ☎ (0386) 853683
Willersey Hill (2m NE)
At the edge of the Cotswolds lies this downland course,
at an altitude of 900 ft above sea level, with extensive
views.
18 holes, 6216yds, Par 72, SSS 69. Membership 700.

Visitors welcome (ex Sat unless with M No ladies Sun
(am)) must contact in advance Societies welcome
(☎early application advised)
Green fees £17 per day (£21 WE & BH)
Facilities ⊗ ⊮ by prior arrangement 🏌 ⚏ (no
catering Mon) ♀ ⌂ 🏠 ⛴ John W Freeman
Hotel ★★★68% Dormy House Hotel, Willersey Hill,
BROADWAY ☎(0386) 852711 26⇌🐾 Annexe:23⇌

DROITWICH   Map 3 H6

Droitwich ☎ (0905) 774344
Ford Ln (1.5m N off A38)
Undulating parkland course. Snooker.
18 holes, 6040yds, Par 70, SSS 69. Membership 768.

Visitors welcome (with M only WE) ✉ Societies
welcome (☎ or by letter)
Green fees £18
Facilities ⊗ ⊮ 🏌 ⚏ ♀ ⌂ 🏠 ⛴ C Thompson
Hotel ★★★★70% Chateau Impney Hotel, DROITWICH
☎(0905) 774411 67⇌🐾

FLADBURY   Map 3 J6

Evesham ☎ Evesham (0386) 860395
Craycombe Links, Old Worcester Rd (.75m N on B4084)
Parkland course with good views.
18 holes, 6415yds, Par 72, SSS 71. Membership 360.

Visitors welcome (ex Tue & comp days. H'cap cert required) ✉ Societies welcome (by letter)
Green fees £15 per day/round
Facilities ⊗ by prior arrangement ⅏ by prior arrangement ⅃ ⅊ ♀ △ ⌂ ⎾ J R Gray
Hotel ★★★66% The Evesham Hotel, Coopers Ln, off Waterside, EVESHAM ☎(0386) 765566 40⇦⅏♠

HEREFORD   Map 3 G7

Belmont Lodge Hotel & Golf Club ☎ (0432) 352666
Belmont House, Belmont (2m S on A4654)
Partly wooded course, the second half of which is on the banks of the River Wye. Accommodation. Tennis, fishing, snooker.
18 holes, 6480yds, Par 71, SSS 71, Course record 70. Membership 500.

Visitors welcome must contact in advance Societies welcome (by letter)
Green fees £16 (£18 WE)
Facilities ⊗ (Sun only) ⅏ ⅃ ⅊ ♀ △ ⌂ ⎾ Mike Welsh
Hotel ★★★68% Hereford Moat House, Belmont Rd, HEREFORD ☎(0432) 354301 28⇦♠ Annexe:32⇦♠

HOLLYWOOD   Map 3 J5

Gay Hill ☎ 021-474 6001
Alcester Rd (N side of village)
A meadowland course, some 7m from Birmingham. Snooker.
18 holes, 6532yds, Par 72, SSS 71, Course record 66. Membership 715.

Visitors welcome (with M only WE) ✉ Societies welcome (by letter)
Green fees £20 per day
Facilities ⊗ ⅏ ⅃ ⅊ ♀ △ ⌂ ⎾ ⎾ Andrew Hill
Hotel ★★★63% George Hotel, High St, SOLIHULL ☎021-711 2121 74⇦♠

KIDDERMINSTER   Map 3 H5

Habberley ☎ (0562) 745756
(2m NW)
Very hilly parkland course.
9 holes, 2736yds, Par 69, SSS 68. Membership 300.

Visitors welcome (ex competition days) must contact in advance Societies welcome (☎)
Green fees Not confirmed
Facilities ⊗ ⅏ ⅃ ⅊ ♀ △ ⌂
Hotel ★★68% Gainsborough House Hotel, Bewdley Hill, KIDDERMINSTER ☎(0562) 820041 42⇦♠

Kidderminster ☎ (0562) 822303
Russel Rd (.5m SE of town centre)
Parkland course with natural hazards and some easy walking.
18 holes, 6223yds, Par 71, SSS 70. Membership 700.

Visitors welcome (with M only WE & BH) ✉ Societies welcome (by letter)
Green fees £18 per day
Facilities ⊗ ⅏ by prior arrangement ⅃ (Tue-Sat) ⅊ ♀ △ ⌂ ⎾ ⎾ N P Underwood
Hotel ★★68% Gainsborough House Hotel, Bewdley Hill, KIDDERMINSTER ☎(0562) 820041 42⇦♠

KINGTON   Map 3 F6

Kington ☎ (0544) 230340
Bradnor Hill (.5m N off B4355)
The highest golf course in England and Wales, with views over seven counties. A natural heathland course with easy walking on mountain turf cropped by sheep. There is bracken to catch any really bad shots but no sand traps.
18 holes, 5840yds, Par 70, SSS 68, Course record 65. Membership 600.

Visitors welcome (ex WE 1015-1200 & 1345-1445 & comp days)
Green fees £11 (£16 WE & BH)
Facilities ⊗ by prior arrangement ⅏ by prior arrangement ⅃ ⅊ ♀ △ ⌂
Hotel ★★★53% Talbot Hotel, West St, LEOMINSTER ☎(0568) 6347 23⇦♠

LEOMINSTER   Map 3 G6

Leominster ☎ (0568) 2863
Ford Bridge (3m S on A49)
Sheltered parkland course. Fishing.
18 holes, 6084yds, Par 69, SSS 69. Membership 600.

Visitors welcome (ex Sun am) must contact in advance ✉ Societies welcome (☎)
Green fees £14 per day (£17 WE & BH)
Facilities ⊗ ⅏ ⅃ ⅊ (no catering Mon) ♀ (ex Mon) △ ⌂ ⎾ ⎾ Russell Price
Hotel ★★60% Royal Oak Hotel, South St, LEOMINSTER ☎(0568) 2610 17⇦♠ Annexe:1⇦

MALVERN WELLS   Map 3 H6

Worcestershire ☎ Malvern (0684) 575992
Wood Farm, Hanley Rd (2m S of Gt Malvern on B4209)
Fairly easy walking on windy downland course with trees, ditches and other natural hazards. Outstanding views of Malvern Hills and Severn Valley. 17th hole (par 5) is approached over small lake. Snooker.
18 holes, 6449yds, Par 71, SSS 71, Course record 66. Membership 800.

Visitors welcome (only after 1000 at WE, or with M) must contact in advance ✉ Societies welcome (☎)
Green fees £16 per day (£20 WE & BH)

Facilities ⊗ ⊞ 🏌 🍺 ⚑ ⛳ 🏌 (Grahame M Harris
Hotel ★★★61% Foley Arms Hotel, Worcester Rd, MALVERN ☎(0684) 573397 26⇨🏠 Annexe:2rm

REDDITCH   Map 3 J6

Abbey Park Golf & Country Club ☎ (0527) 63918
Dagnell End Rd (1.25m N off A441 on B4101)
A newly-built parkland course with rolling fairways. A 'Site of Special Scientific Interest', the course includes two fly-fishing lakes and is pleasant to play. Accommodation, indoor-heated swimming pool, snooker, sauna, solarium, gymnasium.
18 holes, 6411yds, Par 71, SSS 71, Course record 69. Membership 1400.

Visitors welcome (with M only WE) Societies welcome (by letter)
Green fees £6-£7 per day (£10 WE)
Facilities ⊗ ⊞ 🏌 🍺 ⚑ ⛳ 🏠 🏌 (R K Cameron
Hotel ★★★61% Southcrest Hotel, Pool Bank, Southcrest, REDDITCH ☎(0527) 541511 58⇨🏠

Pitcheroak ☎ (0257) 541054
Plymouth Rd (SW side of town centre off A448)
Woodland course, hilly in places.
9 holes, 4527yds, Par 66, SSS 62. Membership 350.

Visitors welcome Societies welcome
Green fees £2.30 (9 holes) £4 (18 holes) (£2.80/£4.50 WE)
Facilities ⊗ ⊞ 🏌 🍺 ⚑ ⛳ 🏠 🏌 (David Stewart
Hotel ★★★61% Southcrest Hotel, Pool Bank, Southcrest, REDDITCH ☎(0527) 541511 58⇨🏠

Redditch ☎ (0527) 543309
Lower Grinsty Ln, Callow Hill (2m SW)
Parkland course, where hazards include woods, ditches and large ponds. The par 4, 14th is a testing hole. Snooker.
18 holes, 6671yds, Par 72, SSS 72. Membership 814.

Visitors welcome (with M only WE & BH) Societies welcome (by letter)
Green fees £20 per day
Facilities ⊗ ⊞ 🏌 🍺 ⚑ ⛳ 🏠 🏌 (F Powell
Hotel ★★★60% Perry Hall Hotel, Kidderminster Rd, BROMSGROVE ☎(0527) 579976 55⇨🏠

ROSS-ON-WYE   Map 3 G7

Ross-on-Wye ☎ Gorsley (098982) 267
Two Park, Gorsley (on B4221 N side of M50 junc 3)
This undulating, parkland course has been cut out of a silver birch forest, the fairways being well-screened from each other. They are tight, the greens good. Snooker.
18 holes, 6500yds, Par 72, SSS 73. Membership 750.

Visitors welcome (restricted WE) must contact in advance Societies welcome (☎)
Green fees £25 per day (£30 WE & BH)

Facilities ⊗ ⊞ 🏌 🍺 ⚑ ⛳ 🏠 (Adrian Clifford
Hotel ★★★60%, Chase Hotel, Gloucester Rd, ROSS-ON-WYE ☎(0989) 763161 40⇨🏠

WORCESTER   Map 3 H6

Tolladine ☎ (0905) 21074
Tolladine Rd (1.5m E)
Parkland type course with excellent views of the surrounding hills and Worcester city.
9 holes, 5619yds, Par 68, SSS 67, Course record 67. Membership 350.

Visitors welcome (with M only WE & BH) Societies welcome (by letter)
Green fees £10 per day
Facilities 🍺 ⛳ 🏠
Hotel ★★★56% Giffard Hotel, High St, WORCESTER ☎(0905) 726262 103⇨

Worcester ☎ (0905) 422555
Boughton Park (SW side of city centre off A4103)
Fine parkland course, many trees, and with views of the Malvern Hills. Tennis squash and snooker.
18 holes, 5946yds, Par 68, SSS 68, Course record 67. Membership 1100.

Visitors welcome (with M only WE) must contact in advance ✉ Societies welcome (☎)
Green fees £18 per day/round
Facilities ⊗ ⊞ 🏌 🍺 ⚑ ⛳ 🏠 (Colin Colenso
Hotel ★★★56% Giffard Hotel, High St, WORCESTER ☎(0905) 726262 103⇨

WORMSLEY   Map 3 G6

Herefordshire ☎ Canon Pyon (0432) 71219
Ravens Causeway (E side of village)
Undulating parkland course with expansive views.
18 holes, 6050yds, Par 70, SSS 69, Course record 62. Membership 900.

Visitors welcome must contact in advance Societies welcome (☎ or by letter)
Green fees £15 per day (£21 WE & BH)
Facilities ⊗ ⊞ 🏌 🍺 ⚑ ⛳ 🏠 🏌 (David Hemming
Hotel ★★★61% The Green Dragon, Broad St, HEREFORD ☎(0432) 272506 88⇨

WYTHALL   Map 3 J5

Fulford Heath ☎ (0564) 822806
Tanners Green Ln (1m SE off A435)
Heathland course in two parts either side of the River Cole.
18 holes, 6216yds, Par 70, SSS 70. Membership 700.

Visitors welcome (one only with M WE & BH) must contact in advance ✉ Societies welcome (by letter)
Green fees Available on request

▶

To see a full range of AA guides and maps, visit your local AA Shop or any good bookshop.

Facilities ⊗ ⵊⵊⵊ ᴸᴸ ⵌ (no catering Mon, dinner not served Sun) ♀ ⵈ 🛏 ⵗ ⵌ
Hotel ★★★64% St John's Swallow Hotel, 651 Warwick Rd, SOLIHULL ☎021-711 3000 206⮎

HERTFORDSHIRE

ALDENHAM   Map 2 E2

Aldenham Golf and Country Club
☎ Watford (0923) 853929
Church Ln (W side of village)
Undulating parkland course. Snooker.
Old Course 18 holes, 6455yds, Par 70, SSS 71. New Course 9 holes, 2400yds. Membership 500.

Visitors welcome (restricted WE after 1300) Societies welcome (☎ or by letter)
Green fees £18 per round (£25 WE/BH)
Facilities ⊗ ⵊⵊⵊ by prior arrangement ᴸᴸ ⵌ ♀ ⵈ 🛏 ⵌ A McKay
Hotel ★★★58% Hilton National Hotel, Elton Way, Watford Bypass, BUSHEY ☎(0923) 35881 196⮎

BERKHAMSTED   Map 2 D2

Berkhamsted ☎ (0442) 865832
The Common (1.5m E)
There are no sand bunkers on this heathland course but this does not make it any easier to play. The natural hazards will test the skill of the most able players, with a particularly testing hole at the 11th, 568 yards, par 5. The clubhouse is very comfortable.
18 holes, 6605yds, Par 71, SSS 72, Course record 69. Membership 700.

Visitors welcome (h'cap cert required) must contact in advance Societies welcome (Wed & Fri only)
Green fees £25 per round, £30 per day (£50 WE & BH)
Facilities ⊗ ⵊⵊⵊ ᴸᴸ ⵌ ♀ ⵈ 🛏 ⵗ ⵌ B J Proudfoot
Hotel ★★★55% Post House Hotel, Breakspear Way, HEMEL HEMPSTEAD ☎(0442) 51122
Annexe:107⮎

BISHOP'S STORTFORD   Map 2 F1

Bishop's Stortford ☎ (0279) 54715
Dunmow Rd (1m W of M11 junc 8 on A1250)
Parkland course, fairly flat.
18 holes, 6440yds, Par 71, SSS 71. Membership 700.

Visitors welcome (ex WE & BH) must contact in advance ✉ Societies welcome (must book)
Green fees Not confirmed
Facilities ⵈ 🛏 ⵌ
Hotel ★★55% The Saracen's Head, High St, GREAT DUNMOW ☎(0371) 873901 24⮎

If you know of a golf course, not in this guide already, which welcomes visitors, we would be pleased to hear about it.

BRICKENDON   Map 2 F2

Brickendon Grange ☎ (099286) 258
(W side of village)
Parkland course.
18 holes, 6315yds, Par 71, SSS 70. Membership 650.

Visitors welcome (with M only WE & BH) Societies welcome (☎)
Green fees Not confirmed
Facilities ⵈ 🛏 ⵗ ⵌ
Hotel ★★★61% White Horse, Hertingfordbury, HERTFORD ☎(0992) 586791 42⮎

BROOKMANS PARK   Map 2 E2

Brookmans Park
☎ Potters Bar (0707) 52487
Golf Club Rd (N side of village off A1000)
Brookman's Park is an undulating parkland course, with several cleverly constructed holes. But it is a fair course, although it can play long. The 11th, par 3, is a testing hole which plays across a lake. Fishing. Snooker.
18 holes, 6231yds, Par 71, SSS 71, Course record 66. Membership 750.

SCORE CARD: White Tees					
Hole	Yds	Par	Hole	Yds	Par
1	434	4	10	395	4
2	384	4	11	168	3
3	484	5	12	426	4
4	200	3	13	499	5
5	479	5	14	329	4
6	141	3	15	182	3
7	503	5	16	405	4
8	411	4	17	428	4
9	151	3	18	435	4
Out	3187	36	In	3267	35
			Totals	6454	71

Visitors welcome (must have h'cap cert; with M WE & BH) must contact in advance Societies welcome (Wed & Thu only ☎)
Green fees £25 per day; £20 per round
Facilities ⊗ ᴸᴸ ⵌ ♀ ⵈ 🛏 ⵌ Mike Plumbridge/ Ian Jelley
Hotel ★★★65% Crest Hotel, Bignells Corner, SOUTH MIMMS ☎(0707) 43311 123⮎

BUNTINGFORD   Map 4 E8

East Herts ☎ Ware (0920) 821978
Hamels Park (1m N of Puckeridge off A10)
An attractive undulating parkland course with magnificent specimen trees.
18 holes, 6449yds, Par 71, SSS 71, Course record 64. Membership 750.

Visitors welcome (ex Wed & WE. Handicap cert required) must contact in advance ✉ Societies welcome (booking form to be completed)
Green fees £26 per day, £21 per round
Facilities ⊗ by prior arrangement ⵊⵊⵊ by prior arrangement ᴸᴸ ⵌ ♀ ⵈ 🛏 ⵌ James Hamilton
Hotel ★★★63% Ware Moat House, Baldock St, WARE ☎(0920) 465011 50rm(43⮎6♙)

Each golf course entry has a recommended hotel. For a wider choice of places to stay, consult *AA Hotels and Restaurants in Britain* or *AA-inspected Bed and Breakfast in Britain*.

BUSHEY
Map 2 E3

Bushey Hall ☎ (0923) 225802
Bushey Hall Dr (1.5m NW on A4008)
Parkland course.
18 holes, 6100yds, Par 70, SSS 69, Course record 66.
Membership 600.

Visitors welcome (h'cap cert required. With M only
WE) must contact in advance Societies welcome (by
letter)
Green fees £25 per day
Facilities ⊗ ⅢL ⅃ ⬛ ♀ ⚲ 🖻 ℓ Danny Fitzsimmons
Hotel ★★★58% Hilton National Hotel, Elton Way,
Watford Bypass, BUSHEY ☎(0923) 35881 196⇥🏠

Hartsbourne Golf & Country Club ☎ 081-950 1133
Hartsbourne Ave (S off A4140)
Parkland course with good views.
18 holes, 6305yds, Par 71, SSS 70. Membership 460.

Visitors welcome Member must accompany ✉
Societies welcome (apply by letter)
Green fees Not confirmed
Facilities Catering by prior arrangement ⚲ 🖻 ⌁
ℓ Geoff Hunt
Hotel ★★★58% Hilton National Hotel, Elton Way,
Watford Bypass, BUSHEY ☎(0923) 35881 196⇥🏠

CHESHUNT
Map 2 F2

Cheshunt ☎ (0992) 29777
Cheshunt Park, Park Ln (1.5m NW off B156)
Municipal parkland course, well-bunkered with ponds,
easy walking.
18 holes, 6604yds, Par 71, SSS 69, Course record 65.
Membership 510.

Visitors welcome Member must accompany must
contact in advance Societies welcome (☎)
Green fees Not confirmed
Facilities ♀ ⚲ 🖻 ⌁ ℓ
Hotel ★★★57% Post House Hotel, High Rd, Bell
Common, EPPING ☎(0378) 73137 Annexe:82⇥🏠

CHORLEYWOOD
Map 2 D2

Chorleywood ☎ (09278) 2009
Common Rd (E side of village off A404)
Heathland course with natural hazards and good views.
9 holes, 2838yds, Par 68, SSS 67, Course record 61.
Membership 300.

Visitors welcome (restricted Tue & Thu am & WE)
must contact in advance Societies welcome (☎)
Green fees £10 per round (£12 WE & BH)
Facilities ⊗ by prior arrangement ⅃L ⅃ ⬛ ♀ (Mon-Sat)
⚲
Hotel ★★★62% Bedford Arms Thistle Hotel, CHENIES
☎(09278) 3301 10⇥🏠

This guide is updated annually – make sure you
use an up-to-date edition.

ESSENDON
Map 2 E2

Hatfield London Country Club
☎ Potters Bar (0707) 42624
Bedwell Park (1m S)
Parkland course with many varied hazards, including
ponds, a stream and a ditch. 19th-century manor
clubhouse. 9-hole pitch and putt. Tennis.
18 holes, 6878yds, Par 72, SSS 72.

Visitors welcome must contact in advance Societies
welcome (by letter)
Green fees £19 per day; £11 per round (£23/24 WE)
Facilities ⅃L ♀ ⚲ 🖻 ⌁ ℓ Norman Greer
Hotel ★★★50% Comet Hotel, 301 St Albans Rd West,
HATFIELD ☎(0707) 265411 57rm(52⇥2🏠)

HARPENDEN
Map 2 E2

Harpenden ☎ (0582) 712580
Hammonds End, Redbourn Ln (1m S on B487)
Gently undulating parkland course, easy walking.
18 holes, 5819meters, Par 70, SSS 70. Membership 800.

Visitors welcome (ex WE) must contact in advance ✉
Societies welcome (by letter)
Green fees Not confirmed
Facilities ⊗ by prior arrangement Ⅲ by prior
arrangement ⅃L ⬛ ♀ ⚲ 🖻 ℓ D Smith
Hotel ★★★66% Harpenden Moat House Hotel, 18
Southdown Rd, HARPENDEN ☎(0582) 764111 18⇥🏠
Annexe:37⇥

Harpenden Common ☎ (0582) 715959
Cravells Rd, East Common (1m S on A1081)
Flat, easy walking, good greens - typical common course.
18 holes, 5560yds, Par 68, SSS 67, Course record 63.
Membership 700.

Visitors welcome (WE with M handicap certificate
required) must contact in advance Societies welcome
(Thu & Fri only ☎)
Green fees £20 per day; £16 per round
Facilities ⊗ Ⅲ by prior arrangement ⅃L ⬛ ♀ ⚲ 🖻
ℓ Nigel Lawrence
Hotel ★★★64% Glen Eagle Hotel, 1 Luton Rd,
HARPENDEN ☎(0582) 760271 51⇥🏠

HEMEL HEMPSTEAD
Map 2 D2

Boxmoor ☎ (0442) 242434
18 Box Ln, Boxmoor (2m SW on B4505)
Challenging moorland course, fine views, hard walking.
Testing holes: 3rd (par 3), 4th (par 4).
9 holes, 4302yds, Par 62, SSS 62. Membership 250.

Visitors welcome (ex Sun) Societies welcome (☎)
Green fees £8 per day (£10 Sat)
Facilities ⚲
Hotel ★★★55% Post House Hotel, Breakspear Way,
HEMEL HEMPSTEAD ☎(0442) 51122 Annexe:107⇥

For an explanation of the symbols and
abbreviations used, see page 33.

Little Hay ☎ (0442) 833798
Box Ln, Bovingdon (1.5m SW on B4505 off A41)
Semi-parkland, inland links. Floodlit golf range. 9-hole pitch and putt.
18 holes, 6678yds, Par 72, SSS 72.

Visitors welcome Societies welcome (☎ or by letter)
Green fees £5.50 per day (£8.50 WE)
Facilities ⊗ ⅢℓＬ ♪ ♀ △ ⌂ ⌁ ℓ
Hotel ★★★55% Post House Hotel, Breakspear Way,
HEMEL HEMPSTEAD ☎(0442) 51122 Annexe:107⇌

KNEBWORTH

Map 2 E1

Knebworth ☎ Stevenage (0438) 812752
Deards End Ln (N side of village off B197)
Parkland course, easy walking.
*18 holes, 6428yds, Par 71, SSS 71, Course record 64.
Membership 900.*

Visitors welcome (wkdays only) must contact in advance handicap certificate required ⊠ Societies welcome (☎)
Green fees £25 per day/round
Facilities ⊗ Ⅲ by prior arrangement ℓ ♪ ♀ △ ⌂ ℓ Bobby Mitchell
Hotel ★★★54% Roebuck Hotel, Old London Rd,
Broadwater, STEVENAGE ☎(0438) 365444 54⇌

LETCHWORTH

Map 4 D8

Letchworth
☎ (0462) 683203
Letchworth Ln (S side of town centre off A505)
Planned more than 50 years ago by Harry Vardon, this adventurous course is set in a peaceful corner of 'Norman' England. To its variety of natural artificial hazards is added an unpredictable wind.
18 holes, 6181yds, Par 70, SSS 69. Membership 1000.

	SCORE CARD				
Hole	Yds	Par	Hole	Yds	Par
1	289	4	10	400	4
2	198	3	11	305	4
3	407	4	12	388	4
4	387	4	13	296	4
5	358	4	14	314	4
6	419	4	15	341	4
7	156	3	16	469	4
8	396	4	17	185	3
9	353	4	18	520	5
Out	2963	34	In	3218	36
			Totals	6181	70

Visitors welcome (WE with M) must contact in advance ⊠ Societies welcome (Wed, Thu & Fri only ☎)
Green fees £30 per day
Facilities ⊗ (Tue-Fri) Ⅲ (Tue-Fri) ℓ ♪ ♀ △ ⌂ ℓ John Mutimer
Hotel ★★★59% Blakemore Thistle, Little Wymondley, HITCHIN ☎(0438) 355821 82⇌

LITTLE GADDESDEN

Map 2 D2

Ashridge ☎ (044284) 2244
Good parkland course, challenging but fair. Excellent clubhouse facilities.
*18 holes, 6508yds, Par 72, SSS 71, Course record 64.
Membership 730.*

Visitors welcome (ex Thu & WE) must contact in advance ⊠ Societies welcome (wkdays ex Thu (Mar-Oct))
Green fees Not confirmed
Facilities ⊗ Ⅲ ℓ ♪ ♀ △ ⌂ ⌁ ℓ Geoff Pook
Hotel ★★★(red)Bell Inn, ASTON CLINTON ☎(0296) 630252 21⇌♠

POTTERS BAR

Map 2 E2

Potters Bar ☎ (0707) 52020
Darkes Ln (N side of town centre)
Parkland course.
*18 holes, 5993yds, Par 71, SSS 69, Course record 65.
Membership 520.*

Visitors welcome (with M only WE) must contact in advance handicap certificate required ⊠ Societies welcome (Mon-Fri ☎)
Green fees £27.50
Facilities ⊗ ℓ ♪ ♀ △ ⌂ ℓ Kevin Hughes
Hotel ★★★65% Crest Hotel, Bignells Corner, SOUTH MIMMS ☎(0707) 43311 123⇌♠

RADLETT

Map 2 E2

Porters Park ☎ (0923) 854127
Shenley Hill (NE side of village off A5183)
A splendid parkland course with fine trees, lush grass and easy walking. The holes are all different and interesting - on many accuracy of shot to the green is of paramount importance.
*18 holes, 6313yds, Par 70, SSS 70, Course record 65.
Membership 700.*

Visitors welcome (with M at WE & Fri pm) must contact in advance ⊠ Societies welcome (Wed & Thu only ☎)
Green fees £35 per day; £25 per round
Facilities ⊗ Ⅲ ℓ ♪ ♀ △ ⌂ ⌁ ℓ David Gleeson
Hotel ★★★71% Noke Thistle Hotel, Watford Rd,
ST ALBANS ☎(0727) 54252 111⇌♠

REDBOURN

Map 2 D2

Redbourn ☎ (0582) 792150
Kinsbourne Green Ln (1m N off A5183)
Testing parkland course (Five par 4's over 400 yds). Also 9-hole par 3 course. Driving range. Snooker.
18 holes, 6407yds, Par 70, SSS 71, Course record 67 or 9 holes, 2722yds, Par 54.

Visitors welcome (with M only WE & BH) Societies welcome (☎)
Green fees £11 (18 holes); £3.50 (9 holes) £5.25 (9 holes twice.
Facilities ⊗ Ⅲ ℓ ♪ ♀ (1100-2300) △ ⌂ ⌁ ℓ Steve Baldwin
Hotel ★★★66% Harpenden Moat House Hotel, 18 Southdown Rd, HARPENDEN ☎(0582) 764111 18⇌♠
Annexe:37⇌

RICKMANSWORTH   Map 2 D3

Moor Park ☏ (0923) 773146
(1.5m SE off A4145)
Two parkland courses.
18 holes, 6675yds, Par 72, SSS 72. West Golf Course 18 holes, 5815yds, Par 69, SSS 68. Membership 1800.

Visitors welcome (☏ for details) Societies welcome (by letter)
Green fees Not confirmed
Facilities ♀ ⛳ 🏠 🍴 ⚷
Hotel ★★★58% Hilton National Hotel, Elton Way, Watford Bypass, BUSHEY ☏(0923) 35881 196⇨🕊

Rickmansworth ☏ (0923) 775278
Moor Ln (2m S of town off A4145)
Undulating, municipal parkland course.
18 holes, 4412yds, Par 63, SSS 62. Membership 220.

Visitors welcome
Green fees Not confirmed
Facilities ♀ ⛳ 🏠 🍴 ⚷
Hotel ★★★58% Hilton National Hotel, Elton Way, Watford Bypass, BUSHEY ☏(0923) 35881 196⇨🕊

ROYSTON   Map 4 E7

Royston ☏ (0763) 242696
Baldock Rd (.5m W of town centre)
Heathland course. Snooker.
18 holes, 6032yds, Par 70, SSS 69. Membership 650.

Visitors welcome (with M only WE) must contact in advance ✉ Societies welcome (☏)
Green fees Not confirmed
Facilities ⊗ �🍴 ⛳ ♀ ⛳ 🏠 🍴 ⚷ Mark Hatcher
Hotel ★★★59% Blakemore Thistle, Little Wymondley, HITCHIN ☏(0438) 355821 82⇨🕊

ST ALBANS   Map 2 E2

Batchwood Halls ☏ (0727) 33349
Batchwood Halls (1m NW off A5183)
Municipal parkland course.
18 holes, 6462yds, Par 71, SSS 71. Membership 300.

Visitors welcome
Green fees Not confirmed
Facilities ♀ ⛳ 🏠 🍴 ⚷
Hotel ★★★63% St Michael's Manor Hotel, Fishpool St, ST ALBANS ☏(0727) 64444 26rm(13⇨9🕊)

Verulam ☏ (0727) 53327
London Rd (1m from junc 22 of M25 off A1081)
Parkland course.
18 holes, 6218yds, Par 72, SSS 70, Course record 65. Membership 600.

Visitors welcome (ex WE) Societies welcome (☏ year in advance)
Green fees £20 per day; £16 per round (reduced Mon)

Facilities ⊗ ⛳ ⬛ ♀ (all day) ⛳ 🏠 🍴 ⚷ Paul Anderson
Hotel ★★★71% Noke Thistle Hotel, Watford Rd, ST ALBANS ☏(0727) 54252 111⇨🕊

STEVENAGE   Map 4 D8

Stevenage Golf Centre ☏ (0438) 88424
Aston Ln (4m SE off B5169)
Natural water hazards designed by John Jacobs, with some wooded areas.
18 holes, 6204yds, Par 72, SSS 71, Course record 65. Membership 590.

Visitors welcome must contact in advance Societies welcome (At least one week's notice)
Green fees Not confirmed
Facilities ⊗ ⛳ ⬛ ♀ (all day) ⛳ 🏠 🍴 ⚷ K Bond
Hotel ★★★54% Roebuck Hotel, Old London Rd, Broadwater, STEVENAGE ☏(0438) 365444 54⇨

WARE   Map 2 F2

Chadwell Springs ☏ (0920) 461447
Hertford Rd (.75m W on A119)
Quick-drying moorland course on high plateau subject to wind. The first two holes are par 5 and notable.
9 holes, 6042yds, Par 72, SSS 69. Membership 400.

Visitors welcome (with M only WE) Societies welcome (by letter)
Green fees Not confirmed
Facilities ⊗ 🍴 by prior arrangement ⛳ ⬛ ♀ ⛳ 🏠 ⚷ A N Shearn
Hotel ★★★63% Ware Moat House, Baldock St, WARE ☏(0920) 465011 50rm(43⇨6🕊)

Hanbury Manor Golf & Country Club
☏ (0920) 487722
Thunderidge
Superb parkland course designed by Jack Nicklaus II. Large oval tees, watered fairways and undulating greens make up first 9 holes. Attractive lakes and deep-faced bunkers are strategically sited. Second 9-holes scheduled to open Spring 1991 and will offer open panoramas and challenging holes. Accommodation and extensive sports and leisure facilities.
18 holes, 6922yds, Par 72, SSS 73. Membership 228.

Visitors welcome (Residents, member's guests/ h'cap cert) must contact in advance
Green fees On application
Facilities ⊗ 🍴 ⛳ ⬛ ♀ (10am-11pm) ⛳ 🏠 🍴 ⚷ Peter Blaze
Hotel Hanbury Manor, Thundridge, WARE ☏(0920) 487722 98⇨🕊

To see a full range of AA guides and maps, visit your local AA Shop or any good bookshop.

WATFORD   Map 2 E2

West Herts ☎ (0923) 36484
Cassiobury Park (W side of town centre off A412)
Another of the many clubs which were inaugurated
in the 1890's when the game of golf was being given
a tremendous boost by the performances of the first
star professionals, Braid, Vardon and Taylor. The
West Herts course is close to Watford but it's setting
is beautiful and tranquil. Set out on a plateau the
course is exceedingly dry. It also has a very severe
finish with the 17th, a hole of 386 yards, the toughest
on the course. The last hole measures over 500 yards.
18 holes, 6488yds, Par 72, SSS 71. Membership 660.

Visitors welcome (wkdays only) Societies welcome
(Wed & Fri only)
Green fees Not confirmed
Facilities ♀ ⌂ 🏠 ⛳ (
Hotel ★★★58% Hilton National Hotel, Elton Way,
Watford Bypass, BUSHEY ☎(0923) 35881 196⇄♠

WELWYN GARDEN CITY   Map 2 E2

Panshanger Golf & Squash Complex ☎ (0707) 333350
Herns Ln (N side of town centre off B1000)
Municipal parkland course overlooking Mimram
Valley. Squash.
18 holes, 6638yds, Par 72, SSS 70.

Visitors welcome Societies welcome (by letter)
Green fees Not confirmed
Facilities ⊗ 🍽 ⓛ 🍺 (catering by prior arrangement)
♀ ⌂ 🏠 ⛳ (
Hotel ★★★61% Crest Hotel, Homestead Ln, WELWYN
GARDEN CITY ☎(0707) 324336 58⇄♠

Welwyn Garden City ☎ (0707) 325243
Mannicotts (W side of town centre off B197)
Undulating parkland course with ravine. The 14th hole
('The Dell') a par 4, crosses the ravine. Course record
holder is Nick Faldo.
*18 holes, 6051yds, Par 70, SSS 69, Course record 63.
Membership 650.*

Visitors welcome (ex Sun) must contact in advance ✉
Societies welcome (Wed & Thu only)
Green fees Not confirmed
Facilities ⊗ 🍽 by prior arrangement ⓛ 🍺 ♀ (1130-
2230) ⌂ 🏠 (Simon Bishop
Hotel ★★★61% Crest Hotel, Homestead Ln, WELWYN
GARDEN CITY ☎(0707) 324336 58⇄♠

WHEATHAMPSTEAD   Map 2 E2

Mid Herts ☎ (058283) 2242
Gustard Wood (1m N on B651)
Commonland, wooded with heather and gorse-lined
fairways.
*18 holes, 6094yds, Par 69, SSS 69, Course record 66.
Membership 600.*

Visitors welcome (not Tue, Wed (pm) & WE) must
contact in advance ✉ Societies welcome (by letter)
Green fees Not confirmed

Facilities ⌂ 🏠 (
Hotel ★★★66% Harpenden Moat House Hotel, 18
Southdown Rd, HARPENDEN ☎(0582) 764111 18⇄♠
Annexe:37⇄

HUMBERSIDE

BEVERLEY   Map 5 H6

Beverley & East Riding ☎ (0482) 867190
The Westwood (1m SW on B1230)
Picturesque parkland course with some hard walking
and natural hazards - trees and gorse bushes. Also cattle
and sheep (spring to autumn), horse-riders occasionally
early morning.
*18 holes, 5605yds, Par 68, SSS 67, Course record 62.
Membership 460.*

Visitors welcome (restricted WE & BH) Societies
welcome (☎ (0482) 868757)
Green fees £10 (£12.50 WE & BH)
Facilities ⌂ 🏠 (
Hotel ★★★67% Beverley Arms Hotel, North Bar
Within, BEVERLEY ☎(0482) 869241 57⇄♠

BRANDESBURTON   Map 5 J5

Hainsworth Park ☎ Hornsea (0964) 542362
Burton Holme (SW side of village on A165)
A parkland course with easy walking. Accommodation.
Additional nine holes under construction.
9 holes, 5400yds, Par 68, SSS 66. Membership 300.

Visitors welcome (ex competition days) must contact in
advance Societies welcome (by letter)
Green fees £7 per day (£10 WE & BH)
Facilities ⌂ 🏠 ⛳
Hotel ★★★66% Tickton Grange Hotel, Tickton,
BEVERLEY ☎(0964) 543666 16⇄♠

BRIDLINGTON   Map 5 J5

Bridlington ☎ (0262) 672092
Belvedere Rd (1m S off A165)
Clifftop, seaside course, windy at times. Snooker.
*18 holes, 6491yds, Par 71, SSS 71, Course record 68.
Membership 640.*

Visitors welcome (ex Sun until 1115) Societies welcome
(7 days notice)
Green fees £12 (£18 WE)
Facilities ⊗ 🍽 by prior arrangement ⓛ 🍺 ♀ ⌂ 🏠
(David Rands
Hotel ★★67% Monarch Hotel, South Marine Dr,
BRIDLINGTON ☎(0262) 674447 40rm(36⇄♠)

BROUGH   Map 5 H6

Brough ☎ (0482) 667374
Cave Rd (.5m N)
Parkland course.
18 holes, 6183yds, Par 68, SSS 69. Membership 650.

Visitors welcome (ex WE or Wed before 1400) must contact in advance Societies welcome (by letter)
Green fees Not confirmed
Facilities ⊗ ⅏ by prior arrangement ⅃ ⬛ ♀ (all day) ⛳ 🏠 ⅂ 𝄢 G Townhill
Hotel ★★★67% Crest Hotel-Hull, Ferriby High Rd, NORTH FERRIBY ☎(0482) 645212 102⇥

CLEETHORPES   Map 5 J7

Cleethorpes ☎ (0472) 814060
Kings Rd (1.5m S off A1031)
Seaside course, with a beck running across it.
18 holes, 6018yds, Par 70, SSS 69, Course record 64. Membership 760.

Visitors welcome (restricted Wed pm) (not WE ☎)
Green fees £12 per day (£15 WE)
Facilities ⊗ ⅏ by prior arrangement ⅃ ⬛ ♀ ⛳ 🏠 𝄢 Eric Sharp
Hotel ★★★70% Kingsway Hotel, Kingsway, CLEETHORPES ☎(0472) 601122 53⇥💈

DRIFFIELD, GREAT   Map 5 H5

Driffield ☎ Driffield (0377) 43116
Sunderlandwick (2m S of off A164)
An easy walking, parkland course.
9 holes, 6202yds, Par 70, SSS 70. Membership 320.

Visitors welcome
Green fees Not confirmed
Facilities ♀ ⛳ 🏠
Hotel ★★⁂57% Wold House Country Hotel, Nafferton, DRIFFIELD ☎(0377) 44242 11rm(7⇥💈) Annexe:1💈

ELSHAM   Map 5 H7

Elsham ☎ Barnetby (0652) 680291
Barton Rd (2m SW on B1206)
Parkland course, easy walking.
18 holes, 6411yds, Par 71, SSS 71, Course record 68. Membership 600.

Visitors welcome (with M only WE & BH) Societies welcome (☎ or letter)
Green fees £15
Facilities ⊗ ⅏ ⅃ ⬛ ♀ (1100-2230) ⛳ 🏠 𝄢
Hotel ★★★65% Wortley House Hotel, Rowland Rd, SCUNTHORPE ☎(0724) 842223 38⇥💈

FLAMBOROUGH   Map 5 J5

Flamborough Head ☎ Bridlington (0262) 850333
Lighthouse Rd (2m E off B1259)
Undulating seaside course. Snooker.
18 holes, 5438yds, Par 66, SSS 66, Course record 63. Membership 380.

Visitors welcome (not before noon on Sun) must contact in advance ✉ Societies welcome (☎ or by letter)
Green fees £10 per day (£13 WE & BH)

Facilities ⊗ ⅏ ⅃ ⬛ (no catering Mon) ♀ ⛳
Hotel ★68%, Flaneburg Hotel, North Marine Rd, FLAMBOROUGH ☎(0262) 850284 13rm(8💈)

GRIMSBY   Map 5 J7

Grimsby ☎ (0472) 342630
Littlecoates Rd (W side of town centre off A1136)
Parkland course with easy walking.
18 holes, 6058yds, Par 70, SSS 69, Course record 66. Membership 725.

Visitors welcome (restricted WE) must contact in advance ✉ Societies welcome (Mon-Fri only ☎)
Green fees Not confirmed
Facilities ⊗ (Tue, Thu, Sun) ⅏ by prior arrangement ⅃ ⬛ ♀ ⛳ 🏠 𝄢 Steve Houltby
Hotel ★★★66% Humber Royal Crest Hotel, Littlecoates Rd, GRIMSBY ☎(0472) 350295 52⇥💈

HESSLE   Map 5 H6

Hessle ☎ Hull (0482) 650171
Westfield Rd, Raywell (4m NW off A164)
Well-wooded downland course, easy walking, windy. Snooker.
18 holes, 6290yds, Par 72, SSS 70, Course record 68. Membership 650.

Visitors welcome (handicap certificate required) must contact in advance Societies welcome (☎)
Green fees Not confirmed
Facilities ⊗ by prior arrangement ⅏ by prior arrangement ⅃ by prior arrangement ⬛ by prior arrangement ♀ ⛳ 🏠 𝄢 Grahame Fieldsend
Hotel ★★★67% Crest Hotel-Hull, Ferriby High Rd, NORTH FERRIBY ☎(0482) 645212 102⇥

HORNSEA   Map 5 J5

Hornsea ☎ (0964) 532020
Rolston Rd (1m S of on B1242)
Parkland course. Snooker.
18 holes, 6461yds, Par 71, SSS 71. Membership 600.

Visitors welcome (WE with M or after 1500) must contact in advance Societies welcome (by letter)
Green fees £20 per day; £15 per round (£30/£25 WE)
Facilities ⊗ ⅏ ⅃ ⬛ ♀ ⛳ 🏠 𝄢 Brian Thompson
Hotel ★★★67% Beverley Arms Hotel, North Bar Within, BEVERLEY ☎(0482) 869241 57⇥💈

HOWDEN   Map 5 H6

Boothferry ☎ (0430) 30364
Spaldington Ln, Goole (2.5m N of Howden off B1228)
A heavily bunkered meadowland course with several dykes.
18 holes, 6600yds, Par 73. Membership 600.

Visitors welcome must contact in advance Societies welcome (by letter)
Green fees Not confirmed

▶

Facilities ♀ ⅄ 🖻 🌱 ⌊
Hotel ★★59% Clifton Hotel, 1 Clifton Gardens,
Boothferry Rd, GOOLE ☎(0405) 761336 10rm(5⟜3🐾)

HULL

Map 5 J6

Ganstead Park ☎ (0482) 874754
Longdales Ln, Coniston (6m NE off A165)
Parkland course, easy walking. Snooker.
18 holes, 6801yds, Par 72, SSS 73, Course record 67.
Membership 700.

Visitors welcome (ex Sun & Wed mornings) Societies
welcome (☎ or by letter)
Green fees £15 per day (£18 WE)
Facilities ⊗ ⅀ ᧒ ⅃ ♀ ⅄ 🖻 🌱 ⌊ Michael J Smee
Hotel ★★71% Waterfront Hotel, Dagger Ln, HULL
☎(0482) 227222 30⟜3🐾

Hull ☎ (0482) 658919
The Hall, 27 Packman Ln (5m W of city centre off A164)
Parkland course. Snooker.
18 holes, 6242yds, Par 70, SSS 70. Membership 758.

Visitors welcome (ex WE) must contact in advance
Societies welcome (by letter)
Green fees £22 per day/round
Facilities ⊗ ⅀ ᧒ ⅃ ♀ ⅄ 🖻 ⌊
Hotel ★★★70% Willerby Manor Hotel, Well Ln,
WILLERBY ☎(0482) 652616 36⟜3🐾

Springhead Park ☎ (0482) 656309
Willerby Rd (5m W off A164)
Municipal parkland course with undulating fairways.
18 holes, 6439yds, Par 73, SSS 71, Course record 65.
Membership 520.

Visitors welcome
Green fees £3.25 per day (£4.50 WE)
Facilities 🖻 🌱 ⌊ B Herrington
Hotel ★★★70% Willerby Manor Hotel, Well Ln,
WILLERBY ☎(0482) 652616 36⟜3🐾

Sutton Park ☎ (0482) 74242
Salthouse Rd (3m NE on B1237 off A165)
Municipal parkland course. Snooker.
18 holes, 6251yds, Par 70, SSS 70, Course record 67.
Membership 450.

Visitors welcome
Green fees Not confirmed
Facilities ⊗ (WE only) ᧒ (WE only) ⅃ ♀ ⅄ 🖻 🌱
⌊ Paul Rushworth
Hotel ★★71% Waterfront Hotel, Dagger Ln, HULL
☎(0482) 227222 30⟜3🐾

NORMANBY

Map 5 H7

Normanby Hall ☎ Scunthorpe (0724) 720226
Normanby Park (5m N of Scunthorpe adj to Normanby
Hall)
Parkland course.
18 holes, 6548yds, Par 72, SSS 71, Course record 68.
Membership 740.

Visitors welcome Societies welcome (ex WE & BH, ☎)
Green fees Not confirmed
Facilities ⊗ ᧒ ⅃ ♀ ⅄ 🖻 🌱 ⌊ C Mann
Hotel ★★63% Royal Hotel, Doncaster Rd,
SCUNTHORPE ☎(0724) 282233 33⟜3🐾

SCUNTHORPE

Map 5 H7

Holme Hall ☎ (0724) 840909
Holme Ln, Bottesford (3m SE)
Heathland course, easy walking. Snooker.
18 holes, 6475yds, Par 71, SSS 71. Membership 675.

Visitors welcome (with M WE & BH) must contact in
advance Societies welcome (☎)
Green fees £8 per round, £12 per day
Facilities ⊗ ⅀ ᧒ ⅃ ♀ ⅄ 🖻 🌱 ⌊ Richard
McKiernon
Hotel ★★63% Royal Hotel, Doncaster Rd,
SCUNTHORPE ☎(0724) 282233 33⟜3🐾

Kingsway ☎ (0724) 840945
Kingsway (W side of town centre off A18)
Parkland course with many par 3's.
9 holes, 1915yds, Par 30, SSS 29.

Visitors welcome
Green fees Not confirmed
Facilities ⅄ 🖻 🌱
Hotel ★★63% Royal Hotel, Doncaster Rd,
SCUNTHORPE ☎(0724) 282233 33⟜3🐾

Scunthorpe ☎ (0724) 866561
Ashby Decoy, Burringham Rd (2.5m SW on B1450)
Very tight parkland course. Snooker.
18 holes, 6028yds, Par 71, SSS 71. Membership 700.

Visitors welcome (ex Sun. Handicap certificate
required) must contact in advance Societies welcome
(by letter)
Green fees £14 per day (Sat only with M)
Facilities ⊗ ⅀ by prior arrangement ᧒ ⅃ ♀ ⅄ 🖻
⌊ Graham Bailey
Hotel ★★63% Royal Hotel, Doncaster Rd,
SCUNTHORPE ☎(0724) 282233 33⟜3🐾

WITHERNSEA

Map 5 J6

Withernsea ☎ (0964) 612258
Chesnut Av (S side of town centre off A1033)
Exposed seaside links with bunkers.
9 holes, 5112yds, Par 66, SSS 64, Course record 62.
Membership 450.

Visitors welcome (ex WE with M only) Societies
welcome (by letter)
Green fees £8 per day (£10 WE with M only)
Facilities ⊗ ⅀ ᧒ ⅃ (also catering by prior
arrangement) ♀ ⅄ 🖻 ⌊ Graham Harrison
Hotel ★★63% Pearson Park Hotel, Pearson Park,
HULL ☎(0482) 43043 35rm(29⟜3🐾)

KENT

ADDINGTON   Map 2 G4

West Malling ☎ (0732) 844785
London Rd (1m S off A20)
Two 18-hole parkland courses. Squash and snooker.
Spitfire 18 holes, 6142yds, Par 70, SSS 70. Hurricane 18 holes, 6011yds, Par 70, SSS 69. Membership 800.

Visitors welcome (restricted WE) ✉ Societies welcome (by letter)
Green fees £20 per day; £14 per round (£16 WE)
Facilities ✕ ℳ by prior arrangement ⅃ ■ ♀ △ 🏠
《 Paul Foston
Hotel ★★★54% Post House, London Rd, Wrotham Heath, WROTHAM ☎Borough Green (0732) 883311 119⇔🐾

ASHFORD   Map 2 J5

Ashford ☎ (0233) 622655
Sandyhurst Ln (1.5m NW off A20)
Parkland course with good views and easy walking.
Narrow fairways and tightly bunkered greens ensure a challenging game.
18 holes, 6246yds, Par 71, SSS 70, Course record 66. Membership 650.

Visitors welcome (Handicap certificate required) must contact in advance ✉ Societies welcome (Tue & Thu only ☎)
Green fees £16 per day (£20 WE & BH)
Facilities ✕ ℳ by prior arrangement ⅃ ■ ♀ △ 🏠
《 H Sherman
Hotel ★★★54% Master Spearpoint Hotel, Canterbury Rd, Kennington, ASHFORD ☎(0233) 636863 36⇔🐾

BARHAM   Map 2 K5

Broome Park ☎ Canterbury (0227) 831701
(1.5m SE on A260)
Parkland course in a valley, with a 350-year-old mansion/clubhouse. Also offers tennis, outdoor heated swimming pool, squash, riding, snooker, sailing, solarium and gymnasium facilities.
18 holes, 6600yds, Par 72, SSS 70, Course record 63. Membership 510.

Visitors welcome must contact in advance ✉ Societies welcome (Mon-Fri only ☎)
Green fees £20 day (£22 WE); £14 per round (£17 WE)
Facilities ✕ ℳ ⅃ ■ ♀ (1100-2300 ex Sun) △ 🏠 🍴 《 Tienie Britz
Hotel ★★★52% Chaucer Hotel, Ivy Ln, CANTERBURY ☎(0227) 464427 45⇔

BEARSTED   Map 2 H4

Bearsted ☎ Maidstone (0622) 38198
Ware St (2.5m E of Maidstone off A20)
Parkland course with fine views of the North Downs.
18 holes, 6278yds, Par 72, SSS 68. Membership 700.

Visitors welcome (ex WE) ✉ Societies welcome (☎)

Green fees £25 per day; £18 per round
Facilities ✕ (ex Mon) ℳ ⅃ (ex Mon) ■ ♀ △ 🏠
《 Tim Simpson
Hotel ★★★68% Great Danes Hotel, Ashford Rd, HOLLINGBOURNE ☎(0622) 30022 126⇔🐾

BOROUGH GREEN   Map 2 G4

Wrotham Heath ☎ (0732) 884800
Seven Mile Ln (2.25m E on B2016)
Parkland course, hilly, good views.
9 holes, 5918yds, Par 69, SSS 68, Course record 66. Membership 380.

Visitors welcome (with M WE) must contact in advance ✉ Societies welcome (Fri only ☎)
Green fees £22 per day; £17 per round
Facilities ✕ ℳ by prior arrangement ⅃ ■ ♀ △ 🏠
《 H Dearden
Hotel ★★★54% Post House, London Rd, Wrotham Heath, WROTHAM ☎Borough Green (0732) 883311 119⇔🐾

BROADSTAIRS   Map 2 K4

North Foreland ☎ Thanet (0843) 62140
Convent Rd, Kingsgate (1.5m N off B2052)
A picturesque course situated where the Thames Estuary widens towards the sea. North Foreland always seems to have a breath of tradition of golf's earlier days about it. Perhaps the ghost of one of its earlier professionals, the famous Abe Mitchell, still haunts the lovely turf of the fairways. Walking is easy and the wind is deceptive. The 8th and 17th, both par 4, are testing holes. There is also an approach and putting course. Tennis.
18 holes, 6400yds, Par 71, SSS 71, Course record 65. Short Course 18 holes, 1752yds, Par 71, SSS 71. Membership 900.

Visitors welcome must contact in advance Societies welcome (Wed & Fri only ☎)
Green fees Short course £4.50 day (£5 WE); Main course £20 per day £15 per round (£20 WE)
Facilities ✕ ℳ ⅃ ■ ♀ △ 🏠 《 Mike Lee
Hotel ★★★62% Castle Keep Hotel, Joss Gap Rd, Kingsgate, BROADSTAIRS ☎(0843) 65222 29⇔🐾

CANTERBURY   Map 2 J4

Canterbury ☎ (0227) 453532
Scotland Hills (1.5m E on A257)
Undulating parkland course, natural hazards.
18 holes, 6249yds, Par 70, SSS 70. Membership 700.

Visitors welcome ✉ Societies welcome
Green fees £24 per day; £18 per round (£25 per round WE & BH not before 1500)
Facilities ✕ ℳ ⅃ ■ ♀ (all day in summer) △ 🏠
《 Paul Everard
Hotel ★★★52% Chaucer Hotel, Ivy Ln, CANTERBURY ☎(0227) 464427 45⇔

CRANBROOK   Map 2 H5

Cranbrook ☎ (0580) 712934
Benenden Rd (2m E)
Scenic, parkland course with easy terrain, backed by
Hemstead Forest and close to Sissinghurst Castle (1m).
Testing hole at 12th (530 yds par 5). Venue for the
County Championships.
18 holes, 6136yds, Par 70, SSS 70. Membership 600.

Visitors welcome Societies welcome
Green fees Not confirmed
Facilities ♀ 👟 🏠 ⛳ ♏
Hotel ★★🏌70% Kennel Holt Country House Hotel,
Goudhurst Rd, CRANBROOK ☎(0580) 712032 9⇥🐾
Annexe:1🐾

DARTFORD   Map 2 G4

Dartford ☎ (0322) 26455
Dartford Heath
Parkland/heathland course.
18 holes, 5914yds, Par 69, SSS 68, Course record 65.
Membership 500.

Visitors welcome (ex WE) ✉ Societies welcome (Mon &
Fri only ☎)
Green fees Not confirmed
Facilities ⊗ �📷 👟 🍺 ♀ ⛳ 🏠 (A Blackburn
Hotel ★★★70% Crest Hotel, Black Prince
Interchange, Southwold Rd, BEXLEY ☎(0322) 526900
106⇥🐾

DEAL   Map 2 K5

Royal Cinque Ports
☎ (0304) 374007
Golf Rd (Along seafront at
N end of Deal)
Famous championship
seaside links, windy but
with easy walking.
Outward nine is generally
considered the easier,
inward nine is longer and
includes the renowned
16th, perhaps the most
difficult hole. On a fine day
there are wonderful views
across the Channel.
18 holes, 6741yds, Par 72, SSS 72. Membership 1200.

SCORE CARD: Championship Tees					
Hole	Yds	Par	Hole	Yds	Par
1	361	4	10	362	4
2	399	4	11	398	4
3	492	5	12	437	4
4	153	3	13	420	4
5	502	5	14	222	3
6	315	4	15	455	4
7	366	4	16	506	5
8	170	3	17	372	4
9	404	4	18	407	4
Out	3162	36	In	3579	36
			Totals	6741	72

Visitors welcome (ex Wed, WE & BH) must contact
in advance ✉ Societies welcome (☎ or by letter)
Green fees £35 per day; £25 per round
Facilities ⊗ 📷 👟 🍺 (catering by prior
arrangement) ♀ (by arrangement) ⛳ 🏠 ♏
(Andrew Reynolds
Hotel ★★★62% Crest Hotel, Singledge Ln,
Whitfield, DOVER ☎(0304) 821222 67⇥🐾

EDENBRIDGE   Map 2 F5

Edenbridge Golf & Country Club ☎ (0732) 865097
Crouch House Rd (1m W of town centre)
Gently undulating course with a driving range.
Fishing.
18 holes, 6604yds, Par 73, SSS 72. Membership 820.

Visitors welcome (restricted WE) must contact in
advance Societies welcome (☎)
Green fees £12 per day (£15 WE)
Facilities ⊗ 📷 👟 🍺 ♀ ⛳ 🏠 ♏ (
Hotel ★★★(red)🏌Gravetye Manor Hotel, EAST
GRINSTEAD ☎(0342) 810567 14⇥🐾

FAVERSHAM   Map 2 J4

Faversham ☎ (079589) 561
Belmont Park (3.5m S)
A beautiful inland course
laid out over part of a large
estate with pheasants
walking the fairways quite
tamely. Play follows two
heavily wooded valleys but
the trees affect only the
loose shots going out of
bounds. Fine views.
18 holes, 6021yds, Par 70,
SSS 69. Membership 800.

SCORE CARD					
Hole	Yds	Par	Hole	Yds	Par
1	476	5	10	370	4
2	299	4	11	398	4
3	156	3	12	445	4
4	421	4	13	182	3
5	336	4	14	397	4
6	358	4	15	330	4
7	544	5	16	140	3
8	355	4	17	302	4
9	139	3	18	373	4
Out	3084	36	In	2937	34
			Totals	6021	70

Visitors welcome (handicap certificate required)
Societies welcome (by letter)
Green fees £25 per day; £16 per round weekdays
only
Facilities ⛳ 🏠 ♏ (
Hotel ★★★72% Throwley House, Ashford Rd,
Sheldwich, FAVERSHAM ☎(0795) 539168 12⇥🐾

GILLINGHAM   Map 2 H4

Gillingham ☎ Medway (0634) 53017
Woodlands Rd (1.5m SE on A2)
Seaside links course.
18 holes, 5900yds, Par 70, SSS 68, Course record 64.
Membership 830.

Visitors welcome (with M only WE & BH) ✉ Societies
welcome (by letter)
Green fees £18 per day/round
Facilities ⊗ 📷 (ex Mon and Tue) 👟 🍺 ♀ ⛳ 🏠 ♏
(Brian Impett
Hotel ★★★66% Crest Hotel, Maidstone Rd,
ROCHESTER ☎(0634) 687111 105⇥🐾

Opening times of bar and catering facilities vary
from place to place – it is wise to check in
advance of your visit.

To see a full range of AA guides and maps, visit
your local AA Shop or any good bookshop.

GRAVESEND
Map 2 G4

Mid Kent ☎ (0474) 568035
Singlewell Rd (S side of town centre off A227)
A well-maintained downland course with some easy
walking and some excellent greens. The first hole is
short, but nonetheless a real challenge. The slightest
hook and the ball is out of bounds or lost.
*18 holes, 6206yds, Par 70, SSS 70, Course record 64.
Membership 1200.*

Visitors welcome (WE with M) must contact in
advance ⊠ Societies welcome (Tue only ☎)
Green fees £30 per day
Facilities ⊗ ⅷ by prior arrangement ᚼ 🍺 ♀ ⅄
🏠 ⅂ ᚎ Robert Lee
Hotel ★★★62% Inn on the Lake, Watling St,
SHORNE ☎(047482) 3333 78⇥🌂

HAWKHURST
Map 2 H6

Hawkhurst ☎ (0580) 752396
High St (W side of village off A268)
Undulating parkland course. Squash.
*9 holes, 5769yds, Par 72, SSS 68, Course record 68.
Membership 350.*

Visitors welcome (with M only WE) must contact in
advance Societies welcome (by letter)
Green fees £12 per day (£15 WE)
Facilities ᚼ 🍺 ♀ ⅄ 🏠 ᚎ Tony Collins
Hotel ★★64% Tudor Court Hotel, Rye Rd,
HAWKHURST ☎(0580) 752312 18⇥🌂

HERNE BAY
Map 2 J4

Herne Bay ☎ (0227) 373964
Thanet Way (1m S on A291)
Parkland course with bracing air.
18 holes, 5466yds, Par 68, SSS 67. Membership 350.

Visitors welcome (ex WE am)
Green fees Not confirmed
Facilities ♀ ⅄ 🏠 ᚎ
Hotel ★★★60% Falstaff Hotel, St Dunstans St,
CANTERBURY ☎(0227) 462138 24⇥🌂

HOLTYE
Map 2 F5

Holtye ☎ Cowden (0342) 850635
(N side of village on A264)
Heathland course with tree-lined fairways providing
testing golf.
*9 holes, 5289yds, Par 66, SSS 66, Course record 64.
Membership 500.*

Visitors welcome (ex WE & Thu am) must contact in
advance Societies welcome (☎ Tue & Fri)
Green fees Not confirmed
Facilities ⊗ by prior arrangement ⅷ by prior
arrangement ᚼ 🍺 ♀ ⅄ 🏠 ᚎ M K Scarles
Hotel ★★★(red)🍴Gravetye Manor Hotel, EAST
GRINSTEAD ☎(0342) 810567 14⇥🌂

HOO
Map 2 H4

Deangate Ridge ☎ Medway (0634) 251180
(4m NE of Rochester off A228)
Parkland, municipal course designed by Fred Hawtree.
18-hole pitch and putt. Tennis.
18 holes, 6300yds, Par 71, SSS 70. Membership 950.

Visitors welcome Societies welcome (by letter)
Green fees £4.50 per day & BH (£6 WE)
Facilities ⊗ ⅷ ᚼ 🍺 ♀ ⅄ 🏠 ⅂ ᚎ Barrie Aram
Hotel ★★★66% Crest Hotel, Maidstone Rd,
ROCHESTER ☎(0634) 687111 105⇥🌂

HYTHE
Map 2 J5

Hythe Imperial Hotel ☎ (0303) 267441 ext 445
Princes Pde (SE side of town)
A 9-hole links course played off alternative tees on the
second nine. Flat but interesting and testing. The large
sea-front hotel provides comfortable accommodation
and an extensive range of sports and leisure facilities.
9 holes, 5421yds, Par 68, SSS 66. Membership 400.

Visitors welcome must contact in advance Societies
welcome (☎)
Green fees £10 per day (No green fees for hotel
residents)
Facilities ⊗ ⅷ ᚼ 🍺 ♀ ⅄ 🏠 ⅂ ᚎ Gordon Ritchie
Hotel ★★★★64% The Hythe Imperial Hotel, Princes
Pde, HYTHE ☎(0303) 267441 100⇥🌂

Located on the A2 easily accessible from the
M25 — Crest offers the very best in modern
comfort and friendly service.
Ideally based for local Golf Clubs; Bexleyheath,
Barnehurst, Dartford and Chislehurst.
All 106 bedrooms offer private bathrooms,
beautifully furnished with modern facilities.
Excellent food from bar lunches in the Black
Prince Pub to more elegant meals in Edwards
Restaurant. Free Parking.

CREST HOTEL
BEXLEY

Black Prince Interchange, Southwold Road, Bexley, Kent DA5 1ND.
Telephone: Crayford (0322) 526900. Fax:(0322)526113. Telex: 8956539.

Sene Valley ☏ (0303) 68513
Sene (1m NE off B2065)
A two-level downland course which provides
interesting golf over an undulating landscape with sea
views. Snooker.
18 holes, 6287yds, Par 71, SSS 70. Membership 650.

Visitors welcome must contact in advance ✉ Societies
welcome (minimum notice one week ☏)
Green fees Not confirmed
Facilities ⊗ (ex Mon) ⫟ (ex Mon) ⊫ (ex Mon) ⚒ ♀
⚎ 🏠 �ʈ T Dungate
Hotel ★★★★64% The Hythe Imperial Hotel, Princes
Pde, HYTHE ☏(0303) 267441 100⇌🐾

KINGSDOWN
Map 2 K5

Walmer & Kingsdown ☏ (0304) 373256
The Leas (.5m S off B2057)
This course near Deal has through the years been
overshadowed by its neighbours at Deal and
Sandwich, yet it is a testing circuit with many
undulations. The course is famous as being the one
on which, in 1964, Assistant Professional, Roger
Game became the first golfer in Britain to hole out
in one at two successive holes; the 7th and 8th. The
course is situated on top of the cliffs, with fine views.
18 holes, 6451yds, Par 72, SSS 71. Membership 600.

Visitors welcome (ex before noon WE & BH) must
contact in advance ✉ Societies welcome (one
month's notice ☏)
Green fees Not confirmed
Facilities ⊗ ⫟ by prior arrangement ⊫ ⚒ ♀ ⚎
🏠 ⁊ ʈ Tim Hunt
Hotel ★★★62% Crest Hotel, Singledge Ln,
Whitfield, DOVER ☏(0304) 821222 67⇌🐾

LAMBERHURST
Map 2 G5

Lamberhurst ☏ (0892) 890241
Church Rd (N side of village on A21)
Parkland course crossing river twice. Fine views.
*18 holes, 6232yds, Par 72, SSS 70, Course record 67.
Membership 700.*

Visitors welcome (restricted WE & BH am) Societies
welcome (Tue, Wed & Thu only ☏)
Green fees £20 per day (£25 WE & BH)
Facilities ⊗ ⊫ ⚒ ♀ ⚎ 🏠 ⁊ ʈ Mike Travers
Hotel ★★71% Star & Eagle Hotel, High St,
GOUDHURST ☏(0580) 211512 11rm(9⇌🐾)

For a full list of the golf courses
included in this book, check
with the index on page 284

Littlestone ☏ New Romney (0679) 63355
St Andrew's Rd (N side of village)
Located in the Romney Marshes, this flattish seaside
links course calls for every variety of shot. The 8th,
15th, 16th and 17th are regarded as classics by
international golfers. Allowance for wind must
always be made. Additional facilities include
hardcourt tennis and an extensive practice area.
*18 holes, 6424yds, Par 71, SSS 71, Course record 66.
Shore Course 9 holes, 1998yds, Par 32, SSS 63.
Membership 500.*

Visitors welcome (restricted all week) must contact
in advance ✉ Societies welcome (☏ one year in
advance)
Green fees £28 per day; £20 per round (£22 WE/BH
after 1500 only)
Facilities ⊗ ⊫ ⚒ ♀ ⚎ 🏠 ⁊ ʈ Stephen
Watkins
Hotel ★★★★64% The Hythe Imperial Hotel,
Princes Pde, HYTHE ☏(0303) 267441 100⇌🐾

MAIDSTONE
Map 2 H4

Cobtree Manor Park ☏ (0622) 681560
Chatham Rd, Sandling (on A229 .25m N of M20 junc 6)
An undulating parkland course with some water
hazards.
18 holes, 5716yds, Par 69, SSS 68. Membership 530.

Visitors welcome must contact in advance Societies
welcome (not WE)
Green fees Not confirmed
Facilities ♀ ⚎ 🏠 ⁊ ʈ
Hotel ★★61% Boxley House Hotel, Boxley Rd, Boxley,
MAIDSTONE ☏(0622) 692269 11⇌🐾 Annexe:7⇌🐾

RAMSGATE
Map 2 K4

St Augustine's ☏ Thanet (0843) 590333
Cottington Rd, Cliffsend
A comfortably flat course in this famous bracing
Championship area of Kent. Neither as long nor as
difficult as its lordly neighbours, St Augustine's will
nonetheless extend most golfers. Dykes run across
the course.
*18 holes, 5138yds, Par 69, SSS 65, Course record 59.
Membership 600.*

Visitors welcome (handicap certificate required)
must contact in advance ✉ Societies welcome (by
letter)
Green fees £18 per day (£20 WE & BH)
Facilities ⊗ (ex Mon) ⫟ (ex Mon) ⊫ ⚒ ♀ ⚎ 🏠
ʈ Derek Scott
Hotel ★★53% Savoy Hotel, Grange Rd, 43 West
Cliff, RAMSGATE ☏(0843) 592637 15rm(1⇌7🐾)
Annexe:11⇌🐾

ROCHESTER   Map 2 G4

Rochester & Cobham Park
☎ Shorne (047 482) 3411
Park Pale (2.5m W on A2)
A first-rate course of
challenging dimensions in
undulating parkland. All
holes differ and each
requires accurate drive
placing to derive the best
advantage. The clubhouse
and course are situated .25
mile from the western end
of the M2.
18 holes, 6467yds, Par 72, SSS 71, Course record 66.
Membership 700.

SCORE CARD: White Tees					
Hole	Yds	Par	Hole	Yds	Par
1	298	4	10	350	4
2	358	4	11	181	3
3	434	4	12	357	4
4	190	3	13	479	5
5	476	5	14	311	4
6	382	4	15	492	5
7	402	4	16	159	3
8	204	3	17	503	5
9	446	4	18	445	4
Out	3190	35	In	3277	37
			Totals	6467	72

Visitors welcome (with M only WE & BH) must
contact in advance ✉ Societies welcome (Tue &
Thu only ☎)
Green fees £30 per day ; £20 per round (£25 WE
after 1600)
Facilities ⊗ ⅲ ┗ ⬛ ♀ ⚲ 🛍 (Matt Henderson
Hotel ★★★62% Inn on the Lake, Watling St,
SHORNE ☎(047482) 3333 78⇾🐾

SANDWICH   Map 2 K4

Prince's ☎ (0304) 611118
Prince's Dr, Sandwich Bay (2m E via toll road)
Championship links of the highest calibre and
comparable to its near neighbour, Royal Cinque
Ports. Typical flat duneland running along the
shore of Sandwich Bay. The ball must be struck well
to attain a good score. Snooker.
Dunes 9 holes, 3343yds, Par 36, SSS 71. Himalayas 9
holes, 3163yds, Par 35, SSS 71. Shore 9 holes,
3347yds, Par 36, SSS 72. Membership 450.

Visitors welcome must contact in advance Societies
welcome (☎)
Green fees £30 per day (£34 Sat & BH, £37 Sun)
Facilities ⊗ ⅲ ┗ ⬛ ♀ ⚲ 🛍 ╅ (Philip Sparks
Hotel ★★69% The Bow Window Inn, High St,
LITTLEBOURNE ☎(0227) 721264 8⇾🐾

Royal St George's See page 127

Each golf course entry has a recommended
hotel. For a wider choice of places to stay,
consult *AA Hotels and Restaurants in Britain* or
AA-inspected Bed and Breakfast in Britain.

SEVENOAKS   Map 2 F5

Knole Park
☎ (0732) 452150
Seal Hollow Rd (SE side of
town centre off B2019)
The course is set in a
majestic park with many
fine trees and deer running
loose. It has a wiry turf
seemingly impervious to
rain. Certainly a pleasure
to play on. Excellent views.
Squash and snooker.
18 holes, 6249yds, Par 70,
SSS 70, Course record 64.
Membership 950.

SCORE CARD					
Hole	Yds	Par	Hole	Yds	Par
1	197	3	10	163	3
2	345	4	11	426	4
3	403	4	12	200	3
4	413	4	13	319	4
5	174	3	14	438	4
6	418	4	15	483	5
7	480	5	16	199	3
8	177	3	17	502	5
9	512	5	18	400	4
Out	3119	35	In	3130	35
			Totals	6249	70

Visitors welcome (wkdays only & with handicap
certificate) must contact in advance Societies
welcome (by letter a year in advance)
Green fees £23
Facilities ⊗ ⅲ by prior arrangement ┗ ⬛ ♀ ⚲
🛍 (P E Gill
Hotel ★★59% Sevenoaks Park Hotel, Seal Hollow
Rd, SEVENOAKS ☎(0732) 454245 16rm(3⇾3🐾)
Annexe:10⇾🐾

SHEERNESS   Map 2 H4

Sheerness ☎ (0795) 662585
Power Station Rd (1.5m E off A249)
Seaside course, subject to wind.
18 holes, 6500yds, Par 72, SSS 71, Course record 68.
Membership 600.

Visitors welcome (with M only WE) Societies welcome
(by letter)
Green fees £18 per day ; £12 per round
Facilities ⊗ ⅲ by prior arrangement ┗ ⬛ ♀ ⚲ 🛍
(Paul King
Hotel ★★★68% Great Danes Hotel, Ashford Rd,
HOLLINGBOURNE ☎(0622) 30022 126⇾🐾

SHOREHAM   Map 2 F4

Darenth Valley ☎ Otford (09592) 2944
Station Rd (1m E on A225)
Easy walking parkland course in beautiful valley.
Testing 12th hole, par 4.
18 holes, 6356yds, Par 72, SSS 71, Course record 68.

Visitors welcome ex WE & PH Societies welcome (☎ or
by letter)
Green fees £7.50 per day (£10 WE & BH)
Facilities ⊗ ⅲ ┗ ⬛ ♀ ⚲ 🛍 ╅ (Paul Edwards
Hotel ★★★65% Royal Oak Hotel, Upper High St,
SEVENOAKS ☎(0732) 451109 23rm(19⇾2🐾)
Annexe:16⇾🐾

We make every effort to provide accurate information, but some details may change after we
go to print.

SITTINGBOURNE   Map 2 H4

Sittingbourne & Milton Regis
☏ Newington (0795) 842261
Wormdale, Newington (3m W off A249)
A downland course with pleasant vistas. There are a few
uphill climbs, but the course is far from difficult. The
166-yard, 2nd hole is a testing par 3.
18 holes, 6121yds, Par 70, SSS 69, Course record 66.
Membership 672.

Visitors welcome (ex WE & restricted Wed) must
contact in advance ✉ Societies welcome (☏)
Green fees £20 per round weekdays only
Facilities ⊗ ℳ ⮐ 🍺 ♀ 🛆 ⌂ 🍴 J Hearn
Hotel ★★★68% Great Danes Hotel, Ashford Rd,
HOLLINGBOURNE ☏(0622) 30022 126⇨🐾

TENTERDEN   Map 2 H6

Tenterden ☏ (05806) 3987
Woodchurch Rd (.75m E on B2067)
Attractive parkland course, last 3 holes are hilly.
Additional 9 holes under construction and due to open
Spring 1991.
9 holes, 5643yds, Par 68, SSS 67. Membership 510.

Visitors welcome (restricted WE & BH until 1200) must
contact in advance Societies welcome (☏)
Green fees not confirmed
Facilities ⊗ by prior arrangement ℳ by prior
arrangement 🍺 ⮐ ♀ 🛆 ⌂ 🍴 Gary Potter
Hotel ★★⚑70% Kennel Holt Country House Hotel,
Goudhurst Rd, CRANBROOK ☏(0580) 712032 9⇨🐾
Annexe:1🐾

TONBRIDGE   Map 2 G5

Poultwood ☏ (0732) 364039
Higham Ln
Public 'pay and play' woodland/parkland course. Easy
but varied walking, water hazards. Squash.
18 holes, 5569yds, Par 68, SSS 67.

Visitors welcome (public course) Societies welcome (☏)
Green fees On application
Facilities ⊗ ℳ 🍺 ⮐ ♀ 🛆 ⌂ 🍴
Hotel ★★64% Rose & Crown Hotel, High St,
TONBRIDGE ☏(0732) 357966 50⇨🐾

TUNBRIDGE WELLS (ROYAL)   Map 2 G5

Nevill ☏ (0892) 25818
Benhall Mill Rd
The county boundary with Kent runs along the
northern perimeter of the course. Open undulating
ground, well-wooded with much heather and gorse
for the first half. The second nine holes slope away
from the clubhouse to a valley where a narrow
stream hazards two holes.
18 holes, 6336yds, Par 71, SSS 70, Course record 65.
Membership 950.

Visitors welcome must contact in advance Societies
welcome
Green fees £24 (£35 WE)
Facilities ⊗ ℳ by prior arrangement 🍺 ⮐ ♀ 🛆
⌂ 🍴 Paul Huggett
Hotel ★★★76% Spa Hotel, Mount Ephraim,
TUNBRIDGE WELLS ☏(0892) 20331 76⇨🐾

Tunbridge Wells ☏ (0892) 25818
Langton Rd (1m W on A264)
Somewhat hilly parkland course with lake; trees form
natural hazards.
18 holes, 6336yds, Par 71, SSS 70. Membership 850.

Visitors welcome must contact in advance Societies
welcome (by letter)
Green fees Not confirmed
Facilities ♀ 🛆 ⌂ 🍴 🍴
Hotel ★★★76% Spa Hotel, Mount Ephraim,
TUNBRIDGE WELLS ☏(0892) 20331 76⇨🐾

WESTGATE ON SEA   Map 2 K4

Westgate and Birchington ☏ Thanet (0843) 31115
176 Canterbury Rd (E side of town centre off A28)
Seaside course.
18 holes, 4926yds, Par 64, SSS 64. Membership 310.

Visitors welcome (restricted WE) must contact in
advance ✉ Societies welcome (three mths in advance)
Green fees £12 per day (£15 WE & BH)
Facilities ⮐ ♀ 🛆 ⌂ 🍴 Roger Game
Hotel ★★53% Savoy Hotel, Grange Rd, 43 West Cliff,
RAMSGATE ☏(0843) 592637 15rm(1⇨7🐾)
Annexe:11⇨🐾

WEST KINGSDOWN   Map 2 G4

Woodlands Manor ☏ (09592) 3806
Woodlands (2m S off A20)
Interesting, undulating parkland course with testing
1st, 9th and 15th holes. Snooker.
18 holes, 5858yds, Par 69, SSS 68. Membership 550.

Visitors welcome (with M only WE pm) Societies
welcome (by letter)
Green fees Not confirmed
Facilities ♀ 🛆 ⌂ 🍴 🍴
Hotel ★★59% Sevenoaks Park Hotel, Seal Hollow Rd,
SEVENOAKS ☏(0732) 454245 16rm(3⇨3🐾)
Annexe:10⇨🐾

WHITSTABLE   Map 2 J4

Chestfield (Whitstable)☏ Chestfield (022779) 4411
103 Chestfield Rd (2m SE off A299)
Parkland course with sea views.
18 holes, 6181yds, Par 70, SSS 70, Course record 66.
Membership 680.

Visitors welcome (ex WE) must contact in advance ✉
Societies welcome (by letter)
Green fees Not confirmed

▶

SCORE CARD:					
Championship tees					
Hole	Yds	Par	Hole	Yds	Par
1	448	4	10	401	4
2	377	4	11	218	3
3	215	3	12	367	4
4	471	4	13	445	4
5	422	4	14	509	5
6	157	3	15	468	4
7	532	5	16	165	3
8	420	4	17	427	4
9	391	4	18	470	4
Out	3421	35	In	3470	35
			Totals	6903	70

SANDWICH   Map2 K4

Royal St George's ☎ (0304) 613090. 1.5m E of town.

Sandwich is one of the most beautiful and unspoiled towns in southern England. Driving to this part of Kent is much like stepping back into history The big golf course here, Royal St Goerge's, is where Sandy Lyle won the Open Championship in 1985, by one shot from that colourful American, Payne Stewart.

Close to the sea, overlooking Pegwell Bay, any kind of wind can make this man-size test even tougher. The sweeping rough at the first can be daunting, so can the bunkers and the huge sandhills. But there are classic shots here; it is the truest links you will find in all England and the R&A, in its wisdom, choose it for major championships knowing it will find the pedigree player at the end of a week.

The clubhouse is old-fashioned and the seats near the window, in the bar, seem to have been there forever. The barstaff may know as much about fishing or lifeboats as they know about beer, and make a visit there a delight, providing you are not looking for modern sophistication.

Off-sea breezes can turn to incredible gales, and it is possible to find the course virtually unplayable. A smooth swing can be blown inside out and stories of three good woods to reach certain greens, into wind, are common-place. Often the problem in high winds is simply to stand up, and address the ball. Putting, too, can be almost impossible with the ball blown off the surface, and maybe into the sand! Christy O'Connor Jnr put together a 64 here, and no wonder it's the record.

18 holes, 6903, Par 70, SSS74. Course record 64, Membership 700

Visitors	welcome (ex WE). Must contact in advance ✉ . Societies welcome (by letter).
Green fees	£45/£46 per day; £31/£32 per round
Facilities	⊗ � (for groups & societies) 🍴 🍺 ♀ ⚒ 🏠 ⚑ ⚐ Naill Cameron

WHERE TO STAY AND EAT NEARBY

HOTELS:

CANTERBURY	★★★ 60% Flagstaff, St Dunstans St ☎ (0227) 462138. 24 ⌁ ♪ . ♀ English & Continental cuisine.
DOVER	★★★ 64% Crest, Singledge Ln, Whitfield (3m NW jct A2/A256) ☎ (0304) 821222. 67 ⌁ ♪ . ♀ International cuisine.
LITTLEBOURNE	★★ 69% The Bow Window Inn, High St. ☎ Canterbury (0227) 721264. 8 ⌁ ♪ . ♀ English & French cuisine.
RAMSGATE	★★ 53% Savoy, Grange Rd, 43 West Cliff. ☎ Thanet (0843) 592637. 15rm (1 ⌁ 7 ♪) Annexe 11 ⌁ ♪ . ♀ French cuisine.

RESTAURANTS:

DEAL	✗ Captain's Table, Cliffe Rd, Kingsdown. ☎ (0304) 373755. ♀ English & French cuisine.
CANTERBURY	✗✗ Michael's Restaurant, 17 Wincheap, ☎ (0227) 767411. ♀ British & French cuisine.

Facilities ⊗))lll by prior arrangement ⅙ ⬛ ♀ ☖ 🖼
𝄐 J J Brotherton
Hotel ★★★52% Chaucer Hotel, Ivy Ln, CANTERBURY
𝄐(0227) 464427 45⤳

Whitstable & Seasalter 𝄐 (0227) 272020
Collingwood Rd (W side of town centre off B2205)
Links course.
9 holes, 5276yds, Par 66, SSS 63. Membership 414.

Visitors welcome (WE with M only)
Green fees £15 per round
Facilities ⅙ ⬛ ♀ ☖ 🖼
Hotel ★★★52% Chaucer Hotel, Ivy Ln, CANTERBURY
𝄐(0227) 464427 45⤳

LANCASHIRE

ACCRINGTON   Map 5 D6

Baxenden & District 𝄐 (0254) 34555
Top o' th' Meadow, Baxenden (1.5m SE off A680)
Moorland course.
18 holes, 5740yds, SSS 68.

Visitors welcome Societies welcome
Green fees Not confirmed
Facilities ♀ ☖
Hotel ★★★61% Dunkenhalgh Hotel, Blackburn Rd,
Clayton le Moors, ACCRINGTON 𝄐(0254) 398021 35⤳▐▜
Annexe:28⤳▐▜

Green Haworth 𝄐 (0254) 37580
Green Haworth (2m S off A680)
Moorland course dominated by quarries.
9 holes, 5513yds, Par 68, SSS 67, Course record 68.
Membership 190.

Visitors welcome (with M only Sun) Societies welcome
(𝄐)
Green fees £8 (£12 WE)
Facilities ☖ 🖼
Hotel ★★★57% Blackburn Moat House, Preston New
Rd, BLACKBURN 𝄐(0254) 64441 98⤳▐▜

BACUP   Map 5 D6

Bacup 𝄐 (0706) 873170
Bankside Ln (W side of town off A671)
Moorland course, predominantly flat except climbs to
1st and 10th holes.
9 holes, 5652yds, Par 68, SSS 67. Membership 400.

Visitors welcome Societies welcome
Green fees Not confirmed
Facilities ⅙ ⬛ ♀ ☖
Hotel ★★★63% Keirby Hotel, Keirby Walk, BURNLEY
𝄐(0282) 27611 49⤳▐▜

Each golf course entry has a recommended
hotel. For a wider choice of places to stay,
consult *AA Hotels and Restaurants in Britain* or
AA-inspected Bed and Breakfast in Britain.

BARNOLDSWICK   Map 5 D6

Ghyll 𝄐 Earby (0282) 842466
Ghyll Brow (1m NE on B6252)
Parkland course with outstanding views, especially
from the 8th tee where you can see the Three Peaks.
Testing 3rd hole is an uphill par 4.
9 holes, 5422yds, Par 68, SSS 66, Course record 64.
Membership 310.

Visitors welcome (ex Tue pm, Fri evening & Sun)
Societies welcome (by letter)
Green fees £8 per day (£12 WE)
Facilities Catering by prior arrangement ♀ (from 1900)
☖
Hotel ★★★65% Stirk House Hotel, GISBURN 𝄐(0200)
445581 36⤳▐▜ Annexe:12⤳

BLACKBURN   Map 5 D6

Blackburn 𝄐 (0254) 51122
Beardwood Brow (1.25m NW of town centre off A677)
Parkland course on a high plateau with stream and
hills. Indoor and outdoor practice facilities.
18 holes, 6140yds, Par 71. Membership 800.

Visitors welcome Societies welcome (𝄐)
Green fees £14 per day (£18 WE & BH)
Facilities ⊗))lll ⅙ ⬛ (no catering Mon other times by
prior arrangement) ♀ ☖ 🖼 𝄐 Alan Rodwell
Hotel ★★★57% Blackburn Moat House, Preston New
Rd, BLACKBURN 𝄐(0254) 64441 98⤳▐▜

BLACKPOOL   Map 5 C6

Blackpool North Shore 𝄐 (0253) 52054
Devonshire Rd (On A587 N of town centre)
Undulating parkland course. Snooker.
18 holes, 6400yds, Par 71, SSS 71. Membership 860.

Visitors welcome (ex Thu & Sat) Societies welcome (𝄐)
Green fees £15 per day (£17 WE)
Facilities ☖ 🖼 ⍟ 𝄐
Hotel ★★67% Brabyns Hotel, Shaftesbury Av, North
Shore, BLACKPOOL 𝄐(0253) 54263 22⤳▐▜
Annexe:3⤳▐▜

BURNLEY   Map 5 D6

Burnley 𝄐 (0282) 21045
Glen View (1.5m S off A646)
Moorland course with hilly surrounds. Snooker.
18 holes, 5891yds, Par 69, SSS 69, Course record 65.
Membership 600.

Visitors welcome (ex WE) must contact in advance
Societies welcome
Green fees £10 per day (£15 WE & BH)
Facilities ⊗))lll ⅙ ⬛ (no catering Mon) ♀ (ex Mon)
☖ 🖼 𝄐 Reg Cade
Hotel ★★★63% Keirby Hotel, Keirby Walk, BURNLEY
𝄐(0282) 27611 49⤳▐▜

Towneley ☎ (0282) 38473
Towneley Park, Todmorden Rd (1m SE of town centre on A671)
Parkland course, with other sporting facilities available.
18 holes, 5812yds, Par 70, SSS 68, Course record 65. Membership 300.

Visitors welcome (☎ WE) Societies welcome
Green fees Not confirmed
Facilities ⊗ (ex Mon) 🍽 by prior arrangement ⬇ (ex Mon) 🏌 ♀ 👔 🖼 ⛳ 🍸
Hotel ★★★71% Oaks Hotel, Colne Rd, Reedley, BURNLEY ☎(0282) 414141 58⇨🐾

CHORLEY   Map 5 C7

Chorley ☎ (0257) 480263
Hall o' th' Hill, Heath Charnock (2.5m SE on A673)
A splendid moorland course with plenty of fresh air. The well-sited clubhouse affords some good views of the Lancashire coast and of Angelzarke, a local beauty spot. Beware of the short 3rd hole with its menacing out-of-bounds. Snooker.
18 holes, 6277yds, Par 71, SSS 70, Course record 65. Membership 400.

Visitors welcome must contact in advance ✉
Societies welcome (☎)
Green fees Not confirmed
Facilities ⊗ 🍽 ⬇ 🏌 ♀ 👔 🖼 🍸 Paul Wesselingh
Hotel ★★★67% Pines Hotel, Clayton-le-Woods, CHORLEY ☎(0772) 38551 25⇨🐾

Duxbury Jubilee Park ☎ (02572) 65380
Duxbury Park (2.5m S off A6)
Municipal parkland course.
18 holes, 6390yds, Par 71, SSS 70, Course record 66. Membership 225.

Visitors welcome (prior booking 6 days in advance) must contact in advance Societies welcome (wkdays only ☎)
Green fees £4.35 per round (£5.95 WE & BH)
Facilities ⬇ 🏌 ♀ 👔 🖼 🍸 David Clarke
Hotel ★★54% Welcome Lodge, Mill Ln, CHARNOCK RICHARD ☎(0257) 791746 103⇨

Shaw Hill Hotel Golf & Country Club ☎ (02572) 69221
Preston Rd, Whittle-Le-Woods (On A6 1.5m N)
A fine course designed by one of Europe's most prominent golf architects and offering a considerable challenge as well as tranquillity and scenic charm. Seven lakes guard par 5 and long par 4 holes. Hotel offers good accommodation, restaurant, snooker, sauna and solarium.
18 holes, 6467yds, Par 72, SSS 71, Course record 68.

Visitors welcome Societies welcome (☎)
Green fees £30 per day; £20 per round (£40/£30 WE & BH)
Facilities ⊗ 🍽 ⬇ 🏌 ♀ 👔 🖼 🍸 Ian Evans

Hotel ★★★61% Shaw Hill Hotel Golf & Country Club, Preston Rd, Whittle-le-Woods, CHORLEY ☎(02572) 69221 22⇨🐾

CLITHEROE   Map 5 D6

Clitheroe ☎ (0200) 22292
Whalley Rd, Pendleton (2m S on A671)
One of the best inland courses in the country. Clitheroe is a parkland-type course with water hazards and good scenic views, particularly on towards Longridge, and Pendle Hill. The Club has been the venue for the Lancashire Amateur Championships.
18 holes, 6322yds, Par 71, SSS 71. Membership 700.

SCORE CARD: White Tees					
Hole	Yds	Par	Hole	Yds	Par
1	464	5	10	372	4
2	346	4	11	406	4
3	447	4	12	445	4
4	298	4	13	518	5
5	144	3	14	187	3
6	345	4	15	379	4
7	434	4	16	317	4
8	161	3	17	151	3
9	379	4	18	522	5
Out	3025	35	In	3297	36
			Totals	6322	70

Visitors welcome (ex WE & Thu) must contact in advance Societies welcome (by letter)
Green fees £17 per day (£21 WE & BH)
Facilities ⊗ 🍽 ⬇ 🏌 ♀ 👔 🖼 🍸
Hotel ★★77% Shireburn Arms Hotel, HURST GREEN ☎(025486) 518 16⇨🐾

COLNE   Map 5 E6

Colne ☎ (0282) 863391
Law Farm, Skipton Old Rd (1m E off A56)
Moorland course. Snooker.
9 holes, 5961yds, Par 70, SSS 69, Course record 67. Membership 300.

Visitors welcome (restricted Thu) must contact in advance Societies welcome (☎)
Green fees £10 per day (£12 WE & BH)
Facilities ⊗ 🍽 ⬇ 🏌 (no catering Mon unless by prior arrangement) ♀ 👔
Hotel ★★★65% Stirk House Hotel, GISBURN ☎(0200) 445581 36⇨🐾 Annexe:12⇨

DARWEN   Map 5 D6

Darwen ☎ (0254) 701287
Winter Hill (1m NW)
Moorland course.
18 holes, 5752yds, Par 68, SSS 68, Course record 64. Membership 600.

Visitors welcome (ex Sat) Societies welcome (☎)
Green fees £12 per day (£18 WE)
Facilities ⊗ 🍽 ⬇ 🏌 (no catering Mon) ♀ (ex Mon) 👔 🖼 🍸 W Lennon
Hotel ★★★56% Whitehall Hotel, Springbank, Whitehall, DARWEN ☎(0254) 701595 18rm(14⇨🐾)

This guide is updated annually – make sure you use an up-to-date edition.

FLEETWOOD

Map 5 C5

Fleetwood ☎ (03917) 3661
Princes Way (W side of town centre)
Long, flat seaside links where the player must always be alert to changes of direction or strength of the wind. Snooker.
18 holes, 6437yds, Par 72, SSS 71. Membership 600.

Visitors welcome (ex competition days) Societies welcome (☎ deposit £2 per player)
Green fees £14 per day (£16 WE & BH)
Facilities ⊗ ⊫ ☕ ♀ ⌂ 🏠 (Clive Thomas Burgess
Hotel ★★★60% North Euston Hotel, The Esplanade, FLEETWOOD ☎(03917) 6525 59rm(55⇨🐾)

HARWOOD, GREAT

Map 5 D6

Great Harwood ☎ Blackburn (0254) 884391
Harwood Bar, Whallwy Rd (E side of town centre on A680)
Flat parkland course with fine views of the Pendle region.
9 holes, 6411yds, Par 73, SSS 71, Course record 68. Membership 325.

Visitors welcome (ex competition days) must contact in advance Societies welcome (by letter)
Green fees £10 per day (£12 WE & BH)
Facilities ⊗ ⊯ ⊫ ☕ (ex Mon) ♀ (ex Mon) ⌂
Hotel ★★77% Shireburn Arms Hotel, HURST GREEN ☎(025486) 518 16⇨🐾

HASLINGDEN

Map 5 D6

Rossendale ☎ Rossendale (0706) 831339
Ewood Ln Head (1.5m S off A56)
Testing, and usually windy meadowland course. Snooker.
18 holes, 6267yds, Par 72, SSS 70, Course record 67. Membership 700.

Visitors welcome (restricted Sun) must contact in advance Societies welcome (☎)
Green fees £15 per day (£20 WE & BH)
Facilities ⊗ ⊯ by prior arrangement ⊫ by prior arrangement ☕ ♀ ⌂ 🏠 (S J Nicholls
Hotel ★★★57% Blackburn Moat House, Preston New Rd, BLACKBURN ☎(0254) 64441 98⇨🐾

HEYSHAM

Map 5 C5

Heysham ☎ Lancaster (0524) 51011
Trumcar Park, Middleton Rd (.75m S off A589)
Seaside course. Course record holder Howard Clark. Snooker.
18 holes, 6258yds, Par 69, SSS 70, Course record 64. Membership 900.

Visitors welcome Societies welcome (by letter)
Green fees Not confirmed
Facilities ⊗ ⊫ ☕ ♀ ⌂ 🏠 ⌐ (Roy Williamson
Hotel ★★60% Clarendon Hotel, Promenade, West End, MORECAMBE ☎(0524) 410180 33rm(20⇨7🐾)

KNOTT END-ON-SEA

Map 5 C5

Knott End ☎ Blackpool (0253) 810576
Wyre-Side (W side of village off B5377)
Pleasant course on banks of River Wyre. Open to sea breezes. Large practise areas. Snooker.
18 holes, 5700yds, Par 69, SSS 68. Membership 680.

Visitors welcome (restricted daily) Societies welcome (by letter)
Green fees £15 (£19 WE)
Facilities ⊗ ⊯ ⊫ ☕ ♀ ⌂ 🏠 (Kevin Short
Hotel ★★★50% Imperial Hotel, North Promenade, BLACKPOOL ☎(0253) 23971 183⇨🐾

LANCASTER

Map 5 C5

Lancaster Golf & Country Club ☎ (0524) 751247
Ashton Hall, Ashton-with-Stodday (3m S on A588)
This course is unusual for parkland golf as it is exposed to the winds coming off the Irish Sea. It is situated on the Lune estuary and has some natural hazards and easy walking. There are, however, several fine holes among woods near the old clubhouse. Accommodation, snooker.
18 holes, 6465yds, Par 71, SSS 71. Membership 925.

Visitors welcome (restricted WE) must contact in advance ✉ Societies welcome (Mon-Fri only ☎)
Green fees £18
Facilities ⊗ ⊯ ⊫ ☕ (catering by prior arrangement) ♀ ⌂ 🏠 (Robert Head
Hotel ★★★67% Royal Kings Arms, Market St, LANCASTER ☎(0524) 32451 55⇨🐾

Lansil ☎ (0532) 685180
Caton Rd (N side of town centre on A683)
Parkland course.
9 holes, 5608yds, Par 70, SSS 67. Membership 375.

Visitors welcome (Not WE before 1300) Societies welcome (wkdays only by letter)
Green fees Not confirmed
Facilities ⌂
Hotel ★★★★59% Post House Hotel, Waterside Park, Caton Rd, LANCASTER ☎(0524) 65999 117⇨🐾

LEYLAND

Map 5 C6

Leyland ☎ (0772) 436457
Wigan Rd (E side of town centre on A49)
Parkland course, fairly flat and usually breezy.
18 holes, 6123yds, Par 70, SSS 69. Membership 860.

Visitors welcome (restricted WE & BH) must contact in advance Societies welcome (☎)
Green fees £15 per day/round
Facilities ⊗ (ex Mon) ⊯ ⊫ ☕ ♀ ⌂ 🏠 (C Burgess
Hotel ★★★67% Pines Hotel, Clayton-le-Woods, CHORLEY ☎(0772) 38551 25⇨🐾

Opening times of bar and catering facilities vary from place to place – it is wise to check in advance of your visit.

LONGRIDGE   Map 5 D6

Longridge ☎ (0772) 783291
Fell Barn, Jeffrey Hill
Moorland course 850 ft high with views of the Ribble Valley, Trough of Bowland, The Fylde and Welsh Mountains. Snooker.
18 holes, 5726 yds, Par 70, SSS 68, Course record 66.
Membership 500.

Visitors welcome Societies welcome (☎)
Green fees £12 Mon-Thu; £15 Fri-Sun
Facilities ⊗ ⅏ ⌊ ⬤ (catering Tue-Sun) ♀ (Tue-Sun) ⌲ 🏠 ⌁
Hotel ★★77% Shireburn Arms Hotel, HURST GREEN ☎(025486) 518 16⊸⋔

LYTHAM ST ANNES   Map 5 C6

Fairhaven ☎ (0253) 736741
Lytham Hall Park, Ansdell (E side of town centre off B5261)
A flat, but interesting course of good standard. There are natural hazards as well as numerous bunkers and players need to produce particularly accurate second shots. Snooker.
18 holes, 6884 yds, Par 74, SSS 73, Course record 65.
Membership 950.

Visitors welcome must contact in advance ✉ Societies welcome (☎ or by letter)
Green fees £25 per day; £20 per round (£25 WE)
Facilities ⊗ ⅏ ⌊ ⬤ ♀ ⌲ 🏠 ⬥ ⌁ I Howieson
Hotel ★★★68% Bedford Hotel, 307-311 Clifton Dr South, LYTHAM ST ANNES ☎(0253) 724636 36⊸⋔

Lytham Green Drive ☎ (0253) 737390
Ballam Rd (E side of town centre off B5259)
Pleasant parkland course, ideal for holidaymakers. Snooker.
18 holes, 6175 yds, Par 70, SSS 69. Membership 760.

Visitors welcome (ex Wed & Sat) must contact in advance Societies welcome (☎)
Green fees £21 per day (£26 Sun & BH)
Facilities ⊗ ⅏ ⌊ (no catering Mon) ⬤ ♀ ⌲ 🏠 ⌁ F W Accleton
Hotel ★★★★50% Clifton Arms, West Beach, Lytham, LYTHAM ST ANNES ☎(0253) 739898 41⊸⋔

Royal Lytham & St Annes See page 133

St Annes Old Links ☎ (0253) 723597
Highbury Rd, St Annes (N side of town centre)
Seaside links qualifying course for Open Championship, compact and of very high standard, particularly greens. Windy, very long 5th, 17th and 18th holes. Famous hole: 9th (171 yds), par 3. Practice ground, exceptional club facilities. Snooker.
18 holes, 6616 yds, Par 72, SSS 72, Course record 66.
Membership 945.

Visitors welcome must contact in advance ✉ Societies welcome (☎)
Green fees £25 per day (£30 WE & BH)

Facilities ⊗ ⅏ ⌊ ⬤ ♀ ⌲ 🏠 ⌁ G G Hardiman
Hotel ★★★68% Bedford Hotel, 307-311 Clifton Dr South, LYTHAM ST ANNES ☎(0253) 724636 36⊸⋔

MORECAMBE   Map 5 C5

Morecambe
☎ (0524) 418050
Bare (N side of town centre on A5105)
Holiday golf at its most enjoyable. The well-maintained, seaside course is not long but full of character. Even so the panoramic views across Morecambe Bay and to the Lake District make concentration difficult. The 4th is a testing hole. Snooker.
18 holes, 5766 yds, Par 67, SSS 68, Course record 64.
Membership 1200.

			SCORE CARD		
Hole	Yds	Par	Hole	Yds	Par
1	338	4	10	194	3
2	451	4	11	326	4
3	143	3	12	183	3
4	439	4	13	366	4
5	194	3	14	412	4
6	372	4	15	419	4
7	387	4	16	174	3
8	351	4	17	336	4
9	386	4	18	295	4
Out	3061	34	In	2705	33
			Totals	5766	67

Visitors welcome (ex 1000-1400 & Sun before 1115) ✉ Societies welcome (☎)
Green fees £14 per day; £11 per round (£18/£15 WE&BH)
Facilities ⊗ ⅏ by prior arrangement ⌊ ⬤ ♀ ⌲ 🏠 ⌁ Donald Helmn
Hotel ★★★52% Elms Hotel, Bare, MORECAMBE ☎(0524) 411501 40⊸⋔

NELSON   Map 5 D6

Marsden Park ☎ (0282) 67525
Nelson Municipal Golf Course, Townhouse Rd (E side of town centre off A56)
18 holes, 5806 yds, Par 70, SSS 68. Membership 150.

Visitors welcome (☎ WE)
Green fees Not confirmed
Facilities ⌲ 🏠 ⬥ ⌁
Hotel ★★★71% Oaks Hotel, Colne Rd, Reedley, BURNLEY ☎(0282) 414141 58⊸⋔

Nelson ☎ (0282) 64583
King's Causeway, Brierfield (1.5m SE)
Hilly moorland course, usually windy, with good views. Testing 8th hole, par 4.
18 holes, 5967 yds, Par 70, SSS 69, Course record 65.
Membership 550.

Visitors welcome (ex Thu pm & Sat Apr-Oct) must contact in advance ✉ Societies welcome (by letter)
Green fees £13 per day (£15 WE & BH)
Facilities ⊗ ⅏ by prior arrangement ⌊ ⬤ ♀ ⌲ 🏠 ⬥ ⌁ R Geddes
Hotel ★★★71% Oaks Hotel, Colne Rd, Reedley, BURNLEY ☎(0282) 414141 58⊸⋔

ORMSKIRK
Map 5 C7

Ormskirk ☎ (0695) 72112
Cranes Ln, Lathom (1.5m NE)
A pleasantly secluded, fairly flat, parkland course
with much heath and silver birch. Accuracy from
the tees will provide an interesting variety of
second shots.
18 holes, 6142yds, Par 70, SSS 70, Course record 63.
Membership 300.

Visitors welcome (restricted Sat) must contact in
advance ✉ Societies welcome (by letter)
Green fees £22.50 per day (£27.50 Wed, WE & BH)
Facilities ⊗ ﷽ ﷽ ﷽ (no catering Mon) ♀ ⚲ 🏠
𝄐 Jack Hammond
Hotel ★★64% Bold Hotel, Lord St, SOUTHPORT
☎(0704) 32578 22rm(15⇘6♠)

PLEASINGTON
Map 5 D6

Pleasington ☎ Blackburn (0254) 202177
(W side of village)
Plunging and rising across lovely moorland turf this
course tests judgement of distance through the air
to greens of widely differing levels. The 11th and
17th are testing holes. Snooker.
18 holes, 6417yds, Par 71, SSS 70. Membership 605.

Visitors welcome (Mon & Wed-Fri only) must
contact in advance ✉ Societies welcome (☎)
Green fees £20 per day (£25 WE & BH)
Facilities ⊗ ﷽ ﷽ ﷽ (catering by prior
arrangement) ♀ ⚲ 🏠𝄐
Hotel ★★★57% Blackburn Moat House, Preston
New Rd, BLACKBURN ☎(0254) 64441 98⇘♠

POULTON-LE-FYLDE
Map 5 C6

Poulton-le-Fylde ☎ (0253) 893150
Breck Rd (N side of town)
Municipal parkland course, with easy walking.
9 holes, 5958yds, Par 70, SSS 69. Membership 200.

Visitors welcome Societies welcome (☎)
Green fees £3.20 (£4.50 WE)
Facilities ⊗ ﷽ ﷽ ♀ 🏠𝄐𝄐 Lewis Ware
Hotel ★★★★50% Imperial Hotel, North Promenade,
BLACKPOOL ☎(0253) 23971 183⇘♠

PRESTON
Map 5 C6

Ashton & Lea ☎ (0772) 726480
Tudor Av, Lea (3m W on A5085)
Semi-parkland course offering pleasant walks and some
testing holes. Snooker.
18 holes, 6289yds, Par 71, SSS 70, Course record 65.
Membership 650.

Visitors welcome (some restricted times) must contact
in advance Societies welcome (Mon, Tue & WE only by
letter)
Green fees £12.50 per day (£17 WE)

Facilities ⊗ ﷽ ﷽ (no catering Thu) ﷽ ♀ ⚲ 🏠𝄐
𝄐 Peter Laugher
Hotel ★★★63% Crest Hotel, The Ringway, PRESTON
☎(0772) 59411 126⇘♠

Fishwick Hall ☎ (0772) 798300
Glenluce Dr, Farringdon Park
Meadowland course overlooking River Ribble. Natural
hazards. Snooker.
18 holes, 6128yds, Par 70, SSS 69, Course record 66.
Membership 650.

Visitors welcome (restricted daily) must contact in
advance Societies welcome (by letter)
Green fees £15 per day (£20 WE & BH)
Facilities ⊗ ﷽ ﷽ ﷽ ♀ ⚲ 🏠𝄐 Stuart Bence
Hotel ★★★63% Crest Hotel, The Ringway, PRESTON
☎(0772) 59411 126⇘♠

Ingol ☎ (0772) 734556
Tanterton Hall Rd, Ingol (2m NW junc 32 of M55 off
B5411)
Long, high course with natural water hazards. Squash
and snooker.
18 holes, 6225yds, Par 71, SSS 70, Course record 67.
Membership 800.

Visitors welcome (ex competition days) must contact in
advance Societies welcome (☎)
Green fees £15 per day (£18 WE & BH)
Facilities ⊗ ﷽ ﷽ ﷽ ♀ ⚲ 🏠𝄐𝄐 Mark Cartwright
Hotel ★★★63% Crest Hotel, The Ringway, PRESTON
☎(0772) 59411 126⇘♠

Penwortham
☎ (0772) 744630
Blundell Ln, Penwortham
(W side of town centre off
A59)
A progressive golf club set
close to the banks of the
River Ribble. The course
has tree-lined fairways,
excellent greens, and
provides easy walking.
Testing holes include the
178-yd, par 3 (3rd), the 480-
yd, par 5 (6th), and the 398-
yd par 4 (16th). Snooker.

SCORE CARD: White Tees					
Hole	Yds	Par	Hole	Yds	Par
1	389	4	10	443	4
2	328	4	11	350	4
3	178	3	12	135	3
4	398	4	13	307	4
5	361	4	14	524	5
6	480	5	15	148	3
7	315	4	16	398	4
8	396	4	17	437	4
9	157	3	18	171	3
Out	3002	35	In	2913	34
			Totals	5915	69

18 holes, 5915yds, Par 69, SSS 68, Course record 62.
Membership 870.

Visitors welcome (restricted daily) must contact in
advance Societies welcome (Mon & Wed-Fri only ☎)
Green fees £19 per day (£25 WE & BH)
Facilities ⊗ ﷽ ﷽ ﷽ ♀ ⚲ 🏠𝄐 John Wright
Hotel ★★★72% Tickled Trout, Preston New Rd,
Samlesbury, PRESTON ☎(0772) 877671 72⇘♠

If you know of a golf course, not in this guide
already, which welcomes visitors, we would be
pleased to hear about it.

SCORE CARD					
Hole	Yds	Par	Hole	Yds	Par
1	206	3	10	334	4
2	420	4	11	485	5
3	458	4	12	189	3
4	393	4	13	339	4
5	188	3	14	445	4
6	486	5	15	468	4
7	551	5	16	356	4
8	394	4	17	413	4
9	162	3	18	386	4
Out	3258	35	In	3415	36
			Totals	6673	71

LYTHAM ST ANNES   Map5 C6

Royal Lytham & St Annes ☎ (0253) 724206. Links Gate (0.5m E of St Annes Town).

Venue for many Open Championships, the most famous winner here was amateur Bobby Jones who, in 1926, put together a four-round total of 291 using wooden clubs and the old-fashioned ball. In the last round, when level with Al Watrous with two to play, Jones bunkered his teeshot at the 17th while Watrous hit a perfect drive and then a fine second onto the green. Jones climbed into the bunker, decided a 175-yard shot was needed if he had any chance, and hit a club similar to today's 4-iron. The shot was brilliant and finished, not only on the green, but nearer than his rival. Shaken, Watrous 3-putted, Jones got his four and finished with a perfect par while Watrous, rattled, had taken six. The club placed a plaque by the famous bunker and it's there, to this day.

Since that time the course, which runs close to the railway but slightly inland from the sea, has staged other historic Opens. Bob Charles of New Zealand, became the only left-hander to win the title while Tony Jacklin, in 1969, signalled the re-awakening of British golf by winning.

This huge links, not far from Blackpool, is not easy. When the wind gets up it can be a nightmare. And not everyone approves a championship course that starts with a par 3 hole and it is, in fact, a rare thing in Britain. Some object to the close proximity of red-bricked houses, and aren't keen on trains that rattle passed. But it's a test full of history and must be played.

18 holes, 6673 yds, Par 71, SSS 73, Course record 65

Visitors	welcome (ex WE). Must contact in advance. Handicap cert required ✉ . Societies welcome (☎).
Green fees	£50 per day; £36 per round
Facilities	⊗ ⏫ ᵇ ■ ♀ (all catering by arrangement) ⛳🏠🖋 (by arrangement) ⸐ E.Birchenough.

WHERE TO STAY AND EAT NEARBY

HOTELS:

BLACKPOOL	★★★★ 67% Pembroke, North Promenade ☎ (0253) 23434.
	278 ↵ᵇⁿ . ♀ English & French cuisine.
LYTHAM ST ANNES	★★★★ 61% Clifton Arms, West Beach. ☎ (0253) 739898.
	41 ↵ᵇⁿ . ♀ English & French cuisine.
	★★★ 68% Bedford, 307-311 Clifton Drive South. ☎ (0253) 724636.
	36 ↵ᵇⁿ . ♀ English & Continental cuisine.
	★★ 69% Chadwick, South Promenade. ☎ (0253) 714455.
	70 ↵ᵇⁿ . ♀ English & French cuisine.
	★★ 66% St Ives, 7-9 South Promenade. ☎ (0253) 724447.
	71rm (61 ↵ᵇ 3 ⁿ). ♀ English & French cuisine.

RESTAURANT:

THORNTON	✗The River House, Skippool Creek. ☎ Poulton-Le-Fylde (0253) 883497 & 883307.
CLEVELEYS	♀ International cuisine.

Preston ☎ (0772) 794234
Fulwood Hall Ln, Fulwood (N side of town centre)
Pleasant inland golf at this course set in very agreeable parkland. There is a well-balanced selection of holes, undulating amongst groups of trees, and not requiring great length. Snooker.
18 holes, 6233yds, Par 71, SSS 70. Membership 600.

Visitors welcome (midweek only) must contact in advance ✉ Societies welcome (by letter)
Green fees £20 day; £17 per round
Facilities ⊗ ⟮ ⮂ ⬛ ♀ ⌂ 🏠 ⌂ P A Wells
Hotel ★★★71% Broughton Park Hotel & Country Club, Garstang Rd, Broughton, PRESTON ☎(0772) 864087 98⇥🛏

RISHTON   Map 5 D6

Rishton ☎ Great Harwood (0254) 884442
Eachill Links, Hawthorn Dr (S side of town off A678)
Moorland course recovered from recent dissection by the M65.
9 holes, 6199yds, Par 70, SSS 69, Course record 66. Membership 250.

Visitors welcome (with M only WE & BH) Societies welcome (☎)
Green fees £8 per day
Facilities ⊗ ⟮ ⮂ ⬛ ♀ ⌂
Hotel ★★★61% Dunkenhalgh Hotel, Blackburn Rd, Clayton le Moors, ACCRINGTON ☎(0254) 398021 35⇥🛏 Annexe:28⇥🛏

SILVERDALE   Map 5 C5

Silverdale ☎ (0524) 701300
Red Bridge Ln (opposite Silverdale Station)
Difficult heathland course with rock outcrops. Excellent views.
9 holes, 5288yds, Par 70, SSS 67, Course record 66. Membership 500.

Visitors welcome (ex Sun in summer unless with M) Societies welcome (by letter)
Green fees £8 per day (£12 WE & BH)
Facilities ⮂ ⬛ (Wed and Fri lunch) ♀ (Wed & Fri lunch) ⌂
Hotel ★62% Wheatsheaf Hotel, BEETHAM ☎(05395) 62123 6⇥🛏

UPHOLLAND   Map 5 C7

Beacon Park ☎ (0695) 622700
Beacon Ln (S of Ashurst Beacon Hill)
Undulating/hilly parkland course designed by Donald Steel. Floodlit driving range.
18 holes, 5996yds, Par 72, SSS 69, Course record 68. Membership 300.

Visitors welcome Societies welcome (by letter)
Green fees £3.50 per day (£4.50 WE & BH)
Facilities ⊗ ⟮ ⮂ ⬛ ♀ ⌂ 🏠 ⌂ ⌂ Ray Peters
Hotel ★★62% Holland Hall Hotel, 6 Lafford Ln, UPHOLLAND ☎(0695) 624426 29⇥🛏 Annexe:5⇥🛏

Dean Wood
☎ (0695) 622219
Lafford Ln (.5m NE off A577)
This parkland course has a varied terrain. Beware the par 4, 17th which has ruined many a card. If there were a prize for the best maintained course in Lancashire, Dean Wood would be a strong contender.
18 holes, 6129yds, Par 71, SSS 70, Course record 66. Membership 850.

SCORE CARD: White Tees					
Hole	Yds	Par	Hole	Yds	Par
1	367	4	10	157	3
2	389	4	11	398	4
3	335	4	12	343	4
4	157	3	13	358	4
5	368	4	14	363	4
6	338	4	15	206	3
7	514	5	16	192	3
8	522	5	17	279	4
9	337	4	18	506	5
Out	3327	37	In	2802	34
			Totals	6129	71

Visitors welcome (restricted WE & BH) must contact in advance Societies welcome (by letter)
Green fees £20 per day (£25 WE & BH)
Facilities ⊗ ⟮ ⮂ ⬛ ♀ ⌂ 🏠 ⌂ Tony Coop
Hotel ★★62% Holland Hall Hotel, 6 Lafford Ln, UPHOLLAND ☎(0695) 624426 29⇥🛏 Annexe:5⇥🛏

WHALLEY   Map 5 D6

Whalley ☎ (0254) 822236
Long Leese Barn, Portfield Ln (1m SE off A671)
Parkland course on Pendle Hill, overlooking the Ribble Valley. 9th hole over pond.
9 holes, 5444mtrs, Par 70, SSS 69, Course record 67. Membership 475.

Visitors welcome (restricted Thu 1230-1600 & Sat Apr-Sep) Societies welcome (☎ 4 wks notice Apr-Sep)
Green fees £9 per day (£12 WE & BH)
Facilities ⊗ ⟮ ⮂ ⬛ ♀ ⌂ 🏠 ⌂ ⌂ H Smith
Hotel ★★★57% Blackburn Moat House, Preston New Rd, BLACKBURN ☎(0254) 64441 98⇥🛏

WHITWORTH   Map 5 D7

Lobden ☎ (0706) 343228
Lobden Moor (E side of town centre off A671)
Moorland couse, with hard walking. Windy.
9 holes, 5770yds, Par 70, SSS 68. Membership 245.

Visitors welcome
Green fees Not confirmed
Facilities ♀
Hotel ★★60% Midway Hotel, Manchester Rd, Castleton, ROCHDALE ☎(0706) 32881 25⇥🛏

WILPSHIRE   Map 5 D6

Wilpshire ☎ Blackburn (0254) 248260
72 Whalley Rd (E side of village off A666)
Semi-moorland course. Testing 17th hole (219 yds) par 3. Good views of Ribble Valley. Snooker.
18 holes, 5911yds, Par 69, SSS 68, Course record 61. Membership 650.

Visitors welcome (ex competition days) must contact in advance ✉ Societies welcome (by letter)
Green fees £13 per day (£21 WE & BH)

Facilities ⊗)╫ ⓑ ⬛ ♀ ⌂ 📦 (W Slaven
Hotel ★★★57% Blackburn Moat House, Preston New Rd, BLACKBURN ☎(0254) 64441 98⇥🐾

LEICESTERSHIRE

ASHBY-DE-LA-ZOUCH   Map 3 K4

Willesley Park ☎ (0530) 411532
Measham Rd (SW side of town centre on A453)
Undulating heathland and parkland course with quick draining sandy sub-soil. Snooker.
18 holes, 6304yds, Par 70, SSS 70, Course record 65.
Membership 600.

Visitors welcome (not before 0930 on WE & BH) must contact in advance ✉ Societies welcome (☎ up to a year in advance)
Green fees £20.50 per day (£27.50 WE & BH)
Facilities ⊗)╫ ⓑ ⬛ (no catering Mon) ♀ (restricted Mon) ⌂ 📦 ⫪ (C J Hancock
Hotel ★★★57% Royal Osprey Hotel, Station Rd, ASHBY-DE-LA-ZOUCH ☎(0530) 412833 31⇥🐾

BIRSTALL   Map 4 A4

Birstall ☎ Leicester (0533) 674322
Station Rd (SW side of town centre off A6)
Parkland course. Snooker.
18 holes, 6203yds, Par 70, SSS 70. Membership 500.

Visitors welcome (with M Tue & WE) Societies welcome
Green fees £12 per day
Facilities ⌂ 📦 (David Clarke
Hotel ★★★62% Hotel Saint James, Abbey St, LEICESTER ☎(0533) 510666 72⇥🐾

COSBY   Map 4 A5

Cosby ☎ Leicester (0533) 864759
Chapel Ln, off Boughton Rd (S side of village off)
Parkland course. Snooker.
18 holes, 6277yds, Par 71, SSS 70, Course record 67.
Membership 650.

Visitors welcome (before 1600 & with M only WE & BH) must contact in advance ✉ Societies welcome (book with secretary)
Green fees £20 per day ; £18 per round
Facilities ⊗)╫ ⓑ ⬛ (no catering Mon) ♀ ⌂ 📦 (David Bowring
Hotel ★★★56% Post House Hotel, Braunstone Ln East, LEICESTER ☎(0533) 630500 172⇥🐾

HINCKLEY   Map 3 K5

Hinckley ☎ (0455) 615124
Leicester Rd (1.5m NE on A47)
Rolling pastureland with lake features, and lined fairways. Snooker.
18 holes, 6592yds, Par 71, SSS 71, Course record 66.
Membership 1000.

Visitors welcome (ex WE) must contact in advance ✉ Societies welcome (by letter)
Green fees £23 per day ; £18 per round
Facilities ⊗)╫ ⓑ (ex Sun) ⬛ ♀ ⌂ 📦 (Richard Jones
Hotel Longshoot Toby Hotel, Watling St, NUNEATON ☎(0203) 329711 Annexe:47⇥🐾

KETTON   Map 4 C4

Luffenham Heath ☎ Stamford (0780) 720205
Stamford (1.5m SW on A6121)
This undulating heathland course with low bushes, much gorse and many trees, lies in a conservation area for flora and fauna. From the higher part of the course there is a magnificent view across the Chater Valley.
18 holes, 6250yds, Par 70, SSS 70, Course record 64.
Membership 555.

Visitors welcome (handicap certificate required) must contact in advance ✉ Societies welcome (☎)
Green fees £25 per day (£30 WE & BH)
Facilities ⊗ by prior arrangement)╫ by prior arrangement ⓑ ⬛ ♀ ⌂ 📦 ⫪ (J A Lawrence
Hotel ★★★72% George of Stamford Hotel, St Martins, STAMFORD ☎(0780) 55171 47⇥🐾

KIBWORTH   Map 4 B5

Kibworth ☎ (0533) 792301
Weir Rd, Beauchamp (S side of village)
Parkland course with easy walking. A brook affects a number of fairways
18 holes, 6282yds, Par 71, SSS 70, Course record 67.
Membership 680.

Visitors welcome (h'cap cert required, with M only WE) Societies welcome (☎)
Green fees £16 per day
Facilities ⊗ ⓑ ⬛ (no catering Sun) ♀ ⌂ 📦 (A Strange
Hotel ★★★61% Three Swans Hotel, 21 High St, MARKET HARBOROUGH ☎(0858) 66644 due to change to 466644 21⇥🐾 Annexe:16⇥🐾

KIRBY MUXLOE   Map 4 A4

Kirby Muxloe ☎ Leicester (0533) 393457
Station Rd (S side of village off B5380)
Parkland course. Snooker.
18 holes, 6303yds, Par 71, SSS 70, Course record 65.
Membership 800.

Visitors welcome (restricted WE) must contact in advance ✉ Societies welcome (☎)
Green fees £15 day ; £12.50 round (£12.50 WE & BH)
Facilities ⊗)╫ by prior arrangement ⓑ ⬛ ♀ ⌂ 📦 (Robert Stephenson
Hotel ★★★★60% Holiday Inn, St Nicholas Circle, LEICESTER ☎(0533) 531161 188⇥🐾

LEICESTER

Map 4 A4

Humberstone Heights ☎ (0533) 764674
Gypsy Ln (2.5m NE of city centre)
Municipal parkland course with 9 hole pitch and putt.
18 holes, 6300yds, Par 70, SSS 71, Course record 67.
Membership 500.

Visitors welcome Societies welcome (☎)
Green fees £4.50 per round (£5.50 WE & BH)
Facilities ⊗ by prior arrangement ⋔ by prior
arrangement ⓛ ⯅ ♀ (ex Mon) ⛳ 🏠 ⸀ (Philip
Highfield
Hotel ★★★60% Park International Hotel,
Humberstone Rd, LEICESTER ☎(0533) 620471 209⇨▐

Leicestershire ☎ (0533) 738825
Evington Ln (2m E of city off A6030)
Pleasantly undulating parkland course.
18 holes, 6312yds, Par 68, SSS 70. Membership 750.

Visitors welcome must contact in advance ✉ Societies
welcome (☎)
Green fees £22 per day (£27 WE)
Facilities ⊗ by prior arrangement ⋔ by prior
arrangement ⓛ ⯅ ♀ ⛳ 🏠 (John R Turnbull
Hotel ★★★65% Leicestershire Moat House, Wigston
Rd, Oadby, LEICESTER ☎(0533) 719441 57⇨▐

Western Park ☎ (0533) 876158
Scudamore Rd, Braunstone Frith (1.5m W of city centre
off A47)
Pleasant, undulating parkland course with open aspect
fairways.
18 holes, 6629yds, Par 72, SSS 72. Membership 350.

Visitors welcome
Green fees Not confirmed
Facilities ♀ ⛳ 🏠 ⸀
Hotel ★★★56% Post House Hotel, Braunstone Ln
East, LEICESTER ☎(0533) 630500 172⇨▐

LOUGHBOROUGH

Map 4 A4

Longcliffe ☎ (0509) 239129
Snell's Nook Ln,
Nanpantan (3m SW off
B5350)
A re-designed course of
natural heathland with
outcrops of granite forming
natural hazards especially
on the 1st and 15th. The
course is heavily wooded
and has much bracken and
gorse. There are a number
of tight fairways and one
blind hole.

SCORE CARD: White Tees					
Hole	Yds	Par	Hole	Yds	Par
1	179	3	10	367	4
2	390	4	11	331	4
3	381	4	12	487	5
4	461	4	13	405	4
5	139	3	14	315	4
6	273	4	15	167	3
7	463	4	16	378	4
8	565	5	17	495	5
9	417	4	18	338	4
Out	3268	35	In	3283	37
			Totals	6551	72

18 holes, 6551yds, Par 71, SSS 72, Course record 68.
Membership 600.

Visitors welcome (with M only WE) must contact in
advance ✉ Societies welcome (☎)
Green fees £25 per day; £20 per round

Facilities ⊗ ⋔ ⓛ ⯅ ♀ ⛳ 🏠 (
Hotel ★★★63% King's Head Hotel, High St,
LOUGHBOROUGH ☎(0509) 233222 78⇨▐

LUTTERWORTH

Map 4 A5

Lutterworth ☎ (0455) 552532
Rugby Rd (.5m S on A426)
Hilly course with River Swift running through.
18 holes, 5570yds, Par 67, SSS 67. Membership 600.

Visitors welcome (ex WE) Societies welcome (Mon-Fri
☎)
Green fees £18 per day; £14 per round
Facilities ⊗ ⋔ ⓛ ⯅ (ex Tue and Thu) ♀ ⛳ 🏠
(Nick Melvin
Hotel ★★★72% Denbigh Arms Hotel, High St,
LUTTERWORTH ☎(0455) 553537 34⇨

MARKET HARBOROUGH

Map 4 B5

Market Harborough ☎ (0858) 463684
Oxendon Rd (1m S on A508)
A parkland course situated close to the town. There are
wide-ranging views over the surrounding countryside.
9 holes, 6080yds, Par 71, SSS 69, Course record 67.
Membership 330.

Visitors welcome (WE with M only) Societies welcome
(☎ (0536) 771771)
Green fees £7 per 9 holes, £12 per 18 holes, £18 per day
Facilities ⊗ ⋔ ⓛ ⯅ (no catering Mon) ♀ ⛳ 🏠 ⸀
(Frazer Baxter
Hotel ★★★61% Three Swans Hotel, 21 High St,
MARKET HARBOROUGH ☎(0858) 66644 due to change to
466644 21⇨▐ Annexe:16⇨▐

MELTON MOWBRAY

Map 4 B4

Melton Mowbray ☎ (0664) 62118
Thorpe Arnold (2m NE on A607)
Downland but flat course providing easy walking. Open
to the wind.
18 holes, 5792yds, Par 70, SSS 70. Membership 447.

Visitors welcome Societies welcome
Green fees £10 per day (£15 WE & BH)
Facilities ⯅ ♀ ⛳
Hotel ★★★55% Harboro' Hotel, Burton St, MELTON
MOWBRAY ☎(0664) 60121 26⇨▐

OADBY

Map 4 A4

Oadby ☎ (0533) 700326
Leicester Rd (West side of town centre off A6)
Municipal parkland course.
18 holes, 6228yds, Par 71, SSS 69. Membership 400.

Visitors welcome Societies welcome (☎)
Green fees Not confirmed
Facilities ♀ ⛳ 🏠 ⸀ (
Hotel ★★★65% Leicestershire Moat House, Wigston
Rd, Oadby, LEICESTER ☎(0533) 719441 57⇨▐

ROTHLEY   Map 4 A4

Rothley Park ☎ Leicester (0533) 302809
Westfield Ln (.75m W on B5328)
Parkland course in picturesque situation.
18 holes, 6482yds, Par 71, Course record 67. Membership 600.

Visitors welcome (restricted Tue & competitions) must contact in advance Societies welcome (by letter)
Green fees Not confirmed
Facilities ⊗ ⅏ ▐ ♨ ♀ △ 🏠 ⊤ 🕯 Peter Dolan
Hotel ★★★70% Rothley Court Hotel, Westfield Ln, ROTHLEY ☎(0533) 374141 15⇥🪶 Annexe:21⇥

SCRAPTOFT   Map 4 A4

Scraptoft ☎ (0533) 418863
Beeby Rd (1m NE)
Pleasant, inland country course.
18 holes, 6166yds, Par 70, SSS 69, Course record 66. Membership 550.

Visitors welcome (with M only WE) ✉ Societies welcome (by letter)
Green fees £16 (£20 WE)
Facilities ⊗ ⅏ (ex Mon) ⅏ (ex Mon and by prior arrangement) ▐ ♨ ♀ △ 🏠 ⊤ 🕯 Simon Sherratt
Hotel ★★★65% Leicestershire Moat House, Wigston Rd, Oadby, LEICESTER ☎(0533) 719441 57⇥🪶

ULLESTHORPE   Map 4 A5

Ullesthorpe ☎ Leire (0455) 209023
Frolesworth Rd (.5m N off B577)
Parkland course. Accommodation and extensive sport and leisure facilities.
18 holes, 6650yds, Par 72, SSS 72, Course record 72. Membership 640.

Visitors welcome (ex WE) must contact in advance Societies welcome (☎)
Green fees On application
Facilities ⊗ ⅏ ▐ ♨ ♀ △ 🏠 🕯 Nick Brown
Hotel ★★★72% Denbigh Arms Hotel, High St, LUTTERWORTH ☎(0455) 553537 34⇥

WHETSTONE   Map 4 A5

Whetstone ☎ (0533) 861424
Cambridge Rd, Cosby (1m S of village)
Small and very flat parkland course adjacent to motorway.
9 holes, 6212yds, Par 72, SSS 69. Membership 70.

Visitors welcome Societies welcome (by letter)
Green fees Not confirmed
Facilities ♀ △ 🏠 ⊤ 🕯
Hotel ★★★56% Post House Hotel, Braunstone Ln East, LEICESTER ☎(0533) 630500 172⇥🪶

Opening times of bar and catering facilities vary from place to place – it is wise to check in advance of your visit.

WOODHOUSE EAVES   Map 4 A4

Charnwood Forest ☎ Loughborough (0509) 890259
Breakback Ln (.75m NW off B591)
Hilly heathland course with hard walking.
9 holes, 5960yds, Par 69, SSS 69, Course record 65. Membership 300.

Visitors welcome (restricted Tue) must contact in advance ✉ Societies welcome (☎)
Green fees £15 day, 18 holes; £18 all day
Facilities △
Hotel ★★★63% King's Head Hotel, High St, LOUGHBOROUGH ☎(0509) 233222 78⇥🪶

Lingdale ☎ (0509) 890703
Joe Moore's Ln (1.5m S off B5330)
Parkland course located in Charnwood Forest with some hard walking at some holes. The par 3, (3rd) and par 5, (8th) are testing holes. The 4th and 5th have water hazards.
9 holes, 6684yds, Par 72, SSS 72, Course record 69. Membership 485.

Visitors welcome (restricted WE & competition days) must contact in advance Societies welcome (☎)
Green fees £12 (£20 WE)
Facilities ⊗ ⅏ by prior arrangement ▐ ♨ △ 🏠 🕯 Peter Sellears
Hotel ★★★63% King's Head Hotel, High St, LOUGHBOROUGH ☎(0509) 233222 78⇥🪶

LINCOLNSHIRE

BLANKNEY   Map 4 C2

Blankney ☎ Metheringham (0526) 20263
(1m SW on B1188)
Peaceful parkland course, fairly flat. Snooker.
18 holes, 6402yds, Par 71, SSS 71. Membership 650.

Visitors welcome (ex Sun & winter wknds, restricted Sat) must contact in advance Societies welcome (by letter with deposit)
Green fees £16 per day; £12 per round
Facilities ⊗ by prior arrangement ⅏ by prior arrangement ▐ ♨ ♀ △ 🏠 🕯 Graham Bradley
Hotel ★★★54% Moor Lodge Hotel, BRANSTON ☎(0522) 791366 25⇥🪶

BOSTON   Map 4 E2

Boston ☎ (0205) 350589
Cowbridge, Horncastle Rd (2m N off B1183)
Parkland course with many water hazards.
18 holes, 5825yds, Par 69, SSS 68. Membership 650.

Visitors welcome (ex WE & BH) must contact in advance Societies welcome (28 days notice ☎)
Green fees £15.50 per day (£24 WE & BH)
Facilities ⊗ ⅏ ▐ ♨ ♀ △ 🏠 ⊤ 🕯 Terry Squires
Hotel ★★61% New England, 49 Wide Bargate, BOSTON ☎(0205) 365255 25⇥

GAINSBOROUGH   Map 5 H8

Gainsborough ☎ (0427) 613088
Thonock (1m N off A159)
Scenic parkland course. Floodlit driving range.
Snooker.
18 holes, 6551yds, Par 73, SSS 71. Membership 600.

Visitors welcome Societies welcome (☎)
Green fees £20 per day; £15 per round
Facilities ⊗ ⅲ 🍺 ♀ ⚘ 🏠 (Steven Cooper
Hotel ★★64% Hickman-Hill Hotel, Cox's Hill,
GAINSBOROUGH ☎(0427) 3639 8rm(3⇆3🐾)

GRANTHAM   Map 4 C3

Belton Park ☎ (0476) 67399
Belton Ln, Londonthorpe Rd (1.5m NE off A607)
Parkland course, wooded, with deer park and Canadian
Geese Reserve. Famous holes: 5th, 12th, 16th and 18th.
A 27-hole championship course, with three 9-hole
combinations.
9 holes, 6420yds, Par 71, SSS 71, Course record 65.
Ancaster 9 holes, 6252yds, Par 70, SSS 70. Belmont 9
holes, 6016yds, Par 69, SSS 69. Membership 950.

Visitors welcome (ex 0830-0930 & 1230-1400) Societies
welcome (by letter)
Green fees £15-£20 per round (£22-£26 WE & BH)
Facilities ⊗ ⅲ 🍺 🍺 ♀ ⚘ 🏠 (
Hotel ★★★65% Angel & Royal Hotel, High St,
GRANTHAM ☎(0476) 65816 24⇆

LINCOLN   Map 5 H8

Canwick Park ☎ (0522) 522166
Canwick Park, Washingborough Rd (2m SE on B1190)
Parkland course. Testing 14th hole (par 3).
18 holes, 6237yds, Par 70, SSS 70. Membership 576.

Visitors welcome (restricted WE) must contact in
advance Societies welcome (☎ months notice)
Green fees £8 per day (£12 WE & BH)
Facilities ⊗ ⅲ by prior arrangement (ex Mon) 🍺 🍺
♀ ⚘ 🏠 (
Hotel ★★★58% Eastgate Post House Hotel, Eastgate,
LINCOLN ☎(0522) 520341 71⇆

Carholme ☎ (0522) 23725
Carholme Rd (1m W of city centre on A57)
Parkland course where prevailing west winds can add
interest. Good views.
18 holes, 6086yds, Par 71, SSS 69. Membership 620.

Visitors welcome (ex Sun 0730-1430)
Green fees Not confirmed
Facilities ♀ ⚘ 🏠 (
Hotel ★★★★63% The White Hart, Bailgate, LINCOLN
☎(0522) 26222 50⇆

Each golf course entry has a recommended
hotel. For a wider choice of places to stay,
consult *AA Hotels and Restaurants in Britain* or
AA-inspected Bed and Breakfast in Britain.

LOUTH   Map 5 J8

Louth ☎ (0507) 603681
Crowtree Ln (SE side of town centre off A157)
Undulating parkland course, fine views. Squash.
18 holes, 6502yds, Par 71, SSS 71. Membership 900.

Visitors welcome must contact in advance ✉ Societies
welcome (one months notice ☎)
Green fees Not confirmed
Facilities ⊗ by prior arrangement ⅲ by prior
arrangement 🍺 🍺 ♀ ⚘ 🏠 ⚓ (A Blundell
Hotel ★★64% Priory Hotel, Eastgate, LOUTH ☎(0507)
602930 12rm(6⇆3🐾)

MARKET RASEN   Map 5 J8

Market Rasen & District ☎ (0673) 842416
Legsby Rd (2m SE)
Picturesque, well-wooded heathland course, easy
walking, breezy with becks forming natural hazards.
Good views of Lincolnshire Wolds.
18 holes, 6043yds, Par 70, SSS 69, Course record 65.
Membership 550.

Visitors welcome (WE with M only) must contact in
advance Societies welcome (Tue & Fri only ☎)
Green fees £18 per day; £12 per round
Facilities ⚘ 🏠 (
Hotel ★★★58% Eastgate Post House Hotel, Eastgate,
LINCOLN ☎(0522) 520341 71⇆

SKEGNESS   Map 4 F1

North Shore ☎ (0754) 3298
North Shore Rd (1m N of town centre off A52)
A half-links, half-parkland course with easy walking
and good sea views.
18 holes, 5913yds, Par 68, SSS 71. Membership 590.

Visitors welcome ✉ Societies welcome (wkdays only)
Green fees Not confirmed
Facilities ♀ ⚘ 🏠 (
Hotel ★★55% County Hotel, North Pde, SKEGNESS
☎(0754) 2461 44⇆🐾

Seacroft ☎ (0754) 3020
Drummond Rd, Seacroft (S side of town centre)
A typical seaside links with flattish fairways
separated by low ridges. Easy to walk round. To the
east are sandhills leading to the shore. Southward
lies 'Gibraltar Point Nature Reserve'.
18 holes, 6490yds, Par 71, SSS 71. Membership 620.

Visitors welcome must contact in advance ✉
Societies welcome
Green fees £25 per day; £18 per round (£30; £25
WE)
Facilities ⊗ ⅲ 🍺 🍺 ♀ ⚘ 🏠 (
Hotel ★★55% County Hotel, North Pde, SKEGNESS
☎(0754) 2461 44⇆🐾

SLEAFORD   Map 4 C2

Sleaford ☎ South Rauceby (05298) 273
South Rauceby (1m W off A153)
Flat, dry course in winter, with the appearance of a
links course.
18 holes, 6443yds, Par 72, SSS 71, Course record 65.
Membership 650.

Visitors welcome (ex Sun in winter) ⊠ Societies
welcome (wkdays only ☎)
Green fees £15 per day (£23 WE & BH)
Facilities ⊗ ⅏ by prior arrangement ﰟ ⬛ (no
catering Mon) ♀ ⌂ 📷 ℮ Steve Harrison
Hotel ★★★65% Angel & Royal Hotel, High St,
GRANTHAM ☎(0476) 65816 24⇨

SPALDING   Map 4 D3

Spalding ☎ (077585) 386 & 474
Surfleet (5m N off A16)
A pretty, well-laid-out course in a fenland area. The
River Glen runs beside the 1st and 2nd holes, and
streams, ponds and new tree plantings add to the
variety of this well-maintained course. The clubhouse
has good modern facilities.
18 holes, 5807yds, Par 68, SSS 68. Membership 500.

Visitors welcome ⊠ Societies welcome (by letter/☎)
Green fees Not confirmed
Facilities ♀ ⌂ 📷 ℮
Hotel ★★66% Woodlands Hotel, 80 Pinchbeck Rd,
SPALDING ☎(0775) 769933 18⇨☊

STAMFORD   Map 4 C4

Burghley Park ☎ (0780) 53789
St Martins (1m S of town on B1081)
Short, flat parkland course with superb greens, situated
in the grounds of Burghley House.
18 holes, 6133yds, Par 70, SSS 69, Course record 65.
Membership 950.

Visitors welcome (with M only WE handicap cert
required) must contact in advance ⊠ Societies welcome
(by letter)
Green fees £18 per day
Facilities ⊗ ⅏ ﰟ ⬛ ♀ ⌂ 📷 ᛁ ℮ Glenn Davies
Hotel ★★★72% George of Stamford Hotel, St Martins,
STAMFORD ☎(0780) 55171 47⇨☊

STOKE ROCHFORD   Map 4 C3

Stoke Rochford ☎ Great Ponton (047683) 275
(off A1 5m S of Grantham)
Parkland course designed by C. Turner.
18 holes, 6251yds, Par 70, SSS 70, Course record 65.
Membership 525.

Visitors welcome (restricted to 0900 wkdays, 1030 WE &
BH) must contact in advance ⊠ Societies welcome (☎
year in advance)
Green fees £21 per day; £14 per round

Facilities ⊗ ⅏ ﰟ ⬛ ♀ ⌂ 📷 ℮ Angus Dow
Hotel ★★56% Kings Hotel, North Pde, GRANTHAM
☎(0476) 590800 23rm(16⇨5☊)

SUTTON BRIDGE   Map 4 E3

Sutton Bridge ☎ Holbeach (0406) 350323
New Rd (E side of village off A17)
Parkland course.
9 holes, 5804yds, Par 70, SSS 68, Course record 63.
Membership 350.

Visitors welcome (ex competition days, WE & BH) must
contact in advance ⊠
Green fees £15 (to rise)
Facilities ⊗ ⅏ ﰟ ⬛ (no catering Mon) ♀ (ex Mon)
⌂ 📷 ᛁ ℮ R Wood
Hotel ★★★60% The Duke's Head, Tuesday Market Pl,
KING'S LYNN ☎(0553) 774996 72⇨

SUTTON ON SEA   Map 5 K8

Sandilands ☎ (0521) 41432
(1.5m S off A52)
Flat seaside course.
18 holes, 5995yds, Par 70, SSS 69, Course record 66.
Membership 350.

Visitors welcome Societies welcome (wkdays only ☎)
Green fees £15 per day; £10 per round (£15 per round
WE & BH)
Facilities ⊗ ⅏ ﰟ ⬛ ♀ ⌂ 📷 ᛁ ℮ David Vernon
Hotel ★★60% Grange & Links Hotel, Sea Ln,
Sandilands, MABLETHORPE ☎(0507) 441334 23⇨☊

TORKSEY   Map 5 H8

Lincoln ☎ (042771) 210
(SW side of village)
A testing inland course with quick-drying sandy subsoil
and easy walking.
18 holes, 6438yds, Par 71, SSS 71. Membership 700.

Visitors welcome (ex 1230-1400, WE & BH) must contact
in advance ⊠ Societies welcome (by letter)
Green fees £20 per day
Facilities ⊗ ⅏ by prior arrangement ﰟ ⬛ ♀ ⌂ 📷
ᛁ ℮
Hotel ★★★★63% The White Hart, Bailgate, LINCOLN
☎(0522) 26222 50⇨

Opening times of bar and catering facilities vary
from place to place – it is wise to check in
advance of your visit.

WOODHALL SPA   Map 4 D1

Woodhall Spa
☎ (0526) 52511
The Broadway (NE side of village off B1191)
One of the country's greatest and most beautiful heathland courses, founded in 1905, and originally laid out by Harry Vardon. It provides flat, easy walking amongst heather and tree-lined fairways, and is renowned for its vast bunkers and clubhouse atmosphere.
18 holes, 6866yds, Par 73, SSS 73. Membership 500.

	SCORE CARD				
Hole	Yds	Par	Hole	Yds	Par
1	363	4	10	333	4
2	408	4	11	442	4
3	417	4	12	152	3
4	415	4	13	437	4
5	155	3	14	489	5
6	506	5	15	325	4
7	435	4	16	398	4
8	193	3	17	322	4
9	560	5	18	516	5
Out	3452	36	In	3414	37
			Totals	6866	73

Visitors welcome must contact in advance ✉ Societies welcome (☎)
Green fees £20 per round (£22 WE & BH)
Facilities ⊗ 🍽 by prior arrangement 💺 ♀ 🛆 📷 ⌇ Peter Fixter
Hotel ★★★59% Petwood House, Stixwould Rd, WOODHALL SPA ☎(0526) 52411 46⇌🏌

LONDON

Courses within the London Postal District area (ie those that have London Postcodes - W1, SW1 etc) are listed here in postal district order commencing **East** then **North, South** and **West.** Courses outside the London postal area, but within Greater London are to be found listed under the county of **Greater London** in the gazetteer (see page 86).

E4 Chingford

Royal Epping Forest ☎ 081-529 2195
Forest Approach, Chingford (300 yds S of Chingford Station)
Woodland course. 'Red' garments must be worn. Snooker.
18 holes, 6620yds, Par 72, SSS 70, Course record 65. Membership 495.

Visitors welcome
Green fees £5.50 per day (£8 WE)
Facilities 🛆 📷 ⌇ R Gowers
Hotel ★★★68% Woodford Moat House, Oak Hill, WOODFORD GREEN ☎081-505 4511 99⇌🏌

West Essex ☎ 081-529 7558
Bury Rd, Sewardstonebury (off N Circular Rd at Chingford on M25)
Testing parkland course within Epping Forest. Notable holes are 8th (par 4), 16th (par 5/4), 18th (par 5).
18 holes, 6289yds, Par 71, SSS 70, Course record 67. Membership 645.

Visitors welcome (ex Tue am, Thu pm & WE) must contact in advance ✉ Societies welcome (☎)
Green fees £30 per day; £25 per round
Facilities ⊗ by prior arrangement 🍽 by prior arrangement 💺 💺 ♀ 🛆 📷 ⌇ C Cox
Hotel ★★57% Roebuck Hotel, North End, BUCKHURST HILL ☎081-505 4636 29⇌

E11 Leytonstone

Wanstead ☎ 081-989 3938
Overton Dr, Wanstead (from central London A11 NE to Wanstead)
A flat, picturesque parkland course with many trees and shrubs and providing easy walking. The par 4, 16th, involves driving across a lake.
18 holes, 6109yds, Par 69, SSS 69, Course record 62. Membership 500.

Visitors welcome (Mon, Tue & Fri only) must contact in advance Societies welcome (☎)
Green fees £25 per day; £20 per round
Facilities ⊗ 🍽 💺 💺 ♀ 🛆 📷 ⌇ Gary Jacom
Hotel ★★★68% Woodford Moat House, Oak Hill, WOODFORD GREEN ☎081-505 4511 99⇌🏌

N2 East Finchley

Hampstead ☎ 081-455 0203
Winnington Rd
Parkland course.
9 holes, 5812yds, Par 68, SSS 68. Membership 500.

Visitors welcome (handicap certificate required) must contact in advance Societies welcome (☎)
Green fees £25 day; £20 per round (£28 WE)
Facilities ⊗ by prior arrangement 💺 (ex Sun) 💺 ♀ 🛆 📷 ⌇ ⌇ Peter Brown
Hotel ★★★58% Post House Hotel, Haverstock Hill, LONDON NW3 ☎071-794 8121 140⇌🏌

N6 Highgate

Highgate ☎ 081-340 1906
Denewood Rd
Parkland course.
18 holes, 5982yds, Par 69, SSS 69, Course record 66. Membership 705.

Visitors welcome (ex Wed & WE) Societies welcome (☎)
Green fees £25 per round
Facilities ⊗ 💺 💺 ♀ 🛆 📷 ⌇ Robin Turner
Hotel ★★★59% Charles Bernard, 5-7 Frognal, Hampstead, LONDON NW3 ☎071-794 0101 57⇌🏌

N9 Lower Edmonton

Leaside ☎ 081-803 3611
Picketts Lock Sports Centre, Edmonton
Flat parkland course with River Lea running alongside several holes.
9 holes, 2496yds, Par 32, SSS 32.

Visitors welcome
Green fees Not confirmed
Facilities ♀ ᗜ 🏠 ⛳ ⸤
Hotel ★★54% Holtwhites Hotel, 92 Chase Side,
ENFIELD ☎081-363 0124 30rm(28⇥🐾)

Picketts Lock ☎ 081-803 3611
Picketts Lock Sports Centre, Edmonton
Short, municipal parkland course with the River Lea
providing a natural hazard. Many other sports and
leisure activities available.
9 holes, 2496yds, Par 64, SSS 64.

Visitors welcome
Green fees Not confirmed
Facilities 🍴 🍺 (lunchtime) ♀ (1⊗0-14🍺0) ᗜ 🏠 ⛳
⸤ Richard Garten
Hotel ★★54% Holtwhites Hotel, 92 Chase Side,
ENFIELD ☎081-363 0124 30rm(28⇥🐾)

N14 Southgate

Trent Park ☎ 081-366 7432
Bramley Rd, Southgate
Parkland course set in 150 acres of green belt area. 7
holes played across Merryhills brook. Testing holes are
2nd (405 yds) over brook, 190 yds from the tee, and up to
plateau green; 7th (435 yds) dog-leg, over brook, par 4.
Considerable practice facilities.
18 holes, 6008yds, Par 69, SSS 69, Course record 65.
Membership 915.

Visitors welcome (restricted WE) must contact in
advance WE Societies welcome (☎)
Green fees £4.50 per round (£6 WE & BH)
Facilities ⊗ by prior arrangement 🍴 by prior
arrangement 🍴 🍺 ♀ ᗜ 🏠 ⸤ Craig Easton
Hotel ★★★★62% West Lodge Park Hotel, Cockfosters
Rd, HADLEY WOOD ☎081-440 8311 48⇥🐾
Annexe:2⇥🐾

N20 Whetstone

North Middlesex ☎ 081-445 1604
The Manor House, Friern Barnet Ln
Short parkland course with tricky greens.
18 holes, 5611yds, Par 69, SSS 67. Membership 600.

Visitors welcome must contact in advance ✉ Societies
welcome (☎)
Green fees £25 per day (£27 WE)
Facilities ⊗ 🍴 by prior arrangement 🍴 🍺 ♀ ᗜ 🏠
⛳ ⸤ Steve Roberts
Hotel ★★★★62% West Lodge Park, Cockfosters Rd,
HADLEY WOOD ☎081-440 8311 48⇥🐾 Annexe: 2⇥🐾

For a full list of the golf courses
included in this book, check
with the index on page 284

South Herts ☎ 081-445 2035
Links Dr, Totteridge
An open, undulating parkland course. It is, perhaps,
most famous for the fact that two of the greatest of
all British professionals, Harry Vardon and Dai
Rees, CBE were professionals at the course. The course
is testing, over rolling fairways, especially in the
prevailing south-west wind.
18 holes, 5748yds, Par 72, SSS 71. Membership 830.

Visitors welcome must contact in advance ✉
Societies welcome (Wed-Fri)
Green fees Not confirmed
Facilities ᗜ 🏠 ⛳ ⸤ R Livingston
Hotel ★★★65% Crest Hotel, Bignells Corner,
SOUTH MIMMS ☎(0707) 43311 123⇥🐾

N21 Winchmore

Bush Hill Park ☎ 081-360 5738
Bush Hill, Winchmore Hill
Pleasant parkland course surrounded by trees.
*18 holes, 5809yds, Par 70, SSS 68 or 5595yds, Par 70, SSS
67. Membership 654.*

Visitors welcome (ex WE & BH) must contact in
advance ✉ Societies welcome (☎)
Green fees Not confirmed
Facilities ⊗ 🍴 🍺 ♀ ᗜ 🏠 ⸤ George W Low
Hotel ★★54% Holtwhites Hotel, 92 Chase Side,
ENFIELD ☎081-363 0124 30rm(28⇥🐾)

N22 Wood Green

Muswell Hill ☎ 081-888 2044
Rhodes Av, Wood Green (off N Circular Rd at Bounds
Green)
Narrow parkland course, popular with societies.
18 holes, 6474yds, Par 71, SSS 71, Course record 65.
Membership 500.

Visitors welcome (restricted Tue am, WE & BH) must
contact in advance Societies welcome (☎)
Green fees £35 per day; £25 per round (£35 WE) £5
reduction with h'cap cert
Facilities ⊗ 🍴 🍺 ♀ ᗜ 🏠 ⛳ ⸤ Iain Roberts
Hotel ★★54% Holtwhites Hotel, 92 Chase Side,
ENFIELD ☎081-363 0124 30rm(28⇥🐾)

NW7 Mill Hill

Finchley ☎ 081-346 2436
Nether Court, Frith Ln, Mill Hill (Near Mill Hill East
Tube Station)
Easy walking on wooded parkland course.
18 holes, 6154yds, Par 72, SSS 69. Membership 450.

Visitors welcome must contact in advance Societies
welcome (☎)
Green fees £31 per day (£36 WE); £26 per round

▶

Facilities ⊗ �🏛 ⬛ ⬛ ♀ ⛴ 🏠 ⛳ 🍴 David Brown
Hotel ★★★★62% West Lodge Park, Cockfosters Rd,
HADLEY WOOD ☎081-440 8311 48⇆🛏 Annexe: 2⇆🛏

Hendon ☎ 081-346 6023
Sanders Ln, Mill Hill
Easy walking, parkland course which provides good
golf.
*18 holes, 6241yds, Par 70, SSS 70, Course record 66.
Membership 500.*

Visitors welcome (restricted WE & BH ☎) must
contact in advance Societies welcome (☎)
Green fees £30 per day; £22 per round (£33 WE & BH)
Facilities ⊗ (ex Mon) ⬛ (am) ♀ (restricted winter)
⛴ 🏠 ⛳ 🍴 Stuart Murray
Hotel ★★★59% Charles Bernard, 5-7 Frognal,
Hampstead, LONDON NW33 ☎071-794 0101 57⇆

Mill Hill ☎ 081-959 2339
100 Barnet Way, Mill Hill (On A1 S bound carriageway)
Parkland course with easy walking. Snooker.
*18 holes, 6286yds, Par 69, SSS 70 or 5952yds, Par 69, SSS
69. Membership 400.*

Visitors welcome (restricted WE & BH) must contact in
advance Societies welcome (☎)
Green fees Not confirmed
Facilities ⊗ 🏛 by prior arrangement ⬛ ⬛ ♀ ⛴ 🏠
⛳ 🍴 A Daniel
Hotel ★★★★62% West Lodge Park, Cockfosters Rd,
HADLEY WOOD ☎081-440 8311 48⇆🛏 Annexe: 2⇆🛏

SE9 Eltham

Eltham Warren ☎ 081-850 1166
Bexley Rd, Eltham
Easy walking on parkland course. Snooker.
*9 holes, 5840yds, Par 69, SSS 68, Course record 66.
Membership 400.*

Visitors welcome (ex WE) must contact in advance ✉
Societies welcome (☎)
Green fees £20 per day
Facilities ⊗ 🏛 by prior arrangement ⬛ ⬛ ♀ ⛴ 🏠
🍴 Ian Coleman
Hotel ★★★58% Bromley Court Hotel, Bromley Hill,
BROMLEY ☎081-464 5011 122⇆🛏

Each golf course entry has a recommended
hotel. For a wider choice of places to stay,
consult *AA Hotels and Restaurants in Britain* or
AA-inspected Bed and Breakfast in Britain.

Royal Blackheath ☎ 081-850 1795
Court Rd
A pleasant, parkland course
of great character as befits
the antiquity of the Club;
the clubhouse dates from
the 17th century. Many
great trees survive. The
18th is quite a gimmick
requiring a pitch to the
green over a thick clipped
hedge.
*18 holes, 6209yds, Par 70,
SSS 70. Membership 750.*

SCORE CARD					
Hole	Yds	Par	Hole	Yds	Par
1	472	4	10	347	4
2	391	4	11	377	4
3	428	4	12	173	3
4	197	3	13	518	5
5	360	4	14	382	4
6	476	5	15	349	4
7	379	4	16	164	3
8	158	3	17	397	4
9	365	4	18	276	4
Out	3226	35	In	2983	35
			Totals	6209	70

Visitors welcome (mid-week only, h'cap cert
required) must contact in advance ✉ Societies
welcome (mid-week only ☎)
Green fees £30 per day; £25 per round
Facilities ⊗ (Tue-Fri) ⬛ (Tue-Fri) ♀ ⛴ 🏠 ⛳
🍴 I McGregor
Hotel ★★★58% Bromley Court Hotel, Bromley
Hill, BROMLEY ☎081-464 5011 122⇆🛏

SE18 Woolwich

Shooters Hill ☎ 081-854 6368
Eaglesfield Rd, Shooters Hill (Shooters Hill Rd from
Blackheath)
Hilly parkland course with good view and natural
hazards. Tennis, snooker.
*18 holes, 5736 yds, Par 69, SSS 68, Course record 62.
Membership 960.*

Visitors welcome (must be M of a golf club with h'cap
cert) ✉ Societies welcome (Tue & Thu only)
Green fees £25 per day; £20 per round
Facilities ⊗ 🏛 ⬛ ⬛ (all catering by prior
arrangement) ♀ (by prior arrangement) ⛴ 🏠
🍴 Michael Ridge
Hotel ★★★70% Crest Hotel, Black Prince
Interchange, Southwold Rd, BEXLEY ☎(0322) 526900
106⇆🛏

SE21 Dulwich

Dulwich & Sydenham Hill ☎ 081-693 3961
Grange Ln, College Rd
Parkland course, overlooking London, hilly with
narrow fairways.
18 holes, 6192yds, Par 69, SSS 69. Membership 850.

Visitors welcome (with M only WE) ✉ Societies
welcome (☎)
Green fees Not confirmed
Facilities ⊗ (ex WE) 🏛 by prior arrangement ⬛ ⬛ ♀
⛴ 🏠 ⛳ 🍴 David Baillie
Hotel ★★★58% Bromley Court Hotel, Bromley Hill,
BROMLEY ☎081-464 5011 122⇆🛏

SE22 East Dulwich

Aquarius ☎ 081-693 1626
Marmora Rd, Honor Oak, Off Forest Hill Rd
Course laid-out on two levels around and over covered
reservoir; hazards include vents and bollards.
9 holes, 5213yds, Par 66, SSS 65, Course record 62.
Membership 440.

Visitors welcome Member must accompany ✉
Green fees £7 per round/day
Facilities ⊗ (Sun only) 🖿 ⏛ ♀ ⏢ 🏠 ⸀
Hotel ★★★58% Bromley Court Hotel, Bromley Hill,
BROMLEY ☎081-464 5011 122⊸🏌

SW15 Putney

Richmond Park ☎ 081-876 1795
Roehampton Gate
Two public parkland courses.
Richmond Park 18 holes, 5909yds, Par 68, SSS 68,
Course record 62. Dukes 18 holes, 5486yds, Par 72.

Visitors welcome (No spectators or caddies)
Societies welcome (☎ or letter)
Green fees £5.50 per day (£8 WE)
Facilities ⊗ 🌑 ⏛ ♀ ⏢ 🏠 ⸙ ⸀
Hotel ★★★64% Richmond Hill, 146-150 Richmond
Hill, RICHMOND ☎081-940 2247 & 081-940 5466
123⊸🏌

SW19 Wimbledon

Royal Wimbledon ☎ 081-946 2125
29 Camp Rd
A club steeped in the history of the game, it is also of great age, dating back to 1865. Of sand and heather like so many of the Surrey courses, its 12th hole (par 4) is rated as the best on the course.
18 holes, 6300yds, Par 70, SSS 70, Course record 64.
Membership 1050.

	SCORE CARD				
Hole	Yds	Par	Hole	Yds	Par
1	405	4	10	476	5
2	426	4	11	421	4
3	382	4	12	455	4
4	401	4	13	161	3
5	164	3	14	455	4
6	261	4	15	421	4
7	500	5	16	390	4
8	221	3	17	138	3
9	282	4	18	341	4
Out	3042	35	In	3258	35
			Totals	6300	70

Visitors welcome (restricted WE & BH) Member
must accompany must contact in advance ✉
Societies welcome (Wed-Fri)
Green fees Not confirmed
Facilities ⊗ 🖿 ⏛ ♀ ⏢ 🏠 ⸙ ⸀ Hugh Boyle
Hotel ★★★64% Richmond Hill, 146-150 Richmond
Hill, RICHMOND ☎081-940 2247 & 081-940 5466
123⊸🏌

Wimbledon Common ☎ 081-946 0294
Camp Rd
Quick-drying course on Wimbledon Common. Well
wooded, with long challenging short holes. All players
must wear plain red upper garments.
18 holes, 5438yds, Par 68, SSS 66, Course record 63.
Membership 250.

Visitors welcome (with M only WE) Societies welcome
Green fees Not confirmed
Facilities ⊗ 🖿 ⏛ ♀ ⏢ 🏠 ⸀ J S Jukes
Hotel ★★★63% Cannizaro House Hotel, West Side,
Wimbledon Common, LONDON ☎081-879 1464 48⊸🏌

Wimbledon Park ☎ 081-946 1250
Home Park Rd, Wimbledon (400 yds from Wimbledon
Park Station)
Easy walking on parkland course. Sheltered lake
provides hazard on 3 holes.
18 holes, 5417yds, Par 66, SSS 66, Course record 60.
Membership 600.

Visitors welcome (restricted WE & BH) must contact in
advance ✉ Societies welcome (☎)
Green fees £25 (£25 per round WE & BH)
Facilities ⊗ (ex Mon) 🌑 by prior arrangement 🖿 ⏛
♀ (to 7pm Mon, 8pm Tue) ⏢ 🏠 ⸀ D Wingrove
Hotel ★★★64% Richmond Hill, 146-150 Richmond
Hill, RICHMOND ☎081-940 2247 & 081-940 5466 123⊸🏌

W7 Hanwell

Brent Valley ☎ 081-567 1287
138 Church Rd, Hanwell
Municipal parkland course with easy walking. The
River Brent winds through the course.
18 holes, 5426yds, Par 67, SSS 66. Membership 350.

Visitors welcome Societies welcome (one month's
notice)
Green fees Not confirmed
Facilities ⊗ (vary with season) 🌑 by prior
arrangement 🖿 ⏛ ♀ ⏢ 🏠 ⸙ ⸀ Peter Byrne
Hotel ★★★60% Master Robert Hotel, Great West Rd,
HOUNSLOW ☎081-570 6261 100⊸

MERSEYSIDE

BEBINGTON   Map 5 C8

Brackenwood ☎ 051-608 3093
Brackenwood Park (.75m N of M53 junc 4 on B5151)
Municipal parkland course with easy walking.
18 holes, 6285yds, Par 70, SSS 70. Membership 320.

Visitors welcome Societies welcome (☎)
Green fees £3.20 per day
Facilities ⏛ ⏢ 🏠 ⸙ ⸀ Colin Disbury
Hotel ★★★61% Bowler Hat Hotel, 2 Talbot Rd, Oxton,
BIRKENHEAD ☎051-652 4931 29⊸🏌

BIRKENHEAD   Map 5 C8

Arrowe Park ☎ 051-677 1527
Woodchurch (1m from M53 junc 3 on A551)
Pleasant municipal parkland course.
18 holes, 6435yds, Par 72, SSS 71. Membership 210.

Visitors welcome Societies welcome (☎)
Green fees Not confirmed

►

Facilities ⓑ ⚲ 🏠 ⚑ (Clive Scanlon
Hotel ★★★61% Bowler Hat Hotel, 2 Talbot Rd, Oxton, BIRKENHEAD ☎051-652 4931 29⟿▐

Prenton ☎ 051-608 1461
Golf Links Rd, Prenton (S side of town centre off B5151)
Parkland course with easy walking and views of the Welsh Hills. Snooker.
18 holes, 5966yds, Par 70, SSS 69. Membership 760.

Visitors welcome (restricted to yellow tees) Societies welcome (Wed & Fri ☎ or by letter)
Green fees £18 per day (£20 WE & BH)
Facilities ⊗ �🏵 ⓑ 🍺 ⚲ ⚲ 🏠 (Robin Thompson
Hotel ★★64% Riverhill Hotel, Talbot Rd, Oxton, BIRKENHEAD ☎051-653 3773 16⟿▐

Wirral Ladies ☎ 051-652 1255
93 Bidston Rd, Oxton (W side of town centre on B5151)
Heathland course with heather and birch.
18 holes, 4966yds, SSS 70. Membership 450.

Visitors welcome must contact in advance ✉ Societies welcome (☎)
Green fees Not confirmed
Facilities ⊗ 🏵 by prior arrangement ⓑ 🍺 ⚲ ⚲ 🏠
(Philip Chandler
Hotel ★★★61% Bowler Hat Hotel, 2 Talbot Rd, Oxton, BIRKENHEAD ☎051-652 4931 29⟿▐

BLUNDELLSANDS Map 5 B7

West Lancashire ☎ 051-924 1076
Hall Rd West (N side of village)
This challenging links with its sandy subsoil provides excellent golf throughout the year. There are many fine holes, particularly the four short ones.
18 holes, Par 70, SSS 70, Course record 66. Membership 650.

Visitors welcome (ex competition days, h'cap cert required) must contact in advance Societies welcome
Green fees £25 per day (£30 WE & BH)
Facilities ⊗ 🏵 ⓑ 🍺 ⚲ ⚲ 🏠 (David Lloyd
Hotel ★★★59% Blundellsands Hotel, Serpentine, BLUNDELLSANDS ☎051-924 6515 41⟿▐

BOOTLE Map 5 C7

Bootle ☎ 051-928 1371
Dunnings Bridge Rd (2m NE on A5036)
Municipal seaside course, with NW wind. Testing holes: 5th (200 yds) Par 3; 7th (415 yds) Par 4.
18 holes, 6362yds, Par 70, SSS 70.

Visitors welcome Societies welcome
Green fees Not confirmed
Facilities ⚲ ⚲ 🏠 ⚑ (
Hotel ★★★54% Park Hotel, Dunnington Rd, Netherton, BOOTLE ☎051-525 7555 58⟿▐

BROMBOROUGH Map 5 C8

Bromborough ☎ 051-334 2155
Raby Hall Rd (.5m W of Station)
Parkland course.
18 holes, 6650yds, Par 72, SSS 73. Membership 700.

Visitors welcome (ex Sun, Tue am & Sat before 1430)
Societies welcome (normal society day Wed ☎)
Green fees Not confirmed
Facilities 🏵 by prior arrangement ⓑ 🍺 ⚲ ⚲ 🏠 (
Hotel ★★★61% Bowler Hat Hotel, 2 Talbot Rd, Oxton, BIRKENHEAD ☎051-652 4931 29⟿▐

CALDY Map 5 B8

Caldy ☎ 051-625 5660
Links Hey Rd (SE side of village)
A parkland course situated on the estuary of the River Dee with many of the fairways running parallel to the river. Of Championship length, the course is subject to variable winds that noticeably alter the day to day playing of each hole. There are excellent views of North Wales and Snowdonia. The clubhouse has good facilities. Snooker.
18 holes, 6675yds, Par 72, SSS 73, Course record 68. Membership 800.

Visitors welcome (wkdays only) must contact in advance ✉ Societies welcome (☎)
Green fees £25 per day (£20 after 1400)
Facilities ⊗ 🏵 ⓑ 🍺 ⚲ ⚲ 🏠 (K Jones
Hotel ★★62% Parkgate Hotel, Boathouse Ln, PARKGATE ☎051-336 5001 27⟿▐

EASTHAM Map 5 C8

Eastham Lodge ☎ 051-327 3003
117 Ferry Rd (1.5m N)
A new parkland course.
15 holes, 5813yds, Par 69, SSS 68. Membership 500.

Visitors welcome (with M only at WE) Societies welcome (Tues only ☎)
Green fees £13 wkdays
Facilities ⊗ 🏵 by prior arrangement ⓑ 🍺 ⚲ (1200-2300) ⚲ 🏠 (Ivor Jones
Hotel ★★★67% Cromwell Hotel, High St, BROMBOROUGH ☎051-334 2917 31⟿

FORMBY Map 5 C7

Formby ☎ (07048) 72164
Golf Rd (N side of town)
Championship seaside links course.
18 holes, 6695yds, Par 72, SSS 73, Course record 66. Membership 600.

Visitors welcome (ex Wed, WE & BH) must contact in advance ✉ Societies welcome (Tues & Thu only ☎)
Green fees £35

Facilities ⊗ (ex Mon) ☕ ♀ ⛳ 🏠 ✆ C Harrison
Hotel ★★★★54% Prince of Wales Hotel, Lord St, SOUTHPORT ☎(0704) 536688 104⇥🐾

Formby Ladies ☎ (07048) 73493
Golf Rd (N side of town)
Seaside links - one of the few independent ladies club in the country. Course has contrasting hard-hitting holes in flat country and tricky holes in sandhills and woods. Fine short 5th hole (par 3).
18 holes, 5374yds, Par 71, SSS 71. Membership 423.

Visitors welcome (ex Thu) must contact in advance
Societies welcome (☎)
Green fees £22 per day (£27.50 WE & BH)
Facilities �)∭ by prior arrangement ⛳ ☕ ♀ ⛳ 🏠 ✆
✆ Clive Harrison
Hotel ★★★★54% Prince of Wales Hotel, Lord St, SOUTHPORT ☎(0704) 536688 104⇥🐾

HESWALL   Map 5 B8

Heswall ☎ (051342) 1237
Cottage Ln (1m S off A540)
A pleasant parkland course in soft undulating country over-looking the estuary of the River Dee. There are excellent views in all directions and a good test of golf. The clubhouse is modern and well-appointed with good facilities. Snooker.
18 holes, 6472yds, Par 72, SSS 72, Course record 66. Membership 900.

SCORE CARD					
Hole	Yds	Par	Hole	Yds	Par
1	421	4	10	435	4
2	393	4	11	148	3
3	337	4	12	490	5
4	209	3	13	330	4
5	494	5	14	431	4
6	396	4	15	327	4
7	434	4	16	151	3
8	160	3	17	520	5
9	509	5	18	287	4
Out	3353	36	In	3119	36
			Totals	6472	72

Visitors welcome (handicap certificate required) must contact in advance Societies welcome (Wed & Fri only ☎)
Green fees £20 per day (£25 WE & BH)
Facilities ⊗ ∭ by prior arrangement ⛳ ☕ ♀
(1100-2300 summer) ⛳ 🏠 ✆ Alan E Thompson
Hotel ★★62% Parkgate Hotel, Boathouse Ln, PARKGATE ☎051-336 5001 27⇥🐾

HOYLAKE   Map 5 B8

Hoylake Municipal ☎ 051-632 2956
Carr Ln (SW side of town off A540)
Flat, generally windy course. Very tricky fairways. Snooker, darts.
18 holes, 3613yds, Par 70, SSS 70, Course record 67. Membership 300.

Visitors welcome must contact in advance WE only
Societies welcome (☎ 051-632 4883 M E Down)
Green fees £3.40 per round
Facilities ⊗ ∭ by prior arrangement ⛳ ☕ ♀ ⛳ 🏠
✆ ✆ Robert Boobyer
Hotel ★★★61% Bowler Hat Hotel, 2 Talbot Rd, Oxton, BIRKENHEAD ☎051-652 4931 29⇥🐾

Royal Liverpool ☎ 051-632 3101
Meols Dr (SW side of town on A540)
A world famous seaside links course, windswept. Snooker.
18 holes, 6804yds, Par 72. Membership 640.

Visitors welcome must contact in advance ✉
Societies welcome (by letter)
Green fees £50 per day; £35 per round (£75/£45 WE)
Facilities ⊗ by prior arrangement ∭ by prior arrangement ⛳ ☕ ♀ (all day in summer) ⛳ 🏠 ✆
✆ John Heggarty
Hotel ★★★61% Bowler Hat Hotel, 2 Talbot Rd, Oxton, BIRKENHEAD ☎051-652 4931 29⇥🐾

HUYTON   Map 5 C8

Bowring ☎ 051-489 1901
Bowring Park, Roby Rd (On A5080 adjacent M62 junc 5)
Flat parkland course.
9 holes, 2009yds, Par 34. Membership 80.

Visitors welcome
Green fees Not confirmed
Facilities ⛳ 🏠 ✆
Hotel ★★★63% Crest Hotel Liverpool-City, Lord Nelson St, LIVERPOOL ☎051-709 7050 150⇥

For an explanation of the symbols and abbreviations used, see page 33.

Huyton & Prescot ☎ 051-489 3948
Hurst Park, Huyton, Huyton Ln (1.5m NE off B5199)
Reconstructed parkland course, easy walking, excellent golf.
18 holes, 5738yds, Par 68, SSS 68. Membership 700.

Visitors welcome (restricted WE) must contact in advance ✉ Societies welcome (☎)
Green fees Not confirmed
Facilities ⊗ ⅏ by prior arrangement ⅃ ☕ ♀ △ ⌂ ☂ ⌇ Ronald Pottage
Hotel ★58% Rockland Hotel, View Rd, RAINHILL ☎051-426 4603 10� Annexe:3➔🐾

LIVERPOOL   Map 5 C8

Allerton Park ☎ 051-428 8510
Allerton Manor Golf Estate, Allerton Rd (5.5m SE of city centre off A562 and B5180)
Parkland course.
18 holes, 5459yds, Par 67, SSS 67, Course record 62. Membership 300.

Visitors welcome
Green fees Not confirmed
Facilities ⅃ ☕ ♀ ⌂ ☂ ⌇
Hotel ★★59% Grange Hotel, Holmfield Rd, Aigburth, LIVERPOOL ☎051-427 2950 25➔🐾

Childwall ☎ 051-487 0654
Naylors Rd, Gateacre (7m E of city centre off B5178)
Parkland golf is played here over a testing course, where accuracy from the tee is well-rewarded. The course is very popular with visiting societies for the clubhouse has many amenities. Course designed by James Braid. Snooker.
18 holes, 6025yds, Par 69, SSS 69, Course record 65. Membership 600.

Visitors welcome (yellow tees only) Societies welcome (☎)
Green fees £15 per day (£21 WE)
Facilities ⊗ ⅏ ⅃ ☕ ♀ △ ⌂ ☂ ⌇ Nigel Parr
Hotel ★58% Rockland Hotel, View Rd, RAINHILL ☎051-426 4603 10➔ Annexe:3➔🐾

Lee Park ☎ 051-487 9861
Childwall Valley Rd (7m E of city centre off B5178)
Flat course with ponds in places. Snooker.
18 holes, 5508mtrs, Par 71, SSS 69. Membership 500.

Visitors welcome must contact in advance ✉ Societies welcome (☎)
Green fees Not confirmed
Facilities ⊗ ⅏ by prior arrangement ⅃ ☕ ♀ △
Hotel ★★★50% Liverpool Moat House Hotel, Paradise St, LIVERPOOL ☎051-709 0181 251➔🐾

Liverpool Municipal ☎ 051-546 5435
Ingoe Ln, Kirkby (7.5m NE of city centre on A506)
Flat easy course.
18 holes, 6588yds, Par 72, SSS 71, Course record 70. Membership 150.

Visitors welcome must contact in advance Societies welcome (☎ wk in advance)
Green fees Not confirmed
Facilities ⊗ by prior arrangement ⅏ by prior arrangement ⅃ ☕ ♀ △ ⌂ ☂ ⌇ Dave Weston
Hotel ★★★54% Park Hotel, Dunnington Rd, Netherton, BOOTLE ☎051-525 7555 58➔🐾

West Derby ☎ 051-228 1540
Yew Tree Ln, West Derby (4.5m E of city centre off A57)
A parkland course always in first-class condition, and so giving easy walking. The fairways are well-wooded. Care must be taken on the first nine holes to avoid the brook which guards many of the greens. A modern well-designed clubhouse with many amenities, overlooks the course. Snooker.
18 holes, 6333yds, Par 72, SSS 70. Membership 550.

Visitors welcome (not before 0930) Societies welcome (ex Sat, Sun & BH ☎)
Green fees £18 per day (£25 WE)
Facilities ⊗ ⅏ ⅃ ☕ ♀ △ ⌂ ☂ ⌇ Nicholas Brace
Hotel ★★★63% Crest Hotel Liverpool-City, Lord Nelson St, LIVERPOOL ☎051-709 7050 150➔

Woolton ☎ 051-486 2298
Speke Rd (7m SE of city centre off A562)
Parkland course providing a good round of golf for all standards. Snooker.
18 holes, 5706yds, Par 69, SSS 68. Membership 650.

Visitors welcome (restricted daily) Societies welcome (☎)
Green fees £17 per day (£25 WE & BH)
Facilities ⊗ ⅏ by prior arrangement ⅃ ☕ ♀ △ ⌂ ⌇
Hotel ★★59% Grange Hotel, Holmfield Rd, Aigburth, LIVERPOOL ☎051-427 2950 25➔🐾

NEWTON-LE-WILLOWS   Map 5 C7

Haydock Park
☎ (0925) 228525
Golborne Park, Rob Ln (.75m NE off A49)
A well-wooded parkland course, close to the well-known racecourse, and always in excellent condition. The pleasant undulating fairways offer some very interesting golf. The clubhouse is very comfortable having all modern facilities. Snooker.

SCORE CARD					
Hole	Yds	Par	Hole	Yds	Par
1	408	4	10	363	4
2	182	3	11	375	4
3	490	5	12	151	3
4	119	3	13	449	4
5	523	5	14	283	4
6	362	4	15	495	5
7	310	4	16	328	4
8	191	3	17	380	4
9	438	4	18	196	3
Out	3023	35	In	3020	35
			Totals	6043	70

18 holes, 6043yds, Par 70, SSS 69, Course record 65. Membership 600.

Visitors welcome must contact in advance Societies welcome (by letter)
Green fees £18 per day

Facilities ⊗ ⅲ ᴸᴸ 💺 ♀ ⅄ 🏠 (Peter Kenwright
Hotel ★★★66% Post House Hotel, Lodge Ln,
Newton-Le-Willows, HAYDOCK ☎(0942) 717878
142↵

ST HELENS   Map 5 C7

Grange Park ☎ (0744) 26318
Toll Bar, Prescot Rd (1.5m W on A58)
A course of Championship length set in plesant
country surroundings - playing the course it is hard
to believe that industrial St Helens lies so close at
hand. The course is a fine test of golf and there are
many attractive holes liable to challenge all grades
of player. Snooker.
*18 holes, 6429yds, Par 72, SSS 71, Course record 65.
Membership 700.*

Visitors welcome must contact in advance ✉
Societies welcome (by letter)
Green fees £18 per day (£25 WE & BH)
Facilities ⊗ ⅲ ᴸᴸ 💺 ♀ ⅄ 🏠 (Paul G Evans
Hotel ★★★66% Post House Hotel, Lodge Ln,
Newton-Le-Willows, HAYDOCK ☎(0942) 717878
142↵

Sherdley Park ☎ (0744) 813149
Sherdley Rd (2m S off A570)
Fairly hilly course with ponds in places.
18 holes, 5941yds, Par 70, SSS 69. Membership 160.

Visitors welcome
Green fees Not confirmed
Facilities ⅄ 🏠 ⅌ (
Hotel ★★★66% Post House Hotel, Lodge Ln, Newton-
Le-Willows, HAYDOCK ☎(0942) 717878 142↵

SOUTHPORT   Map 5 C7

The Hesketh ☎ (0704) 536897
Cockle Dick's Ln, off Cambridge Rd (1m NE of town
centre off A565)
Hesketh is the senior club in Southport, founded in
1885. The championship course comprises much of
the original territory plus a large area of reclaimed
land on the seaward side - essentially 'Links' in
character. Snooker.
*18 holes, 6478yds, Par 71, SSS 72, Course record 66.
Membership 580.*

Visitors welcome ✉ Societies welcome
Green fees £25 per day; £20 per round (£30 WE)
Facilities ⊗ ⅲ ᴸᴸ 💺 ♀ ⅄ 🏠 ⅌ (John
Donoghue
Hotel ★★64% Bold Hotel, Lord St, SOUTHPORT
☎(0704) 32578 22rm(15↵6♠)

Hillside ☎ (0704) 67169
Hastings Rd, Hillside (2m SW of town centre on A565)
Championship links course with natural hazards open
to strong wind. Course record holder, P. Way.
*18 holes, 6850yds, Par 72, SSS 72, Course record 66.
Membership 750.*

Visitors welcome (restricted Tue am, WE & BH) must
contact in advance Societies welcome (☎)
Green fees £30 per day
Facilities ⊗ ⅲ ᴸᴸ 💺 (catering by prior arrangement)
♀ ⅄ 🏠 (Brian Seddon
Hotel ★★★57% Royal Clifton Hotel, Promenade,
SOUTHPORT ☎(0704) 33771 107↵♠

Park ☎ (0704) 530133
Park Rd (N side of town centre off A565)
Very flat, municipal parkland course.
18 holes, 6200yds, Par 70, SSS 70. Membership 400.

Visitors welcome (restricted WE, ☎ for details)
Green fees Not confirmed
Facilities ♀ (M only) 🏠 ⅌
Hotel ★★★★54% Prince of Wales Hotel, Lord St,
SOUTHPORT ☎(0704) 536688 104↵♠

Royal Birkdale See page 148

Southport & Ainsdale
☎ (0704) 78000
Bradshaws Ln, Ainsdale
(3m S off A565)
'S and A', as it is known in
the North is another of the
fine Championship courses
for which this part of the
country is famed. This Club
has staged many important
events and offers golf of the
highest order. Snooker.
*18 holes, 6603yds, Par 72,
SSS 73. Membership 815.*

SCORE CARD: White Tees					
Hole	Yds	Par	Hole	Yds	Par
1	200	3	10	160	3
2	520	5	11	447	4
3	418	4	12	401	4
4	316	4	13	145	3
5	447	4	14	383	4
6	386	4	15	353	4
7	480	5	16	510	5
8	157	3	17	443	4
9	482	5	18	355	4
Out	3406	37	In	3197	72
			Totals	6603	72

Visitors welcome (ex Wed, Thu, WE & BH) must
contact in advance ✉ Societies welcome (☎)
Green fees £30 per day; £20 per round
Facilities ⊗ by prior arrangement ⅲ by prior
arrangement ᴸᴸ 💺 ♀ ⅄ 🏠 ⅌ (M Houghton
Hotel ★★★★54% Prince of Wales Hotel, Lord St,
SOUTHPORT ☎(0704) 536688 104↵♠

Southport Municipal ☎ (0704) 535286
Park Rd West (N side of town centre off A565)
Municipal seaside links course. Played over by Alt Golf
Club. Snooker.
18 holes, 6400yds, Par 70, SSS 69. Membership 750.

Visitors welcome must contact in advance Societies
welcome (☎ 6 days in advance)
Green fees £3.50 per round (£5 WE & BH)
Facilities ⊗ ᴸᴸ 💺 ♀ ⅄ 🏠 ⅌ (Bill Fletcher
Hotel ★★★★54% Prince of Wales Hotel, Lord St,
SOUTHPORT ☎(0704) 536688 104↵♠

Southport Old Links ☎ (0704) 28207
Moss Ln, Churchtown (NW side of town centre off
A5267)
Seaside course, easy walking.
*9 holes, 6486yds, Par 72, SSS 71, Course record 68.
Membership 400.*

▶

SCORE CARD: White Tees					
Hole	Yds	Par	Hole	Yds	Par
1	447	4	10	372	4
2	416	4	11	374	4
3	407	4	12	181	3
4	202	3	13	436	4
5	341	4	14	198	3
6	488	5	15	542	5
7	150	3	16	344	4
8	414	4	17	502	5
9	413	4	18	476	5
Out	3278	35	In	3425	37
			Totals	6703	72

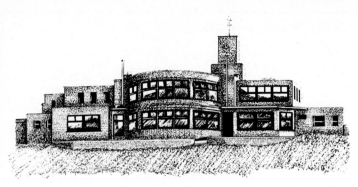

SOUTHPORT   **Map5 C7**

Royal Birkdale ☎ (0704) 67920. Waterloo Road, Birkdale (1.75m S of town).

There are a few seaside links in the world that can be described as 'great'. And Royal Birkdale, with its expanse of sandhills and willow scrub, is one of them. Founded in 1889, there have been some changes, even since Arnold Palmer hit that wondrous recovery shot which helped him win an Open in the early 'sixties, and led to a plaque being erected at the spot from which the divot was taken.

Well bunkered, the sandhills run along the edges of the fairways and make ideal platforms from which to view the Open Championship, played frequently here because the examination is supreme in the United Kingdom. Maybe the links, in a wind, is too difficult for the weekender.

Certainly it found out Dai Rees in 1961 when he was chasing Palmer for the title. In the last round the course struck at the very first hole. Rees had hit his teeshot a might to the left, and then had to wait for the players to hole out on the green ahead, before attempting a powerful shot with a lofted wood from the fairway. The ball smacked into the back of a bunker, and fell back into sand. Rees took an awful seven and Palmer beat him for the trophy - by one shot. The Welshman had stormed back in 31 but his chance to win an Open had gone forever. But Rees still touched his hat to the links, and held it in great respect as, indeed, does Arnold Palmer.

But for the amateur, another problem is simply hitting the ball far enough because, if you play it from the Open Championship back tees, it measures 7080 yards and par 73 takes some getting, even with your handicap allowance.

They have hosted everything that matters here, including the Ryder Cup and will probably get the match again, soon.

18 holes, 6703 yds, Par 72, SSS73, Course record 64-Mark O'Meara. Membership 850

Visitors   welcome. Must contact in advance to pre-book. Handicap cert required ✉. Societies welcome (by letter) or (☎).

Green fees   £48 per day; £32 per round (£50 WE)

Facilities   ⊗ ▥   (parties over 20 only)   ⌑ ☕ ♀ ⛲ 🏠 ⛳ ❢ Richard Bradbeer

WHERE TO STAY AND EAT NEARBY

HOTELS:

SOUTHPORT   ★★★★ 54% Prince of Wales, Lord St. ☎ (0704) 536688. 104 ⊲ ❢ . ♀ English & French cuisine.

★★★ 62% Royal Clifton, Promenade. ☎ (0704) 33771. 107 ⊲ ❢ . ♀ English & French cuisine.

★★★ 61% Scarisbrick, Lord St. ☎ (0704) 33335. 66 ⊲ ❢ . ♀ English & French cuisine.

★★ 68% Balmoral Lodge, 41 Queens Rd. ☎ (0704) 544298. 15 ⊲ ❢

★★ 61% Stutelea Hotel & Leisure Club, Alexandra Rd. ☎ (0704) 544220. 18 ⊲ ❢

RESTAURANT:

WRIGHTINGTON✕ ✕ ✕High Moor, Highmoor Ln (jct 27 off M6, take B5239).   Appleby Bridge ☎ (02575) 2364.   ♀ English & French cuisine.

Visitors welcome (ex Wed, Sun & BH) must contact in advance ✉ Societies welcome (ex Wed & Sun ☎)
Green fees £15 per day (£20 WE)
Facilities ⊗ ≡ by prior arrangement ㄴ ♣ ♀ △
Hotel ★★64%, Bold Hotel, Lord St, SOUTHPORT ☎(0704) 32578 22rm(15⇨6♠)

WALLASEY   Map 5 C7

Bidston ☎ 051-638 3412
Scoresby Rd, Leasowe, Moreton (.5m W of M53 junc 1 entrance off A551)
Parkland course, with westerly winds. Snooker.
18 holes, 5827yds, Par 70, SSS 69. Membership 550.

Visitors welcome (restricted WE) must contact in advance Societies welcome (by letter)
Green fees Not confirmed
Facilities ⊗ ≡ ㄴ ♣ ♀ △ 🏠 ⊄ Mike Adams
Hotel ★★★61% Bowler Hat Hotel, 2 Talbot Rd, Oxton, BIRKENHEAD ☎051-652 4931 29⇨♠

Leasowe ☎ 051-677 5852
Moreton (2m W on A551)
Rather flat seaside course.
18 holes, 6204yds, Par 71, SSS 71, Course record 63. Membership 500.

Visitors welcome (ex 1300-1400) Societies welcome (14 days notice ☎)
Green fees £15 per day (£17.50 WE)
Facilities ⊗ ≡ ㄴ ♣ ♀ △ 🏠 ⊄ M Adams
Hotel ★★★61% Bowler Hat Hotel, 2 Talbot Rd, Oxton, BIRKENHEAD ☎051-652 4931 29⇨♠

Wallasey ☎ 051-691 1024
Bayswater Rd (N side of town centre off A554)
A well-established sporting links with huge sandhills and many classic holes where the player's skills are often combined with good fortune.
18 holes, 6607yds, Par 72, SSS 73. Membership 700.

Visitors welcome Societies welcome (by letter)
Green fees Not confirmed
Facilities ⊗ ≡ by prior arrangement ㄴ ♣ ♀ △ 🏠 ⊄ Mike Adams
Hotel ★★★61% Bowler Hat Hotel, 2 Talbot Rd, Oxton, BIRKENHEAD ☎051-652 4931 29⇨♠

Warren ☎ 051-691 1024
Grove Rd (N side of town centre off A554)
Short, undulating links course with first-class greens.
9 holes, 2927yds, Par 72, SSS 70, Course record 69. Membership 150.

Visitors welcome
Green fees Not confirmed
Facilities ♀ △ 🏠 ⊄ Ken Lamb
Hotel ★★★61% Bowler Hat Hotel, 2 Talbot Rd, Oxton, BIRKENHEAD ☎051-652 4931 29⇨♠

To see a full range of AA guides and maps, visit your local AA Shop or any good bookshop.

NORFOLK

BARNHAM BROOM   Map 4 H4

Barnham Broom Golf and Country Club
☎ (060545) 393
Honingham Rd (1m N, S of A47)
Attractive river valley courses with modern hotel and leisure complex. Accommodation, tennis, swimming pool (heated), squash, sauna, solarium, gymnasium and snooker.
Hill Course 18 holes, 6628yds, Par 72, SSS 72. Valley Course 18 holes, 6470yds, Par 72, SSS 71. Membership 700.

Visitors welcome (WE with M, handicap certificate required) must contact in advance Societies welcome (☎)
Green fees £25 per day ; £20 per round
Facilities ⊗ ≡ ㄴ ♣ ♀ △ 🏠 ⊬ ⊄ Steve Beckham
Hotel ★★★65% Barnham Broom Hotel Conference & Leisure, Centre, BARNHAM BROOM ☎(060545) 393 52⇨♠
See advertisement on page 151

BAWBURGH   Map 4 H4

Bawburgh ☎ (0603) 746390
Norwich Golf Centre, Long Ln
An open-links. Driving range available.
9 holes, 2639yds, Par 33, SSS 66, Course record 66. Membership 300.

Visitors welcome must contact in advance Societies welcome (☎)
Green fees Not confirmed
Facilities △ 🏠 ⊄ Robert Waugh
Hotel ★★★70% Park Farm Hotel, HETHERSETT ☎(0603) 810264 6⇨♠ Annexe :29⇨♠

BRANCASTER   Map 4 G2

Royal West Norfolk
☎ (0485) 210087
If you want to see what golf courses were like years ago, then go to the Royal West Norfolk where tradition exudes from both clubhouse and course. Close by the sea, the links are characterised by sleepered greens, superb cross-bunkering and salt marshes.
18 holes, 6428yds, Par 71, SSS 71, Course record 69. Membership 767.

SCORE CARD					
Hole	Yds	Par	Hole	Yds	Par
1	410	4	10	151	3
2	449	4	11	478	5
3	407	4	12	386	4
4	128	3	13	317	4
5	421	4	14	432	4
6	186	3	15	188	3
7	486	5	16	346	4
8	478	5	17	377	4
9	404	4	18	384	4
Out	3369	36	In	3059	35
			Totals	6428	71

Visitors welcome (after 1000 WE with permission) must contact in advance Societies welcome (☎ then letter)
Green fees £22 per day (£27 WE)

▶

Facilities ⊗ ᾘ 堕 ⬤ ♀ ⌂ 🏮 ᴵ ʃ R E Kimber
Hotel ★★71% Titchwell Manor Hotel, TITCHWELL
☎(0485) 210221 & 210284 11rm(7⇨🦶🏮) Annexe:4⇨🏮

CROMER   Map 4 J2

Royal Cromer ☎ (0263) 512884
145 Overstrand Rd (1m E on B1159)
Seaside course set out on cliff edge, hilly and subject to
wind.
18 holes, 6508yds, Par 72, SSS 71, Course record 68.
Membership 700.

Visitors welcome (handicap certificate required) must
contact in advance Societies welcome (☎)
Green fees £20 per day (£25 WE & BH)
Facilities ⊗ ᾘ 堕 ⬤ ♀ ⌂ 🏮 ᴵ R J Page
Hotel ★★★65% Links Country Park Hotel & Golf
Club, Sandy Ln, WEST RUNTON ☎(026375) 691 22⇨🏮
Annexe:10⇨

DENVER   Map 4 F5

Ryston Park ☎ Downham Market (0366) 383834
(.5m S on A10)
Parkland course.
9 holes, 6292yds, Par 70, SSS 70. Membership 320.

Visitors welcome (ex WE & BH) Societies welcome (☎
not WE)
Green fees £15 per day
Facilities ⊗ ᾘ 堕 ⬤ ♀ ⌂ 🏮
Hotel ★★61% Crown Hotel, Bridge St, DOWNHAM
MARKET ☎(0366) 382322 10rm(5⇨2🏮)

DISS   Map 4 H5

Diss ☎ (0379) 642847
Stuston (1.5m SE on B1118)
Commonland course with natural hazards. Course is
being extended to 18 holes and should be opened summer
1991.
9 holes, 5900yds, Par 69, SSS 68, Course record 68.
Membership 500.

Visitors welcome (ex WE & BH) must contact in
advance Societies welcome (☎)
Green fees Not confirmed
Facilities ⌂ 🏮 ᴵ ʃ
Hotel ★★60% Scole Inn, SCOLE ☎(0379) 740481 12⇨🏮
Annexe:11⇨🏮

EAST DEREHAM   Map 4 H4

Dereham ☎ Dereham (0362) 695900
Quebec Rd (N side of town centre off B1110)
Parkland course.
9 holes, 6225yds, Par 71, SSS 70, Course record 67.
Membership 520.

Visitors welcome (with M only WE, handicap cert
required) must contact in advance ✉ Societies welcome
(☎)
Green fees £14 per day (£8.50 WE with M)

Facilities ⊗ ᾘ 堕 ⬤ ♀ ⌂ 🏮 ᴵ ʃ S Fox
Hotel ★★55% The Phoenix, Church St, DEREHAM
☎(0362) 692276 23⇨

GORLESTON-ON-SEA   Map 4 K4

Gorleston ☎ Great Yarmouth (0493) 661911
Warren Rd (S side of town centre)
Seaside course. Snooker.
18 holes, 6400yds, Par 71, SSS 71. Membership 860.

Visitors welcome (handicap certificate required) ✉
Societies welcome (☎)
Green fees £15 per day (£20 WE & BH)
Facilities ⊗ ᾘ 堕 ⬤ ♀ ⌂ 🏮 ᴵ Ralph Moffitt
Hotel ★★★70% Cliff Hotel, Gorleston, GREAT
YARMOUTH ☎(0493) 662179 30⇨🏮

HUNSTANTON   Map 4 F3

Hunstanton ☎ (0485) 532811
(1.5m N off A149)
Links course.
18 holes, 6670yds, Par 72, SSS 72, Course record 65.
Membership 650.

Visitors welcome (ex WE & BH, must be club M
with h'c cert) must contact in advance Societies
welcome (by letter)
Green fees £25 per day (£27 WE)
Facilities ⊗ by prior arrangement ᾘ by prior
arrangement 堕 ⬤ ♀ ⌂ 🏮 ᴵ ʃ John Carter
Hotel ★★67% Caley Hall Motel, Old Hunstanton
Rd, HUNSTANTON ☎(04853) 33486
Annexe:29rm(27⇨)

KING'S LYNN   Map 4 F4

King's Lynn ☎ Castle Rising (0553) 631654
Castle Rising (4m NE off A148)
Challenging parkland course. Snooker.
18 holes, 6646yds, Par 72, SSS 72, Course record 68.
Membership 945.

Visitors welcome (handicap cert required) must contact
in advance Societies welcome (h'cap cert required ☎)
Green fees £25 per day (£30 WE)
Facilities ⊗ ᾘ 堕 ⬤ ♀ ⌂ 🏮 ʃ Chris Hanlon
Hotel ★★★60% The Duke's Head, Tuesday Market Pl,
KING'S LYNN ☎(0553) 774996 72⇨

MIDDLETON   Map 4 F4

Middleton Hall ☎ King's Lynn (0553) 841800
(4m from King's Lynn off A47)
The 9-hole King's course (played off 18 tees) is a pleasant
parkland course constructed with conservation in mind
around numerous mature trees, pond and reservoir.
Additional par 3 pitch and putt Queen's course.
9 holes, 5570yds, Par 68, SSS 67. Membership 300.

Visitors welcome Societies welcome (☎)
Green fees £10 per round (£12 WE & BH)

Facilities ⊗ ⅢⅢ by prior arrangement 🄻 💻 ♀ ⚘ 🄼
🄿 (John Laing
Hotel ★★★64% Butterfly Hotel, Beveridge Way,
Hardwick Narrows, KING'S LYNN ☎(0553) 771707
50⇔🄼

MUNDESLEY   Map 4 J3

Mundesley ☎ (0263) 720279
Links Rd (W side of village off B1159)
Seaside course, good views, windy.
9 holes, 5410yds, Par 68, SSS 66. Membership 400.

Visitors welcome (restricted Wed & WE) must contact
in advance Societies welcome (one months prior notice
☎)
Green fees £12 per day (£20 WE & BH)
Facilities ⚘ 🄼 (T G Symmons
Hotel ★★♨74% Felmingham Hall Country House
Hotel, FELMINGHAM ☎(069269) 631 12⇔🄼
Annexe :6⇔🄼

NORWICH   Map 4 J4

Eaton ☎ (0603) 51686
Newmarket Rd (2.5m SW of city centre off A11)
An undulating, tree-lined parkland course.
18 holes, 6135yds, Par 70, SSS 69, Course record 65.
Membership 885.

Visitors welcome (before 1130 Sat & Sun) Member must
accompany ✉
Green fees Not confirmed
Facilities 🄼
Hotel ★★★56% Arlington Hotel, 10 Arlington Ln
Newmarket Rd, NORWICH ☎(0603) 617841 44⇔

Royal Norwich ☎ (0603) 49928
Hellesdon (2.5m NW of city centre on A1067)
Undulating parkland course.
18 holes, 6603yds, Par 72, SSS 72. Membership 650.

Visitors welcome (ex WE & BH) ✉
Green fees Not confirmed
Facilities ♀ ⚘ 🄼 🄿
Hotel ★★★65% Hotel Norwich, 121-131 Boundary Rd,
NORWICH ☎(0603) 787260 102⇔🄼

SHERINGHAM   Map 4 H2

Sheringham
☎ (0263) 822038
Weybourne Rd (W side of
town centre on A149)
Splendid cliff-top links with
good 'seaside turf' and
plenty of space. Straight
driving is essential for a low
score. The course is close to
the shore and can be very
windswept.
Accommodation.
18 holes, 6464yds, Par 70,
SSS 71, Course record 69.
Membership 750.

SCORE CARD: White Tees					
Hole	Yds	Par	Hole	Yds	Par
1	335	4	10	444	4
2	543	5	11	163	3
3	424	4	12	425	4
4	327	4	13	351	4
5	452	4	14	354	4
6	217	3	15	195	3
7	490	5	16	349	4
8	157	3	17	405	4
9	410	4	18	423	4
Out	3355	36	In	3109	34
			Totals	6464	70

Visitors welcome (handicap certificate required)
must contact in advance ✉ Societies welcome (by
letter)
Green fees £23 per day (£28 WE & BH)
Facilities ⊗ ⅢⅢ 🄻 💻 (all catering restricted Mon
& Tue) ♀ ⚘ 🄼 🄿 (
Hotel ★★64% Beaumaris Hotel, South St,
SHERINGHAM ☎(0263) 822370 24rm(22⇔🄼)

We make every effort to provide accurate information, but some details may change after we
go to print.

Each golf course entry has a recommended
hotel. For a wider choice of places to stay,
consult *AA Hotels and Restaurants in Britain* or
AA-inspected Bed and Breakfast in Britain.

SWAFFHAM
Map 4 G4

Swaffham ☎ (0760) 721611
Cley Rd (1.5m SW)
Heathland course.
9 holes, 6252yds, Par 72, SSS 70. Membership 450.

Visitors welcome (with M only WE) must contact in advance Societies welcome (one month's notice)
Green fees £20 per day; £15 per round
Facilities ⊗ (ex Mon-Tue) �🍽 (ex Mon-Tue) ⬛ ▣ ♀ ⛳ 🏠 ℂ Chris Norton
Hotel ★★★71% George Hotel, Station Rd, SWAFFHAM ☎(0760) 721238 27rm(24⇋1🏠)

THETFORD
Map 4 G5

Thetford ☎ (0842) 752169
Brandon Rd (.75m W on B1107)
This is a course with a good pedigree. It was laid-out by a fine golfer, C H Mayo, later altered by James Braid and then again altered by another famous course designer, Mackenzie Ross. It is a testing heathland course with a particularly stiff finish.
18 holes, 6879yds, Par 72, SSS 73, Course record 68. Membership 650.

SCORE CARD: White Tees					
Hole	Yds	Par	Hole	Yds	Par
1	195	3	10	546	5
2	365	4	11	205	3
3	157	3	12	369	4
4	407	4	13	522	5
5	380	4	14	429	4
6	495	5	15	375	4
7	417	4	16	157	3
8	451	4	17	521	5
9	421	4	18	467	4
Out	3288	35	In	3591	37
			Totals	6879	72

Visitors welcome (with M WE, handicap certificate required) must contact in advance ✉ Societies welcome (by letter)
Green fees £25 per day
Facilities ⊗ 🍽 ⬛ ▣ ♀ ⛳ 🏠 ℂ Norman Arthur
Hotel ★★★59% Bell Hotel, King St, THETFORD ☎(0842) 754455 47⇋🏠

WEST RUNTON
Map 4 J2

Links Country Park Hotel & Golf Club
☎ (026375) 691
(S side of village off A149)
Parkland course 500 yds from the sea, superb views overlooking West Runton. Accommodation, indoor-heated pool, tennis (hardcourt), riding stables, sauna and solarium.
9 holes, 4814yds, Par 66, SSS 64. Membership 250.

Visitors welcome (handicap certificate required) Societies welcome (☎)
Green fees Not confirmed
Facilities ⊗ 🍽 ⬛ ▣ ♀ ⛳ 🏠 ℂ Mike Jubb
Hotel ★★★65% Links Country Park Hotel & Golf Club, Sandy Ln, WEST RUNTON ☎(026375) 691 22⇋🏠 Annexe:10⇋

For an explanation of the symbols and abbreviations used, see page 33.

YARMOUTH, GREAT
Map 4 K4

Great Yarmouth & Caister ☎ (0493) 728699
Beach House, Caister on Sea (.5m N off A149)
This great old club, which celebrated its centenary in 1982, has played its part in the development of the game. It is a fine old-fashioned links where not many golfers have bettered the SSS in competitions. The 468-yard 8th (par 4), is a testing hole.
18 holes, 6235yds, Par 70, SSS 70. Membership 650.

Visitors welcome (restricted Sun until 1130) ✉ Societies welcome (by letter)
Green fees Not confirmed
Facilities ♀ ⛳ 🏠 ⚐ ℂ
Hotel ★★69% Imperial Hotel, North Dr, GREAT YARMOUTH ☎(0493) 851113 41⇋🏠

NORTH YORKSHIRE

BEDALE
Map 5 F4

Bedale ☎ (0677) 22451
Leyburn Rd (N side of town on A684)
Secluded parkland course with many trees.
18 holes, 5737yds, Par 69, SSS 68. Membership 800.

Visitors welcome must contact in advance Societies welcome (☎)
Green fees £14 per day (£20 WE)
Facilities ⊗ 🍽 ⬛ ▣ ♀ ⛳ 🏠 ℂ Tony Johnson
Hotel ★★63% Motel Leeming, BEDALE ☎(0677) 23611 40⇋

BENTHAM
Map 5 D5

Bentham ☎ (05242) 62455
Robin Ln (N side of High Bentham)
Moorland course with glorious views.
9 holes, 5752yds, Par 70, SSS 69. Membership 430.

Visitors welcome Societies welcome (☎)
Green fees £8 per day (£10 WE & BH)
Facilities ♀ ⛳ 🏠
Hotel ★★★55% Royal Hotel, Main St, KIRKBY LONSDALE ☎(05242) 71217 20rm(15⇋1🏠)

CATTERICK GARRISON
Map 5 F4

Catterick Garrison ☎ Richmond (0748) 833268
Leyburn Rd (1m W)
Parkland/moorland course with good views of the Pennines and Cleveland hills. Testing 1st and 3rd holes.
18 holes, 6312yds, Par 71, SSS 70, Course record 65. Membership 670.

Visitors welcome (handicap certificate may be required) must contact in advance Societies welcome (by letter)
Green fees £12 per day (£16 WE & BH)
Facilities ⊗ 🍽 by prior arrangement ⬛ ▣ ♀ ⛳ 🏠 ⚐ ℂ Steve Bradley
Hotel ★★58% Bridge House Hotel, CATTERICK BRIDGE ☎(0748) 818331 15rm(4⇋9🏠)

COPMANTHORPE   Map 5 G6

Pike Hills ☎ York (0904) 706566
Tadcaster Rd (3m N of York on A64)
Parkland course surrounding nature reserve.
18 holes, 6100yds, Par 71, SSS 69, Course record 65.
Membership 820.

Visitors welcome (with M only WE & BH) must contact
in advance Societies welcome (☎)
Green fees £16 per day summer (£10 winter)
Facilities ⊗ ⅢⅢ by prior arrangement 🛍 🍺 ♀ ⚑ 🎒
🥄 Ian Gradwell
Hotel ★★★70% Swallow Chase Hotel, Tadcaster Rd,
YORK ☎(0904) 701000 112⇌🐾

EASINGWOLD   Map 5 G5

Easingwold ☎ (0347) 21964
Stillington Rd (1m S)
Parkland course with easy walking. On 6 holes there are
water hazards which come into play. Pool table.
18 holes, 6041yds, Par 72, SSS 69, Course record 65.
Membership 550.

Visitors welcome (with M only WE & BH (winter))
must contact in advance Societies welcome (ex WE ☎)
Green fees £17 per day (£20 WE & BH)
Facilities ⊗ by prior arrangement ⅢⅢ by prior
arrangement 🛍 🍺 ♀ (1130-2200) ⚑ 🎒 🥄
Hotel ★★69% Beechwood Close Hotel, 19 Shipton Rd,
Clifton, YORK ☎(0904) 658378 14⇌🐾

FILEY   Map 5 J4

Filey ☎ Scarborough (0723) 513293
West Av (.5m S)
Parkland course with good views, windy. Stream runs
through course. Testing 9th and 13th holes. Snooker.
18 holes, 6030yds, Par 69, SSS 69, Course record 64.
Membership 950.

Visitors welcome (ex BH & special competition days)
must contact in advance Societies welcome (via booking
form)
Green fees £10-£13 (£12.50-£16 WE)
Facilities ⊗ (seasonal) ⅢⅢ (seasonal) 🛍 🍺 ♀ ⚑ 🎒 🍴
🥄 David England
Hotel ★★69% Wrangham House Hotel, 10 Stonegate,
Hunmanby, FILEY ☎(0723) 891333 9⇌🐾 Annexe:4⇌🐾

GANTON   Map 5 H4

Ganton ☎ Sherburn (0944) 70329
(.25m NW off A64)
Championship course, heathland, gorse and heavily
bunkered, variable winds.
18 holes, 6455yds, Par 71, SSS 71. Membership 580.

Visitors welcome (ex WE) must contact in advance
Societies welcome (☎)
Green fees £30 per day (£35 WE & PH)

▶

Facilities ⊗ by prior arrangement ⅲ by prior arrangement 🛍 💻 ♀ 🛆 🏨 ⛳ ℂ Gary Brown
Hotel ★★62% Downe Arms Hotel, WYKEHAM
☎(0723) 862471 10⇨🏨

HARROGATE

Map 5 F5

Harrogate ☎ (0423) 862999
Forest Ln Head, Starbeck
(2.25m on A59)
One of Yorkshire's oldest
and best courses was
designed in 1897 by 'Sandy'
Herd. A perfect example of
golf architecture, its greens
and fairways offer an
interesting but fair
challenge. The course once
formed part of the ancient
Forest of Knaresborough.
Snooker.
18 holes, 6241yds, Par 69, SSS 70. Membership 650.

SCORE CARD: White Tees					
Hole	Yds	Par	Hole	Yds	Par
1	315	4	10	343	4
2	429	4	11	509	5
3	171	3	12	179	3
4	274	4	13	467	4
5	219	3	14	175	3
6	382	4	15	406	4
7	514	5	16	455	4
8	373	4	17	392	4
9	227	3	18	411	4
Out	2904	34	In	3337	35
			Totals	6241	69

Visitors welcome (handicap certificate required)
must contact in advance Societies welcome (by
letter)
Green fees £22 per day ; (£30 WE)
Facilities ⊗ by prior arrangement ⅲ by prior
arrangement 🛍 💻 ♀ 🛆 🏨 ℂ Paul Johnson
Hotel ★★★69% Balmoral Hotel & Restaurant,
Franklin Mount, HARROGATE ☎(0423) 508208
20⇨🏨

Oakdale ☎ (0423) 567162
Oakdale (N side of town centre off A61)
A pleasant, undulating parkland course which
provides a good test of golf for the low handicap
player without intimidating the less proficient. A
special feature is an attractive stream which comes
in to play on four holes. Excellent views from the
clubhouse which has good facilities. Snooker.
18 holes, 6456yds, Par 71, SSS 71, Course record 66.
Membership 850.

Visitors welcome (ex 0800-0930 & 1230-1330) must
contact in advance Societies welcome (☎ 1 mth
notice)
Green fees £16 per day (£21 WE)
Facilities ⊗ ⅲ by prior arrangement 🛍 💻 ♀ 🛆
🏨 ⛳ ℂ Richard Jessop
Hotel ★★★68% Grants Hotel, 3-11 Swan Rd,
HARROGATE ☎(0423) 560666 37⇨🏨

KIRKBYMOORSIDE

Map 5 G4

Kirkbymoorside ☎ (0751) 31525
Manor Vale (N side of village)
Parkland course.
18 holes, 6016yds, Par 69, SSS 69, Course record 67.
Membership 600.

Visitors welcome (☎ for details) Societies welcome (☎
or letter)

Green fees £12 daily (£16 WE & BH)
Facilities ⊗ by prior arrangement ⅲ by prior
arrangement 🛍 by prior arrangement 💻 ♀ 🛆
Hotel ★★68% George & Dragon Hotel, 17 Market
Place, KIRKBYMOORSIDE ☎(0751) 31637 14⇨🏨
Annexe:8⇨🏨

KNARESBOROUGH

Map 5 F5

Knaresborough ☎ Harrogate (0423) 862690
Boroughbridge Rd (1.25 N on A6055)
Undulating parkland course with mature trees.
18 holes, 6232yds, Par 70, SSS 70, Course record 65.
Membership 750.

Visitors welcome (☎ for details) Societies welcome (At
least 2 weeks notice)
Green fees £12 round ; £16 day (£20 round/day WE)
Facilities ⊗ ⅲ 🛍 💻 ♀ 🛆 🏨 ℂ K I Johnstone
Hotel ★★★69% Dower House Hotel, Bond End,
KNARESBOROUGH ☎(0423) 863302 28⇨🏨
Annexe:4⇨🏨

MALTON

Map 5 H5

Malton & Norton ☎ (0653) 692959
Welham Park, Norton (1m S)
Parkland course with fine view from 4th tee. Very
testing 1st hole (564 yds dog-leg, left).
18 holes, 6426yds, Par 72, SSS 71. Membership 700.

Visitors welcome must contact in advance Societies
welcome (☎)
Green fees £15.50 (£20 WE & PH)
Facilities ⊗ ⅲ 🛍 💻 ♀ 🛆 🏨 ℂ M L Henderson
Hotel ★★67% Talbot Hotel, Yorkersgate, MALTON
☎(0653) 694031 29⇨🏨

MASHAM

Map 5 F4

Masham ☎ Ripon (0765) 89379
Burnholme, Swinton Rd (1m SW off A6108)
Flat parkland course crossed by stream, easy walking.
9 holes, 5244yds, Par 66, SSS 66, Course record 69.
Membership 305.

Visitors welcome (with M only WE & BH) Societies
welcome (☎)
Green fees £10 per day
Facilities ⊗ ⅲ 🛍 💻 ♀ 🛆
Hotel ★★⬆74% Jervaulx Hall Hotel, MASHAM
☎(0677) 60235 10⇨

PANNAL

Map 5 F5

Pannal ☎ Harrogate (0423) 872628
Follifoot Rd (E side of village off A61)
A fine championship course. Moorland turf but well-
wooded with the trees closely involved with the
play.
18 holes, 6659yds, Par 72, SSS 72, Course record 66.
Membership 815.

Visitors welcome (restr' 0800-0930&1200-1330; WE after 1430) must contact in advance Societies welcome (Several months notice required)
Green fees Not confirmed
Facilities ⊗ ⍙ by prior arrangement ⬛ 🍺 ♀ ⬠
🏠 ☂ ⌇ Murray Burgess
Hotel ★★★★62% The Majestic, Ripon Rd, HARROGATE ☎(0423) 568972 156⇥🐾

RICHMOND   Map 5 F4

Richmond ☎ (0748) 2457
Bend Hagg (.75m N)
Parkland course.
18 holes, 5704yds, Par 70, SSS 68, Course record 64. Membership 470.

Visitors welcome (restricted WE) Societies welcome (by letter)
Green fees Not confirmed
Facilities ⊗ (ex Mon) ⍙ (ex Sun and Mon) ⬛ 🍺 ♀ ⬠ 🏠 ☂ ⌇ Paul Jackson
Hotel ★★67% King's Head Hotel, Market Square, RICHMOND ☎(0748) 850220 23⇥🐾 Annexe:4⇥🐾

RIPON   Map 5 F5

Ripon City ☎ (0765) 3640
Palace Rd (1m N on A6108)
Hard-walking on parkland course; two testing par 3's at 5th and 7th.
9 holes, 5700yds, Par 70, SSS 68, Course record 65. Membership 430.

Visitors welcome
Green fees £10 (£15 WE & BH)
Facilities ⬠ 🏠 ☂ ⌇ T Davis
Hotel ★★★67% Ripon Spa Hotel, Park St, RIPON ☎(0765) 2172 40⇥🐾

SCARBOROUGH   Map 5 H4

Scarborough North Cliff ☎ (0723) 360786
North Cliff Av (2m N of town centre off A165)
Seaside parkland course with good views.
18 holes, 6425yds, Par 71, SSS 71. Membership 835.

Visitors welcome (must be M of a club with h'cap cert) must contact in advance Societies welcome (by letter)
Green fees £17 per day (£21 WE & BH)
Facilities ⊗ by prior arrangement ⍙ (Sun only) ⬛ 🍺 ♀ ⬠ 🏠 ☂ ⌇ S N Deller
Hotel ★★★63% Esplanade Hotel, Belmont Rd, SCARBOROUGH ☎(0723) 360382 73⇥🐾

Scarborough South Cliff ☎ (0723) 374737
Deepdale Av (1m S on A165)
Parkland/seaside course designed by Dr Mackenzie.
18 holes, 6085yds, Par 70, SSS 69. Membership 650.

Visitors welcome (☎ for details) ✉ Societies welcome (advance notice required ☎)
Green fees Not confirmed

Facilities ⊗ ⍙ ⬛ 🍺 ♀ ⬠ 🏠 ☂ ⌇ David Edwards
Hotel ★★66% Bradley Court, 7-9 Filey Rd, South Cliff, SCARBOROUGH ☎(0723) 360476 40rm(22⇥17🐾)

SELBY   Map 5 G6

Selby ☎ (0757) 228622
Brayton Barff
Mainly flat links course, prevailing SW wind. Testing holes including the 3rd, 7th and 16th. Snooker.
18 holes, 6246yds, Par 70, SSS 70, Course record 64. Membership 780.

Visitors welcome (restricted 1100-1300. WE with M only) must contact in advance ✉ Societies welcome (Wed, Thu & Fri ☎)
Green fees £18 per day; £15 per round
Facilities ⊗ ⍙ by prior arrangement ⬛ 🍺 (no catering Mon) ♀ ⬠ 🏠 ⌇ C A C Smith
Hotel ★★★68% Monk Fryston Hall, MONK FRYSTON ☎(0977) 682369 29⇥🐾

SETTLE   Map 5 D5

Settle ☎ (07292) 3912
Buckhaw Brow, Giggleswick (1m N on A65)
Picturesque parkland course.
9 holes, 4596yds, Par 64, SSS 62. Membership 170.

Visitors welcome (restricted Sun) Societies welcome (by letter)
Green fees Not confirmed
Facilities ♀
Hotel ★★★62% Falcon Manor Hotel, Skipton Rd, SETTLE ☎(07292) 3814 15⇥🐾

SKIPTON   Map 5 E5

Skipton ☎ (0756) 793922
Off North West By-Pass (1m N on A65)
Grassland course with panoramic views.
18 holes, 5771yds, Par 69, SSS 68, Course record 70. Membership 740.

Visitors welcome (ex competition days) must contact in advance Societies welcome (☎)
Green fees £15 per day (£20 WE & BH)
Facilities ⊗ ⍙ ⬛ 🍺 (no catering Mon) ♀ ⬠ 🏠 ☂ ⌇ John Hammond
Hotel ★★★75% Devonshire Arms Country House Hotel, BOLTON ABBEY ☎(075671) 441 40⇥

THIRSK   Map 5 F4

Thirsk & Northallerton ☎ (0845) 522170
Thornton-le-Street (2m N on A168)
The course has good views of the nearby Hambleton Hills. Testing course, mainly flat land.
9 holes, 6257yds, Par 72, SSS 70, Course record 69. Membership 340.

Visitors welcome (with M only Sun) must contact in advance ✉ Societies welcome (by letter)
Green fees Not confirmed

▶

Facilities ⊗ by prior arrangement ⅏ by prior arrangement 𝕃 💺 ⬱ (restricted winter) 🛆 🏠 ⛳ 𝄢 E Pullan
Hotel ★★66% Golden Fleece Hotel, Market Place, THIRSK ☎(0845) 523108 22rm(6⇦)

WHITBY

Map 5 H3

Whitby ☎ (0947) 602768
Low Straggleton, Sandsend Rd (1.5m NW on A174)
Seaside course on cliff top. Good views and fresh sea breeze.
18 holes, 5706yds, Par 69, SSS 67. Membership 800.

Visitors welcome (ex competition days) Societies welcome (by letter)
Green fees Not confirmed
Facilities ⊗ (ex Mon) ⅏ (ex Mon) 𝕃 (ex Mon) 💺 (ex Mon) ⬱ 🛆 🏠 ⛳ 𝄢 Andrew Brook
Hotel ★★65% White House Hotel, Upgang Lane, West Cliff, WHITBY ☎(0947) 600469 12rm(7⇦4🐾)

YORK

Map 5 G5

Fulford ☎ (0904) 413579
Heslington Ln (2m SE)
A flat, parkland/moorland course well-known for the superb quality of its turf, particularly the greens, and now famous as the venue for some of the best golf tournaments in the British Isles.
18 holes, 6775yds, Par 72, SSS 72, Course record 62. Membership 600.

SCORE CARD: White Tees					
Hole	Yds	Par	Hole	Yds	Par
1	412	4	10	165	3
2	438	4	11	504	5
3	189	3	12	321	4
4	458	4	13	473	4
5	167	3	14	175	3
6	561	5	15	443	4
7	415	4	16	361	4
8	371	4	17	356	4
9	486	5	18	480	5
Out	3496	36	In	3278	36
			Totals	6775	72

Visitors welcome must contact in advance ✉ Societies welcome (by letter)
Green fees £25 (£30 WE & BH)
Facilities ⊗ ⅏ 𝕃 💺 ⬱ 🛆 🏠 ⛳ 𝄢 Bryan Hessay
Hotel ★★★★63% Viking Hotel, North St, YORK ☎(0904) 659822 188⇦🐾

Heworth ☎ (0904) 424618
Muncaster House, Muncaster Gate (1.5m NE of city centre on A1036)
Parkland course, easy walking.
11 holes, 6141yds, Par 70, SSS 69. Membership 460.

Visitors welcome (ex winter-Sun (am)) must contact in advance ring pro Societies welcome (by letter to secretary)
Green fees £12 per day (£14 WE & BH)
Facilities ⊗ ⅏ 𝕃 💺 (catering by prior arrangement no catering Mon) ⬱ 🛆 🏠 ⛳ 𝄢 Steve Robinson
Hotel ★★★71% Dean Court Hotel, Duncombe Place, YORK ☎(0904) 625082 41⇦🐾

This guide is updated annually – make sure you use an up-to-date edition.

York ☎ (0904) 491840
Lords Moor Ln, Strensall (6m NE, E of Strensall village)
A pleasant, well-designed, heathland course with easy walking. The course is of good length but being flat the going does not tire. There are two testing pond holes.
18 holes, 6285yds, Par 70, SSS 70, Course record 65. Membership 700.

Visitors welcome (after 0900 & not between 1200-1330) must contact in advance Societies welcome (☎)
Green fees £20 per day (£24 WE & BH)
Facilities ⊗ ⅏ 𝕃 💺 ⬱ 🛆 🏠 𝄢 A D Mason
Hotel ★★★71% Dean Court Hotel, Duncombe Place, YORK ☎(0904) 625082 41⇦🐾

NORTHAMPTONSHIRE

CHACOMBE

Map 3 K6

Cherwell Edge ☎ (0295) 711591
(.5m S off B4525)
Parkland course.
18 holes, 5322mtrs, Par 70, SSS 68, Course record 71. Membership 500.

Visitors welcome Societies welcome (by letter)
Green fees £8.50 per day; £4.60 per round (£6 WE)
Facilities ⊗ ⅏ 𝕃 💺 ⬱ 🛆 🏠 ⛳ 𝄢 Richard Davies
Hotel ★★★66% Whately Hall Hotel, Banbury Cross, BANBURY ☎(0295) 263451 74⇦🐾

COLD ASHBY

Map 4 B6

Cold Ashby ☎ Northampton (0604) 740099
Stanford Rd (1m W)
Undulating parkland course, nicely matured, with superb views. Ski-ing in suitable conditions.
18 holes, 5957yds, Par 70, SSS 69, Course record 62. Membership 600.

Visitors welcome (restricted WE) Societies welcome (☎)
Green fees £16 per day; £12 per round (£14 WE)
Facilities ⊗ ⅏ 𝕃 💺 ⬱ 🛆 🏠 ⛳ 𝄢 Tony Skingle
Hotel ★★★65% Post House Hotel, CRICK ☎(0788) 822101 96⇦🐾

For a full list of the golf courses included in this book, check with the index on page 284

COLLINGTREE
Map 4 B7

Collingtree Park
☎ (0604) 700000
Windingbrook Ln (M1-junc
15 on A508 to
Northampton)
Superb 18-hole resort
course designed by former
U.S. and British Open
champion Johnny Miller.
Stunning island green at
the 18th hole. Green fee
includes buggy cart and
range balls. The Golf

SCORE CARD: White Tees					
Hole	Yds	Par	Hole	Yds	Par
1	348	4	10	348	4
2	386	4	11	387	4
3	431	4	12	192	3
4	533	5	13	423	4
5	179	3	14	542	5
6	367	4	15	170	3
7	388	4	16	392	4
8	166	3	17	401	4
9	498	5	18	541	5
Out	3296	36	In	3396	36
			Totals	6692	72

Academy includes a driving
range, practice holes, indoor video teaching room,
golf custom-fit centre. **See colour feature.**
18 holes, 6692yds, Par 72, SSS 72, Course record 68.
Membership 600.

Visitors welcome (handicap certificate required)
must contact in advance Societies welcome (contact
Irene Kilbane)
Green fees £40 includes buggy cart & range balls
(£45 WE)
Facilities ⊗ ⊮ ⓛ ▆ ♀ ⌂ 🏠 ⌁ ₵ John Cook
Hotel ★★★★59% Swallow Hotel, Eagle Dr,
NORTHAMPTON ☎(0604) 768700 122⇉♦♠

CORBY
Map 4 C5

Priors Hall ☎ (0536) 60756
Stamford Rd, Weldon (4m NE on A43)
Municipal course laid out on made-up quarry ground
and open to prevailing wind.
18 holes, 6677yds, Par 72, SSS 72. Membership 400.

Visitors welcome Societies welcome (☎)
Green fees Not confirmed
Facilities ⓛ ▆ ♀ ⌂ 🏠 ⌁ ₵
Hotel ★★★62% The Talbot, New St, OUNDLE ☎(0832)
273621 38rm(18⇉17♠)

DAVENTRY
Map 4 A6

Daventry & District ☎ (0327) 702829
Norton Rd (1m NE)
A hilly course with hard walking.
18 holes, 5555yds, Par 69, SSS 67. Membership 300.

Visitors welcome (restricted Sun am & WE (Oct-
Mar)☎)
Green fees Not confirmed
Facilities ♀ ⌂ 🏠 ⌁ ₵
Hotel ★★★67% Northampton Moat House, Silver
Street, Town Centre, NORTHAMPTON ☎(0604) 22441
142⇉♠

Each golf course entry has a recommended
hotel. For a wider choice of places to stay,
consult *AA Hotels and Restaurants in Britain* or
AA-inspected Bed and Breakfast in Britain.

FARTHINGSTONE
Map 4 A7

Woodlands ☎ (032736) 291
(1m W)
Pleasant rambling course with open aspect and
widespread views. Accommodation, four championship
squash courts and two snooker tables.
18 holes, 6248yds, Par 71, SSS 71, Course record 66.
Membership 600.

Visitors welcome must contact in advance Societies
welcome (by letter)
Green fees £25 per day; £15 per round (£30/£20 WE)
Facilities ⊗ ⊮ ⓛ ▆ ♀ ⌂ 🏠 ⌁ ₵ Mike Gallagher
Hotel ★★★70% Crossroads Hotel, WEEDON ☎(0327)
40354 10⇉ Annexe:40⇉

KETTERING
Map 4 C6

Kettering ☎ (0536) 512074
Headlands (S side of town centre)
A very pleasant, mainly flat meadowland course with
easy walking.
18 holes, 6035yds, Par 69, SSS 69, Course record 65.
Membership 500.

Visitors welcome (WE & BH with M) ✉ Societies
welcome (☎)
Green fees £20
Facilities ⊗ ⊮ ⓛ ▆ ♀ ⌂ 🏠 ⌁ ₵ Kevin Theobald
Hotel ★★58% High View Hotel, 156 Midland Rd,
WELLINGBOROUGH ☎(0933) 78733 due to change to
278733 14⇉♠ Annexe:3rm

NORTHAMPTON
Map 4 B6

Delapre Golf Complex ☎ (0604) 764036
Eagle Dr, Nene Valley Way (2m SE)
Municipal golf complex, also includes two 9-hole, par 3
courses, pitch-and-putt and 33 bay driving-range.
18 holes, 6356yds, Par 70, SSS 70, Course record 66.
Membership 800.

Visitors welcome Societies welcome
Green fees £5.75 per round (£7.25 WE & BH)
Facilities ⊗ ⊮ ⓛ ▆ ♀ ⌂ 🏠 ⌁ ₵ John Corby
Hotel ★★★63% Westone Moat House, Ashley Way,
Weston Favell, NORTHAMPTON ☎(0604) 406262 30⇉
Annexe:36⇉

Kingsthorpe ☎ (0604) 710610
Kingsley Rd (N side of town centre on A5095)
Parkland course.
18 holes, 6006yds, Par 69, SSS 69, Course record 63.
Membership 450.

Visitors welcome (with M only WE & BH, h'cap cert
required) must contact in advance ✉ Societies welcome
(☎)
Green fees £16 per day/round
Facilities ⊗ ⊮ ⓛ ▆ ♀ ⌂ 🏠 ⌁ ₵ Paul Smith
Hotel ★★★63% Westone Moat House, Ashley Way,
Weston Favell, NORTHAMPTON ☎(0604) 406262 30⇉
Annexe:36⇉

Northampton ☎ (0604) 845155
Harlestone (NW of town centre on A428)
New course open to visitors from May 1991.
18 holes, 6534yds, Par 72, SSS 71. Membership 700.

Visitors welcome (with M only WE, h'cap cert
required) must contact in advance ✉ Societies welcome
(☎)
Green fees £25 per day/round
Facilities ⊗ ⒨ by prior arrangement ⒧ ⒧ ⒴ ⒧ ⒧
⒧ Mark Chamberlaine
Hotel ★★★67% Northampton Moat House, Silver
Street, Town Centre, NORTHAMPTON ☎(0604) 22441
142⇨⒧

Northamptonshire County ☎ (0604) 843025
Church Brampton (4m NW of town centre off A50)
Undulating heathland course with gorse, heather and
fine pine woods.
18 holes, 6602yds, Par 70, SSS 71. Membership 850.

Visitors welcome (Ladies at WE) must contact in
advance ✉ Societies welcome (Mon, Thu & Fri only ☎)
Green fees £30 day/round
Facilities ⊗ ⒨ ⒧ ⒧ ⒴ ⒧ ⒧ ⒧ ⒧
Hotel ★★★63% Westone Moat House, Ashley Way,
Weston Favell, NORTHAMPTON ☎(0604) 406262 30⇨
Annexe:36⇨

OUNDLE

Map 4 C5

Oundle ☎ (0832) 273267
Benefield Rd (1m W on A427)
Undulating parkland course close to the town. A small
brook affects some of the approaches to the greens.
18 holes, 5507yds, Par 70, SSS 67. Membership 605.

Visitors welcome (not before 1030 WE unless with M)
Societies welcome (☎)
Green fees £10 per day (£12 WE)
Facilities ⊗ ⒨ ⒧ ⒧ ⒴ ⒧ ⒧ ⒧ ⒧ C M Cunningham
Hotel ★★★62% The Talbot, New St, OUNDLE ☎(0832)
273621 38rm(18⇨17⒧)

STAVERTON

Map 4 A6

Staverton Park ☎ Daventry (0327) 705911
(.75m NE of Staverton on A425)
Open course, fairly testing with good views.
Accommodation, snooker, sauna and solarium.
*18 holes, 6634yds, Par 71, SSS 71, Course record 65.
Membership 478.*

Visitors welcome (restricted WE) must contact in
advance Societies welcome (☎)
Green fees £24.50 per day; £15 per round (£28.50/£19.50
WE & BH)
Facilities ⊗ ⒨ ⒧ ⒧ ⒴ ⒧ ⒧ ⒧ ⒧ Brian & Richard
Mudge
Hotel ★★★70% Crossroads Hotel, WEEDON ☎(0327)
40354 10⇨ Annexe:40⇨

WELLINGBOROUGH

Map 4 C6

Rushden ☎ Rushden (0933) 312581
Kimbolton Rd, Chelveston (2m E of Higham Ferrers on
A45)
Parkland course.
*9 holes, 6381yds, Par 71, SSS 70, Course record 67.
Membership 400.*

Visitors welcome (ex Wed pm; WE with M) Societies
welcome (by letter)
Green fees £12 per round
Facilities ⊗ ⒨ ⒧ ⒧ ⒴ ⒧
Hotel ★★★50% Hind Hotel, Sheep St,
WELLINGBOROUGH ☎(0933) 222827 34⇨⒧

Wellingborough ☎ (0933) 677234
Gt Harrowden Hall (2m N on A509)
An undulating parkland course with many trees. The
514-yd, 14th is a testing hole. Outdoor-heated swimming
pool, fishing and snooker.
*18 holes, 6054mtrs, Par 72, SSS 72, Course record 69.
Membership 850.*

Visitors welcome (ex WE & BH-handicap certificate
required) must contact in advance Societies welcome
(by letter)
Green fees £25 per day; £20 per round
Facilities ⊗ (ex Sun) ⒨ (ex Sun and Mon) ⒧ ⒧ ⒴ ⒧
⒧ ⒧ ⒧ David Clifford
Hotel ★★★50% Hind Hotel, Sheep St,
WELLINGBOROUGH ☎(0933) 222827 34⇨⒧

NORTHUMBERLAND

ALLENDALE

Map 6 J6

Allendale ☎ 091-267 5875
Thornley Gate (.75m W)
Slightly hilly, rural course with fine views. Club room
available to picnickers. Riding stables.
*9 holes, 2244yds, Par 66, SSS 63, Course record 65.
Membership 120.*

Visitors welcome (restricted Sun am & Aug BH till
1600) Societies welcome (2-3 wks in advance in advance)
Green fees £4 (£5 WE)
Facilities ⒧ ⒧ ⒧
Hotel ★★62% County Hotel, Priestpopple, HEXHAM
☎(0434) 602030 9⇨⒧

ALNMOUTH

Map 6 K4

Alnmouth ☎ (0665) 830368
Foxton Hall (1m NE)
Coastal course. Accommodation.
*18 holes, 6414yds, Par 71, SSS 71, Course record 65.
Membership 600.*

Visitors welcome (ex Wed, Fri, WE & BH) must contact
in advance Societies welcome (by letter)
Green fees £18 per day (£22 WE & BH)

Facilities ⊗ ⋔ 🏌 💺 ♀ ⛳ 🏠 ⛳

Hotel ★★★59% White Swan Hotel, Bondgate Within, ALNWICK ☎(0665) 602109 43⇆🏌

Alnmouth Village ☎ (0665) 830370
Marine Rd (E side of village)
Seaside course with part coastal view.
9 holes, 6078 yds, Par 70, SSS 70. Membership 480.

Visitors welcome Societies welcome
Green fees Not confirmed
Facilities ♀ ⛳
Hotel ★★★59% White Swan Hotel, Bondgate Within, ALNWICK ☎(0665) 602109 43⇆🏌

ALNWICK   Map 6 K4

Alnwick ☎ (0665) 602632
Swansfield Park (S side of town)
Parkland course offering a fair test of golfing skills.
9 holes, 5387 yds, Par 66, SSS 66, Course record 62. Membership 402.

Visitors welcome (ex competition days) Societies welcome (☎)
Green fees £8 per day; £6 per round (£10/£8 WE & BH)
Facilities ⋔ by prior arrangement 🏌 💺 ♀ ⛳
Hotel ★★★59% White Swan Hotel, Bondgate Within, ALNWICK ☎(0665) 602109 43⇆🏌

BAMBURGH   Map 6 K3

Bamburgh Castle
☎ (06684) 378
(6m E of A1 via B1341 or B1342)
This is not a long course, but there are those who have played golf all over the world who say that for sheer breathtaking beauty this northern seaside gem cannot be bettered. And the course itself is the greatest fun to play.
18 holes, 5465 yds, Par 68, SSS 67, Course record 63. Membership 650.

SCORE CARD					
Hole	Yds	Par	Hole	Yds	Par
1	182	3	10	196	3
2	213	3	11	334	4
3	510	5	12	413	4
4	476	5	13	406	4
5	314	4	14	149	3
6	224	3	15	404	4
7	279	4	16	268	4
8	162	3	17	260	4
9	361	4	18	314	4
Out	2721	34	In	2744	34
			Totals	5465	68

Visitors welcome (with M BH & comp days, h'cap cert reqd) must contact in advance Societies welcome (☎)
Green fees £12 per day (£16 WE)
Facilities ⊗ ⋔ 🏌 💺 ♀ ⛳
Hotel ★★69% Lord Crewe Arms, Front St, BAMBURGH ☎(06684) 243 25rm(14⇆6🏌)

Each golf course entry has a recommended hotel. For a wider choice of places to stay, consult *AA Hotels and Restaurants in Britain* or *AA-inspected Bed and Breakfast in Britain.*

BEDLINGTON   Map 6 K5

Bedlingtonshire ☎ (0670) 822087
Acorn Bank (1m SW on A1068)
Parkland course with easy walking. Under certain
conditions the wind can be a distinct hazard.
18 holes, 6813ydss, Par 73, SSS 73, Course record 65.
Membership 829.

Visitors welcome (restricted in summer) must contact
in advance Societies welcome (book: Wansbeck DC,
Ashington)
Green fees £8 per day (£10 WE)
Facilities ⊗ ⅏ ⓛ ♨ by prior arrangement ♀ ⌂ ⌂
⚐ ☪ Marcus Webb
Hotel ★★★★54% Holiday Inn Newcastle, Great
North Rd, SEATON BURN ☎091-236 5432 150⇔⅃🅜

BELLINGHAM   Map 6 J5

Bellingham ☎ (0434) 220530
Boggle Hole (N side of village on B6320)
Downland course with natural hazards.
9 holes, 5245yds, Par 67, SSS 66, Course record 63.
Membership 250.

Visitors welcome (by appointment only on Sun)
Societies welcome (☎ or by letter)
Green fees £6 per round (£7.50 WE & BH)
Facilities ⊗ by prior arrangement ⓛ ♨ ♀ ⌂
Hotel ★★64% Riverdale Hall Hotel, BELLINGHAM
☎(0434) 220254 20⇔⅃🅜

BERWICK-UPON-TWEED   Map 6 J3

Berwick-upon-Tweed (Goswick)☎ (0289) 87256
Goswick (6m S off A1)
Seaside links course playable all year round.
18 holes, 6425yds, Par 72, SSS 71, Course record 64.
Membership 458.

Visitors welcome (after 1000-1200 & after 1400 WE)
must contact in advance Societies welcome (Party 8 +
by prior arrangement)
Green fees £16 per day; £12.50 per round (£22/£16 WE)
Facilities ⊗ by prior arrangement ⅏ by prior
arrangement ⓛ ♨ ♀ ⌂ ⌂ ☪ Malcolm Leighton
Hotel ★★★63% Turret House Hotel, Etal Rd,
Tweedmouth, BERWICK-UPON-TWEED ☎(0289) 330808
13⇔⅃🅜

Magdalene Fields ☎ (0289) 306384
Magdalene Fields (E side of town centre)
Seaside course with natural hazards formed by sea bays.
Last 9 holes open to winds. Testing 18th hole over bay
(par 3).
18 holes, 6551yds, Par 72, SSS 71, Course record 69.
Membership 200.

Visitors welcome (must possess individual sets of clubs)
must contact in advance ✉ Societies welcome
Green fees Not confirmed
Facilities ⊗ by prior arrangement ⓛ ♨ ♀ ⌂ ⚐

Hotel ★★★63% Turret House Hotel, Etal Rd,
Tweedmouth, BERWICK-UPON-TWEED ☎(0289) 330808
13⇔⅃🅜

BLYTH   Map 6 K5

Blyth ☎ (0670) 367728
New Delaval (6m N of Whitley Bay)
Course built over old colliery. Parkland with water
hazards.
18 holes, 6533yds, Par 72, SSS 71, Course record 66.
Membership 815.

Visitors welcome (with M WE) Societies welcome (by
letter)
Green fees £12 per day, £10 per round
Facilities ⊗ ⓛ ♨ ♀ ⌂ ⌂ ☪ Brian Rumney
Hotel ★★63% Windsor Hotel, South Pde, WHITLEY
BAY ☎091-252 3317 55rm(38⇔5🅜)

CRAMLINGTON   Map 6 K6

Arcot Hall ☎ 091-236 2794
(2m SW off A1)
A wooded parkland course, reasonably flat. Snooker.
18 holes, 6389yds, Par 70, SSS 70, Course record 65.
Membership 700.

Visitors welcome (midweek only must be M of a golf
club) must contact in advance Societies welcome
(midweek only ☎)
Green fees £18 per day (£22 WE & BH)
Facilities ⊗ ⅏ ⓛ ♨ ♀ ⌂ ⌂ ⚐ ☪ Graham Cant
Hotel ★★★★54% Holiday Inn Newcastle, Great
North Rd, SEATON BURN ☎091-236 5432 150⇔⅃🅜

EMBLETON   Map 6 K4

Dunstanburgh Castle ☎ (066576) 562
(.5m E)
Rolling links with castle and bird sanctuary either side,
superb views.
18 holes, 6039yds, Par 70, SSS 69. Membership 350.

Visitors welcome Societies welcome (☎ or letter)
Green fees £8.50 per day; £10.50 per round WE & BH,
£12.75 per day WE & BH
Facilities ⊗ ⅏ ⓛ ♨ ♀ ⌂ ⌂ ⚐
Hotel ★★Dunstanburgh Castle Hotel, EMBLETON
☎(066576) 203 17rm(9⇔)

HEXHAM   Map 6 J6

Hexham ☎ (0434) 603072
Spital Park (1m NW on B6531)
A very pretty, undulating parkland course with
interesting natural contours. From parts of the
course, particularly the elevated 6th tee, there are
the most exquisite views of the valley below. As good
a parkland course as any in the North of England.
Squash and snooker.
18 holes, 6044yds, Par 70, SSS 68, Course record 65.
Membership 700.

Visitors welcome must contact in advance Societies welcome (ex WE ☎)
Green fees £16 per day ; £12 per round (£20/£16 WE)
Facilities ⊗ by prior arrangement ⋔ by prior arrangement 🛏 🍺 ♀ 🏌 🏠 ⛳ 🏃 Ian Waugh
Hotel ★★★70% Beaumont Hotel, Beaumont St, HEXHAM ☎(0434) 602331 23⇨🏠

Tynedale ☎ No telephone
Tyne Green (N side of town)
Flat, easy moorland course. Bounded by river and railway.
9 holes, 5643yds, Par 69, SSS 67. Membership 275.

Visitors welcome (ex Sun)
Green fees Not confirmed
Hotel ★★★70% Beaumont Hotel, Beaumont St, HEXHAM ☎(0434) 602331 23⇨🏠

MORPETH   Map 6 K5

Morpeth ☎ (0670) 519980
The Common (S side of town centre on A197)
Parkland course with views of the Cheviots.
18 holes, 6206yds, Par 72, SSS 70, Course record 67. Membership 700.

Visitors welcome (restricted WE & BH) must contact in advance ✉ Societies welcome (☎)
Green fees £15 per day ; £10 per round (£20/£15 WE)
Facilities 🏌 🏠 ⛳ 🏃 Martin Jackson
Hotel ★★★★74% Linden Hall Hotel, LONGHORSLEY ☎(0670) 516611 45⇨🏠

NEWBIGGIN-BY-THE-SEA   Map 6 K5

Newbiggin-by-the-Sea ☎ (0670) 817344
(N side of town)
Seaside course. Snooker.
18 holes, 6452yds, Par 72, SSS 71, Course record 67. Membership 500.

Visitors welcome (not before 1000) must contact in advance Societies welcome (by letter)
Green fees £6 (£9 WE & BHs)
Facilities ⊗ ⋔ by prior arrangement 🛏 🍺 ♀ 🏌 🏠 ⛳ 🏃 David Fletcher
Hotel ★★★★74% Linden Hall Hotel, LONGHORSLEY ☎(0670) 516611 45⇨🏠

PONTELAND   Map 6 K6

Ponteland ☎ (0661) 22689
53 Bell Villas (.5m E on A696)
Open parkland course, good views and testing golf.
18 holes, 6512yds, Par 72, SSS 71. Membership 720.

Visitors welcome (with M only WE & BH) ✉ Societies welcome
Green fees Not confirmed
Facilities ♀ 🏌 🏠 ⛳ 🏃

Hotel ★★★64% Airport Moat House Hotel, Woolsington, NEWCASTLE UPON TYNE AIRPORT ☎(0661) 24911 100⇨🏠

PRUDHOE   Map 6 K6

Prudhoe ☎ (0661) 32466
Eastwood Park (E side of town centre off A695)
Parkland course with natural hazards, easy walking.
18 holes, 5812yds, Par 69, SSS 68. Membership 390.

Visitors welcome must contact in advance by letter Societies welcome (by letter)
Green fees Not confirmed
Facilities ♀ 🏌 🏠
Hotel ★★62% County Hotel, Priestpopple, HEXHAM ☎(0434) 602030 9⇨🏠

ROTHBURY   Map 6 K5

Rothbury ☎ (0669) 20718
Old Race Course (S side of town off B6342)
Very flat downland course with natural hazards. Snooker.
9 holes, 5560yds, Par 68, SSS 67. Membership 230.

Visitors welcome (ex WE) Societies welcome (ex WE)
Green fees Not confirmed
Facilities ♀ (Fri & WE only) 🏌
Hotel ★★★59% White Swan Hotel, Bondgate Within, ALNWICK ☎(0665) 602109 43⇨🏠

SEAHOUSES   Map 6 K4

Seahouses ☎ Alnwick (0665) 720794
Beadnell Rd (S side of village on B1340)
Seaside course. Easy walking.
18 holes, 5400yds, Par 66, SSS 66, Course record 64. Membership 350.

Visitors welcome Societies welcome (by letter)
Green fees £11 per day (£14 & £12 round WE & BH, £40 per week)
Facilities ⊗ (ex Tue) ⋔ (ex Tue) 🛏 🍺 ♀ 🏌 🏠 ⛳
Hotel ★★69% Olde Ship Hotel, SEAHOUSES ☎(0665) 720200 14⇨🏠

STOCKSFIELD   Map 6 K6

Stocksfield ☎ (0661) 843041
New Ridley Rd (2.5m SE off A695)
Challenging course: parkland (9 holes), woodland (9 holes).
18 holes, 5594yds, Par 68, SSS 68, Course record 65. Membership 700.

Visitors welcome (ex WE until 4pm) must contact in advance Societies welcome (☎ or by letter)
Green fees £10-£15 per day
Facilities ⊗ by prior arrangement ⋔ by prior arrangement 🛏 🍺 ♀ 🏌 🏠 ⛳ 🏃 Ken Driver
Hotel ★★★70% Beaumont Hotel, Beaumont St, HEXHAM ☎(0434) 602331 23⇨🏠

WARKWORTH
Map 6 K4

Warkworth ☎ (0665) 711596
The Links (.5m E of village off A1068)
Seaside course, good views.
9 holes, 5817yds, Par 70, SSS 68, Course record 67.
Membership 400.

Visitors welcome (ex Tue & Sat) Societies welcome (by letter)
Green fees Not confirmed
Facilities ⌚ ▥ ▣ ♀ ⌂
Hotel ★★★59% White Swan Hotel, Bondgate Within, ALNWICK ☎(0665) 602109 43⇔♪♠

NOTTINGHAMSHIRE

EAST LEAKE
Map 4 A3

Rushcliffe ☎ (0509) 852209
Stocking Ln (1m N)
Parkland course. Snooker.
18 holes, 3057yds, Par 70, SSS 69. Membership 700.

Visitors welcome (with M only WE) must contact in advance Societies welcome (☎ for details)
Green fees Not confirmed
Facilities ♀ ⌂ ⌂ ♪♦ ┇
Hotel ★★★58% Novotel Nottingham Derby, Bostock Ln, LONG EATON ☎(0602) 720106 110⇔♪♠

KEYWORTH
Map 4 A3

Stanton on the Wolds ☎ Plumtree (06077) 2006
(E side of village)
Parkland course.
18 holes, 6437yds, Par 73, SSS 71, Course record 66.
Membership 1000.

Visitors welcome (restricted Tue & competition days) must contact in advance ✉ Societies welcome (apply in Oct)
Green fees £14 per day; £12 per round;(£15 WE & BH)
Facilities ⊗ ▥ ▥ ▣ ♀ ⌂ ⌂ ♪♦ ┇ Nick Hernon
Hotel ★★65% Rufford Hotel, 53 Melton Road, West Bridgford, NOTTINGHAM ☎(0602) 814202 35♠

KIRKBY IN ASHFIELD
Map 4 A2

Notts ☎ Mansfield (0623) 753225
Hollinwell (1.5m SE off A611)
Undulating heathland Championship course.
Driving range.
18 holes, 6609yds, Par 72, SSS 72. Membership 500.

Visitors welcome (ex WE & BH unless with M) must contact in advance ✉ Societies welcome (☎)
Green fees £33 per day; £28 per round
Facilities ⊗ ▥ ▥ ▣ ♀ ⌂ ⌂ ♪♦ ┇ Brian Waites
Hotel ★★★62% Swallow Hotel, Carter Ln East, SOUTH NORMANTON ☎(0773) 812000 123⇔♪♠

MANSFIELD
Map 4 A2

Sherwood Forest ☎ (0623) 26689
Eakring Rd (2.5m E)
As the name suggests, the Forest is the main feature of this heathland course with heather-lined fairways. The homeward nine holes are particularly testing. The 11th and 14th are notable par 4 holes on this well-bunkered course.
18 holes, 6307yds, Par 71, SSS 73, Course record 67.
Membership 800.

Visitors welcome (ex Mon, Thu & Fri) must contact in advance ✉ Societies welcome (Mon, Thu & Fri only ☎)
Green fees £25 per round (£30 WE); £30 per day
Facilities ⊗ ▥ ▥ ▣ ♀ (during golf season) ⌂
⌂ ┇ Ken Hall
Hotel ★★★52% Post House Hotel, Bostocks Ln, SANDIACRE ☎(0602) 397800 107⇔♪♠

MANSFIELD WOODHOUSE
Map 4 A1

Mansfield Woodhouse ☎ Mansfield (0623) 23521
Leeming Ln North (N side of town centre off A60)
Easy walking on heathland.
9 holes, 2150yds, Par 62, SSS 60 or 2411yds, Par 68, SSS 65. Membership 100.

Visitors welcome Societies welcome (by letter)
Green fees Not confirmed
Facilities ⊗ ▥ ▥ ▣ ♀ ⌂ ⌂ ♪♦ ┇ Leslie Highfield
Hotel ★★61% Pine Lodge Hotel, 281-283 Nottingham Rd, MANSFIELD ☎(0623) 22308 21rm(13⇔3♠)

NEWARK-ON-TRENT
Map 4 B2

Newark ☎ (0636) 626282
Coddington (4m E on A17)
Parkland course in secluded situation with easy walking.
18 holes, 6486yds, Par 71, SSS 71, Course record 70.
Membership 660.

Visitors welcome must contact in advance Societies welcome (by letter)
Green fees £16 (£20 WE)
Facilities ⊗ ▥ ▥ ▣ ♀ ⌂ ⌂ ♪♦ ┇ H A Bennett
Hotel ★★66% Grange Hotel, 73 London Rd, NEWARK ☎(0636) 703399 9⇔♪♠

NOTTINGHAM
Map 4 A3

Beeston Fields ☎ (0602) 257062
Beeston (4m SW off A52)
Parkland course with sandy subsoil and wide, tree-lined fairways. The par 3, 14th has elevated tee and small bunker-guarded green. Snooker.
18 holes, 6414yds, Par 71, SSS 71. Membership 700.

Visitors welcome must contact in advance Societies welcome (☎)
Green fees £17 per day; £15 per round (£17 WE & BH)

Facilities ⛳ 🏠 (Alun Wardle
Hotel ★★★52% Post House Hotel, Bostocks Ln,
SANDIACRE ☎(0602) 397800 107⇥🐾

Bulwell Forest ☎ (0602) 278008
Hucknall Rd, Bulwell (4m NW of city centre on A611)
Municipal heathland course with many natural
hazards. Very tight fairways and subject to wind.
18 holes, 5606yds, Par 68, SSS 67. Membership 420.

Visitors welcome
Green fees Not confirmed
Facilities ♀ 🏠 (
Hotel ★★★★56% Nottingham Moat House, Mansfield
Rd, NOTTINGHAM ☎(0602) 602621 172⇥🐾

Chilwell Manor ☎ (0602) 258958
Meadow Ln, Chilwell (4m SW on A6005)
Flat parkland course.
18 holes, 6379yds, Par 70, SSS 69. Membership 777.

Visitors welcome (with M only WE) ✉ Societies
welcome (Mon only by arrangement)
Green fees £20
Facilities ⊗ 🍴 💺 ♀ ⛳ 🏠 (Edward McCausland
Hotel ★★57% Europa Hotel, 20 Derby Rd, LONG
EATON ☎(0602) 728481 19rm(14⇥🐾)

Mapperley ☎ (0602) 265611
Central Av, Mapperley Plains (3m NE of city centre off
B684)
Hilly meadowland course but with easy walking.
18 holes, 6283yds, Par 71, SSS 70. Membership 600.

Visitors welcome Societies welcome
Green fees £12.50 per round (£14 WE)
Facilities ⊗ (ex Wed) 🍴 by prior arrangement 💺 💺
♀ ⛳ 🏠 (Richard Daibell
Hotel ★★★★59% Albany Hotel, Saint James's St,
NOTTINGHAM ☎(0602) 470131 139⇥

Nottingham City ☎ (0602) 278021
Bulwell Hall Park (4m NW of city centre off A6002)
A pleasant, municipal parkland course on the city
outskirts.
18 holes, 6218yds, Par 69, SSS 70. Membership 400.

Visitors welcome must contact in advance ☎ Societies
welcome (ex WE)
Green fees £4 (£5 WE)
Facilities ⊗ 🍴 by prior arrangement 💺 💺 ♀ ⛳ 🏠
🍴 (Cyril Jepson
Hotel ★★★★56% Nottingham Moat House, Mansfield
Rd, NOTTINGHAM ☎(0602) 602621 172⇥🐾

Wollaton Park ☎ (0602) 787574
Wollaton Park (2.5m W of city centre off A52)
A pleasant, fairly level course set in a park close to
the centre of Nottingham, with deer. The fairways
are tree-lined. The 525-yard dog-leg 15th is a notable
hole. Stately home - Wollaton Hall - is situated in
the park. Snooker.
*18 holes, 6494yds, Par 71, SSS 71, Course record 65.
Membership 770.*

Visitors welcome must contact in advance Societies
welcome (Tue & Fri only ☎)
Green fees £12 per round (£14.50 WE & BH)
Facilities ⊗ 🏠 🍴 (
Hotel ★★★59% Waltons Hotel, 2 North Road, The
Park, NOTTINGHAM ☎(0602) 475215 13⇥🐾

OXTON
Map 4 A2

Oxton ☎ (0602) 653545
Oaks Ln (1m NW off A6097)
Exposed and very testing, quick-drying heathland
course with easy walking. The par 3 (16th) and par 4
(1st) are notable. Thirty-bay floodlit driving range.
*North Course 18 holes, 5681mtrs, Par 72, SSS 72, Course
record 65. South Course 9 holes, 3193mtrs, Par 37.
Membership 520.*

Visitors welcome Societies welcome (by letter)
Green fees North £10 per wkday (£15 WE & BH);
South £6 per wkday (£7.50 WE & BH)
Facilities ⊗ 🍴 💺 💺 ♀ ⛳ 🏠 🍴 (G C Norton
Hotel ★★★62% Saracen's Head Hotel, Market Place,
SOUTHWELL ☎(0636) 812701 27⇥🐾

RADCLIFFE-ON-TRENT
Map 4 A3

Radcliffe-on-Trent ☎ (06073) 3000
Drewberry Ln, Cropwell Rd (1m SE off A52)
Parkland course with three good finishing holes: 16th
(427 yds) par 4; 17th (180 yds) through spinney, par 3;
18th (331 yds) dog-leg par 4.
18 holes, 6381yds, Par 70, SSS 71. Membership 650.

Visitors welcome (ex Tue) ✉ Societies welcome (Wed
only)
Green fees £20 per day (£25 WE)
Facilities ⛳ 🏠 (
Hotel ★★★59% Waltons Hotel, 2 North Road, The
Park, NOTTINGHAM ☎(0602) 475215 13⇥🐾

SERLBY
Map 5 G8

Serlby Park ☎ (0777) 818268
(E side of village off A638)
Parkland course.
9 holes, 5325yds, Par 66, SSS 66. Membership 300.

Visitors welcome Member must accompany
Green fees Not confirmed
Facilities ♀ (WE & special occ) ⛳ 🏠
Hotel ★★★61% Charnwood Hotel, Sheffield Rd,
BLYTH ☎(0909) 591610 20⇥🐾

We make every effort to provide accurate information, but some details may change after we
go to print.

SUTTON IN ASHFIELD   Map 4 A2

Coxmoor
☎ Mansfield (0623) 557359
Coxmoor Rd (2m SE off
A611)
Undulating moorland
course with easy walking
and excellent views. The
clubhouse is modern with a
well-equipped games room.
The course lies adjacent to
Forestry Commission land
over which there are
several footpaths and
extensive views. Snooker.
18 holes, 6501yds, Par 73, SSS 71. Membership 650.

SCORE CARD: Medal Tees					
Hole	Yds	Par	Hole	Yds	Par
1	438	4	10	161	3
2	185	3	11	352	4
3	493	5	12	389	4
4	300	4	13	535	5
5	414	4	14	328	4
6	487	5	15	300	4
7	136	3	16	533	5
8	390	4	17	195	3
9	355	4	18	510	5
Out	3198	36	In	3303	37
			Totals	6501	73

Visitors welcome must contact in advance Societies welcome (☎)
Green fees Not confirmed
Facilities ⊗ ∭ ⅃ ➤ ♀ ⌂ ⌂ ⌊ David Ridley
Hotel ★★★62% Swallow Hotel, Carter Ln East, SOUTH NORMANTON ☎(0773) 812000 123⇥⋔

WORKSOP   Map 5 G8

Kilton Forest ☎ (0909) 472488
Blyth Rd (1m NE of town centre on B6045)
On the north edge of Sherwood Forest.
*18 holes, 6569yds, Par 73, SSS 72, Course record 69.
Membership 400.*

Visitors welcome (ex Sun & competition days) must
contact in advance Societies welcome (by letter)
Green fees £6 per round (£7 WE)
Facilities ⊗ by prior arrangement ∭ by prior
arrangement ⅃ ➤ ♀ ⌂ ⌂ ⌊ P W Foster
Hotel ★★★60% Ye Olde Bell Hotel, BARNBY MOOR
☎(0777) 705121 55⇥⋔

Lindrick ☎ (0909) 475282
Lindrick Common (3m NW on A57)
Heathland course with some trees and masses of
gorse. Snooker.
18 holes, 6615yds, Par 71, SSS 72. Membership 500.

Visitors welcome (ex Tue or WE) must contact in
advance Societies welcome (ex Tue am & WE)
Green fees summer £30 round/day; winter £20
Facilities ⊗ ∭ by prior arrangement ➤ ♀ ⌂ ⌂
⌐ ⌊
Hotel ★★★60% Ye Olde Bell Hotel, BARNBY MOOR
☎(0777) 705121 55⇥⋔

Worksop ☎ (0909) 472696
Windmill Ln (1.75m S off A620)
Adjacent to Clumber Park this course has a sandy
subsoil and drains well, a valuable asset for winter
golfers. Snooker.
*18 holes, 6651yds, Par 72, SSS 72, Course record 67.
Membership 500.*

Visitors welcome must contact in advance Societies
welcome (by letter)

Green fees £16.50 round (£22.50 WE & BH);£22 day
(wkday)
Facilities ⊗ ∭ ⅃ ➤ (no catering Mon Nov-Mar) ♀
⌂ ⌂ ⌊ John R King
Hotel ★★★60% Ye Olde Bell Hotel, BARNBY MOOR
☎(0777) 705121 55⇥⋔

OXFORDSHIRE

BURFORD   Map 3 J7

Burford ☎ (099382) 2583
Swindon Rd (.5m S off A361)
Created out of open-farmland, this parkland course has
high quality fairways and greens.
18 holes, 6083yds, Par 71, SSS 71. Membership 800.

Visitors welcome must contact in advance Societies
welcome (book in advance)
Green fees Not confirmed
Facilities ⊗ ∭ ⅃ ➤ ♀ ⌂ ⌂ ⌐ ⌊ Norman Allen
Hotel ★★63% Golden Pheasant Hotel, High St,
BURFORD ☎(099382) 3223 12⇥⋔

CHESTERTON   Map 2 B1

Chesterton Country ☎ Bicester (0869) 241204
(.5m W on A4095)
Laid out over one-time farmland. Well-bunkered, and
water hazards increase the difficulty of the course.
Snooker.
*18 holes, 6224yds, Par 71, SSS 70, Course record 68.
Membership 700.*

Visitors welcome must contact in advance WE & BH
only Societies welcome (ex WE & BH deposit required)
Green fees £12 per day (£18 WE & BH)
Facilities ⊗ ∭ ⅃ ➤ ♀ (1200-1700 winter) ⌂ ⌂
⌊ J W Wilkshire
Hotel ★★65% Jersey Arms Hotel, MIDDLETON STONEY
☎(086989) 234 & 505 6⇥ Annexe:10⇥

CHIPPING NORTON   Map 3 K7

Chipping Norton ☎ (0608) 642383
Southcombe (1.5m E on A44)
Pleasant course open to winds.
*18 holes, 6280yds, Par 71, SSS 70, Course record 67.
Membership 825.*

Visitors welcome (WE with M only) must contact in
advance Societies welcome (by letter)
Green fees £18 per weekday
Facilities ⊗ ∭ ⅃ ➤ ♀ ⌂ ⌂ ⌐ ⌊ Bob Gould
Hotel ★★62% Chadlington House Hotel,
CHADLINGTON ☎(060876) 437 11rm(5⇥5⋔)

For an explanation of the symbols and
abbreviations used, see page 33.

FRILFORD

Map 2 A3

Frilford Heath ☎ (0865) 390864
Abingdon (1m N off A338)
There are two, 18-hole heathland courses. Both the
Red and the Green courses are of outstanding
interest and beauty. Heather, pine, birch and, in
particular, a mass of flowering gorse enhance the
terrain. The greens are extensive.
18 holes, 6768yds, Par 73, SSS 73, Course record 65.
Membership 900.

Visitors welcome (restricted WE & BH) must
contact in advance ✉ Societies welcome (Mon, Wed
& Fri only ☎)
Green fees Not confirmed
Facilities ⊗ ⑂ ♨ ♎ ♀ ⚲ 🏠 ⚐ ⅃ Derek Craik
Hotel ★★★61% Abingdon Lodge Hotel, Marcham
Rd, ABINGDON ☎(0235) 553456 63⇥

HENLEY-ON-THAMES

Map 2 C3

Badgemore Park ☎ (0491) 572206
(1m W)
Parkland course with many trees and easy walking.
Squash.
18 holes, 6112yds, Par 69, SSS 69. Membership 890.

Visitors welcome (handicap certificate required) must
contact in advance Societies welcome (by letter)
Green fees £22 per day (£26 WE & BH)
Facilities ♨ ♎ ♀ ⚲ 🏠 ⅃ Mark Wright
Hotel ★★★62% Red Lion Hotel, Hart St, HENLEY-ON-
THAMES ☎(0491) 572161 26rm(22⇥)

Henley ☎ (0491) 575742
Harpsden (1.25m S off A4155)
Undulating parkland course. 6th hole, blind (par 4),
with steep hill.
18 holes, 6329yds, Par 70, SSS 70, Course record 65.
Membership 830.

Visitors welcome (Mon-Fri ex BH, h'cap cert required)
must contact in advance ✉ Societies welcome (☎)
Green fees Not confirmed
Facilities ⊗ ⑂ ♨ ♎ (catering by prior arrangement)
♀ (by prior arrangement) ⚲ 🏠 ⚐ ⅃ Mark Howell
Hotel ★★★62% Red Lion Hotel, Hart St, HENLEY-ON-
THAMES ☎(0491) 572161 26rm(22⇥)

Each golf course entry has a recommended
hotel. For a wider choice of places to stay,
consult *AA Hotels and Restaurants in Britain* or
AA-inspected Bed and Breakfast in Britain.

NUFFIELD

Map 2 C3

Huntercombe
☎ (0491) 641207
(N off A423)
This heathland/woodland
course overlooks the
Oxfordshire plain and has
many attractive and
interesting fairways and
greens. Walking is easy
after the 3rd hole which is a
notable hole. The course is
subject to wind and grass
pot bunkers are interesting
hazards.

SCORE CARD: White Tees					
Hole	Yds	Par	Hole	Yds	Par
1	150	3	10	184	3
2	394	4	11	336	4
3	366	4	12	409	4
4	335	4	13	408	4
5	396	4	14	432	4
6	525	5	15	175	3
7	214	3	16	492	5
8	436	4	17	279	4
9	369	4	18	401	4
Out	3185	35	In	3116	35
			Totals	6301	70

18 holes, 6301yds, Par 70, SSS 70, Course record 64.
Membership 600.

Visitors welcome (after 1000 wkdays, not at WE)
must contact in advance ✉ Societies welcome (by
letter)
Green fees £25 per day
Facilities ⊗ ⑂ ♨ ♎ ♀ ⚲ 🏠 ⚐ ⅃ J B Draycott
Hotel ★★★59% Shillingford Bridge Hotel,
Shillingford, WALLINGFORD ☎(086732) 8567 25⇥

OXFORD

Map 2 B2

North Oxford ☎ (0865) 54415
Banbury Rd (3m N of city centre on A423)
Parkland course with easy walking.
18 holes, 5805yds, Par 67, SSS 67, Course record 64.
Membership 600.

Visitors welcome (Sun am with M only) must contact in
advance Societies welcome (by letter or ☎)
Green fees £20 per day (£25 WE)
Facilities ⊗ ⑂ ♨ ♎ ♀ ⚲ 🏠 ⅃ Bob Harris
Hotel ★★★63% Oxford Moat House, Godstow Rd,
Wolvercote Rbt, OXFORD ☎(0865) 59933 155⇥

Southfield ☎ (0865) 242158
Hill Top Rd (1.5m SE of city centre off B480)
Home of both the City and University Clubs and
well-known to graduates throughout the world. A
challenging course, in varied parkland setting,
providing a real test for players.
18 holes, 5945yds, Par 69, SSS 69. Membership 850.

Visitors welcome (WE only with M) Societies
welcome (by letter)
Green fees £20 per day
Facilities ⊗ ⑂ ♨ ♎ ♀ ⚲ 🏠 ⚐ ⅃ A Rees
Hotel ★★★55% Eastgate Hotel, The High, Merton
St, OXFORD ☎(0865) 248244 43⇥

SHRIVENHAM

Map 2 A3

Shrivenham Park ☎ (0793) 783853
Pennyhooks (.5m NE of town centre)
Parkland course with easy walking. The par 4, 15th is a
difficult dog-leg through woods.
18 holes, 5500yds, Par 68, SSS 68.

▶

Visitors welcome must contact in advance Societies welcome (by letter)
Green fees £12.50 per day; £5 per 9 holes, £7.50 per 18 holes (£15/£6/£10 WE)
Facilities ⊗ ℳ ㏇ ♨ ♀ ♨ 🏠 ⚐ ℓ Roger Male
Hotel ★★★60% Crest Hotel, Oxford Rd, Stratton St Margaret, SWINDON ☎(0793) 831333 94⇨🕯

TADMARTON

Map 3 K7

Tadmarton Heath ☎ Hook Norton (0608) 737278 (1m SW of Lower Tadmarton off B4035)
A mixture of heath and sandy land, the course, which is open to strong winds, incorporates the site of an old Roman encampment. There is an annual open 36-hole scratch competition. The clubhouse is an old farm building with a 'holy well' from which the greens are watered. The 7th is a testing hole over water. Fishing.
18 holes, 5917yds, Par 69, SSS 69, Course record 63. Membership 600.

Visitors welcome (with M only WE, Thu by arrangement) must contact in advance ✉ Societies welcome (☎)
Green fees Not confirmed
Facilities ⊗ ℳ ㏇ ♨ ♀ ♨ 🏠 ⚐ ℓ Les Bond
Hotel ★★64% Olde School Hotel, Church St, BLOXHAM ☎(0295) 720369 11⇨🕯 Annexe:27⇨🕯

SHROPSHIRE

BRIDGNORTH

Map 3 H5

Bridgnorth ☎ (0746) 763315
Stanley Ln (1m N off B4373)
A pleasant course laid-out on meadowland on the bank of the River Severn.
18 holes, 6627yds, Par 73, SSS 72. Membership 550.

Visitors welcome Societies welcome
Green fees Not confirmed
Facilities ⊗ (ex Mon) ℳ (ex Mon) ㏇ (ex Mon) ♨ (ex Mon) ♀ (ex Mon) ♨ 🏠 ℓ
Hotel ★★61% Falcon Hotel, St John St, Lowtown, BRIDGNORTH ☎(0746) 763134 15rm(5⇨7🕯)

CHURCH STRETTON

Map 3 G5

Church Stretton ☎ (0694) 722281
Trevor Hill (NW side of village off B4370)
Moorland course with very fine turf.
18 holes, 5008yds, Par 66, SSS 65, Course record 63. Membership 500.

Visitors welcome (not before 1030, WE & BH) must contact in advance ✉ Societies welcome (☎)
Green fees £10 (£15 WE & BH)
Facilities ⊗ ℳ ㏇ ♨ (catering Apr-Oct) ♀ ♨ 🏠
Hotel ★★★58% Stretton Hall Hotel, All Stretton, CHURCH STRETTON ☎(0694) 723224 13⇨🕯

LILLESHALL

Map 3 H4

Lilleshall Hall ☎ Telford (0952) 603840
Newport (3m SE)
Heavily wooded parkland course.
18 holes, 5906yds, Par 68, SSS 68, Course record 65. Membership 650.

Visitors welcome (with M only WE) must contact in advance Societies welcome (☎)
Green fees £15 (£25 BH & following day)
Facilities ⊗ ℳ by prior arrangement ㏇ ♨ ♀ ♨ 🏠 ℓ
Hotel ★★64% Royal Victoria Hotel, St Mary's St, NEWPORT ☎(0952) 820331 24rm(16⇨7🕯)

LUDLOW

Map 3 G5

Ludlow ☎ (058477) 285
Bromfield (2m N off A49)
A long-established parkland course in the middle of the racecourse. Very flat, quick drying, with little variance between summer and winter play.
18 holes, 6239yds, Par 70, SSS 70. Membership 650.

Visitors welcome (with M only WE) must contact in advance ✉ Societies welcome (by letter)
Green fees £14 per day (£18 WE)
Facilities ⊗ ℳ ㏇ ♨ (no catering Mon) ♀ ♨ 🏠 ℓ G J Farr
Hotel ★★★65% The Feathers at Ludlow, Bull Ring, LUDLOW ☎(0584) 875261 40⇨🕯

MARKET DRAYTON

Map 3 G3

Market Drayton ☎ (0630) 652266
Sutton (1m SW)
Parkland course in quiet, picturesque surroundings providing a good test of golf. Bungalow on course is made available for golfing holidays.
18 holes, 6400yds, Par 71, SSS 70, Course record 69. Membership 450.

Visitors welcome (Sat with M only, Sun no visitors) must contact in advance Societies welcome (☎)
Green fees £15 per day (summer);£15 per round (winter)
Facilities ⊗ ℳ ㏇ ♨ ♀ ♨ 🏠 ℓ Russel Clewes
Hotel ★★52% Corbet Arms, High St, MARKET DRAYTON ☎(0630) 2037 12rm(8⇨2🕯)

MEOLE BRACE

Map 3 G4

Meole Brace ☎ (0743) 64050
(NE side of village off A49)
Pleasant municipal course.
12 holes, 3066yds, Par 43, SSS 42.

Visitors welcome
Green fees Not confirmed
Facilities ♨ 🏠 ⚐ ℓ
Hotel ★★★60% Lion Hotel, Wyle Cop, SHREWSBURY ☎(0743) 53107 59⇨

OSWESTRY   Map 3 F3

Oswestry ☏ Queens Head (069188) 535
Aston Park (2m SE on A5)
Parkland course laid-out on undulating ground.
Snooker.
18 holes, 6038yds, Par 70, SSS 69, Course record 62.
Membership 700.

Visitors welcome (must be M of recognised golf club)
must contact in advance ✉ Societies welcome (Wed &
Fri only ☏)
Green fees £12 per day (£16 WE)
Facilities ⊗ ⅲ � ⅃ ♀ ⌂ ♿ ℓ David Skelton
Hotel ★★★67% Wynnstay Hotel, Church St,
OSWESTRY ☏(0691) 655261 26⇦♦

PANT   Map 3 F3

Llanymynech ☏ Llanymynech (0691) 830983
(.5m SW off A483)
Upland course on the site of an early British
encampment with far-reaching views. The 4th fairway
crosses the Welsh border.
18 holes, 6114yds, Par 70, SSS 69, Course record 65.
Membership 790.

Visitors welcome (with M only after 1630) must contact
in advance Societies welcome (by letter)
Green fees £15 per day; £11 per round (£18/£16.50 WE
& BH)
Facilities ⊗ ⅲ ⅷ ⅃ ♀ ⌂ ♿ ℓ Andrew Griffiths
Hotel ★★★67% Wynnstay Hotel, Church St,
OSWESTRY ☏(0691) 655261 26⇦♦

SHIFNAL   Map 3 H4

Shifnal ☏ Telford (0952) 460330
Decker Hill (1m N off B4379)
Well-wooded parkland course. Walking is easy and an
attractive country mansion serves as the clubhouse.
Snooker.
18 holes, 6260yds, Par 71, SSS 71, Course record 66.
Membership 560.

Visitors welcome (with M only WE & BH) must contact
in advance ✉ Societies welcome (☏)
Green fees £22 per day
Facilities ⊗ ⅲ ⅷ ⅃ ♀ ⌂ ♿ ℓ Justin Flanagan
Hotel ★★★63% Park House Hotel, Silvermere Park,
Park St, SHIFNAL ☏(0952) 460128 54⇦♦

SHREWSBURY   Map 3 G4

Shrewsbury ☏ Bayston Hill (074372) 2976
Condover (4m S off A49)
Parkland course. Snooker.
18 holes, 6212yds, Par 70, SSS 70, Course record 60.
Membership 610.

Visitors welcome must contact in advance ✉ Societies
welcome
Green fees £16 per day; £10 per round (£18 WE)

Facilities ⊗ ⅲ ⅷ ⅃ ♀ ⌂ ♿ ℓ Peter Seal
Hotel ★★★61% Radbrook Hall Hotel, Radbrook Rd,
SHREWSBURY ☏(0743) 236676 28⇦♦

TELFORD   Map 3 H4

Telford Hotel Golf & Country Club ☏ (0952) 585642
Sutton Hill (4m S of town centre off A442)
Parkland course with easy walking. Three lakes and
large sand traps are hazards to the fine greens.
Accommodation. Indoor-heated swimming pool, squash,
snooker and sauna.
18 holes, 6766yds, Par 72, SSS 72, Course record 62.
Membership 500.

Visitors welcome (handicap certificate required) must
contact in advance ✉ Societies welcome (by letter)
Green fees £20 per day (£25 WE & BH)
Facilities ⊗ ⅲ ⅷ ⅃ ♀ ⌂ ♿ ♔ ℓ Steve Marr
Hotel ★★65% Charlton Arms Hotel, Wellington,
TELFORD ☏(0952) 251351 26rm(22⇦1♦)

WELLINGTON   Map 3 G4

Wrekin ☏ Telford (0952) 244032
Ercall Woods (1.25m S off B5061)
Downland course with some hard walking but
rewarding views.
18 holes, 5699yds, Par 66, SSS 67, Course record 65.
Membership 700.

Visitors welcome must contact in advance Societies
welcome (☏)
Green fees £12 per day (£20 WE & BH)
Facilities ⊗ ⅲ ⅷ ⅃ (no catering on Mon) ♀ ⌂ ⌂
ℓ K Housden
Hotel ★★★63% Buckatree Hall Hotel, Wellington,
TELFORD ☏(0952) 641821 37⇦♦

WESTON-UNDER-REDCASTLE   Map 3 G3

Hawkstone Park Hotel ☏ (093924) 611
(N side of village .75m E of A49)
Two courses in a beautiful setting, both with
natural hazards and good views. Hawkstone Course
has been established for over 50 years and enjoys a
superb setting whilst the Weston course has
developed well over the last 10 years.
Accommodation.
18 holes, 6203yds, Par 72, SSS 70. Membership 450.

Visitors welcome (☏ for details)
Green fees Not confirmed
Facilities ⅃ ⌂ ♔ ℓ
Hotel ★★★53% Hawkstone Park Hotel, WESTON
☏(093924) 611 43⇦♦ Annexe:16⇦

This guide is updated annually – make sure you
use an up-to-date edition.

WHITCHURCH

Map 3 G3

Hill Valley ☎ (0948) 3584
Terrick Rd (1m N)
This parkland course, opened in 1975, was designed to championship standard by Peter Alliss and Dave Thomas. The hilly terrain is enhanced by many glorious views. There are natural water hazards on seven holes. Accommodation. Tennis, squash, snooker and sauna.
Championship 18 holes, 6050yds, Par 72, SSS 69. Northern 9 holes, 5106yds, Par 68, SSS 66. Par 3 9 holes, 793yds, Par 27. Membership 400.

SCORE CARD: White Tees					
Hole	Yds	Par	Hole	Yds	Par
1	490	5	10	380	4
2	404	4	11	388	4
3	403	4	12	339	4
4	181	3	13	449	4
5	518	5	14	346	4
6	183	3	15	157	3
7	491	5	16	489	5
8	403	4	17	169	3
9	349	4	18	378	4
Out	3422	37	In	3095	35
			Totals	6517	72

Visitors welcome must contact in advance Societies welcome (deposit required)
Green fees Package :9 + 18 holes coffee, soup, sandwiches & evening meal £25 (£30 WE)
Facilities ⊗ �𝄞 ⯊ 🍺 ♀ 🛆 🏠 ♬ A R Minshall
Hotel ★★★62% Terrick Hall Country Hotel, Hill Valley, WHITCHURCH ☎(0948) 3031 10⊶ Annexe:7⊶♜

SOMERSET

BURNHAM-ON-SEA

Map 1 G4

Brean ☎ Brean Down (0278) 751570
Coast Rd, Brean (6m N on coast rd)
Moorland/meadowland course with water hazards. Facilities of 'Brean Leisure Park' adjoining.
18 holes, 5200yds, Par 69, SSS 67. Membership 550.

Visitors welcome (ex Sat & Sun) ✉ Societies welcome (wkdays only ☎)
Green fees £10 per round
Facilities ⯊ 🍺 ♀ 🛆 🏠 ♬ ♬ Malcolm Coombes
Hotel ★★62% Battleborough Grange Country Hotel, Bristol Rd, BRENT KNOLL ☎(0278) 760208 18rm(8⊶6♜)

Burnham & Berrow
☎ Burham-on-Sea (0278) 783137
St Christopher's Way (N side of town off B3140)
Links championship course with large sandhills. Accommodation.
18 holes, 6327yds, Par 71, SSS 72, Course record 68 or 9 holes, 6550yds, Par 72. Membership 940.

Visitors welcome (handicap certificate required) must contact in advance Societies welcome (members of a golf club only)
Green fees £30 per day (£40 WE & BH); 9 hole £7
Facilities ⊗ �𝄞 ⯊ 🍺 (catering 11am-6pm or by prior arrangement) ♀ 🛆 🏠 ♬ ♬ Nigel Blake
Hotel ★★62% Battleborough Grange Country Hotel, Bristol Rd, BRENT KNOLL ☎(0278) 760208 18rm(8⊶6♜)

CHARD

Map 1 G5

Windwhistle Golf, Squash & Country Club ☎ (046030) 231
Cricket St Thomas (3m E on A30)
Parkland course at 735 ft above sea level with outstanding views of the Bristol Channel and South Wales. Squash.
West Course 18 holes, 6442yds. West Course 9 holes. Membership 450.

Visitors welcome (jeans & denims not acceptable) must contact in advance Societies welcome (☎)
Green fees £12 (£15 per round WE)
Facilities ⊗ �𝄞 ⯊ 🍺 ♀ 🛆 🏠 ♬
Hotel ★★60% Shrubbery Hotel, ILMINSTER ☎(0460) 52108 12⊶

ENMORE

Map 1 G4

Enmore Park ☎ Spaxton (0278) 67481 (1m E)
Parkland course on foothills of Quantocks. Wooded countryside and views of Quantocks and Mendips. 1st and 10th are testing holes.
18 holes, 6423yds, Par 71, SSS 71. Membership 730.

Visitors welcome (restricted competition days) Societies welcome (by letter)
Green fees £16 per day (£20 WE)
Facilities ⊗ �𝄞 ⯊ 🍺 ♀ (restricted at WE) 🛆 🏠 ♬ ♬
Hotel ★★★68% Walnut Tree Inn, North Petherton, BRIDGWATER ☎(0278) 662255 28⊶

GURNEY SLADE

Map 1 H3

Mendip ☎ Oakhill (0749) 840570 (1.5m S off A37)
Undulating downland course offers an interesting test of golf on superb fairways.
18 holes, 5958yds, Par 69, SSS 69, Course record 65. Membership 800.

Visitors welcome (handicap certificate required) must contact in advance Societies welcome (☎)
Green fees £15 (£30 WE)
Facilities ⊗ �𝄞 ⯊ 🍺 ♀ 🛆 🏠 ♬ ♬ Ron Lee
Hotel ★★55% Crown Hotel, Market Place, WELLS ☎(0749) 73457 15⊶♜

Each golf course entry has a recommended hotel. For a wider choice of places to stay, consult *AA Hotels and Restaurants in Britain* or *AA-inspected Bed and Breakfast in Britain.*

MINEHEAD

Map 1 F4

Minehead & West Somerset ☎ (0643) 702057
The Warren (E side of town centre)
Flat seaside links, very exposed to wind, with good turf set on a shingle bank. The last five holes adjacent to the beach are testing. The 215-yard 18th is wedged between the beach and the club buildings and provides a good finish.
18 holes, 6228yds, Par 71, SSS 71. Membership 475.

SCORE CARD: White Tees					
Hole	Yds	Par	Hole	Yds	Par
1	276	4	10	133	3
2	379	4	11	493	5
3	384	4	12	424	4
4	218	3	13	354	4
5	476	5	14	149	3
6	310	4	15	310	4
7	541	5	16	425	4
8	392	4	17	332	4
9	417	4	18	215	3
Out	3393	37	In	2835	34
			Totals	6228	71

Visitors welcome Societies welcome (by letter)
Green fees £17 per day (£20 WE & BH)
Facilities ⊗ ⅲ ᒻ ⬤ ♀ ⚲ 🏠 ⊣ℾ ⊏ I M Read
Hotel ★★★67% Northfield Hotel, Northfield Rd, MINEHEAD ☎(0643) 705155 24⇨🏠

TAUNTON

Map 1 G4

Taunton & Pickeridge ☎ (082342) 537
Corfe (4m S off B3170)
Downland course with extensive views. Snooker.
18 holes, 5927yds, Par 69, SSS 68, Course record 66. Membership 600.

Visitors welcome must contact in advance ⊠ Societies welcome (☎)
Green fees Not confirmed
Facilities ⊗ ⅲ ᒻ ⬤ ♀ ⚲ 🏠 ⊏ Graham Glew
Hotel ★★★56% County Hotel, East St, TAUNTON ☎(0823) 337651 67⇨

Vivary Park Municipal ☎ (0823) 333875
Fons George (S side of town centre off A38)
A parkland course, tight and narrow with ponds. Tennis, riding stables.
18 holes, 4620yds, Par 63, SSS 63.

Visitors welcome must contact in advance Societies welcome (by letter)
Green fees Not confirmed
Facilities ⚲ 🏠 ⊣ℾ ⊏
Hotel ★★61% Falcon Hotel, Henlade, TAUNTON ☎(0823) 442502 11⇨🏠

WELLS

Map 1 H4

Wells (Somerset) ☎ (0749) 75005
East Horrington Rd (1.5m E off B3139)
Beautiful wooded course. The prevailing SW wind complicates the 445-yd, 3rd.
18 holes, 5354yds, Par 67, SSS 66, Course record 64. Membership 790.

Visitors welcome (after 0930 & handicap cert needed WE) Societies welcome (☎)
Green fees £13.50 per day (£17.50 WE)
Facilities ⊗ ⅲ ᒻ (ex Sun) ⬤ ♀ ⚲ 🏠 ⊣ℾ ⊏ Andrew England
Hotel ★★★62% Swan Hotel, Sadler St, WELLS ☎(0749) 78877 32⇨🏠

YEOVIL

Map 1 H5

Yeovil ☎ (0935) 22965
Sherborne Rd (1m E on A30)
The opener lies by the River Yeo before the gentle climb to high downs with good views. The outstanding 14th and 15th holes present a challenge, being below the player with a deep railway cutting on the left of the green. Snooker.
18 holes, 6144yds, Par 72, SSS 69, Course record 66. Membership 720.

SCORE CARD: White Tees					
Hole	Yds	Par	Hole	Yds	Par
1	324	4	10	159	3
2	158	3	11	523	5
3	405	4	12	288	4
4	333	4	13	136	3
5	518	5	14	469	5
6	382	4	15	232	3
7	347	4	16	497	5
8	388	4	17	310	4
9	316	4	18	359	4
Out	3171	36	In	2973	36
			Totals	6144	72

Visitors welcome must contact in advance ⊠ Societies welcome (wkdays only)
Green fees Not confirmed
Facilities ⊗ ⅲ ᒻ ⬤ ♀ ⚲ 🏠 ⊣ℾ ⊏ Geoff Kite
Hotel ★★★65% Manor Crest Hotel, Hendford, YEOVIL ☎(0935) 23116 20⇨🏠 Annexe:21⇨🏠

SOUTH YORKSHIRE

BARNSLEY Map 5 F7

Barnsley ☎ (0226) 382856
Wakefield Rd, Staincross (3m N on A61)
Undulating meadowland course with easy walking
apart from last 4 holes. Testing 8th and 18th holes.
18 holes, 6042yds, Par 69, SSS 69, Course record 64.
Membership 800.

Visitors welcome (Sat 0700-1530, Sun 0700-1200) must
contact in advance Societies welcome (☎ 1 wk prior
notice)
Green fees £5 per day (£6 WE)
Facilities ⊗ ⍟ � � ♀ △ 🏠 ⵂ (M Melling
Hotel ★50% Royal Hotel, Church St, BARNSLEY
☎(0226) 203658 17rm(1⇌)

BAWTRY Map 5 G7

Austerfield Park ☎ Doncaster (0302) 710841
Cross Ln (2m NE on A640)
Long moorland course with postage stamp 8th and
testing 618 yd-7th. Driving range attached.
18 holes, 6457yds, Par 73, SSS 73, Course record 71.
Membership 600.

Visitors welcome Societies welcome (☎)
Green fees £11 per day (£15 WE & BH)
Facilities ⊗ ⍟ � � ♀ △ 🏠 ⵂ (Jason Taylor
Hotel ★★★66% Crown Hotel & Posting House, High
Street, BAWTRY ☎Doncaster (0302) 710341 57⇌

CONISBROUGH Map 5 G7

Crookhill Park Municipal ☎ (0709) 862979
(1.5m SE on B6094)
A rolling parkland course.
18 holes, 5846yds, Par 70, SSS 68.

Visitors welcome (restricted WE before 0900) Societies
welcome
Green fees Not confirmed
Facilities ♀ △ 🏠 ⵂ
Hotel ★★★55% Danum Swallow Hotel, High St,
DONCASTER ☎(0302) 342261 66⇌

DONCASTER Map 5 G7

Doncaster ☎ (0302) 868316
278 Bawtry Rd, Bessacarr (5m SE on A638)
Pleasant, undulating heathland course with wooded
surroundings. Quick drying, ideal autumn, winter and
spring.
18 holes, 6230yds, Par 69, SSS 70, Course record 66.
Membership 600.

Visitors welcome (not before 1100 WE & BH) Societies
welcome (☎)
Green fees Not confirmed
Facilities ⊗ ⍟ � � ♀ △ 🏠 ⵂ (S Fox
Hotel ★★★64% Mount Pleasant Hotel, Great North
Rd, ROSSINGTON ☎(0302) 868696 & 868219
38rm(23⇌10ℝ)

Doncaster Town Moor ☎ (0302) 535286
The Bell Vue Club, Belle Vue (1.5m E, at racecourse, on
A638)
Easy walking, but testing, heathland course with good
true greens. Friendly club. Notable hole is 11th (par 4),
474 yds.
18 holes, 6112yds, Par 69, SSS 69, Course record 63.
Membership 500.

Visitors welcome (ex Sun am) Societies welcome (☎)
Green fees £10 (£12 WE & BH)
Facilities ⊗ � � ♀ △ 🏠 ⵂ (Steve Poole
Hotel ★★★55% Danum Swallow Hotel, High St,
DONCASTER ☎(0302) 342261 66⇌ℝ

Wheatley ☎ (0302) 831655
Armthorpe Rd (NE side of town centre off A18)
Fairly flat, well-bunkered, lake-holed, parkland course.
18 holes, 6169yds, Par 70, SSS 69. Membership 600.

Visitors welcome must contact in advance ✉ Societies
welcome (☎)
Green fees Not confirmed
Facilities ⊗ ⍟ � � ♀ △ 🏠 (T C Parkinson
Hotel ★★★64% Mount Pleasant Hotel, Great North
Rd, ROSSINGTON ☎(0302) 868696 & 868219
38rm(23⇌10ℝ)

HICKLETON Map 5 G7

Hickleton ☎ Rotherham (0709) 895170
(.5m W on B6411)
Undulating parkland course with stream running
through, designed by Neil Coles and Brian Huggett.
18 holes, 6231yds, Par 71, SSS 70. Membership 500.

Visitors welcome (ex 1000-1100 Sat & after 1430 WE)
must contact in advance Societies welcome (☎)
Green fees £15 per day (£20 WE & BH)
Facilities ⊗ ⍟ � � (no catering Mon) ♀ △ 🏠
(Paul Shepherd
Hotel ★★★55% Danum Swallow Hotel, High St,
DONCASTER ☎(0302) 342261 66⇌ℝ

HIGH GREEN Map 5 F7

Tankersley Park ☎ Sheffield (0742) 468247
(1m NE)
Parkland course, hilly, windy, with good views.
18 holes, 6212yds, Par 70, SSS 70, Course record 66.
Membership 505.

Visitors welcome (with M at WE) must contact in
advance Societies welcome (by letter)
Green fees £17 per day ; £14 per round
Facilities ⊗ ⍟ � � ♀ △ 🏠 (I Kirk
Hotel ★★69% Rutland Hotel, 452 Glossop Rd,
Broomhill, SHEFFIELD ☎(0742) 664411 73rm(68⇌1ℝ)
Annexe:17⇌ℝ

Opening times of bar and catering facilities vary
from place to place – it is wise to check in
advance of your visit.

RAWMARSH
Map 5 F7

Wath ☎ (0709) 878677
Abdy (2.5m N off A633)
Parkland course, not easy in spite of short length; 17th
hole a difficult 240 yds with narrow driving area.
18 holes, 5776yds, Par 68, SSS 68. Membership 600.

Visitors welcome (with M only WE) must contact in
advance ✉ Societies welcome (☎)
Green fees £10 per day/round
Facilities ⊗ (not WE) ⬛ ⬛ ⬛ ♀ △ 🏠 (Chris
Bassett
Hotel ★★69% Brentwood Hotel, Moorgate Rd,
ROTHERHAM ☎(0709) 382772 37rm(32⇨⬛)
Annexe:10⇨⬛

ROTHERHAM
Map 5 F7

Grange Park ☎ (0709) 558884
Upper Wortley Rd (3m NW off A629)
Parkland/meadowland course, with panoramic views
especially from the back nine. The golf is testing,
particularly at the 1st, 4th and 18th holes (par 4), and
8th, 12th and 15th (par 5).
18 holes, 6461yds, Par 71, SSS 70. Membership 325.

Visitors welcome
Green fees Not confirmed
Facilities ⊗ (ex Mon) ⬛ (ex Mon) ⬛ ♀ △ 🏠 ⬛
(Eric Clark
Hotel ★★69% Brentwood Hotel, Moorgate Rd,
ROTHERHAM ☎(0709) 382772 37rm(32⇨⬛)
Annexe:10⇨⬛

Phoenix ☎ (0709) 363864
Pavilion Ln, Brinsworth (SW side of town centre off
A630)
Undulating meadowland course with variable wind.
Tennis (hardcourt), squash, snooker.
*18 holes, 6145yds, Par 71, SSS 69, Course record 66.
Membership 750.*

Visitors welcome Societies welcome (by letter)
Green fees £12 per day (£16 WE & BH)
Facilities ⊗ ⬛ by prior arrangement ⬛ by prior
arrangement ⬛ ♀ △ 🏠 ⬛ (Andrew Limb
Hotel ★★69% Brentwood Hotel, Moorgate Rd,
ROTHERHAM ☎(0709) 382772 37rm(32⇨⬛)
Annexe:10⇨⬛

Rotherham Golf Club Ltd ☎ (0709) 850812
Thrybergh Park, Thrybergh (3.5m E on A630)
Parkland course with easy walking along tree-lined
fairways. Snooker and gymnasium.
*18 holes, 6324yds, Par 70, SSS 70, Course record 66.
Membership 400.*

Visitors welcome must contact in advance Societies
welcome (☎ or letter)
Green fees £20 per day (£25 WE & BH)
Facilities ⊗ ⬛ ⬛ ⬛ ♀ △ 🏠 (Simon Thornhill

Hotel ★★69% Brentwood Hotel, Moorgate Rd,
ROTHERHAM ☎(0709) 382772 37rm(32⇨⬛)
Annexe:10⇨⬛

Sitwell Park ☎ (0709) 541046
Shrogs Wood Rd
Parkland course with easy walking.
*18 holes, 6203yds, Par 71, SSS 70, Course record 67.
Membership 500.*

Visitors welcome must contact in advance Societies
welcome (☎ or letter)
Green fees £18 per day; £14 per round (£20/£16 WE &
BH)
Facilities ⊗ ⬛ by prior arrangement ⬛ ⬛ ♀ △ 🏠
(N J Taylor
Hotel ★★69% Brentwood Hotel, Moorgate Rd,
ROTHERHAM ☎(0709) 382772 37rm(32⇨⬛)
Annexe:10⇨⬛

SHEFFIELD
Map 5 F8

Abbeydale ☎ (0742) 360743
Twentywell Ln, Dore (4m SW of city centre off A621)
Parkland course, well-kept, wooded. Testing hole; 12th,
par 3. Snooker.
*18 holes, 6410yds, Par 72, SSS 71, Course record 69.
Membership 750.*

Visitors welcome (restricted Wed 1000-1330) must
contact in advance (☎)
Green fees Not confirmed
Facilities ⊗ ⬛ ⬛ ⬛ ♀ △ 🏠 (Stephen Cooper
Hotel ★★★64% Hallam Tower Post House Hotel,
Manchester Rd, Broomhill, SHEFFIELD ☎(0742) 670067
135⇨⬛

Beauchief Municipal ☎ (0742) 367274
Abbey Ln (4m SW of city centre off A621)
Municipal course with natural water hazards. The
rolling land looks west to the Pennines and a 12th-
century abbey adorns the course.
*18 holes, 5452yds, Par 67, SSS 66, Course record 63.
Membership 350.*

Visitors welcome must contact in advance Societies
welcome (by letter)
Green fees £5.50 per day (concessions for pensioners)
Facilities ⊗ ⬛ ⬛ (cafe closed Tue) ♀ (ex Tue) △ 🏠
⬛ (Brian English
Hotel ★★53% Manor Hotel, 10 High St, DRONFIELD
☎(0246) 413971 10⇨⬛

Birley Wood ☎ (0742) 647262
Birley Ln (4.5m SE of city centre off A621)
Undulating meadowland course with well-varied
features, easy walking and good views. Practice range
and green.
*18 holes, 5452yds, Par 68, SSS 67, Course record 61.
Membership 100.*

Visitors welcome Societies welcome (by letter)
Green fees £6 for 18 holes, £3 for 9 holes

▶

Facilities ⛏ 🏠 ⚐ (Peter Ball
Hotel ★★★★53% Grosvenor House Hotel, Charter Square, SHEFFIELD ☎(0742) 720041 103⇨

Concord Park ☎ (0742) 456806
Shiregreen Ln (3.5m N of city centre on B6086 off A6135)
Hilly, municipal parkland course with some fairways wood-flanked, good views, often windy.
18 holes, 4321yds, Par 65, SSS 62, Course record 61.
Membership 170.

Visitors welcome
Green fees £5 per round
Facilities ⛏ ⚐
Hotel ★★★64% Hallam Tower Post House Hotel, Manchester Rd, Broomhill, SHEFFIELD ☎(0742) 670067 135⇨🐾

Dore & Totley ☎ (0742) 360492
Bradway Rd, Bradway (7m S of city centre on B6054 off A61)
Flat parkland course. Snooker.
18 holes, 6265yds, Par 70, SSS 70. Membership 580.

Visitors welcome (ex Wed; before 0930 & 1200-1430) must contact in advance ✉ Societies welcome (by letter)
Green fees £20 per day; £17 per round
Facilities ⊗ ⅲ ᴸ ⬛ (no catering on Mon) ♀ (ex Mon) ⛏ 🏠 ⚐ (Mark Pearson
Hotel ★★★64% Hallam Tower Post House Hotel, Manchester Rd, Broomhill, SHEFFIELD ☎(0742) 670067 135⇨🐾

Hallamshire ☎ (0742) 302153
Redmires Rd, Sandygate (3m W of city centre off A57)
Situated on a shelf of land at a height of 850 ft.
Magnificent view to the west. Moorland turf. Good natural drainage. Snooker.
18 holes, 6396yds, Par 71, SSS 71, Course record 63.
Membership 550.

Visitors welcome Societies welcome (☎)
Green fees £25 per day (£30 WE & BH)
Facilities ♀ ⛏ 🏠 ⚐ (
Hotel ★★★64% Hallam Tower Post House Hotel, Manchester Rd, Broomhill, SHEFFIELD ☎(0742) 670067 135⇨🐾

Hillsborough ☎ (0742) 343608
Worrall Rd (3m NW of city centre off A616)
Beautiful moorland/woodland course 500 ft above sea-level, reasonable walking.
18 holes, 6204yards, Par 71, SSS 70. Membership 500.

Visitors welcome (restricted WE) must contact in advance ✉ Societies welcome (by letter)
Green fees Not confirmed
Facilities ⊗ by prior arrangement ⅲ by prior arrangement ᴸ ⬛ ♀ ⛏ 🏠 (Graham Walker
Hotel ★★69% Rutland Hotel, 452 Glossop Rd, Broomhill, SHEFFIELD ☎(0742) 664411 73rm(68⇨1🐾)
Annexe:17⇨🐾

Lees Hall ☎ (0742) 554402
Hemsworth Rd, Norton (3.5m S of city centre off A6102)
Parkland/meadowland course with panoramic view of city. Snooker.
18 holes, 6137yds, Par 71, SSS 69, Course record 63.
Membership 500.

Visitors welcome (restricted Wed) Societies welcome (by letter)
Green fees £16 per day (£25 WE)
Facilities ⊗ ⅲ ᴸ ⬛ (no catering on Tue) ♀ ⛏ 🏠 ⚐ (J Ray Wilkinson
Hotel ★★★64% Hallam Tower Post House Hotel, Manchester Rd, Broomhill, SHEFFIELD ☎(0742) 670067 135⇨🐾

Tinsley Park Municipal Golf ☎ (0742) 560237
High Hazels Park (4m E of city centre off A630)
Wooded course.
18 holes, 6000yds, Par 69, SSS 69. Membership 475.

Visitors welcome
Green fees Not confirmed
Facilities ♀ ⛏ 🏠 ⚐
Hotel ★★★★53% Grosvenor House Hotel, Charter Square, SHEFFIELD ☎(0742) 720041 103⇨

SILKSTONE
Map 5 F7

Silkstone ☎ Barnsley (0226) 790328
Field Head, Elmhurst Ln (1m E off A628)
Parkland/downland course, fine views over the Pennines. Testing golf. Snooker.
18 holes, 6078yds, Par 70, SSS 70. Membership 450.

Visitors welcome (with M only WE) Societies welcome (by letter)
Green fees £10 per day/round
Facilities ⊗ ⅲ ᴸ ⬛ ♀ ⛏ 🏠 (Kevin Guy
Hotel ★★★66% Ardsley Moat House, Doncaster Rd, Ardsley, BARNSLEY ☎(0226) 289401 73⇨🐾

STOCKSBRIDGE
Map 5 F7

Stocksbridge & District ☎ Sheffield (0742) 882003
30 Royd Ln, Townend (S side of town centre)
Hilly moorland course.
18 holes, 5200yds, Par 66, SSS 65, Course record 61.
Membership 450.

Visitors welcome Societies welcome (apply to secretary)
Green fees £10 per day (£15 WE & BH)
Facilities ⊗ ᴸ (lunch time) ⬛ ♀ ⛏
Hotel ★★★64% Hallam Tower Post House Hotel, Manchester Rd, Broomhill, SHEFFIELD ☎(0742) 670067 135⇨🐾

WORTLEY
Map 5 F7

Wortley ☎ Sheffield (0742) 885294
Hermit Hill Ln (.5m NE of village off A629)
Well-wooded, parkland course sheltered from prevailing wind, undulating.
18 holes, 5983yds, Par 68, SSS 69. Membership 300.

Visitors welcome must contact in advance ⊠ Societies welcome (Wed & Fri only)
Green fees £14 per day/round (£20 WE & BH)
Facilities ⊗ by prior arrangement ⅲ by prior arrangement 🔼 💺 ♀ 🔼 🏠 ⅎ ⎰ J Tilson
Hotel ★★★64% Hallam Tower Post House Hotel, Manchester Rd, Broomhill, SHEFFIELD ☎(0742) 670067 135⇆🏠

STAFFORDSHIRE

BROCTON   Map 3 H4

Brocton Hall ☎ (0785) 661901
(NW side of village off A34)
Parkland course undulating in places, easy walking. Snooker.
18 holes, 6095yds, Par 69, SSS 69. Membership 750.

Visitors welcome (ex competition days) must contact in advance Societies welcome (☎)
Green fees £20 per day (£22 WE & BH)
Facilities ⊗ ⅲ 🔼 💺 (all catering by prior arrangement) ♀ 🔼 🏠 ⅎ ⎰ R G Johnson
Hotel ★★65% Garth Hotel, Wolverhampton Rd, Moss Pit, STAFFORD ☎(0785) 56124 60⇆🏠

BURTON-UPON-TRENT   Map 3 J3

Branston ☎ (0283) 43207
Burton Rd, Branston (1.5m SW on A5121)
Adjacent to River Trent on undulating ground with natural water hazards.
18 holes, 6480yds, Par 72, SSS 71. Membership 600.

Visitors welcome (with M only WE) must contact in advance Societies welcome (by letter)
Green fees £8 per day (£10 WE)
Facilities ⊗ ⅲ 🔼 💺 ♀ 🔼 🏠 ⅎ ⎰ S D Warner
Hotel ★★★63% Riverside Inn, Riverside Dr, Branston, BURTON UPON TRENT ☎(0283) 511234 21⇆

Burton-upon-Trent ☎ (0283) 44551
43 Ashby Rd East (2m E on A50)
Parkland course.
18 holes, 6555yds, Par 71, SSS 71. Membership 420.

Visitors welcome
Green fees Not confirmed
Facilities ♀ 🔼 🏠 ⅎ ⎰
Hotel ★★★52% Newton Park Hotel, NEWTON SOLNEY ☎(0283) 703568 46⇆

ENVILLE   Map 3 H5

Enville ☎ Kinver (0384) 872074
Highgate Common (2m NE)
Easy walking on two fairly flat parkland/moorland courses - the 'Highgate' and the 'Lodge'.
Highgate 18 holes, 6541yds, Par 72, SSS 72, Course record 68. Lodge 18 holes, 6207yds, Par 72, SSS 72, Course record 68. Membership 900.

Visitors welcome (WE with M only) must contact in advance ⊠ Societies welcome (by letter)
Green fees £20 per round; £25 per 27 holes; £30 per 36 holes
Facilities ⊗ ⅲ 🔼 💺 by prior arrangement ♀ 🔼 🏠 ⎰ Sean Power
Hotel ★★65% Talbot Hotel, High St, STOURBRIDGE ☎(0384) 394350 25rm(13⇆7🏠)

HAZELSLADE   Map 3 J4

Beau Desert ☎ Hednesford (0543) 422626
(.5m NE of village)
Woodland course.
18 holes, 6300yds, Par 70, SSS 71, Course record 64. Membership 500.

Visitors welcome (restricted WE) must contact in advance ⊠ Societies welcome (by letter)
Green fees £25 per day (£37 WE)
Facilities ⊗ ⅲ 🔼 💺 ♀ 🔼 🏠 ⎰ Barrie Stevens
Hotel ★★★59% Roman Way Hotel, Watling St, Hatherton, CANNOCK ☎(0543) 572121 56⇆🏠

HIMLEY   Map 3 H5

Himley Hall Golf Centre
☎ Wolverhampton (0902) 895207
Log Cabin, Himley Hall Park (.5m E on B4176)
Parkland course set in 70 acres, with lovely views. Large practice area including a pitch-and-putt.
9 holes, 3145yds, Par 36, SSS 71. Membership 140.

Visitors welcome (☎ at WE)
Green fees £4per round (£4.50 WE) (18 holes)
Facilities 🔼 💺 🏠
Hotel ★★★66% Himley Country Club & Hotel, School Rd, HIMLEY ☎(0902) 896716 76⇆🏠

LEEK   Map 3 J2

Leek ☎ (0538) 384779
Birchall (.75m S on A520)
Undulating, challenging moorland course. Snooker.
18 holes, 6240yds, Par 70, SSS 70, Course record 63. Membership 750.

Visitors welcome (before 1500) must contact in advance ⊠ Societies welcome (☎)
Green fees £20 per day (£25 WE & BH)
Facilities ⊗ ⅲ 🔼 💺 ♀ 🔼 🏠 ⎰ Peter A Stubbs
Hotel ★★★67% Stakis Grand Hotel, 66 Trinity St, Hanley, STOKE-ON-TRENT ☎(0782) 202361 128⇆🏠

Opening times of bar and catering facilities vary from place to place – it is wise to check in advance of your visit.

LICHFIELD

Map 3 J4

Whittington Barracks ☎ (0543) 432317
Tamworth Rd (2.5m SE on A51)
18 magnificent holes winding their way through
heathland and trees, presenting a good test for the
serious golfer. Leaving the fairway can be severely
punished. The dog-legs are most tempting, inviting
the golfer to chance his arm. Local knowledge is a
definite advantage. Clear views of the famous three
spires of Lichfield Cathedral. Snooker.
18 holes, 6457yds, Par 70, SSS 71. Membership 750.

Visitors welcome (with M only WE) must contact in
advance ✉ Societies welcome (☎)
Green fees £18 (£20 winter)
Facilities ⊗ ⫟ by prior arrangement ⮢ ⬤ ♀ △
🏠 ⫪ (Adrian Sadler
Hotel ★★★59% George Hotel, Bird St, LICHFIELD
☎(0543) 414822 38⇔⋔

NEWCASTLE-UNDER-LYME

Map 3 H3

Newcastle Municipal ☎ (0782) 627596
Keele Rd (2m W on A525)
An open course on the side of a hill without any mature
trees.
18 holes, 6302yds, Par 72, SSS 70. Membership 195.

Visitors welcome
Green fees Not confirmed
Facilities △ 🏠 ⫪
Hotel ★★★62% Clayton Lodge, Clayton Rd,
NEWCASTLE-UNDER-LYME ☎(0782) 613093 50⇔⋔

Newcastle-Under-Lyme ☎ (0782) 617006
Whitmore Rd (1m SW on A53)
Parkland course.
18 holes, 6229yds, Par 72, SSS 71. Membership 550.

Visitors welcome (h'cap cert required, with M only
WE) must contact in advance Societies welcome (Mon &
Wed only ☎)
Green fees £20 per day
Facilities ⊗ ⮢ ⬤ ♀ △ 🏠 ⫪ (Paul Symonds
Hotel ★★★62% Clayton Lodge, Clayton Rd,
NEWCASTLE-UNDER-LYME ☎(0782) 613093 50⇔⋔

ONNELEY

Map 3 H3

Onneley ☎ Stoke-on-Trent (0782) 750577
(2m from Woore on A525)
A tight, undulating, picturesque meadowland course.
*9 holes, 5584yds, Par 67, SSS 70, Course record 67.
Membership 375.*

Visitors welcome (ex WE & BH) Societies welcome (by
letter)
Green fees £10 per round
Facilities ⮢ ⬤ (Tue-Fri evening only) ♀ (Tue-Fri pm
only) △
Hotel ★★★58% Crewe Arms Hotel, Nantwich Rd,
CREWE ☎(0270) 213204 53⇔⋔

PATTINGHAM

Map 3 H4

Patshull Park Hotel Golf & Country Club
☎ Burnhill Green (0902) 700342
(off A464)
Picturesque woodland course. Accommodation, indoor-
heated swimming pool, fishing, snooker, sauna, solarium
and gymnasium. Clay shooting and horse riding by
arrangement.
*18 holes, 6412yds, Par 72, SSS 71, Course record 66.
Membership 500.*

Visitors welcome (h'cap preferred) must contact in
advance Societies welcome (☎ or by letter)
Green fees £20 per round ; £30 per day (£25/£35 WE &
BH)
Facilities ⊗ ⫟ ⮢ ⬤ ♀ △ 🏠 ⫪ (Duncan J
McDowall
Hotel ★★★⮢68% Old Vicarage Hotel, WORFIELD
☎(07464) 497 11⇔⋔ Annexe:4⇔⋔

STAFFORD

Map 3 H4

Stafford Castle ☎ (0785) 223821
Newport Rd (SW side of town centre off A518)
Meadowland course.
*9 holes, 6073yds, Par 71, SSS 69, Course record 70.
Membership 400.*

Visitors welcome (restricted WE am) Societies welcome
(wkdays only ☎)
Green fees £10 per day (£14 WE & BH, handicap
certificate required)
Facilities ⊗ ⫟ by prior arrangement ⮢ by prior
arrangement ⬤ (early evenings) ♀ △ 🏠
Hotel ★★63% Swan Hotel, Greengate St, STAFFORD
☎(0785) 58142 32⇔⋔

STOKE-ON-TRENT

Map 3 H3

Burslem ☎ (0782) 837006
Wood Farm, High Ln, Tunstall (4m N of city centre on
B5049)
A moorland course on the outskirts of Tunstall with
hard walking.
*9 holes, 5354yds, Par 66, SSS 66, Course record 64.
Membership 250.*

Visitors welcome (ex Sun & with M only Sat & BH)
Societies welcome (☎)
Green fees Not confirmed
Facilities ⫟ by prior arrangement ⮢ by prior
arrangement ⬤ ♀ △
Hotel ★★★67% Stakis Grand Hotel, 66 Trinity St,
Hanley, STOKE-ON-TRENT ☎(0782) 202361 128⇔⋔

Greenway Hall ☎ (0782) 503158
Stanley Rd, Stockton Brook (5m NE off A53)
Moorland course with fine views of the Pennines.
*18 holes, 5678yds, Par 70, SSS 67, Course record 64.
Membership 400.*

Visitors welcome (ex Sat & Sun am) Societies welcome
(☎)

Green fees Not confirmed
Facilities ♀ ☖
Hotel ★★★67% Stakis Grand Hotel, 66 Trinity St, Hanley, STOKE-ON-TRENT ☎(0782) 202361 128⇆🛉

Trentham ☎ (0782) 658109
14 Barlaston Old Rd, Trentham (3m S off A5035)
Parkland course. The par 3, 4th is a testing hole. Squash courts and snooker.
18 holes, 6644yds, Par 72, SSS 72, Course record 64.
Membership 680.

Visitors welcome (ex Sat. H'cap cart required) must contact in advance ✉ Societies welcome (☎ a year in advance)
Green fees £20-£25
Facilities ⊗ ⅲ ⅲ ⬛ (by prior arrangement for all catering) ♀ ☖ 🏠 ⅊ (D McDonald
Hotel ★★★79% Hanchurch Manor Hotel, HANCHURCH ☎(0782) 643030 7⇆ Annexe:5⇆🛉

Trentham Park ☎ (0782) 658800
Trentham Park (3m SW off A34)
Fine parkland course. Snooker.
18 holes, 6403yds, Par 71, SSS 71, Course record 67.
Membership 600.

Visitors welcome Societies welcome (Wed & Fri only ☎)
Green fees £17 per day (£22 WE & BH)
Facilities ⊗ ⅲ ⅲ ⬛ ♀ ☖ 🏠 (R Clarke
Hotel ★★★60% Post House Hotel, Clayton Rd, NEWCASTLE-UNDER-LYME ☎(0782) 717171 126⇆🛉

STONE   Map 3 H3

Stone ☎ (0785) 813103
Filleybrooks (.5m W on A34)
Parkland course with easy walking. Snooker.
9 holes, 6299yds, Par 71, SSS 70, Course record 64.
Membership 350.

Visitors welcome (with M only WE & BH) Societies welcome (by letter)
Green fees £10
Facilities ⊗ ⅲ ⅲ ⬛ ♀ ☖
Hotel ★★★63% Stone House Hotel, STONE ☎(0785) 815531 50⇆🛉

TAMWORTH   Map 3 J4

Drayton Park ☎ (0827) 251139
Drayton Park (2m S on A4091)
Parkland course designed by James Braid. Club established since 1897. Snooker.
18 holes, 6214yds, Par 71, SSS 71, Course record 65.
Membership 450.

Visitors welcome (wkdays only) must contact in advance Societies welcome (by letter)
Green fees £21 per day/round

For an explanation of the symbols and abbreviations used, see page 33.

Facilities ⊗ ⅲ ⅲ ⬛ (all catering by prior arrangement) ♀ ☖ 🏠 (M W Passmore
Hotel ★★★★66% The Belfry, Lichfield Rd, WISHAW ☎(0675) 70301 219⇆

Tamworth Municipal ☎ (0827) 53850
Eagle Dr (2.5m E off B5000)
First-class parkland course and a good test of golf.
18 holes, 6083yds, Par 73, SSS 72, Course record 66.
Membership 700.

Visitors welcome must contact in advance Societies welcome (by letter)
Green fees £6 per 18 holes
Facilities ⊗ ⅲ ⅲ ⬛ ♀ ☖ 🏠 ⅊ (Barry Jones
Hotel ★★72% Angel Croft Hotel, Beacon St, LICHFIELD ☎(0543) 258737 11rm(3⇆6🛉) Annexe:8⇆🛉

UTTOXETER   Map 3 J3

Uttoxeter ☎ (0889) 564884
Wood Ln (1m SE off B5017)
Downland course with open aspect.
18 holes, 5456yds, Par 69, SSS 67. Membership 350.

Visitors welcome Societies welcome
Green fees Not confirmed
Facilities ♀ ☖
Hotel ★★★66% Ye Olde Dog & Partridge Hotel, High St, TUTBURY ☎(0283) 813030 3⇆ Annexe:14⇆🛉

WESTON   Map 3 J3

Ingestre Park ☎ (0889) 270304
(2m SE off A51)
Parkland course set in the grounds of Ingestre Hall, former home of the Earl of Shrewsbury.
18 holes, 6334yds, Par 71, SSS 70, Course record 67.
Membership 650.

Visitors welcome (with M only WE & BH) Societies welcome (☎)
Green fees £20
Facilities ⊗ ⅲ ⅲ ⬛ ♀ ☖ 🏠 (Danny Scullion
Hotel ★★★64% Tillington Hall, Eccleshall Rd, STAFFORD ☎(0785) 53531 90⇆🛉

SUFFOLK

ALDEBURGH   Map 4 K7

Aldeburgh ☎ (0728) 452890
Saxmundham Rd (1m W on A1094)
A most enjoyable and not unduly difficult seaside course; ideal for golfing holidaymakers. A bracing and fairly open terrain with some trees and heathland.
18 holes, 6330yds, Par 68, SSS 71. River Course 9 holes, 4228yds, Par 64, SSS 64. Membership 750.

Visitors welcome (h'cap cert needed for 18 hole course) must contact in advance ✉ Societies welcome (☎)

▶

Green fees £22.50 per day ; £16 per round (£27.50/
£20 WE & BH)
Facilities ⊗ ╚ ♨ ♀ △ 🛏 ⚑ ⌇ K R Preston
Hotel ★★★65% Wentworth Hotel, Wentworth Rd,
ALDEBURGH ☎(0728) 452312 31rm(24⇆4♠)

BECCLES
Map 4 K5

Beccles ☎ (0502) 712244
The Common (NE side of town)
Heathland course with natural hazards and particularly
exposed to wind.
9 holes, 2781yds, Par 68, SSS 67. Membership 200.

Visitors welcome (with M only Sun) Societies welcome
Green fees Not confirmed
Facilities ♀ △ 🛏 ⌇
Hotel ★★61% Waveney House Hotel, Puddingmoor,
BECCLES ☎(0502) 712270 13⇆♠

BUNGAY
Map 4 J5

Bungay & Waveney Valley ☎ (0986) 892337
Outney Common (.5m NW on A143)
Heathland course partly comprising Neolithic stone
workings, easy walking.
18 holes, 5950yds, Par 69, SSS 68, Course record 64.
Membership 709.

Visitors welcome (with M WE & BH) must contact in
advance Societies welcome (by letter)
Green fees £18 per day (or round)
Facilities ⊗ ╟ ╚ ♨ (no catering Mon) ♀ (ex Mon)
△ 🛏 ⚑ ⌇ N Whyte
Hotel ★★61% Swan Hotel, The Thoroughfare,
HARLESTON ☎(0379) 852221 14⇆♠

BURY ST EDMUNDS
Map 4 G6

Bury St Edmunds ☎ (0284) 755979
Tuthill (2m NW on B1106 off A45)
Undulating parkland course with easy walking and
attractive short holes. Snooker.
18 holes, 6615yds, Par 72, SSS 72, Course record 67.
Membership 830.

Visitors welcome (WE only with M) Societies welcome
(☎ Secretary)
Green fees £20 per day
Facilities ⊗ ╟ by prior arrangement ╚ ♨ ♀ △ 🛏
⚑ ⌇ Mark Jillings
Hotel ★★★76% Angel Hotel, Angel Hill, BURY ST
EDMUNDS ☎(0284) 753926 41⇆♠

Fornham Park ☎ (0284) 706777
St John's Hill Plantation, The Street, Fornham All
Saints (2m N off A134)
Downland course with many water hazards. Also a
country club where facilities include sauna, snooker,
bars and restaurant.
18 holes, 6218yds, Par 72, SSS 70. Membership 500.

Visitors welcome Societies welcome (☎)
Green fees Not confirmed

Facilities ⊗ ╟ ╚ ♨ ♀ △ 🛏 ⚑ ⌇ Stewart Wright
Hotel ★★★⚑75% Ravenwood Hall Hotel, Rougham,
BURY ST EDMUNDS ☎(0359) 70345 7⇆

CRETINGHAM
Map 4 J6

Cretingham ☎ Earl Soham (072882) 275
Grove Farm (2m from A1120 at Earl Soham)
Parkland course. Tennis (hardcourt), outdoor
swimming pool and snooker.
9 holes, 1955yds, Par 30, SSS 60, Course record 28.
Membership 360.

Visitors welcome Societies welcome (☎)
Green fees £8 per day (£10 WE & BH)
Facilities ♨ △ 🛏 ⚑
Hotel ★★68% Crown Hotel, Market Hill,
FRAMLINGHAM ☎(0728) 723521 14⇆

FELIXSTOWE
Map 4 J8

Felixstowe Ferry ☎ (0394) 286834
(NE side of town centre)
Seaside links course, pleasant views, easy walking.
Testing 491-yd, 7th hole. Accommodation.
18 holes, 6324yds, Par 72, SSS 70, Course record 65.
Membership 700.

Visitors welcome (not before 0900) Member must
accompany ✉ Societies welcome (by booking form)
Green fees £18 per day (£21 WE)
Facilities ⊗ ╟ by prior arrangement ╚ ♨ ♀ △ 🛏
⌇ Ian MacPherson
Hotel ★★★69% Orwell Moat House Hotel, Hamilton
Rd, FELIXSTOWE ☎(0394) 285511 58⇆♠

FLEMPTON
Map 4 G6

Flempton ☎ (028484) 291
(.5m W on A1101)
Breckland course.
9 holes, 6080yds, Par 70, SSS 69, Course record 64.
Membership 300.

Visitors welcome (with M only WE & BH) must contact
in advance ✉
Green fees £20 per day ; £15 per round
Facilities ⊗ ╟ ╚ ♨ (all catering and bar by prior
arrangement) ♀ △ 🛏 ⌇ Alistair Curry
Hotel ★★66% Suffolk Hotel, 38 The Buttermarket,
BURY ST EDMUNDS ☎(0284) 753995 33⇆♠

HAVERHILL
Map 4 F7

Haverhill ☎ (0440) 61951
Coupals Rd (1m SE off A604)
Private parkland course with small river crossing each
9 holes three times.
9 holes, 5707yds, Par 68, SSS 68, Course record 67.
Membership 395.

Visitors welcome (ex competition days) Societies
welcome (by letter)
Green fees £12 per day (£17 WE & BH)

Facilities 🏌 🏌 ♀ ⛳ 🏠 ⛳ 🏌 Simon Mayfield
Hotel ★★70% Bell Hotel, Market Hill, CLARE ☎(0787) 277741 10rm(3⇋4🏠) Annexe:11⇋

HINTLESHAM   Map 4 H7

Hintlesham Hall ☎ (047387) 334 or 671
(In village on A1071)
Magnificent new 18-hole championship length course, opening in Summer 1991, and blending harmoniously with the ancient parkland surrounding this exclusive hotel. The 6,835 yd parkland course was designed by Hawtree and Son, one of the oldest established firms of golf course architects in the world. The course is fair but challenging for low and high handicappers alike. Hotel offers beautiful accommodation, excellent cuisine and many sports and leisure facilities.
18 holes, 6835yds, Par 72.

Visitors welcome (Hotel residents or member's guests)
Green fees Not confirmed
Facilities ⊗ 🏌 🏌 ♀ ⛳ 🏠
Hotel ★★★(red)⛳Hintlesham Hall Hotel, HINTLESHAM ☎(047387) 334 & 268 33⇋🏠

IPSWICH   Map 4 H7

Ipswich ☎ (0473) 728941
Purdis Heath (E side of town centre off A1156)
Many golfers are suprised when they hear that Ipswich has, at Purdis Heath, a first-class golf course. In some ways it resembles some of Surrey's better courses; a beautiful heathland/parkland course with two lakes and easy walking.
18 holes, 6405yds, Par 71, SSS 71, Course record 64 or 9 holes, 1930yds, Par 31, SSS 31. Membership 850.

SCORE CARD					
Hole	Yds	Par	Hole	Yds	Par
1	330	4	10	153	3
2	512	5	11	531	5
3	163	3	12	363	4
4	425	4	13	406	4
5	433	4	14	440	4
6	182	3	15	141	3
7	437	4	16	298	4
8	373	4	17	497	5
9	308	4	18	413	4
Out	3163	35	In	3242	36
			Totals	6405	71

Visitors welcome (h'cap cert required for 18 hole coures) must contact in advance ✉ Societies welcome (☎ or by letter)
Green fees £20-£25, 18 hole; £7.50-£10, 9hole
Facilities ⊗ 🏌 🏌 🏌 ♀ (all day) ⛳ 🏠 🏌 Stephen Whymark
Hotel ★★★71% Marlborough Hotel, Henley Rd, IPSWICH ☎(0473) 257677 22⇋🏠

Rushmere ☎ (0473) 725648
Rushmere Heath (2m E off A12)
Heathland course with much gorse, prevailing winds. Testing 5th hole - dog leg, 419 yards (par 4).
18 holes, 6287yds, Par 70, SSS 70, Course record 66. Membership 750.

Visitors welcome (ex after 1630 & before 1430 WE & BH) Societies welcome (☎)

Green fees £15 per day
Facilities ⊗ 🏌 🏌 ♀ ⛳ 🏠 🏌 🏌 N T J McNeill
Hotel ★★★71% Marlborough Hotel, Henley Rd, IPSWICH ☎(0473) 257677 22⇋🏠

LOWESTOFT   Map 4 K5

Rookery Park ☎ (0502) 560380
Carlton Colville (3.5m SW on A146)
Parkland course. 9-hole , par 3, course adjacent. Snooker.
18 holes, 6602yds, Par 72, SSS 72, Course record 71. Membership 600.

Visitors welcome ✉ Societies welcome (☎)
Green fees Not confirmed
Facilities ⊗ 🏌 🏌 🏌 ♀ ⛳ 🏠 🏌 🏌 Martin Elsworthy
Hotel ★★★59% Broadlands Hotel, Bridge Rd, Oulton Broad, LOWESTOFT ☎(0502) 516031 52⇋

NEWMARKET   Map 4 F6

Links ☎ (0638) 663000
Cambridge Rd (1m SW on A1034)
Gently undulating parkland.
18 holes, 6424yds, Par 72, SSS 71, Course record 68. Membership 700.

Visitors welcome (restricted Sun after 1130 h'cap cert) ✉ Societies welcome (☎)
Green fees £18 per day (£25 WE & BH)
Facilities ⊗ 🏌 by prior arrangement (ex Mon) 🏌 (ex Mon) 🏌 ♀ ⛳ 🏠 🏌 Derek Thomson
Hotel ★★58% White Hart Hotel, High St, NEWMARKET ☎(0638) 663051 23⇋🏠

NEWTON   Map 4 G7

Newton Green ☎ Newton Green (0787) 77217
Sudbury Rd (W side of village on A134)
Flat, commonland course.
9 holes, 5488yds, Par 68, SSS 67, Course record 60. Membership 360.

Visitors welcome (ex Tue, WE & BH) Member must accompany must contact in advance
Green fees £10 per round/day
Facilities ⊗ 🏌 by prior arrangement 🏌 🏌 ♀ ⛳ 🏠 🏌 Kevin Lovelock
Hotel ★★★59% Bull Hotel, Hall St, LONG MELFORD ☎(0787) 78494 25⇋

SOUTHWOLD   Map 4 K6

Southwold ☎ (0502) 723234
The Common (.5m W off A1095)
Commonland course with 4-acre practice ground and panoramic views of the sea.
9 holes, 6001yds, Par 70, SSS 69. Membership 450.

Visitors welcome (restricted Sun, BH & competition days) must contact in advance Societies welcome (by letter)
Green fees Not confirmed

▶

Facilities ⊗ 🏌 💺 ♀ 🏖 🏠 ⛳ 𝄃 Brian Allen
Hotel ★★★69% Swan Hotel, Market Place,
SOUTHWOLD ☎(0502) 722186 27⇌🏠 Annexe:18⇌

STOWMARKET
Map 4 H6/7

Stowmarket ☎ Rattlesden (0449) 736473
Lower Rd, Onehouse (2.5m SW off B115)
Parkland course.
18 holes, 6101yds, Par 69, SSS 69, Course record 66.
Membership 600.

Visitors welcome (ex Wed am) must contact in advance
✉ Societies welcome (Thu & Fri only)
Green fees £15 per day (£25 WE)
Facilities ⊗ by prior arrangement 🏌 by prior
arrangement 🏌 💺 ♀ 🏖 🏠 𝄃 C Aldred
Hotel ★★64% Limes Hotel, NEEDHAM MARKET
☎(0449) 720305 11⇌

THORPENESS
Map 4 K6

Thorpeness
☎ Aldeburgh (0728) 452176
(W side of village off B1353)
The holes of this moorland
course are pleasantly varied
with several quite difficult
par 4's. Natural hazards
abound. The 15th, with its
sharp left dog-leg, is one of
the best holes.
Accommodation.
18 holes, 6241yds, Par 69,
SSS 71, Course record 66.
Membership 350.

SCORE CARD: White Tees					
Hole	Yds	Par	Hole	Yds	Par
1	324	4	10	179	3
2	186	3	11	312	4
3	394	4	12	370	4
4	449	4	13	424	4
5	420	4	14	499	5
6	377	4	15	416	4
7	145	3	16	191	3
8	402	4	17	280	4
9	439	4	18	434	4
Out	3136	34	In	3105	35
			Totals	6241	69

Visitors welcome must contact in advance Societies
welcome (☎)
Green fees £30 per day (£40 WE)
Facilities ⊗ 🏌 🏌 💺 ♀ 🏖 🏠 ⛳ 𝄃 T Pennock
Hotel ★67% White Horse Hotel, Station Rd,
LEISTON ☎(0728) 830694 10rm(1⇌5🏠) Annexe:3🏠

WOODBRIDGE
Map 4 J7

Woodbridge
☎ (03943) 2038
Bromeswell Heath (2.5m NE
off A1152)
A beautiful course, one of
the best in East Anglia. It is
situated on high ground
and in different seasons
present golfers with a great
variety of colour. Some say
that of the many good holes
the 14th is the best.
18 holes, 6314yds, Par 70,
SSS 70, Course record 64 or
9 holes, 2243yds, Par 31, SSS 31. Membership 900.

SCORE CARD: White Tees					
Hole	Yds	Par	Hole	Yds	Par
1	346	4	10	431	4
2	329	4	11	392	4
3	529	5	12	184	3
4	330	4	13	310	4
5	371	4	14	425	4
6	401	4	15	188	3
7	149	3	16	460	4
8	514	5	17	400	4
9	198	3	18	357	4
Out	3167	36	In	3147	34
			Totals	6314	70

Visitors welcome (with M only WE & BH) must
contact in advance ✉ Societies welcome (by letter
up to 1 year ahead)
Green fees £23 per day; £18 per round
Facilities ⊗ 🏌 🏌 💺 ♀ 🏖 🏠 𝄃 Leslie Jones
Hotel ★★★♨73% Seckford Hall Hotel,
WOODBRIDGE ☎(0394) 385678 24⇌🏠
Annexe:10⇌🏠

WORLINGTON
Map 4 F6

Royal Worlington & Newmarket ☎ (0638) 712216
(.5m SE)
9-hole 'links' course inland. Favourite 9-hole course
of many golf writers and home to Cambridge
University Golf Club.
9 holes, 3105yds, Par 70, SSS 70. Membership 325.

Visitors welcome (with M only at WE) must contact
in advance ✉ Societies welcome (by letter)
Green fees Not confirmed
Facilities ⊗ by prior arrangement 🏌 💺 ♀ (all
day) 🏖 🏠 ⛳ 𝄃 Malcolm Hawkins
Hotel ★★★63% Riverside Hotel, Mill St,
MILDENHALL ☎(0638) 717274 19rm(10⇌5🏠)

SURREY

ASHFORD
Map 2 D4

Ashford Manor ☎ (0784) 252049
Fordbridge Rd (2m E of Staines via A308 Staines bypass)
Parkland course, looks easy but is difficult.
18 holes, 6343yds, Par 70, SSS 70. Membership 600.

Visitors welcome must contact in advance ✉ Societies
welcome
Green fees Not confirmed
Facilities 🏖 🏠 ⛳ 𝄃
Hotel ★★★57% Thames Lodge Hotel, Thames St,
STAINES ☎(0784) 464433 44⇌

BANSTEAD
Map 2 E4

Banstead Downs ☎ 081-642 2284
Burdon Ln, Belmont, Sutton (1.5m N on A217)
Downland course with narrow fairways and hawthorns.
18 holes, 6169yds, Par 69, SSS 69, Course record 63.
Membership 542.

Visitors welcome (h'cap cert required, only with M at
WE) ✉ Societies welcome
Green fees Not confirmed
Facilities ⊗ (ex Mon) 🏌 by prior arrangement 🏌 💺
♀ 🏖 🏠 𝄃 Ian Marr
Hotel ★★59% Heathside Hotel, Brighton Rd, BURGH
HEATH ☎(0737) 353355 47⇌🏠

To see a full range of AA guides and maps, visit
your local AA Shop or any good bookshop.

Cuddington ☎ 081-393 0952
Banstead Rd (N of Banstead station on A2022)
Parkland course with easy walking and providing good views.
18 holes, 6352yds, Par 70, SSS 70. Membership 790.

Visitors welcome must contact in advance ✉ Societies welcome (☎ Thu only)
Green fees £24 per day (£30 per round WE)
Facilities ⊗ ⅷ by prior arrangement ⅃ ⬛ ♀ � ⌂
⟨ R Gardner
Hotel ★★59% Heathside Hotel, Brighton Rd, BURGH HEATH ☎(0737) 353355 47⇥↾

BRAMLEY   Map 2 D5

Bramley ☎ Guildford (0483) 892696
(.5 m N on A281)
Downland course, fine views from top.
18 holes, 5966yds, Par 69, SSS 68, Course record 63. Membership 780.

Visitors welcome (with M only WE & BH) must contact in advance Societies welcome (☎)
Green fees £22 per day, £17.50 per round
Facilities ⊗ ⅷ by prior arrangement ⅃ ⬛ ♀ � ⌂
⅂⟨ Gary Peddie
Hotel ★★★70% The Manor at Newlands, Newlands Corner, GUILDFORD ☎(0483) 222624 20⇥↾

BROOKWOOD   Map 2 D4

West Hill ☎ (04867) 4365
Bagshot Rd (E side of village on A332)
Worplesdon's next-door neighbour and a comparably great heath-and-heather course. Slightly tighter than Worplesdon with more opportunities for getting into trouble - but a most interesting and challenging course with wonderful greens. The 15th is a testing par 3. Course record holder Neil Coles.
18 holes, 6368yds, Par 69, SSS 70, Course record 66. Membership 535.

SCORE CARD: White Tees					
Hole	Yds	Par	Hole	Yds	Par
1	395	4	10	422	4
2	377	4	11	392	4
3	454	4	12	297	4
4	193	3	13	149	3
5	532	5	14	462	4
6	419	4	15	212	3
7	170	3	16	384	4
8	387	4	17	512	5
9	171	3	18	440	4
Out	3098	34	In	3270	35
			Totals	6368	69

Visitors welcome (ex WE & BH) must contact in advance ✉ Societies welcome (by letter)
Green fees £38.50 per day ; £27.50 per round
Facilities ⊗ ⅷ ⅃ ⬛ ♀ ⚘ ⌂ ⅂⟨ John Clements
Hotel ★★★★70% Pennyhill Park Hotel, London Rd, BAGSHOT ☎(0276) 71774 22⇥↾
Annexe:41⇥↾

If you know of a golf course, not in this guide already, which welcomes visitors, we would be pleased to hear about it.

CAMBERLEY   Map 2 C4

Camberley Heath ☎ (0276) 23258
Golf Dr (1.25m SE of town centre off A325)
One of the great 'heath and heather' courses so frequently associated with Surrey. Several very good short holes - especially the 8th. The 10th is a difficult and interesting par 4, as also is the 17th, where the drive must be held well to the left as perdition lurks on the right.
18 holes, 6402yds, Par 72, SSS 71. Membership 700.

Visitors welcome (with M only WE) must contact in advance ✉ Societies welcome
Green fees Not confirmed
Facilities ⊗ ⅷ ⅃ ⬛ ♀ ⚘ ⌂ ⅂⟨ Gary Smith
Hotel ★★★★70% Pennyhill Park Hotel, London Rd, BAGSHOT ☎(0276) 71774 22⇥↾
Annexe:41⇥↾

CHERTSEY   Map 2 D4

Barrow Hills ☎ (0932) 848117
Longcross (3m W on B386)
Parkland course with natural hazards.
18 holes, 3090yds, Par 56, SSS 53, Course record 58. Membership 235.

Visitors welcome (restricted WE & BH pm) Member must accompany
Green fees Not confirmed
Facilities ⬛
Hotel ★★★57% Thames Lodge Hotel, Thames St, STAINES ☎(0784) 464433 44⇥

Laleham ☎ (0932) 564211
Laleham Reach (1.5m N)
Well-bunkered parkland/meadowland.
18 holes, 6210yds, Par 70, SSS 70. Membership 600.

Visitors welcome (Mon-Fri & after 0930 Tue & Thu) must contact in advance ✉ Societies welcome (by letter)
Green fees £20 per day or per round
Facilities ⊗ ⅷ by prior arrangement ⅃ ⬛ ♀ ⚘ ⌂
⟨ T Whitton
Hotel ★★★57% Thames Lodge Hotel, Thames St, STAINES ☎(0784) 464433 44⇥

CHIPSTEAD   Map 2 E4

Chipstead ☎ Downland (0737) 555781
How Ln (.5m N of village)
Hilly downland course, hard walking, good views. Testing 18th hole.
18 holes, 5454yds, Par 67, SSS 67. Membership 630.

Visitors welcome (wkdays only) Societies welcome
Green fees £20 (£15 after 1400)
Facilities ⊗ ⅷ (Societies only) ⅃ ⬛ ♀ ⚘ ⌂⟨ Gary Torbett
Hotel ★★★★62% Selsdon Park Hotel, Sanderstead, CROYDON ☎081-657 8811 170⇥↾

COBHAM

Map 2 D4

Silvermere ☎ (0932) 66007
Redhill Rd (2.25m NW off A245)
Parkland course with many very tight holes through woodland, 17th has 170 yds carry-over lake. Driving range. Fishing.
18 holes, 6333yds, Par 71, SSS 71, Course record 65.
Membership 850.

Visitors welcome (ex WE until 1300) must contact in advance Societies welcome (☎)
Green fees £12.50 per day (£16 WE)
Facilities ⊗ ⅷ ㋐ 및 ♀ ♨ ⌂ ⅋ (Doug McClelland
Hotel ★★★63% Thatchers Resort Hotel, Epsom Rd, EAST HORSLEY ☎(04865) 4291 36↩🐾 Annexe:23↩🐾

CRANLEIGH

Map 2 D5

Fernfell Golf & Country Club ☎ (0483) 268855
Barhatch Ln (1m N)
Scenic woodland/parkland course at the base of the Surrey hills, easy walking. Clubhouse in 400-year-old barn. Tennis (hardcourt), outdoor-heated swimming pool, snooker and sauna.
18 holes, 5071yds, Par 68, SSS 67, Course record 68.
Membership 1000.

Visitors welcome (ex WE) must contact in advance Societies welcome (☎)
Green fees £28 per day ; £20 per round
Facilities ⊗ ⅷ ㋐ 및 ♀ ♨ ⌂ ⅋ (Trevor Longmuir
Hotel ★★★70% The Manor at Newlands, Newlands Corner, GUILDFORD ☎(0483) 222624 20↩🐾

DORKING

Map 2 E5

Betchworth Park ☎ (0306) 882052
Reigate Rd (1m E on A25)
Parkland course, with hard walking.
18 holes, 6266yds, Par 69, SSS 70, Course record 66.
Membership 725.

Visitors welcome (ex WE, Tue/Wed am & limited Fri) must contact in advance Societies welcome (Mon-Thu ☎)
Green fees £25 weekdays (£35 Sun)
Facilities ⊗ ㋐ 및 ♀ ♨ ⌂ ⅋ (Alex King
Hotel ★★★50% The White Horse, High St, DORKING ☎(0306) 881138 36↩🐾 Annexe:32↩

Dorking ☎ (0306) 889786
Chart Park (1m S on A24)
Dry, undulating parkland course, easy slopes, wind-sheltered. Testing holes: 5th 'Tom's Puddle' (par 4); 7th 'Rest and Be Thankful' (par 4); 9th 'Double Decker' (par 4).
9 holes, 5120yds, Par 66, SSS 65, Course record 62.
Membership 400.

Visitors welcome (ex WE & BH) must contact in advance Societies welcome (☎)
Green fees £12, 18 holes; £16 all day

Facilities ㋐ 및 (meals by arrangement) ♀ ♨ ⌂ ⅋ (P Napier
Hotel ★★★57% The Burford Bridge, Burford Bridge, Box Hill, DORKING ☎(0306) 884561 48↩

EAST HORSLEY

Map 2 D5

Drift ☎ (04865) 4641
(1.5m N off B2039)
Woodland course with sheltered fairways and many ponds.
18 holes, 6414yds, Par 74, SSS 71, Course record 68 or 18 holes, 5957yds, Par 71.

Visitors welcome (with M only at WE & BH) must contact in advance Societies welcome (☎)
Green fees Not confirmed
Facilities ⊗ ㋐ 및 ♀ (all day) ♨ ⌂ ⅋ (Joe Hagen
Hotel ★★★63% Thatchers Resort Hotel, Epsom Rd, EAST HORSLEY ☎(04865) 4291 36↩🐾 Annexe:23↩🐾

EFFINGHAM

Map 2 E5

Effingham ☎ Bookham (0372) 452203
Guildford Rd (W side of village on A246)
Easy-walking downland course laid out on 27- acres with tree-lined fairways. It is one of the longest of the Surrey courses with wide subtle greens that provide a provocative but by no means exhausting challenge. Facilities include 4 tennis courts and 2 squash courts.
18 holes, 6488yds, Par 71, SSS 71. Membership 1200.

Visitors welcome (with M only WE & BH) must contact in advance Societies welcome (☎ for details)
Green fees £30 per day ; £25 pm only
Facilities ⊗ ⅷ ㋐ 및 ♀ ♨ ⌂ ⅋ (Steve Hoatson
Hotel ★★★63% Thatchers Resort Hotel, Epsom Rd, EAST HORSLEY ☎(04865) 4291 36↩🐾 Annexe:23↩🐾

ENTON GREEN

Map 2 D5

West Surrey ☎ Godalming (04868) 21275
(S side of village)
A good parkland-type course in rolling, well-wooded setting. Some fairways are tight with straight driving at a premium. The 17th is a testing hole with a long hill walk. Snooker.
18 holes, 6259yds, Par 71, SSS 70, Course record 66.
Membership 600.

Visitors welcome (must be M of a club with h'cap cert) must contact in advance ✉ Societies welcome (by letter)
Green fees £30 per day ; £20 per round (£40 WE & BH)
Facilities ⊗ ⅷ by prior arrangement ㋐ 및 ♀ ♨ ⌂ (J Hoskison
Hotel ★★★64% Hog's Back Hotel, Hog's Back, SEALE ☎(02518) 2345 75↩🐾

EPSOM

Map 2 E4

Epsom ☎ (03727) 21666
Longdown Ln South, Epsom Downs (SE side of town centre on B288)
Downland course.
*18 holes, 5118yds, Par 67, SSS 65, Course record 65.
Membership 660.*

Visitors welcome (restricted WE & BH) Societies welcome (☎)
Green fees £10 per round (£15 WE & BH)
Facilities ⊗ ⅲ ﹝ ﹏ (no catering all day Mon or Sun evening) ♀ ⌂ 🖿 ⟨
Hotel ★★59% Heathside Hotel, Brighton Rd, BURGH HEATH ☎(0737) 353355 47⇨🖢

ESHER

Map 2 E4

Moore Place ☎ (0372) 463533
Portsmouth Rd (SW side of town centre on A244)
Public course on attractive, undulating parkland laid out 60 years ago by Harry Vardon. Examples of most of the trees that will survive in the UK are to be found on the course. Testing short holes at 4th, 5th and 7th.
*9 holes, 2049yds, Par 32, SSS 30, Course record 25.
Membership 100.*

Visitors welcome Societies welcome
Green fees £4, 9 holes (£5 WE & BH, 9 holes)
Facilities ⊗ ⅲ ﹝ ﹏ ♀ (all day) ⌂ 🖿 ⑂ ⟨ David Allen
Hotel ★★★64% Ship Thistle Hotel, Monument Green, WEYBRIDGE ☎(0932) 848364 39⇨🖢

Sandown Golf Centre ☎ (0372) 463340
Sandown Park, More Ln (1m NW off A307)
Parkland course. Additional facilities include a driving range, and a pitch-and-putt course.
New Course 9 holes, 2828yds, Par 70, SSS 67. Par 3 9 holes, 1193yds, Par 27. Membership 300.

Visitors welcome (restricted WE & BH) must contact in advance at WE Societies welcome (☎)
Green fees 9 holes: New course £4 (£5 WE); Par 3 course £2.70 (£3.30 WE); P & P £1.50
Facilities ⊗ ﹝ ﹏ ♀ ⌂ 🖿 ⑂
Hotel ★★62% Haven Hotel, Portsmouth Rd, ESHER ☎081-398 0023 16⇨🖢 Annexe:4⇨🖢

Thames Ditton & Esher ☎ 081-398 1551
Marquis of Granby, Portsmouth Rd (1m NE on A307)
Commonland course, public right of way.
*18 holes, 5190yds, Par 66, SSS 65, Course record 61.
Membership 400.*

Visitors welcome (ex Sun am) Societies welcome (☎)
Green fees Not confirmed
Facilities ﹝ (ex Thu and Sun) ﹏ (ex Thu and Sun) ♀ ⌂ 🖿 ⟨ Rodney Hutton
Hotel ★★62% Haven Hotel, Portsmouth Rd, ESHER ☎081-398 0023 16⇨🖢 Annexe:4⇨🖢

FARNHAM

Map 2 C5

Farnham ☎ Runfold (02518) 2109
The Sands (3m E off A31)
A mixture of meadowland and heath with quick drying sandy subsoil. Several of the earlier holes have interesting features, the finishing holes rather less.
*18 holes, 6325yds, Par 72, SSS 70, Course record 67.
Membership 800.*

Visitors welcome (with M only WE) Member must accompany must contact in advance Societies welcome (book one year in advance)
Green fees £23.50 per day; £20 per round
Facilities ⊗ ⅲ by prior arrangement ﹝ ﹏ ♀ ⌂ 🖿 ⟨ G Cowlishaw
Hotel ★★★56%, Bush Hotel, The Borough, FARNHAM ☎(0252) 715237 68⇨🖢

Farnham Park ☎ (0252) 715216
Folly Hill, Farnham Park (N side of town centre on A287)
Municipal parkland course in Farnham Park.
9 holes, 1163yds, Par 27, SSS 27.

Visitors welcome Societies welcome (☎)
Green fees £2.40 per day (£3 WE)
Facilities ⊗ ﹏ 🖿 ⑂ ⟨ Peter Chapman
Hotel ★★★56% Bush Hotel, The Borough, FARNHAM ☎(0252) 715237 68⇨🖢

GUILDFORD

Map 2 D5

Guildford ☎ (0483) 66765
High Path Rd, Merrow (E side of town centre off A246)
A downland course but with some trees and much scrub. The holes provide an interesting variety of play, an invigorating experience. Snooker.
*18 holes, 6080yds, Par 69, SSS 70, Course record 64.
Membership 700.*

Visitors welcome (with M only WE & BH) must contact in advance Societies welcome (☎)
Green fees £30 per day; £24 per round
Facilities ﹝ ﹏ ♀ ⌂ 🖿 ⟨ Peter Hollington
Hotel ★★★70% The Manor at Newlands, Newlands Corner, GUILDFORD ☎(0483) 222624 20⇨🖢

For an explanation of the symbols and abbreviations used, see page 33.

HINDHEAD

Map 2 D5

Hindhead ☎ (0428) 604614
Churt Rd (1.5m NW on A287)
A good example of a Surrey heath-and-heather course, and most picturesque. Players must be prepared for some hard walking. The first nine fairways follow narrow valleys requiring straight hitting; the second nine are much less restricted. Snooker.
18 holes, 6349yds, Par 70, SSS 70, Course record 65. Membership 820.

SCORE CARD: White Tees					
Hole	Yds	Par	Hole	Yds	Par
1	410	4	10	177	3
2	478	5	11	431	4
3	182	3	12	415	4
4	526	5	13	274	4
5	389	4	14	387	4
6	142	3	15	130	3
7	384	4	16	513	5
8	238	3	17	411	4
9	420	4	18	442	4
Out	3169	35	In	3180	35
			Totals	6349	70

Visitors welcome must contact in advance Societies welcome (Wed & Thu only)
Green fees £30 per day (£34 WE)
Facilities ⊗ ⬥ 🍺 ♀ ⛳ 🖼 ✝ ⟨
Hotel ★★★65% Frensham Pond Hotel, CHURT ☎(025125) 3175 7⟲ 🏚 Annexe:12⟲🏚

KINGSWOOD

Map 2 E5

Kingswood ☎ Mogador (0737) 832188
Sandy Ln (5m S of village off A217)
Flat parkland course, easy walking. Squash, snooker.
18 holes, 6855yds, Par 72, SSS 73, Course record 71. Membership 640.

Visitors welcome (after 1200 at WE) Member must accompany Societies welcome (☎)
Green fees £40 per day; £28 per round (£40 WE)
Facilities ⊗ ⬥ 🍺 ♀ ⛳ 🖼 ✝ ⟨ Rick Blackie
Hotel ★★59% Heathside Hotel, Brighton Rd, BURGH HEATH ☎(0737) 353355 47⟲🏚

LEATHERHEAD

Map 2 E4

Leatherhead ☎ Oxshott (037284) 3966
Kingston Rd (1.25m N on A244)
Parkland course with numerous ditches and only two hills, so walking is easy. Snooker and sauna.
18 holes, 6107yds, Par 71, SSS 69, Course record 68. Membership 600.

Visitors welcome (ex Thu, Sat or Sun am) must contact in advance Societies welcome (by letter)
Green fees £32.50 per two rounds (£37.50 WE & BH one round)
Facilities ⊗ ⬥ 🍺 ♀ ⛳ 🖼 ✝ ⟨ Richard Hurst
Hotel ★★★63% Thatchers Resort Hotel, Epsom Rd, EAST HORSLEY ☎(04865) 4291 36⟲🏚 Annexe:23⟲🏚

Tyrrells Wood ☎ (0372) 376025
(1.25m N on A244)
Parkland course with easy walking. Snooker.
18 holes, 6246yds, Par 71, SSS 70, Course record 65. Membership 744.

This guide is updated annually – make sure you use an up-to-date edition.

Visitors welcome (Yellow tee markers only. Restricted WE) must contact in advance ⊠ Societies welcome (by letter)
Green fees £30 per day (£36 WE & BH)
Facilities ⊗ 🍺 by prior arrangement ⬥ 🍺 ♀ ⛳ 🖼 ✝
⟨ Philip Taylor
Hotel ★★★★57% The Burford Bridge, Burford Bridge, Box Hill, DORKING ☎(0306) 884561 48⟲

LIMPSFIELD

Map 2 F5

Limpsfield Chart ☎ (0883) 722106
(1m E on A25)
Tight inland course set in National Trust land.
9 holes, 5718yds, Par 70, SSS 68. Membership 350.

Visitors welcome (WE with M only, Thu not before 1530) Societies welcome (by arrangement)
Green fees £15
Facilities ⊗ by prior arrangement 🍺 by prior arrangement ⬥ 🍺 ♀ ⛳
Hotel ★★★64% Reigate Manor Hotel, Reigate Hill, REIGATE ☎(0737) 240125 51⟲🏚

OCKLEY

Map 2 E5

Gatton Manor Hotel & Golf Club ☎ (030679) 555
(1.5m SW off A29)
Undulating course through woods and over many challenging water holes. Games room. Accommodation. Fishing, grasscourt tennis and bowls.
18 holes, 6145yds, Par 72, SSS 69. Membership 300.

Visitors welcome (2 weeks prior notice) must contact in advance Societies welcome (☎)
Green fees £12 per round (£17 WE)
Facilities ⊗ 🍺 ⬥ 🍺 ♀ ⛳ 🖼 ✝ ⟨
Hotel ★★★50% The White Horse, High St, DORKING ☎(0306) 881138 36⟲🏚 Annexe:32⟲

OTTERSHAW

Map 2 D4

Foxhills ☎ (093287) 2050
Stonehill Rd (1m NW)
A pair of parkland courses designed in the grand manner and with American course-design in mind. One course is tree-lined, the other, as well as trees, has massive bunkers and artificial lakes which contribute to the interest. Both courses offer testing golf and they finish on the same long 'double green'. Par 3 'Manor' course also available.
Accommodation, tennis, outdoor and indoor- heated swimming pool, squash, snooker, sauna, solarium, gymnasium.
Chertsey 18 holes, 6658yds, Par 71, SSS 72. Longcross 18 holes, 6406yds, Par 71, SSS 71. Manor Par 3 9 holes, 2250yds, Par 27. Membership 1100.

Visitors welcome must contact in advance Societies welcome (weekdays only by reservation)
Green fees £25 per day; £18 pe round (£30 WE)

Facilities ⊗ 〼 ᒪ ᴍ ♀ ⚊ 🏠 ⵢ 𝄐 Bernard Hunt MBE
Hotel ★★★57% Thames Lodge Hotel, Thames St, STAINES ☎(0784) 464433 44⇨

PIRBRIGHT   Map 2 D5

Goal Farm ☎ (04867) 3183 & 3205
Gole Rd (1.5m NW on B3012)
Beautiful lanscaped parkland 'Pay and Play' course with excellent greens.
9 holes, 1273yds, Par 54, SSS 54. Membership 400.

Visitors welcome (ex Sat am) Member must accompany
Green fees Not confirmed
Facilities 🏠 ⵢ
Hotel ★★★60% Queens Hotel, Lynchford Rd, FARNBOROUGH ☎(0252) 545051 110⇨

PUTTENHAM   Map 2 D5

Puttenham ☎ Guildford (0483) 810498
(1m SE on B3000)
Picturesque, tree-lined heathland course offering testing golf, easy walking.
18 holes, 6070yds, Par 71, SSS 69. Membership 630.

Visitors welcome (with M only WE) must contact in advance ⊠ Societies welcome (☎)
Green fees £18 per round ; £23 per day
Facilities ⊗ ᒪ ᴍ ♀ ⚊ 🏠 𝄐 Gary Simmons
Hotel ★★★64% Hog's Back Hotel, Hog's Back, SEALE ☎(02518) 2345 75⇨🐾

REDHILL   Map 2 E5

Redhill & Reigate ☎ Reigate (0737) 240777
Clarence Rd, Pendelton Rd (1m S on A23)
Parkland course.
18 holes, 5238yds, Par 67, SSS 66. Membership 500.

Visitors welcome (after 1100 WE, ex Sun Jun-Sep) must contact in advance Societies welcome (by letter)
Green fees £20 per day ; £12 per round (£15 per round WE)
Facilities ⊗ (ex Mon) 〼 (ex Mon) ᒪ ᴍ ♀ ⚊ 🏠 ⵢ
𝄐 B Davies
Hotel ★★★64% Reigate Manor Hotel, Reigate Hill, REIGATE ☎(0737) 240125 51⇨🐾

REIGATE   Map 2 E5

Reigate Heath ☎ (0737) 242610
(1.5m W off A25)
Heathland course.
9 holes, 5202yds, Par 66, SSS 66. Membership 300.

Visitors welcome (with M only WE & BH) must contact in advance Societies welcome (by letter)
Green fees £22 day ; £16 round
Facilities ⊗ (Tue-Sat) 〼 by prior arrangement ᒪ (Tue-Sat) ᴍ ♀ ⚊ 🏠 𝄐 W H Carter
Hotel ★★★64% Reigate Manor Hotel, Reigate Hill, REIGATE ☎(0737) 240125 51⇨🐾

TANDRIDGE   Map 2 F5

Tandridge ☎ Oxted (0883) 712274
(1m NE off A25)
Rolling parkland course, good views.
18 holes, 6250yds, Par 70, SSS 70. Membership 650.

Visitors welcome (Mon, Wed, Thu only) must contact in advance ⊠ Societies welcome (☎ or by letter)
Green fees £35 per day
Facilities ⊗ ᴍ ♀ ⚊ 🏠 ⵢ 𝄐 Allan Farquhar
Hotel ★★★74% Nutfield Priory, NUTFIELD ☎(0737) 822066 34⇨🐾

TILFORD   Map 2 C5

Hankley Common ☎ Frensham (025125) 2493
(.75m SE)
A natural heathland course subject to wind. Greens are first rate. The 18th, a long par 4, is most challenging, the green being beyond a deep chasm which traps any but the perfect second shot. The 7th is a spectacular one-shotter.
18 holes, 6418yds, Par 71, SSS 71, Course record 62. Membership 700.

Visitors welcome (h'cap reqd, restricted Wed & alternate WE) must contact in advance ⊠ Societies welcome (by letter)
Green fees £30 per day ; £25 per round (£30 per round after 1400 WE)
Facilities ⊗ ᒪ ᴍ ♀ ⚊ 🏠 𝄐 Peter Stow
Hotel ★★★65% Frensham Pond Hotel, CHURT ☎(025125) 3175 7⇨🐾 Annexe:12⇨🐾

VIRGINIA WATER   Map 2 D4

Wentworth See page 184

WALTON-ON-THAMES   Map 2 D4

Burhill ☎ (0932) 227345
Burwood Rd (2m S)
A relatively short and easy parkland course with some truly magnificent trees. The 18th is a splendid par 4 requiring a well-placed drive and a long firm second. This course is always in immaculate condition. Badminton and squash.
18 holes, 6224yds, Par 69, SSS 70, Course record 65. Membership 1100.

SCORE CARD					
Hole	Yds	Par	Hole	Yds	Par
1	433	4	10	209	3
2	376	4	11	382	4
3	382	4	12	325	4
4	284	4	13	153	3
5	406	4	14	530	5
6	128	3	15	441	4
7	374	4	16	152	3
8	410	4	17	440	4
9	370	4	18	429	4
Out	3163	35	In	3061	34
			Totals	6224	69

Visitors welcome (ex WE) must contact in advance ⊠ Societies welcome (by letter)
Green fees £30 before noon, £18 afternoons
Facilities ⊗ 〼 by prior arrangement ᒪ ᴍ (no catering Mon) ♀ ⚊ 🏠 𝄐 Lee Johnson
Hotel ★★★64% Ship Thistle Hotel, Monument Green, WEYBRIDGE ☎(0932) 848364 39⇨🐾

SCORE CARD: West Course					
Hole	Yds	Par	Hole	Yds	Par
1	471	4	10	186	3
2	155	3	11	376	4
3	452	4	12	483	5
4	501	5	13	441	4
5	191	3	14	179	3
6	344	4	15	466	4
7	399	4	16	380	4
8	398	4	17	571	5
9	450	4	18	502	5
Out	3361	35	In	3584	37
			Totals	6945	72

VIRGINIA WATER   **Map2 D4**

Wentworth ☎ (09904) 2201. W side of town, off B389.

Among the famous inland courses in England you have to name Woodhall Spa, Sunningdale, Swinley Forest - and Wentworth. The attraction at Wentworth is that the great players, including Ben Hogan and Sam Snead, have played here. The challenge, in terms of sheer yards, is enormous. But the qualities go beyond this, and include the atmosphere, the silver birch and fairway-side homes.

The West Course is the one every visitor wishes to play. You can't possibly name the best hole. Bernard Gallacher the local pro has his view, but you may select the seventh where the drive rolls downhill, and the second shot has to be played high up to a stepped green. The closing holes really sort out the best of them too.

The clubhouse offers Country Club facilities not typical of British golf courses. The pro shop resembles a plush city store; evening hospitality events are frequent and society meetings here are catered for as at few other centres for sport, and it's all done in five-star style.

Probably it is during the World Match-Play championship when Wentworth can be seen at its best. The tents are up, the superstars pile in and out of huge cars and the air is one of luxury and opulence.

Gary Player has won marvellously at Wentworth, beating Tony Lema after being seven down in the 36-hole match! Great competitors from the past have stamped their mark here. Arnold Palmer, back in the 1960s, beat Neil Coles in the Match-Play final but then, a generation later, faced young Seve Ballesteros. The Spaniard saved his bacon by pitching in for an eagle three at the last against Palmer, to take the clash into extra holes, where he won.

54 holes. West Course 18 holes, 6945 yds, Par 72, SSS 74, Course record 64. East Course 18 holes, 6176 yds, Par 68, SSS 70, Course record 62. Edinburgh 18 holes, 6979 yds, Par 72, SSS 73. Membership 2,200

Visitors   welcome weekdays only. Must contact in advance ✉. Societies welcome but handicap restriction (men 20, ladies 30)

Green fees   West Course £80 (with M £25; WE £35) East Course £55 (with M £25; WE £35) Edinburgh Course £65

Facilities   ⊗ ⓑ ▬ ♀(all day) ⚒ 🗒 ⛳ ℓ Bernard Gallacher

WHERE TO STAY AND EAT NEARBY

HOTELS:

ASCOT   ★★★★ 56% The Royal Berkshire, London Rd, Sunninghil ☎ (0990) 23322. 64 ⌐⅔ℓ Annexe 18 ⌐⅔

            ★★★★ 50% Berystede, Bagshot Rd, Sunninghill ☎ (0990) 23311.

            91 ⌐⅔ℓ . ♀ French & English cuisine.

            (Note: During the currency of this publication Ascot telephone numbers are liable to change).

MAIDENHEAD ★★★★ 71% Fredrick's Shoppenhangers Rd ☎ (0628) 35934.   37 ⌐⅔ℓ . ♀ French & English cuisine.

RESTAURANTS:

BRAY   ✗✗✗ The Waterside, River Cottage, Ferry Rd ☎ Maidenhead (0628) 20691 & 22941. ♀ French cuisine.

EGHAM   ✗✗ La Bonne Franquette, 5 High Street ☎ (0784) 439494. ♀ French cuisine.

WALTON-ON-THE-HILL
Map 2 E5

Walton Heath See page 186

WEST BYFLEET
Map 2 D4

West Byfleet
☎ Byfleet (0932) 343433
Sheerwater Rd (W side of village on A245)
An attractive course set against a background of woodland and gorse. The 13th is the famous 'pond' shot with a water hazard and two bunkers fronting the green. No less than five holes of 420 yards or more. Snooker.
18 holes, 6211yds, Par 70, SSS 70, Course record 64. Membership 650.

SCORE CARD					
Hole	Yds	Par	Hole	Yds	Par
1	405	4	10	452	4
2	378	4	11	159	3
3	425	4	12	392	4
4	123	3	13	160	3
5	307	4	14	365	4
6	430	4	15	421	4
7	499	5	16	425	4
8	276	4	17	173	3
9	322	4	18	499	5
Out	3165	36	In	3046	34
			Totals	6211	70

Visitors welcome (not WE unless with M, not Thu Ladies day) must contact in advance Societies welcome (by letter)
Green fees £27 per day; £33 per round
Facilities ⊗ ⅲ by prior arrangement Ⅼⅎ 🍴 ⌣ 🏠 (David Regan
Hotel ★★★63% Thatchers Resort Hotel, Epsom Rd, EAST HORSLEY ☎(04865) 4291 36⇨🐾
Annexe:23⇨🐾

WEST END
Map 2 D4

Windlemere ☎ (0276) 858727
Windlesham Rd (N side of village off A319)
A parkland course, undulating in parts with natural water hazards, there is a floodlit driving range also.
9 holes, 2673yds, Par 34.

Visitors welcome Societies welcome (☎ or by letter)
Green fees Not confirmed
Facilities Ⅼⅎ 🍴 ⌣ 🏠 (David Thomas & Alistair Kelso
Hotel ★★★★♨70% Pennyhill Park Hotel, London Rd, BAGSHOT ☎(0276) 71774 22⇨🐾 Annexe:41⇨🐾

WEYBRIDGE
Map 2 D4

St George's Hill ☎ (0932) 842406
(2m S off B374)
Comparable and similar to Wentworth, a feature of this course is the number of long and difficult par 4s. To score well it is necessary to place the drive - and long driving pays handsomely. Walking is hard on the undulating, heavily-wooded course.
18 holes, 6492yds, Par 70, SSS 71. Membership 435.

Visitors welcome Societies welcome (by letter)
Green fees Not confirmed
Facilities ⅎ ⌣ 🏠 (
Hotel ★★★64% Ship Thistle Hotel, Monument Green, WEYBRIDGE ☎(0932) 848364 39⇨🐾

WOKING
Map 2 D4

Hoebridge Golf Centre ☎ (0483) 722611
Old Woking Rd, Old Woking (1m SE of Woking Rd)
This public course is set in parkland. Snooker. Three courses.
Main Course 18 holes, 6536yds, Par 72, SSS 71. Intermediate Course 9 holes, 2294yds, Par 33. Par 3 Course 18 holes, 2230yds, Par 54. Membership 400.

Visitors welcome must contact in advance Societies welcome (Mon-Fri only ☎)
Green fees Not confirmed
Facilities ⊗ ⅲ Ⅼ ⅎ 🍴 ⌣ 🏠 ⅌ (Tim Powell
Hotel ★★★★♨70% Pennyhill Park Hotel, London Rd, BAGSHOT ☎(0276) 71774 22⇨🐾 Annexe:41⇨🐾

Worplesdon ☎ (04867) 2277
Heath House Rd (3.5m SW off B380)
The scene of the celebrated mixed-foursomes competition. Accurate driving is essential. The short 10th across a lake from tee to green is a notable hole, and the 18th provides a wonderfully challenging par-4 finish.
18 holes, 6440yds, Par 71, SSS 71, Course record 64. Membership 570.

Visitors welcome (with M only WE & BH) must contact in advance ✉ Societies welcome (by letter)
Green fees Not confirmed
Facilities ⊗ Ⅼ ⅎ 🍴 ⌣ 🏠 ⅌ (J Christine
Hotel ★★★★♨70% Pennyhill Park Hotel, London Rd, BAGSHOT ☎(0276) 71774 22⇨🐾 Annexe:41⇨🐾

WOLDINGHAM
Map 2 F5

North Downs ☎ (0883) 652057
Northdown Rd (.75m S)
Downland course, 850 ft above sea-level, with several testing holes.
18 holes, 5787yds, Par 69, SSS 68, Course record 66. Membership 700.

Visitors welcome (with M only WE & BH) must contact in advance ✉ Societies welcome (by letter)
Green fees £25
Facilities ⊗ ⅲ Ⅼ ⅎ 🍴 ⌣ 🏠 (Peter Ellis
Hotel ★★59% Sevenoaks Park Hotel, Seal Hollow Rd, SEVENOAKS ☎(0732) 454245 16rm(3⇨3🐾) Annexe:10⇨🐾

TYNE & WEAR

BACKWORTH
Map 6 K6

Backworth ☎ 091-268 1048
The Hall (W side of town on B1322)
Parkland course, easy walking, natural hazards, good scenery.
9 holes, 5930yds, Par 71, SSS 69, Course record 64. Membership 400.

Visitors welcome (ex Tue-Thu after 1700 & Sun am) Societies welcome (by letter)

▶

SCORE CARD: Old Course (Medal Tees)					
Hole	Yds	Par	Hole	Yds	Par
1	298	4	10	395	4
2	439	4	11	189	3
3	289	4	12	371	4
4	443	4	13	507	5
5	391	4	14	517	5
6	422	4	15	404	4
7	174	3	16	510	5
8	489	5	17	181	3
9	390	4	18	404	4
Out	3335	36	In	3478	37
			Totals	6813	73

WALTON-ON-THE-HILL — Map2 E5

Walton Heath ☎ (0737) 812060. (SE side of village, off B2032)

Several historic names are etched on the Honours Board at Walton Heath, almost 700 feet above sea level. The rare atmosphere here is justified because this Surrey course can claim to be the toughest inland examination in Britain. Based on sand, the fairways equal the best on any seaside links and quickly dry out, even after a severe storm.

Weekend players are tormented in awful fashion. Erratic shots, wide of the prepared surface, are wickedly punished. Nobody escapes undamaged from the gorse and bracken but it is the heather, with those tough stems, that really snarl up any attempt at an over-ambitious recovery shot. So be advised - if you're caught off the fairway, don't attempt anything fancy. Play back on the shortest route to comparative security.

The course is famous for staging the Ryder Cup but older players will remember it best for the Match-Play Championship battles that involved Sir Henry Cotton and Dai Rees as well as huge money matches that brought names such as Bobby Locke and Fred Daly to public prominence.

Once owned by the News of the World newspaper, MP's, Lords and significant members of the press would be invited down to Walton Heath by Sir Emsley Carr one of the first to employ a lady as secretary and manager of a well-known championship venue.

While the Old Course is most frequently played by visitors, the New Course also offers classic silver birch trees, and all the subtle shots required if you are to get the ball near the hole. And, in the clubhouse, they serve a spectacular lunch.

36 holes. Old Course 18 holes, 6883 yds, Par 73, SSS 73, Course record 65. New Course 18 holes, 6659 yds, Par 72, SSS 72, Course record 64. Membership 900

Visitors welcome weekdays only. Must contact in advance ✉ . Societies welcome (by letter).

Green fees £45

Facilities ⊗ ⅃ ⬛ ♀ (closes 8.30pm) ⬥ 🏠 ⚐ ╭Ken Macpherson

WHERE TO STAY AND EAT NEARBY

HOTELS:

BURGH HEATH ★★ 58% Heathside, Brighton Rd. ☎ (0737) 353355. 47 ⌁ ╭ . ♀ English & French cuisine.

DORKING ★★★★ 65% The Burford Bridge, Burford Bridge, Box Hill (2m NE A24). ☎ (0306) 884561. 48 ⌁ . ♀ English & French cuisine.

REIGATE ★★★ 56% Bridge House, Reigate Hill. ☎ (0737) 246801 & 244821. 40 ⌁ ╭ . ♀ English & French cuisine.

STOKE D'ABERNON ★★★ 75% Woodlands Park, Woodlands Ln. ☎ Oxshott (037284) 3933. 59 ⌁ ╭

RESTAURANTS:

DORKING Partners, West Sreet 2-4 West St. ☎ (0306) 882826. ♀ English & French cuisine.

WALTON ON THE HILL ✕✕ Ebenezer Cottage, 36 Walton St. ☎ Tadworth (0737) 813166. ♀ English & French cuisine.

Green fees Not confirmed
Facilities ⊗ by prior arrangement ⦨ by prior
arrangement ⬩ ⬛ ♀ ⬠
★★★57% Newcastle Moat House, Coast Rd,
WALLSEND ☏091-262 8989 & 091-262 7044 150⇥🐾

BIRTLEY   Map 6 K6

Birtley ☏ 091-410 2207
Portobello Rd
Parkland course.
9 holes, 5660, Par 66, SSS 67, Course record 64.
Membership 270.

Visitors welcome (with M only at WE) Societies
welcome (one mth notice in summer)
Green fees Not confirmed
Facilities ⬛ ♀ (after 19.⬛0 & WE) ⬠
Hotel ★★★61% Post House Hotel, Emerson Distrist 5,
WASHINGTON ☏091-416 2264 138⇥🐾

BOLDON   Map 5 F1

Boldon ☏ 091-536 5360 & 091-536 4182
Dipe Ln, East Boldon (S side of village off A184)
Meadowland links course, easy walking, distant sea
views, windy. Snooker.
18 holes, 6348yds, Par 72, SSS 70, Course record 67.
Membership 700.

Visitors welcome (ex WE) Societies welcome (by letter)
Green fees Not confirmed
Facilities ⊗ ⦨ ⬩ ⬛ ♀ ⬠ 📠 ⁓ ⁏
Hotel ★★★63% Swallow Hotel, Queen's Pde, Seaburn,
SUNDERLAND ☏091-529 2041 65⇥

CHOPWELL   Map 6 K6

Garesfield ☏ (0207) 561278
(.5m N)
Undulating parkland course with good views and
picturesque woodland surroundings.
18 holes, 6203yds, Par 72, SSS 70. Membership 615.

Visitors welcome (WE after 1600 only unless with M)
must contact in advance for WE only Societies welcome
(☏)
Green fees Not confirmed
Facilities ⊗ ⦨ by prior arrangement ⬩ ⬛ ♀ ⬠ 📠
Hotel ★★★63% Swallow Hotel, Newgate Arcade,
NEWCASTLE UPON TYNE ☏091-232 5025 93⇥🐾

FELLING   Map 6 K6

Heworth ☏ (0632) 692137
Gingling Gate, Heworth (On A195, .5m NW of junc with
A1(M))
Fairly flat, downland course.
18 holes, 6462yds, Par 71, SSS 71. Membership 500.

Visitors welcome (ex WE & BH (am))
Green fees Not confirmed
Facilities ♀ ⬠ 📠
Hotel ★★★61% Post House Hotel, Emerson Distrist 5,
WASHINGTON ☏091-416 2264 138⇥🐾

GATESHEAD   Map 6 K6

Ravensworth ☏ 091-487 6014
Moss Heaps, Wrekenton (3m SE off A6127)
Moorland/parkland course 600 ft above sea-level with
fine views. Testing 13th hole (par 3).
18 holes, 5872yds, Par 68, SSS 68. Membership 600.

Visitors welcome Societies welcome (☏)
Green fees £12 per round (£20 WE & BH)
Facilities ⊗ ⦨ ⬩ ⬛ (catering by prior arrangement
Mon & Wed) ♀ ⬠ 📠
Hotel ★★★66% Swallow Hotel-Gateshead, High West
St, GATESHEAD ☏091-477 1105 103⇥🐾

GOSFORTH   Map 6 K6

Gosforth ☏ 091-285 3495
Broadway East (N side of town centre off A6125)
Parkland course with natural water hazards, easy
walking.
18 holes, 6043yds, Par 69, SSS 69. Membership 480.

Visitors welcome (ex Tue & competition days) must
contact in advance Societies welcome (☏)
Green fees £12 per day (£20 WE)
Facilities ⦨ (ex Mon) ⦨ (ex Mon, Tue and Fri) ⬩ ⬛
♀ ⬠ 📠 ⁓ ⁏ David Race
Hotel ★★★★65% Swallow Gosforth Park Hotel, High
Gosforth Park, Gosforth, NEWCASTLE UPON TYNE
☏091-236 4111 178⇥🐾

Gosforth Park ☏ 091-236 4480
Parklands Golf Club, High Gosforth Park (2m N on
B1318 off A6125)
A very flat course, short in length, tree-lined with a
burn running through many holes. There is also a 30-
bay covered floodlit driving range and a 9-hole pitch-
putt course.
18 holes, 6200yds, Par 70, SSS 69, Course record 66.
Membership 650.

Visitors welcome must contact in advance Societies
welcome (☏)
Green fees £8.50 (£10 WE)
Facilities ⊗ ⦨ by prior arrangement ⬩ ⬛ ♀ ⬠ 📠
⁏ Grahame Garland
Hotel ★★★★65% Swallow Gosforth Park Hotel, High
Gosforth Park, Gosforth, NEWCASTLE UPON TYNE
☏091-236 4111 178⇥🐾

HOUGHTON-LE-SPRING   Map 5 F2

Houghton-le-Spring ☏ 091-845 1198
Copt Hill (.5m E on B1404)
Hilly, downland course with natural slope hazards.
18 holes, 6416yds, Par 72, SSS 71. Membership 600.

Visitors welcome (ex WE & BH) Societies welcome
Green fees Not confirmed
Facilities ⬩ ⬛ ♀ ⬠ 📠 ⁓ ⁏
Hotel ★★★69% Ramside Hall Hotel, Belmont,
DURHAM ☏091-386 5282 82⇥🐾

NEWCASTLE UPON TYNE   Map 6 K6

City of Newcastle ☎ 091-285 1775
Three Mile Bridge, Great North Rd (3m N on A1)
A well-manicured parkland course in the Newcastle
suburbs, subject to wind. Snooker.
18 holes, 6508yds, Par 72, SSS 71, Course record 67.
Membership 570.

Visitors welcome (ex competition days) Societies
welcome (☎)
Green fees £11 per day (£15 WE & BH)
Facilities ⊗ 🏌 🏡 ⌇ A J Matthew
Hotel ★★★64% Airport Moat House Hotel,
Woolsington, NEWCASTLE UPON TYNE AIRPORT
☎(0661) 24911 100⇨🏌

Newcastle United ☎ 091-286 4693
Ponteland Rd, Cowgate (1.25m NW of city centre off
A6127)
Moorland course with natural hazards. Snooker and
pool.
18 holes, 6484yds, Par 72, SSS 71, Course record 64.
Membership 500.

Visitors welcome (WE with M) Societies welcome (by
letter)
Green fees £7.50 wkday
Facilities ⊗ 🏌 🍺 ♀ 🏌 🏡
Hotel ★★★59% Imperial Hotel, Jesmond Rd,
NEWCASTLE UPON TYNE ☎091-281 5511 129⇨

Northumberland ☎ 091-236 2009
High Gosforth Park (4m N of city centre off A1)
Many golf courses have been sited inside
racecourses, although not so many survive today.
One which does is the Northumberland Club's
course at High Gosforth Park. Naturally the course
is flat but there are plenty of mounds and other
hazards to make it a fine test of golf. It should be said
that not all the holes are within the confines of the
racecourse, but both inside and out there are some
good holes. This is a Championship course.
18 holes, 6629yds, Par 72, SSS 72. Membership 550.

Visitors welcome (restricted competition days)
must contact in advance ✉ Societies welcome (☎)
Green fees Not confirmed
Facilities ⊗ (ex Mon) 🍴 (Wed and Sat) 🏌 🍺 ♀
🏌
Hotel ★★★★65% Swallow Gosforth Park Hotel,
High Gosforth Park, Gosforth, NEWCASTLE UPON
TYNE ☎091-236 4111 178⇨🏌

Westerhope ☎ 091-286 9125
Bowerbank, Whorlton Grange, Westerhope (4.5m NW of
city centre off B6324)
Attractive parkland course with tree-lined fairways,
and easy walking. Good open views towards the airport.
18 holes, 6468yds, Par 72, SSS 71. Membership 750.

Visitors welcome (only with M Sat & Sun) Societies
welcome (☎)
Green fees Not confirmed

Facilities ⊗ 🍴 🏌 🍺 ♀ 🏌 🏡 ⌇
Hotel ★★★★65% Swallow Gosforth Park Hotel, High
Gosforth Park, Gosforth, NEWCASTLE UPON TYNE
☎091-236 4111 178⇨🏌

RYTON   Map 6 K6

Ryton ☎ 091-413 3737
Clara Vale (NW side of town off A695)
Parkland course.
18 holes, 5968yds, Par 70, SSS 68. Membership 400.

Visitors welcome (with M only WE)
Green fees Not confirmed
Facilities ♀ 🏌
Hotel ★★62% County Hotel, Priestpopple, HEXHAM
☎(0434) 602030 9⇨🏌

Tyneside ☎ 091-413 2177
Westfield Ln (NW side of town off A695)
Open parkland course, not heavily bunkered. Water
hazard, hilly, practice area.
18 holes, 6042yds, Par 70, SSS 69, Course record 65.
Membership 660.

Visitors welcome Societies welcome (by letter)
Green fees £12 per day (£16 WE & BH)
Facilities ⊗ 🍴 🏌 🍺 ♀ 🏌 🏡 ⌇ Malcolm Gunn
Hotel ★★62% County Hotel, Priestpopple, HEXHAM
☎(0434) 602030 9⇨🏌

SOUTH SHIELDS   Map 5 F2

South Shields ☎ 091-456 8942
Cleadon Hills (SE side of town centre off A1300)
A slightly undulating downland course on a limestone
base ensuring good conditions underfoot. Open to
strong winds, the course is testing but fair. There are
fine views of the coastline.
18 holes, 6264yds, Par 71, SSS 70, Course record 64.
Membership 800.

Visitors welcome must contact in advance ✉ Societies
welcome (☎)
Green fees £14 per day (£19 WE & BH)
Facilities ⊗ 🍴 🏌 🍺 ♀ 🏌 🏡 🍴 ⌇ Gary Parsons
Hotel ★★63% New Crown Hotel, Mowbray Rd, SOUTH
SHIELDS ☎091-455 3472 11rm(6⇨1🏌)

Whitburn ☎ 091-529 2144
Lizard Ln (2.5m SE off A183)
Parkland course. Snooker.
18 holes, 6046yds, Par 70, SSS 69, Course record 65.
Membership 500.

Visitors welcome (restricted on competition days &
Sun) Societies welcome (☎)
Green fees Not confirmed
Facilities ⊗ 🏌 🍺 ♀ (restricted Sun) 🏌 🏡 ⌇ David
Stephenson
Hotel ★★★63% Swallow Hotel, Queen's Pde, Seaburn,
SUNDERLAND ☎091-529 2041 65⇨

SUNDERLAND   Map 5 F2

Wearside ☎ 091-534 2518
Coxgreen (3.5m W off A183)
Open, undulating parkland course rolling down to
the River Wear and beneath the shadow of the
famous Penshaw Monument, built on the lines of an
Athenian temple it is a well-known landmark. Two
ravines cross the course presenting a variety of
challenging holes.
*18 holes, 6373yds, Par 71, SSS 70, Course record 67.
Membership 729.*

Visitors welcome (ex before 0930 & after 1600) ✉
Societies welcome (by letter)
Green fees £12 per day (£18 WE & BH)
Facilities ⊗ Ⅲ by prior arrangement ᒥᒪ ᒻ ♀ ᐱ
🏠 (Steven Wynn
Hotel ★★★63% Swallow Hotel, Queen's Pde,
Seaburn, SUNDERLAND ☎091-529 2041 65⇨

TYNEMOUTH   Map 5 F1

Tynemouth ☎ 091-257 4578
Spital Dene (.5m W)
Well-drained parkland/downland course, easy walking.
18 holes, 6082yds, Par 70, SSS 69. Membership 810.

Visitors welcome (restricted WE & BH) Societies
welcome (by letter)
Green fees £12 (£14 WE)
Facilities ⊗ ᒥᒪ ᒻ ♀ ᐱ 🏠 (J P McKenna
Hotel ★★★61% Park Hotel, Grand Pde, TYNEMOUTH
☎091-257 1406 49rm(41⇨2🐾)

WALLSEND   Map 6 K6

Wallsend ☎ 091-262 1973
Rheydt Av, Bigges Main (NW side of town centre off
A193)
Parkland course.
*18 holes, 6608yds, Par 72, SSS 72, Course record 68.
Membership 750.*

Visitors welcome (ex after 1230 WE) must contact in
advance Societies welcome (by letter)
Green fees Not confirmed
Facilities ⊗ by prior arrangement Ⅲ by prior
arrangement ᒥᒪ ᒻ ♀ ᐱ 🏠 (Ken Phillips
Hotel ★★★57% Newcastle Moat House, Coast Rd,
WALLSEND ☎091-262 8989 & 091-262 7044 150⇨🐾

WASHINGTON   Map 5 F2

Washington Moat House ☎ (091) 4172626
Stone Cellar Rd, High Usworth
Championship course. Also a 9-hole (par 3) course,
putting green and 21-bay floodlit driving range.
'Bunkers Bar' at the 10th tee is one of the few 'spike'
bars in the country. Accommodation. Indoor-heated
swimming pool, squash, snooker, sauna, solarium and
gymnasium.
*18 holes, 6604yds, Par 73, SSS 71, Course record 66.
Membership 650.*

Visitors welcome must contact in advance Societies
welcome (by letter)
Green fees £10 (£16 WE & BH)
Facilities ⊗ Ⅲ ᒥᒪ ᒻ ♀ ᐱ 🏠 ᆔ (
Hotel ★★★68% Washington Moat House, Stone
Cellar Rd, District 12, WASHINGTON ☎091-417 2626
106⇨🐾

WHICKHAM   Map 6 K6

Whickham ☎ 091-488 7309
Hollinside Park (1.5m S)
Parkland course, some uphill walking, fine views.
*18 holes, 6129yds, Par 68, SSS 69, Course record 61.
Membership 600.*

Visitors welcome ✉ Societies welcome (☎)
Green fees Not confirmed
Facilities ⊗ by prior arrangement Ⅲ by prior
arrangement ᒥᒪ ᒻ ♀ ᐱ 🏠 ᆔ
Hotel ★★★66% Swallow Hotel-Gateshead, High West
St, GATESHEAD ☎091-477 1105 103⇨🐾

WHITLEY BAY   Map 5 F1

Whitley Bay ☎ 091-252 0180
Claremont Rd (NW side of town centre off A1148)
Downland course close to the sea. A stream runs
through the undulating terrain.
*18 holes, 6717yds, Par 71, SSS 72, Course record 66.
Membership 700.*

Visitors welcome (with M only WE & BH) Societies
welcome (not WE, ☎)
Green fees £15
Facilities ᐱ 🏠 (W J Light
Hotel ★★63% Holmedale Hotel, 106 Park Av, WHITLEY
BAY ☎091-251 3903 & 091-253 1162 18rm(7⇨9🐾)

WARWICKSHIRE

ATHERSTONE   Map 3 K4

Atherstone ☎ (0827) 713110
The Outwoods, Coleshill Rd (.5m S on B4116)
Ninety-year-old parkland course, laid out on some hilly
ground.
*18 holes, 6235yds, Par 73, SSS 70, Course record 66.
Membership 350.*

Visitors welcome (h'cap cert required, with M only
WE) Societies welcome (with h'cap cert, wkdays only)
Green fees £15 per day (£20 BH)
Facilities ⊗ Ⅲ ᒥᒪ ᒻ ♀ ᐱ 🏠
Hotel ★★61% Chase Hotel, Higham Ln, NUNEATON
☎(0203) 341013 28⇨🐾

Purley Chase ☎ (0203) 393118
Ridge Ln (2m S off B4114)
Meadowland course with tricky water hazards and
undulating greens.
*18 holes, 6604yds, Par 71, SSS 71, Course record 64.
Membership 600.*

▶

Visitors welcome (ex WE (am)) Societies welcome (☎ 1 mth in advance)
Green fees Not confirmed
Facilities ⊗ Ⅲ ⓛ 💺 ♀ ♨ 🏠 ℂ David Llewelyn
Hotel Longshoot Toby Hotel, Watling St, NUNEATON
☎(0203) 329711 Annexe:47⊸🏌

BRANDON Map 3 K5

City of Coventry-Brandon Wood
☎ Coventry (0203) 543141
Brandon Ln (1m W)
Municipal parkland course surrounded by fields and bounded by River Avon on east side.
18 holes, 6530yds, Par 72, SSS 71, Course record 68.
Membership 800.

Visitors welcome Societies welcome (by letter)
Green fees £5.40 per round (£6.90 WE & BH)
Facilities ⊗ Ⅲⓛ 💺 ♀ ♨ 🏠 ℸℂ Chris Gledhill
Hotel ★★★60% Chace Crest Hotel, London Rd, Willenhall, COVENTRY ☎(0203) 303398 68⊸🏌

COLESHILL Map 3 J5

Maxstoke Park ☎ (0675) 464915
Castle Ln (2m E)
Parkland course with easy walking. Numerous trees and a lake form natural hazards.
18 holes, 6151yds, Par 71, SSS 69, Course record 65.
Membership 450.

Visitors welcome (with M only WE & BH) Societies welcome (☎)
Green fees £25 per day; £20 per round
Facilities ⊗ Ⅲⓛ 💺 ♀ ♨ 🏠 ℸℂ R A Young
Hotel ★★63% Swan Hotel, High St, COLESHILL
☎(0675) 464107 32⊸🏌

KENILWORTH Map 3 K5

Kenilworth ☎ (0926) 58517
Crew Ln (.5m NE)
Parkland course in open hilly situation. Modern clubhouse. Snooker.
18 holes, 6263yds, Par 72, SSS 70. Membership 875.

Visitors welcome (ex competition days) Societies welcome (☎ for details)
Green fees Not confirmed
Facilities ♀ ♨ 🏠 ℸℂ
Hotel ★★64% Clarendon House Hotel, Old High St, KENILWORTH ☎(0926) 57668 31⊸🏌

LEAMINGTON SPA Map 3 K6

Leamington & County ☎ (0926) 425961
Golf Ln, Whitnash (S side of town centre)
Undulating parkland course with extensive views. Snooker.
18 holes, 6424yds, Par 71, SSS 71, Course record 64.
Membership 700.

Visitors welcome Societies welcome (☎)

Green fees £23 per day; £20 per round (£60/£30 WE)
Facilities ⊗ Ⅲ ⓛ 💺 ♀ ♨ 🏠 ℂ I A Grant
Hotel ★★★57% Manor House Hotel, Avenue Rd, LEAMINGTON SPA ☎(0926) 423251 53⊸🏌

Newbold ☎ (0296) 21157
Newbold Ter East (.75m E of town centre off B4099)
Municipal parkland course with hard walking in parts. The par 4, 9th is a 467-yd testing hole.
18 holes, 6221yds, Par 70, SSS 70. Membership 350.

Visitors welcome
Green fees Not confirmed
Facilities ♀ ♨ 🏠 ℸℂ
Hotel ★★★57% Manor House Hotel, Avenue Rd, LEAMINGTON SPA ☎(0926) 423251 53⊸🏌

NUNEATON Map 3 K5

Nuneaton ☎ (0203) 347810
Golf Dr, Whitestone (2m SE off B4114)
Parkland course.
18 holes, 5431yds, Par 71, SSS 71. Membership 550.

Visitors welcome (with M only WE)
Green fees Not confirmed
Facilities ♀ ♨ 🏠 ℂ
Hotel ★★61% Chase Hotel, Higham Ln, NUNEATON
☎(0203) 341013 28⊸🏌

RUGBY Map 3 K5

Rugby ☎ (0788) 542306
Clifton Rd (1m NE on B5414)
Parkland course with brook running through the middle and crossed by a viaduct. Snooker.
18 holes, 5457yds, Par 68, SSS 67. Membership 550.

Visitors welcome (WE & BH with M) must contact in advance ✉ Societies welcome (by letter)
Green fees £14 per day
Facilities ⊗ by prior arrangement (ex Tue) Ⅲ by prior arrangement (ex Tue) ⓛ 💺 ♀ ♨ 🏠 ℸℂ D Sutherland
Hotel ★★★60% Grosvenor Hotel, Clifton Rd, RUGBY
☎(0788) 535686 21⊸🏌

STRATFORD-UPON-AVON Map 3 J6

Stratford-upon-Avon ☎ (0789) 205749
Tiddington Rd (0.75m E on B4086)
Beautiful parkland course. The par 3, 16th is tricky and the par 5, 17th and 18th, provide a tough end.
18 holes, 6309yds, Par 72, SSS 70, Course record 64.
Membership 750.

Visitors welcome (restricted Wed) must contact in advance Societies welcome (☎)
Green fees £20 per day (£30 WE)
Facilities ⊗ Ⅲ ⓛ 💺 ♀ ♨ 🏠 ℸℂ N D Powell
Hotel ★★★59% Alveston Manor Hotel, Clopton Bridge, STRATFORD-UPON-AVON ☎(0789) 204581 108⊸

Welcombe Hotel ☎ (0789) 295252
Warwick Rd (1.5m NE off A46)
This wooded parkland course has great character and
boasts superb views of the River Avon, Stratford and
the Cotswolds. It is a good test for all standards.
Accommodation, tennis, fishing, snooker.
18 holes, 6202yds, Par 70, SSS 70, Course record 67.
Membership 300.

Visitors welcome (ex before 1100 WE) must contact in
advance ✉ Societies welcome (booking via Hotel)
Green fees £25 day (£30 WE & BH)
Facilities ⊗ ⫬ ⤬ ⬙ ⬚ ⬛ ⬚
Hotel ★★★★62% Welcombe Hotel and Golf Course,
Warwick Rd, STRATFORD-UPON-AVON ☎(0789) 295252
76⇌

TANWORTH-IN-ARDEN   Map 3 J5

Ladbrook Park ☎ (05644) 2264
Poolhead Ln (1m NW on A4023)
Parkland course lined with trees.
18 holes, 6407yds, Par 71, SSS 71, Course record 61.
Membership 750.

Visitors welcome (WE with M handicap certificate
required) must contact in advance ✉ Societies welcome
(☎)
Green fees Not confirmed

Facilities ⊗ ⫬ ⤬ ⬙ ⬚ ⬛ ⬚ Graham Taylor
Hotel ★★★64% St John's Swallow Hotel, 651
Warwick Rd, SOLIHULL ☎021-711 3000 206⇌

WARWICK   Map 3 K6

Warwick ☎ (0926) 494316
The Racecourse (W side of town centre)
Parkland course with easy walking. Driving range with
floodlit bays. Snooker.
9 holes, 2682yds, Par 34, SSS 66, Course record 67.
Membership 150.

Visitors welcome (ex Sun am)
Green fees £3 per day (£4 WE)
Facilities ⬙ ⬚ ⬛ ⬚ ⬚ Phil Sharp
Hotel ★★★57% Hilton National, A46, Stratford Rd,
WARWICK ☎(0926) 499555 180⇌🐾

WEST MIDLANDS

ALDRIDGE   Map 3 J4

Druids Heath ☎ (0922) 55595
Stonnal Rd (NE side of town centre off A454)
Testing undulating heathland course.
18 holes, 6914yds, Par 72, SSS 73. Membership 500.

Visitors welcome (with M only WE) must contact in
advance ✉ Societies welcome
Green fees Not confirmed

Facilities 🍸 △ ⌂ ⛳ ℓ
Hotel ★★★66% Fairlawns Hotel, 178 Little Aston Road, Aldridge, WALSALL ☏(0922) 55122 36⇨⛆

BIRMINGHAM

Map 3 J5

Brandhall ☏ 021-552 2195
Heron Rd, Oldbury, Warley (5.5m W of city centre off A4123)
Private golf club on municipal parkland course, easy walking, good hazards. Testing holes: 1st-516 yds (par 5); 10th-497 yds dog-leg (par 5). Snooker.
18 holes, 5813yds, Par 70, SSS 68. Membership 320.

Visitors welcome must contact in advance Societies welcome (☏)
Green fees Not confirmed
Facilities 🍸 (M & guest only) ⛳
Hotel ★★★58% Post House Hotel, Chapel Ln, GREAT BARR ☏021-357 7444 204⇨

Cocks Moors Woods Municipal ☏ 021-444 3584
Alcester Rd South, Kings Heath (5m S of city centre on A435)
Tree-lined, parkland course.
18 holes, 5888yds, Par 69, SSS 68. Membership 250.

Visitors welcome Societies welcome
Green fees Not confirmed
Facilities △ ⌂ ⛳
Hotel ★★★★51% Albany Hotel, Smallbrook Queensway, BIRMINGHAM ☏021-643 8171 254⇨

Edgbaston ☏ 021-454 1736
Church Rd, Edgbaston (1m S of city centre on B4217 off A38)
Parkland course in lovely country. Snooker.
18 holes, 6118yds, Par 69, SSS 69. Membership 835.

Visitors welcome (handicap certificate required) Societies welcome (by letter)
Green fees £24 per day (£30 WE & BH)
Facilities ⊗ ☽ ♨ ☕ 🍸 △ ⌂ ⛳ ℓ Andrew H Bownes
Hotel ★★★★67% Plough & Harrow, Hagley Rd, Edgbaston, BIRMINGHAM ☏021-454 4111 44⇨⛆

Great Barr ☏ 021-358 4376
Chapel Ln, Great Barr (6m N of city centre off A 34)
Parkland course with easy walking. Pleasant views of Barr Beacon National Park. Snooker.
18 holes, 6545yds, Par 73, SSS 72. Membership 600.

Visitors welcome (restricted WE) ✉ Societies welcome (by letter)
Green fees £20 per day (£25 WE)
Facilities ⊗ by prior arrangement ☽ by prior arrangement ♨ ☕ 🍸 △ ⌂ ⛳ ℓ S Doe
Hotel ★★★58% Post House Hotel, Chapel Ln, GREAT BARR ☏021-357 7444 204⇨

For an explanation of the symbols and abbreviations used, see page 33.

Handsworth ☏ 021-554 0599
Sunningdale Close, Handsworth Wood (3.5m NW of city centre off A4040)
Undulating parkland course with some tight fairways but subject to wind. Squash and snooker.
18 holes, 6312yds, Par 70, SSS 70. Membership 850.

Visitors welcome (restricted WE, BH & Xmas) must contact in advance ✉ Societies welcome (by letter, not WE)
Green fees Not confirmed
Facilities ⊗ (ex Mon) ☽ (ex Mon) ♨ (ex Mon) ☕ (ex Mon) 🍸 △ ⌂ ⛳ ℓ M J Hicks
Hotel ★★★63% West Bromwich Moat House, Birmingham Rd, WEST BROMWICH ☏021-553 6111 180⇨⛆

Harborne ☏ 021-427 3058
40 Tennal Rd, Harborne (3.5 m SW of city centre off A4040)
Parkland course in hilly situation. Snooker.
18 holes, 6240yds, Par 70, SSS 70, Course record 65. Membership 500.

Visitors welcome (ex WE, BH & 27 Dec-1 Jan h'cap cert) must contact in advance ✉ Societies welcome (☏)
Green fees £20 per day
Facilities ⊗ (Tue-Fri) ☽ (Tue-Fri) ♨ (Tue-Sat) ☕ (ex Mon) 🍸 △ ⌂ ℓ Alan Quarterman
Hotel ★★★★67% Plough & Harrow, Hagley Rd, Edgbaston, BIRMINGHAM ☏021-454 4111 44⇨⛆

Harborne Church Farm ☏ 021-427 1204
Vicarage Rd, Harborne (3.5m SW of city centre off A4040)
Parkland course with water hazards and easy walking. Some holes might prove difficult.
9 holes, 4732yds, Par 66, SSS 63, Course record 63. Membership 250.

Visitors welcome
Green fees £4.20, 18 holes; £2.20, 9 holes
Facilities ⊗ ☽ ☕ △ ⌂ ⛳ ℓ Mark J Hampton
Hotel ★★★53% Apollo Hotel, 243-247 Hagley Rd, Edgbaston, BIRMINGHAM ☏021-455 0271 128⇨⛆

Hatchford Brook ☏ 021-743 9821
Coventry Rd, Sheldon (6m E of city centre on A45)
Fairly flat, municipal parkland course.
18 holes, 6164yds, Par 69, SSS 69. Membership 400.

Visitors welcome
Green fees Not confirmed
Facilities △ ⌂ ⛳ ℓ
Hotel ★★★54% Excelsior Hotel, Coventry Rd, Elmdon, BIRMINGHAM AIRPORT ☏021-782 8141 141⇨⛆

Hilltop ☏ 021-554 4463
Park Ln, Handsworth (3.5m N of city centre off A4040)
Testing and hilly municipal parkland course.
18 holes, 6114yds, Par 71, SSS 69. Membership 280.

Visitors welcome Societies welcome (☏)
Green fees £4.40 per round (£4.90 WE)

Facilities ⊗ ⋔ ⬛ ⛺ 🏠 ⅋ ℓ Kevin Highfield
Hotel ★★★63% West Bromwich Moat House,
Birmingham Rd, WEST BROMWICH ☎021-553 6111
180⇌🐾

Lickey Hills ☎ 021-453 3159
Rednal (10m SW of city centre on B4096)
Hilly municipal course overlooking the city.
18 holes, 6610yds, Par 69, SSS 69. Membership 300.

Visitors welcome Societies welcome
Green fees Not confirmed
Facilities ⅋ ⛺ 🏠 ⅋ ℓ
Hotel ★★★60% Perry Hall Hotel, Kidderminster Rd,
BROMSGROVE ☎(0527) 579976 55⇌🐾

Moseley ☎ 021-444 2115
Springfield Rd, Kings Heath (4m S of city centre on
B4146 off A435)
Parkland course with a lake, pond and stream to provide
natural hazards. The par-3, 5th goes through a cutting
in woodland to a tree and garden-lined amphitheatre,
and the par-4, 6th entails a drive over a lake to a dog-leg
fairway.
18 holes, 6285yds, Par 70, SSS 70, Course record 64.
Membership 560.

Visitors welcome (ex WE) must contact in advance ✉
Societies welcome
Green fees Not confirmed
Facilities ⊗ (ex Mon) ⋔ by prior arrangement �📍 ⬛
⅋ ⛺ 🏠 ℓ G Edge
Hotel ★★63% New Cobden Hotel, 166 Hagley Rd,
Edgbaston, BIRMINGHAM ☎021-454 6621 230⇌🐾

Warley ☎ 021-429 2440
Lightswood Hill, Bearwood (4m W of city centre off
A456)
Municipal parkland course in Warley Woods. One of the
nearest courses to Birmingham centre.
9 holes, 2606yds, Par 33, SSS 64, Course record 62.
Membership 150.

Visitors welcome
Green fees Not confirmed
Facilities ⊗ 📍 ⬛ ⛺ 🏠 ⅋ ℓ David Owen
Hotel ★★50% Norfolk Hotel, 257/267 Hagley Rd,
Edgbaston, BIRMINGHAM ☎021-454 8071
175rm(32⇌56🐾)

COVENTRY   Map 3 K5

Coventry ☎ (0203) 414152
Finham Park (3m S of city centre on A444)
The scene of several major professional events, this
undulating parkland course has a great deal of
quality. More than that, it usually plays its length,
and thus scoring is never easy, as many
professionals have found to their cost. Snooker.
18 holes, 6613yds, Par 73, SSS 72, Course record 66.
Membership 760.

Visitors welcome (wkdays only, h'cap cert required)
must contact in advance Societies welcome (☎)

Green fees £30 per day
Facilities ⊗ ⋔ 📍 ⬛ ⅋ ⛺ 🏠 ℓ P Weaver
Hotel ★★★57% Hylands Hotel, Warwick Rd,
COVENTRY ☎(0203) 501600 55rm(54⇌)

The Grange ☎ (0203) 451465
Copsewood, Binley Rd (2m E of city centre on A428)
Flat parkland course with very tight out of bounds on a
number of holes, and a river which affects play on five of
them. Well-bunkered, with plenty of trees.
9 holes, 6002yds, Par 72, SSS 69. Membership 300.

Visitors welcome (not before 1400 wkdays; after 1200
Sun) Societies welcome (Limited. ☎)
Green fees Not confirmed
Facilities ⅋ ⛺
Hotel ★★★60% Chace Crest Hotel, London Rd,
Willenhall, COVENTRY ☎(0203) 303398 68⇌🐾

Hearsall ☎ (0203) 713470
Beechwood Av (1.5m SW of city centre off A429)
Parkland course with fairly easy walking. A brook
provides an interesting hazard.
18 holes, 5603yds, Par 70, SSS 68, Course record 70.
Membership 600.

Visitors welcome (with M only Sat & Sun) Societies
welcome (☎)
Green fees £19 per day
Facilities ⊗ ⋔ 📍 ⬛ ⅋ ⛺ 🏠 ℓ Mark Jennings
Hotel ★★★57% Hylands Hotel, Warwick Rd,
COVENTRY ☎(0203) 501600 55rm(54⇌)

DUDLEY   Map 3 H5

Dudley ☎ (0384) 233877
Turner's Hill (2m S of town centre off B4171)
Exposed and very hilly parkland course. Snooker.
18 holes, 5832yds, Par 69, SSS 68. Membership 300.

Visitors welcome (ex WE) Societies welcome (☎)
Green fees Not confirmed
Facilities ⊗ ⋔ by prior arrangement 📍 ⬛ ⅋ ⛺ 🏠
ℓ David Down
Hotel ★★60% Station Hotel, Birmingham Rd, DUDLEY
☎(0384) 253418 38⇌🐾

Swindon ☎ Wombourne (0902) 897031
Bridgnorth Rd, Swindon
Attractive, undulating woodland course. Fishing,
snooker.
Old Course 18 holes, 6042yds, Par 71, SSS 69, Course
record 68. New Course 9 holes, 1135yds, Par 27.
Membership 500.

Visitors welcome (no jeans, wide wheel trolleys)
Societies welcome (☎ weekdays only)
Green fees £12 per day (£18 WE & BH)
Facilities ⊗ ⋔ 📍 ⬛ ⅋ ⛺ 🏠 ⅋ ℓ P Lester
Hotel ★★60% Station Hotel, Birmingham Rd, DUDLEY
☎(0384) 253418 38⇌🐾

HALESOWEN   Map 3 H5

Halesowen ☎ 021-501 3606
The Leasowes (1m E)
Parkland course in convenient position. Snooker.
18 holes, 5754yds, Par 69, SSS 68, Course record 65.
Membership 600.

Visitors welcome (ex WE) Societies welcome (☎)
Green fees £12 per round
Facilities ⊗ ⅧⅢ ⅃ ⅃ ♀ ⚲ 🛏 ⅋ ℂ Mark Crowther-Smith
Hotel ★★50% Norfolk Hotel, 257/267 Hagley Rd,
Edgbaston, BIRMINGHAM ☎021-454 8071
175rm(32⇌56♠)

KNOWLE   Map 3 J5

Copt Heath ☎ (0564) 772650
1220 Warwick Rd (On A41 .25m S of junc 5 of M42)
Parkland course designed by H. Vardon.
18 holes, 6170yds, Par 71, SSS 71, Course record 65.
Membership 700.

Visitors welcome (Yellow tees only) must contact in
advance Societies welcome (☎)
Green fees £30 per round
Facilities ⊗ ⅧⅢ ⅃ ⅃ (no catering Mon) ♀ ⚲ 🛏 ℂ
Hotel ★★★64% St John's Swallow Hotel, 651
Warwick Rd, SOLIHULL ☎021-711 3000 206⇌

MERIDEN   Map 3 J5

Forest of Arden Hotel Golf and Country Club
☎ Meridan (0676) 22335
Maxstoke Ln (1m SW on B4102)
Two parkland and moorland courses offering a fine test
of golf. Accommodation, tennis, indoor-heated
swimming pool, squash, fishing, snooker, sauna,
solarium and gymnasium.
Arden Course 18 holes, 6915yds, Par 72, SSS 73, Course
record 67. Aylesford Course 18 holes, 6475yds, Par 72,
SSS 71. Membership 700.

Visitors welcome (ex WE (unless hotel resident) h'cap
cert) must contact in advance ✉ Societies welcome (☎)
Green fees Arden £22 per day (£25 WE). Aylesford £18
per day (£20 WE)
Facilities ⊗ ⅧⅢ ⅃ ⅃ ♀ ⚲ 🛏 ⅋ ℂ Michael Tarn
Hotel ★★★68% Manor Hotel, MERIDEN ☎(0676) 22735
74⇌♠

North Warwickshire ☎ (0676) 22259
Hampton Ln (1m SW on B4102)
Downland course with easy walking.
9 holes, 3186yds, Par 72, SSS 70. Membership 450.

Visitors welcome (restricted Thu, WE & BH) must
contact in advance Societies welcome
Green fees Not confirmed
Facilities ♀ ⚲ 🛏 ℂ
Hotel ★★★68% Manor Hotel, MERIDEN ☎(0676) 22735
74⇌♠

SOLIHULL   Map 3 J5

Olton ☎ 021-705 1083
Mirfield Rd (1m NW off A41)
Parkland course, prevailing SW wind. Snooker.
18 holes, 5694metres, Par 69, SSS 71. Membership 600.

Visitors welcome (with M only WE) Societies welcome
(☎)
Green fees £23 per day
Facilities ⊗ by prior arrangement ⅧⅢ by prior
arrangement ⅃ ⅃ ♀ ⚲ 🛏 ℂ D Playdon
Hotel ★★★64% St John's Swallow Hotel, 651
Warwick Rd, SOLIHULL ☎021-711 3000 206⇌

Robin Hood ☎ 021-706 0061
St Bernards Rd (2m W off B4025)
Pleasant parkland course with easy walking and open to
good views. Snooker.
18 holes, 6609yds, Par 72, SSS 72, Course record 68.
Membership 640.

Visitors welcome (with M only WE) must contact in
advance Societies welcome
Green fees Not confirmed
Facilities ⊗ by prior arrangement ⅧⅢ by prior
arrangement ⅃ (Tue-Sat) ⅃ ♀ ⚲ 🛏 ℂ F E Miller
Hotel ★★★64% St John's Swallow Hotel, 651
Warwick Rd, SOLIHULL ☎021-711 3000 206⇌

Shirley ☎ 021-744 6001
Stratford Rd, Monkpath (3m SW off A34)
Fairly flat parkland course. Snooker.
18 holes, 6510yds, Par 72, SSS 71, Course record 68 or
6084yds, Par 72, SSS 69. Membership 500.

Visitors welcome (ex BH, with M only WE) Societies
welcome (☎)
Green fees Not confirmed
Facilities ⊗ ⅧⅢ ⅃ ⅃ ♀ ⚲ 🛏 ℂ C J Wicketts
Hotel ★★★63% George Hotel, High St, SOLIHULL
☎021-711 2121 74⇌♠

STOURBRIDGE   Map 3 H5

Hagley Country Club ☎ (0562) 883701
Wassell Grove, Pedmore (1m E of Hagley off A456)
Parkland course set beneath the Clent Hills; there are
superb views. Squash courts.
18 holes, 6353yds, Par 72, SSS 72, Course record 72.
Membership 640.

Visitors welcome (restricted Wed (with M only WE))
Societies welcome (ex WE; by letter)
Green fees £20 per day; £15 per round
Facilities ⊗ ⅧⅢ ⅃ ⅃ ♀ ⚲ 🛏 ⅋ ℂ Iain Clark
Hotel ★★65% Talbot Hotel, High St, STOURBRIDGE
☎(0384) 394350 25rm(13⇌7♠)

Stourbridge ☎ (0384) 395566
Worcester Ln, Pedmore (2m from town centre)
Parkland course. Snooker.
18 holes, 6178yds, Par 69, SSS 69, Course record 65.
Membership 720.

Visitors welcome (ex WE & Wed pm) ✉ Societies welcome (by letter)
Green fees £20 day/round
Facilities ✗ (Tue-Fri) ⵊ by prior arrangement ⌊ (ex Sun) ⬤ ♀ ⌂ ⌸ ☂ ⟨
Hotel ★★65% Talbot Hotel, High St, STOURBRIDGE ☎(0384) 394350 25rm(13⇌7🛏)

SUTTON COLDFIELD   Map 3 J5

Belfry
☎ Curdworth (0675) 70301
Lichfield Rd, Wishaw (exit junc 4 M42 4m E)
Famed for hosting recent Ryder Cup matches. The two 18-hole courses here, the Brabazon and Derby have been designed by Peter Alliss and Dave Thomas. The Brabazon, a demanding championship course, has eleven holes on which one has to negotiate water.

SCORE CARD: Brabazon Course					
Hole	Yds	Par	Hole	Yds	Par
1	408	4	10	301	4
2	340	4	11	365	4
3	455	4	12	225	3
4	569	5	13	364	4
5	389	4	14	184	3
6	386	4	15	540	5
7	173	3	16	400	4
8	476	5	17	555	5
9	390	4	18	455	4
Out	3586	37	In	3389	36
			Totals	6975	73

Accommodation and many sports facilities. Course record holder is Eamon Darcey.
Brabazon 18 holes, 6975yds, Par 73, SSS 73, Course record 63. Derby 18 holes, 5953yds, Par 69, SSS 69.

Visitors welcome (handicap certificate for Brabazon course) must contact in advance Societies welcome (☎)
Green fees Not confirmed
Facilities ✗ ⵊ ⌊ ⬤ ♀ ⌂ ⌸ ☂ ⟨ G Laidlow & P McGovern
Hotel ★★★★66% The Belfry, Lichfield Rd, WISHAW ☎(0675) 70301 219⇌

Little Aston ☎ 021-353 2066
Streetly (3.5m NW off A454)
18 holes, 6724yds, Par 72, SSS 73. Membership 250.

Visitors welcome must contact in advance ✉ Societies welcome (by letter)
Green fees £30 per person
Facilities ⌊ ⬤ (ex Mon) ♀ ⌂ ⌸ ⟨
Hotel ★★60% Parson & Clerk Motel, Chester Rd, STREETLY ☎021-353 1747 30⇌🛏

Moor Hall ☎ 021-308 6130
Moor Hall Dr (2.5 m N of town centre off A453)
Parkland course. The 14th is a notable hole.
18 holes, 6249yds, Par 70, SSS 70. Membership 600.

Visitors welcome (with M only WE & BH) must contact in advance Societies welcome (by letter)
Green fees £26 per day ; £20 per round
Facilities ✗ (Tue-Fri) ⵊ (Tue-Fri) ⌊ (Tue-Fri) ⬤ ♀ ⌂ ⌸ ☂ ⟨ Alan Partridge
Hotel ★★★68% Moor Hall Hotel, Moor Hall Dr, Four Oaks, SUTTON COLDFIELD ☎021-308 3751 75⇌🛏

Pype Hayes ☎ 021-351 1014
Eachelhurst Rd, Walmley (2.5m S off B4148)
Attractive, fairly flat course with excellent greens.
18 holes, 5811yds, Par 70. Membership 300.

Visitors welcome Societies welcome
Green fees £4.90 per 18 holes
Facilities ✗ ⬤ ⌂ ⌸ ☂ ⟨ James Bayliss
Hotel ★★★★55% Penns Hall Hotel, Penns Ln, Walmley, SUTTON COLDFIELD ☎021-351 3111 114⇌🛏

Sutton Coldfield ☎ 021-353 9633
Thornhill Rd, Streetly (3m NW on B4138)
A fine natural, heathland course, which is surprising as the high-rise buildings of Birmingham are not far away. Snooker.
18 holes, 6541yds, Par 72, SSS 70, Course record 64. Membership 500.

Visitors welcome (☎ for details, h'cap cert required) must contact in advance Societies welcome (at least 3 months notice)
Green fees £25 per day (£25 WE)
Facilities ✗ by prior arrangement ⵊ by prior arrangement ⌊ ⬤ ♀ ⌂ ⟨ J M Hayes
Hotel ★★60% Parson & Clerk Motel, Chester Rd, STREETLY ☎021-353 1747 30⇌🛏

To see a full range of AA guides and maps, visit your local AA Shop or any good bookshop.

Walmley ☎ 021-373 0029
Brooks Rd, Wylde Green (2m S off A5127)
Pleasant parkland course with many trees. The hazards
are not difficult. Snooker.
18 holes, 6281yds, Par 71, SSS 71. Membership 703.

Visitors welcome (with M only WE) must contact in
advance ✉ Societies welcome (☎)
Green fees £25 per day; £18 per round
Facilities ⊗ (ex Mon) ▥ by prior arrangement (ex
Mon) ▙ ⬤ ♀ ⚲ 🏠 (M J Skerritt
Hotel ★★★★55% Penns Hall Hotel, Penns Ln,
Walmley, SUTTON COLDFIELD ☎021-351 3111 114⇌🏌

WALSALL
Map 3 J4

Bloxwich ☎ Bloxwich (0922) 405724
Stafford Rd, Bloxwich (3m N of town centre on A34)
Undulating parkland course with natural hazards and
subject to strong north wind. Snooker.
*18 holes, 5401yds, Par 71, SSS 70, Course record 65.
Membership 500.*

Visitors welcome (WE with M) must contact in advance
✉ Societies welcome (by letter)
Green fees £16 per day (fees to rise)
Facilities ⊗ ▥ ▙ ⬤ ♀ ⚲ 🏠 ⌐ (Brian Janes
Hotel ★★★61% Baron's Court Hotel, Walsall Rd,
Walsall Wood, WALSALL ☎(0543) 452020 100⇌

Walsall ☎ (0922) 613512
The Broadway (1m S of town centre off A34)
Parkland course with easy walking. The greens are very
extensive.
18 holes, 6243yds, Par 70, SSS 70. Membership 700.

Visitors welcome (ex WE & BH) Societies welcome (by
letter)
Green fees Not confirmed
Facilities ♀ ⚲ 🏠 (
Hotel ★★★62% Crest Hotel-Birmingham/Walsall,
Birmingham Rd, WALSALL ☎(0922) 33555 101⇌🏌

WEST BROMWICH
Map 3 J5

Dartmouth ☎ 021-588 2131
Vale St (E side of town centre off A4041)
Well-wooded parkland course with undulating but easy
walking. The 615 yd (par 5) first hole is something of a
challenge. Snooker.
9 holes, 6060yds, Par 71, SSS 69. Membership 230.

Visitors welcome (with M only WE) must contact in
advance Societies welcome (by letter)
Green fees Not confirmed
Facilities ♀ ⚲ 🏠 ⌐ (
Hotel ★★★63% West Bromwich Moat House,
Birmingham Rd, WEST BROMWICH ☎021-553 6111
180⇌🏌

Sandwell Park ☎ 021-553 4637
Birmingham Rd (SE side of town centre off A4040)
Undulating heathland course close to the motorway.
Snooker.
18 holes, 6500yds, Par 71, SSS 71. Membership 500.

Visitors welcome (wkdays with M) must contact in
advance Societies welcome (by letter)
Green fees £20 per day; £14 per round
Facilities ⊗ ▥ ▙ ⬤ ♀ ⚲ 🏠 ⌐ (A W Mutton
Hotel ★★★63% West Bromwich Moat House,
Birmingham Rd, WEST BROMWICH ☎021-553 6111
180⇌🏌

WOLVERHAMPTON
Map 3 H4

Oxley Park ☎ (0902) 20506
Stafford Rd, Bushbury (N of town centre off A449)
Parkland course with easy walking on the flat. Snooker.
18 holes, 6168yds, Par 71, SSS 69. Membership 530.

Visitors welcome (☎ for details) Societies welcome (by
letter)
Green fees £20 per day; £16 per round (£22/£18 WE &
BH)
Facilities ⊗ ▥ by prior arrangement ▙ by prior
arrangement ⬤ ♀ ⚲ 🏠 (Les Burlison
Hotel ★★★59% Mount Hotel, Mount Road, Tettenhall
Wood, WOLVERHAMPTON ☎(0902) 752055 49⇌🏌

Penn ☎ (0902) 341142
Penn Common, Penn (SW side of town centre off A449)
Heathland course just outside the town. Snooker.
18 holes, 6465yds, Par 70, SSS 71. Membership 570.

Visitors welcome (wkdays only) Societies welcome (☎)
Green fees £16 per day
Facilities ⊗ ▥ ▙ ⬤ (times vary) ♀ ⚲ 🏠 ⌐ (
Alistair Briscos
Hotel ★★★61% Park Hall Hotel, Park Drive,
Goldthorn Park, WOLVERHAMPTON ☎(0902) 331121
57⇌🏌

South Staffordshire ☎ (0902) 751065
Danescourt Rd, Tettenhall (3m NW off A41)
A parkland course. Snooker.
*18 holes, 6621yds, Par 72, SSS 72, Course record 67.
Membership 600.*

Visitors welcome (ex Tue until 1400 & WE) Societies
welcome (ex Tue am & WE)
Green fees £26 per day; £20 per round
Facilities ⊗ ▥ ▙ ⬤ ♀ ⚲ 🏠 ⌐ (Jim Rhodes
Hotel ★★★59% Mount Hotel, Mount Road, Tettenhall
Wood, WOLVERHAMPTON ☎(0902) 752055 49⇌🏌

For an explanation of the symbols and
abbreviations used, see page 33.

We make every effort to provide accurate information, but some details may change after we
go to print.

WEST SUSSEX

ANGMERING
Map 2 D7

Ham Manor ☎ (0903) 783288
(.75m SW)
Two miles from the sea and easily reached from
London, this parkland course has fine springy turf
and provides an interesting test in two loops of nine
holes each. Snooker.
18 holes, 6216yds, Par 70, SSS 70, Course record 64.
Membership 850.

Visitors welcome must contact in advance ✉
Societies welcome (☎)
Green fees Not confirmed
Facilities ⊗ (ex Mon) ⊞ by prior arrangement ⓑ
⬛ ♀ (ex Sun) ⛳ 🏠 ſ Simon Buckley
Hotel ★★★62% Chatsworth Hotel, Steyne,
WORTHING ☎(0903) 36103 105⇥🌂

BOGNOR REGIS
Map 2 D7

Bognor Regis ☎ (0243) 865867
Downview Rd, Felpham (1.5m NE off A259)
This flattish, parkland course has more variety than
is to be found on some of the South Coast courses.
The club is also known far and wide for its
enterprise in creating a social atmosphere. The
course is open to the prevailing wind.
18 holes, 6238yds, Par 70, SSS 70. Membership 725.

Visitors welcome (restricted Tue, with M only WE
Apr-Oct) must contact in advance ✉ Societies
welcome (☎)
Green fees £18 per day (£24 WE)
Facilities ⛳ 🏠 ſ Robin P Day
Hotel ★★★±72% Bailiffscourt, CLIMPING
☎(0903) 723511 18⇥ Annexe:2⇥🌂

CHICHESTER
Map 2 C7

Goodwood ☎ (0243) 774968
(4.5m NE off A27)
Originally designed by James Braid, this mixed
downland/parkland course has superb views of the
downs and the coast. Snooker.
18 holes, 6383yds, Par 72, SSS 70, Course record 68.
Membership 900.

Visitors welcome (handicap certificate required)
must contact in advance Societies welcome (by
letter)
Green fees £20 per day/round (£30 WE & BH)
Facilities ⊗ by prior arrangement ⊞ by prior
arrangement ⓑ ⬛ ♀ ⛳ 🏠 🍴 ſ K R MacDonald
Hotel ★★★65% Goodwood Park Hotel, Golf &
Country Club, GOODWOOD ☎(0243) 775537 89⇥🌂

Opening times of bar and catering facilities vary
from place to place – it is wise to check in
advance of your visit.

COPTHORNE
Map 2 F5

Copthorne ☎ (0342) 712033
Borers Arms Rd (E side of
village junc 10 of M23 off
A264)
Despite it having been in
existence since 1892, this
club remains one of the
lesser known Sussex
courses. It is hard to know
why because it is most
attractive with plenty of
trees and much variety
18 holes, 6505yds, Par 71,
SSS 71, Course record 68.
Membership 550.

SCORE CARD: White Tees					
Hole	Yds	Par	Hole	Yds	Par
1	370	4	10	354	4
2	396	4	11	395	4
3	199	3	12	156	3
4	332	4	13	485	5
5	400	4	14	399	4
6	485	5	15	185	3
7	186	3	16	471	4
8	488	5	17	370	4
9	440	4	18	394	4
Out	3296	36	In	3209	35
			Totals	6505	71

Visitors welcome (restricted WE after 1300) must
contact in advance Societies welcome (Thu & Fri☎
well in advance)
Green fees £30 per day (£35 WE & BH); £20 per
round
Facilities ⊗ ⊞ (Wed evening) ⓑ ⬛ ♀ ⛳ 🏠 ſ
Joe Burrell
Hotel ★★★★66% Copthorne Hotel, Copthorne
Road, Copthorne, COPTHORNE ☎(0342) 714971 225⇥

Effingham Park ☎ (0342) 716528
(2m E on B2028)
Parkland course. Indoor-heated swimming pool, sauna,
solarium and gymnasium.
9 holes, 1749yds, Par 30, Course record 26. Membership
430.

Visitors welcome (after 1300 WE)
Green fees £7 per 9 holes; £10 per 18 holes (£8/£12 WE)
Facilities ⊗ ⓑ ⬛ ♀ ⛳ 🏠 🍴 ſ Ian Dryden
Hotel ★★★★66% Copthorne Hotel, Copthorne Road,
Copthorne, COPTHORNE ☎(0342) 714971 225⇥

CRAWLEY·
Map 2 E5

Cottesmore ☎ (0293) 28256
Buchan Hill, Pease Pottage (3m SW 1m W of M23 junc
11)
The old North Course is undulating with birch and
rhododendrons. Four holes are over water. The new
South Course is short parkland. Accommodation.
Squash.
Old Course 18 holes, 6100yds, Par 71, SSS 70, Course
record 66. New South Course 18 holes, 5800yds, Par 68,
SSS 66. Membership 1600.

Visitors welcome (after 1200 WE on Old Course) must
contact in advance Societies welcome (wkdays only ☎)
Green fees Not confirmed
Facilities ⊗ ⊞ ⓑ ⬛ ♀ ⛳ 🏠 🍴 ſ Paul Webster
Hotel ★★★63% Goffs Park Hotel, 45 Goffs Park Road,
Crawley, CRAWLEY ☎(0293) 35447 37⇥🌂
Annexe:28⇥🌂

Gatwick Manor ☎ (0293) 24470
Lowfield Heath (2m N on A23)
Interesting short course. Expert tuition.
9 holes, 1109yds, Par 27, SSS 27.

Visitors welcome Societies welcome
Green fees Not confirmed
Facilities ♀ 📧
Hotel ★★63% Gatwick Manor Hotel, London Rd,
Lowfield Heath, Crawley, CRAWLEY ☎(0293) 26301 &
35251 30⇔♠

Ifield Golf & Country Club ☎ (0293) 20222
Rusper Rd, Ifield (1m W side of town centre off A23)
Parkland course. Squash and snooker.
*18 holes, 6314yds, Par 70, SSS 70, Course record 65 or
5901yds, Par 70, SSS 70. Membership 800.*

Visitors welcome (ex after 1530 Fri & with M only WE)
must contact in advance ✉ Societies welcome (Mon-
Wed (pm) & Thu)
Green fees Not confirmed
Facilities ⊗ ⅏ by prior arrangement ♨ ♀ ⌂ 📧 ♪
Colin Strathearn
Hotel ★★★62% George Hotel, High St, CRAWLEY
☎(0293) 24215 86⇔♠

HAYWARDS HEATH   Map 2 F6

Haywards Heath ☎ (0444) 414866
High Beech Ln (1.25m N off B2028)
Parkland/heathland course.
18 holes, 6202yds, Par 71, SSS 70. Membership 800.

Visitors welcome (outside tee reservation times) ✉
Societies welcome (Wed & Thu only)
Green fees £13 per day (£17 WE & BH)
Facilities ⊗ ♨ ♨ ♀ ⌂ 📧 ♪ Michael Henning
Hotel ★★★72% Ockenden Manor, Ockenden Ln,
CUCKFIELD ☎(0444) 416111 22⇔♠

LITTLEHAMPTON   Map 2 D7

Littlehampton ☎ (0903) 717170
Rope Walk, West Beach (1m W off A259)
A delightful seaside links in an equally delightful
setting - and the only links course in the area.
18 holes, 6202yds, Par 70, SSS 70. Membership 650.

Visitors welcome Societies welcome (Mon Tue & Fri)
Green fees Not confirmed
Facilities ♀ ⌂ 📧 ♪
Hotel ★★★67% Norfolk Arms Hotel, High St,
ARUNDEL ☎(0903) 882101 21⇔ Annexe:13⇔

If you know of a golf course, not in this guide
already, which welcomes visitors, we would be
pleased to hear about it.

MANNINGS HEATH   Map 2 E6

Mannings Heath ☎ Horsham (0403) 210228
Goldings Ln (N side of village)
The course meanders up hill and down dale over
heathland with streams affecting 11 of the holes.
Wooded valleys protect the course from strong winds.
Famous holes at 12th (the 'Waterfall', par 3), 13th (the
'Valley', par 4).
*18 holes, 6402yds, Par 73, SSS 71, Course record 66.
Membership 710.*

Visitors welcome (not WE, BH & after 1700 in summer)
must contact in advance ✉ Societies welcome (ex Mon
& WE ☎)
Green fees £25 per day; £17 per round
Facilities ⊗ by prior arrangement ⅏ by prior
arrangement ♨ ♨ ♀ (Mon-Sat) ⌂ 📧 ♪ Mike Denny
Hotel ★★★★⩐63%, South Lodge Hotel, Brighton Rd,
LOWER BEEDING ☎(0403) 891711 39⇔

MIDHURST   Map 2 D6

Cowdray Park ☎ (0730) 813599
(1m E on A272)
Parkland course, hard walking up to 4th green; 4th and
11th very good par 4's.
*18 holes, 6212yds, Par 70, SSS 70, Course record 68.
Membership 700.*

Visitors welcome (after 0900 wkdys, 1100 Sat & 1500
Sun) must contact in advance ✉ Societies welcome (☎)
Green fees £20 per day (£30 WE & BH)
Facilities ⊗ ⅏ ♨ ♨ ♀ ⌂ 📧 ♔ ♪ Stephen Hall
Hotel ★★★66% Spread Eagle Hotel, South St,
MIDHURST ☎(0730) 816911 37⇔ Annexe:4♠

PULBOROUGH   Map 2 D6

West Sussex ☎ (07982) 2563
Hurston Ln (1.5m E off A283)
Heathland course.
*18 holes, 6221yds, Par 68, SSS 70, Course record 61.
Membership 800.*

Visitors welcome (after 0930, h'cap cert required)
must contact in advance ✉ Societies welcome (Wed
& Thu only ☎)
Green fees Not confirmed
Facilities ⊗ ⅏ by prior arrangement ♨ ♨ ♀ ⌂
📧 ♪
Hotel ★★★61% Roundabout Hotel, Monkmead Ln,
WEST CHILTINGTON ☎(0798) 813838 23⇔

PYECOMBE   Map 2 E6

Pyecombe ☎ Hassocks (07918) 5372
Clayton Hill (E side of village on A273)
Typical downland course on the inland side of the South
Downs.
*18 holes, 6234yds, Par 71, SSS 70, Course record 67.
Membership 650.*

Visitors welcome (after 0915 wkdays, 1400 Sat & 1500
Sun) ✉ Societies welcome (☎)

Green fees £25 per day; £20 per round (£25 per round WE)
Facilities ⊗ ⅏ ⅃ ⅃ (no catering Sun) ⅃ ⅃ ⅃ ⅃
⅃ C White
Hotel ★★★58% Courtlands Hotel, 19-27 The Drive, HOVE ☎(0273) 731055 53⤳🛏 Annexe:5⤳

SELSEY
Map 2 C7

Selsey ☎ (0243) 602203
Golf Links Ln (1m N off B2145)
Fairly difficult seaside course, exposed to wind and has natural ditches. Tennis.
9 holes, 5932yds, Par 68, SSS 68, Course record 66. Membership 450.

Visitors welcome (ex WE & BH) ✉ Societies welcome (by letter)
Green fees Not confirmed
Facilities ⊗ ⅏ by prior arrangement ⅃ ⅃ ⅃ ⅃ ⅃
⅃ Peter Grindley
Hotel ★★★61% The Dolphin & Anchor, West St, CHICHESTER ☎(0243) 785121 51⤳🛏

WORTHING
Map 2 E7

Hill Barn Municipal ☎ (0903) 37301
Hill Barn Ln (N side of town at junction of A24/A27)
Downland course with views of both Isle of Wight and Brighton.
18 holes, 6400yds, Par 70, SSS 70, Course record 63. Membership 1000.

Visitors welcome Societies welcome (☎)
Green fees £9 (£11 WE & BH)
Facilities ⊗ ⅏ ⅃ ⅃ ⅃ ⅃ ⅃ ⅃ P Higgins
Hotel ★★★62% Chatsworth Hotel, Steyne, WORTHING ☎(0903) 36103 105⤳🛏

Worthing ☎ (0903) 60801
Links Rd (N side of town centre off A27)
The Upper Course, short and tricky with entrancing views, will provide good entertainment. 'Lower Course' is considered to be one of the best downland courses in the country. Snooker.
Lower Course 18 holes, 6519yds, Par 71, SSS 72, Course record 66. Upper Course 18 holes, 5243yds, Par 66, SSS 66. Membership 1146.

Visitors welcome must contact in advance ✉ Societies welcome (by letter 6mths in advance)
Green fees £24 day (£30 WE & BH)
Facilities ⊗ ⅏ (Fri) ⅃ ⅃ ⅃ ⅃ ⅃ S Rolley
Hotel ★★59% Ardington Hotel, Steyne Gardens, WORTHING ☎(0903) 30451 55rm(22⤳22🛏)

To see a full range of AA guides and maps, visit your local AA Shop or any good bookshop.

WEST YORKSHIRE

ALWOODLEY
Map 5 F6

Alwoodley ☎ Leeds (0532) 681680
Wigton Ln (5m N off A61)
A fine heathland course with length, trees and abundant heather. Many attractive situations - together a severe test of golf.
18 holes, 6686yds, Par 72, SSS 72. Membership 250.

Visitors welcome (ex WE & BH) must contact in advance Societies welcome (☎)
Green fees £30 per day, Apr-Oct; (£25, Nov-Mar)
Facilities ⊗ by prior arrangement ⅏ by prior arrangement ⅃ by prior arrangement ⅃ ⅃
⅃ J Green
Hotel ★★★65% Parkway Hotel, Otley Rd, LEEDS ☎(0532) 672551 103⤳🛏

BAILDON
Map 5 E6

Baildon ☎ (0274) 595162
Moorgate (N off A6038)
Moorland course with much bracken rough. The 5th is a hard climb.
18 holes, 6225yds, Par 70, SSS 70, Course record 64. Membership 600.

Visitors welcome (restricted Tue & WE) Societies welcome (ex Tue & WE ☎)
Green fees £12 per day (£15 WE)
Facilities ⊗ ⅏ by prior arrangement ⅃ ⅃ (no catering Mon) ⅃ (ex Mon) ⅃ ⅃ ⅃ R Masters
Hotel ★★★64% Bankfield Hotel, Bradford Rd, BINGLEY ☎(0274) 567123 103⤳🛏

BINGLEY
Map 5 E6

Bingley St Ives ☎ Bradford (0274) 562436
The Mansion, St Ives, Harden (.75m W off B6429)
Parkland/heathland course. Snooker.
18 holes, 6312yds, Par 71, SSS 71, Course record 62. Membership 650.

Visitors welcome (restricted wkdays after 1630) Societies welcome
Green fees £12.50 per day (£20 WE & BH)
Facilities ⊗ ⅏ by prior arrangement ⅃ ⅃ (Clubhouse closed Mon) ⅃ (ex Mon) ⅃ ⅃ ⅃ Raymond K Firth
Hotel ★★★64% Bankfield Hotel, Bradford Rd, BINGLEY ☎(0274) 567123 103⤳🛏

BRADFORD
Map 5 E6

Bradford Moor ☎ (0274) 638313
Scarr Hall, Pollard Ln (2m NE of city centre off A658)
Parkland course, hard walking.
9 holes, 5854yds, Par 70, SSS 68. Membership 376.

Visitors welcome Societies welcome
Green fees Not confirmed

▶

Facilities ♀ ♨ 🏠 ⛳ ⬧
Hotel ★★★★52% Stakis Norfolk Gardens Hotel, Hall
Ings, BRADFORD ☎(0274) 734734 126⇨🏌

Clayton ☎ (0274) 880047
Thornton View Rd, Clayton (2.5m W of city centre on
A647)
Moorland course, windy. Snooker.
9 holes, 5407yds, Par 68, SSS 66. Membership 350.

Visitors welcome (after 1600 on Sun) Societies welcome
(☎)
Green fees £10 per day; £8 per round (£10 WE & BH)
Facilities ⊗ ⧚ by prior arrangement ♨ ⬧ ♀ ♨
Hotel ★★★57% Novotel Bradford, Merrydale Rd,
BRADFORD ☎(0274) 683683 132⇨🏌

East Bierley ☎ (0274) 681023
South View Rd, East Bierley (4m SE of city centre off
A650)
Downland course with narrow fairways, easy walking.
Two par 3 holes over 200 yds.
9 holes, 4700yds, Par 64, SSS 63. Membership 200.

Visitors welcome (restricted Sat (am), Sun & Mon
evening) must contact in advance Societies welcome
(☎)
Green fees Not confirmed
Facilities ⊗ ⧚ ♨ ⬧ ♀ (evenings only) ♨
Hotel ★★★59% Victoria Hotel, Bridge St, BRADFORD
☎(0274) 728706 59⇨🏌

Headley ☎ (0274) 833481
Headley Ln, Thornton (4m W of city centre off B6145 at
Thornton)
Hilly moorland course, short but very testing, windy,
fine views.
*9 holes, 4914yds, Par 64, SSS 64, Course record 61.
Membership 200.*

Visitors welcome (with M Sun) must contact in
advance Societies welcome (☎)
Green fees £5 per day (£10 WE)
Facilities ⊗ by prior arrangement ⧚ by prior
arrangement ♨ ⬧ ♀ ♨
Hotel ★★★★52% Stakis Norfolk Gardens Hotel, Hall
Ings, BRADFORD ☎(0274) 734734 126⇨🏌

Phoenix Park ☎ (0274) 667573
Phoenix Park, Thornbury (E side of city centre on A647)
Very short, tight, moorland course, rather testing.
9 holes, 4776yds, Par 66, SSS 64. Membership 150.

Visitors welcome (Mon-Fri only) Societies welcome
Green fees Not confirmed
Facilities ♨ ⬧ ♀ ♨ ⬧ Ferguson
Hotel ★★★★52% Stakis Norfolk Gardens Hotel, Hall
Ings, BRADFORD ☎(0274) 734734 126⇨🏌

Queensbury ☎ (0274) 882155
Brighouse Rd, Queensbury (4m from Bradford on A647)
Undulating parkland course. Snooker.
*9 holes, 5024yds, Par 66, SSS 65, Course record 63.
Membership 300.*

Visitors welcome (ex WE) Societies welcome (☎)
Green fees £8 per day (£15 WE & BH)
Facilities ⊗ ⧚ ♨ ⬧ ♀ ♨ 🏠 ⛳ ⬧ S Yearsleyer
Hotel ★★★★52% Stakis Norfolk Gardens Hotel, Hall
Ings, BRADFORD ☎(0274) 734734 126⇨🏌

South Bradford ☎ (0274) 679195
Pearson Rd, Odsal (2m S of city centre off A638)
Testing meadowland course with trees and ditches.
Interesting short 2nd hole (par 3) 200 yds, well-bunkered
and played from an elevated tee. Snooker.
9 holes, 6004yds, Par 70, SSS 69. Membership 305.

Visitors welcome (ex competition days) Societies
welcome (by letter)
Green fees Not confirmed
Facilities ♀ ♨ 🏠 ⬧
Hotel ★★★57% Novotel Bradford, Merrydale Rd,
BRADFORD ☎(0274) 683683 132⇨🏌

West Bowling ☎ (0274) 724449
Newall Hall, Rooley Ln (S side of city centre off A638)
Parkland course, easy going. Testing hole: 'the coffin'
short par 3, very narrow. Snooker.
*18 holes, 5657yds, Par 69, SSS 67, Course record 66.
Membership 400.*

Visitors welcome (ex before 0930, 1200-1330 & restricted
WE) must contact in advance ✉ Societies welcome (☎)
Green fees £15 (£25 WE)
Facilities ⊗ ⧚ ♨ by prior arrangement ⬧ ♀ ♨ 🏠
⬧ A P Swaine
Hotel ★★★59% Victoria Hotel, Bridge St, BRADFORD
☎(0274) 728706 59⇨🏌

West Bradford ☎ West Bradford (0274) 542767
Chellow Grange Rd (W side of city centre off B6269)
Parkland course, windy, especially 3rd, 4th, 5th and 6th
holes. Hilly but not hard. Snooker.
*18 holes, 5752yds, Par 69, SSS 68, Course record 63.
Membership 444.*

Visitors welcome (ex Sat) Societies welcome (by letter)
Green fees £14 per day (£20 WE)
Facilities ⊗ ⧚ ♨ ⬧ ♀ ♨ 🏠 ⬧ N M Barber
Hotel ★★★64% Bankfield Hotel, Bradford Rd,
BINGLEY ☎(0274) 567123 103⇨🏌

CLECKHEATON Map 5 F6

Cleckheaton & District ☎ (0274) 851266
Bradford Rd (1.5m NW on A638 junc 26 M62)
Parkland course with gentle hills.
18 holes, 5847yds, Par 71, SSS 69. Membership 500.

Visitors welcome must contact in advance ✉ Societies
welcome (ex WE ☎)
Green fees Not confirmed
Facilities ⊗ (ex Mon) ⧚ (ex Mon) ♨ (ex 2pm-4pm) ⬧
(ex 2pm-4pm) ♀ (ex Mon) ♨ 🏠 ⛳ ⬧ M B Ingham
Hotel ★★★57% Novotel Bradford, Merrydale Rd,
BRADFORD ☎(0274) 683683 132⇨🏌

DEWSBURY   Map 5 F6

Hanging Heaton ☎ (0924) 461606
White Cross Rd (.75m NE off A653)
Arable land course, easy walking, fine views. Testing
4th hole (par 3).
9 holes, 5400mtrs, Par 69, SSS 67. Membership 550.

Visitors welcome (with M only WE & BH) must contact
in advance Societies welcome (☎)
Green fees £10 per day
Facilities ⊗ ⊾ ⊒ ♀ ⟁ 📷 ℓ G Hutchinson
Hotel ★★★61% Post House, Queen's Dr, Ossett,
WAKEFIELD ☎(0924) 276388 99⇔🏌

ELLAND   Map 5 E6

Elland ☎ (0422) 72505
Hammerstones, Leach Ln (1m SW)
Parkland course.
9 holes, 2815yds, Par 66, SSS 66. Membership 250.

Visitors welcome
Green fees £8 per day (£12 WE & BH)
Facilities ⊗ ⊤ ⊾ ⊒ ♀ ⟁ 📷 ℓ Jeremy Tindall
Hotel ★★★67% Pennine Hilton National,
HUDDERSFIELD ☎(0422) 375431 118⇔🏌

FENAY BRIDGE   Map 5 F7

Woodsome Hall ☎ Huddersfield (0484) 602971
(1.5m SW off A629)
Historic clubhouse; parkland course with views.
Snooker.
18 holes, 6080yds, Par 70, SSS 69. Membership 800.

Visitors welcome (restricted WE & comps) must contact
in advance Societies welcome (☎)
Green fees £18 per round/day (£22 WE & BH)
Facilities ⊗ ⊤ ⊾ ⊒ (all catering by prior
arrangement) ♀ ⟁ 📷 🏌 ℓ
Hotel ★★★65% The George, St George's Square,
HUDDERSFIELD ☎(0484) 515444 60⇔🏌

GARFORTH   Map 5 F6

Garforth ☎ (0532) 862021
(1m N)
Moorland course with fine views, easy walking.
Snooker.
*18 holes, 6000yds, Par 70, SSS 70, Course record 64.
Membership 400.*

Visitors welcome (with M only WE & BH) must contact
in advance Societies welcome (☎)
Green fees Not confirmed
Facilities ⊗ ⊤ ⊾ ⊒ ♀ ⟁ 📷 🏌 ℓ K Findlater
Hotel ★★★66% Hilton National, Wakefield Rd,
Garforth Rdbt, GARFORTH ☎(0532) 866556 144⇔🏌

Each golf course entry has a recommended
hotel. For a wider choice of places to stay,
consult *AA Hotels and Restaurants in Britain* or
AA-inspected Bed and Breakfast in Britain.

GUISELEY   Map 5 F6

Bradford ☎ (0943) 75570
Hawksworth Ln (SW side of town centre off A6038)
Moorland course with eight par 4 holes of 360 yds or
more. Snooker.
*18 holes, 6259yds, Par 71, SSS 70, Course record 67.
Membership 600.*

Visitors welcome (wkdays only) ✉ Societies welcome
(wkdays only)
Green fees £16 per day (£20 WE)
Facilities ⊗ ⊤ ⊾ ⊒ ♀ (restricted Sun) ⟁ 📷 🏌
ℓ Sydney Weldon
Hotel ★★★58% Cow & Calf Hotel, Moor Top, ILKLEY
☎(0943) 607335 17⇔🏌

HALIFAX   Map 5 E6

Halifax ☎ (0422) 244171
Bob Hall, Union Ln, Ogden (4m NW off A629)
Moorland course crossed by streams, natural hazards,
and offering fine views. Testing 172-yd 17th hole (par 3).
Snooker.
*18 holes, 6037yds, Par 70, SSS 70, Course record 66.
Membership 500.*

Visitors welcome (ex competition days) must contact in
advance Societies welcome (☎)
Green fees £12 (£20 WE & BH)
Facilities ⊗ ⊤ ⊾ ⊒ (no catering Mon) ♀ (ex Mon)
⟁ 📷 🏌 ℓ Steven Foster
Hotel ★★★73% Holdsworth House Hotel, Holmfield,
HALIFAX ☎(0422) 240024 40⇔🏌

Lightcliffe ☎ (0422) 202459
Knowle Top Rd, Lightcliffe (3.5m E on A58)
Heathland course.
9 holes, 5368yds, Par 68, SSS 68. Membership 235.

Visitors welcome Societies welcome (☎ 21 days notice)
Green fees Not confirmed
Facilities ♀ (all day) ⟁ 📷 ℓ R Parry
Hotel ★★★73% Holdsworth House Hotel, Holmfield,
HALIFAX ☎(0422) 240024 40⇔🏌

West End ☎ (0422) 53608
Paddock Ln, Highroad Well (W side of town centre off
A646)
Semi-moorland course. Snooker.
*18 holes, 6003yds, Par 68, SSS 69, Course record 65.
Membership 450.*

Visitors welcome (ex 1000-1330) must contact in
advance Societies welcome (by letter)
Green fees £10 per day (£12-£14 WE)
Facilities ⊗ ⊤ ⊾ ⊒ ♀ ⟁ 📷 ℓ David Rishworth
Hotel ★★★73% Holdsworth House Hotel, Holmfield,
HALIFAX ☎(0422) 240024 40⇔🏌

If you know of a golf course, not in this guide
already, which welcomes visitors, we would be
pleased to hear about it.

HEBDEN BRIDGE   Map 5 E6

Hebden Bridge ☎ (0422) 842896
Mount Skip, Wadsworth (1.5m E off A6033)
Moorland course with splendid views.
9 holes, 5112yds, Par 68, SSS 65, Course record 63.
Membership 200.

Visitors welcome (ex competition days) Societies
welcome (by arrangment with directors)
Green fees £7.50 per day (£10 WE)
Facilities ⊗ by prior arrangement ⫚ by prior
arrangement ⮱ 🍺 ⛳ ⛳ 🏠
Hotel ★★67% Hebden Lodge Hotel, New Rd, HEBDEN
BRIDGE ☎(0422) 845272 13⇨🏌

HOLYWELL GREEN   Map 5 E7

Halifax Bradley Hall ☎ Halifax (0422) 374108
(S on A6112)
Moorland course, tightened by recent tree planting,
easy walking. Snooker.
18 holes, 6213yds, Par 70, SSS 70, Course record 65.
Membership 608.

Visitors welcome Societies welcome (☎)
Green fees £12 per day (£20 WE & BH)
Facilities ⊗ ⫚ ⮱ 🍺 (catering by prior arrangement
Mon-Tue) ⛳ ⛳ 🏠 ⛳ Peter Wood
Hotel ★★★67% Pennine Hilton National,
HUDDERSFIELD ☎(0422) 375431 118⇨🏌

HUDDERSFIELD   Map 5 E7

Bradley Park ☎ (0484) 539988
Off Bradley Rd (3m N on A6107)
Parkland course, challenging with good mix of long and
short holes. Also 14-bay floodlit driving range and 9-hole
par 3 course, ideal for beginners. Superb views.
18 holes, 6202yds, Par 70, SSS 70, Course record 64. Par 3
9 holes, 1180yds, Par 27, SSS 27. Membership 300.

Visitors welcome (contact for WE play) Societies
welcome (midweek only by letter)
Green fees £6 (£7.50 WE)
Facilities ⊗ ⫚ ⮱ 🍺 ⛳ 🏠 ⛳ ⛳ Parnell E Reilly
Hotel ★★★65% The George, St George's Square,
HUDDERSFIELD ☎(0484) 515444 60⇨🏌

Crosland Heath ☎ (0484) 653216
Felk Stile Rd, Crosland Heath (SW off A62)
Moorland course with fine views over valley.
18 holes, 5972yds, Par 70, SSS 70. Membership 350.

Visitors welcome (☎ for details) must contact in
advance ✉
Green fees Not confirmed
Facilities ⊗ ⫚ ⮱ 🍺 ⛳ ⛳ 🏠 ⛳ Richard Jessop
Hotel ★★★65% The George, St George's Square,
HUDDERSFIELD ☎(0484) 515444 60⇨🏌

We make every effort to provide accurate information, but some details may change after we
go to print.

Huddersfield ☎ (0484) 426203
Fixby Hall, Lightridge Rd, Fixby (2m N off A641)
A testing parkland/moorland course of championship
standard laid out in 1891. Snooker. Conference
facilities.
18 holes, 6402yds, Par 71, SSS 71, Course record 67.
Membership 730.

Visitors welcome (ex Tue (ladies day)) must contact in
advance Societies welcome (ex WE by letter)
Green fees £20.50 per day (£22.50 WE & BH)
Facilities ⊗ ⫚ ⮱ 🍺 (catering by prior arrangement)
⛳ (by prior arrangement) ⛳ 🏠 ⛳ Paul Carman
Hotel ★★★67% Pennine Hilton National,
HUDDERSFIELD ☎(0422) 375431 118⇨🏌

Longley Park ☎ (0484) 422304
Maple St, Off Somerset Rd (.5m SE of town centre off
A629)
Lowland course.
9 holes, 5269yds, Par 66, SSS 66, Course record 66.
Membership 400.

Visitors welcome (restricted Thu & WE) must contact
in advance ✉ Societies welcome (☎ (ex Thu))
Green fees £8 per day (£10 WE)
Facilities ⊗ ⫚ by prior arrangement ⮱ 🍺 ⛳ ⛳ 🏠
⛳ ⛳ Neil Suckling
Hotel ★★★65% The George, St George's Square,
HUDDERSFIELD ☎(0484) 515444 60⇨🏌

ILKLEY   Map 5 E6

Ben Rhydding ☎ (0943) 608759
High Wood, Ben Rhydding (SE side of town)
Moorland course with splendid views over the Wharfe
valley.
9 holes, 4711yds, Par 65, SSS 64. Membership 300.

Visitors welcome (ex Sat & Sun)
Green fees Not confirmed
Facilities ⛳
Hotel ★★76% Rombalds Hotel & Restaurant, 11 West
View, Wells Rd, ILKLEY ☎(0943) 603201 16⇨🏌

Ilkley ☎ (0943) 600214
Middleton (W side of town
centre off A65)
This beautiful parkland
course is situated in
Wharfedale and the Wharfe
is a hazard on each of the
first five holes. In fact, the
3rd is laid out entirely on
an island in the middle of
the river. Snooker, fishing.
18 holes, 6262yds, Par 69,
SSS 70. Membership 500.

SCORE CARD: Medal Tees					
Hole	Yds	Par	Hole	Yds	Par
1	410	4	10	316	4
2	166	3	11	443	4
3	206	3	12	400	4
4	504	5	13	153	3
5	200	3	14	433	4
6	497	5	15	146	3
7	423	4	16	426	4
8	351	4	17	416	4
9	395	4	18	377	4
Out	3152	35	In	3110	34
			Totals	6262	69

Visitors welcome must contact in advance Societies
welcome (ex Tue, Fri & WE)
Green fees Not confirmed

Facilities ⊗ 〣 by prior arrangement ⮭ ⬛ ♀ △
🏠 ⸨ J L Hammond
Hotel ★★76% Rombalds Hotel & Restaurant, 11
West View, Wells Rd, ILKLEY ☎(0943) 603201
16⊶❀

KEIGHLEY
Map 5 E6

Branshaw
☎ Haworth (0535) 43235 due to change to 643235
Branshaw Moor (2m SW on B6143)
Picturesque moorland course.
18 holes, 5858yds, Par 69, SSS 69, Course record 65.
Membership 460.

Visitors welcome (ex competition days (Sun)) Societies
welcome (☎)
Green fees £10 per day (£15 WE)
Facilities ⊗ by prior arrangement 〣 by prior
arrangement ⮭ (ex Mon) ⬛ ♀ (ex Mon) △
Hotel ★★66% Dalesgate Hotel, 406 Skipton Rd, Utley,
KEIGHLEY ☎(0535) 664930 21⊶❀

Keighley ☎ (0535) 604778
Howden Park, Utley (1m NW of town centre off B6143)
Parkland course.
18 holes, 6150yds, Par 69, SSS 70, Course record 66.
Membership 600.

Visitors welcome (restrictions Sat & Sun) must contact
in advance Societies welcome (☎)
Green fees £17 per day (£20 WE & BH)
Facilities ⊗ 〣 ⮭ ⬛ ♀ △ 🏠 ⸨
Hotel ★★66% Dalesgate Hotel, 406 Skipton Rd, Utley,
KEIGHLEY ☎(0535) 664930 21⊶❀

LEEDS
Map 5 F6

Gotts Park ☎ (0532) 638232
Armley Ridge Rd (3m E of city centre off A647)
Municipal parkland course.
18 holes, 4960yds, Par 65, SSS 64. Membership 250.

Visitors welcome
Green fees £4.20 (£4.50 WE & BH)
Facilities ⊗ ⬛ ♀ (ex Thu) △ 🏠 ⫿ ⸨ John F
Simpson
Hotel ★★★65% Parkway Hotel, Otley Rd, LEEDS
☎(0532) 672551 103⊶❀

Headingley ☎ (0532) 675100
Back Church Ln, Adel (5.5m N of city centre off A660)
An undulating course with a wealth of natural features
offering fine views from higher ground. Leeds's oldest
course, founded in 1892. Snooker.
18 holes, 6298yds, Par 69, SSS 70, Course record 64.
Membership 650.

Visitors welcome (ex before 0930 & 1200-1330) must
contact in advance Societies welcome (by letter)
Green fees £25 per day ; £20 per round (£30 per day/
round WE & BH)

▶

Facilities ⊗ by prior arrangement ⅏ by prior arrangement ⌷ ⏻ ♀ △ 🖻 ℓ Andrew Dyson
Hotel ★★★69% Post House Hotel, Otley Rd, BRAMHOPE ☎(0532) 842911 129⇥

Horsforth ☎ (0532) 586819
Layton Rise, Layton Rd, Horsforth (6.5m NW of city centre off A65)
Moorland course overlooking airport. Snooker.
18 holes, 6243yds, Par 71, SSS 70, Course record 67. Membership 700.

Visitors welcome (ex Sat & with M only Sun) Societies welcome (☎)
Green fees £20 per day (£24 WE & BH)
Facilities ⊗ ⅏ ⌷ ⏻ ♀ △ 🖻 ⍑ ℓ
Hotel ★★★69% Post House Hotel, Otley Rd, BRAMHOPE ☎(0532) 842911 129⇥

Leeds ☎ (0532) 658775
Elmete Ln (5m NE of city centre on A6120 off A58)
Parkland course with pleasant views. Snooker.
18 holes, 6097yds, Par 69, SSS 69, Course record 63. Membership 600.

Visitors welcome (with M only WE, yellow tees only) must contact in advance Societies welcome (by letter)
Green fees £20 per day; £15 per round
Facilities ⊗ ⅏ by prior arrangement ⌷ ⏻ ♀ △ 🖻 ⍑ ℓ S Longster
Hotel ★★★★64% Hilton International Hotel, Neville St, LEEDS ☎(0532) 442000 210⇥

Middleton Park Municipal ☎ (0532) 700449
Middleton Park, Middleton (3m S off A653)
Parkland course.
18 holes, 5263yds, Par 68, SSS 66. Membership 300.

Visitors welcome
Green fees £4.50
Facilities △ 🖻 ⍑ ℓ David Bulmer
Hotel ★★★★64% Hilton International Hotel, Neville St, LEEDS ☎(0532) 442000 210⇥

Moor Allerton
☎ (0532) 661154
Coal Rd, Wike (5.5m N of city centre on A61)
The Moor Allerton Club has 27 holes set in 220 acres of undulating parkland, with magnificent views extending across the Vale of York. The Championship Course was designed by Robert Trent Jones, the famous American course architect, and is the only course of his design in the British Isles. Tennis, snooker, sauna.
Lakes 9 holes, 6045yds, SSS 72. Blackmoor 9 holes, 6224yds, SSS 72. High Course 9 holes, 6930yds, SSS 73. Membership 1000.

SCORE CARD: The Lakes (Championship Tees)					
Hole	Yds	Par	Hole	Yds	Par
1	448	4	10	449	4
2	409	4	11	359	4
3	358	4	12	388	4
4	143	3	13	182	3
5	483	5	14	499	5
6	316	4	15	353	4
7	190	3	16	388	4
8	562	5	17	154	3
9	404	4	18	385	4
Out	3313	36	In	3157	35
			Totals	6470	71

Visitors welcome (ex WE) ✉ Societies welcome (☎)
Green fees 18 holes £30, 27 holes £33, 36 holes £36
Facilities ⊗ ⅏ ⌷ ⏻ ♀ △ 🖻 ⍑ ℓ
Hotel ★★★66% Harewood Arms Hotel, Harrogate Rd, HAREWOOD ☎(0532) 886566 24⇥🌳

Moortown ☎ (0532) 686521
Harrogate Rd, Alwoodley (6m N of city centre on A61)
Championship course, tough but fair. Springy moorland turf, natural hazards of heather, gorse and streams, cunningly placed bunkers and immaculate greens.
18 holes, 6544yds, Par 71, SSS 72, Course record 69. Membership 550.

Visitors welcome (WE by prior arrangement) must contact in advance Societies welcome (☎)
Green fees £32 per day; £25 per round (£37/£32 WE & BH)
Facilities ⊗ ⅏ ⌷ ⏻ (all catering by prior arrangement) ♀ △ 🖻 ℓ Bryon Hutchinson
Hotel ★★★66% Harewood Arms Hotel, Harrogate Rd, HAREWOOD ☎(0532) 886566 24⇥🌳

Roundhay ☎ (0532) 662695
Park Ln (4m NE of city centre off A58)
Attractive municipal parkland course, natural hazards, easy walking.
9 holes, 5166yds, Par 65, SSS 68. Membership 300.

Visitors welcome Societies welcome (☎)
Green fees £4.20 per round (£4.50 Sun & BH)
Facilities △ 🖻 ⍑
Hotel ★★★64% Stakis Windmill Hotel, Mill Green View, Seacroft, LEEDS ☎(0532) 732323 100⇥🌳

Sand Moor
☎ (0532) 685180
Alwoodley Ln (5m N of city centre off A61)
A beautiful, undulating course overlooking Lord Harewood's estate and the Eccup Reservoir. The course is wooded with some holes adjacent to water. The 12th is perhaps the most difficult where the fairway falls away towards the reservoir. Snooker.
18 holes, 6429yds, Par 71, SSS 71, Course record 65. Membership 551.

SCORE CARD: White Tees					
Hole	Yds	Par	Hole	Yds	Par
1	491	5	10	173	3
2	258	4	11	381	4
3	413	4	12	522	5
4	379	4	13	339	4
5	358	4	14	464	4
6	472	4	15	160	3
7	383	4	16	548	5
8	186	3	17	156	3
9	364	4	18	382	4
Out	3304	36	In	3125	35
			Totals	6429	71

Visitors welcome (ex WE & BH) must contact in advance ✉ Societies welcome (☎)
Green fees £25 per round
Facilities ⊗ ⅏ by prior arrangement ⌷ ⏻ ♀ △ 🖻 ℓ
Hotel ★★★69% Post House Hotel, Otley Rd, BRAMHOPE ☎(0532) 842911 129⇥

South Leeds ☎ (0542) 700479
Gipsy Ln, Beeston (3m S of city centre off A653)
Parkland couse, windy, hard walking, good views.
18 holes, 5835yds, Par 69, SSS 68. Membership 650.

Visitors welcome must contact in advance Societies welcome (☎)
Green fees £12 per day (£16 WE & BH)
Facilities ⊗ �aeqₗ ⓛ ◪ ♀ ⌂ ⌖ ┌ Mike Lewis
Hotel ★★★★61% The Queen's, City Square, LEEDS ☎(0532) 431323 188⊸↰

Temple Newsam ☎ (0532) 645624
Temple-Newsam Rd (3.5m E of city centre off A63)
Two parkland courses. Testing long 13th (563 yds) on second course. Snooker.
Lord Irwin 18 holes, 6448yds, Par 69, SSS 71, Course record 65. Lady Dorothy 18 holes, 6029yds, Par 70, SSS 70, Course record 65. Membership 450.

Visitors welcome Societies welcome (☎)
Green fees £4 per day (£5 WE)
Facilities ⊗ (WE only) ◪ ◪ (WE only) ♀ ⌂ ⌖ ┌ D Bulmer
Hotel ★★★★64% Hilton International Hotel, Neville St, LEEDS ☎(0532) 442000 210⊸

MARSDEN
Map 5 E7

Marsden ☎ (0484) 844253
Mount Rd, Hemplow (S side off A62)
Moorland course with good views, natural hazards, windy. Hardcourt tennis.
9 holes, 5702yds, Par 68, SSS 68. Membership 185.

Visitors welcome (with M only WE) Societies welcome (Mon-Fri ☎)
Green fees £10 per day (£15 BH)
Facilities ⊗ ◪ ◪ ♀ ⌂
Hotel ★★★62% Briar Court Hotel, Halifax Road, Birchencliffe, HUDDERSFIELD ☎(0484) 519902 48⊸↰

MELTHAM
Map 5 E7

Meltham ☎ Huddersfield (0484) 850227
Thick Hollins Hall (SE side of village off B6107)
Parkland course with good views. Testing 548 yd, 13th hole (par 5). Snooker.
18 holes, 6145yds, Par 70, SSS 70. Membership 600.

Visitors welcome (ex Tue & Wed) Societies welcome
Green fees Not confirmed
Facilities ♀ ⌂ ⌖ ┌
Hotel ★★★65% The George, St George's Square, HUDDERSFIELD ☎(0484) 515444 60⊸↰

MIRFIELD
Map 5 F6

Dewsbury District ☎ (0924) 492399
Sands Ln (1m S off A644)
Heathland/parkland course with panoramic view from top, hard walking. Ponds in middle of 3rd fairway, left of 5th green and 17th green. Snooker.
18 holes, 6248yds, Par 71, SSS 71, Course record 68. Membership 500.

Visitors welcome (restricted WE & BH) must contact in advance Societies welcome (☎)
Green fees £11 per day
Facilities ⊗ �aeqₗ ◪ ◪ (catering Tue-Fri) ♀ ⌂ ⌂ ⌖ ┌ Nigel Hirst
Hotel ★★★65% The George, St George's Square, HUDDERSFIELD ☎(0484) 515444 60⊸↰

MORLEY
Map 5 F6

Howley Hall ☎ Batley (0924) 478417
Scotchman Ln (1.5m S on B6123)
Parkland course with easy walking and good views.
18 holes, 6029yds, Par 71, SSS 69. Membership 500.

Visitors welcome (standard course only) must contact in advance Societies welcome (by letter)
Green fees Not confirmed
Facilities ⊗ �aeqₗ ◪ ◪ (no catering Mon) ♀ ⌂ ⌂ ⌖ ┌ Stephen A Spinks
Hotel ★★65% Alder House Hotel, Towngate Rd, off Healey Ln, BATLEY ☎(0924) 444777 22rm(20⊸↰)

NORMANTON
Map 5 F6

Normanton ☎ Wakefield (0924) 892943
Snydale Rd (.5m SE on B6133)
A pleasant, flat 9-hole course with tight fairways in places and an internal out of bounds requiring accuracy.
9 holes, 5288yds, Par 66, SSS 66. Membership 250.

Visitors welcome (ex Sun) Societies welcome (mid-week only)
Green fees £5 per day (£9 Sat & BH)
Facilities ⊗ �aeqₗ ◪ ◪ ♀ ⌂ ⌂ ⌖ ┌ Martin Evans
Hotel ★★★61% Swallow Hotel, Queens St, WAKEFIELD ☎(0924) 372111 64⊸↰

OSSETT
Map 5 F7

Low Laithes ☎ (0924) 273275
Parkmill Ln, Flushdyke (1.5m SE off A128)
Testing parkland course. Short holes.
18 holes, 6448yds, Par 71, SSS 71. Membership 450.

Visitors welcome must contact in advance Societies welcome (Mon-Fri ☎)
Green fees Not confirmed
Facilities ⊗ �aeqₗ ◪ ◪ (catering by prior arrangement) ♀ ⌂ ⌂ ⌖ ┌ Paul Browning
Hotel ★★65% Alder House, Towngate Rd, off Healey Ln, BATLEY ☎(0924) 444777 22rm (20⊸↰)

We make every effort to provide accurate information, but some details may change after we go to print.

OTLEY
Map 5 F6

Otley ☎ (0943) 461015
Off West Busk Ln (1.5m SW off A6038)
An expansive course with magnificent views across Wharfedale. It is well-wooded with streams crossing the fairway. The 4th is a fine hole which generally needs two woods to reach the plateau green. The 17th is a good short hole. Snooker.
18 holes, 6225yds, Par 70, SSS 70, Course record 62. Membership 650.

SCORE CARD: White Tees					
Hole	Yds	Par	Hole	Yds	Par
1	423	4	10	276	4
2	169	3	11	402	4
3	398	4	12	392	4
4	444	4	13	420	4
5	208	3	14	264	4
6	490	5	15	131	3
7	387	4	16	368	4
8	480	5	17	180	3
9	361	4	18	432	4
Out	3360	36	In	2865	34
			Totals	6225	70

Visitors welcome (ex Sat) Societies welcome (☎)
Green fees Not confirmed
Facilities ⊗ ᛗ by prior arrangement ⊫ ⬤ ♀ ⌲ 📧 ⫟ 𝄢 Stephen McNally
Hotel ★★★69% Post House Hotel, Otley Rd, BRAMHOPE ☎(0532) 842911 129⏎

OUTLANE
Map 5 E7

Outlane ☎ Halifax (0422) 374762
Slack Ln (S side of village off A640)
Moorland course.
18 holes, 5735yds, Par 71, SSS 68. Membership 500.

Visitors welcome (restricted Thu) must contact in advance ✉ Societies welcome (14 days notice ☎)
Green fees Not confirmed
Facilities ⊗ (ex Mon) ᛗ (ex Mon & Sun) ⊫ (ex Mon & Sun) ⬤ (ex Mon) ♀ (ex Mon) ⌲ 📧 ⫟ 𝄢 David Chapman
Hotel ★★★67% Pennine Hilton National, HUDDERSFIELD ☎(0422) 375431 118⏎🌂

PONTEFRACT
Map 5 F6

Pontefract & District ☎ (0977) 792241
Park Ln (1.5m W on B6134)
Parkland course.
18 holes, 6067yds, Par 69, SSS 69, Course record 63. Membership 800.

Visitors welcome (ex Wed & WE) must contact in advance ✉ Societies welcome (ex Wed & WE)
Green fees £20 per day (£25 BH)
Facilities ⊗ ᛗ ⊫ ⬤ ♀ ⌲ 📧 𝄢 J Coleman
Hotel ★★★⏴67% Wentbridge House Hotel, WENTBRIDGE ☎(0977) 620444 12⏎🌂

PUDSEY
Map 5 F6

Fulneck ☎ (0532) 565191
(S side of town centre)
Picturesque, hilly parkland course. Compact but strenuous.
9 holes, 5432yds, Par 66, SSS 67, Course record 64. Membership 275.

Visitors welcome (☎ for details) Societies welcome (☎)
Green fees £8
Facilities ♀ ⌲
Hotel ★★★57% Novotel Bradford, Merrydale Rd, BRADFORD ☎(0274) 683683 132⏎🌂

Woodhall Hills ☎ (0532) 564771
Calverley (2.5m NW off A647)
Meadowland course, prevailing SW winds, fairly hard walking. Testing holes: 8th, 377 yd (par 4); 14th, 233 yd (par 3). Snooker.
18 holes, 6102yds, Par 71, SSS 69, Course record 66. Membership 315.

Visitors welcome (restricted wkdays until 0930)
Societies welcome (by letter)
Green fees £15 per round (£20 WE & BH)
Facilities ⊗ ᛗ ⊫ ⬤ ♀ ⌲ 📧 𝄢 Darren Tear
Hotel ★★★★52% Stakis Norfolk Gardens Hotel, Hall Ings, BRADFORD ☎(0274) 734734 126⏎🌂

RAWDON
Map 5 F6

Rawdon Golf & Lawn Tennis Club ☎ (0532) 506040
Buckstone Dr (S side of town off A65)
Undulating parkland course. Grass and hard tennis courts. Snooker.
9 holes, 5980yds, Par 72, SSS 69, Course record 64. Membership 700.

Visitors welcome (with M only WE) must contact in advance ✉ Societies welcome (☎ or by letter)
Green fees £15
Facilities ⊗ ᛗ ⊫ ⬤ ♀ (ex Mon) ⌲ 📧 𝄢 John Clapham
Hotel ★★★69% Post House Hotel, Otley Rd, BRAMHOPE ☎(0532) 842911 129⏎

RIDDLESDEN
Map 5 E6

Riddlesden ☎ Keighley (0535) 602148
Howden Rough (1m NW)
Undulating moorland course with two quarry hazards, prevailing W winds, some hard walking and beautiful views. Short, par-3 course, with some very testing holes.
18 holes, 4247yds, Par 61, SSS 60. Membership 200.

Visitors welcome (restricted WE) Societies welcome (by letter)
Green fees £5 per day (£10 WE & BH)
Facilities ⊫ (WE/summer evenings) ⬤ ♀ (WE & summer eves) ⌲
Hotel ★★66% Dalesgate Hotel, 406 Skipton Rd, Utley, KEIGHLEY ☎(0535) 664930 21⏎🌂

SCARCROFT
Map 5 F6

Scarcroft ☎ Leeds (0532) 892263
Syke Ln (.5m N of village off A58)
Undulating parkland course, prevailing west wind, easy walking. Snooker.
18 holes, 6031yds, Par 71, SSS 69. Membership 667.

Visitors welcome (no parties Fri-Sun & BH) must contact in advance Societies welcome (by letter)
Green fees £27 per day ; £22 per round (£32 WE)
Facilities ⊗ (ex Mon) ⋔ (ex Mon) ⌕ ⬛ ♀ ⌂ 🏠 ⛳ ⌞ Martin Ross
Hotel ★★★64% Stakis Windmill Hotel, Mill Green View, Seacroft, LEEDS ☎(0532) 732323 100⇨🛏️

SHIPLEY   Map 5 E6

Northcliffe ☎ Bradford (0274) 584085
High Bank Ln (1.25m SW off A650)
Parkland course with magnificent views of moors. Testing 1st hole (18th green 100 feet below tee). Snooker.
18 holes, 6067yds, Par 71, SSS 69, Course record 67. Membership 657.

Visitors welcome Societies welcome (by letter)
Green fees £16 per day (£25 WE & BH)
Facilities ⊗ (by prior arrangement ex Mon) ⋔ (by prior arrangement ex Mon) ⌕ (ex Mon) ⬛ (ex Mon) ♀ (ex Mon) ⌂ 🏠 ⛳ ⌞ Simon Poot
Hotel ★★★64% Bankfield Hotel, Bradford Rd, BINGLEY ☎(0274) 567123 103⇨🛏️

SILSDEN   Map 5 E6

Silsden ☎ Steeton (0535) 52998
High Brunthwaite (1m E)
Tight downland course which can be windy. Good views of the Aire Valley.
14 holes, 4870yds, Par 65, SSS 64. Membership 300.

Visitors welcome Societies welcome
Green fees Not confirmed
Facilities ♀ ⌂
Hotel ★★66% Dalesgate Hotel, 406 Skipton Rd, Utley, KEIGHLEY ☎(0535) 664930 21⇨🛏️

SOWERBY   Map 5 E6

Ryburn ☎ Halifax (0422) 831355
The Shaw, Norland (1m S of Sowerby Bridge off A58)
Moorland course, easy walking.
9 holes, 4996yds, Par 66, SSS 64. Membership 200.

Visitors welcome must contact in advance Societies welcome
Green fees Not confirmed
Facilities ♀ ⌂
Hotel ★★★67% Pennine Hilton National, HUDDERSFIELD ☎(0422) 375431 118⇨🛏️

TODMORDEN   Map 5 E6

Todmorden ☎ (070681) 298681
Rive Rocks, Cross Stone Rd (NE off A646)
Pleasant moorland course.
9 holes, 5818yds, Par 68, SSS 68. Membership 140.

Visitors welcome (restricted Sat pm & competition days)
Green fees Not confirmed

Facilities ♀ ⌂ 🏠
Hotel ★★★⚘70% Scaitcliffe Hall, Burnley Rd, TODMORDEN ☎(0706) 818888 13⇨🛏️

WAKEFIELD   Map 5 F6

City of Wakefield ☎ (0924) 374316
Lupset Park, Horbury Rd (1.5m W of city centre on A642)
Parkland course.
18 holes, 6299yds, Par 72, SSS 70, Course record 66. Membership 825.

Visitors welcome (ex WE) Societies welcome (☎ or letter)
Green fees £4.10 per round (£6.20 WE & BH)
Facilities ⊗ by prior arrangement ⋔ by prior arrangement ⌕ ⬛ ♀ ⌂ 🏠 ⛳ ⌞ Roger Holland
Hotel ★★★61% Post House, Queen's Dr, Ossett, WAKEFIELD ☎(0924) 276388 99⇨🛏️

Painthorpe House ☎ (0924) 255083
Painthorpe Ln, Painthorpe, Crigglestone (2m S off A636)
Undulating meadowland course, easy walking. Bowling green.
9 holes, 4520yds, Par 62, SSS 62, Course record 64. Membership 150.

Visitors welcome (ex Sun) must contact in advance Societies welcome (☎)
Green fees £3 per day (£5 Sat)
Facilities ⊗ ⋔ ⌕ ⬛ ♀ ⌂ 🏠
Hotel ★★★61% Post House, Queen's Dr, Ossett, WAKEFIELD ☎(0924) 276388 99⇨🛏️

Wakefield ☎ (0924) 255104
Woodthorpe Ln, Sandal (3m S off A61)
A well-sheltered parkland course with easy walking. Good views. Snooker.
18 holes, 6626yds, Par 72, SSS 72, Course record 67. Membership 500.

Visitors welcome Societies welcome (by letter)
Green fees £18 per day (£20 WE & BH)
Facilities ⊗ ⋔ ⌕ ⬛ ♀ ⌂ 🏠 ⌞ I M Wright
Hotel ★★★61% Post House, Queen's Dr, Ossett, WAKEFIELD ☎(0924) 276388 99⇨🛏️

WETHERBY   Map 5 F5

Wetherby ☎ (0937) 62527
Linton Ln (1m W off A661)
Parkland course with fine views.
18 holes, 6235yds, Par 71, SSS 70, Course record 66. Membership 700.

Visitors welcome Societies welcome (by letter)
Green fees £20 per day ; £15 per round
Facilities ⌕ ⬛ ♀ ⌂ 🏠 ⌞ David Padgett
Hotel ★★★57% Penguin Hotel, Leeds Rd, WETHERBY ☎(0937) 63881 72⇨🛏️

This guide is updated annually – make sure you use an up-to-date edition.

WIGHT, ISLE OF

COWES
Map 2 B7

Cowes ☎ (0983) 292303
Crossfield Av (NW side of town)
Small but tight parkland course with testing 8th hole.
9 holes, 2967yds, Par 70, SSS 68, Course record 67.
Membership 265.

Visitors welcome (restricted Thu, Fri & Sun (am))
Societies welcome (☎)
Green fees £12 (£15 WE)
Facilities ⊗ ╚ ▣ ♀ △ ⛳
Hotel ★★55% Fountain Hotel, High St, COWES
☎(0983) 292397 20⇌

EAST COWES
Map 2 B7

Osborne ☎ (0983) 295421
Osborne (E side of town centre off A3021)
Undulating parkland course in the grounds of Osborne
House. Quiet and peaceful situation.
9 holes, 5934yds, Par 70, SSS 69. Membership 350.

Visitors welcome (restricted Tue 0900-1300, WE before
1200) ✉ Societies welcome (☎)
Green fees £14 per day
Facilities ⊗ ⫼ by prior arrangement ╚ ▣ ♀ △ 🏠
⛳ ⛏ Ian Taylor
Hotel ★★63% Cowes Hotel, 260 Artic Rd, COWES
☎(0983) 291541 15⇌⚑

FRESHWATER
Map 2 A8

Freshwater Bay ☎ (0983) 752955
Afton Down (.5m E of village off A3055)
A downland/seaside links with wide fairways and
spectacular coastal views of the Solent and Channel.
18 holes, 5662yds, Par 68, SSS 68, Course record 64.
Membership 500.

Visitors welcome (after 0930 wkdays & 1000 Sun) must
contact in advance Societies welcome (by letter)
Green fees £15 per day (£20 WE & BH)
Facilities ⊗ ╚ ▣ ♀ △ ⛳
Hotel ★★★56% Albion Hotel, FRESHWATER ☎(0983)
753631 42rm(39⇌⚑)

NEWPORT
Map 2 B8

Newport ☎ (0983) 525076
St George's Down (1.5m S off A3020)
Downland course, fine views.
9 holes, 5218yds, Par 68, SSS 68. Membership 300.

Visitors welcome (ex after 1500 Sat, 1200 Sun) Societies
welcome (☎)
Green fees Not confirmed
Facilities ╚ ▣ ♀ △ 🏠 ⛳
Hotel ★★★57% Melville Hall Hotel, Melville St,
SANDOWN ☎(0983) 406526 33⇌⚑

RYDE
Map 2 B8

Ryde ☎ (0983) 614809
Binstead Rd (1m W on A3054)
Parkland course with wide views over the Solent.
9 holes, 5200yds, Par 66, SSS 66. Membership 350.

Visitors welcome (ex Wed pm & Sun am) ✉ Societies
welcome (☎)
Green fees £15 per day (£18 WE & BH)
Facilities ╚ ▣ ♀ △ 🏠 ⛳
Hotel ★★67% Biskra House Beach Hotel, 17 Saint
Thomas's St, RYDE ☎(0983) 67913 9⇌⚑

SANDOWN
Map 2 B8

Shanklin & Sandown ☎ (0983) 403217
Fairway, Lake (1m NW)
Links course.
18 holes, 6000yds, Par 69, SSS 69, Course record 65.
Membership 720.

Visitors welcome (must be M of a club with h'cap cert)
must contact in advance ✉ Societies welcome (limited
booking ☎)
Green fees £18 per day (£20 WE & BH)
Facilities ⊗ ⫼ by prior arrangement ╚ ▣ ♀ △ 🏠
⛳ ⛏ Peter Hammond
Hotel ★★★58% Cliff Tops Hotel, Park Rd, SHANKLIN
☎(0983) 863262 88⇌⚑

VENTNOR
Map 2 B8

Ventnor ☎ (0983) 853326
Steep Hill Down Rd, Upper Ventnor (1m NW off B3327)
Downland course subject to wind. Fine seascapes.
9 holes, 5752yds, Par 70, SSS 68, Course record 73.
Membership 200.

Visitors welcome (ex Sun am) Societies welcome (☎ or
letter)
Green fees £10 per day (£10 WE & BH)
Facilities ▣ ♀ △ ⛳
Hotel ★★★64% Ventnor Towers Hotel, Madeira Rd,
VENTNOR ☎(0983) 852277 27rm(17⇌5⚑)

WILTSHIRE

BISHOPS CANNINGS
Map 1 K3

North Wilts ☎ (038086) 627
(2m NW)
High, downland course with fine views.
18 holes, 6450yds, Par 72, SSS 71. Membership 500.

Visitors welcome Societies welcome
Green fees Not confirmed
Facilities ♀ △ 🏠 ⛏
Hotel ★★★61% Bear Hotel, Market Place, DEVIZES
☎(0380) 722444 24⇌

Opening times of bar and catering facilities vary
from place to place – it is wise to check in
advance of your visit.

CHIPPENHAM   Map 1 J3

Chippenham ☎ (0249) 652040
Malmesbury Rd (1.5m N on A429)
Easy walking on downland course. Testing holes at 1st and 15th.
18 holes, 5559yds, Par 69, SSS 67. Membership 650.

Visitors welcome (handicap certificate required) must contact in advance ✉ Societies welcome (by letter with handicap cert)
Green fees £18 per day (£24 WE & BH)
Facilities ⊗ (ex Mon) ⅏ (ex Sun and Mon) ⅃ ⬛ ♀ ⌓ 🏠 ⥾ ⋐ Bill Creamer
Hotel ★★★★⚑70% Manor House Hotel, CASTLE COMBE ☎(0249) 782206 12⇨⁵🐾 Annexe:24⇨⁵🐾

DURNFORD, GREAT   Map 1 K4

High Post ☎ Middle Woodford (072273) 356
(1.75m SE on A345)
An interesting course on Wiltshire chalk with good turf and splendid views over the southern area of Salisbury Plain. The par 3, 17th and the two-shot 18th require good judgement.
18 holes, 5473yds, Par 69, SSS 69. Membership 600.

Visitors welcome (handicap certificate required at WE) must contact in advance Societies welcome (not WE)
Green fees £20 per day; £16 per round (£25/£20 WE)
Facilities ⊗ ⅏ ⬛ ♀ ⌓ 🏠 ⋐ Anthony John Harman
Hotel ★★★60% Rose & Crown Hotel, Harnham Road, Harnham, SALISBURY ☎(0722) 27908 due to change to 327908 28⇨⁵🐾

KINGSDOWN   Map 1 J3

Kingsdown ☎ Box (0225) 742530
(W side of village)
Fairly flat heathland course with surrounding wood.
18 holes, 6445yds, Par 72, SSS 71, Course record 68. Membership 620.

Visitors welcome (ex at WE, h'cap cert reqd) must contact in advance ✉ Societies welcome (by letter)
Green fees £20 per day
Facilities ⊗ ⅏ ⅃ ⬛ ♀ ⌓ 🏠 ⥾ ⋐ R H Emery
Hotel ★★67% Methuen Arms Hotel, High St, CORSHAM ☎(0249) 714867 19rm(17⇨⁵1🐾) Annexe:6⇨⁵🐾

MARLBOROUGH   Map 1 K3

Marlborough ☎ (0672) 512147
The Common (N side of town centre on A345)
Downland course open to prevailing wind. Extensive views.
18 holes, 6526yds, Par 72, SSS 71. Membership 920.

Visitors welcome (restricted times & h'cap cert reqd WE) must contact in advance Societies welcome (☎)
Green fees £20 per day; £15 per round (£30 WE)

Facilities ⊗ ⅏ ⅃ ⬛ ♀ ⌓ 🏠 ⋐ L Ross, B McAdams, G Clough
Hotel ★★★59% Castle & Ball Hotel, High St, MARLBOROUGH ☎(0672) 515201 36⇨⁵

OGBOURNE ST GEORGE   Map 1 K2

Swindon ☎ (067284) 327
(N side of village on A3459)
Downland turf and magnificent greens.
18 holes, 6226yds, Par 71, SSS 70, Course record 65. Membership 700.

Visitors welcome (wkdays only, h'cap cert reqd) must contact in advance Societies welcome (by letter)
Green fees Not confirmed
Facilities ⊗ ⅏ by prior arrangement ⅃ ⬛ ♀ ⌓ 🏠 ⥾ ⋐ Colin Harraway
Hotel ★★★60% Crest Hotel, Oxford Rd, Stratton St Margaret, SWINDON ☎(0793) 831333 94⇨⁵🐾

SALISBURY   Map 1 K4

Salisbury & South Wilts ☎ (0722) 742645
Netherhampton (2m W on A3094)
Gently undulating downland course in country setting.
18 holes, 6130yds, Par 70, SSS 70, Course record 66. Membership 900.

Visitors welcome (ex competitions days) must contact in advance Societies welcome (by letter)
Green fees £15 per day (£22 WE & BH)
Facilities ⊗ ⅏ ⅃ ⬛ ♀ ⌓ 🏠 ⥾ ⋐ Gary Emerson
Hotel ★★★60% Rose & Crown Hotel, Harnham Road, Harnham, SALISBURY ☎(0722) 27908 due to change to 327908 28⇨⁵🐾

SWINDON   Map 1 K2

Broome Manor Golf Complex ☎ (0793) 532403
Pipers Way (1.75m SE of town centre off B4006)
Two courses and a 20-bay floodlit driving range.
Parkland course with water hazards, requires accuracy. Walking is easy on gentle slopes.
18 holes, 6359yds, Par 71, SSS 70, Course record 68 or 9 holes, 2745yds, Par 33, SSS 67. Membership 1300.

Visitors welcome must contact in advance Societies welcome (Mon-Thu only)
Green fees £6.20 per round (£6.80 WE & BH)
Facilities ⊗ ⅏ ⅃ ⬛ ♀ ⌓ 🏠 ⥾ ⋐ Barry Sandry
Hotel ★★★60% Crest Hotel, Oxford Rd, Stratton St Margaret, SWINDON ☎(0793) 831333 94⇨⁵🐾

UPAVON   Map 1 K3

RAF Upavon ☎ Stonehenge (0980) 630787
York Rd (2m E on A342)
Downland course set on sides of valley, with some wind affecting play. The 2nd, 9th, 11th and 18th are all par 3 to small greens.
18 holes, 5116mtrs, Par 69, SSS 67, Course record 66. Membership 300.

▶

Visitors welcome must contact in advance Societies
welcome (by letter)
Green fees £12 per day (£15 WE)
Facilities ⛳ 🏠
Hotel ★★★61% Bear Hotel, Market Place, DEVIZES
☎(0380) 722444 24⇄

WARMINSTER   Map 1 J4

West Wilts ☎ (0985) 212702
Elm Hill (N side of town centre off A350)
A hilltop course among the Wiltshire downs without
trees and somewhat windswept. First-class springy turf
with many interesting holes.
18 holes, 5701yds, Par 70, SSS 68, Course record 62.
Membership 600.

Visitors welcome (with M only WE, h'cap cert
required) must contact in advance Societies welcome
(by letter)
Green fees £17 per day (£28 WE)
Facilities ⊗ �🍽 ⛳ 🍺 ♀ ⛳ 🏠 ℓ Alan Harvey
Hotel ★★★★🏌67% Bishopstrow House Hotel,
WARMINSTER ☎(0985) 212312 32⇄🏌

CHANNEL ISLANDS

ALDERNEY

ALDERNEY   Map 1 B3

Alderney ☎ (048182) 2835
Route des Carrières (1m E of St Annes)
Undulating seaside course with sea on all sides. Course
designed by Frank Pennink.
9 holes, 2528yds, Par 32, SSS 33, Course record 28.
Membership 525.

Visitors welcome (ex before 1000 WE) Societies
welcome (book for parties of 4)
Green fees £8 per day (£14 WE & BH)
Facilities ⊗ ⛳ 🍺 ♀ ⛳ 🏠 🏌
Hotel ★★57% Inchalla Hotel, St Anne, ALDERNEY
☎(048182) 3220 11rm(8⇄)

Each golf course entry has a recommended
hotel. For a wider choice of places to stay,
consult *AA Hotels and Restaurants in Britain* or
AA-inspected Bed and Breakfast in Britain.

GUERNSEY

L'ANCRESSE VALE   Map 1 A4

Royal Guernsey ☎ (0481) 47022
(3m N of St Peter Port)
Not quite as old as its neighbour Royal Jersey, Royal
Guernsey is a sporting course which was re-
designed after World War II by Mackenzie Ross,
who has many fine courses to his credit. It is a
pleasant links, well-maintained, and administered
by the States of Guernsey in the form of the States
Tourist Committee. The 8th hole, a good par 4,
requires an accurate second shot to the green set
amongst the gorse and thick rough. The 18th, with
lovely views, needs a strong shot to reach the green
well down below. The course is windy, with hard
walking. There is a junior section. Snooker.
18 holes, 6206yds, Par 70, SSS 70. Membership 1500.

Visitors welcome (ex Thu & Sat (pm) & Sun h'cap
cert) ✉ Societies welcome (Oct-Apr ☎)
Green fees £15 per day/round
Facilities ⊗ ⍟ (ex Sun and Mon) ⛳ 🍺 ♀ ⛳ 🏠
🏌 ℓ Norman Wood
Hotel ★★★★67% St Pierre Park Hotel, Rohais, ST
PETER PORT ☎(0481) 28282 135⇄🏌

ST PETER PORT   Map 1 A4

St Pierre Park Golf Club ☎ (0481) 27039 & 28282
Rohais (1m W off Rohais Rd)
Parkland course with delightful setting, lakes, streams
and many tricky holes. Accommodation (see below).
9 holes, 1136yds, Par 27.

Visitors welcome
Green fees Not confirmed
Facilities ♀ ⛳ 🏠 🏌
Hotel ★★★★67% St Pierre Park Hotel, Rohais, ST
PETER PORT ☎(0481) 28282 135⇄🏌

JERSEY

GROUVILLE   Map 1 C5

Royal Jersey ☎ Jersey (0534) 54416
(4m E of St Helier off coast rd)
A seaside links, historic because of its age: its
centenary was celebrated in 1978. It is also famous
for the fact that Britian's greatest golfer, Harry
Vardon, was born in a little cottage on the edge of
the course and learned his golf here. Snooker.
18 holes, 6051yds, Par 70, SSS 70, Course record 64.
Membership 1364.

Visitors welcome (restricted to 1000-1200 & 1400-
1600) Societies welcome (Mon-Fri afternoons only)
Green fees £25 per round (£30 WE)
Facilities ⊗ ⍟ ⛳ 🍺 ♀ ⛳ 🏠 🏌 ℓ T A Horton
Hotel ★★★★(red)🏌Longueville Manor Hotel, ST
SAVIOUR ☎(0534) 25501 33⇄

LA MOYE
Map 1 B5

La Moye
☎ Jersey (0534) 43401
(W side of village off A13)
Seaside championship links
course situated in an
exposed position on the
south western corner of the
island overlooking St
Ouens Bay. Offers
spectacular views, two start
points, full course all year -
no temporary greens,
indoor practice nets and
snooker.
18 holes, 6512yds, Par 72, SSS 71, Course record 69.
Membership 1300.

SCORE CARD: White Tees					
Hole	Yds	Par	Hole	Yds	Par
1	158	3	10	370	4
2	522	5	11	502	5
3	185	3	12	163	3
4	437	4	13	396	4
5	449	4	14	190	3
6	482	5	15	345	4
7	379	4	16	482	5
8	415	4	17	419	4
9	407	4	18	397	4
Out	3434	36	In	3264	36
			Totals	6698	72

Visitors welcome must contact in advance ✉
Societies welcome (☎)
Green fees £40 per day (lunch incl); £25 per round
(£30 per round WE & BH)
Facilities ⊗ ∭ 🏌 ♨ ♀ ♨ 🏠 ⚑ ℂ David
Melville
Hotel ★★67% Les Arches Hotel, Archirondel Bay,
ARCHIRONDEL ☎(0534) 53839 54⇒🐾

ST CLEMENT
Map 1 B5

St Clement ☎ Jersey (0534) 21938
Jersey Recreation Grounds (E side of St Helier on A5)
Very tight moorland course. Holes cross over fairways,
impossible to play to scratch. Suitable for middle to high
handicaps. Tennis.
9 holes, 2244yds, Par 30. Membership 500.

Visitors welcome must contact in advance
Green fees Not confirmed
Facilities ♨
Hotel ★★★★(red)⛴Longueville Manor Hotel, ST
SAVIOUR ☎(0534) 25501 33⇒

ISLE OF MAN

DOUGLAS
Map 5 A6

Pulrose ☎ (0624) 75952
(1m W off A1)
Hilly, mainly moorland course under the control of
Douglas Corporation.
18 holes, 6080yds, Par 70, SSS 69. Membership 430.

Visitors welcome
Green fees Not confirmed
Facilities ♀ ♨ 🏠 ⚑ ℂ
Hotel ★★★64% Empress Hotel, Central Promenade,
DOUGLAS ☎(0624) 27211 102⇒🐾

ONCHAN
Map 5 A6

King Edward Bay Golf & Country Club
☎ Douglas (0624) 20430
Howstrake, Groudle Rd (E side of town off A11)
Hilly seaside course, perfect for beginners, with natural
hazards. Good views. Snooker, sauna, solarium.
18 holes, 5367yds, Par 68, SSS 66. Membership 400.

Visitors welcome Societies welcome (☎)
Green fees £5 per day (£7 WE)
Facilities ⊗ ∭ 🏌 ♨ ♀ ♨ 🏠 ⚑
Hotel ★★★64% Sefton Hotel, Harris Promenade,
DOUGLAS ☎(0624) 26011 80⇒🐾

PEEL
Map 5 A6

Peel ☎ (062484) 2227
Rheast Ln (SE side of town centre on A1)
Moorland course, with natural hazards and easy
walking. Good views. 11th hole is a par 4, dog-leg.
18 holes, 5914yds, Par 69, SSS 68, Course record 64.
Membership 600.

Visitors welcome (not before 1030 WE & BH) Societies
welcome (☎)
Green fees £10 per day (£12 WE & BH)
Facilities ⊗ ∭ by prior arrangement 🏌 ♨ ♀ ♨
Hotel ★★★64% Empress Hotel, Central Promenade,
DOUGLAS ☎(0624) 27211 102⇒🐾

PORT ERIN
Map 5 A6

Rowany ☎ Isle of Man (0624) 834108
Rowany Dr (N side of village off A32)
Undulating seaside course with testing later holes.
18 holes, 5840yds, Par 70, SSS 69, Course record 67.
Membership 600.

Visitors welcome (restricted WE) must contact in
advance ✉ Societies welcome (WE only ☎)
Green fees £8 per day (£12 WE & BH)
Facilities ⊗ ∭ 🏌 ♨ ♀ ♨ 🏠
Hotel ★★★66% Castletown Golf Links Hotel, Fort
Island, CASTLETOWN ☎(0624) 822201 58rm(44⇒12🐾)

RAMSEY
Map 5 B5

Ramsey ☎ (0624) 812244
Brookfield (SW side of town)
Parkland course, with easy walking. Windy. Good
views. Testing holes : 1st, par 5; 18th, par 3. Snooker.
18 holes, 6019yds, Par 70, SSS 69, Course record 64.
Membership 860.

Visitors welcome (restricted Tue am, Sat & Sun)
Societies welcome (not Sat & Sun ☎)
Green fees £10 per day (£12 WE)
Facilities ⊗ 🏌 ♨ ♀ ♨ 🏠 ⚑ ℂ Peter Lowrey
Hotel ★★★★60% Grand Island Hotel, Bride Rd,
RAMSEY ☎(0624) 812455 54⇒🐾

WALES

CLWYD

ABERGELE　　　　　　　　　　　Map 3 E2

Abergele & Pensarn ☎ (0745) 824034
Tan-y-Goppa Rd (.5m W off A547/A55)
A beautiful parkland course with views of the Irish Sea
and Gwyrch Castle. There are splendid finishing holes, a
testing par 5, 16th; a 185 yd, 17th to an elevated green,
and a superb par 5 18th with out of bounds just behind
the green. Snooker.
18 holes, 6520yds, Par 72, SSS 71, Course record 70.
Membership 1200.

Visitors welcome (restricted Tue) Societies welcome (by
letter)
Green fees £14.50 per day (£16.50 WE & BH)
Facilities ⊗ ⅢⅢ ⅃⅄ ⅊⅊ ♀ △ 🏠 ⌆ Iain R Runcie
Hotel ★★63% Kinmel Manor Hotel, St Georges Rd,
ABERGELE ☎(0745) 832014 25⇨🟊

COLWYN BAY　　　　　　　　　　Map 3 E2

Old Colwyn ☎ (0492) 515581
Woodland Av, Old Colwyn (E side of town centre on
B5383)
Hilly, meadowland course with sheep and cattle grazing
on it in parts.
9 holes, 5000yds, Par 68, SSS 66. Membership 300.

Visitors welcome Societies welcome (☎ for details)
Green fees Not confirmed
Facilities ♀ (WE) △
Hotel ★★70% Hopeside Hotel, Princes Dr, West End,
COLWYN BAY ☎(0492) 533244 19⇨🟊

DENBIGH　　　　　　　　　　　　Map 3 E2

Denbigh ☎ (0745) 814159
Henllan Rd (1.5m NW on B5382)
Parkland course, giving a testing and varied game.
Good views.
18 holes, 5581yds, Par 68, SSS 67, Course record 64.
Membership 550.

Visitors welcome (not before 1030 WE) must contact in
advance Societies welcome (☎)
Green fees £11 per day (£15 WE & BH)
Facilities ⊗ ⅢⅢ ⅃⅄ ⅊ (no catering Mon) ♀ △ 🏠 ⌆
⌆ M D Jones
Hotel ★★63% Kinmel Manor Hotel, St Georges Rd,
ABERGELE ☎(0745) 832014 25⇨🟊

FLINT　　　　　　　　　　　　　　Map 3 F2

Flint ☎ (03526) 2327
Cornist Park (1m W)
Parkland course incorporating woods and streams.
Hardcourt tennis, snooker.
9 holes, 5819yds, Par 68, SSS 68, Course record 67.
Membership 330.

Visitors welcome (with M only WE) Societies welcome
(☎ or letter)
Green fees £6 per day
Facilities ⊗ by prior arrangement ⅢⅢ by prior
arrangement ⅃⅄ ⅊ ♀ △ ⌆ M Station
Hotel ★★★64% The Chequers Country House Hotel,
Chester Rd, NORTHOP HALL ☎(0244) 816181 27⇨🟊

HAWARDEN　　　　　　　　　　Map 3 F2

Hawarden ☎ (0244) 531447
Groomsdale Ln (W side of town off B5125)
Parkland course with comfortable walking and good
views.
9 holes, 5620yds, Par 68, SSS 67, Course record 65.
Membership 430.

Visitors welcome Member must accompany must
contact in advance ✉ Societies welcome (by letter)
Green fees £10 per day
Facilities ⊗ ⅢⅢ ⅃⅄ ⅊ ♀ △ 🏠 ⌆
Hotel ★★★64% The Chequers Country House Hotel,
Chester Rd, NORTHOP HALL ☎(0244) 816181 27⇨🟊

HOLYWELL　　　　　　　　　　　Map 3 F2

Holywell ☎ (0352) 710040
Brynford (1.25m SW off B5121)
Exposed moorland course, with easy walking. 720 ft
above sea level. Snooker.
18 holes, 5951yds, Par 70, SSS 71. Membership 370.

Visitors welcome (WE & BH with M) Societies welcome
(☎)
Green fees £8 per day (£10 WE & BH)
Facilities ⊗ by prior arrangement ⅢⅢ by prior
arrangement ⅃⅄ ⅊ ♀ △
Hotel ★★66% Stamford Gate Hotel, Halkyn Rd,
HOLYWELL ☎(0352) 712942 & 712968 12⇨🟊

LLANGOLLEN　　　　　　　　　Map 3 F3

Vale of Llangollen ☎ (0978) 860040
Holyhead Rd (1.5m E on A5)
Parkland course, set in superb scenery by the River Dee.
18 holes, 6661yds, SSS 72. Membership 660.

Visitors welcome must contact in advance Societies
welcome (☎)
Green fees £15 per day (£18 WE & BH)
Facilities ⊗ by prior arrangement ⅢⅢ by prior
arrangement ⅃⅄ ⅊ ♀ △ 🏠 ⌆ ⌆
Hotel ★★★⚑64% Bryn Howel Hotel & Restaurant,
LLANGOLLEN ☎(0978) 860331 38⇨🟊

For an explanation of the symbols and
abbreviations used, see page 33.

MOLD
Map 3 F2

Old Padeswood ☎ Buckley (0244) 547401
Station Rd, Padeswood (3m SE off A5118)
Meadowland course, undulating in parts. Fishing, riding stables.
18 holes, 6639yds, Par 72, SSS 72, Course record 69 or 6138yds, Par 72, SSS 70 or 5596yds, Par 73, SSS 73. Membership 600.

Visitors welcome must contact in advance ✉ Societies welcome (☎)
Green fees Not confirmed
Facilities ⊗ ⫴ by prior arrangement ⛳ ⬤ ♀ ⚲ 🛍
〖 Tony Davies
Hotel ★★★64% The Chequers Country House Hotel, Chester Rd, NORTHOP HALL ☎(0244) 816181 27⇨🐾

Padeswood & Buckley ☎ (0244) 550537
The Caia, Station Ln (3m SE off A5118)
Gently undulating parkland course, with natural hazards and good views of the Welsh Hills.
18 holes, 5823yds, Par 68, SSS 68, Course record 66. Membership 600.

Visitors welcome (☎ for details) Societies welcome (☎)
Green fees £14.50 per day ; £13 per round (£15 WE & BH)
Facilities ⊗ ⫴ by prior arrangement ⛳ ⬤ ♀ ⚲ 🛍
⫛ 〖 David Ashton
Hotel ★★★64% The Chequers Country House Hotel, Chester Rd, NORTHOP HALL ☎(0244) 816181 27⇨🐾

PANTYMWYN
Map 3 F2

Mold ☎ (0352) 740318
(E side of village)
Meadowland course with some hard walking and natural hazards. Fine views.
18 holes, 5521yds, Par 67, SSS 67, Course record 62. Membership 350.

Visitors welcome Societies welcome (by letter)
Green fees £10 (£14 WE)
Facilities ⊗ by prior arrangement ⫴ by prior arrangement ⛳ ⬤ ♀ ⚲ 🛍 ⫛ 〖 Martin Carty
Hotel ★★★64% The Chequers Country House Hotel, Chester Rd, NORTHOP HALL ☎(0244) 816181 27⇨🐾

PRESTATYN
Map 3 E1

Prestatyn ☎ (0745) 854320
Marine Rd East (.5m N off A548)
Very flat seaside links exposed to stiff breeze. Testing holes : 9th, par 4, bounded on 3 sides by water ; 10th, par 4 ; 16th, par 4.
18 holes, 6792yds, Par 72, SSS 73, Course record 70. Membership 650.

Visitors welcome (ex Sat) must contact in advance ✉ Societies welcome (☎ & booking form)
Green fees £12 per day (£16 Sun & BH)
Facilities ⊗ ⫴ ⛳ ⬤ ♀ ⚲ 🛍 ⫛ 〖 M Staton
Hotel ★★63% Kinmel Manor Hotel, St Georges Rd, ABERGELE ☎(0745) 832014 25⇨🐾

St Melyd ☎ (0745) 854914
The Paddock, Meliden Rd (.5m S on A547)
Parkland course with good views of mountains and Irish Sea. Testing 1st hole (415 yds) par 4.
9 holes, 5600yds, Par 68, SSS 67, Course record 65. Membership 400.

Visitors welcome (ex competitions days) ✉ Societies welcome (☎)
Green fees £9 (£14 WE & BH)
Facilities ⊗ ⫴ by prior arrangement ⛳ ⬤ ♀ ⚲ 🛍
〖 Nigel H Lloyd
Hotel ★★★61% Oriel House Hotel, Upper Denbigh Rd, ST ASAPH ☎(0745) 582716 19⇨🐾

RHOS-ON-SEA
Map 3 E1

Rhos-on-Sea ☎ Llandudno (0492) 49641
Penryhn Bay, Llandudno (.5m W off A546)
Seaside course, with easy walking and panoramic views. Accommodation. Snooker.
18 holes, 6064yds, Par 69, SSS 69.

Visitors welcome must contact in advance Societies welcome (☎)
Green fees Not confirmed
Facilities ♀ ⚲ 🛍 ⫛ 〖
Hotel ★★★64% Gogarth Abbey Hotel, West Shore, LLANDUDNO ☎(0492) 76211 40⇨🐾

RHUDDLAN
Map 3 E2

Rhuddlan ☎ (0745) 590217
Meliden Rd (E side of town on A547)
Parkland course with easy walking and both artificial and natural hazards. Snooker.
18 holes, 6477yds, Par 71, SSS 71, Course record 68. Membership 929.

Visitors welcome wkdays (with M Sun) must contact in advance ✉ Societies welcome (by letter)
Green fees £16 per day (£20 Sat & BH)
Facilities ⊗ ⫴ ⛳ ⬤ ♀ ⚲ 🛍 ⫛ 〖 Ian Worsley
Hotel ★★★61% Oriel House Hotel, Upper Denbigh Rd, ST ASAPH ☎(0745) 582716 19⇨🐾

RHYL
Map 3 E1

Rhyl ☎ (0745) 353171
Coast Rd (1m E on A548)
Seaside course. Snooker.
9 holes, 3109yds, Par 35, SSS 35. Membership 350.

Visitors welcome (restricted Sun in summer) must contact in advance Societies welcome (☎ for WE)
Green fees Not confirmed
Facilities ⊗ ⫴ ⛳ ⬤ (no catering Mon) ♀ (ex Mon) ⚲ 🛍 ⫛
Hotel ★★★61% Oriel House Hotel, Upper Denbigh Rd, ST ASAPH ☎(0745) 582716 19⇨🐾

For an explanation of the symbols and abbreviations used, see page 33.

RUTHIN

Map 3 F2

Ruthin-Pwllglas ☏ (08242) 4658
Pwllglas (2.5m S off A494)
Moorland course in elevated position with panoramic views. Undulating, except for stiff climb to 3rd and 9th holes.
10 holes, 5362yds, Par 66, SSS 66, Course record 64. Membership 370.

Visitors welcome (ex competition days) Societies welcome (ex WE ☏)
Green fees £8 per day (£12 WE & BH)
Facilities ⌂
Hotel ★★★63% Ruthin Castle, RUTHIN ☏(08242) 2664 58⊐🏠

WREXHAM

Map 3 F3

Wrexham ☏ (0978) 261033
Holt Rd (1.75m NE on A534)
Inland, sandy course with easy walking. Testing dog-legged 7th hole (par 4), and short 14th hole (par 3) with full carry to green. Snooker.
18 holes, 6078yds, Par 70, SSS 69, Course record 66. Membership 650.

Visitors welcome (ex competition days) must contact in advance ✉ Societies welcome (ex Tue, Wed & WE)
Green fees Not confirmed
Facilities ⊗ ⍫ ⅃ 🍺 ♀ ⌂ 📷 ⴹ (D A Larvin
Hotel ★★★63% Wynnstay Arms, High Street/Yorke St, WREXHAM ☏(0978) 291010 75⊐🏠

DYFED

ABERYSTWYTH

Map 3 D5

Aberystwyth ☏ (0970) 615104
Brynymor Rd (N side of town)
Undulating meadowland course. Testing holes: 16th (The Loop) par 3; 17th, par 4; 18th, par 3. Good views over Cardigan Bay.
18 holes, 5835yds, Par 68, SSS 68, Course record 63. Membership 400.

Visitors welcome (☏ WE & BH) ✉ Societies welcome (☏)
Green fees £10-£12 (£12-£15 WE & BH)
Facilities ⊗ ⍫ ⅃ 🍺 ♀ ⌂ 📷 ⴹ (Graeme Brownlie
Hotel ★★61% Belle Vue Royal Hotel, Marine Ter, ABERYSTWYTH ☏(0970) 617558 42rm(16⊐8🏠)

BORTH

Map 3 D5

Borth & Ynslas ☏ (0970) 871202
(.5m N on B4353)
Seaside links with strong winds at times. Some narrow fairways.
18 holes, 5776yds, Par 70, SSS 69. Membership 410.

Visitors welcome (ex WE before 1000 or 1300-1430) ✉ Societies welcome (by letter)
Green fees £12 per day (£15 WE & BH)

Facilities ⊗ ⍫ ⅃ 🍺 ♀ ⌂ 📷 ⴹ (John G Lewis
Hotel ★★64% Court Royale Hotel, Eastgate, ABERYSTWYTH ☏(0970) 611722 10⊐🏠

BURRY PORT

Map 1 D2

Ashburnham
☏ (05546) 2269
Cliffe Ter (W side of town on B4311)
This course has a lot of variety. In the main it is of the seaside type although the holes in front of the clubhouse are of an inland character. They are, however, good holes which make a very interesting finish. Course record holder, Sam Torrance.

SCORE CARD: Championship Tees					
Hole	Yds	Par	Hole	Yds	Par
1	188	3	10	553	5
2	447	4	11	434	4
3	325	4	12	372	4
4	401	4	13	140	3
5	496	5	14	556	5
6	189	3	15	471	5
7	389	4	16	169	3
8	536	5	17	435	4
9	438	4	18	377	4
Out	3409	36	In	3507	36
			Totals	6916	72

18 holes, 6916yds, Par 72, SSS 72, Course record 67. Membership 750.

Visitors welcome (special times available) must contact in advance ✉ Societies welcome (by letter)
Green fees £20 per day; £15 per round (£25/£20 WE & BH)
Facilities ⊗ ⍫ ⅃ 🍺 ♀ ⌂ 📷 ⴹ (Richard J Playle
Hotel ★★★59% Diplomat Hotel, Felinfoel, LLANELLI ☏(0554) 756156 31⊐ Annexe:8rm

CARDIGAN

Map 3 B6

Cardigan ☏ (0239) 612035
Gwbert-on Sea (3m N off B4548)
A links course, very dry in winter, with wide fairways, light rough and gorse. Every hole overlooks the sea. Squash.
18 holes, 6641yds, Par 72, SSS 72, Course record 66. Membership 300.

Visitors welcome (ex 1300-1400) ✉ Societies welcome (☏)
Green fees £12 per day (£15 WE)
Facilities ⊗ ⍫ ⅃ 🍺 ♀ ⌂ 📷 ⴹ (
Hotel ★★★54% Cliff Hotel, GWBERT ☏(0239) 613241 75⊐🏠

CARMARTHEN

Map 3 C7

Carmarthen ☏ (026787) 493
Blaenycoed Rd (4m NW)
Mixed downland and heathland type course.
18 holes, 6210yds, Par 71, SSS 71, Course record 68. Membership 700.

Visitors welcome Societies welcome (☏ or by letter)
Green fees £15 per day (£20 WE)
Facilities ⊗ ⍫ ⅃ 🍺 ♀ ⌂ 📷 ⴹ (
Hotel ★★★64% The Ivy Bush Royal, Spilman St, CARMARTHEN ☏(0267) 235111 79⊐🏠

HAVERFORDWEST
Map 3 B7

Haverfordwest ☎ (0437) 764523
Arnolds Down (1m E on A40)
Parkland course in attractive surroundings.
18 holes, 6000yds, Par 70, SSS 70, Course record 68.
Membership 720.

Visitors welcome (ex WE) Societies welcome (by letter)
Green fees £12 per day (£16 WE); (£40 5 day ticket)
Facilities ⊗ ⅏ by prior arrangement ⭙ ⬛ ♀ ⌂ 🏠
⬥ 𝄪 Alex J Pile
Hotel ★★60% Mariners Inn, NOLTON HAVEN ☎(0437)
710469 14⇌🏃

LLANDYBIE
Map 3 D7

Glynhir ☎ (0269) 850472
Glynhir Rd (2m NE)
Parkland course with good views, latter holes close to
Upper Loughor River. The 14th is a 405-yd dog leg.
Accommodation.
18 holes, 6090yds, Par 69, SSS 70. Membership 450.

Visitors welcome must contact in advance ✉ Societies
welcome (wkdays only ☎)
Green fees Not confirmed
Facilities ⊗ (ex Mon) ⅏ (ex Mon) ⭙ (ex Mon) ⬛ (ex
Mon) ♀ (ex Mon) ⌂ 🏠 𝄪 Steve Rastal
Hotel ★★67% Mill at Glynhir, Glyn-Hir, Llandybie,
AMMANFORD ☎(0269) 850672 9⇌🏃 Annexe:2⇌🏃

LLANGYBI
Map 3 D6

Cilgwyn ☎ (0570) 45286
(.5m NW off A485)
Parkland course.
9 holes, 5318yds, Par 68, SSS 67, Course record 66.
Membership 150.

Visitors welcome Societies welcome (☎)
Green fees £6.50 per day (£7.50 WE)
Facilities ⬛ ♀ ⌂ ⬥
Hotel ★★★63% Falcondale Country House Hotel,
LAMPETER ☎(0570) 422910 21⇌🏃

MILFORD HAVEN
Map 3 A8

Milford Haven ☎ (0646) 692368
Woodbine House, Hubberstone (1.5m W)
Parkland course.
18 holes, 6071yds, Par 71, SSS 70, Course record 68.
Membership 300.

Visitors welcome Societies welcome (☎)
Green fees £10 per day (£12 WE & BH)
Facilities ⊗ ⅏ ⭙ ⬛ ♀ ⌂ 🏠
Hotel ★★60% Lord Nelson Hotel, Hamilton Ter,
MILFORD HAVEN ☎(0646) 695341 32⇌🏃

Each golf course entry has a recommended
hotel. For a wider choice of places to stay,
consult *AA Hotels and Restaurants in Britain* or
AA-inspected Bed and Breakfast in Britain.

NEWPORT — Map 3 B7

Newport (Pemb)☎ (0239) 820244
The Golf Club (1.25m N)
Seaside course, with easy walking and good view.
Accommodation.
9 holes, 6178yds, Par 72, SSS 69, Course record 67.
Membership 220.

Visitors welcome Societies welcome (☎)
Green fees £8 per day
Facilities ⊗ ⅲ ⅙ ⅙ ♀ ⚲ 🏠 ⚐ ⟨ Colin Parsons
Hotel ★★61% Cartref Hotel, 15-19 High St,
FISHGUARD ☎(0348) 872430 12rm(4♠)

PEMBROKE DOCK — Map 3 B8

South Pembrokeshire ☎ (0646) 683817
Defensible Barracks (SW side of town centre off B4322)
Downland course overlooking Milford Haven, with easy
walking and little rough. Suitable for beginners.
9 holes, 5804yds, Par 70, SSS 69. Membership 305.

Visitors welcome Societies welcome (by letter)
Green fees Not confirmed
Facilities ⊗ (ex Mon) ⅲ by prior arrangement ⅙ ⅙
♀ ⚲
Hotel ★★59% Old Kings Arms, Main St, PEMBROKE
☎(0646) 683611 21↩

ST DAVID'S — Map 3 A7

St David's City ☎ Croeseoch (0437) 721620
c/o 39 Penygarn
The course overlooks Whitesands beach and bay.
9 holes, 5572yds, Par 70, SSS 70, Course record 67.
Membership 200.

Visitors welcome Societies welcome (☎)
Green fees £8 per round
Facilities ⅙ ⚲
Hotel ★★★64% Warpool Court Hotel, ST DAVID'S
☎(0437) 720300 25↩♠

TENBY — Map 1 C2

Tenby ☎ (0834) 2978
The Burrows
A fine old seaside links, with sea views and natural
hazards. It provides good golf, and is a popular
holiday course. Snooker.
18 holes, 6330yds, Par 69, SSS 71. Membership 650.

Visitors welcome (subject to competition & tee
reservation) Societies welcome (☎)
Green fees £15 per day (£20 WE & BH)
Facilities ⊗ ⅲ ⅙ ⅙ ♀ ⚲ 🏠 ⚐ ⟨ T Mountford
Hotel ★★69% Atlantic Hotel, Esplanade, TENBY
☎(0834) 2881 & 4176 35↩♠

If you know of a golf course, not in this guide
already, which welcomes visitors, we would be
pleased to hear about it.

GWENT

ABERGAVENNY — Map 3 F7

Monmouthshire ☎ (0873) 3171
Gypsy Ln, Llanfoist (2m S off B4269)
This parkland course is very picturesque, with the
beautifully wooded River Usk running alongside.
There are a number of par 3 holes and a testing par 4
at the 15th. Fishing.
18 holes, 5961yds, Par 69, SSS 69, Course record 64.
Membership 700.

Visitors welcome (with M only WE) must contact in
advance ✉ Societies welcome (by letter)
Green fees £18 per day (£23 WE & BH)
Facilities ⊗ ⅲ ⅙ ⅙ ♀ ⚲ 🏠 ⚐ ⟨ P Worthing
Hotel ★★★57% Angel, Cross St, ABERGAVENNY
☎(0873) 7121 29↩

BLACKWOOD — Map 1 G2

Blackwood ☎ (0495) 223152
Cwmgelli (.75m N off A4048)
Heathland course with sand bunkers. Undulating, with
hard walking. Testing 2nd hole par 4. Good views.
9 holes, 5304yds, Par 66, SSS 66, Course record 65.
Membership 250.

Visitors welcome (with M only WE & BH) must contact
in advance ✉ Societies welcome (ex WE & BH)
Green fees £8 (£10 WE & BH)
Facilities ⚲
Hotel ★★★50% Maes Manor Hotel, BLACKWOOD
☎(0495) 224551 & 220011 8↩ Annexe:14↩

CHEPSTOW — Map 1 H2

**St Pierre Hotel Golf and
Country Club**
☎ (0291) 625261
St Pierre Park (3m SW off
A48)
Parkland/meadowland
championship course. The
Old is home to the Epson
Grand Prix of Europe, and
is one of Britain's major
courses. Its long par 5, 12th
hole of 545 yds, tests even
the finest golfers.
Accommodation and a wide
range of sports and leisure facilities are available.
*Old Course 18 holes, 6748yds, Par 71, SSS 73, Course
record 63. Mathern Course 18 holes, 5762yds, Par 68,
SSS 68. Membership 800.*

SCORE CARD: Old Course (White Tees)					
Hole	Yds	Par	Hole	Yds	Par
1	576	5	10	362	4
2	388	4	11	393	4
3	135	3	12	545	5
4	379	4	13	219	3
5	420	4	14	521	5
6	165	3	15	375	4
7	442	4	16	426	4
8	309	4	17	412	4
9	444	4	18	237	3
Out	3258	35	In	3490	36
			Totals	6748	71

Visitors welcome must contact in advance Societies
welcome (☎)
Green fees from £30
Facilities ⊗ ⅲ ⅙ ⅙ ♀ ⚲ 🏠 ⚐ ⟨ Renton Doig

Hotel ★★★69% St Pierre Hotel, Golf & Country Club, St Pierre Park, CHEPSTOW ☎(0291) 625261 107⇨🏠 Annexe:43⇨🏠

CWMBRAN
Map 1 G2

Pontnewydd ☎ (06333) 2170
Maesgwyn Farm, West Pontnewydd (N side of town centre)
Mountainside course, with hard walking. Good views across the Severn Estuary.
10 holes, 5321yds, Par 68, SSS 67, Course record 63.
Membership 250.

Visitors welcome (with M only WE & BH)
Green fees Not confirmed
Facilities ⊗ by prior arrangement 〗 by prior arrangement 🔁 ♀ 🛆
Hotel ★★61% Priory Hotel, High St, Caerleon, NEWPORT ☎(0633) 421241 16⇨🏠 Annexe:5⇨🏠

LLANWERN
Map 1 G2

Llanwern ☎ (0633) 412029
Tennyson Av (.5m S off A455)
Meadowland course. Snooker.
New Course 18 holes, 6202yds, Par 70, SSS 69.
Membership 829.

Visitors welcome (must be M of recognised club)
Societies welcome (☎)
Green fees £15 per 18 holes, £10 per 9 holes (£20/£17 WE & BH)
Facilities ⊗ 〗 🔁 🍺 ♀ 🛆 🏠 🎵 Stephen Price
Hotel ★★★57% Hilton National, The Coldra, NEWPORT ☎(0633) 412777 119⇨🏠

MONMOUTH
Map 3 G7

Monmouth ☎ (0600) 2212
Leasebrook Ln (1.5m NE off A40)
Downland course in scenic setting. High, undulating land with good views. Testing 1st and 4th holes.
9 holes, 5523yds, Par 68, SSS 66. Membership 380.

Visitors welcome (ex before 1115 on Sun) Societies welcome (☎)
Green fees £10 per day (£15 WE & BH)
Facilities ⊗ (ex Mon) 〗 (ex Mon) 🔁 🍺 ♀ 🛆 🏠
Hotel ★★★63% Kings Head Hotel, Agincourt Square, MONMOUTH ☎(0600) 2177 29⇨🏠

Rolls of Monmouth
☎ (0600) 5353 due to change to 715353
The Hendre (4m W on B4233)
This spacious parkland course has an arboretum close to the first tee and a natural division between the first and second 9 holes. Several lakes and ponds add interest.
18 holes, 6723yds, Par 72, SSS 72, Course record 68.
Membership 220.

Visitors welcome (ex open day) Societies welcome (☎)
Green fees £20 per day (£26 WE & BH)
Facilities ⊗ 〗 🔁 🍺 ♀ 🛆 🏠 🎵
Hotel ★★★63% Kings Head Hotel, Agincourt Square, MONMOUTH ☎(0600) 2177 29⇨🏠

NANTYGLO
Map 3 F8

West Monmouthshire ☎ (0495) 310233
Pond Rd (.25m W off A467)
Mountain and heathland course with hard walking and natural hazards. Testing 3rd hole, par 5, and 7th hole, par 4.
18 holes, 6118yds, Par 71, SSS 69, Course record 65.
Membership 500.

Visitors welcome Societies welcome (1 wk notice ☎)
Green fees £8 wkdays & BH (£15 WE)
Facilities ⊗ 〗 🔁 🍺 ♀ 🛆
Hotel ★★★57% Angel Hotel, Cross St, ABERGAVENNY ☎(0873) 7121 29⇨

NEWPORT
Map 1 G2

Newport ☎ (0633) 896794
Great Oak, Rogerstone (3m NW of city centre off B4591)
An undulating downland course, part-wooded. The 2nd hole is surrounded by bunkers - a difficult hole. The 11th hole is a bogey 4 and the fairway runs through an avenue of trees, making a straight drive preferable. Practice grounds available.
18 holes, 6314yds, Par 72, SSS 71, Course record 64. Membership 700.

SCORE CARD					
Hole	Yds	Par	Hole	Yds	Par
1	324	4	10	391	4
2	142	3	11	356	4
3	459	4	12	486	5
4	475	5	13	404	4
5	507	5	14	147	3
6	175	3	15	360	4
7	476	5	16	177	3
8	228	3	17	388	4
9	342	4	18	477	5
Out	3128	36	In	3186	36
			Totals	6314	72

Visitors welcome must contact in advance ✉ Societies welcome (by letter)
Green fees £25 (£30 WE)
Facilities ⊗ 〗 🔁 🍺 ♀ 🛆 🏠 🎵 🎵 R F Skuse
Hotel ★★★★63% Celtic Manor Hotel, Coldra Woods, NEWPORT ☎(0633) 413000 73⇨🏠

Tredegar Park ☎ (0633) 895219
Bassaleg Rd (2m SW off A467 exit 276 of M4)
A parkland course with river and streams as natural hazards. The ground is very flat with narrow fairways and small greens. The 17th hole (par 3) is played on to a plateau where many players spoil their medal round. Snooker.
18 holes, 6097mtrs, Par 71, SSS 70, Course record 67.
Membership 800.

Visitors welcome (must be M of a golf club) must contact in advance ✉ Societies welcome (☎)
Green fees £15 per day (£20 WE & BH)

▶

Facilities ⊗ ⌲ ⅃ ▬ ♀ ⌂ ☞ ⌇ M L Morgan
Hotel ★★★57% Hilton National, The Coldra,
NEWPORT ☎(0633) 412777 119⇆♠

PONTYPOOL

Map 1 G2

Pontypool ☎ (0495) 763655
Trevethin (1.5m N off A4043)
Undulating, hill-course with magnificent views.
Snooker.
18 holes, 6013yds, Par 69, SSS 69. Membership 626.

Visitors welcome (handicap certificate required) must
contact in advance ✉ Societies welcome (☎)
Green fees £12 per day (£17.50 WE & BH)
Facilities ⊗ ⌲ ⅃ ▬ ♀ ⌂ ☞ ⌇ Jim Howard
Hotel ★★74% Glen-yr-Afon Hotel, Pontypool Rd, USK
☎(02913) 2302 16rm(10⇆5♠)

TREDEGAR

Map 3 F8

Tredegar and Rhymney ☎ Rhymney (0685) 840743
Cwmtysswg, Rhymney (1.75m SW on B4256)
Mountain course with lovely views of the surrounding
area.
9 holes, 5504yds, Par 68. Membership 194.

Visitors welcome Societies welcome (by letter)
Green fees £7.50 per day
Facilities ♀ ⌂
Hotel ★★64% Tregenna Hotel, Park Ter, MERTHYR
TYDFIL ☎(0685) 723627 & 82055 14⇆♠ Annexe:7⇆♠

GWYNEDD

ABERDOVEY

Map 3 D4

Aberdovey ☎ (065472) 210
(.5m W on A493)
A beautiful championship course at the mouth of the
Dovey estuary, Aberdovey has all the true
characteristics of a seaside links. It has some fine
holes among them the 3rd, the 12th, an especially
good short hole, and the 15th. There are some
striking views to be had from the course. Snooker.
18 holes, 6445yds, Par 71, SSS 71, Course record 67.
Membership 650.

Visitors welcome (M have priority 0800-1000 &
1230-1400) ✉ Societies welcome
Green fees £15-£20 per day; £10-£18 per round
(£18-£25 WE)
Facilities ⊗ ⌲ by prior arrangement ⅃ ▬ ♀ ⌂
⌂ ⌇ John Davies
Hotel ★★★65% Trefeddian Hotel, ABERDOVEY
☎(065472) 213 46rm(37⇆5♠)

For a full list of the golf courses
included in this book, check
with the index on page 284

ABERSOCH

Map 3 C3

Abersoch ☎ (075881) 2622
(S side of village)
Seaside links, with easy walking and several holes
notable for scenic beauty.
18 holes, 5892yds, Par 70, SSS 68. Membership 650.

Visitors welcome Member must accompany Societies
welcome
Green fees Not confirmed
Facilities ♀ ⌂ ⌂ ⌇
Hotel ★★★62% Abersoch Harbour Hotel, ABERSOCH
☎(075881) 2406 & 3632 9rm(7⇆1♠) Annexe:5⇆♠

AMLWCH

Map 3 C1

Bull Bay ☎ (0407) 830960
(1m NW on A5025)
Pleasant seaside course with natural meadow, rock,
gorse and wind hazards. Views from all tees across Irish
Sea to Isle of Man.
18 holes, 6160yds, Par 70, SSS 70, Course record 66.
Membership 800.

Visitors welcome (ex WE) Societies welcome (☎)
Green fees £7.50 per day (£10.50 WE)
Facilities ⊗ (ex Tue) ⌲ by prior arrangement ⅃ ▬ ♀
⌂ ⌂ ⌇ Neil Dunroe
Hotel ★★57% Trecastell Hotel, Bull Bay, AMLWCH
☎(0407) 830651 12rm(8⇆3♠)

BALA

Map 3 E3

Bala ☎ (0678) 520359
Penlan (.5m SW off A494)
Mountainous course with natural hazards.
10 holes, 4990yds, Par 66, SSS 64, Course record 64.
Membership 250.

Visitors welcome (☎ BH) Societies welcome (☎)
Green fees £8 per day (£10 WE & BH); £25 wkly
Facilities ♀ ⌂ ⌂ ☞
Hotel ★★57% Plas Coch Hotel, High St, BALA ☎(0678)
520309 10⇆♠

BANGOR

Map 3 D2

St Deiniol ☎ (0248) 353098
Penybryn (E side of town centre off A5122)
Elevated parkland course with panoramic views of
Snowdonia, Menai Straits, and Anglesey.
18 holes, 5068mtrs, Par 68, SSS 67, Course record 63.
Membership 500.

Visitors welcome (restricted WE) Societies welcome (by
letter)
Green fees £8 (£10 WE)
Facilities ⊗ ⌲ ⅃ ▬ (no catering Mon) ♀ ⌂ ⌂ ⌇
Paul Lovell
Hotel ★★68% Menai Court Hotel, Craig y Don Rd,
BANGOR ☎(0248) 354200 12⇆♠

BEAUMARIS   Map 3 D2

Baron Hill ☎ (0286) 810231
(1m SW off A545)
Undulating course with natural hazards of rock and gorse. Testing 3rd and 4th holes (par 4's).
9 holes, 2396mtrs, Par 68, SSS 67, Course record 64. Membership 400.

Visitors welcome Societies welcome (by letter)
Green fees Not confirmed
Facilities ⓑ ⓔ ♀ ⚲ ⓕ Peter Maton
Hotel ★★67% Bishopsgate House Hotel, 54 Castle St, BEAUMARIS ☎(0248) 810302 10⇔↟

BETWS-Y-COED   Map 3 D2

Betws-y-Coed ☎ (06902) 556
(NE side of village off A5)
Attractive parkland course set between two rivers in Snowdonia National Park.
9 holes, 4996yds, Par 64, SSS 64, Course record 63. Membership 350.

Visitors welcome Societies welcome
Green fees £10 per day (£12 WE)
Facilities ⊗ ⓜ ⓑ ⓔ ♀ ⚲ ⓕ
Hotel ★★★63% Royal Oak, Holyhead Rd, BETWS-Y-COED ☎(06902) 219 due to change to (0690) 710219 27⇔↟

CAERNARFON   Map 3 C2

Caernarfon ☎ (0286) 3783
Llanfaglan (1.75m SW)
Parkland course with gentle gradients.
18 holes, 5870yds, Par 69, SSS 69, Course record 67. Membership 600.

Visitors welcome (ex competition days) must contact in advance Societies welcome (by letter or ☎)
Green fees £12 per day
Facilities ⊗ (ex Mon) ⓜ ⓑ ⓔ ♀ ⚲
Hotel ★★★61% Stables Hotel, LLANWNDA ☎(0286) 830711 & 830935 Annexe:14⇔↟

CONWY   Map 3 D2

Conwy ☎ Aberconwy (0492) 593400
The Morfa (1m W of town centre on A55)
This course close by the old town of Conwy is a real seaside links with gorse, rushes, sandhills and fine old turf. There are plenty of natural hazards, the gorse providing more than its share. The course has a spectacular setting between sea and mountains.
18 holes, 6458yds, Par 72, SSS 71. Membership 960.

Visitors welcome (restricted WE & competitions) Societies welcome (☎)
Green fees £15 per day (£20 WE & BH)

For an explanation of the symbols and abbreviations used, see page 33.

Facilities ⊗ (ex Tue) ⓜ (ex Mon and Tue) ⓑ (ex Tue) ⓔ ♀ ⚲ ⓕ ⓣ ⓕ Peter Lees
Hotel ★★66% Bryn Cregin Garden Hotel, Ty Mawr Rd, DEGANWY ☎(0492) 585266 16⇔↟

CRICCIETH   Map 3 C3

Criccieth ☎ (0766) 522154
Ednyfed Hill (1m NE)
Hilly course on Lleyn Peninsula. Good views.
18 holes, 5587yds, Par 69, SSS 68. Membership 234.

Visitors welcome Societies welcome
Green fees £7.50
Facilities ⊗ by prior arrangement ⓜ by prior arrangement ⓑ ⓔ ♀ ⚲ ⓕ
Hotel ★★57% George IV Hotel, CRICCIETH ☎(0766) 522168 37rm(28⇔6↟)

DOLGELLAU   Map 3 D4

Dolgellau ☎ (0341) 422603
Pencefn Rd (.5m N)
Undulating parkland course. Ideal course for middle/high handicap players. Good views of mountains and Mawddach estuary.
9 holes, 4671yds, Par 66, SSS 63, Course record 64. Membership 280.

Visitors welcome (ex Sat) Societies welcome (☎)
Green fees £8 per day (£10 WE & BH)

Facilities ⊗ by prior arrangement ⫴ by prior arrangement 🗲 ⬛ ♀ 🚲 🏠 🍴
Hotel ★★63% Royal Ship Hotel, Queens Square, DOLGELLAU ☎(0341) 422209 24rm(13⇨3🛏)

FFESTINIOG   Map 3 D3

Ffestiniog ☎ (076676) 2637
Y Cefn (1m E on B4391)
Moorland course set in Snowdonia National Park.
9 holes, 4570yds, Par 68, SSS 66, Course record 77.
Membership 120.

Visitors welcome (ex competitions) Societies welcome (☎)
Green fees £5 per day
Facilities ♀ 🚲
Hotel ★★(red)⚑Maes y Neuadd Hotel, TALSARNAU ☎(0766) 780200 12⇨🛏 Annexe:4⇨🛏

HARLECH   Map 3 D3

Royal St Davids ☎ (0766) 780361
(W side of town on A496)
Championship links, with easy walking and natural hazards.
18 holes, 6427yds, Par 69, SSS 71, Course record 64.
Membership 750.

Visitors welcome must contact in advance ✉ Societies welcome (by letter)
Green fees £16 per day (£20 WE & BH)
Facilities ⊗ ⫴ 🗲 ⬛ (catering restricted in winter) ♀ 🚲 🏠 🍴 John Barnett
Hotel ★★62% Ty Mawr Hotel, LLANBEDR ☎(034123) 440 10⇨🛏

HOLYHEAD   Map 3 C1

Holyhead ☎ (0407) 763279
Trearddur Bay (1.25m S on B4545)
Treeless, undulating seaside course which provides a varied and testing game, particularly in a south wind. The fairways are bordered by gorse, heather and rugged outcrops of rock. Designed by James Braid. Accommodation, indoor driving range, snooker.
18 holes, 6086yds, Par 70, SSS 70, Course record 64.
Membership 1309.

Visitors welcome (h'cap certificate required) must contact in advance Societies welcome (☎)
Green fees Not confirmed
Facilities ⊗ ⫴ 🗲 ⬛ ♀ 🚲 🏠 🍴 P Capper
Hotel ★★★62% Trearddur Bay Hotel, TREARDDUR BAY ☎(0407) 860301 27rm(20⇨)

To see a full range of AA guides and maps, visit your local AA Shop or any good bookshop.

LLANDUDNO   Map 3 D1

Llandudno (Maesdu)☎ (0492) 76450
Hospital Rd (S side of town centre on A546)
Part links, part meadowland, this championship course starts and finishes on one side of the main road, the remaining holes, more seaside in nature, being played on the other side. The holes are pleasantly undulating and present a pretty picture when the gorse is in bloom. Often windy, this varied and testing course is not for beginners. Snooker.
18 holes, 6513yds, Par 73, SSS 72, Course record 65.
Membership 950.

Visitors welcome (must be M of club with h'cap cert) Societies welcome (☎)
Green fees £15 per day (£20 WE & BH)
Facilities ⊗ ⫴ by prior arrangement 🗲 ⬛ ♀ 🚲 🏠 🍴 🍴 Simon Boulden
Hotel ★★★64% Imperial Hotel, The Promenade, LLANDUDNO ☎(0492) 77466 100⇨🛏

North Wales ☎ (0492) 75325
72 Bryniau Rd, West Shore (W side of town on A546)
This course is across the railway from Maesdu and is more of a seaside links with several extremely fine holes. Snooker.
18 holes, 6132yds, Par 71, SSS 69, Course record 65.
Membership 690.

Visitors welcome (restricted wkdays) must contact in advance ✉ Societies welcome (☎)
Green fees £15.50 per day (£20 WE & BH)
Facilities ⊗ ⫴ 🗲 ⬛ ♀ 🚲 🏠 🍴 🍴 Richard Bradbury
Hotel ★★(red)St Tudno Hotel, Promenade, LLANDUDNO ☎(0492) 874411 21⇨🛏

LLANFAIRFECHAN   Map 3 D2

Llanfairfechan ☎ (0248) 680144
Fford Llannerch (W side of town on A55)
· Hillside course with panoramic views of coast.
9 holes, 3119yds, Par 54, SSS 57, Course record 53.
Membership 130.

Visitors welcome (☎ for details) Societies welcome (☎)
Green fees Not confirmed
Facilities 🚲
Hotel ★★★65% Sychnant Pass Hotel, Sychnant Pass Rd, CONWY ☎(0492) 596868 & 596869 13⇨🛏

LLANGEFNI (Anglesey)   Map 3 C2

Llangefni (Public)☎ (0248) 722193
(1.5m off A5)
Picturesque parkland course designed by Hawtree & Son.
9 holes, 1342yds, Par 28, SSS 28.

Visitors welcome Societies welcome (☎)
Green fees Not confirmed
Facilities 🚲 🏠 🍴 🍴
Hotel ★★65% Anglesey Arms, MENAI BRIDGE ☎(0248) 712305 17rm(10⇨6🛏)

MORFA NEFYN   Map 3 C3

Nefyn & District ☎ (0758) 720218
(.75m NW)
Seaside course, with parkland fairways and good
views. Testing golf along cliff edge. Large clubhouse
with excellent facilities. Snooker. Course record
holder Ian Woosnam.
18 holes, 6294yds, Par 72, SSS 71. Membership 750.

Visitors welcome (handicap certificate required)
must contact in advance Societies welcome (☎)
Green fees £15 per day (£20 WE & BH)
Facilities ⊗ 业 ﾚ ⬛ ♀ ㊁ 🛏 ⼻ ⌇ J R
Pilkington
Hotel ★★58% Linksway Hotel, MORFA NEFYN
☎(0758) 720258 26rm(11⇔10♒)

PENMAENMAWR   Map 3 D2

Penmaenmawr ☎ (0492) 623330
Cae Maen Pavilion (1.5m NE off A55)
Hilly course with magnificent views across the bay to
Llandudno and Anglesey. Dry-stone wall natural
hazards.
*9 holes, 5229yds, Par 67, SSS 66, Course record 64.
Membership 500.*

Visitors welcome Societies welcome (☎)
Green fees £8 per day (£10 WE & BH)
Facilities ﾚ ⬛ ♀ ㊁
Hotel ★★58% Lion Hotel, Y Maes, CRICCIETH ☎(0766)
522460 36rm(27⇔♒)

PORTHMADOG   Map 3 D3

Porthmadog ☎ (0766) 512037
Morfa Bychan (1.5m SW)
Seaside links, with easy walking and good views.
Snooker.
18 holes, 6020yds, Par 70, SSS 70. Membership 500.

Visitors welcome must contact in advance Societies
welcome (☎)
Green fees £15 per day
Facilities ⊗ 业 ﾚ ⬛ ♀ ㊁ 🛏 ⌇ Peter Bright
Hotel ★★57% Madoc Hotel, TREMADOG ☎(0766)
512021 21rm(1⇔3♒)

PWLLHELI   Map 3 C3

Pwllheli ☎ (0758) 612520
Golf Rd (.5m SW off A497)
Easy walking on flat seaside course with outstanding
views of Snowdon, Cadar Idris and Cardigan Bay.
Snooker.
*18 holes, 6105yds, Par 69, SSS 69, Course record 66.
Membership 650.*

Visitors welcome (restricted Tue, Thu & WE) Societies
welcome (☎)
Green fees £12 per day (£15 WE & BH)
Facilities ⊗ 业 ﾚ ⬛ ♀ ㊁ 🛏 ⌇ G D Verity
Hotel ★60% Caeau Capel Hotel, Rhodfar Mor, NEFYN
☎(0758) 720240 20rm(6⇔4♒)

RHOSNEIGR (Anglesey)   Map 3 C2

Anglesey ☎ Rhosneigr (0407) 810219
Station Rd (NE side of village on A4080)
Seaside course with easy walking.
18 holes, 5700yds, Par 69, SSS 69. Membership 400.

Visitors welcome Societies welcome (by letter)
Green fees Not confirmed
Facilities ♀ ㊁ 🛏 🛏 ⌇
Hotel ★★★62% Trearddur Bay Hotel, TREARDDUR
BAY ☎(0407) 860301 27rm(20⇔♒)

MID GLAMORGAN

ABERDARE   Map 3 E8

Aberdare ☎ (0685) 871188
Abernant (.75m E)
Pleasant, parkland course with outstanding valley
views. Snooker.
*18 holes, 5875yds, Par 69, SSS 69, Course record 63.
Membership 500.*

Visitors welcome (ex Sat unless with M) must contact
in advance ✉ Societies welcome (☎)
Green fees Not confirmed
Facilities ⊗ 业 ﾚ ⬛ (no catering Mon) ♀ ㊁ 🛏
⌇ Alan Palmer
Hotel ★★★50% Maes Manor Hotel, BLACKWOOD
☎(0495) 224551 & 220011 8⇔ Annexe:14⇔

BARGOED   Map 1 G2

Bargoed ☎ (0443) 830143
Heolddu (NW side of town)
Mountain parkland course, testing par 4, 13th hole.
18 holes, 5836yds, Par 70, SSS 70, Course record 65.
Membership 452.

Visitors welcome (Mon-Fri (with M only WE)) ✉
Societies welcome (☎)
Green fees £12 per day
Facilities ⊗ ⅏ by prior arrangement ⅃ 🍺 ♀ ⌂
Hotel ★★★50% Maes Manor Hotel, BLACKWOOD
☎(0495) 224551 & 220011 8⌐ Annexe:14⌐

BRIDGEND   Map 1 F2

Southerndown ☎ (0656) 880476
Ewenny (3m SW on B4524)
A unique course standing on high downs close to the
sea. The views are entrancing, and the golf
completely natural. Well worth a visit. Snooker.
18 holes, 6615yds, Par 70, SSS 73. Membership 598.

Visitors welcome (Sun only with M) must contact
in advance ✉ Societies welcome (Tue & Thu)
Green fees Not confirmed
Facilities ⊗ ⅏ by prior arrangement ⅃ 🍺 ♀ ⌂
🏠 (Dennis McMonagle
Hotel ★★★64% Heronston Hotel, Ewenny,
BRIDGEND ☎(0656) 668811 76⌐

CAERPHILLY   Map 1 G2

Caerphilly ☎ (0222) 883481
Pencapel Mountain Rd (.5m S on A469)
Undulating mountain course. Good views especially
from 10th hole, 700 ft above sea level. Snooker.
14 holes, 6023yds, Par 71, SSS 71, Course record 65.
Membership 773.

Visitors welcome (WE & BH with M only, h'cap cert
required) ✉ Societies welcome (☎ or letter)
Green fees £14 per round
Facilities ⅃ ♀ ⌂ 🏠 (Graeme Brownlee
Hotel ★★62% Griffin Inn Motel, Rudry, CAERPHILLY
☎(0222) 869735 Annexe:20⌐

Castell Heights ☎ (0222) 886666
Blaengwynlais (2m SW)
'Pay as you play' course.
9 holes, 2688yds, Par 34, SSS 33. Membership 500.

Visitors welcome Societies welcome
Green fees Not confirmed
Facilities ♀ ⌂ 🏠 ⌐
Hotel ★★62% Griffin Inn Motel, Rudry, CAERPHILLY
☎(0222) 869735 Annexe:20⌐

Each golf course entry has a recommended
hotel. For a wider choice of places to stay,
consult *AA Hotels and Restaurants in Britain* or
AA-inspected Bed and Breakfast in Britain.

CREIGIAU (CREIYIAU)   Map 1 F2

Creigiau ☎ Cardiff (0222) 890263
(6m NW of Cardiff on A4119)
Downland course, with small greens.
18 holes, 5955yds, Par 69, SSS 68. Membership 800.

Visitors welcome (with M only WE) Societies welcome
(☎)
Green fees £18 per day
Facilities ⊗ ⅏ by prior arrangement ⅃ 🍺 ♀ ⌂ 🏠
(Colin Thomas
Hotel ★★★64% Crest Hotel, Castle St, CARDIFF
☎(0222) 388681 159⌐⌐

MAESTEG   Map 1 F2

Maesteg ☎ (0656) 732037
Mount Pleasant (.5m W off B4282)
Mountainside course.
18 holes, 5845yds, Par 69, SSS 69, Course record 64.
Membership 650.

Visitors welcome (must have membership card/h'cap
cert) Societies welcome (wkdays only ☎)
Green fees £12 (£15 WE)
Facilities ⊗ ⅏ ⅃ 🍺 ♀ (ex Thu) ⌂ 🏠 (Gary
Hopkins
Hotel ★★★58% Aberafan Beach Hotel, Princess
Margaret Way, PORT TALBOT ☎(0639) 884949 66⌐

MAESYCWMMER   Map 2 D3

Bryn Meadows ☎ Blackwood (0495) 225590
The Bryn (on the A4048 Blackwood to Ystrad Mynach
rd)
A heavily-wooded parkland course with panoramic
views. Testing 3rd, 12th and 15th holes.
Accommodation.
18 holes, 6200yds, Par 71, SSS 69, Course record 66.
Membership 540.

Visitors welcome (ex Sun am) must contact in advance
Societies welcome (Tue & Thu only)
Green fees £16 (£20 WE)
Facilities ⊗ ⅏ ⅃ 🍺 ♀ ⌂ 🏠 (
Hotel ★★★50% Maes Manor Hotel, BLACKWOOD
☎(0495) 224551 & 220011 8⌐ Annexe:14⌐

MERTHYR TYDFIL   Map 3 E8

Merthyr Tydfil (Cilanws) ☎ (0685) 3308
Cilsanws, Cefn Coed (2m NW off A470)
Hilly, mountain course with good views and water
hazards.
11 holes, 5820yds, Par 70, SSS 68, Course record 66.
Membership 240.

Visitors welcome (ex Sun)
Green fees £10 (£12 WE)
Facilities ⌂
Hotel ★★61% Nant Ddu Lodge, Cwm Taf, MERTHYR
TYDFIL ☎(0685) 79111 15⌐

Morlais Castle ☎ (0685) 722822
Pant, Dowlais (2.5m N off A465)
Beautiful course in National Park adjacent to Brecon
Beacons. Testing course since it is rocky off the
fairways.
18 holes, 6320yds, Par 71, SSS 71. Membership 400.

Visitors welcome (ex Sat 1200-1600, Sun 0800-1200)
Societies welcome (wkdays only ☎)
Green fees Not confirmed
Facilities ⊗ ⫿ by prior arrangement ☖ ⬛ by prior
arrangement ⛛ ⌂
Hotel ★★61% Nant Ddu Lodge, Cwm Taf, MERTHYR
TYDFIL ☎(0685) 79111 15⇥⬩

MOUNTAIN ASH   Map 1 F2

Mountain Ash ☎ (0443) 472265
Cefnpennar (1m NW off A4059)
Mountain course.
*18 holes, 5553yds, Par 69, SSS 68, Course record 63.
Membership 500.*

Visitors welcome (WE with M only) ✉ Societies
welcome (by letter)
Green fees £14
Facilities ⌂ ⌂ ⎰ Jeff Sim
Hotel ★★61% Nant Ddu Lodge, Cwm Taf, MERTHYR
TYDFIL ☎(0685) 79111 15⇥⬩

NELSON   Map 1 G2

Whitehall ☎ (0443) 740245
The Pavilion (2m W off A470)
Windy mountain course. Testing 4th hole (235 yds) par
3, and 6th hole (408 yds) par 4.
9 holes, 5400yds, Par 68, SSS 68. Membership 300.

Visitors welcome
Green fees Not confirmed
Facilities ⛛ (1200-1600 ex Wed) ⌂
Hotel ★★62% Griffin Inn Motel, Rudry, CAERPHILLY
☎(0222) 869735 Annexe:20⇥

PONTYGWAITH   Map 1 F2

Rhondda ☎ Tonypandy (0443) 433204
Golf Club House (.5m W off B4512)
Mountain course with good views. Snooker.
*18 holes, 6428yds, Par 70, SSS 71, Course record 69.
Membership 430.*

Visitors welcome (restricted Sun) Societies welcome
(☎)
Green fees £10 per day
Facilities ⊗ ⫿ ☖ ⬛ ⛛ ⌂ ⌂
Hotel ★★54% Wyndham Hotel, Dunraven Place,
BRIDGEND ☎(0656) 652080 & 57431 28rm(25⇥)

For a full list of the golf courses
included in this book, check
with the index on page 284

PONTYPRIDD   Map 1 F2

Pontypridd ☎ (0443) 409904
Ty Gwyn Rd (E side of town centre off A470)
Well-wooded mountain course with springy turf. Good
views of the Rhondda Valleys and coast. Snooker.
*18 holes, 5650yds, Par 69, SSS 68, Course record 66.
Membership 730.*

Visitors welcome (with M only WE & BH, h'cap cert
required) ✉ Societies welcome (wkdays only ☎)
Green fees Not confirmed
Facilities ⊗ (ex Thu) ⫿ by prior arrangement ☖ ⬛ ⛛
⌂ ⌂ ⎰ K Gittins
Hotel ★★★64% Crest Hotel, Castle St, CARDIFF
☎(0222) 388681 159⇥⬩

PORTHCAWL   Map 1 F2

Royal Porthcawl ☎ (065671) 2251
(1.5m NW of town centre)
This championship-standard heathland/downland
links course is always in sight of the sea.
*18 holes, 6691yds, Par 72, SSS 74, Course record 65.
Membership 800.*

Visitors welcome (with M only WE & BH, h'cap cert
required) must contact in advance ✉ Societies
welcome (by letter)
Green fees Not confirmed
Facilities ⊗ ⫿ by prior arrangement ☖ ⬛ ⛛ ⌂
⌂ �🛈 ⎰ Graham Poor
Hotel ★★★58% Seabank Hotel, The Promenade,
PORTHCAWL ☎(065671) 2261 62⇥⬩

PYLE   Map 1 F2

Pyle & Kenfig ☎ Porthcawl (065671) 3093
Waun-Y-Mer (S side of Pyle off A4229)
Links course, with sand-dunes. Easy walking. Often
windy.
*18 holes, 6081yds, Par 71, SSS 73, Course record 67.
Membership 1045.*

Visitors welcome (with M only WE) ✉ Societies
welcome (wkdays only ☎)
Green fees £25 per day; £20 per round
Facilities ⊗ ⫿ ☖ ⬛ ⛛ ⌂ ⎰ Robert Evans
Hotel ★★★58% Seabank Hotel, The Promenade,
PORTHCAWL ☎(065671) 2261 62⇥⬩

TALBOT GREEN   Map 1 F2

Llantrisant & Pontyclun ☎ Llantrisant (0443) 222148
Llanelry Rd (N side of village off A473)
Parkland course.
12 holes, 5712yds, Par 68, SSS 68. Membership 600.

Visitors welcome (with club membership card & h'cap
cert) Member must accompany ✉ Societies welcome (by
letter)
Green fees £15 per day

▶

Facilities ⊗)Ⅲ by prior arrangement ⅃ ⬛ ♀ 스 🏠 ⚑ ꙭ Nick Watson
Hotel ★★54% Wyndham Hotel, Dunraven Place, BRIDGEND ☎(0656) 652080 & 57431 28rm(25⇨)

POWYS

BRECON
Map 3 E7

Brecon ☎ (0874) 2004
Newton Park (.75m W of town centre on A40)
Parkland course, with easy walking. Natural hazards include two rivers on boundary of course. Good river and mountain scenery.
9 holes, 5218yds, Par 66, SSS 66, Course record 61. Membership 420.

Visitors welcome (restricted on competition days)
Societies welcome (☎)
Green fees £8 per day (WE included)
Facilities ♀ 스
Hotel ★★58% Castle of Brecon Hotel, Castle Square, BRECON ☎(0874) 4611 34⇨ꙮ Annexe:12ꙮ

Cradoc ☎ (0874) 3658
Penoyre Park, Cradoc (2m NW)
Parkland with wooded areas, lakes, spectacular views over the Brecon Beacons and challenging golf.
18 holes, 6301yds, Par 71, SSS 71, Course record 65. Membership 600.

Visitors welcome must contact in advance Societies welcome (☎ 7 days in advance)
Green fees £13 (£16 WE & BH)
Facilities ⊗ (ex Mon))Ⅲ (ex Mon) ⅃ ⬛ ♀ 스 🏠 ꙭ Douglas Beattie
Hotel ★★58% Castle of Brecon Hotel, Castle Square, BRECON ☎(0874) 4611 34⇨ꙮ Annexe:12ꙮ

KNIGHTON
Map 3 F5

Knighton ☎ (0547) 528646
Frydd Wood (.5m S off B4355)
Hill course with hard walking.
9 holes, 2660yds, Par 68, SSS 66, Course record 62. Membership 130.

Visitors welcome (ex Sun pm) Societies welcome (☎)
Green fees £5 per day (£7 WE & BH)
Facilities ⅃ ⬛ ♀ 스
Hotel ★★64% Radnorshire Arms Hotel, High St, PRESTEIGNE ☎(0544) 267406 8⇨ Annexe:8⇨

LLANDRINDOD WELLS
Map 3 E6

Llandrindod Wells ☎ (0597) 823873
(1m SE off A483)
Moorland course with easy walking and panoramic views. One of the highest courses in Wales (1,100 ft above sea level).
18 holes, 5800yds, Par 69, SSS 68, Course record 65. Membership 550.

Visitors welcome Societies welcome (☎ for details)

Green fees Not confirmed
Facilities ⊗ (ex Tue))Ⅲ ⅃ ⬛ ♀ 스 🏠 ꙭ
Hotel ★★★63% Hotel Metropole, Temple St, LLANDRINDOD WELLS ☎(0597) 822881 121⇨ꙮ

LLANGATTOCK
Map 3 F7

Old Rectory ☎ (0873) 810373
Sheltered course with easy walking. Swimming pool.
9 holes, 2225yds, Par 53, SSS 54 or 53yds. Membership 200.

Visitors welcome
Green fees Not confirmed
Facilities ♀ 스
Hotel ★★⬤70% Gliffaes Country House Hotel, CRICKHOWELL ☎(0874) 730371 19rm(15⇨3ꙮ) Annexe:3⇨ꙮ

LLANIDLOES
Map 3 E5

St Idloes ☎ (05512) 2559
Penrhallt (1m N off B4569)
Hill-course which is undulating but walking is easy. Good views.
9 holes, 5320yds, Par 66, SSS 66. Membership 150.

Visitors welcome (ex Sun am)
Green fees Not confirmed
Facilities ♀ (evenings only) 스
Hotel ★61% Red Lion Hotel, Longbridge St, LLANIDLOES ☎(05512) 2270 6rm

MACHYNLLETH
Map 3 D4

Machynlleth ☎ (0654) 702000
Ffordd Drenewydd (.5m E off A489)
Lowland course with mostly natural hazards.
9 holes, 5726yds, Par 68, SSS 67, Course record 65. Membership 233.

Visitors welcome (ex competitions & Thu 1300-1400)
Societies welcome (☎ or letter)
Green fees £10 per day
Facilities ⊗ ⅃ ⬛ ♀ 스 ⚑
Hotel ★★61% Wynnstay Arms Hotel, Maengwyn St, MACHYNLLETH ☎(0654) 702941 20⇨

NEWTOWN
Map 3 F5

St Giles ☎ (0686) 625844
Pool Rd (.5m NE on A483)
Inland country course with easy walking. Testing 2nd hole, par 3, and 4th hole, par 4. River Severn skirts 4 holes. Fishing.
9 holes, 5864yds, Par 70, SSS 68. Membership 250.

Visitors welcome (restricted Sat pm, Sun am & Thu pm)
✉ Societies welcome (☎)
Green fees £7 per day (£10 WE & BH)
Facilities ⊗)Ⅲ ⅃ ⬛ ♀ 스 🏠 ⚑ ꙭ
Hotel ★★63% Elephant & Castle, Broad St, NEWTOWN ☎(0686) 626271 25⇨ꙮ Annexe:11⇨ꙮ

WELSHPOOL
Map 3 F4

Welshpool ☎ Castle Caerinion (0938) 83249
Golfa Hill (3m W off A458)
Undulating heathland course with bracing air. Testing holes are 2nd (par 5), 14th (par 3), 17th (par 3).
18 holes, 5708yds, Par 70, SSS 69. Membership 250.

Visitors welcome must contact in advance Societies welcome (booking required)
Green fees £8 (£15 WE & BH)
Facilities ⊗ (ex Mon) 💺 (ex Mon) ♀ (ex Mon) ⛳ 🏠
Hotel ★★64% Royal Oak Hotel, WELSHPOOL ☎(0938) 552217 24🛏🐾

SOUTH GLAMORGAN

BARRY
Map 1 G3

Brynhill ☎ (0446) 735061
Port Rd (1.25m N on B4050)
Meadowland course with some hard walking. Prevailing west wind.
18 holes, 5511mtrs, Par 71, SSS 69, Course record 67. Membership 450.

Visitors welcome (ex Sun) ✉ Societies welcome (wkdays only)
Green fees £15
Facilities ⊗ ⅏ 🍴 💺 ♀ ⛳ 🏠 ⛏ ⌇ P Fountain
Hotel ★★★53% Mount Sorrell Hotel, Porthkerry Rd, BARRY ☎(0446) 740069 45🛏🐾 Annexe:4🛏

CARDIFF
Map 1 G3

Cardiff ☎ (0222) 753320
Sherborne Av, Cyncoed (3m N of city centre)
Parkland course, trees form natural hazards. Interesting variety of holes, mostly bunkered.
18 holes, 6016yds, Par 70, SSS 70. Membership 930.

Visitors welcome (with M only WE) ✉ Societies welcome (Thu only)
Green fees Not confirmed
Facilities ⊗ ⅏ by prior arrangement 🍴 💺 ♀ ⛳ 🏠 ⌇ Terry Hanson
Hotel ★★★59% Post House Hotel, Pentwyn Rd, Pentwyn, CARDIFF ☎(0222) 731212 150🛏

Llanishen ☎ (0222) 755078
Cwm Lisvane (5m N of city centre off A469)
Undulating, parkland course, with hard walking.
18 holes, 5296yds, Par 68, SSS 66, Course record 63. Membership 900.

Visitors welcome (Mon-Fri only ex BH) must contact in advance ✉ Societies welcome (Thu only)
Green fees £20 per day (subject to review)
Facilities ⊗ (ex Mon) ⅏ (ex Mon) 🍴 💺 ♀ ⛳ 🏠 ⌇ R A Jones
Hotel ★★★59% Post House Hotel, Pentwyn Rd, Pentwyn, CARDIFF ☎(0222) 731212 150🛏

Radyr ☎ (0222) 842408
Drysgol Rd, Radyr (4.5m NW of city centre off A4119)
Hillside, parkland course which can be windy. Good views.
18 holes, 6031yds, Par 69, SSS 70, Course record 63. Membership 900.

Visitors welcome (with M only WE) must contact in advance ✉ Societies welcome (☎)
Green fees £22 per day
Facilities ⊗ ⅏ 🍴 💺 (no catering Thu) ♀ ⛳ 🏠 ⌇ Steve Gough
Hotel ★★★★54% Park Hotel, Park Place, CARDIFF ☎(0222) 383471 119🛏🐾

St Mellons ☎ (0633) 680408
St Mellons (5m NE off A48)
This parkland course comprises quite a few par-3 holes and provides some testing golf. It is indeed a challenge to the single handicap golfer. The 12th hole runs over a stream, making an accurate drive virtually essential.
18 holes, 6080yds, Par 70, SSS 69. Membership 800.

SCORE CARD: White Tees					
Hole	Yds	Par	Hole	Yds	Par
1	333	4	10	454	4
2	421	4	11	135	3
3	199	3	12	556	5
4	320	4	13	493	5
5	172	3	14	160	3
6	470	4	15	280	4
7	477	5	16	357	4
8	186	3	17	437	4
9	361	4	18	464	4
Out	2939	34	In	3336	36
			Totals	6275	70

Visitors welcome (with M only WE) must contact in advance ✉ Societies welcome (☎ or letter)
Green fees Not confirmed
Facilities ⊗ ⅏ 🍴 💺 ♀ ⛳ 🏠 ⌇ Barry Thomas
Hotel ★★★59% Post House Hotel, Pentwyn Rd, Pentwyn, CARDIFF ☎(0222) 731212 150🛏

Whitchurch ☎ (0222) 620985
Whitchurch (4m N of city centre on A470)
Parkland course, with easy walking. Snooker.
18 holes, 6319yds, Par 71, SSS 70, Course record 62. Membership 930.

Visitors welcome (restricted Sat (Apr-Oct), Sun (Oct-Apr)) ✉ Societies welcome (by letter)
Green fees £20 (£25 WE & BH)
Facilities ⊗ ⅏ by prior arrangement 🍴 💺 ♀ ⛳ 🏠 ⛏ ⌇ E Clark
Hotel ★★★★54% Park Hotel, Park Place, CARDIFF ☎(0222) 383471 119🛏🐾

DINAS POWIS
Map 1 G3

Dinas Powis ☎ (0222) 512727
Old High Walls (NW side of village)
Parkland/downland course with views over the Bristol Channel and the seaside resort of Barry.
18 holes, 5377yds, Par 67, SSS 66, Course record 65. Membership 620.

Visitors welcome (with M only WE) ✉ Societies welcome (☎or letter)
Green fees £15 per day (£20 WE & BH)

▶

Facilities ⊗ ⫟ ⫼ 🛏 ♀ ⛳ 🏠 (G Bennett
Hotel ★★★53% Mount Sorrell Hotel, Porthkerry Rd,
BARRY ☎(0446) 740069 45⇔🛏 Annexe:4⇔

PENARTH

Map 1 G3

Glamorganshire ☎ Cardiff (0222) 701185
Lavernock Rd (S side of town centre on B4267)
Parkland course, overlooking the Bristol Channel.
Squash and snooker.
18 holes, 6150yds, Par 70, SSS 70, Course record 65.
Membership 1000.

Visitors welcome (ex competition days) must contact in
advance ✉ Societies welcome (Mon, Wed-Fri only ☎)
Green fees £15 per day (£20 WE & BH)
Facilities ⊗ ⫟ ⫼ 🛏 ♀ ⛳ 🏠 (Andrew Kerr Smith
Hotel ★65% Walton House Hotel, 37 Victoria Rd,
PENARTH ☎(0222) 707782 12rm(9⇔🛏)

WENVOE

Map 1 G3

Wenvoe Castle ☎ Cardiff (0222) 594371
(1m S off A4050)
Parkland course which is hilly for first 9 holes. Pond,
situated 280 yds from tee at 10th hole, is a hazard.
18 holes, 6422yds, Par 72, SSS 71. Membership 600.

Visitors welcome (WE with M only) must contact in
advance ✉ Societies welcome (by letter)
Green fees £20 per day
Facilities ⊗ ⫟ ⫼ 🛏 ♀ ⛳ 🏠 (M Pycroft
Hotel ★★★64% Crest Hotel, Castle St, CARDIFF
☎(0222) 388681 159⇔🛏

WEST GLAMORGAN

CLYDACH

Map 1 E2

Inco ☎ (0792) 844216
(.75m SE on B4291)
Flat meadowland course.
18 holes, 5976yds, Par 71, SSS 69. Membership 300.

Visitors welcome Societies welcome
Green fees Not confirmed
Facilities ♀ ⛳
Hotel ★★62% Oak Tree Parc Hotel, Birchgrove Rd,
BIRCHGROVE ☎(0792) 817781 10⇔🛏

GLYNNEATH

Map 3 E8

Glynneath ☎ (0639) 720452
Pen-y-graig (2m NE on B4242)
Attractive hillside course overlooking the Vale of
Neath. Snooker.
18 holes, 5456yds, Par 68, SSS 67, Course record 66.
Membership 450.

Visitors welcome (restricted during starting times at
WE) Societies welcome (Mid-week-4 weeks notice)
Green fees £10 per day (£20 WE & BH)
Facilities 🛏 ⫼ 🛏 ♀ ⛳
Hotel ★★62% Oak Tree Parc Hotel, Birchgrove Rd,
BIRCHGROVE ☎(0792) 817781 10⇔🛏

NEATH

Map 1 E2

Neath ☎ (0639) 643615
Cadoxton (2m NE off A4230)
Mountain course, with spectacular views. Testing
holes: 10th par 4; 12th par 5; 15th par 4. Snooker.
18 holes, 6492yds, Par 72, SSS 72, Course record 67.
Membership 650.

Visitors welcome (restricted WE) Societies welcome
(☎)
Green fees £12 per day (£18 WE & BH)
Facilities ⊗ ⫟ ⫼ 🛏 ♀ ⛳ 🏠 ⚑ (M E E Bennett
Hotel ★★64% Castle Hotel, The Parade, NEATH
☎(0639) 641119 & 643581 28⇔🛏

Swansea Bay ☎ Skewen (0792) 814153
Jersey Marine (4m SW off A48)
Fairly level seaside links with part-sand dunes.
Snooker.
18 holes, 6302yds, Par 71, SSS 70, Course record 67.
Membership 500.

Visitors welcome ✉ Societies welcome (☎)
Green fees £13 per day (£18 WE & BH)
Facilities ⊗ ⫟ ⫼ 🛏 ♀ ⛳ 🏠 ⚑ (Mike Day
Hotel ★★64% Castle Hotel, The Parade, NEATH
☎(0639) 641119 & 643581 28⇔🛏

PONTARDAWE

Map 3 D8

Pontardawe ☎ (0792) 863118
Cefn Llan (N side of town centre M4 junc 45 off A406)
Meadowland course situated on plateau 600 ft above sea-
level with good views over Bristol Channel and Brecon
Beacons. Snooker.
18 holes, 6162yds, Par 70, SSS 70. Membership 700.

Visitors welcome must contact in advance ✉ Societies
welcome (ex WE ☎)
Green fees Not confirmed
Facilities ⫟ by prior arrangement ⛳ 🏠 ⚑
(R A Ryder
Hotel ★★62% Oak Tree Parc Hotel, Birchgrove Rd,
BIRCHGROVE ☎(0792) 817781 10⇔🛏

SOUTHGATE

Map 1 E2

Pennard ☎ Bishopston (044128) 3131
2 Southgate Rd (NW side of village)
Undulating seaside links with good coastal views.
Squash and snooker.
18 holes, 6275yds, Par 71, SSS 71, Course record 66.
Membership 800.

Visitors welcome (ex WE & BH handicap certificate
required) Societies welcome (ex WE & BH apply by
letter)
Green fees £13 per day
Facilities ⊗ ⫟ ⫼ 🛏 ♀ ⛳ 🏠 ⚑
(Michael V Bennett
Hotel ★73% Windsor Lodge Hotel, Mount Pleasant,
SWANSEA ☎(0792) 642158 & 652744 19rm(11⇔4🛏)

SWANSEA

Map 1 E2

Clyne ☎ (0792) 401989
120 Owls Lodge Ln, The Mayals, Blackpyl (3.5m SW on B4436 off A4067)
Course of heath and moor, very open to the wind. Snooker.
18 holes, 6344yds, Par 70, SSS 71, Course record 64.
Membership 700.

Visitors welcome (must be M of a club with h'cap cert) must contact in advance ⊠ Societies welcome (☎)
Green fees £15 per day (£20 WE & BH)
Facilities ⊗ ⫟ ⓛ ⬛ (all catering by prior arrangement) ♀ △ 🖻 ⎰ Mark Bevan
Hotel ★★64% Langland Court, Langland Court Rd, LANGLAND ☎(0792) 361545 16⇔⋔ Annexe:5⇔⋔

Langland Bay ☎ (0792) 366023
Langland Bay (6m W on A4067)
Parkland course overlooking Gower coast. The par 4, 6th is an uphill dog-leg open to the wind, and the par 3, 16th (151 yds) is aptly named 'Death or Glory'.
18 holes, 5830yds, Par 70, SSS 70. Membership 850.

Visitors welcome ⊠ Societies welcome (☎)
Green fees £15 per day (£17 WE & BH)
Facilities ⊗ ⫟ ⓛ ⬛ ♀ △ 🖻 ⎰
Hotel ★★★59% Osborne Hotel, Rotherslade Rd, LANGLAND ☎(0792) 366274 36rm(32⇔⋔)

Morriston ☎ (0792) 796528
160 Clasemont Rd (5m N on A48)
Parkland course.
18 holes, 5785yds, Par 68, SSS 68. Membership 580.

Visitors welcome (☎ for details) must contact in advance ⊠ Societies welcome (☎)
Green fees £10 + VAT per day (£16 + VAT WE & BH)
Facilities ⊗ ⫟ by prior arrangement ⓛ ⬛ ♀ △ 🖻 ⎴ ⎰ Deryl Rees
Hotel ★★62% Oak Tree Parc Hotel, Birchgrove Rd, BIRCHGROVE ☎(0792) 817781 10⇔⋔

UPPER KILLAY

Map 1 E2

Fairwood Park ☎ Swansea (0792) 203648
Blackhills Ln (1.5m S off A4118)
Parkland course on Gower coast with good views and easy walking. Snooker.
18 holes, 6608yds, Par 72, SSS 72. Membership 750.

Visitors welcome Societies welcome (☎)
Green fees Not confirmed
Facilities ⊗ by prior arrangement ⫟ by prior arrangement ⓛ by prior arrangement ⬛ ♀ △ 🖻 ⎰ Mark Evans
Hotel ★73% Windsor Lodge Hotel, Mount Pleasant, SWANSEA ☎(0792) 642158 & 652744 19rm(11⇔4⋔)

Opening times of bar and catering facilities vary from place to place – it is wise to check in advance of your visit.

YSTALYFERA

Map 3 D8

Palleg ☎ (0639) 842193
Lower Cwm-twrch (1.5m N off A4068)
Heathland course liable to become heavy going after winter rain.
9 holes, 6400yds, Par 36, SSS 72, Course record 71.
Membership 200.

Visitors welcome (no jeans, tee shirts or trainers)
Societies welcome (two months in advance)
Green fees £8 (£10 WE & BH)
Facilities ⊗ ⫟ ⓛ ⬛ (catering by arrangement) ♀ △
Hotel ★★62% Oak Tree Parc Hotel, Birchgrove Rd, BIRCHGROVE ☎(0792) 817781 10⇔⋔

SCOTLAND

BORDERS

COLDSTREAM

Map 6 J3

Hirsel ☎ (0890) 2678
Kelso Rd (SW side of town off A678)
Parkland course, with hard walking and sheltered trees. Testing 3rd and 6th holes.
9 holes, 5860yds, Par 70, SSS 68, Course record 64.
Membership 280.

Visitors welcome (restricted during competitions)
Societies welcome (☎ for details)
Green fees £6 per day (£8 WE)
Facilities ⓛ ⬛ ♀ (Apr-Sep) △ 🖻
Hotel ★★★64% Ednam House Hotel, Bridge St, KELSO ☎(0573) 24168 32⇔⋔

DUNS

Map 6 J3

Duns ☎ (0361) 82717
Longformacus Rd (1m W off A6105)
Interesting course, natural hazards of water and hilly slopes.
9 holes, 5826yds, Par 68, SSS 68, Course record 66.
Membership 260.

Visitors welcome (ex competition days & Tue evenings)
Societies welcome (by letter)
Green fees £6 per day
Facilities ♀ (May-Sep WE & lunch) △
Hotel ★★★63% Turret House Hotel, Etal Rd, Tweedmouth, BERWICK-UPON-TWEED ☎(0289) 330808 13⇔⋔

EYEMOUTH

Map 6 J2

Eyemouth ☎ (08907) 50551
Gunsgreen House (E side of town)
With the exception of a steep climb to the 1st tee, this is a compact, flat and popular seaside course. Snooker.
9 holes, 2369mtrs, Par 33. Membership 189.

Visitors welcome (after 1400 WE) Societies welcome
Green fees Not confirmed

▶

Facilities ♀ ⌂ 🏠 ƒ Graig Maltman
Hotel ★★★63% Turret House Hotel, Etal Rd,
Tweedmouth, BERWICK-UPON-TWEED ☎(0289) 330808
13⇌🐾

GALASHIELS
Map 6 H3

Galashiels ☎ (0896) 3724
Ladhope Recreation Ground (N side of town centre off
A7)
Hillside course, superb views from the top, 10th hole
very steep.
18 holes, 5311yds, Par 68, SSS 67. Membership 250.

Visitors welcome Societies welcome (☎)
Green fees £5 (Sun £5.70)
Facilities ⊗ (Sun only) ∭ (Sun only) 🍴 (Sat-Sun) ♀
⌂

Hotel ★★★65% Kingsknowes Hotel, Selkirk Rd,
GALASHIELS ☎(0896) 58375 11rm(8⇌2🐾)

Torwoodlee ☎ (0896) 2260
(1.75m NW off A7)
Parkland course with natural hazards designed by
James Braid. Testing 3rd hole (par 3).
*9 holes, 5800yds, Par 68, SSS 68, Course record 64.
Membership 290.*

Visitors welcome (ex Sat & Thu evenings) Societies
welcome (☎ & letter)
Green fees £10 per day ; £8 per round WE
Facilities ⊗ ∭ 🍴 🍺 (no catering Tue) ♀ (ex Tue) ⌂
🏠

Hotel ★★64% Burt's Hotel, The Square, MELROSE
☎(089682) 2285 21⇌🐾

HAWICK
Map 6 H4

Hawick ☎ (0450) 72293
Vertish Hill (SW side of town)
Hill course with good views.
18 holes, 5929yds, Par 68, SSS 69. Membership 690.

Visitors welcome (by arrangement WE) Societies
welcome (by letter)
Green fees £10 per day, £7 per round (£12 WE)
Facilities ⊗ 🍴 🍺 ♀ 🏠
Hotel ★★69% Kirklands Hotel, West Stewart Place,
HAWICK ☎(0450) 72263 6rm(2⇌1🐾) Annexe:7⇌🐾

INNERLEITHEN
Map 6 G3

Innerleithen ☎ (0896) 830951
Leithen Water, Leithen Rd (1.5m N on B709)
Moorland course, with easy walking. Burns and rivers
as natural hazards. Testing 5th hole (100 yds) par 3.
*9 holes, 2910yds, Par 34, SSS 68, Course record 67.
Membership 175.*

Visitors welcome Societies welcome (☎)
Green fees £5 per day

Facilities ⊗ by prior arrangement 🍴 by prior
arrangement 🍺 ♀ ⌂
Hotel ★★🍴66% Tweed Valley Hotel & Restaurant,
Galashiels Rd, WALKERBURN ☎(089687) 636 15⇌🐾

JEDBURGH
Map 6 H4

Jedburgh ☎ (08356) 3587
Dunion Rd (1m W on B6358)
Parkland course, windy, easy walking.
9 holes, 2760yds, Par 68, SSS 67. Membership 300.

Visitors welcome
Green fees Not confirmed
Facilities Catering Sat and Sun ♀ (Sat & Sun) ⌂ 🏠
Hotel ★★69% Kirklands Hotel, West Stewart Place,
HAWICK ☎(0450) 72263 6rm(2⇌1🐾) Annexe:7⇌🐾

KELSO
Map 6 H3

Kelso ☎ (0573) 23009
Racecourse Rd (N side of town centre off B6461)
Parkland course. Easy walking.
18 holes, 6066yds, Par 70, SSS 69. Membership 310.

Visitors welcome Societies welcome (☎)
Green fees Not confirmed
Facilities ♀ ⌂ 🏠 ⍻
Hotel ★★★63% Cross Keys Hotel, 36-37 The Square,
KELSO ☎(0573) 23303 24⇌🐾

MELROSE
Map 6 H3

Melrose ☎ (089682) 2855
Dingleton (S side of town centre on B6359)
Undulating, tree-lined fairways with spendid views.
*18 holes, 5579yds, Par 70, SSS 68, Course record 62.
Membership 350.*

Visitors welcome (ex Sat, Apr-Oct) Societies welcome
(☎)
Green fees Not confirmed
Facilities 🍴 (WE only) 🍺 (WE only) ♀ (Apr-Oct) ⌂
Hotel ★★64% Burt's Hotel, The Square, MELROSE
☎(089682) 2285 21⇌🐾

MINTO
Map 6 H4

Minto ☎ Denholm (045087) 220
Denholm (S side of village)
Parkland course in wooded surroundings, easy walking.
*18 holes, 5460yds, Par 68, SSS 68, Course record 66.
Membership 400.*

Visitors welcome (restricted during a club medal)
Societies welcome (WE only if more than 8 ☎)
Green fees Not confirmed
Facilities 🍴 🍺 ♀ ⌂
Hotel ★★69% Kirklands Hotel, West Stewart Place,
HAWICK ☎(0450) 72263 6rm(2⇌1🐾) Annexe:7⇌🐾

This guide is updated annually – make sure you
use an up-to-date edition.

We make every effort to provide accurate information, but some details may change after we
go to print.

NEWCASTLETON   Map 6 H5

Newcastleton ☎ Liddesdale (03873) 75257
Holm Hill (W side of village)
Hill course.
9 holes, 5748yds, Par 70, SSS 68, Course record 64.
Membership 70.

Visitors welcome Societies welcome (☎)
Green fees £3 per round
Facilities ▥
Hotel ★★56% Eskdale Hotel, Market Place,
LANGHOLM ☎(03873) 80357 16rm(3⇨7♦)

PEEBLES   Map 6 G3

Peebles Municipal ☎ (0721) 20197
Kirkland St (W side of town centre off A72)
Parkland course with fine views.
18 holes, 6137yds, Par 70, SSS 69. Membership 600.

Visitors welcome must contact in advance ✉ Societies
welcome (Pre-booked with deposit)
Green fees £8 per day (£10 WE); £6 per round (£8WE)
Facilities ⊗ ⅢⅠ ╚ ⬛♂ ♀ ⛳ ⋒ ☂
Hotel ★★★50% The Tontine, High St, PEEBLES
☎(0721) 20892 37⇨♦

ST BOSWELLS   Map 6 H4

St Boswells ☎ (0835) 22359
(N side of village off B6404)
Attractive parkland course by the banks of the River
Tweed, easy walking.
9 holes, 2625yds, Par 66, SSS 65, Course record 62.
Membership 310.

Visitors welcome (ex competition days) Societies
welcome (by letter)
Green fees £5 per day (£6 WE)
Facilities ⬛♂ ⛳
Hotel ★★65% Buccleuch Arms Hotel, The Green, ST
BOSWELLS ☎(0835) 22243 19rm(18⇨♦)

SELKIRK   Map 6 H4

Selkirk ☎ (0750) 20621
Selkirk Hills (1m S on A7)
Heathland course, windy, fine views.
9 holes, 5620yds, Par 68, SSS 67. Membership 305.

Visitors welcome (ex Mon evening, competition/match
days) Societies welcome (☎)
Green fees £9 per day
Facilities ♀ (evenings in summer)
Hotel ★62% Heatherlie House Hotel, Heatherlie Park,
SELKIRK ☎(0750) 21200 7rm(6♦)

WEST LINTON   Map 6 F3

West Linton ☎ (0968) 60970
(NW side of village off A702)
Moorland course with beautiful views of Pentland Hills.
18 holes, 6132yds, Par 69, SSS 69, Course record 67.
Membership 600.

Visitors welcome (ex competition days) Societies
welcome (by letter)
Green fees £12 per day; £10 per round (£16/£13 WE)
Facilities ⊗ ╚ ⬛♂ ♀ ⛳ ⋒ ↿ Douglas Stewart
Hotel ★★★50% The Tontine, High St, PEEBLES
☎(0721) 20892 37⇨♦

CENTRAL

ABERFOYLE   Map 6 D1

Aberfoyle ☎ (08772) 493
Braeval (1m E on A81)
Heathland course with mountain views.
18 holes, 5205yds, Par 66, SSS 66. Membership 350.

Visitors welcome (not allowed to tee off before 0930)
Societies welcome
Green fees £12 per day; £8 per round
Facilities ♀ (Apr-Sep daily) ⛳ ☂
Hotel ★★★✦69% Roman Camp Hotel, CALLANDER
☎(0877) 30003 14⇨♦

ALLOA   Map 6 E1

Alloa ☎ (0259) 722745
Schawpark, Sauchie (1.5m NE on A908)
Parkland course. Snooker.
18 holes, 6240yds, Par 70, SSS 70, Course record 63.
Membership 700.

Peebles Hotel Hydro ★★★

Peebles Hotel Hydro

Set in the heart of the Scottish Borders, the
Peebles Hydro is the perfect place for a
golfing holiday. With a choice of excellent
courses nearby, you can enjoy both a splendid
day's golf together with the comfort and
relaxation of the Hydro with its many indoor
and outdoor facilities. And if your choice is
for real peace and quiet, why not stay at our
sister hotel – The Park – just 400 yards from
the Hydro.
Whichever your choice, Park or Hydro, we
can guarantee excellent golf, good food and
comfort, and a golfing holiday to remember.
Please telephone 0721 20602 for full details.

Visitors welcome must contact in advance Societies welcome (ex WE)
Green fees £15 per day; £9 per round
Facilities ⊗ ⏃ ⮴ 🖳 ♀ ⌂ 🖾 ⚑ 𝄃
Hotel ★★★62% Royal Hotel, Henderson St, BRIDGE OF ALLAN ☎(0786) 832284 32⇥🛈

Braehead ☎ (0259) 722078
Cambus (1.5m NE on A908)
Attactive, long-holed parkland course at the foot of the Ochil Hills.
18 holes, 6013yds, Par 70, SSS 69, Course record 64.
Membership 700.

Visitors welcome must contact in advance Societies welcome (☎ or by letter)
Green fees £10/£15 per round/day (£15/£20 WE)
Facilities ⊗ ⮴ 🖳 ♀ ⌂
Hotel ★★55% King Robert Hotel, Glasgow Rd, Bannockburn, STIRLING ☎(0786) 811666 24rm(21⇥)

BONNYBRIDGE   Map 6 E2

Bonnybridge ☎ (0324) 812822
Larbert Rd (1m NE off A883)
Testing heathland course, with tightly guarded greens. Easy walking.
9 holes, 6060yds, Par 72, SSS 69. Membership 325.

Visitors welcome Member must accompany must contact in advance Societies welcome
Green fees Not confirmed
Facilities ♀ ⌂ 🖾
Hotel ★★★67% Inchyra Grange Hotel, Grange Rd, POLMONT ☎(0324) 711911 33⇥🛈

BRIDGE OF ALLAN   Map 6 E1

Bridge of Allan ☎ (0786) 832332
Sunnylaw (.5m N off A9)
Parkland course, very hilly with good views. Testing 1st hole; 221 yds (par 3) uphill, 6 ft wall 25 yds before green.
9 holes, 4932yds, Par 66, SSS 65, Course record 62.
Membership 300.

Visitors welcome (ex Sat) Societies welcome (☎ or letter)
Green fees £7 per round 18 holes (£10 WE)
Facilities ♀ (summer) ⌂
Hotel ★★★62% Royal Hotel, Henderson St, BRIDGE OF ALLAN ☎(0786) 832284 32⇥🛈

CALLANDER   Map 6 E1

Callander ☎ (0877) 30090
Aveland Rd (E side of town off A84)
Parkland course, with fairly tightly guarded greens. Testing 6th hole (par 4) and 15th (par 3).
18 holes, 5125yds, Par 66, SSS 66, Course record 62.
Membership 580.

Visitors welcome Societies welcome (☎)
Green fees £11 per day; £9 per round (£17 per day WE)

Facilities ⊗ high tea ⮴ 🖳 ♀ ⌂ 🖾 ⚑ 𝄃 William Kelly
Hotel ★★★🏊69% Roman Camp Hotel, CALLANDER ☎(0877) 30003 14⇥🛈

DOLLAR   Map 6 F1

Dollar ☎ (0259) 42400
Brewlands House (.5m N off A91)
Compact hillside course. Snooker.
18 holes, 5144yds, SSS 66. Membership 350.

Visitors welcome Societies welcome (☎)
Green fees £8 per day (£10 WE) ;£6 per round
Facilities ⮴ 🖳 (no catering Tue) ♀ ⌂ ⚑
Hotel ★★55% King Robert Hotel, Glasgow Rd, Bannockburn, STIRLING ☎(0786) 811666 24rm(21⇥)

DRYMEN   Map 6 D2

Buchanan Castle ☎ (0360) 60307
(1m W)
Parkland course, with easy walking and good views.
18 holes, 6086yds, Par 70, SSS 69. Membership 830.

Visitors welcome Member must accompany must contact in advance ✉ Societies welcome (☎)
Green fees Not confirmed
Facilities ⊗ by prior arrangement ⏃ by prior arrangement ⮴ 🖳 ♀ ⌂ 🖾 ⚑ 𝄃 Charles Dernie
Hotel ★★★65% Buchanan Highland Hotel, DRYMEN ☎(0360) 60588 51⇥🛈

DUNBLANE   Map 6 E1

Dunblane New Golf Club ☎ (0786) 823711
Perth Rd (E side of town on A9)
Parkland course, with reasonably hard walking. Testing 6th and 9th holes.
18 holes, 5863yds, Par 69, SSS 68, Course record 63.
Membership 800.

Visitors welcome (ex WE) must contact in advance ✉ Societies welcome (by letter)
Green fees £20 per day; £13 per round
Facilities ⊗ ⏃ ⮴ 🖳 ♀ ⌂ 🖾 ⚑ 𝄃 R M Jamieson
Hotel ★★★(red)🏊Cromlix House Hotel, Kinbuck, DUNBLANE ☎(0786) 822125 14⇥🛈

FALKIRK   Map 6 F2

Falkirk ☎ (0324) 611061
Stirling Rd, Camelon (1.5m W on A9)
Parkland course with trees, gorse and streams.
18 holes, 6257yds, Par 71, SSS 70. Membership 700.

Visitors welcome (with M only WE) Societies welcome (☎ (0324) 6122)
Green fees £12 per day; £7.50 per round
Facilities ⊗ ⏃ ⮴ 🖳 ♀ ⌂ 🖾
Hotel ★★★62% Stakis Park Hotel, Arnot Hill, Camelon Rd, FALKIRK ☎(0324) 28331 55⇥🛈

KILLIN   Map 7 F8

Killin ☎ (05672) 312
(1m N on A827)
Parkland course with good views.
9 holes, 2508yds, Par 66, SSS 65. Membership 180.

Visitors welcome Societies welcome (☎)
Green fees £10 per day
Facilities ⊗ ⑂ ᒪ ◖ ♀ ᐃ 🖻 ⫟
Hotel ★★65% Morenish Lodge Hotel, Loch Tayside,
KILLIN ☎(05672) 258 13rm(4⇆8⋔)

LARBERT   Map 6 F2

Falkirk Tryst ☎ (0324) 562415
86 Burnhead Rd (1m NE off A88/B905)
Moorland course, fairly level and well-bunkered. Winds
can affect play.
18 holes, 6053yds, Par 70, SSS 69. Membership 450.

Visitors welcome (with M only Wed & WE) must
contact in advance Societies welcome (by letter)
Green fees Not confirmed
Facilities ⊗ ⑂ by prior arrangement ᒪ ◖ ♀ ᐃ 🖻
⫔
Hotel ★★★67% Inchyra Grange Hotel, Grange Rd,
POLMONT ☎(0324) 711911 33⇆⋔

Glenbervie Clubhouse ☎ (0324) 562605
Stirling Rd (2m NW on A9)
Parkland course with good views.
*18 holes, 6469yds, Par 71, SSS 71, Course record 63.
Membership 900.*

Visitors welcome (restricted WE) must contact in
advance Societies welcome (by letter)
Green fees £20 per day ; £15 per round
Facilities ⊗ ⑂ ᒪ ◖ ♀ ᐃ 🖻 ⫟ ⫔ George McKay
Hotel ★★★62% Stakis Park Hotel, Arnot Hill,
Camelon Rd, FALKIRK ☎(0324) 28331 55⇆⋔

MUCKHART   Map 6 F1

Muckhart ☎ (025981) 423
(SW of village off A91)
Heathland/downland course. Testing 5th, 'Firehill'
(par 4).
*18 holes, 6192yds, Par 71, SSS 70, Course record 66.
Membership 700.*

Visitors welcome (ex before 0945 & 1200-1430 WE) must
contact in advance Societies welcome (☎ deposit
required)
Green fees £15 per day ; £10 per round (£18/£12 WE)
Facilities ⊗ ⑂ ᒪ ◖ ♀ (all day) ᐃ 🖻 ⫔ K Salmoni
Hotel ★★★62% Green Hotel, 2 The Muirs, KINROSS
☎(0577) 63467 40⇆⋔

Each golf course entry has a recommended
hotel. For a wider choice of places to stay,
consult *AA Hotels and Restaurants in Britain* or
AA-inspected Bed and Breakfast in Britain.

POLMONT   Map 6 F2

Grangemouth ☎ (0324) 711500
Polmont Hill (on unclass rd .5m N of M9 junc 4)
Windy parkland course. Testing holes: 3rd, 4th (par 4's);
5th (par 5) ; 7th (par 3) 216 yds over reservoir (elevated
green); 8th, 9th, 18th (par 4's).
*18 holes, 6314yds, Par 71, SSS 71, Course record 67.
Membership 700.*

Visitors welcome must contact in advance Societies
welcome (by letter)
Green fees Not confirmed
Facilities ⊗ by prior arrangement ⑂ by prior
arrangement ᒪ ◖ ♀ ᐃ 🖻 ⫔ Stuart J Campbell
Hotel ★★★67% Inchyra Grange Hotel, Grange Rd,
POLMONT ☎(0324) 711911 33⇆⋔

Polmont ☎ (0324) 711277
Manuelrigg, Maddiston (E side of village off A803)
Parkland course, hilly with few bunkers. Views of the
River Forth and Ochil Hills.
9 holes, 3044yds, Par 36, SSS 35. Membership 200.

Visitors welcome (restricted Sat) Societies welcome
(☎)
Green fees £5 per day (£7 WE)
Facilities ⊗ ⑂ ᒪ ◖ (all catering by prior
arrangement) ♀ ᐃ
Hotel ★★★67% Inchyra Grange Hotel, Grange Rd,
POLMONT ☎(0324) 711911 33⇆⋔

STIRLING   Map 6 E1

Stirling ☎ (0786) 64098
Queens Rd (W side of town on B8051)
Undulating parkland course with magnificent views.
Testing 15th, 'Cotton's Fancy', 395 yds (par 4).
*18 holes, 6095yds, Par 72, SSS 69, Course record 64.
Membership 950.*

Visitors welcome (ex Sat & restricted Sun) Societies
welcome (☎)
Green fees £21 per day ; £15 per round (£20 WE)
Facilities ⊗ ⑂ by prior arrangement ᒪ ◖ ♀ (all day)
ᐃ 🖻 ⫔ John Chillas
Hotel ★★55% King Robert Hotel, Glasgow Rd,
Bannockburn, STIRLING ☎(0786) 811666 24rm(21⇆)

TILLICOULTRY   Map 6 F1

Tillicoultry ☎ (0259) 50741/51337
Alva Rd
Parkland course at foot of the Ochil Hills entailing some
hard walking.
*18 holes, Par 68, SSS 66, Course record 63 or 18 holes.
Membership 400.*

Visitors welcome (ex during club competitions)
Societies welcome (☎)
Green fees Not confirmed

For an explanation of the symbols and
abbreviations used, see page 33.

Facilities ⊗ (May-Oct) 🍴 by prior arrangement 🏌 by prior arrangement 🏌 by prior arrangement 🏌 (by prior arrangement) ⛏

Hotel ★★★62% Royal Hotel, Henderson St, BRIDGE OF ALLAN ☎(0786) 832284 32⇨🌂

DUMFRIES & GALLOWAY

CASTLE DOUGLAS
Map 6 E6

Castle Douglas ☎ (0556) 2801
Abercromby Rd (W side of town)
Parkland course, one severe hill.
9 holes, 2704yds, Par 34, SSS 33 or , SSS 62. Membership 300.

Visitors welcome (ex Tue eves & Sun competitions)
Societies welcome (by letter)
Green fees Not confirmed
Facilities ⊗ (in season) 🏌 (in season) 🏌 ⛏
Hotel ★★King's Arms Hotel, St Andrew's St, CASTLE DOUGLAS ☎(0556) 2626 15rm(5⇨3🌂)

COLVEND
Map 6 F6

Colvend ☎ Rockcliffe (055663) 398
Sandyhills (6m from Dalbeattie on A710 Solway Coast Rd)
Picturesque and challenging course on solway coast.
9 holes, 2322yds, Par 66, SSS 63, Course record 63. Membership 480.

Visitors welcome (restricted Tue & Thu in summer)
Societies welcome (☎)
Green fees £7 per day
Facilities ⊗ 🍴 🏌 🍺 (catering daily Apr-Sep, Sat and Sun Oct-Mar) 🏌 (Oct-Mar WE only) ⛏ 🍴
Hotel ★★★🏌68% Baron's Craig Hotel, ROCKCLIFFE ☎(055663) 225 27rm(20⇨)

CUMMERTREES
Map 6 F6

Powfoot ☎ (04617) 227
C/O 27 Bank St (.5m off B724)
The Cumberland Hills, away beyond the Solway Firth, and from time to time a sight of the Isle of Man, make playing at this delightfully compact seaside course a scenic treat. Lovely holes include the 2nd, the 8th and the 11th.
18 holes, 6283yds, Par 71, SSS 70, Course record 65. Membership 820.

SCORE CARD: White Tees					
Hole	Yds	Par	Hole	Yds	Par
1	352	4	10	430	4
2	477	5	11	313	4
3	445	4	12	154	3
4	358	4	13	339	4
5	272	4	14	501	5
6	351	4	15	201	3
7	155	3	16	432	4
8	359	4	17	336	4
9	402	4	18	406	4
Out	3171	36	In	3112	35
			Totals	6283	71

Visitors welcome (restricted WE) Societies welcome (☎ 7 days in advance)
Green fees £13 per day/round in summer (£10 per round WE); £8 winter

Facilities ⊗ 🍴 🏌 🍺 🏌 ⛏ 🍴 (Gareth Dick
Hotel ★★61% Golf Hotel, Links Av, POWFOOT ☎(04617) 254 21rm(7⇨7🌂)

DUMFRIES
Map 6 F6

Dumfries & County ☎ (0387) 53585
Edinburgh Rd (1m NE off A701)
Parkland course.
18 holes, 5928yds, Par 69, SSS 68, Course record 63. Membership 600.

Visitors welcome (ex WE) Societies welcome (☎ or letter)
Green fees £12.00 per day (£15 WE)
Facilities ⊗ 🍴 🏌 🍺 🏌 ⛏ 🍴 🍴 (Gordon Gray
Hotel ★★★68% Station Hotel, 49 Lovers Walk, DUMFRIES ☎(0387) 54316 32⇨🌂

Dumfries & Galloway ☎ (0387) 63848
2 Laurieston Av (W side of town centre on A75)
Parkland course. Snooker.
18 holes, 5803yds, Par 68, SSS 68. Membership 800.

Visitors welcome Societies welcome (☎ for details)
Green fees Not confirmed
Facilities 🏌 ⛏ 🍴 🍴 (
Hotel ★★★68% Station Hotel, 49 Lovers Walk, DUMFRIES ☎(0387) 54316 32⇨🌂

GATEHOUSE-OF-FLEET
Map 6 E6

Gatehouse
Laurieston Rd (N side of village)
Set against a background of rolling hills with scenic views of Fleet Bay and the Solway Firth. Tennis.
9 holes, 2398yds, Par 33, SSS 31. Membership 250.

Visitors welcome Societies welcome (☎ (05574) 252)
Green fees Not confirmed
Facilities ⛏
Hotel ★★★65% Murray Arms Hotel, GATEHOUSE OF FLEET ☎(05574) 207 12⇨ Annexe:1⇨

GLENLUCE
Map 6 C6

Wigtownshire County ☎ (05813) 420
Mains of Park (1.5m W off A75)
Seaside links course on the shores of Luce Bay, easy walking.
18 holes, 5715yds, Par 70, SSS 68, Course record 66. Membership 250.

Visitors welcome (ex Wed eve) Societies welcome (☎ (05813) 277)
Green fees £14 per day ; £10 per round (£15/£12 WE)
Facilities ⊗ 🍴 🏌 🍺 Catering Apr-Sep only 🏌 ⛏ 🍴
Hotel ★★★69% North West Castle Hotel, STRANRAER ☎(0776) 4413 74⇨🌂

To see a full range of AA guides and maps, visit your local AA Shop or any good bookshop.

KIRKCUDBRIGHT
Map 6 E6

Kirkcudbright ☎ (0557) 30314
Stirling Crescent (NE side of town off A711)
Parkland course. Hilly, with hard walking. Good views.
*18 holes, 5598yds, Par 67, SSS 67, Course record 63.
Membership 400.*

Visitors welcome (ex club competitions) Societies
welcome (☎)
Green fees £8 per day or round
Facilities ⊗ Ⅲↂ by prior arrangement ⅃ ◤ (no
catering Mon) ♀ ♨
Hotel ★★65% Selkirk Arms Hotel, Old High St,
KIRKCUDBRIGHT ☎(0557) 30402 14⇨▚ Annexe:1⇨

LANGHOLM
Map 6 G5

Langholm
Whiteside (E side of village off A7)
Hillside course with fine views, hard walking.
*9 holes, 5744yds, Par 70, SSS 68, Course record 67.
Membership 130.*

Visitors welcome (restricted Sat) Societies welcome
Green fees £5 per round
Facilities ♨
Hotel ★★56% Eskdale Hotel, Market Place,
LANGHOLM ☎(03873) 80357 16rm(3⇨7▚)

LOCHMABEN
Map 6 F5

Lochmaben ☎ (0387) 810552
Castlehill Gate (S side of village off A709)
Comfortable-walking parkland course between two
lochs with fine old trees and fast greens all year round.
*9 holes, 5304yds, Par 66, SSS 66, Course record 60.
Membership 550.*

Visitors welcome (restricted wkdays & competitions)
Societies welcome (☎)
Green fees £8 per day/round (£10 WE)
Facilities ♨
Hotel ★★★66% Dryfesdale Hotel, LOCKERBIE
☎(05762) 2427 & 2121 15⇨▚

LOCKERBIE
Map 6 F5

Lockerbie ☎ (05762) 3363
Corrie Rd (E side of town centre off B7068)
Parkland course with fine views.
18 holes, 5434yds, Par 67, SSS 66. Membership 350.

Visitors welcome
Green fees Not confirmed
Facilities ♀ ♨
Hotel ★★★62% Lockerbie Manor Country Hotel,
Boreland Rd, LOCKERBIE ☎(05762) 2610 26⇨▚

Each golf course entry has a recommended
hotel. For a wider choice of places to stay,
consult *AA Hotels and Restaurants in Britain* or
AA-inspected Bed and Breakfast in Britain.

MOFFAT
Map 6 F4

Moffat ☎ (0683) 20020
Coatshill (1m SW off A701)
Scenic hill course. Testing 9th, 'Port Arthur' (par 3).
*18 holes, 5218yds, Par 69, SSS 66, Course record 60.
Membership 350.*

Visitors welcome (restricted Wed pm) Societies
welcome
Green fees £11 per day (£17 WE)
Facilities ⊗ Ⅲↂ by prior arrangement ⅃ ◤ ♀ ♨ ☔
Hotel ★★★62% Moffat House Hotel, High St, MOFFAT
☎(0683) 20039 16⇨▚

MONREITH
Map 6 D7

St Medan ☎ Port William (09887) 358
(1m SE off A747)
Moorland/seaside course, fine views.
*9 holes, 2227yds, Par 64, SSS 62, Course record 60.
Membership 300.*

Visitors welcome (ex competition days) Societies
welcome (☎ or letter)
Green fees £4 (9 holes) £7 (18 holes) £10 per day
Facilities ⊗ Ⅲ ⅃ ◤ ♀ ♨
Hotel ★★★63% Corsemalzie House Hotel, PORT
WILLIAM ☎(098886) 254 15⇨▚

NEW GALLOWAY
Map 6 E5

New Galloway ☎ No telephone
(S side of town on A762)
Set on the edge of the Galloway Hills and overlooking
Loch Ken, the course is located in the smallest Royal
Burgh in Scotland.
9 holes, 5058yds, Par 68, SSS 65, Course record 66.
Membership 215.

Visitors welcome (resticted competition days) Societies
welcome (by letter)
Green fees £7.50 per day/round (£10 Sun)
Facilities ♀ ⌣
Hotel ★★★♨59% Culgruff House Hotel, CROSSMICHAEL
☎(055667) 230 16rm(4⇨)

NEWTON STEWART
Map 6 D6

Newton Stewart ☎ (0671) 2172
Kirroughtree Av, Minnigaff (.5m N of town centre)
Parkland course in picturesque setting. Short but quite
tight.
9 holes, 5362yds, Par 68, SSS 66, Course record 64.
Membership 300.

Visitors welcome (☎ for details) Societies welcome (☎)
Green fees £5 per day (£6 WE)
Facilities ⊗ ♨ ♨ (all catering by prior arrangement)
♀ (by prior arrangement) ⌣ ✉
Hotel ★★★★♨55% Kirroughtree Hotel, Minnigaff,
NEWTON STEWART ☎(0671) 2141 20⇨ Annexe:2⇨

PORTPATRICK
Map 6 C6

Portpatrick ☎ (077681) 273
Golf Course Rd (NW side of village)
Seaside course with some natural hazards, easy
walking, fine views.
18 holes, 5663yds, Par 70, SSS 67, Course record 64 or 9
holes, 1442yds, Par 27, SSS 27. Membership 430.

Visitors welcome (ex competition days, h'cap cert
required) must contact in advance Societies welcome
(☎)
Green fees £15 per day ; £10 per round (£20/£12 WE)
Facilities ⊗ ⦀ ♨ ♨ ♀ (all day) ⌣ ✉ ⌕
Hotel ★★★63% Fernhill Hotel, PORTPATRICK
☎(077681) 220 15rm(14⇨) Annexe:4⇨

SANQUHAR
Map 6 E4

Sanquhar ☎ (0659) 50577
Euchan Golf Course (.5m SW off A76)
Moorland course, fine views. Snooker.
9 holes, 5144mtr, Par 70, SSS 68, Course record 66.
Membership 180.

Visitors welcome (ex competition days) Societies
welcome (by letter)
Green fees £6 per day/round (£8 WE)
Facilities ⊗ ⦀ ♨ ♨ (all catering by prior
arrangement) ⌣
Hotel ★★64% Mennockfoot Lodge Hotel, Mennock,
SANQUHAR ☎(0659) 50382 & 50477 1⇨ Annexe:8⇨

SOUTHERNESS
Map 6 F6

Southerness ☎ Kirkbean (038788) 677
(3.5m S of Kirkbean off A710)
Seaside course, windy and flat, with magnificent views.
18 holes, 6554yds, Par 71, SSS 72, Course record 65.
Membership 680.

Visitors welcome (some restricted times) Societies
welcome (☎ or letter)
Green fees £15 per day (£20 WE & BH)
Facilities ⊗ ⦀ by prior arrangement ♨ ♨ ♀ ⌣
Hotel ★★★♨68%, Baron's Craig Hotel, ROCKCLIFFE
☎(055663) 225 27rm(20⇨)

STRANRAER
Map 6 C6

Stranraer ☎ Leswalt (077687) 245
Creachmore by Stranraer (2.5m NW on A718)
Parkland course with beautiful view of Lochryan.
Snooker.
18 holes, 6300yds, Par 70, SSS 71, Course record 66.
Membership 550.

Visitors welcome (restricted WE) must contact in
advance Societies welcome (☎)
Green fees £12.50 per day ; £10 per round (£17/£12.50
WE)
Facilities ⊗ by prior arrangement ⦀ by prior
arrangement ♨ ♨ ♀ ⌣ ✉
Hotel ★★★69% North West Castle Hotel, STRANRAER
☎(0776) 4413 74⇨

THORNHILL
Map 6 F5

Thornhill ☎ Dumfries (0848) 30546
Blacknest (1m E of town off A92)
Course with fine views.
18 holes, 6011yds, Par 71, SSS 69. Membership 580.

Visitors welcome Societies welcome (☎)
Green fees Not confirmed
Facilities ♨ ♨ ♀ ⌣
Hotel ★★72% Trigony House Hotel, Closeburn,
THORNHILL ☎(0848) 31211 9rm(2⇨6)

WIGTOWN
Map 6 D6

Wigtown & Bladnoch ☎ (09884) 3354
Lightlands Av (SW on A714)
Slightly hilly parkland course with fine views over
Wigtown Bay to Galloway Hills.
9 holes, 5462yds, Par 68, SSS 67, Course record 63.
Membership 130.

Visitors welcome (ex competitions, most evenings &
Sun) Societies welcome (by letter)
Green fees £7 per day (£10 Sun)
Facilities ⊗ ⦀ ♨ (catering by prior arrangement) ♀
(evenings & WE) ⌣
Hotel ★★★★♨55% Kirroughtree Hotel, Minnigaff,
NEWTON STEWART ☎(0671) 2141 20⇨ Annexe:2⇨

FIFE

ABERDOUR
Map 6 G2

Aberdour ☎ (0383) 860256
Seaside Place (S side of village)
Parkland course with lovely views over the Firth of
Forth.
*18 holes, 5001 mtrs, Par 67, SSS 67, Course record 63.
Membership 580.*

Visitors welcome (wkdays only) must contact in
advance Societies welcome (☎)
Green fees £14 per day; £10 per round
Facilities ⊗ ⅲ � ⬛ ♀ △ 🗄 ⅍ Alan Hope
Hotel ★★66% Woodside Hotel, High St, ABERDOUR
☎(0383) 860328 21⇨🏴

ANSTRUTHER
Map 6 H1

Anstruther ☎ (0333) 310956
Shore Rd, 'Marsfield' (SW off A917)
Seaside course with some excellent par 3 holes, always
in good condition.
*9 holes, 4144 mtrs, Par 62, SSS 63, Course record 62.
Membership 500.*

Visitors welcome (restricted Jul & Aug) Societies
welcome (ex Jun-Aug)
Green fees £6 per day (£8 WE)
Facilities ⊗ � ⬛ (catering May-Sep) ♀ (May-Sep)
△
Hotel ★★★60% Craws Nest Hotel, Bankwell Rd,
ANSTRUTHER ☎(0333) 310691 31⇨🏴 Annexe:19⇨🏴

BURNTISLAND
Map 6 G2

Burntisland ☎ (0592) 874093
Dodhead (1m E on B923)
This parkland course has fine sea views.
18 holes, 5897 yds, Par 70, SSS 69. Membership 750.

Visitors welcome (max 24 per party-WE) must contact
in advance Societies welcome (by letter)
Green fees £14 per day (£19 WE)
Facilities ⊗ ⅲ � ⬛ ♀ △ 🗄 ⅍ ⅍ Sandy Walker
Hotel ★★★65% Dean Park Hotel, Chapel Level,
KIRKCALDY ☎(0592) 261635 20⇨🏴 Annexe:12🏴

CRAIL
Map 6 H1

Crail Golfing Society ☎ (0333) 50278
Balcomie Clubhouse, Fifeness (2m NE off A917)
Perched on the edge of the North Sea on the very
point of the golfing county of Fife, the Crail Golfing
Society's course at Balcomie is picturesque and
sporting. And here again golf history has been made
for Crail Golfing Society began its life in 1786. The
course is highly thought of by students of the game
both for its testing holes and the stardard of its
greens.
*18 holes, 5202 yds, Par 67, SSS 68, Course record 64.
Membership 950.*

Visitors welcome must contact in advance Societies
welcome (☎)
Green fees £18 per day; £12 per round (£22.50/£15
WE)
Facilities ⊗ ⅲ � ⬛ (catering during high
season) ♀ △ 🗄 ⅍ ⅍ Graheme Lennie
Hotel ★★★60% Craws Nest Hotel, Bankwell Rd,
ANSTRUTHER ☎(0333) 310691 31⇨🏴
Annexe:19⇨🏴

CUPAR
Map 7 H8

Cupar ☎ (0334) 53549
Hilltarvit (.75m S off A92)
Hillside course with fine views.
*9 holes, 5074 yds, Par 68, SSS 65, Course record 61.
Membership 420.*

Visitors welcome (with M only WE) Societies welcome
Green fees Not confirmed
Facilities ⊗ � ⬛ ♀ △
Hotel ★★★⅐64% Fernie Castle Hotel, LETHAM
☎(033781) 381 16⇨🏴

DUNFERMLINE
Map 6 F2

Canmore ☎ (0383) 724969
Venturefair Av (1m N on A823)
Undulating parkland course affording excellent views.
18 holes, 5474 yds, Par 67, SSS 66. Membership 620.

Visitors welcome
Green fees Not confirmed
Facilities ♀ △ 🗄 ⅍
Hotel ★★★67% King Malcolm Thistle Hotel,
Queensferry Rd, Wester Pitcorthie, DUNFERMLINE
☎(0383) 722611 48⇨🏴

Dunfermline ☎ (0383) 723534
Pitfirrane, Crossford (2m W on A994)
Parkland course. The clubhouse is an old historic
mansion. Snooker.
*18 holes, 5813 yds, Par 72, SSS 72, Course record 64. Par 3
course 9 holes, 1144 yds, Par 27. Membership 675.*

Visitors welcome (Mon-Fri) must contact in advance
Societies welcome (ex Sat & Sun ☎ for details)
Green fees £20 per day; £12 per round
Facilities ⊗ (ex Mon) ⅲ by prior arrangement � ⬛
♀ △ 🗄 ⅍ Jacky Montgomory
Hotel ★★★67% King Malcolm Thistle Hotel,
Queensferry Rd, Wester Pitcorthie, DUNFERMLINE
☎(0383) 722611 48⇨🏴

Pitreavie ☎ (0383) 722591
Queensferry Rd (SE side of town on A823)
Picturesque woodland course with panoramic view of
the River Forth Valley. Testing golf.
*18 holes, 6086 yds, Par 70, SSS 69, Course record 65.
Membership 700.*

Visitors welcome (ex competition days)

▶

Green fees £14 per day; £10 per round (£20/£13 WE)
Facilities ⊗ � ⅃ ╘ ♨ ♀ ⚘ 🏠 ⚓ ⚑ ℓ Jim Forrester
Hotel ★★★67% King Malcolm Thistle Hotel,
Queensferry Rd, Wester Pitcorthie, DUNFERMLINE
☎(0383) 722611 48⇔🛏

ELIE   Map 6 H1

Golf House Club
☎ (0333) 330301
(W side of village off A917)
One of Scotland's most
delightful holiday courses
with panoramic views over
the Firth of Forth. Some of
the holes out towards the
rocky coastline are spledid.
This is the course which
has produced many good
professionals, including the
immortal James Braid.
*18 holes, 6241yds, Par 70,
SSS 70, Course record 62. Membership 650.*

SCORE CARD					
Hole	Yds	Par	Hole	Yds	Par
1	420	4	10	267	4
2	284	4	11	120	3
3	214	3	12	466	4
4	378	4	13	380	4
5	365	4	14	414	4
6	316	4	15	338	4
7	252	4	16	407	4
8	382	4	17	439	4
9	440	4	18	359	4
Out	3051	35	In	3190	35
			Totals	6241	70

Visitors welcome (no play before 1000, no parties at
WE) Societies welcome (mid week only, except Jun-
Aug)
Green fees £24 per day; £16 per round (£30/£22
WE)
Facilities ⊗ by prior arrangement ╘ ♨ ♀ ⚘ 🏠
ℓ Robin Wilson
Hotel ★★★60% Craws Nest Hotel, Bankwell Rd,
ANSTRUTHER ☎(0333) 310691 31⇔🛏
Annexe:19⇔🛏

FALKLAND   Map 6 G1

Falkland ☎ (0337) 57404
The Myre (N side of town on A912)
A well kept 'L'-shaped course with excellent greens.
*9 holes, 4768mtrs, Par 68, SSS 66, Course record 67.
Membership 240.*

Visitors welcome Societies welcome (☎)
Green fees £5 per day (£7 WE)
Facilities ╘ (WE only) ♨ ♀ (evening & WE) ⚘
Hotel ★★★72% Balgeddie House Hotel, Balgeddie
Way, GLENROTHES ☎(0592) 742511 18⇔🛏

GLENROTHES   Map 6 G1

Glenrothes ☎ (0592) 758686
Golf Course Rd (W side of town off B921)
Testing and hilly parkland course with burn crossed
four times. Good views.
*18 holes, 6449yds, Par 71, SSS 71, Course record 65.
Membership 800.*

Visitors welcome Societies welcome (☎ month in
advance)
Green fees £3.20 per round (£4.40 WE)
Facilities ⊗ ⅃ ╘ ♨ ♀ ⚘
Hotel ★★★72% Balgeddie House Hotel, Balgeddie
Way, GLENROTHES ☎(0592) 742511 18⇔🛏

KINCARDINE   Map 6 F1

Tulliallan ☎ (0259) 30396
Alloa Rd (1m NW on A977)
Partially hilly parkland course with testing 3rd hole
(par 4).
18 holes, 5982yds, Par 69, SSS 69. Membership 525.

Visitors welcome (restricted WE) Societies welcome (ex
Sat ☎)
Green fees Not confirmed
Facilities ⊗ ⅃ ╘ ♨ ♀ ⚘ 🏠 ⚑ ℓ Steven Kelly
Hotel ★★★67% Inchyra Grange Hotel, Grange Rd,
POLMONT ☎(0324) 711911 33⇔🛏

KINGHORN   Map 6 G2

Kinghorn ☎ (0592) 890345
Macduff Cres (S side of town on A921)
Municipal course, 300 ft above sea level with views over
Firth of Forth and North Sea. Undulating and quite
testing. Facilities shared by Kinghorn Ladies.
18 holes, 5269yds, Par 65, SSS 67. Membership 190.

Visitors welcome Societies welcome (by letter)
Green fees Not confirmed
Facilities ♀ ⚘
Hotel ★★★65% Dean Park Hotel, Chapel Level,
KIRKCALDY ☎(0592) 261635 20⇔🛏 Annexe:12🛏

KIRKCALDY   Map 6 G1

Dunnikier Park ☎ (0592) 261599
Dunnikier Way (2m N off A988)
Parkland, rolling fairways, not heavily bunkered, views
of Firth of Forth.
*18 holes, 6601yds, Par 72, SSS 72, Course record 65.
Membership 600.*

Visitors welcome Societies welcome (by letter to Sec.)
Green fees £3.50 per round (£4.75 WE)
Facilities ⊗ ⅃ ╘ ♨ ♀ ⚘ 🏠
Hotel ★★★65% Dean Park Hotel, Chapel Level,
KIRKCALDY ☎(0592) 261635 20⇔🛏 Annexe:12🛏

Kirkcaldy ☎ (0592) 260370
Balwearie Rd (SW side of town off A910)
Parkland course.
18 holes, 6004yds, Par 71, SSS 70. Membership 700.

Visitors welcome Societies welcome (☎)
Green fees Not confirmed
Facilities ♀ ⚘ 🏠 ℓ
Hotel ★★★65% Dean Park Hotel, Chapel Level,
KIRKCALDY ☎(0592) 261635 20⇔🛏 Annexe:12🛏

LADYBANK   Map 6 G1

Ladybank ☎ (0337) 30814
Annsmuir (N side of village off B9129)
Picturesque heath/moorland course, popular with
visitors. Used as a qualifying course for the British
Open.
*18 holes, 6641yds, Par 71, SSS 72, Course record 66.
Membership 770.*

Visitors welcome must contact in advance Societies welcome (☎)
Green fees £25 per day; £18 per round (£28/£20 WE)
Facilities ⊗ ⅲ 🇲 💻 ♀ ⌂ 🏠 ⍳ ⟨ Martin Gray
Hotel ★★★♨64% Fernie Castle Hotel, LETHAM
☎(033781) 381 16⇒🐾

LESLIE   Map 6 G1

Leslie
Balsillie Laws (N side of town off A911)
Challenging parkland course, par unbroken throughout
course's long history.
9 holes, 2470yds, Par 62, SSS 64, Course record 62.
Membership 250.

Visitors welcome Societies welcome (apply to
Secretary)
Green fees £4 per day (£6 WE)
Facilities ♀ ⌂
Hotel ★★★72% Balgeddie House Hotel, Balgeddie
Way, GLENROTHES ☎(0592) 742511 18⇒🐾

LEUCHARS   Map 7 H8

St Michaels ☎ (0334) 839365
(NW side of village on A919)
Parkland course with open views over Fife and Tayside.
9 holes, 5158yds, Par 70, SSS 66, Course record 66.
Membership 450.

Visitors welcome (ex Sun am Mar-Oct) Societies
welcome (☎)
Green fees £10 per day
Facilities ⊗ 🇲 💻 ♀ ⌂ ⍳
Hotel ★★58% Sandford Hill Hotel, WORMIT ☎(0382)
541802 15rm(13⇒🐾)

LEVEN   Map 6 G1

Leven Golfing Society ☎ (0333) 26096
Links Rd
Plays over Leven Links. Snooker.
18 holes, 6435yds, Par 71, SSS 71. Membership 470.

Visitors welcome (ex Sat) Societies welcome (☎)
Green fees Not confirmed
Facilities ⊗ ⅲ by prior arrangement 🇲 💻 ♀ ⌂ 🏠
⍳ ⟨ George Finlayson
Hotel ★★★72% Old Manor Hotel, Leven Rd, LUNDIN
LINKS ☎(0333) 320368 20rm(15⇒🐾)

To see a full range of AA guides and maps, visit
your local AA Shop or any good bookshop.

Leven Thistle
☎ (0333) 26397
3 Balfour St
Leven has the classic
ingredients which make up
a golf links in Scotland;
undulating fairways with
hills and hallows, out of
bounds and a 'burn' or
stream. A top class
championship links course
used for British Open final
qualifying stages.
18 holes, 6434yds, Par 71,
SSS 71, Course record 64. Membership 400.

SCORE CARD: Leven Links (Medal Tees)					
Hole	Yds	Par	Hole	Yds	Par
1	413	4	10	325	4
2	376	4	11	369	4
3	343	4	12	482	5
4	449	4	13	484	5
5	157	3	14	330	4
6	567	5	15	188	3
7	184	3	16	386	4
8	348	4	17	412	4
9	164	3	18	457	4
Out	3001	34	In	3433	37
			Totals	6434	71

Visitors welcome (no parties Sat) Societies welcome
(☎ month in advance)
Green fees £18 per day; £14 per round (£21/£16
WE)
Facilities ⊗ ⅲ 🇲 💻 ♀ ⌂ 🏠 ⟨ G Finlayson
Hotel ★★★72% Old Manor Hotel, Leven Rd,
LUNDIN LINKS ☎(0333) 320368 20rm(15⇒🐾)

LOCHGELLY   Map 6 G1

Lochgelly ☎ (0592) 780174
Cartmore Rd (W side of town off A910)
Parkland course with easy walking and often windy.
18 holes, 5491yds, Par 68, SSS 67. Membership 400.

▶

FERNIE CASTLE ★ ★ ★ C/H
Letham, Fife.
Telephone: (033781) 381 Fax: (033781) 422

*Imposing to look at, luxurious to live in, one would never
guess that Fernie Castle started its career in the 12th century when it was owned by Duncan, 13th Earl of Fife.
Situated west of Cupar in its own secluded grounds, it
offers considerable comfort and an atmosphere of quiet
ambience. The decor of the drawing room upstairs is
delightful, and all the bedrooms have every modern
facility — including a mini bar. The Conference Room,
with its own entrance, is suitable for many functions.
Outside there is an excellent example of an ice house,
probably one of the best in Scotland. For golfers,
Ladybank is two miles away and the home of golf — St
Andrews — is less than half an hour away by car.*

Visitors welcome (ex competition days) Societies welcome (☎)
Green fees £5 per round (£9 WE)
Facilities ⊗ ⅲ ᴌ 🍺 (catering by prior arrangement) 𝚈 ⌂
Hotel ★★★65% Dean Park Hotel, Chapel Level, KIRKCALDY ☎(0592) 261635 20⇥ Annexe:12

Lochore Meadows ☎ Ballingry (0592) 860086
Lochore Meadows Country Park, Crosshill (2m N off B920)
Lochside course with natural stream running through, and woodland nearby. Fishing and riding stables. Country park also offers sailing, canoeing, windsurfing, trim trail and picnic sites.
9 holes, 5554yds, Par 72, SSS 71, Course record 68. Membership 200.

Visitors welcome Societies welcome (☎)
Green fees £4.10 per day (£5.40 WE)
Facilities ⊗ ᴌ 🍺 ⌂
Hotel ★★★62% Green Hotel, 2 The Muirs, KINROSS ☎(0577) 63467 40⇥

LUNDIN LINKS Map 6 G1

Lundin ☎ (0333) 320202
(W side of village off A915)
The Leven Links and the course of the Lundin Club adjoin each other. This course is part seaside and part inland. The holes, which can be described as seaside holes, are excellent. The others no less so, but of a different nature.
18 holes, 6377yds, Par 71, SSS 71, Course record 63. Membership 850.

SCORE CARD					
Hole	Yds	Par	Hole	Yds	Par
1	424	4	10	353	4
2	346	4	11	466	4
3	335	4	12	133	3
4	452	4	13	512	5
5	140	3	14	175	3
6	330	4	15	418	4
7	273	4	16	314	4
8	364	4	17	345	4
9	555	5	18	442	4
Out	3219	36	In	3158	35
			Totals	6377	71

Visitors welcome (with member only on Sun)
Societies welcome (by letter)
Green fees £22.50 per day; £15 per round (£18 Sat visitors after 1430)
Facilities ⊗ ⅲ ᴌ 🍺 𝚈 ⌂ 🏠 ⚐ ᶜ David K Webster
Hotel ★★★72% Old Manor Hotel, Leven Rd, LUNDIN LINKS ☎(0333) 320368 20rm(15⇥)

Lundin Ladies ☎ (0333) 320022
Woodilea Rd (W side of village off A915)
Short, lowland course with Roman stones on the second fairway, and coastal views.
9 holes, 4730yds, Par 68, SSS 67, Course record 67. Membership 260.

Visitors welcome
Green fees £3.50 (£4.50 WE)
Hotel ★★★72% Old Manor Hotel, Leven Rd, LUNDIN LINKS ☎(0333) 320368 20rm(15⇥)

ST ANDREWS Map 7 J8

British Golf Museum ☎ (0334)78880
(Situated opposite Royal &Ancient Golf Club)
Tells the fascinating history of golf. Highly visual displays are complemented by the use of visitor-activated touch screens throughout the galleries. Exhibits take the visitor from the misty origins of the game to the present day. You will see amazing images, fascinating collections of clubs, balls, fashion and memorabilia, two period workshops and historic documents. An audio-visual theatre shows historic golfing moments. Shop.
   Open All year. Days and hours vary according to season. Opening hours may also vary during major St Andrews golfing events. ☎ to confirm.
   Admission ☎ for details (1990 prices: Adult £2.50; Child (5-18) £1; Pensioners £1.50; Family ticket £6.)
See advertisements for St Andrews on page 241

St Andrews Links See page 239

SALINE Map 6 F1

Saline ☎ (0383) 852591
Kinneddar Hill (.5m E at junc B913/914)
Hillside course with panoramic view of the Forth Valley.
9 holes, 5302yds, Par 68, SSS 66, Course record 60. Membership 350.

SCORE CARD: Old Course					
Hole	Yds	Par	Hole	Yds	Par
1	370	4	10	318	4
2	411	4	11	172	3
3	352	4	12	316	4
4	419	4	13	398	4
5	514	5	14	523	5
6	374	4	15	401	4
7	359	4	16	351	4
8	166	3	17	461	4
9	307	4	18	354	4
Out	3272	36	In	3294	36
			Totals	6566	72

ST ANDREWS   Map7 J8

St Andrews Links ☎ (0334) 75757

If golf has a mother, then without doubt it is St Andrews, the most famous links in all the world. Sir Winston Churchill is said to have claimed golf was invented by the Devil, and if this is so then the famous Old Course must be the Devil's playground. How can one reconcile these two thoughts; the birthplace and mother of the game - and yet the very Devil of a test?

The great Bobby Jones started by hating St Andrews, and shredded his card into a hundred pieces, letting it blow in the wind. But eventually he came to love the place, and earn the affection of all golf. However you view St Andrews, you cannot ignore it. That master shot-maker from America, Sam Snead took one look and claimed they should plant cattle fodder on the bumpy acres. Gary Player once said is should be towed out to sea, and sunk. But Jack Nicklaus loved it so much that when he won an Open title here, he threw his putter into the air. And he went away, and copied several of the St Andrews features in other courses that now decorate this earth.

St Andrews is much more than an 18-hole test. It is a whole experience and a walk in history. Name the famous players of yesteryear, and they played here, taking divots from the very spot that you can take divots - merely by paying for a ticket and wandering out with your clubs to conquer some holes, maybe, and to be brought to a humbling halt by others.

Jack Nicklaus won his most remarkable victory on this course, thanks to an historic missed putt of just 3 feet 6 inches by Doug Sanders who had needed a final hole par 4 to win the 1970 Open Championship. The all-time course record is 62, shot by Curtis Strange in the 1987 Dunhill Cup. Surely nobody can ever beat that?

81 holes. Old Course 18 holes, 6566 yds, Par 72, SSS 72. New (West Sands Rd) 18 holes, 6604 yds, Par 71, SSS 72. Jubilee (West Sands Rd) 18 holes, 6284 yds, Par 69, SSS 70. Eden (Dundee Rd) 18 holes, 5971 yds, Par 69, SSS 69. Balgrove (Dundee Rd) 9 holes, 3546 yds, Par 60, SSS61

Visitors   welcome (☎ for details). Must contact in advance. Societies welcome (☎).

Green fees   Not confirmed

Facilities   ♀ 🏌 🍴 🏨

WHERE TO STAY AND EAT NEARBY

HOTELS:

Sᴛ Aɴᴅʀᴇᴡs   ★★★★ 72% St Andrews Old Course, Old Station Rd. ☎ (0334) 74371.

                 125 🛏 🍴 . ♀ Scottich & French cuisine.

                 ★★★★ 60% Rusacks's, Pilmour Links. ☎ (0334) 74321. 50 🛏 🍴 .

                 ★★★ 68% Rufflets Country House, Strathkinness Low Rd. ☎ (0334) 72594. 18 🛏 🍴 Annexe 3 🛏 🍴

RESTAURANTS:

Aɴsᴛʀᴜᴛʜᴇʀ   ✗✗ Cellar, 24 East Green. ☎ (0333) 310378. ♀ French cuisine.

Cᴜᴘᴀʀ   ✗   Ostlers Close, Bonnygate. ☎ (0334) 55574. ♀ French & Swiss cuisine.

Pᴇᴀᴛ Iɴɴ   ✗✗ The Peat Inn ☎ (033484) 206. ♀ French cuisine.

Visitors welcome (ex Sat) Societies welcome (☎ 2 wks advance)
Green fees £5 per day (£7 Sun)
Facilities ⊗ by prior arrangement ⫙ by prior arrangement ⊯ ⬛ ♀ ⚲
Hotel ★★★67% King Malcolm Thistle Hotel, Queensferry Rd, Wester Pitcorthie, DUNFERMLINE ☎(0383) 722611 48⇨🏠

TAYPORT
Map 7 J8

Scotscraig ☎ Dundee (0382) 552515
(S side of village off B945)
A rather tight course on downland-type turf with an abundance of gorse. The sheltered position of the course ensures good weather throughout the year.
18 holes, 6496yds, Par 71, SSS 71, Course record 61. Membership 600.

Visitors welcome (restricted at WE) must contact in advance Societies welcome (by letter)
Green fees On application
Facilities ⊗ ⫙ ⊯ ⬛ ♀ ⚲ 🏠 ⚑
Hotel ★★★59% Queens Hotel, 160 Nethergate, DUNDEE ☎(0382) 22515 47⇨🏠

THORNTON
Map 6 G1

Thornton ☎ Glenrothes (0592) 771111
Station Rd (1m E of town off A92)
Undulating and fairly difficult parkland course.
18 holes, 5589yds, Par 70, SSS 69, Course record 64. Membership 600.

Visitors welcome (restricted WE before 0930, PH 1230-1400) Societies welcome (by letter & deposit)
Green fees £12 per day ; £8 per round (£18/£12 WE)
Facilities ⊗ ⊯ ⬛ ♀ (all day in summer) ⚲ 🏠
Hotel ★★★72% Balgeddie House Hotel, Balgeddie Way, GLENROTHES ☎(0592) 742511 18⇨🏠

GRAMPIAN

ABERDEEN
Map 7 K6

Balnagask ☎ (0224) 876407
St Fitticks Rd (2m E of city centre)
Links course.
18 holes, 5486mtrs, SSS 69.

Visitors welcome Societies welcome
Green fees Not confirmed
Facilities ♀ ⚲
Hotel ★★★57% Swallow Imperial Hotel, Stirling St, ABERDEEN ☎(0224) 589101 108rm(104⇨🏠)

Bon Accord ☎ (0224) 633464
19 Golf Rd (.75 NE of city centre)
Links coastal course. Municipal, used by three private clubs. Snooker.
18 holes, 6384yds, Par 71, SSS 70. Membership 800.

Visitors welcome Societies welcome
Green fees Not confirmed
Facilities ⊯ ♀ (all day) ⚲ 🏠 ⚑ Bruce Davidson
Hotel ★★★68% Caledonian Thistle Hotel, 10 Union Ter, ABERDEEN ☎(0224) 640233 80⇨🏠

Deeside ☎ (0224) 867697
Bielside (3m W of city centre off A93)
Scenic parkland course. Snooker.
18 holes, 6000yds, Par 69, SSS 69, Course record 64. Membership 800.

Visitors welcome (ex Sat before 1600 & medal days) must contact in advance ✉ Societies welcome (Thu only)
Green fees £12 per round, (£15 WE & BH)
Facilities ⊗ ⫙ ⊯ (Tue-Sun) ⬛ (Tue-Sun) ♀ ⚲ 🏠 ⚑ ⚑
Hotel ★★★63% Stakis Treetops Hotel, 161 Springfield Rd, ABERDEEN ☎(0224) 313377 113⇨🏠

Hazelhead Public ☎ No telephone
Hazelhead (4m W of city centre off A944)
A tree-lined course.
18 holes, 6595yds, Par 70, SSS 70.

Visitors welcome Societies welcome
Green fees Not confirmed
Facilities ⚲ 🏠 ⚑
Hotel ★★★63% Stakis Treetops Hotel, 161 Springfield Rd, ABERDEEN ☎(0224) 313377 113⇨🏠

Murcar ☎ (0224) 704370
Bridge of Don (5m NE of city centre off A92)
Seaside course, prevailing NE wind, hard-walking. Testing 4th and 14th holes.
18 holes, 6240yds, Par 71, SSS 70, Course record 65. Strabatie 9 holes, 2680yds, Par 35, SSS 35. Membership 830.

Visitors welcome (ex Sat) must contact in advance Societies welcome (by letter)
Green fees £17 per day (£19 WE & BH) ;£12 per round
Facilities ⊗ (ex Tue) ⫙ (ex Tue) ♀ ⚲ 🏠 ⚑ ⚑ Alan White
Hotel ★★★63% Skean Dhu Dyce Hotel, Farburn Ter, DYCE ☎(0224) 723101 Annexe:220⇨🏠

Nigg Bay ☎ (0224) 871286
St Fitticks Rd
Seaside course, hard walking. Plays over Balnagask Course.
18 holes, 5984yds, Par 69, SSS 69. Membership 800.

Visitors welcome Member must accompany Societies welcome
Green fees Not confirmed
Facilities ♀ ⚲
Hotel ★★★63% Skean Dhu Dyce Hotel, Farburn Ter, DYCE ☎(0224) 723101 Annexe:220⇨🏠

This guide is updated annually – make sure you use an up-to-date edition.

Northern ☎ (0224) 636440
22 Gold Rd (adjacent to beach)
Exposed and windy seaside course, testing 10th hole.
One of 3 clubs playing over King's Links municipal
course.
18 holes, Par 72, SSS 72. Membership 1000.

Visitors welcome Societies welcome
Green fees Not confirmed
Facilities ♀ ⌂
Hotel ★★★65% Bucksburn Moat House Hotel,
Oldmeldrum Rd, Bucksburn, ABERDEEN ☎(0224) 713911
98⌁🐾

Royal Aberdeen ☎ (0224) 702571
Balgownie, Bridge of Don (2.5m N of city centre off A92)
Championship links course. Windy, easy walking. (Also
short course.)
*Balgownie 18 holes, 6372yds, Par 70, SSS 71, Course
record 64. Silverburn 18 holes, 4066yds, Par 64, SSS 60.
Membership 640.*

Visitors welcome (not before 1530 Sat) must contact in
advance ✉ Societies welcome (☎)
Green fees £25 per day, £20 per round
Facilities ⊗ �𝕄 by prior arrangement ⊾ � ♀ (all day)
⌂ 🏠 ⚐ ⎰ Ronnie MacAskill
Hotel ★★★65% Bucksburn Moat House Hotel,
Oldmeldrum Rd, Bucksburn, ABERDEEN ☎(0224) 713911
98⌁🐾

Westhill ☎ (0224) 740159
Westhill Heights, Westhill, Skene (6m NW of city centre
off A944)
A highland course.
18 holes, 5921yds, Par 69, SSS 69. Membership 600.

Visitors welcome (restricted Mon-Fri 4pm-7pm & Sat all
day) must contact in advance Societies welcome
Green fees Not comfirmed·
Facilities ⊗ by prior arrangement 𝕄 by prior
arrangement ⊾ ▪ ♀ ⌂ 🏠 ⎰ Nigel Hamilton
Hotel ★★★61%, Westhill Hotel, WESTHILL ☎(0224)
740388 38⌁ Annexe:14⌁🐾

ABOYNE   Map 7 J6

Aboyne ☎ (03398) 86328
Formaston Park (E side of village, N of A93)
Parkland/heathland course with outstanding views.
*18 holes, 5350yds, Par 66, SSS 66, Course record 62.
Membership 725.*

Visitors welcome Societies welcome (prior booking
essential)
Green fees £9 per day (£13 WE)
Facilities ⊗ high tea ⊾ ▪ ♀ (all day) ⌂ 🏠 ⚐
⎰ Innes Wright
Hotel ★★61% Birse Lodge Hotel, Charleston Rd,
ABOYNE ☎(03398) 86253 & 86254 11⌁🐾 Annexe:4⌁🐾
See advertisement on page 243

AUCHINBLAE
Map 7 J7

Auchinblae ☎ (05612) 407
(.5m NE)
Picturesque, small parkland/heathland course, good views.
9 holes, 2174mtrs, Par 32, SSS 30, Course record 61. Membership 60.

Visitors welcome (restricted Wed & Fri evenings)
Societies welcome (☎)
Green fees Not confirmed
Facilities 🖿
Hotel ★★55% County Hotel, Arduthie Rd, STONEHAVEN ☎(0569) 64386 14⇨🏊🏌

BALLATER
Map 7 H6

Ballater ☎ (03397) 55567
Victoria Rd (W side of town)
Moorland course with testing long holes and beautiful scenery. Tennis, snooker, bowling and putting green.
18 holes, 6094yds, Par 70, SSS 69, Course record 64. Membership 600.

Visitors welcome must contact in advance Societies welcome (☎)
Green fees £15 per day; £10 per round (£18/£12 WE)
Facilities ⊗ ⏏ ⚑ 🍺 (Nov-Mar by prior arrangement) ♀ (Apr-Oct) ⚓ 📦 🏌 ℂ Fraser Mann
Hotel ★★58% The Highland Haven, Shore St, MACDUFF ☎(0261) 32408 20⇨🏌

BANCHORY
Map 7 J6

Banchory ☎ (03302) 2365
Kinneskie Rd (A93 300 yds from W end of High St)
Sheltered parkland course, with easy walking and woodland scenery. 11th and 12th holes are testing.
18 holes, 5246yds, Par 67, SSS 66, Course record 60. Membership 1000.

Visitors welcome must contact in advance Societies welcome
Green fees £12 per day (£14 WE)
Facilities ⊗ ⚑ 🍺 ♀ ⚓ 📦 🏌 ℂ D W Smart
Hotel ★★★(red)🏨Banchory Lodge Hotel, BANCHORY ☎(03302) 2625 23⇨🏌

BANFF
Map 7 J4

Duff House Royal ☎ (02612) 2062
The Barnyards (.5m S on A98)
Well-manicured flat parkland, bounded by woodlands and River Deveron.
18 holes, 6161yds, Par 68, SSS 69, Course record 63. Membership 1000.

Visitors welcome Societies welcome
Green fees Not confirmed
Facilities ⊗ ⏏ ⚑ 🍺 ♀ ⚓ 📦 🏌 ℂ Bob Strachan
Hotel ★★★56% Banff Springs Hotel, Golden Knowes Rd, BANFF ☎(02612) 2881 30⇨🏌

BRAEMAR
Map 7 H6

Braemar ☎ (03397) 41618
Cluniebank Rd (.5m S)
Set amid beautiful countryside on Royal Deeside, the course is within easy walking distance of the village. Highest 18-hole course in U.K. (1, 200 ft above sea level).
18 holes, 4918yds, Par 65, SSS 64, Course record 61. Membership 280.

Visitors welcome must contact in advance Societies welcome (by letter)
Green fees £9 per day (£11 wknds)
Facilities ⊗ ⏏ ⚑ 🍺 ♀ ⚓ 📦 🏌
Hotel ★★67% Darroch Learg Hotel, Braemar Rd, BALLATER ☎(03397) 55443 15⇨🏌 Annexe:8rm(3⇨2🏌)

BUCKIE
Map 7 H4

Buckpool ☎ (0542) 32236
Barhill Rd, Buckpool (W side of town off A990)
Windy, seaside course, with easy walking. Overlooking Moray Firth. Squash and snooker.
18 holes, 6257yds, Par 70, SSS 70, Course record 64. Membership 600.

Visitors welcome (ex competition days) Societies welcome (☎)
Green fees £7 per day (£10 WE)
Facilities ⊗ ⏏ ⚑ 🍺 (Sat-Sun, other days by prior arrangement) ♀ ⚓
Hotel ★★57% Cluny Hotel, 2 High St, BUCKIE ☎(0542) 32922 10⇨🏌 Annexe:4rm

Strathlene ☎ (0542) 31798
Strathlene Rd (3m E on A942)
Windy seaside course with magnificent view, offering testing golf, including difficult 4th (par 3).
18 holes, 5925yds, Par 68, SSS 68. Membership 200.

Visitors welcome Societies welcome (☎)
Green fees Not confirmed
Facilities ♀ ⚓
Hotel ★★57% Cluny Hotel, 2 High St, BUCKIE ☎(0542) 32922 10⇨🏌 Annexe:4rm

CAIRNBULG
Map 7 K4

Inverallochy ☎ No telephone
24 Shore St (E side of village off B9107)
Windy seaside course, natural hazards, easy walking. Panoramic views of North Sea at every hole.
18 holes, 5137yds, Par 64, SSS 65, Course record 60. Membership 200.

Visitors welcome Societies welcome (☎)
Green fees £5
Facilities ⚑ (evenings and WE) 🍺 (evenings and WE)
Hotel ★★61% Tufted Duck Hotel, ST COMBS ☎(03465) 2481 2482/3 18⇨🏌

Opening times of bar and catering facilities vary from place to place – it is wise to check in advance of your visit.

CRUDEN BAY   Map 7 K5

Cruden Bay ☎ (0779) 812285
(SW side of village on A975)
A seaside links which provides golf of a high order.
It was designed by a master architect, Tom Simpson,
and although changed somewhat from his original
design it is still a great golf course.
*18 holes, 6370yds, Par 70, SSS 71, Course record 63. St
Olaf 9 holes, 4710yds, Par 64, SSS 62. Membership
1050.*

Visitors welcome (ex competition days & restricted
Weds) ✉ Societies welcome (☎)
Green fees Main course £16 per day (£22 WE); St
Olaf £8.50 per day (£12 WE)
Facilities ⊗ ⫙ ⌿ ⫿ ♀ ⚐ 🏠 ⛳ ⚑ David
Symington
Hotel ★★★67% Waterside Inn, Fraserburgh Rd,
PETERHEAD ☎(0779) 71121 70�’🏠 Annexe:40➙🏠

CULLEN   Map 7 J4

Cullen ☎ (0542) 40685
The Links (.5m W off A98)
Interesting links on two levels with rocks and ravines
offering some challenging holes. Spectacular scenery.
*18 holes, 4610yds, Par 63, SSS 62, Course record 58.
Membership 520.*

Visitors welcome Societies welcome (apply by letter)
Green fees Not confirmed
Facilities ⊗ (Jun-Sep) ⫙ by prior arrangement ⌿ ⫿
♀ ⚐ 🏠
Hotel ★★57% Cluny Hotel, 2 High St, BUCKIE ☎(0542)
32922 10➙🏠 Annexe:4rm

DUFFTOWN   Map 7 H5

Dufftown ☎ (0340) 20325
(.75m SW off B9009)
Hilly, heathland course with good views. Highest hole
over 1000 ft above sea level. It is hard to play to
handicap here.
18 holes, 5308yds, Par 67, SSS 66. Membership 150.

Visitors welcome Societies welcome (☎)
Green fees Not confirmed
Facilities ♀ (Thu, Fri, Sat, Sun ev) ⚐
Hotel ★★★⚑64% Rothes Glen Hotel, ROTHES
☎(03403) 254 16rm(13➙)

If you know of a golf course, not in this guide
already, which welcomes visitors, we would be
pleased to hear about it.

ELGIN   Map 7 H4

Elgin ☎ (0343) 2338
Hardhillock, Birnie Rd,
New Elgin (1m S off A941)
Possibly the finest inland
course in the north of
Scotland, with undulating
greens and compact holes
that demand the highest
accuracy. There are
thirteen par 4's and one par
5 hole.
*18 holes, 6401yds, Par 69,
SSS 71, Course record 64.
Membership 900.*

SCORE CARD					
Hole	Yds	Par	Hole	Yds	Par
1	459	4	10	428	4
2	438	4	11	375	4
3	368	4	12	278	4
4	155	3	13	325	4
5	484	5	14	462	4
6	222	3	15	188	3
7	167	3	16	417	4
8	453	4	17	334	4
9	408	4	18	440	4
Out	3154	34	In	3247	35
			Totals	6401	69

Visitors welcome (restricted from 0930 wkdays &
1000 WE) Societies welcome (by letter)
Green fees £18 per day (£25 WE)
Facilities ⊗ ⌿ ⫿ ♀ ⚐ 🏠 ⛳ ⚑ Ian P Rodger
Hotel ★★★57% Eight Acres Hotel, Sheriffmill,
ELGIN ☎(0343) 543077 57➙🏠

ELLON   Map 7 K5

McDonald ☎ (0358) 20576
Hospital Rd (.25m N on A948)
Tight, parkland course with streams and a pond.
18 holes, 5986yds, Par 70, SSS 69. Membership 710.

Visitors welcome
Green fees Not confirmed
Facilities ♀ △
Hotel ★66% Meldrum Arms Hotel, The Square, OLD
MELDRUM ☎(06512) 2238 & 2505 7♦

FORRES   Map 7 G4

Forres ☎ (0309) 72949
Muiryshade (SE side of town centre off B9010)
An all-year parkland course laid on light, well-drained soil in wooded countryside. Walking is easy despite some undulations. The holes are tests for the best golfers.
18 holes, 6141 yds, Par 70, SSS 69, Course record 63. Membership 800.

Visitors welcome Societies welcome (☎ 2-3 weeks in advance)
Green fees £12 per day; £8 per round
Facilities ⊗ ⬟ ♣ ♀ △ 🏠 ♦ ⌇ Sandy Aird
Hotel ★★63% Ramnee Hotel, Victoria Rd, FORRES
☎(0309) 72410 20⇔♦

FRASERBURGH   Map 7 K4

Fraserburgh ☎ (0346) 28287
Corbie Hill (1m SE on B9033)
Testing seaside course. 4 hole course for children.
18 holes, 6217 yds, Par 70, SSS 70. Membership 500.

Visitors welcome Societies welcome (☎)
Green fees Not confirmed
Facilities ⊗ ⬟ ⬟ ♀ (1100-2300) △ 🏠
Hotel ★★61% Tufted Duck Hotel, ST COMBS ☎(03465)
2481 2482/3 18⇔♦

GARMOUTH   Map 7 H4

Garmouth & Kingston ☎ Spey Bay (034387) 388
(In village on B9015)
Seaside/parkland course with tidal waters. 5 miles from Fochabers. Snooker, fishing.
18 holes, 5656 yds, Par 67, SSS 67, Course record 64. Membership 350.

Visitors welcome Societies welcome (☎)
Green fees £10 per day; £6 per round
Facilities △
Hotel ★★58% Gordon Arms Hotel, High St,
FOCHABERS ☎(0343) 820508 13⇔♦

HOPEMAN   Map 7 H4

Hopeman ☎ (0343) 830578
(E side of village off B9012)
Links course.
18 holes, 5511 yds, Par 67, SSS 67, Course record 66. Membership 490.

Visitors welcome (restricted Tue 1700-1800 & WE)
Societies welcome (by letter 2 wks in advance)
Green fees £6 per day (£9 WE)

Facilities ⊗ (WE only Oct-Mar) ⬟ (WE only Oct-Mar)
⬟ ♀ △ ♦
Hotel ★★★57% Eight Acres Hotel, Sheriffmill, ELGIN
☎(0343) 543077 57⇔♦

HUNTLY   Map 7 J5

Huntly ☎ (0466) 2643
Cooper Park (.25m through School Arch N side of Huntly)
A parkland course lying between the Rivers Deveron and Bogie.
18 holes, 5650 yds, Par 67, SSS 66, Course record 61. Membership 600.

Visitors welcome Societies welcome (by letter)
Green fees £6 per day (£8 WE)
Facilities ⊗ ⬟ ⬟ ♣ ♀ △ 🏠
Hotel ★★⚑53% Castle Hotel, HUNTLY ☎(0466) 2696
23rm(7⇔2♦)

INVERURIE   Map 7 J5

Inverurie ☎ (0467) 24080
Davah Wood, Blackhall Rd (W side of town off A96)
Parkland course, part of which is exposed and windy, and part through wooded area.
18 holes, 5096 yds, Par 66, SSS 65. Membership 560.

Visitors welcome
Green fees £8 (£10 WE)
Facilities △ 🏠 ♦
Hotel ★★56% Gordon Arms Hotel, Market Place,
INVERURIE ☎(0467) 20314 11rm(6♦)

KEITH   Map 7 H4

Keith ☎ (05422) 2469
Fife Park (NW side of town centre off A96)
Parkland course, with natural hazards over first 9 holes. Testing 7th hole, 232 yds, par 3.
18 holes, 5767 yds, Par 69, SSS 68. Membership 250.

Visitors welcome Societies welcome (☎ for details)
Green fees Not confirmed
Facilities ♀ △
Hotel ★★58% Gordon Arms Hotel, High St,
FOCHABERS ☎(0343) 820508 13⇔♦

KEMNAY   Map 7 J5

Kemnay ☎ (0467) 42225
Monymusk Rd (W side of village on B993)
9 holes, 5502 yds, Par 68, SSS 64, Course record 66. Membership 270.

Visitors welcome (ex Mon, Tues & Thu evenings)
Societies welcome
Green fees £5 (£6 WE)
Facilities ⬟ ♀ △
Hotel ★★★61% Westhill Hotel, WESTHILL ☎(0224)
740388 38⇔ Annexe:14⇔♦

LOSSIEMOUTH   Map 7 H4

Moray ☎ (034381) 2018
Stotfield Rd (N side of town)
Two fine Scottish championship links courses,
known as Old and New (Moray), and situated on the
Moray Firth where the weather is unusually mild.
*Old Course 18 holes, 6643yds, Par 71, SSS 72, Course
record 67. New Course 18 holes, 6005yds, Par 69, SSS
69, Course record 67. Membership 1300.*

Visitors welcome (restricted WE) must contact in
advance Societies welcome (☎ or letter)
Green fees £15 per day (£20 WE)
Facilities ⊗ ⅷ by prior arrangement ᥨ ▙ ♀ ⊿
🖻 ⎰ Alistair Thomson
Hotel ★★★71% Mansion House Hotel, The Haugh,
ELGIN ☎(0343) 548811 18ᗕ ⋔

MACDUFF   Map 7 J4

Royal Tarlair ☎ (0261) 32897
Buchan St (.75m E off A98)
Seaside clifftop course, can be windy. Testing 13th,
'Clivet' (par 3).
18 holes, 5866yds, Par 71, SSS 68. Membership 400.

Visitors welcome (☎ for parties) Societies welcome (by
letter)
Green fees Not confirmed
Facilities ♀ ⊿ 🖻
Hotel ★★58% County Hotel, 32 High St, BANFF
☎(02612) 5353 7rm(5ᗕ)

NEWBURGH ON YTHAN   Map 7 K5

Newburgh on Ythan ☎ Newburgh (03586) 89438
(E side of village on A975)
Seaside course adjacent to bird sanctuary. Testing 550-
yd dog leg (par 5).
*9 holes, 6300yds, Par 72, SSS 70, Course record 70.
Membership 300.*

Visitors welcome (restricted Tue & Sat) Societies
welcome
Green fees £8 per day (£9 WE)
Hotel ★66% Meldrum Arms Hotel, The Square, OLD
MELDRUM ☎(06512) 2238 & 2505 7⋔

OLD MELDRUM   Map 7 J5

Old Meldrum ☎ (06512) 2648
(E side of village off A947)
Generally narrow downland course requiring accuracy
rather than long hitting, superb views.
*18 holes, 5988yds, Par 70, SSS 69, Course record 71.
Membership 500.*

Visitors welcome Societies welcome (apply in writing)
Green fees £8 per day (£10 WE)
Facilities ᥨ and ▙ (Mon-Fri evening, Sat-Sun all day)
♀ (evenings & Sat-Sun) ⊿
Hotel ★66% Meldrum Arms Hotel, The Square, OLD
MELDRUM ☎(06512) 2238 & 2505 7⋔

PETERHEAD   Map 7 K5

Peterhead ☎ (0779) 72149
Craigewan Links (N side of town centre off A952)
Seaside course. Children's 9-hole course.
*Old Course 18 holes, 6173yds, Par 70, SSS 70, Course
record 64. New Course 9 holes, 2450yds, Par 62, SSS 62.
Membership 550.*

Visitors welcome (☎ for details) Societies welcome (by
letter)
Green fees £7 per day (£11 WE)
Facilities ⊗ by prior arrangement ⅷ by prior
arrangement ᥨ ▙ ♀ ⊿
Hotel ★★★67%, Waterside Inn, Fraserburgh Rd,
PETERHEAD ☎(0779) 71121 70ᗕ⋔ Annexe:40ᗕ⋔

SPEY BAY   Map 7 H4

Spey Bay ☎ Fochabers (0343) 820424
(4.5m N of Fochabers on B9104)
Seaside course, easy walking, good views.
Accommodation, tennis (hardcourt) and fishing.
18 holes, 6059yds, Par 71, SSS 69. Membership 320.

Visitors welcome (☎ for details) Societies welcome (☎)
Green fees Not confirmed
Facilities ⊗ ⅷ ᥨ ▙ ♀ ⊿ 🖻
Hotel ★★58% Gordon Arms Hotel, High St,
FOCHABERS ☎(0343) 820508 13ᗕ⋔

STONEHAVEN   Map 7 K6

Stonehaven ☎ (0569) 62124
Cowie (1m N off A92)
Challenging meadowland course overlooking sea with
three gullies and splendid views. Snooker.
18 holes, 4804yds, Par 64, SSS 64. Membership 800.

Visitors welcome (restricted WE) must contact in
advance Societies welcome
Green fees £10 per day (£12.50 WE)
Facilities ⊗ ⅷ by prior arrangement ᥨ ▙ ♀ ⊿ 🖻
Hotel ★★55% County Hotel, Arduthie Rd,
STONEHAVEN ☎(0569) 64386 14ᗕ⋔

TARLAND   Map 7 J6

Tarland ☎ (03398) 81413
Aberdeen Rd (E side of village off B9119)
Difficult parkland course, but easy walking.
*9 holes, 5816yds, Par 66, SSS 68, Course record 69.
Membership 260.*

Visitors welcome (ex competition days) Societies
welcome (by letter)
Green fees £6 per day (£8 WE)
Facilities ⊗ ᥨ ▙ ♀ ⊿
Hotel ★★61% Birse Lodge Hotel, Charleston Rd,
ABOYNE ☎(03398) 86253 & 86254 11ᗕ⋔ Annexe:4ᗕ⋔

If you know of a golf course, not in this guide
already, which welcomes visitors, we would be
pleased to hear about it.

TORPHINS

Map 7 J6

Torphins ☎ (033982) 493
Golf Rd (.25m W of village off A980)
Heathland course built on hill with views of Cairngorms
and Grampians.
9 holes, 2317 yds, Par 64, SSS 63, Course record 64.
Membership 365.

Visitors welcome (ex competition days) must contact in
advance Societies welcome (by letter)
Green fees £5 per day (£7 WE)
Facilities ⚑ (WE and evenings) ⛏
Hotel ★★★66% Tor-na-Coille Hotel, BANCHORY
☎(03302) 2242 24�🡡

TURRIFF

Map 7 J4

Turriff ☎ (0888) 62982
Rosehall (1m W off B9024)
A well-maintained inland course alongside the River
Deveron in picturesque surroundings. Friendly
clubhouse.
18 holes, 6145 yds, Par 69, SSS 69, Course record 63.
Membership 750.

Visitors welcome (not before 1000 WE) must contact in
advance Societies welcome (☎)
Green fees £10 per day ; £7 per round (£12/£10 WE)
Facilities ⊗ ⅲ ⅃ ⚑ ♀ ⛏ 🖮 ⛾ ℓ Alan Hemsley
Hotel ★★★56% Banff Springs Hotel, Golden Knowes
Rd, BANFF ☎(02612) 2881 30⇄🡡

HIGHLAND

ALNESS

Map 7 F4

Alness ☎ (0349) 883877
Ardross Rd (.5m N off A9)
A short, but testing, 9-hole parkland course with
beautiful views over Moray Firth. First 7 holes guarded
by walls and fences which are out of bounds.
9 holes, 2436 yds, Par 66, SSS 63, Course record 62.
Membership 150.

Visitors welcome Societies welcome (☎)
Green fees Not confirmed
Facilities ⅃ ♀ ⛏
Hotel ★★★65% Morangie House Hotel, Morangie Rd,
TAIN ☎(0862) 2281 11⇄🡡

BOAT OF GARTEN

Map 7 G5

Boat of Garten
☎ (047983) 282
(E side of village)
This parkland course was
cut out from a silver birch
forest though the fairways
are adequately wide. There
are natural hazards of
broom and heather, good
views and walking is easy.
A round provides great
variety. Tennis.
18 holes, 5720 yds, Par 69,
SSS 68, Course record 65.
Membership 400.

SCORE CARD					
Hole	Yds	Par	Hole	Yds	Par
1	186	3	10	265	4
2	347	4	11	369	4
3	146	3	12	339	4
4	484	5	13	436	4
5	333	4	14	274	4
6	403	4	15	305	4
7	382	4	16	167	3
8	353	4	17	346	4
9	150	3	18	435	4
Out	2784	34	In	2936	35
			Totals	5720	69

Visitors welcome must contact in advance Societies
welcome (☎)
Green fees £10 per day (£12 WE)
Facilities ⊗ ⅃ ⚑ ♀ ⛏ 🖮
Hotel ★★★63% Boat Hotel, BOAT OF GARTEN
☎(047983) 258 32⇄🡡

BONAR BRIDGE

Map 7 F3

Bonar Bridge-Ardgay ☎ Invershin (054982) 248
(.5m E)
Wooded moorland course with picturesque views of hills
and loch.
9 holes, 4626 yds, Par 66, SSS 63, Course record 66.
Membership 140.

Visitors welcome
Green fees £4 per day
Facilities ⚑ (summer only) ⛏
Hotel ★★51% Bridge Hotel, BONAR BRIDGE ☎(08632)
204 & 685 15rm(5⇄5🡡)

BRORA

Map 7 G3

Brora ☎ (0408) 21417
Golf Rd (E side of village)
Fairly easy seaside links with little rough and fine
views. Some testing holes.
18 holes, 6110 yds, Par 69, SSS 69, Course record 61.
Membership 388.

Visitors welcome (ex competition days) Societies
welcome (☎)
Green fees £10 per day
Facilities ⊗ (May-Sep) ⅲ ⅃ ⚑ ♀ ⛏ 🖮 ⛾
Hotel ★★★59% The Links Hotel, Golf Rd, BRORA
☎(0408) 21225 22⇄

CARRBRIDGE

Map 7 G5

Carrbridge ☎ (047984) 674
(N side of village)
Part-parkland, part-moorland 'family' course with good
views of the Cairngorms.
9 holes, 5300 yds, Par 71, SSS 66, Course record 67.
Membership 470.

Visitors welcome (restricted Sun & competition days)
Societies welcome (☎ or letter)
Green fees £6 per day (£7 WE)
Facilities ⅃ ⬛ ⌂ ⛳
Hotel ★★⊈67%, Muckrach Lodge Hotel, DULNAIN
BRIDGE ☎(047985) 257 10⇌

DORNOCH   Map 7 G3

Royal Dornoch ☎ (0862) 810219
Golf Rd (E side of town)
Very challenging seaside links, rated in the top ten
of the one-hundred greatest courses in the world.
Superb sea views. Tennis, fishing, riding stables.
*18 holes, 6577yds, Par 70, SSS 72 or 18 holes, 5242yds,
Par 68, SSS 66. Membership 900.*

Visitors welcome (handicap of 24 (women 35)) must
contact in advance ⊠ Societies welcome (☎)
Green fees £25 per round (£30 WE)
Facilities ⊗ ⅲ ⅃ ⬛ ⅄ (all day) ⌂ ⛱ ⛳ ⟨
Wllliam Skinner ⬛
Hotel ★★65% Dornoch Castle Hotel, Castle St,
DORNOCH ☎(0862) 810216 17⇌⋔

Each golf course entry has a recommended
hotel. For a wider choice of places to stay,
consult *AA Hotels and Restaurants in Britain* or
AA-inspected Bed and Breakfast in Britain.

DURNESS

Map 7 F1

Durness ☎ (097181) 364
Balnakeil (1m W of village)
A 9-hole course set in tremendous scenery overlooking
Balnakeil Bay. Part links and part inland with water
hazards. Off alternative tees for second 9 holes giving
surprising variety. Tremendous last hole across the sea.
9 holes, 5545yds, Par 70, SSS 68, Course record 73.
Membership 100.

Visitors welcome (restricted 1000-1200 Sun) Societies
welcome (☎)
Green fees £5 per day; £20 per wk
Facilities ☒ ♿ 🏠 ⛳
Hotel ★★★60% Kinlochbervie Hotel,
KINLOCHBERVIE ☎(097182) 275 14⇔

FORT AUGUSTUS

Map 7 F6

Fort Augustus ☎ (0320) 6460
Markethill (1m SW on A82)
Moorland course, with narrow fairways and good views
adjacent to the Caledonian Canal.
9 holes, 5454yds, Par 67, SSS 68, Course record 69.
Membership 100.

Visitors welcome (ex competition days) Societies
welcome (☎)
Green fees £5 per day
Facilities ♿ ⛳
Hotel ★★66% Lovat Arms Hotel, FORT AUGUSTUS
☎(0320) 6206 26rm(22⇔2♟)

FORTROSE

Map 7 F4

Fortrose & Rosemarkie ☎ (0381) 20733
Ness Rd East (W side of town centre)
Seaside course, with sea on three sides. Easy walking.
Suitable as a holiday course. Testing 4th hole, par 5.
Good views.
18 holes, 5973yds, Par 71, SSS 69, Course record 64.
Membership 730.

Visitors welcome Societies welcome (☎ (0381) 20529)
Green fees £12.50 per day (£12 per round WE) Apr-Oct
Facilities ⊗ (Apr-Oct) ∭ ♿ ☒ ♀ ♿ 🏠 ⛳ ∮ George
Hampton
Hotel ★52% Royal Hotel, Union St, FORTROSE ☎(0381)
20236 11rm(3⇔1♟)

FORT WILLIAM

Map 7 E7

Fort William ☎ (0397) 704464
(3m NE on A82)
Moorland course with fine views. Tees and greens very
good, but fairways can be very soft in wet weather.
18 holes, 5640yds, Par 70, SSS 68. Membership 200.

Visitors welcome Societies welcome (by letter)
Green fees Not confirmed
Facilities ⊗ ♿ ☒ ♀ ♿ ⛳
Hotel ★★★65% Moorings Hotel, Banavie, FORT
WILLIAM ☎(03977) 797 due to change to (0397772) 797
21⇔♟ Annexe:3♟

GAIRLOCH

Map 7 D4

Gairloch ☎ (0445) 2407
(1m S on A832)
Fine seaside course running along Gairloch Sands with
good views over the sea to Skye.
9 holes, 3884yds, Par 62. Membership 250.

Visitors welcome
Green fees £7 per day; £35 weekly
Facilities ☒ ♿ ⛳
Hotel ★★62% The Old Inn, Flowerdale, GAIRLOCH
☎(0445) 2006 14⇔♟

GOLSPIE

Map 7 G3

Golspie ☎ (04083) 3266
Ferry Rd (.5m S off A9)
Seaside course, with easy walking and natural hazards
including beach heather and whins. Spectacular
scenery.
18 holes, 5836yds, Par 68, SSS 68, Course record 65.
Membership 450.

Visitors welcome (ex competition days) Societies
welcome (☎)
Green fees £10 per day
Facilities ⊗ ♿ ☒ (May-Sep or by prior arrangement)
♀ (Apr-Sep) ♿ 🏠
Hotel ★★57% Golf Links Hotel, GOLSPIE ☎(04083)
3408 9⇔♟

GRANTOWN-ON-SPEY

Map 7 G5

Grantown-on-Spey ☎ (0479) 2079 (summer)
Golf Course Rd (E side of town centre)
Moorland and woodland course. Part easy walking,
remainder hilly. Ideal holiday centre.
18 holes, 5745yds, Par 70, SSS 67, Course record 60.
Membership 380.

Visitors welcome Societies welcome (☎ or by letter in
winter)
Green fees £9 per day (£11 WE)
Facilities ⊗ ♿ ☒ (Apr-Oct) ♀ (Apr-Oct) ♿ 🏠 ⛳
∮ W Mitchell
Hotel ★★65% Seafield Lodge Hotel, Woodside Av,
GRANTOWN-ON-SPEY ☎(0479) 2152 14⇔♟

HELMSDALE

Map 7 G3

Helmsdale ☎ (04312) 240
Golf Rd (NW side of town on A896)
Sheltered, undulating 9-hole course following the line of
the Helmsdale River.
9 holes, 1825yds, Par 62, SSS 62, Course record 58.
Membership 137.

Visitors welcome Societies welcome (by letter)
Green fees £3 per day; £10 wkly
Facilities ♿
Hotel ★★★59% The Links Hotel, Golf Rd, BRORA
☎(0408) 21225 22⇔

INVERGORDON
Map 7 F4

Invergordon ☎ (0349) 852715
King George St (W side of town centre on B817)
Fairly easy but windy parkland course, with good views
over Cromarty Firth. Very good greens. Clubhouse
situated 1m from course close to middle of town.
9 holes, 6028yds, Par 68, SSS 69, Course record 65.
Membership 300.

Visitors welcome Societies welcome (☎)
Green fees £4 (£5 WE)
Facilities ┺ (Sat only) ┻ (Sat only) ♀ (Sat, Tue &
Thu eve) ┷
Hotel ★★63% Royal Hotel, Marine Ter, CROMARTY
☎(03817) 217 10rm(5┹2┡)

INVERNESS
Map 7 F5

Inverness ☎ (0463) 239882
Culcabock (1m S of town centre on B9006)
Fairly flat parkland course with burn running through.
Windy in winter.
18 holes, 6226yds, Par 69, SSS 70, Course record 64.
Membership 1050.

Visitors welcome (restricted WE) ✉ Societies welcome
(☎)
Green fees £16 per day; £12 per round (£18/£14 WE &
PH)
Facilities ♀ ┷ ┮ ┱ ┝ A P Thomson
Hotel ★★★64% Kingsmills Hotel, Culcabock Rd,
INVERNESS ☎(0463) 237166 78┹┡ Annexe:6┹┡

Torvean ☎ (0463) 237543
Glenurquhart Rd (1.5m SW on A82)
Municipal parkland course, easy walking, good views.
18 holes, 5784yds, Par 69, SSS 68, Course record 67.
Membership 403.

Visitors welcome (ex competition days.) must contact
in advance Societies welcome (☎)
Green fees Not confirmed
Facilities ⊗ ┺ ┻ ♀ ┷ ┮
Hotel ★★⚑74% Dunain Park Hotel, INVERNESS
☎(0463) 230512 12rm(10┹┡)

KINGUSSIE
Map 7 G6

Kingussie ☎ (0540) 661374
Gynack Rd (.25m N off A86)
Hilly moorland course with natural hazards and
magnificent views.
18 holes, 5555yds, Par 66, SSS 67, Course record 64.
Membership 620.

Visitors welcome Societies welcome (☎)
Green fees £11 per day; £8 per round
Facilities ┺ ┻ ♀ ┷ ┮
Hotel ★65% Osprey Hotel, Ruthven Rd, KINGUSSIE
☎(0540) 661510 8rm(1┹3┡)

For an explanation of the symbols and
abbreviations used, see page 33.

LYBSTER
Map 7 H2

Lybster
Main St (E side of village)
Picturesque, short heathland course, easy walking.
9 holes, 1896yds, Par 62, SSS 62. Membership 80.

Visitors welcome Societies welcome (by letter)
Green fees Not confirmed
Facilities ┷ ┮
Hotel ★★58% Portland Arms, LYBSTER ☎(05932) 208
19┹┡

MUIR OF ORD
Map 7 F4

Muir of Ord ☎ (0463) 870825
Great North Rd (S side of village on A862)
Old established (1875), heathland/moorland course with
tight fairways, easy walking. Testing 11th, 'Castle Hill'
(par 3). Snooker.
18 holes, 5129yds, Par 63, SSS 65, Course record 62.
Membership 687.

Visitors welcome Societies welcome (by letter)
Green fees £8 per day (£9 WE) summer; (£7/£7 winter)
Facilities ┺ ┻ ♀ ┷ ┮ ┱ ┝ James Hamilton
Hotel ★★57% Ord Arms Hotel, Great North Rd, MUIR
OF ORD ☎(0463) 870286 11rm(4┹3┡)

NAIRN

Map 7 G4

Nairn ☎ (0667) 53208
Seabank Rd
Championship, seaside links founded in 1887 and
extended by Tom Morris and James Braid. Opening
holes stretch out along the shoreline with the turn
for home at the 10th. Regularly chosen for national
championships.
18 holes, 6556yds, Par 71, SSS 71, Course record 65.
Membership 1000.

Visitors welcome (after 1030 Sat & Sun) Societies
welcome (min 2 weeks notice ☎)
Green fees £22 per day; £18 per round (£26/£22
WE)
Facilities ⊗ ⅏ ⅃ ♨ ♀ △ ☖ ⅂ ⅃
Hotel ★★★★58% Golf View Hotel, Seabank Rd,
NAIRN ☎(0667) 52301 55⊸◗
See advertisement on page 249

Nairn Dunbar ☎ (0667) 52741
Lochloy Rd (E side of town off A96)
Seaside course with sea views and breezy at holes 6, 7
and 8. Testing hole: 'Long Peter' (527 yds).
18 holes, 6431yds, Par 71, SSS 71, Course record 68.
Membership 500.

Visitors welcome must contact in advance ✉ Societies
welcome
Green fees £12 per day (£15 WE)
Facilities ⊗ ⅃ ♨ ♀ △ ☖ ⅂ ⅃ Brian Mason
Hotel ★★★59% Newton Hotel, Inverness Rd, NAIRN
☎(0667) 53144 30⊸◗ Annexe:14⊸◗

NETHY BRIDGE

Map 7 G5

Abernethy ☎ (047982) 305
(N side of village on B970)
Picturesque moorland course.
9 holes, 2493yds, Par 66, SSS 66, Course record 61.
Membership 250.

Visitors welcome (ex club matches) Societies welcome
(☎)
Green fees £7 per day
Facilities ⊗ snacks ♨ △ ⅂
Hotel ★★⅃67% Muckrach Lodge Hotel, DULNAIN
BRIDGE ☎(047985) 257 10⊸

NEWTONMORE

Map 7 F6

Newtonmore ☎ (05403) 328
Golf Course Rd (E side of town off A9)
Inland course beside the River Spey. Beautiful views
and easy walking. Testing 17th hole (par 3).
18 holes, 5880yds, Par 70, SSS 68. Membership 370.

Visitors welcome Societies welcome (☎)
Green fees Not confirmed
Facilities ⊗ ⅃ ♨ ♀ △ ☖
Hotel ★★67% Columba House Hotel, Manse Rd,
KINGUSSIE ☎(0540) 661402 7⊸◗

PORTMAHOMACK

Map 7 G3

Tarbat ☎ (086287) 236
(E side of village)
Easy seaside links course with magnificent views.
9 holes, 4658yds, Par 66, SSS 63. Membership 180.

Visitors welcome Societies welcome
Green fees £4 per day
Facilities △
Hotel ★★★62% Royal Hotel, High St, TAIN ☎(0862)
2013 25rm(9⊸13◗)

REAY

Map 7 G1

Reay ☎ (084781) 288
(.5m E off A836)
Picturesque seaside links with natural hazards. Junior
tees. Testing 1st, 4th, 6th, 7th and 14th holes.
18 holes, 5865yds, Par 69, SSS 68. Membership 300.

Visitors welcome (restricted competition days)
Green fees £6 per day
Facilities ♀ △
Hotel ★★61% Pentland Hotel, Princes St, THURSO
☎(0847) 63202 53rm(20⊸16◗)

STRATHPEFFER

Map 7 F4

Strathpeffer Spa ☎ (0997) 21219
(.25m N of village off A834)
Moorland course with many natural hazards (no sand
bunkers), hard walking, fine views. Testing 3rd hole
(par 3) across loch.
18 holes, 4792yds, Par 65, SSS 65, Course record 60.
Membership 400.

Visitors welcome Societies welcome (☎)
Green fees £10 per day; £8 per round
Facilities ⊗ ⅃ ♨ (no catering Mon) ♀ △ ☖ ⅂
Hotel ★★64% Holly Lodge Hotel, STRATHPEFFER
☎(0997) 21254 7rm(3⊸3◗)

TAIN

Map 7 G4

Tain ☎ (0862) 2314
Golf Links (E side of town centre off B9174)
Heathland/seaside course with river affecting 3 holes,
easy walking, fine views.
18 holes, 6222yds, Par 70, SSS 70, Course record 66.
Membership 500.

Visitors welcome must contact in advance Societies
welcome (☎)
Green fees £11 day (£13 WE); £8 per round (£9 WE)
Facilities ⅃ ♨ ♀ △ ☖
Hotel ★★★62% Royal Hotel, High St, TAIN ☎(0862)
2013 25rm(9⊸13◗)

This guide is updated annually – make sure you
use an up-to-date edition.

THURSO
Map 7 H1

Thurso ☏ (0847) 63807
Newlands of Geise (2m SW on B874)
Parkland course, windy, fine views.
18 holes, 5818yds, Par 69, SSS 69, Course record 63.
Membership 310.

Visitors welcome Societies welcome (☏)
Green fees £7
Facilities ⬛ by prior arrangement ♀ ⛳ 🏠
Hotel ★★61% Pentland Hotel, Princes St, THURSO
☏(0847) 63202 53rm(20⇨16♠)

WICK
Map 7 H2

Wick ☏ (0955) 2726
Reiss (3.5m N off A9)
Seaside course, windy, easy walking.
18 holes, 5976yds, Par 69, SSS 69, Course record 63.
Membership 250.

Visitors welcome
Green fees Not confirmed
Facilities ⬛ by prior arrangement ♀ ⛳
Hotel ★★58% Mackay's Hotel, Union St, WICK
☏(0955) 2323 26rm(23⇨1♠)

LOTHIAN

ABERLADY
Map 6 H2

Kilspindie ☏ (08757) 358
(W side of village off A198)
Seaside course, short but tight and well-bunkered.
Testing holes: 2nd, 3rd, 4th and 7th.
18 holes, 5410yds, Par 69, SSS 66. Membership 600.

Visitors welcome Societies welcome (☏)
Green fees £15 per day; £10.50 per round (£17.50/£12.50
WE)
Facilities ⊗ high tea (Apr-Oct) ⬛ ♂ ♀ ⛳ 🏠
Ⅼ Graham J Sked
Hotel ★★64% Kilspindie House Hotel, Main St,
ABERLADY ☏(08757) 682 26⇨♠

Luffness New ☏ Gullane (0620) 843336
(1m E on A198)
Seaside course.
18 holes, 6122yds, Par 69, SSS 69, Course record 63.
Membership 700.

Visitors welcome (ex WE & PH) must contact in
advance ✉ Societies welcome (by letter)
Green fees £25 per day; £20 per round
Facilities ⊗ ⅏ by prior arrangement ⬛ ♂ ♀ ⛳ 🏠
Hotel ★★★🚩81% Greywalls Hotel, Duncar Rd,
GULLANE ☏(0620) 842144 17⇨♠ Annexe:5⇨♠

*Opening times of bar and catering facilities vary
from place to place – it is wise to check in
advance of your visit.*

BATHGATE
Map 6 F2

Bathgate ☏ (0506) 52232
Edinburgh Rd (E side of town off A89)
Moorland course. Easy walking. Testing 11th, par 3.
18 holes, 6328yds, Par 71, SSS 70, Course record 64.
Membership 600.

Visitors welcome must contact in advance Societies
welcome (☏)
Green fees £10 per day (£15 WE)
Facilities ⊗ ⅏ (Thu-Sat in season) ⬛ ♂ ♀ ⛳ 🏠 ⍭
Ⅼ
Hotel ★★★60% Hilton National, Almondvale East,
LIVINGSTON ☏(0506) 31222 120♠

BONNYRIGG
Map 6 G2

Broomieknowe ☏ 031-663 9317
36 Golf Course Rd (.5m NE off B704)
Easy walking parkland course laid out by Ben Sayers
and extended by James Braid. Elevated site with
excellent views.
18 holes, 5754yds, Par 68, SSS 68, Course record 64.
Membership 450.

Visitors welcome (restricted Wed WE & BH) Societies
welcome
Green fees Not confirmed
Facilities ⊗ ⅏ ⬛ ♂ ♀ ⛳ 🏠 ⍭ Ⅼ Mark Patchett
Hotel ★★★63% Donmaree Hotel, 21 Mayfield
Gardens, EDINBURGH ☏031-667 3641 9⇨♠
Annexe:8rm(3⇨2♠)

DALKEITH
Map 6 G2

Newbattle ☏ 031-663 2123
Abbey Rd (SW side of town off A68)
Undulating parkland course on three levels, surrounded
by woods.
18 holes, 6012yds, Par 69, SSS 69, Course record 64.
Membership 650.

Visitors welcome (ex WE & restricted until 1600
wkdays) ✉ Societies welcome (☏)
Green fees £15 per day; £9 per round
Facilities ⛳ 🏠 Ⅼ John Henderson
Hotel ★★64% Eskbank Motor Hotel, 29 Dalhousie Rd,
DALKEITH ☏031-663 3234 16⇨♠

Each golf course entry has a recommended
hotel. For a wider choice of places to stay,
consult *AA Hotels and Restaurants in Britain* or
AA-inspected Bed and Breakfast in Britain.

DUNBAR

Map 6 H2

Dunbar ☎ (0368) 62317
East Links (.5m E off A1087)
Another of Scotland's old
links. It is said that it was
some Dunbar members who
first took the game of golf to
the North of England. The
club dates back to 1856. The
wind, if blowing from the
sea, is a problem.
*18 holes, 6426yds, Par 71,
SSS 71, Course record 64.
Membership 650.*

SCORE CARD					
Hole	Yds	Par	Hole	Yds	Par
1	477	5	10	202	3
2	494	5	11	417	4
3	172	3	12	459	4
4	349	4	13	378	4
5	148	3	14	433	4
6	350	4	15	343	4
7	386	4	16	166	3
8	369	4	17	339	4
9	507	5	18	437	4
Out	3252	37	In	3174	34
			Totals	6426	71

Visitors welcome (☎ for details) must contact in
advance Societies welcome (☎)
Green fees £15 per day (£25 WE & BH)
Facilities ⊗ Ⅻ ᴸᴸ ⬛ ♀ (all day) △ 🏠 ⌇
Hotel ★★65% Bayswell Hotel, Bayswell Park,
DUNBAR ☎(0368) 62225 13⇔�—

Winterfield ☎ (0368) 63562
North Rd (W side of town off A1087)
Seaside course with superb views.
18 holes, 5220yds, SSS 64. Membership 200.

Visitors welcome must contact in advance
Green fees Not confirmed
Facilities ♀ △ 🏠 ⌇
Hotel ★★65% Bayswell Hotel, Bayswell Park, DUNBAR
☎(0368) 62225 13⇔�—

EDINBURGH

Map 6 G2

Baberton ☎ 031-453 4911
Juniper Green (5m W of city centre off A70)
Parkland course.
*18 holes, 6098yds, Par 69, SSS 69, Course record 62.
Membership 800.*

Visitors welcome Member must accompany Societies
welcome (☎)
Green fees £18 per day; £12 per round
Facilities ⊗ Ⅻ by prior arrangement ᴸᴸ ⬛ ♀ △ 🏠
⌇ Ken Kelly
Hotel ★★★65% Bruntsfield Hotel, 69/74 Bruntsfield
Place, EDINBURGH ☎031-229 1393 51⇔�—

Braid Hills ☎ 031-447 6666
Braid Hills Approach (2.5m S of city centre off A702)
Municipal heathland course with good views of
Edinburgh and the Firth of Forth.
18 holes, 5731yds, Par 70, SSS 68.

Visitors welcome (ex Sat mornings and evenings)
Green fees Not confirmed
Facilities ♀ △ 🏠 ⌇ ⌇
Hotel ★★★56% Braid Hills Hotel, 134 Braid Rd, Braid
Hills, EDINBURGH ☎031-447 8888 68⇔�—

This guide is updated annually – make sure you
use an up-to-date edition.

Bruntsfield Links Golfing Society ☎ 031-336 1479
32 Barnton Av, Davidsons-Mains (4m NW of city centre
off A90)
Parkland course with good views of Forth Estuary. 4th
and 14th holes are testing.
18 holes, 6407yds, Par 71, SSS 71. Membership 1000.

Visitors welcome (ex WE) must contact in advance ✉
Societies welcome (☎)
Green fees £30 per day; £22 per round
Facilities ⊗ ⅫᎸ (summer only) ⬛ ♀ △ 🏠 ⌇
Hotel ★★★67% Barnton Thistle Hotel, Queensferry
Rd, Barnton, EDINBURGH ☎031-339 1144 50⇔�—

Carrick Vale ☎ 031-337 1096
Carricknowe Municipal, Glendevon Park (3m W of city
centre, S of A8)
Flat parkland course suitable for beginners.
18 holes, 6299yds, Par 71, SSS 70. Membership 450.

Visitors welcome ✉
Green fees Not confirmed
Facilities ⌇
Hotel ★★★65% Post House Hotel, Corstorphine Rd,
EDINBURGH ☎031-334 0390 207⇔

Craigmillar Park ☎ 031-667 0047
Observatory Rd (2m S of city centre off A7)
Parkland course, with good views.
*18 holes, 5846yds, Par 70, SSS 68, Course record 65.
Membership 520.*

Visitors welcome (with M only WE & after 1500) ✉
Societies welcome (by letter)
Green fees £15 per day; £10 per round
Facilities ⊗ ⅫᎸ by prior arrangement ᴸᴸ ⬛ ♀ △ 🏠
⌇ ⌇ Brian McGhee
Hotel ★★★63% Donmaree Hotel, 21 Mayfield
Gardens, EDINBURGH ☎031-667 3641 9⇔�—
Annexe:8rm(3⇔2�—)

Dalmahoy Country ☎ 031-333 1845
Kirknewton (7m W of city centre on A71)
Two upland courses, one championship.
Accommodation, squash.
18 holes, 6664yds, Par 72, SSS 72. Membership 700.

Visitors welcome must contact in advance Societies
welcome (☎ for details)
Green fees Not confirmed
Facilities ♀ △ 🏠 ⌇ ⌇
Hotel ★★★65% Post House Hotel, Corstorphine
Rd, EDINBURGH ☎031-334 0390 207⇔

Duddingston ☎ 031-661 7688
Duddingston Rd West (2.5m SE of city centre off A1)
Parkland, semi-seaside course with burn as a natural
hazard. Testing 11th hole. Easy walking and windy.
*18 holes, 6647yds, Par 72, SSS 72, Course record 64.
Membership 700.*

Visitors welcome (ex WE) Societies welcome (☎ Tue &
Thu only)
Green fees £21 per day; £16 per round

Facilities ⊗ 〽 by prior arrangement 🏌 🍺 ♀ ⌂ 🏠 ⛳ 🕯

Hotel ★★★63% Donmaree Hotel, 21 Mayfield Gardens, EDINBURGH ☎031-667 3641 9⇨🐾 Annexe:8rm(3⇨2🐾)

Kingsknowe ☎ 031-441 1145
326 Lanark Rd (4m SW of city centre on A70)
Hilly parkland course with prevailing SW winds. Snooker.
18 holes, 5979yds, Par 69, SSS 69, Course record 64. Membership 705.

Visitors welcome must contact in advance Societies welcome (☎ or by letter)
Green fees £10 per day; £7.50 per round (£15/£10 WE)
Facilities ⊗ 〽 by prior arrangement 🏌 🍺 ♀ ⌂ 🏠 ⛳ 🕯 William Bauld
Hotel ★★★65% Bruntsfield Hotel, 69/74 Bruntsfield Place, EDINBURGH ☎031-229 1393 51⇨🐾

Liberton ☎ 031-664 3009
297 Gilmerton Rd (3m SE of city centre on A7)
Undulating, wooded parkland course.
18 holes, 5299yds, Par 67, SSS 66. Membership 700.

Visitors welcome
Green fees Not confirmed
Facilities ♀ ⌂ 🏠 🕯
Hotel ★★56% Suffolk Hall Hotel, 10 Craigmillar Park, EDINBURGH ☎031-668 4333 12rm(11⇨🐾)

Lothianburn ☎ 031-445 2206
106b Biggar Rd, Fairmilehead (4.5m S of city centre on A702)
Hilly, with a 'T' shaped wooded-area, the course is situated in the Pentland foothills. Sheep on course.
18 holes, 5750yds, Par 71, SSS 69, Course record 64. Membership 700.

Visitors welcome (ex competition days) Societies welcome (☎)
Green fees £11 per day; £8 per round (£14/£10 WE)
Facilities ⊗ 〽 🏌 🍺 (no catering Wed) ♀ ⌂ 🏠 ⛳ 🕯 Paul Morton
Hotel ★★★56% Braid Hills Hotel, 134 Braid Rd, Braid Hills, EDINBURGH ☎031-447 8888 68⇨🐾

Merchants of Edinburgh ☎ 031-447 1219
10 Craighill Gardens (2m SW of city centre off A702)
Testing hill course. Snooker.
18 holes, 4889yds, Par 64, SSS 64, Course record 61. Membership 680.

Visitors welcome Member must accompany ✉ Societies welcome (by letter)
Green fees £8 per day; £6 per round (£8 WE)
Facilities ⊗ (ex Wed and Thu) 〽 by prior arrangement 🏌 🍺 ♀ ⌂ 🏠 🕯 Craig Imlah
Hotel ★★★56% Braid Hills Hotel, 134 Braid Rd, Braid Hills, EDINBURGH ☎031-447 8888 68⇨🐾

Mortonhall ☎ 031-447 6974
Braid Rd (3m S of city centre off A702)
Moorland course with views over Edinburgh.
18 holes, 6557yds, Par 72, SSS 71. Membership 650.

Visitors welcome ✉ Societies welcome (☎)
Green fees £16 per day; £13 per round (£16 WE)
Facilities ⊗ (ex Mon and Sat) 🏌 🍺 ♀ ⌂ 🏠 🕯 D B Horn
Hotel ★★★56% Braid Hills Hotel, 134 Braid Rd, Braid Hills, EDINBURGH ☎031-447 8888 68⇨🐾

Murrayfield ☎ 031-337 1009
43 Murrayfield Rd (2m W of city centre off A8)
Parkland course with fine views.
18 holes, 5727yds, Par 70, SSS 68, Course record 64. Membership 775.

Visitors welcome (ex WE) Member must accompany must contact in advance ✉
Green fees £21 per day; £15 per round
Facilities ⊗ 〽 by prior arrangement 🏌 🍺 ♀ ⌂ 🏠 ⛳ 🕯 James Fisher
Hotel ★★★65% Post House Hotel, Corstorphine Rd, EDINBURGH ☎031-334 0390 207⇨

Portobello ☎ 031-669 4361
Stanley St (3m E of city centre off A1)
Public parkland course, easy walking.
9 holes, 2400yds, Par 32, SSS 32. Membership 70.

Visitors welcome (ex Sat 0830-1000 & 1230-1400) Societies welcome
Green fees £1.80 per round
Facilities 🕯
Hotel ★★★63% Donmaree Hotel, 21 Mayfield Gardens, EDINBURGH ☎031-667 3641 9⇨🐾 Annexe:8rm(3⇨2🐾)

Prestonfield ☎ 031-667 1273
Priestfield Rd North (1.5m S of city centre off A68)
Parkland course with beautiful views.
18 holes, 5685yds, Par 70, SSS 70, Course record 62. Membership 700.

Visitors welcome (ex 1200-1330 Sat & before 1130 Sun) Societies welcome (☎)
Green fees £14 per day; £11 per round (£15/£20 WE & BH)
Facilities ⊗ 〽 by prior arrangement 🏌 🍺 ♀ ⌂ 🏠 🕯 Brian M Commins
Hotel ★★★63% Donmaree Hotel, 21 Mayfield Gardens, EDINBURGH ☎031-667 3641 9⇨🐾 Annexe:8rm(3⇨2🐾)

Ravelston ☎ 031-332 2486
24 Ravelston Dykes Rd (3m W of city centre off A90)
Parkland course.
9 holes, 5322yds, Par 66, SSS 66, Course record 66. Membership 610.

Visitors welcome (ex WE & BH) must contact in advance ✉
Green fees Not confirmed

▶

Facilities 🏌 💷 ⛱

Hotel ★★★67% Holiday Inn, Queensferry Rd,
EDINBURGH ☎031-332 2442 118⇨🛏🐾

Royal Burgess ☎ 031-339 2075
181 Whitehouse Rd, Barnton (5m W of city centre off
A90)
No mention of golf clubs would be complete without
reference to the Royal Burgess, which was
instituted in 1735, thus being the oldest golfing
society in the world. Its course is a pleasant
parkland, and one with much variety. A club which
all those interested in the history of the game should
visit.
18 holes, 6167yds, Par 68, SSS 69. Membership 620.

Visitors welcome (☎ for details) must contact in
advance ✉ Societies welcome (☎)
Green fees Not confirmed
Facilities ⊗ (Tue-Fri) 🏌 💷 ♀ 📦 ⛳ 🍴 George
Yuille
Hotel ★★★67% Barnton Thistle Hotel,
Queensferry Rd, Barnton, EDINBURGH ☎031-339
1144 50⇨🛏🐾

Silverknowes ☎ 031-336 3843
Silverknowes, Parkway (4m NW of city centre N of
A902)
Links course on coast overlooking the Firth of Forth.
18 holes, 6210yds, Par 72, SSS 71. Membership 500.

Visitors welcome
Green fees Not confirmed
Facilities ♀ ⛱ 📦 ⛳
Hotel ★★63% Murrayfield Hotel, 18 Corstorphine Rd,
EDINBURGH ☎031-337 1844 23⇨🐾 Annexe:13rm

Swanston ☎ 031-445 2239
111 Swanston Rd, Fairmilehead (4m S of city centre off
B701)
Hillside course with steep climb at 12th & 13th holes.
*18 holes, 5024yds, Par 66, SSS 65, Course record 63.
Membership 500.*

Visitors welcome (ex competition days) must contact in
advance Societies welcome (☎ for details)
Green fees £8 per day; £6 per round (£12/£8 WE & PH)
Facilities ⊗ 🏌 💷 ♀ ⛱ 📦 🍴 Ian Seith
Hotel ★★★56% Braid Hills Hotel, 134 Braid Rd, Braid
Hills, EDINBURGH ☎031-447 8888 68⇨🐾

Torphin Hill ☎ 031-441 1100
Torphin Rd, Colinton (5m SW of city centre S of A720)
Beautiful hillside course.
18 holes, 4597mtrs, Par 67, SSS 66. Membership 410.

Visitors welcome (ex competition days) must contact in
advance Societies welcome (☎)
Green fees Not confirmed
Facilities ⊗ (ex Tue) 🎗 (ex Tue) 🏌 💷 ♀ ⛱ 📦 ⛳
Hotel ★★★56% Braid Hills Hotel, 134 Braid Rd, Braid
Hills, EDINBURGH ☎031-447 8888 68⇨🐾

Turnhouse ☎ 031-339 5937
Turnhouse Rd (6m W of city centre N of A8)
Parkland/heathland course, good views.
*18 holes, 6171yds, Par 69, SSS 69, Course record 65.
Membership 750.*

Visitors welcome (ex WE or competition days) Member
must accompany must contact in advance Societies
welcome (by letter)
Green fees £18 per day; £12 per round
Facilities ♀ ⛱ 📦 ⛳ 🍴 Kevin Whitson
Hotel ★★★67% Barnton Thistle Hotel, Queensferry
Rd, Barnton, EDINBURGH ☎031-339 1144 50⇨🐾

GIFFORD
Map 6 H2

Gifford ☎ (062081) 267
Calroust (1m SW off B6355)
Parkland course, with easy walking.
9 holes, 6138yds, Par 71, SSS 69. Membership 450.

Visitors welcome (restricted Tue, Wed & WE)
Green fees Not confirmed
Facilities ⛱
Hotel ★★71% Tweeddale Arms Hotel, GIFFORD
☎(062081) 240 15⇨🐾

GULLANE
Map 6 H2

Gullane ☎ (0620) 843115
(On A198)
Gullane is a delightful village and one of Scotland's
great golf centres. Gullane club was formed in 1882.
There are three Gullane courses and the No 1 is of
championship standard. It differs from most Scottish
courses in as much as it is of the downland type and
really quite hilly. The first tee is literally in the
village. The views from the top of the course are
magnificent and stretch far and wide in every
direction - in fact, it is said that 14 counties can be
seen from the highest spot.
*Course No 1 : 18 holes, 6466yds, Par 71, SSS 71,
Course record 64. Course No 2 : 18 holes, 6219yds, Par
70, SSS 70, Course record 64. Course No 3 : 18 holes,
5128yds, Par 65, SSS 65. Membership 1200.*

Visitors welcome must contact in advance
Green fees £12-£39 per day; £8-£26 per round (£15-
£42/£10-£35 WE) according to course/s
Facilities ⊗ 🎗 🏌 💷 ♀ ⛱ 📦 ⛳ 🍴 Jinny Hume
Hotel ★★★★81% Greywalls Hotel, Duncar Rd,
GULLANE ☎(0620) 842144 17⇨🐾 Annexe:5⇨🐾

**Muirfield (Honourable Company of Edinburgh
Golfers)** See page 255

HADDINGTON
Map 6 H2

Haddington ☎ (062082) 3627
Amisfield Park (E side off A613)
Inland course with trees and bushes.
18 holes, 6280yds, Par 71, SSS 70. Membership 500.

▶

SCORE CARD					
Hole	Yds	Par	Hole	Yds	Par
1	444	4	10	471	4
2	345	4	11	350	4
3	374	4	12	376	4
4	174	3	13	146	3
5	506	5	14	442	4
6	436	4	15	391	4
7	151	3	16	181	3
8	439	4	17	501	5
9	460	4	18	414	4
Out	3329	35	In	3272	35
			Totals	6601	70

GULLANE   Map6 H2

Muirfield (Honourable Company of Edinburgh Golfers). ☎ (062084) 2123. NE side of village.

Ask an American superstar to name the best golf course in Great Britain, or maybe even in the entire world, and the likely answer will be Muirfield. It certainly features in the top ten of any meaningful selection.

Purely on shape and balance, the course has everything. Ask competitors in the Open Championship what they think of the last nine holes, and they will tell you it can wreck the stoutest heart. But ask Isoa Aoki of Japan what he thinks, and he will smile and maybe tell of his course record 63 here.

Established in 1744, it is just ten years older than the R&A itself but not as old as Royal Blackheath. However, these dates show that Muirfield certainly has seniority and tradition. Quite simply, it is exclusive and entirely excellent, and has staged some outstanding Open Championships with one, I suspect, standing out in people's minds more than any other.

Back in 1972, Tony Jacklin was Europe's best player and looked set to prove it again at Muirfield when he had appeared to wear down Lee Trevino, the defending champion. At the 71st hole, Trevino seemed to be frittering away strokes as he mishit a shot downwind through the dry, fast, green. In the next few minutes, hair stood on end. 'I was mad' recalled Trevino. 'My next shot from the bank was strictly a give-up one. And the ball went straight in the hole.' Jacklin had chipped up, well short. Then he missed his put, turned for the return putt, and missed again. We all did mental arithmetic. Jacklin had blown it and when he bogeyed the last, furious at himself, he suddenly wasn't the winner - Trevino was.

Those of us there recall Trevino had holed one bunker shot, and chipped in three times. Muirfield looked on his brilliance with favour and sad Jacklin never won an Open again.

18 holes, 6610 yards, Par 70, SSS73. Membership 625

Visitors   welcome only on Tue & Thu, also Fri am (ex during Jul & Aug). Must contact in advance ✉ . Societies welcome but restricted as above.

Green fees   £60 per day; £45 per round

Facilities   ⊗ ⬛ ♀ ♨ ⚐

WHERE TO STAY AND EAT NEARBY

HOTELS:

ABERLADY   ★★ 58% Weem, Weem (1m NW B846). ☎ (0887) 20381. 14 ⌂🍴 . ♡ European cuisine.

GULLANE   ★★★ ⚑ 81% Greywalls, Duncar Rd. ☎ (0620) 842144.   17 ⌂🍴   Annexe 5 ⌂🍴

NORTH BERWICK ★★★ 64% The Marine, Cromwell Rd. ☎ (0620) 2406. 83 ⌂🍴 . ♡ International cuisine.

                 ★★ 61% Nether Abbey, 20 Dirleton Ave. ☎ (0620) 2802. 16rm (4 ⌂ 🍴 6🍴   )

                 ★★56% Point Garry, West Bay Rd. ☎ (0620) 2380. 16rm (5 ⌂ 🍴 6🍴   ). ♡ International cuisine.

RESTAURANT:

GULLANE   ✗ La Potinière, Main St. ☎ (0620) 843214. ♡ French cuisine.

Visitors welcome (ex WE 0700-1000; 1200-1400; 1600-1800) must contact in advance Societies welcome (☎ deposits required)
Green fees £12 per day; £7.50 per round (£15/£9 WE)
Facilities ⊗ �🏌 🦶 🍺 ♀ ⛳ 🏠 (John Sandilands
Hotel ★★71% Tweeddale Arms Hotel, GIFFORD
☎(062081) 240 15⇨🐦

LINLITHGOW
Map 6 F2

Linlithgow ☎ (0506) 842585
Braehead (1m S off Bathgate Road off A803)
Parkland course in beautiful setting.
18 holes, 5278yds, Par 70, SSS 68. Membership 550.

Visitors welcome (ex Sat. Prior booking Sun) must contact in advance Societies welcome (☎)
Green fees £12 per day; £9 per round (£15/£12 WE)
Facilities Catering by prior arrangement ♀ ⛳ 🏠
(Derek Smith
Hotel ★★★67% Inchyra Grange Hotel, Grange Rd,
POLMONT ☎(0324) 711911 33⇨🐦

West Lothian ☎ (0506) 826030
Airngath Hill (1m S off A706)
Hilly parkland course with superb views of River Forth.
18 holes, 6578yds, Par 71, SSS 71. Membership 500.

Visitors welcome must contact in advance Societies welcome (☎)
Green fees Not confirmed
Facilities ♀ ⛳
Hotel ★★★67% Inchyra Grange Hotel, Grange Rd,
POLMONT ☎(0324) 711911 33⇨🐦

LIVINGSTON
Map 6 F2

Deer Park ☎ (0506) 38843
Carmowdean (N side of town off A809)
Long testing course, fairly flat, championship standard.
18 holes, 6636yds, Par 71, SSS 72. Membership 500.

Visitors welcome
Green fees Not confirmed
Facilities ♀ ⛳ 🏠 ⛳ (
Hotel ★★★⚑65% Houstoun House Hotel, UPHALL
☎(0506) 853831 28⇨🐦 Annexe:2⇨

Pumpherston ☎ (0506) 32869
Drumshoreland Rd, Pumpherston (1m E between A71 & A89)
Undulating parkland course with testing 6th hole (par 3), and view of Pentland Hills.
9 holes, 5154yds, Par 64, SSS 65, Course record 61. Membership 350.

Visitors welcome Member must accompany
Green fees £4 per day (£6 WE)
Facilities ⊗ 🦶 🍺 ♀ ⛳
Hotel ★★★⚑65% Houstoun House Hotel, UPHALL
☎(0506) 853831 28⇨🐦 Annexe:2⇨

LONGNIDDRY
Map 6 G2

Longniddry
☎ (0875) 52141
Links Rd (W side of village off A198)
Seaside and parkland undulating course. One of the numerous courses which stretch east from Edinburgh right to Dunbar. The inward half is more open and less testing than the wooded outward half.
18 holes, 6219yds, Par 68, SSS 70, Course record 63. Membership 980.

			SCORE CARD		
Hole	Yds	Par	Hole	Yds	Par
1	398	4	10	364	4
2	416	4	11	333	4
3	461	4	12	381	4
4	199	3	13	174	3
5	314	4	14	403	4
6	168	3	15	425	4
7	430	4	16	145	3
8	367	4	17	434	4
9	374	5	18	433	4
Out	3127	34	In	3092	34
			Totals	6219	68

Visitors welcome (ex PH & competition days, WE with M only) must contact in advance handicap cert required Societies welcome (by letter)
Green fees £27 per day; £18 per round
Facilities ⊗ 🏌 🦶 🍺 ♀ ⛳ 🏠 ⛳ (John Gray
Hotel ★★64% Kilspindie House Hotel, Main St,
ABERLADY ☎(08757) 682 26⇨🐦

MUSSELBURGH
Map 6 G2

Musselburgh ☎ 031-665 2005
Monktonhall (1m S on B6415)
Testing parkland course with natural hazards including trees and a burn, easy walking.
18 holes, 6600yds, Par 72, SSS 72, Course record 65. Membership 500.

Visitors welcome must contact in advance Societies welcome (☎)
Green fees £14 per day (£18 WE)
Facilities ⊗ 🦶 🍺 ♀ ⛳ 🏠 ⛳ (Tom Stangoe
Hotel ★★★63% Donmaree Hotel, 21 Mayfield
Gardens, EDINBURGH ☎031-667 3641 9⇨🐦
Annexe:8rm(3⇨2🐦)

Musselburgh Old Course ☎ 031-655 2005
Millhill (1m E of town off A1)
A links type course.
9 holes, 2371yds, Par 33, SSS 33, Course record 67. Membership 70.

Visitors welcome (ex WE) Societies welcome (☎)
Green fees Not confirmed
Facilities ♀ ⛳
Hotel ★★★63% Donmaree Hotel, 21 Mayfield
Gardens, EDINBURGH ☎031-667 3641 9⇨🐦
Annexe:8rm(3⇨2🐦)

NORTH BERWICK
Map 6 H2

East Links ☎ (0620) 2726
(E side of town off A198)
Coastal course on the south shores of Firth of Forth, opposite the famous Bass Rock Island.
18 holes, 6086yds, Par 69, SSS 69. Membership 500.

Visitors welcome Societies welcome

Green fees £9.50 per day; £6 per round (£12.50/£8.50 WE)
Facilities ⊗ ⓑ ▣ ♀ △ 🏠 ⛳
Hotel ★★56% Point Garry Hotel, West Bay Rd, NORTH BERWICK ☎(0620) 2380 16rm(5⇄6🏠)

Glen ☎ (0620) 2221
East Links, Tantallon Ter (E side of town centre)
An interesting course with a good variety of holes. The view of the town, the Firth of Forth and the Bass Rock are breathtaking.
18 holes, 6079yds, Par 69, SSS 69, Course record 65. Membership 500.

Visitors welcome Societies welcome (☎)
Green fees £9 per day; £6 per round (£12.50/£8.50 WE)
Facilities ⊗ ⓑ ▣ ♀ △ 🏠 ⛳
Hotel ★★61% Nether Abbey Hotel, 20 Dirleton Av, NORTH BERWICK ☎(0620) 2802 16rm(4⇄6🏠)

North Berwick
☎ (0620) 2135
New Clubhouse, Beach Rd (W side of town on A198)
Another of East Lothian's famous courses, the links at North Berwick, is still popular. The great hole on the course is the 15th, the famous 'Redan', selected for televisions best 18 in the UK. There is also a 9-hole course for children.
18 holes, 6315yds, Par 71, SSS 70. Membership 500.

SCORE CARD: White Tees					
Hole	Yds	Par	Hole	Yds	Par
1	328	4	10	161	3
2	431	4	11	499	5
3	460	4	12	389	4
4	171	3	13	365	4
5	373	4	14	376	4
6	160	3	15	192	3
7	354	4	16	381	4
8	488	5	17	421	4
9	492	5	18	274	4
Out	3257	36	In	3058	35
			Totals	6315	71

Visitors welcome (ex Sat) must contact in advance Societies welcome (☎)
Green fees Not confirmed
Facilities ⊗ ⓜ by prior arrangement ⓑ ▣ ♀ △ 🏠 ⛳ ⓕ D Huish
Hotel ★★★64% The Marine Hotel, Cromwell Rd, NORTH BERWICK ☎(0620) 2406 83⇄🏠

Glencorse ☎ (0968) 77177
Milton Bridge (1.5m N on A701)
Picturesque parkland course with burn running through and many interesting holes. Testing 5th hole (237 yds) par 3.
18 holes, 5205yds, Par 64, SSS 66, Course record 61. Membership 620.

Visitors welcome (restricted WE) must contact in advance Societies welcome (Tue-Thu only ☎)
Green fees £15 per day; £10 per round
Facilities ⊗ ⓜ by prior arrangement ⓑ ▣ ♀ △ 🏠 ⛳ ⓕ Cliffe Jones
Hotel ★★★56% Braid Hills Hotel, 134 Braid Rd, Braid Hills, EDINBURGH ☎031-447 8888 68⇄🏠

Royal Musselburgh ☎ (0875) 810276
Prestongrange House (W side of town centre off A59)
Parkland course overlooking Firth of Forth. Snooker.
18 holes, 6237yds, Par 70, SSS 70. Membership 900.

Visitors welcome (restricted WE) must contact in advance Societies welcome (by letter)
Green fees £20 per day; £12 per round
Facilities ⊗ ⓜ by prior arrangement ⓑ ▣ ♀ △ 🏠 ⛳ ⓕ Allan Minto
Hotel ★★64% Kilspindie House Hotel, Main St, ABERLADY ☎(08757) 682 26⇄🏠

Ratho Park ☎ 031-333 1252
(.75m E, N of A71)
Undulating parkland course, easy walking. Snooker.
18 holes, 5900yds, Par 69, SSS 68, Course record 63. Membership 720.

Visitors welcome must contact in advance Societies welcome (by letter)
Green fees £20 per day (£27 WE)
Facilities ⊗ ⓜ ⓑ ▣ ♀ △ 🏠 ⓕ Alan Pate
Hotel ★★★65% Post House Hotel, Corstorphine Rd, EDINBURGH ☎031-334 0390 207⇄

Dundas Parks ☎ 031-331 1601
3 Loch Place (1m S on B8000)
Parkland course situated on the estate of Lady Jane Stewart-Clark. For 18 holes, the 9 are played twice, yardage and par doubled.
9 holes, 6024yds, Par 70, SSS 69, Course record 65. Membership 500.

Visitors welcome Member must accompany must contact in advance Societies welcome (☎ or by letter)
Green fees £2.50 per day
Facilities △
Hotel ★★★60% Forth Bridges Moat House, Forth Bridge, SOUTH QUEENSFERRY ☎031-331 1199 108⇄🏠

Uphall ☎ (0506) 852414
(W side of village on A899)
Windy parkland course, easy walking.
18 holes, 5567yds, Par 69, SSS 67. Membership 500.

Visitors welcome (restricted WE until 1100)
Green fees Not confirmed
Facilities ♀ △
Hotel ★★★65% Houstoun House Hotel, UPHALL ☎(0506) 853831 28⇄🏠 Annexe:2⇄

Each golf course entry has a recommended hotel. For a wider choice of places to stay, consult *AA Hotels and Restaurants in Britain* or *AA-inspected Bed and Breakfast in Britain*.

WEST CALDER
Map 6 F2

Harburn ☎ (0506) 871256
Moorland, reasonably flat.
18 holes, 5853yds, Par 69, SSS 68, Course record 62.
Membership 600.

Visitors welcome (no tee after 1430) Societies welcome
(by letter)
Green fees £12.50 per day (£17.50 WE)
Facilities ⊗ ﷽ (Fri and Sat only) ⓛ ⓟ ♀ ⏃ 📷
ⓕ Roy Redpath
Hotel ★★★60% Hilton National, Almondvale East,
LIVINGSTON ☎(0506) 31222 120⋔

WHITBURN
Map 6 F2

Polkemmet Country Park ☎ (0501) 43905
(2m W off B7066)
Public course. Parkland and very picturesque. Fifteen
bay floodlit driving range.
9 holes, 2969mtrs, Par 37.

Visitors welcome Societies welcome (☎)
Green fees £1.70 per round (£2.20 Sun)
Facilities ⊗ ﷽ ⓛ ⓟ ♀
Hotel ★★★⋔65% Houstoun House Hotel, UPHALL
☎(0506) 853831 28⋍⋔ Annexe:2⋍

STRATHCLYDE

AIRDRIE
Map 6 E2

Airdrie ☎ (0236) 62195
Rochsoles (1m N on B802)
Picturesque parkland course. Snooker.
18 holes, 6004yds, Par 69, SSS 69, Course record 64.
Membership 640.

Visitors welcome (with M only WE & BH) must contact
in advance ✉ Societies welcome (by letter)
Green fees £15 per day; £10 per round
Facilities ⊗ ﷽ ⓛ ⓟ ♀ ⏃ 📷 ⓕ A McCloskey
Hotel ★★64% Garfield House Hotel, Cumbernauld Rd,
STEPPS ☎041-779 2111 27⋍⋔

Easter Moffat ☎ (0236) 842878
Mansion House, Plains (2m E on old Edinburgh-Glasgow
road)
Moorland/parkland course.
18 holes, 6221yds, Par 72, SSS 70, Course record 67.
Membership 450.

Visitors welcome (wkdays only) Societies welcome (☎)
Green fees Not confirmed
Facilities ⊗ ﷽ by prior arrangement ⓛ and ⓟ (all
day) ♀ ⏃ 📷 ⓕ Brian Dunbar
Hotel ★★64% Garfield House Hotel, Cumbernauld Rd,
STEPPS ☎041-779 2111 27⋍⋔

We make every effort to provide accurate information, but some details may change after we
go to print.

AYR
Map 6 D4

Belleisle ☎ (0292) 41258
Belleisle Park (2m S on A719)
Parkland course with beautiful sea views. First-class
conditions. Accommodation.
Belleisle Course 18 holes, 6540yds, Par 70, SSS 71.
Seafield Course 18 holes, 5244yds, Par 66, SSS 66.

Visitors welcome must contact in advance Societies
welcome
Green fees Not confirmed
Facilities ♀ ⏃ 📷 ⓣ ⓕ
Hotel ★★★61% Pickwick Hotel, 19 Racecourse Rd,
AYR ☎(0292) 260111 15⋍⋔

Dalmilling ☎ (0292) 263893
Westwood Av (1.5m E of town centre off A719)
Meadowland course, with easy walking.
18 holes, 5752yds, Par 69, SSS 68. Membership 140.

Visitors welcome must contact in advance Societies
welcome
Green fees £8.80 per day; £5.50 per round (£11/£7.50
WE)
Facilities ⊗ ﷽ ⓛ ⓟ (no catering Tue) ♀ ⏃ 📷 ⓣ ⓕ
Hotel ★★★60% Carlton Toby Hotel, PRESTWICK
☎(0292) 76811 39⋍⋔

Seafield ☎ (0292) 41258
Doonfoot Rd (2m S on A719)
Public self-starting course of parkland type.
Accommodation.
18 holes, 5457yds, Par 66, SSS 66, Course record 64.

Visitors welcome Societies welcome (by letter)
Green fees Not confirmed
Facilities ⊗ ﷽ ⓛ ⓟ ♀ ⏃ 📷 ⓣ ⓕ J S Easey
Hotel ★★★64% Caledonian Hotel, Dalblair Rd, AYR
☎(0292) 269331 114⋍

BALMORE
Map 6 E2

Balmore ☎ (0360) 20240
(N off A807)
Parkland course with fine views.
18 holes, 5516yds, Par 66, SSS 67. Membership 700.

Visitors welcome Member must accompany must
contact in advance Societies welcome
Green fees £12 per day; £10 per round
Facilities ⊗ ﷽ ⓛ ⓟ ♀ ⏃ 📷
Hotel ★★★59% Black Bull Thistle Hotel, Main St,
MILNGAVIE ☎041-956 2291 27⋍⋔

BARASSIE
Map 6 D4

Kilmarnock (Barassie)☎ Troon (0292) 313920
29 Hillhouse Rd (E side of village on B746)
A magnificent seaside course, relatively flat with
much heather. The turf and greens are quite
unequalled. The 15th is a testing par 3 at 220 yards.
18 holes, 6473yds, Par 71, SSS 71, Course record 63.
Membership 500.

Visitors welcome (with M only Wed & WE) must contact in advance Societies welcome (bookings to Club Secretary)
Green fees £27 per day (Apr-Sep), £16 (Oct-Mar)
Facilities ⊗ ⫛ by prior arrangement ⮂ ⬤ ♀ ⌂
🏠 ⚑ (William R Lockie
Hotel ★★★★65% Marine Highland Hotel, TROON
☎(0292) 314444 72⇱

BARRHEAD   Map 6 D3

Fereneze ☎ 041-881 1519
Fereneze Av (NW side of town off B774)
Moorland course, good view at the end of a hard climb.
18 holes, 5821yds, Par 70, SSS 68, Course record 64.
Membership 700.

Visitors welcome (ex WE) Member must accompany must contact in advance ✉ Societies welcome (by letter)
Green fees £11/£12 per day (wkdays)
Facilities ⊗ ⫛ ⮂ ⬤ ♀ ⌂ 🏠 ⚑ (Andrew Armstrong
Hotel ★★55% Dalmeny Park Hotel, Lochlibo Rd, BARRHEAD ☎041-881 9211 18rm(3⇱10🐾)

BEARSDEN   Map 6 D2

Bearsden ☎ 041-942 2351
Thorn Rd (1m W off A809)
Parkland course, with easy walking and views over city.
9 holes, 6014yds, Par 68, SSS 69, Course record 64.
Membership 550.

Visitors welcome Member must accompany must contact in advance Societies welcome (by letter at least 1 mth prior)
Green fees Not confirmed
Facilities ⊗ ⮂ ⬤ ♀ ⌂ 🏠
Hotel ★★★59% Black Bull Thistle Hotel, Main St, MILNGAVIE ☎041-956 2291 27⇱🐾

Douglas Park ☎ 041-942 2220
Hillfoot (E side of town on A81)
Parkland course.
18 holes, 5957yds, Par 69, SSS 69, Course record 64.
Membership 900.

Visitors welcome (ex Mon & Fri) Member must accompany must contact in advance Societies welcome (☎)
Green fees £15 per day; £12 per round
Facilities ⊗ ⫛ by prior arrangement ⮂ ⬤ ♀ ⌂ 🏠 ⚑ (David Scott
Hotel ★★★59% Black Bull Thistle Hotel, Main St, MILNGAVIE ☎041-956 2291 27⇱🐾

For a full list of the golf courses included in this book, check with the index on page 284

Glasgow ☎ 041-942 2011
Killermont (SE side off A81)
One of the finest parkland courses in Scotland. Private members club.
18 holes, 5968yds, Par 70, SSS 69, Course record 63.
Membership 760.

Visitors welcome Member must accompany must contact in advance ✉
Green fees £30 per round
Facilities ♀ (M guests only) ⌂ 🏠 (J Steven
Hotel ★★★59% Black Bull Thistle Hotel, Main St, MILNGAVIE ☎041-956 2291 27⇱🐾

Windyhill ☎ 041-942 2349
Windyhill (2m NW off B8050)
Hard walking moorland course; testing hole: 12th (par 4).
18 holes, 6257yds, Par 71, SSS 70, Course record 66.
Membership 675.

Visitors welcome (ex WE) must contact in advance Societies welcome (apply to secretary in writing)
Green fees Day ticket £10
Facilities ⊗ ⫛ ⮂ ⬤ ♀ ⌂ 🏠 (R Collinson
Hotel ★★★59% Black Bull Thistle Hotel, Main St, MILNGAVIE ☎041-956 2291 27⇱🐾

BEITH   Map 6 D3

Beith ☎ (05055) 3166
Threepwood Rd (1.5m NE off A737)
Moorland course, with panoramic views over 7 counties.
9 holes, 5580yds, Par 68, SSS 67. Membership 400.

Visitors welcome (ex WE) Societies welcome
Green fees Not confirmed
Facilities ♀ ⌂
Hotel ★★★▲75% Chapeltoun House Hotel, STEWARTON ☎(0560) 82696 8⇱🐾

BELLSHILL   Map 6 E3

Bellshill ☎ (0698) 745124
Community Rd, Orbiston (1m SE off A721)
Parkland course.
18 holes, 6604yds, Par 72, SSS 72, Course record 68.
Membership 600.

Visitors welcome Societies welcome
Green fees £11 per day (£15 WE & BH)
Facilities ⊗ ⫛ by prior arrangement ⮂ ⬤ ♀ ⌂
Hotel ★★58% Silvertrees Hotel, Silverwells Crescent, BOTHWELL ☎(0698) 852311 7⇱ Annexe:19⇱🐾

BIGGAR   Map 6 F3

Biggar Municipal ☎ (0899) 20618
The Park, Broughton Rd (S side of town)
Flat parkland course, easy walking and fine views. Tennis.
18 holes, 5400yds, Par 67, SSS 66, Course record 61.
Membership 200.

▶

Visitors welcome must contact in advance Societies welcome (☎ (0899) 20319)
Green fees £5.50 per day (£7.50 WE)
Facilities ⊗ ⑂ (parties by prior arrangement) 占 ▆ (catering daily Apr-Sep, WE in winter) ♀ (WE only in winter) 占 ▥
Hotel ★★★64% Peebles Hydro Hotel, PEEBLES ☎(0721) 20602 134⇔♠

BISHOPBRIGGS Map 6 E2

Bishopbriggs ☎ 041-772 1810
Brackenbrae Rd (.5m NW off A803)
Parkland course. Snooker.
18 holes, 6041yds, Par 69, SSS 69. Membership 659.

Visitors welcome Member must accompany must contact in advance ⊠ Societies welcome (by letter)
Green fees Not confirmed
Facilities ⊗ ⑂ 占 ▆ ♀ (1100-2300) 占 ▥
Hotel ★★★59% Black Bull Thistle Hotel, Main St, MILNGAVIE ☎041-956 2291 27⇔♠

Cawder ☎ 041-772 5167
Cadder Rd (1m NE off A803)
Two parkland courses; Cawder course hilly, with 5th, 9th, 10th, 11th-testing holes. Keir course flat.
Cawder Course 18 holes, 6295yds, Par 70, SSS 71, Course record 65. Keir Course 18 holes, 5877yds, Par 68, SSS 68. Membership 1150.

Visitors welcome (wkdays only) must contact in advance Societies welcome (by letter)
Green fees £18.50 per day
Facilities ⊗ ⑂ 占 ▆ ♀ 占 ▥ ⚐ ⟨
Hotel ★★★59% Black Bull Thistle Hotel, Main St, MILNGAVIE ☎041-956 2291 27⇔♠

BISHOPTON Map 6 D2

Erskine ☎ (0505) 862302
(.75 NE off B815)
Parkland course.
18 holes, 6287yds, Par 71, SSS 70. Membership 700.

Visitors welcome Member must accompany Societies welcome
Green fees Not confirmed
Facilities ♀ 占 ▥ ⚐ ⟨
Hotel ★★★64% Crest Hotel-Erskine Bridge, North Barr, ERSKINE ☎041-812 0123 168⇔♠

BONHILL Map 6 D2

Vale of Leven ☎ Alexandria (0389) 52351
North Field Rd (E side of town off A813)
Moorland course, very scenic, tricky with many natural hazards - gorse, burns, trees.
18 holes, 5162yds, Par 67, SSS 66, Course record 60. Membership 550.

Visitors welcome (ex Sat Apr-Sep) Societies welcome (by letter)

Green fees £10 per day; £6 per round (£12.50/£10 WE)
Facilities ⊗ ⑂ 占 ▆ ♀ 占 ▥
Hotel ★★69% Dumbuck Hotel, Glasgow Rd, DUMBARTON ☎(0389) 34336 22⇔♠

BOTHWELL Map 6 E3

Bothwell Castle ☎ (0698) 853177
Blantyre Rd (NW of village off B7071)
Flat parkland course.
18 holes, 6243yds, Par 71, SSS 70, Course record 64. Membership 1200.

Visitors welcome (Mon-Fri 0800-1530) Societies welcome (by letter)
Green fees £18 per day, £12 per round
Facilities ⊗ ⑂ 占 ▆ ♀ 占 ▥ ⚐ ⟨ W Walker
Hotel ★★58% Silvertrees Hotel, Silverwells Crescent, BOTHWELL ☎(0698) 852311 7⇔ Annexe:19⇔♠

BURNSIDE Map 6 E3

Blairbeth ☎ 041-634 3355
(S off A749)
Parkland course.
18 holes, 5481yds, Par 70, SSS 67, Course record 64. Membership 400.

Visitors welcome (introduced by M or arrangement with Sec) Member must accompany Societies welcome (by letter)
Green fees £9 per day; £5 per round
Facilities ⊗ ⑂ 占 ▆ ♀ 占
Hotel ★★★67% Macdonald Thistle Hotel, Eastwood Toll, GIFFNOCK ☎041-638 2225 56⇔♠

Cathkin Braes ☎ 041-634 6605
Cathkin Rd (1m S on B759)
Moorland course, prevailing westerly wind, small loch hazard at 5th hole.
18 holes, 6266yds, Par 70, SSS 71, Course record 65. Membership 900.

Visitors welcome (ex WE) must contact in advance ⊠ Societies welcome (by letter)
Green fees £20 per day; £14 per round
Facilities ⊗ ⑂ 占 ▆ ♀ 占 ▥ ⚐ ⟨ Stephen Bree
Hotel ★★61% Royal Hotel, 1 Glaisnock St, CUMNOCK ☎(0290) 20822 11rm(2⇔1♠)

CAMBUSLANG Map 6 E2

Cambuslang ☎ 041-641 3130
Westburn Dr (.25m N off A724)
Parkland course.
9 holes, 6072yds, Par 70, SSS 69, Course record 65. Membership 200.

Visitors welcome must contact in advance ⊠ Societies welcome (ex WE apply by letter)
Green fees £7.50 per day
Facilities ⊗ 占 ▆ ♀ 占
Hotel ★★58% Silvertrees Hotel, Silverwells Crescent, BOTHWELL ☎(0698) 852311 7⇔ Annexe:19⇔♠

CARDROSS   Map 6 D2

Cardross ☎ (0389) 841213
Main Rd (In centre of village on A814)
Undulating parkland course, testing with good views.
18 holes, 6496yds, Par 71, SSS 71, Course record 65.
Membership 800.

Visitors welcome (ex WE unless introduced by M)
Societies welcome (by letter)
Green fees £20 per day ; £13 per round
Facilities ⊗ ⅲ by prior arrangement Ⅼ ⲙ ♀ ⌂ 🛅
🍴 ⌡ Robert Craig
Hotel ★★★61% Commodore Toby Hotel, 112 West
Clyde St, HELENSBURGH ☎(0436) 76924 45⊶

CARLUKE   Map 6 E3

Carluke ☎ (0555) 71070
Mauldslie Rd, Hallcraig (1m W off A73)
Parkland course with views over the Clyde Valley.
Testing 11th hole, par 3.
18 holes, 5805yds, Par 70, SSS 68, Course record 64.
Membership 460.

Visitors welcome (until 1630 weekdays only) must
contact in advance ✉ Societies welcome (by letter)
Green fees £12 per day ; £8 per round
Facilities ⊗ ⅲ by prior arrangement Ⅼⲙ♀⌂🛅
🍴 ⌡ Andrew Brooks
Hotel ★★★61% Popinjay Hotel, Lanark Rd,
ROSEBANK ☎(055586) 441 40⊶🐾

CARNWATH   Map 6 F3

Carnwath ☎ (0555) 840251
1 Main St (W side of village on A70)
Picturesque parkland course slightly hilly but easy
walking.
18 holes, 5955yds, Par 70, SSS 69, Course record 65.
Membership 380.

Visitors welcome (restricted after 1700) Societies
welcome (☎)
Green fees £13 (£15 Sun & BH)
Facilities ⊗ high tea Ⅼⲙ♀ (all day) ⌂🛅
Hotel ★★★61% Popinjay Hotel, Lanark Rd,
ROSEBANK ☎(055586) 441 40⊶🐾

CARRADALE   Map 6 B3

Carradale ☎ (05833) 387
(S side of village)
Pleasant and not too testing seaside holiday course with
extensive views. Natural terrain and small greens are
the most difficult natural hazards. Described as the most
sporting 9-hole golf course in Britain. Testing 7th hole
(240 yds), par 3. Accommodation.
9 holes, 2387yds, Par 66, SSS 63, Course record 62.
Membership 212.

Visitors welcome Societies welcome
Green fees £4 per day

Facilities 🛅
Hotel ★★65% Carradale Hotel, CARRADALE ☎(05833)
223 12rm(10⊶🐾) Annexe :5⊶🐾

CLARKSTON   Map 6 D3

Cathcart Castle ☎ 041-638 0082
Mearns Rd (.75m SW off A726)
Parkland course, with undulating terrain.
18 holes, 5832yds, Par 68, SSS 68. Membership 990.

Visitors welcome Member must accompany Societies
welcome (Tue & Thu only)
Green fees Not confirmed
Facilities ⌂ 🛅 🍴 ⌡ D Naylor
Hotel ★★★67% Macdonald Thistle Hotel, Eastwood
Toll, GIFFNOCK ☎041-638 2225 56⊶🐾

CLYDEBANK   Map 6 D2

Clydebank Municipal ☎ 041-952 6372
Overtoun Rd (2m NW of town centre)
Hilly, parkland course with tough finishing holes, not
suitable for carts and trolleys.
18 holes, 5349yds, Par 67, SSS 66.

Visitors welcome Societies welcome
Green fees £3 (£4 Sun & BH)
Facilities Cafeteria ⌂ 🛅 🍴 ⌡ Richard Bowman
Hotel ★★★64% Stakis Normandy Hotel, Inchinnan
Rd, RENFREW ☎041-886 4100 141⊶🐾

COATBRIDGE   Map 6 E2

Drumpellier ☎ (0236) 24139
Drumpellier Av (.75m W off A89)
Parkland course.
18 holes, 6227yds, Par 71, SSS 70, Course record 63.
Membership 700.

Visitors welcome (ex WE & PH) must contact in
advance Societies welcome (☎ for details)
Green fees £20 per day ; £14 per round
Facilities ⊗ ⅲ Ⅼⲙ♀⌂🛅⌡ I Collins
Hotel ★★★60% Bothwell Bridge Hotel, 89 Main St,
BOTHWELL ☎(0698) 852246 41⊶🐾

CUMBERNAULD   Map 6 E2

Dullatur ☎ (0236) 723230
Dullatur (1.5m N)
Parkland course, with natural hazards and wind.
Testing 17th hole, par 5. Snooker.
18 holes, 6219yds, Par 70, SSS 70. Membership 570.

Visitors welcome (ex competition days, with M only
WE) must contact in advance Societies welcome (by
letter)
Green fees £10 per day ; £6 per round
Facilities ⊗ ⅲ by prior arrangement Ⅼⲙ♀⌂🛅
🍴 ⌡ Duncan Sinclair
Hotel ★★★62% Stakis Park Hotel, Arnot Hill,
Camelon Rd, FALKIRK ☎(0324) 28331 55⊶🐾

Palacerigg ☎ (0236) 734969
Palacerigg Country Park (2m S)
Parkland course.
18 holes, 6444yds, Par 72, SSS 71, Course record 66.
Membership 400.

Visitors welcome (ex WE) must contact in advance ✉
Societies welcome (☎)
Green fees £6 per day (£7 WE)
Facilities ⊗ ⫪ ⪢ 💻 (catering daily ex Mon-Tue Nov-Mar) ♀ △
Hotel ★★★62% Stakis Park Hotel, Arnot Hill,
Camelon Rd, FALKIRK ☎(0324) 28331 55↩︎🛄

Westerwood Hotel Golf & Country Club
☎ (0236) 457171
St Andrews Dr (adjacent to A80)
Undulating parkland/woodland course designed by
Dave Thomas and Seve Ballesteros. Hotel
accommodation and numerous sports and leisure
facilities.
18 holes, 6721yds, Par 73, SSS 73. Membership 400.

Visitors welcome must contact in advance Societies
welcome (☎)
Green fees £30 per day; £20 per round (£40/£25 WE)
Facilities ⊗ ⫪ ⪢ 💻 ♀ △ 🔒 ⌇ ⌇
Hotel ★★★62% Stakis Park Hotel, Arnot Hill,
Camelon Rd, FALKIRK ☎(0324) 28331 55↩︎🛄

DUMBARTON

Map 6 D2

Dumbarton ☎ (0389) 32830
Broadmeadow (.25m N off A814)
Flat parkland course. Testing holes: 4th (par 4), 15th
(par 5).
18 holes, 5992yds, Par 71, SSS 69, Course record 62.
Membership 500.

Visitors welcome (ex WE & PH) Societies welcome
(advance booking with secretary)
Green fees £10 per day
Facilities ⊗ ⫪ by prior arrangement ⪢ ♀ △
Hotel ★★69% Dumbuck Hotel, Glasgow Rd,
DUMBARTON ☎(0389) 34336 22↩︎

DUNOON

Map 6 C2

Cowal ☎ (0369) 5673
Ardenslate Rd (1m N)
Moorland course. Panoramic views of Clyde Estuary
and surrounding hills.
18 holes, 6251yds, Par 70, SSS 70, Course record 64.
Membership 500.

Visitors welcome (h'cap cert preferred or club
membership) Societies welcome (☎)
Green fees £12 per day; £8.50 per round (£16.50/£13
WE)
Facilities ⊗ ⫪ ⪢ 💻 ♀ △ 🔒 ⌇ ⌇ Russell D Weir
Hotel ★★78% Enmore Hotel, Marine Pde, Kirn,
DUNOON ☎(0369) 2230 & 2148 12↩︎🛄

EAGLESHAM

Map 6 D3

Bonnyton ☎ (03553) 2781
(.25m SW off B764)
Windy, moorland turf course.
18 holes, 6252yds, Par 72, SSS 71. Membership 950.

Visitors welcome (☎ for details) must contact in
advance Societies welcome (☎)
Green fees £14 per day
Facilities △ 🔒 ⌇ ⌇
Hotel ★★★62% Bruce Hotel, Cornwall St, EAST
KILBRIDE ☎(03552) 29771 80↩︎🛄

EAST KILBRIDE

Map 6 E3

East Kilbride ☎ (03552) 20913
Chapelside Rd, Nerston (.5m N off A7)
Parkland course, with hard walking. Very windy.
Testing 7th, 9th and 14th holes.
18 holes, 6419yds, Par 71, SSS 71. Membership 750.

Visitors welcome Member must accompany Societies
welcome (☎)
Green fees £15 per day; £10 per round
Facilities ⊗ ⫪ ⪢ 💻 ♀ △ 🔒 ⌇ Alastair R Taylor
Hotel ★★★62% Bruce Hotel, Cornwall St, EAST
KILBRIDE ☎(03552) 29771 80↩︎🛄

Torrance House ☎ (03552) 48638
Calderglen Country Park, Strathaven Rd (1.5m SE of
Kilbride on A726)
A parkland course.
18 holes, 6415yds, Par 72, Course record 64. Membership
1000.

Visitors welcome (Booking system - 6 days notice
required)
Green fees £8 per round
Facilities Catering by prior arrangement ♀ 🔒 ⌇ John
D Dunlop
Hotel ★★★62% Bruce Hotel, Cornwall St, EAST
KILBRIDE ☎(03552) 29771 80↩︎🛄

GALSTON

Map 6 D3

Loudoun ☎ (0563) 821993
Edinburgh Rd (NE side of town on A71)
Pleasant, testing parkland course.
18 holes, 5800yds, Par 67, SSS 68, Course record 61.
Membership 750.

Visitors welcome (ex WE) must contact in advance
Societies welcome (☎)
Green fees £16 per day; £12 per round
Facilities ⊗ ⫪ by prior arrangement ⪢ 💻 ♀ (times
vary) △
Hotel ★★★55% Howard Park Hotel, Glasgow Rd,
KILMARNOCK ☎(0563) 31211 46↩︎

Opening times of bar and catering facilities vary
from place to place – it is wise to check in
advance of your visit.

GARTCOSH   Map 6 E2

Mount Ellen ☎ (0236) 872277
(.75m N off A752)
Downland course with 73 bunkers. Testing hole: 10th
('Bedlay'), 156 yds, par 3.
18 holes, 5525yds, Par 68, SSS 68, Course record 60.
Membership 500.

Visitors welcome (Mon-Fri 0900-1600) must contact in
advance Societies welcome (☎)
Green fees £7 per round
Facilities ⊗ ⫫ (Fri and Sat) ⌂ 🍺 ♀ 🛆 🏠 𝄋 Gary
Brooks
Hotel ★★64% Garfield House Hotel, Cumbernauld Rd,
STEPPS ☎041-779 2111 27🛌🐾

GIRVAN   Map 6 C5

Girvan ☎ (0465) 4272
Golf Course Rd (N side of town off A77)
Municipal seaside and parkland course (private club).
Testing 17th hole (223-yds) uphill, par 3. Good views.
18 holes, 5098yds, Par 64, SSS 65. Membership 175.

Visitors welcome Societies welcome (☎ ex Jul & Aug)
Green fees Not confirmed
Facilities ♀ 🛆
Hotel ★★63% King's Arms Hotel, Dalrymple St,
GIRVAN ☎(0465) 3322 25🛌🐾

GLASGOW   Map 6 E2

Alexandra ☎ 041-556 3211
Alexandra Park, Alexandra Pde (2m E of city centre off
M8/A8)
Parkland course. Designed by Graham McArthur.
9 holes, 2800yds, Par 34. Membership 250.

Visitors welcome Societies welcome
Green fees £1.40 per day (£1.70 WE)
Facilities 🛆
Hotel ★★★★63% Stakis Grosvenor Hotel, 1/10
Grosvenor Ter, Great Western Rd, GLASGOW ☎041-339
8811 95🛌🐾

Cowglen ☎ 041-632 0556
Barrhead Rd (4.5m SW of city centre on B762)
Parkland course with good views over Clyde valley to
Campsie Hills.
18 holes, 5976yds, Par 69, SSS 69, Course record 64.
Membership 775.

Visitors welcome (visitors play on shorter course) must
contact in advance ✉ Societies welcome (☎)
Green fees £18 per day; £12 per round
Facilities ⊗ ⫫ ⌂ 🍺 ♀ 🛆 🏠 𝄋 John McTear
Hotel ★★★67% Macdonald Thistle Hotel, Eastwood
Toll, GIFFNOCK ☎041-638 2225 56🛌🐾

If you know of a golf course, not in this guide
already, which welcomes visitors, we would be
pleased to hear about it.

Haggs Castle ☎ 041-427 0480
70 Dumbreck Rd, Dumbreck (2.5m SW of city centre
on B768)
Wooded, parkland course where Scottish National
Championships and the Glasgow and Scottish Open
have been held. Quite difficult.
18 holes, 6464yds, Par 72, SSS 71. Membership 1000.

Visitors welcome Member must accompany must
contact in advance ✉ Societies welcome (☎)
Green fees £24 per day; £16 per round
Facilities ⊗ ⫫ ⌂ 🍺 ♀ 🛆 🏠 ⚐ 𝄋 Jim McAlister
Hotel ★★58% Sherbrooke Hotel, 11 Sherbrooke
Av, Pollokshields, GLASGOW ☎041-427 4227 10🛌🐾
Annexe:11🛌🐾

Kirkhill ☎ 041-641 8499
Greenless Rd, Cambuslang (5m SE of city centre off
A749)
Meadowland course designed by James Braid.
18 holes, 5889yds, Par 69, SSS 69, Course record 63.
Membership 650.

Visitors welcome (with M only WE) must contact in
advance Societies welcome (☎)
Green fees £15 per day; £10 per round
Facilities ⊗ (ex Mon) ⫫ by prior arrangement ⌂ (ex
Mon and Thu) 🍺 ♀ 🛆
Hotel ★★★60% Stuart Hotel, 2 Cornwall Way, EAST
KILBRIDE ☎(03552) 21161 39🛌🐾

Knightswood Park ☎ 041-959 2131
Lincoln Av (4m W of city centre off A82)
Parkland course within easy reach of Glasgow. Two dog
legs.
9 holes, 2700yds, Par 33, SSS 33, Course record 29.
Membership 60.

Visitors welcome Societies welcome
Green fees £1.70
Facilities 🛆
Hotel ★★★60% Jurys Pond Hotel, Great Western Rd,
GLASGOW ☎041-334 8161 132🛌🐾

Lethamhill ☎ 041-770 6220
1240 Cumbernauld Rd, Millerston (3m NE of city centre
on A80)
Municipal parkland course.
18 holes, 5859yds, Par 70, SSS 68.

Visitors welcome ✉ Societies welcome
Green fees Not confirmed
Facilities 🛆
Hotel ★★64% Garfield House Hotel, Cumbernauld Rd,
STEPPS ☎041-779 2111 27🛌🐾

Linn Park ☎ 041-637 5871
Simshill Rd (4m S of city centre off B766)
Municipal parkland course with six par 3's in outward
half.
18 holes, 4952yds, Par 65, SSS 65, Course record 61.
Membership 80.

Visitors welcome

▶

Green fees £2.75 per day (£3.25 WE)
Facilities △
Hotel ★★★62% Bruce Hotel, Cornwall St, EAST
KILBRIDE ☎(03552) 29771 80⇥↑

Pollok ☎ 041-632 1080
90 Barrhead Rd (4m SW of city centre on A762)
Parkland course with woods and river.
18 holes, 6257yds, Par 71, SSS 70. Membership 460.

Visitors welcome (with M only wkdays) must contact
in advance ⊠ Societies welcome (by letter, Mon-Fri
only)
Green fees £23 per round
Facilities ⊗ ⊪ by prior arrangement ⊾ ⊒ ♀ △
Hotel ★★★66% Tinto Firs Thistle Hotel, 470
Kilmarnock Rd, GLASGOW ☎041-637 2353 28⇥↑

Williamwood ☎ 041-637 2715
Clarkston Rd (5m S of city centre on B767)
Inland course, fairly hilly with wooded areas, a small
lake and pond.
18 holes, 5878yds, SSS 68, Course record 61. Membership 450.

Visitors welcome Member must accompany ⊠
Green fees Not confirmed
Facilities ☎ ℓ J Gardner
Hotel ★★★67% Macdonald Thistle Hotel, Eastwood
Toll, GIFFNOCK ☎041-638 2225 56⇥↑

Gourock ☎ (0475) 31001
Cowal View (SW side of town off A770)
Moorland course. Testing 8th hole, par 5. Magnificent
views over Firth of Clyde.
*18 holes, 6492yds, Par 73, SSS 71, Course record 64.
Membership 650.*

Visitors welcome (introduction or with M)
Green fees Not confirmed
Facilities ⊪ ⊾ ⊒ ♀ △ ☎ ⊓ ℓ R M Collinson
Hotel ★★★⊭60% Manor Park Hotel, SKELMORLIE
☎(0475) 520832 7rm(5⇥1↑)

Greenock ☎ (0475) 20793
Forsyth St (SW side of town off A770)
Testing heathland course with panoramic views of
Clyde Estuary. There is also a 9-hole course.
*18 holes, 5383yds, Par 68, SSS 68, Course record 64.
Membership 730.*

Visitors welcome (ex Sat) must contact in advance ⊠
Societies welcome (☎)
Green fees £12 per day (£15 Sun & BH)
Facilities ⊗ ⊪ ⊾ ⊒ ♀ △ ☎ ℓ Graham Ross
Hotel ★★★⊭60% Manor Park Hotel, SKELMORLIE
☎(0475) 520832 7rm(5⇥1↑)

For an explanation of the symbols and
abbreviations used, see page 33.

Whinhill ☎ (0475) 21064
Beith Rd (1.5m SW off B7054)
Picturesque heathland public course.
18 holes, 5454yds, Par 66, SSS 68.

Visitors welcome (Club facilities only with member)
Green fees Not confirmed
Hotel ★★★⊭60% Manor Park Hotel, SKELMORLIE
☎(0475) 520832 7rm(5⇥1↑)

Hamilton ☎ (0698) 282872
Riccarton, Ferniegair (1.5m SE on A72)
Beautiful parkland course.
18 holes, 6281yds, Par 70, SSS 70. Membership 480.

Visitors welcome Member must accompany
Green fees Not confirmed
Facilities ♀ △ ☎ ℓ
Hotel ★★58% Silvertrees Hotel, Silverwells Crescent,
BOTHWELL ☎(0698) 852311 7⇥ Annexe:19⇥↑

Strathclyde Park ☎ (0698) 66155
Mote Hill (N side of town off B7071)
Municipal parkland course.
9 holes, 3147yds, Par 36, SSS 70. Membership 120.

Visitors welcome Societies welcome (☎)
Green fees Not confirmed
Facilities ⊗ ⊪ ⊾ ⊒ ♀ △ ☎ ℓ Ken Davidson
Hotel ★★58% Silvertrees Hotel, Silverwells Crescent,
BOTHWELL ☎(0698) 852311 7⇥ Annexe:19⇥↑

Helensburgh ☎ (0436) 74173
25 East Abercromby St (NE side of town off B832)
Sporting moorland course with superb views of Loch
Lomond and River Clyde.
*18 holes, 6058yds, Par 69, SSS 69, Course record 64.
Membership 845.*

Visitors welcome (ex WE) must contact in advance
Societies welcome (by letter)
Green fees £15 per day, £10 per round
Facilities ⊪ (Sat evening only) ⊾ ⊒ ♀ △ ☎ ⊓
ℓ Robert Farrell
Hotel ★★★61% Commodore Toby Hotel, 112 West
Clyde St, HELENSBURGH ☎(0436) 76924 45⇥

Glasgow ☎ (0294) 311347
(2m S off A737)
A lovely seaside links. The turf of the fairways and
all the greens is truly glorious and provides tireless
play. Established in 1787, this is the ninth oldest
course in the world and is a qualifying course for the
Open Championship.
18 holes, 6493yds, Par 71, SSS 71. Membership 1150.

Visitors welcome (ex WE & BH) must contact in advance ✉ Societies welcome (apply by letter)
Green fees £30 per day ; £25 per round
Facilities 🏋 💪 ♀ 🛎 🏨 ⌊ J Steven
Hotel ★★★★63% Hospitality Inn, Annick Rd, Annickwater, IRVINE ☎(0294) 74272 128⇨🏌

Irvine ☎ (0294) 78139
Bogside (N side of town off A737)
Testing links course.
18 holes, 6408yds, Par 71, SSS 71. Membership 450.

Visitors welcome must contact in advance Societies welcome (wkdays ☎)
Green fees Not confirmed
Facilities ⊗ 🍽 by prior arrangement 🏋 💪 ♀ 🛎 🏨 ⌊ Keith Erskine
Hotel ★★★★63% Hospitality Inn, Annick Rd, Annickwater, IRVINE ☎(0294) 74272 128⇨🏌

Irvine Ravenspark ☎ (0294) 79550
(N side of town on A737)
Parkland course.
18 holes, 6702yds, Par 71, SSS 71, Course record 66. Membership 400.

Visitors welcome (ex Sat 0700-1000 & 1200-1400) Societies welcome (☎)
Green fees £8 per day (£14.50 WE)
Facilities ⊗ 🍽 🏋 💪 (no catering Tue and Thu) ♀ 🛎 🏨 ⌊ Peter Bond
Hotel ★★★♨75% Chapeltoun House Hotel, STEWARTON ☎(0560) 82696 8⇨🏌

Western Gailes ☎ (0294) 311649
Gailes by Irvine (2m S off A737)
A magnificent seaside links with glorious turf and wonderful greens. The view is open across the Firth of Clyde to the neighbouring islands. It is a well-balanced course crossed by 3 burns. There are 2 par 5's, the 6th and 14th, and the 11th is a testing 445-yd, par 4, dog-leg.
18 holes, 6800yds, Par 71, SSS 72. Membership 390.

Visitors welcome (Mon, Tue, Wed & Fri) must contact in advance Societies welcome (☎ for details)
Green fees Not confirmed
Facilities ♀ 🛎
Hotel ★★★★65% Marine Highland Hotel, TROON ☎(0292) 314444 72⇨

JOHNSTONE   Map 6 D2

Cochrane Castle ☎ (0505) 20146
Scott Av (.5m W off A737)
Moorland and parkland in places, also wooded with two small streams running through the course.
18 holes, 6226yds, Par 70, SSS 70, Course record 66. Membership 580.

Visitors welcome (ex WE) must contact in advance Societies welcome (ex WE)
Green fees £14 per day ; £9 per round.

Facilities ⊗ 🍽 (ex Mon and Thu) 🏋 💪 ♀ 🛎 🏨 ⌊ Stuart Campbell
Hotel ★★★58% Glynhill Hotel & Leisure Club, Paisley Road, Renfrew, RENFREW ☎041-886 5555 125⇨🏌

Elderslie ☎ (0505) 22835
63 Main Rd, Elderslie (E side of town on A737)
Parkland course, undulating, with good views. Snooker.
18 holes, 6037yds, Par 70, SSS 69. Membership 700.

Visitors welcome (ex WE & PH) must contact in advance ✉ Societies welcome (by letter)
Green fees Not confirmed
Facilities ♀ 🛎 🏨 ⌊
Hotel ★★★58% Glynhill Hotel & Leisure Club, Paisley Road, Renfrew, RENFREW ☎041-886 5555 125⇨🏌

KILBIRNIE   Map 6 D3

Kilbirnie Place ☎ (0505) 684444
Largs Rd (1m W on A760)
Easy walking parkland course.
18 holes, 5400yds, Par 69, SSS 67. Membership 300.

Visitors welcome
Green fees Not confirmed
Facilities ♀ 🛎
Hotel ★★55% Elderslie Hotel, John St, Broomfields, LARGS ☎(0475) 686460 25rm(9⇨4🏌)

KILMACOLM   Map 6 D2

Kilmacolm ☎ (050587) 2139
Porterfield Rd (SE side of town off A761)
Moorland course, easy walking, fine views. Testing 7th, 13th and 14th holes.
18 holes, 5964yds, Par 69, SSS 68. Membership 800.

Visitors welcome must contact in advance Societies welcome (☎)
Green fees £20 per day ; £15 per round
Facilities ⊗ by prior arrangement 🍽 by prior arrangement 🏋 💪 ♀ (all day) 🛎 🏨 ⌊
Hotel ★★★♨70% Gleddoch House Hotel, LANGBANK ☎(047554) 711 33⇨🏌

KILMARNOCK   Map 6 D3

Annanhill ☎ (0563) 21644
Irvine Rd (1m W on A71)
Private golf club and municipal parkland course.
18 holes, 6270yds, Par 71, SSS 70. Membership 280.

Visitors welcome (restricted WE) Societies welcome (☎)
Green fees Not confirmed
Facilities ⊗ by prior arrangement 🏋 💪 ♀ 🛎
Hotel ★★★55% Howard Park Hotel, Glasgow Rd, KILMARNOCK ☎(0563) 31211 46⇨
See advertisement on page 267

This guide is updated annually – make sure you use an up-to-date edition.

Caprington ☎ (0563) 23702
Ayr Rd (1.5m S on B7038)
Municipal parkland course.
18 holes, 5718yds, Par 69, SSS 68. Membership 400.

Visitors welcome (ex Fri pm) must contact in advance
✉

Green fees Not confirmed
Facilities ♀ ⌂ 🏠 ⌡
Hotel ★★★55% Howard Park Hotel, Glasgow Rd,
KILMARNOCK ☎(0563) 31211 46⇔

KILSYTH   Map 6 E2

Kilsyth Lennox ☎ (0236) 822190
Tak Ma Doon Rd (N side of town off A803)
Hilly moorland course, hard walking.
*9 holes, 5944yds, Par 70, SSS 69, Course record 65.
Membership 400.*

Visitors welcome (with M only WE) Societies welcome
(by letter)
Green fees Not confirmed
Facilities ⓑ ⚑♀ ⌂ 🏠
Hotel ★★66% Kirkhouse Inn, STRATHBLANE ☎(0360)
70621 15⇔🐾

KIRKINTILLOCH   Map 6 E2

Hayston ☎ 041-776 1244
Campsie Rd (1m NW off A803)
An undulating course with a sandy subsoil and some
wooded areas.
*18 holes, 6042yds, Par 70, SSS 69, Course record 62.
Membership 440.*

Visitors welcome Member must accompany must
contact in advance ✉ Societies welcome (by letter)
Green fees £18 per day; £12 per round
Facilities ⊗ ⫻ by prior arrangement ⓑ ⚑♀
(restricted winter) ⌂ 🏠 ⌡ Steven Barnett
Hotel ★★★59% Black Bull Thistle Hotel, Main St,
MILNGAVIE ☎041-956 2291 27⇔🐾

Kirkintilloch ☎ 041-776 1256
Campsie Rd (1m NW off A803)
Parkland course.
18 holes, 5269yds, Par 70, SSS 66. Membership 650.

Visitors welcome Member must accompany
Green fees Not confirmed
Facilities ⊗ ⫻ ⓑ ⚑ (catering times vary) ♀ ⌂
Hotel ★★★59% Black Bull Thistle Hotel, Main St,
MILNGAVIE ☎041-956 2291 27⇔🐾

Opening times of bar and catering facilities vary
from place to place – it is wise to check in
advance of your visit.

LANARK   Map 6 F3

Lanark ☎ (0555) 3219
The Moor (E side of town
centre off A73)
Chosen as one of the pre-
qualifying tests for the
Open Championship held at
Lanark from 1977 to 1983.
The address of the club,
'The Moor', gives some
indication as to the kind of
golf to be found there. Golf
has been played at Lanark
for well over a century and
the Club dates from 1851.

SCORE CARD					
Hole	Yds	Par	Hole	Yds	Par
1	360	4	10	152	3
2	467	4	11	397	4
3	409	4	12	362	4
4	457	4	13	362	4
5	318	4	14	399	4
6	377	4	15	470	4
7	141	3	16	337	4
8	530	5	17	309	4
9	360	4	18	216	3
Out	3419	36	In	3004	34
			Totals	6423	70

*18 holes, 6423yds, Par 70, SSS 71, Course record 64 or
9 holes, 1562yds. Membership 850.*

Visitors welcome (restricted until 1600 wkdays
only) must contact in advance ✉ Societies welcome
(ex WE ☎)
Green fees £20 per day; £14 per round
Facilities ⊗ ⫻ ⓑ ⚑ (daily summer) ♀ ⌂ 🏠 🐾
⌡ Ron Wallace
Hotel ★★★61% Popinjay Hotel, Lanark Rd,
ROSEBANK ☎(055586) 441 40⇔🐾

LANGBANK   Map 6 D2

Gleddoch Golf and Country Club ☎ (047554) 304
Parkland and heathland course with other sporting
facilities available to temporary members. Good views
over Firth of Clyde. Accommodation and leisure/sports
facilities including swimming, squash, riding, sauna and
satellite television.
18 holes, 5661yds, Par 68, SSS 67. Membership 300.

Visitors welcome (with M only WE) must contact in
advance ✉ Societies welcome
Green fees £15 per day/round
Facilities ⊗ ⫻ ⓑ ⚑ ♀ ⌂ 🏠 🐾 ⌡ Keith Campbell
Hotel ★★★♨70% Gleddoch House Hotel, LANGBANK
☎(047554) 711 33⇔🐾

LARGS   Map 6 C3

Largs ☎ (0475) 673594
Irvine Rd (1m S of town centre on A78)
A parkland, tree-lined course with views to the Clyde
coast and Arran Isles.
*18 holes, 6220yds, Par 70, SSS 70, Course record 64.
Membership 850.*

Visitors welcome must contact in advance Societies
welcome (☎)
Green fees £20 per day; £14 per round (£20 WE)
Facilities ⊗ ⫻ ⓑ ⚑ ♀ ⌂ 🏠 🐾 ⌡ Robbie Stewart
Hotel ★★55% Elderslie Hotel, John St, Broomfields,
LARGS ☎(0475) 686460 25rm(9⇔4🐾)

Routenburn ☎ (0475) 673230
Routenburn Rd (1m N off A78)
Heathland course with magnificent view over Firth of
Clyde.
18 holes, 5675 yds, Par 68, SSS 67. Membership 350.

Visitors welcome
Green fees Not confirmed
Facilities ♀ ⌂ 📷
Hotel ★★★♨60% Manor Park Hotel, SKELMORLIE
☎(0475) 520832 7rm(5⇨1🐾)

LARKHALL   Map 6 E3

Larkhall ☎ (0698) 881113
Burnhead Rd (E side of town on B7019)
Small inland hill course.
*9 holes, 7754 yds, Par 72, SSS 72, Course record 69.
Membership 250.*

Visitors welcome (restricted Tue & Sat)
Green fees Not confirmed
Facilities ⊾ (WE only) ♀ ⌂
Hotel ★★★61% Popinjay Hotel, Lanark Rd,
ROSEBANK ☎(055586) 441 40⇨🐾

LEADHILLS   Map 6 F4

Leadhills ☎ (0659) 74222
(E side of village off B797)
Testing, hilly course with high winds. It is the highest
9-hole golf course in Great Britain (1,500 ft).
*9 holes, 4354 yds, Par 64, SSS 62, Course record 60.
Membership 80.*

Visitors welcome Societies welcome
Green fees £3 per day/round (£4 WE)
Hotel ★★64% Mennockfoot Lodge Hotel, Mennock,
SANQUHAR ☎(0659) 50382 & 50477 1⇨ Annexe:8⇨🐾

LENNOXTOWN   Map 6 E2

Campsie ☎ (0360) 310244
Crow Rd (.5m N on B822)
Scenic hillside course.
*18 holes, 5515 yds, Par 70, SSS 67, Course record 65.
Membership 560.*

Visitors welcome (after 1600) Societies welcome (☎ one
month in advance)
Green fees £7 per day (£10 WE)
Facilities ⊗ 🍴 ⊾ 🎯 ♀ ⌂ 📷
Hotel ★★66% Kirkhouse Inn, STRATHBLANE ☎(0360)
70621 15⇨🐾

LENZIE   Map 6 E2

Lenzie ☎ 041-776 1535
19 Crosshill Rd (S side of town on B819)
Parkland course near Glasgow.
*18 holes, 5982 yds, Par 69, SSS 69, Course record 64.
Membership 700.*

▶

Visitors welcome Member must accompany must contact in advance Societies welcome (☎)
Green fees Not confirmed
Facilities ⊗ ⫼ ♨ ☕ ♀ ⌂ ⊟ ☾ Jim McCallum
Hotel ★★64% Garfield House Hotel, Cumbernauld Rd, STEPPS ☎041-779 2111 27⇐⌐

LESMAHAGOW
Map 6 E3

Holland Bush ☎ (0555) 893484
Acretophead
Fairly difficult, tree-lined municipal parkland and moorland course. 1st half is flat, while 2nd half is hilly. No bunkers.
18 holes, 6110yds, Par 72, SSS 70, Course record 63. Membership 500.

Visitors welcome Societies welcome
Green fees £7 per day; £4.50 per round (£9/£6.50 WE)
Facilities ⊗ ⫼ ♨ ☕ ♀ ⌂ ⊟ ϒ ☾ Ian Rae
Hotel ★★★61% Popinjay Hotel, Lanark Rd, ROSEBANK ☎(055586) 441 40⇐⌐

LOCHWINNOCH
Map 6 D3

Lochwinnoch ☎ (0505) 842153
Burnfoot Rd (W side of town off A760)
Parkland course with hard walking and testing golf. Overlooks bird sanctuary and boating loch.
18 holes, 6223yds, Par 70, SSS 70, Course record 63. Membership 500.

Visitors welcome (ex WE & restricted comp days) must contact in advance Societies welcome (☎)
Green fees £8 per day ;£6 per round
Facilities ⊗ ⫼ ♨ ☕ ♀ ⌂ ⊟ ϒ ☾ Gerry Reilly
Hotel ★★55% Elderslie Hotel, John St, Broomfields, LARGS ☎(0475) 686460 25rm(9⇐4⌐)

MACHRIHANISH
Map 6 A4

Machrihanish ☎ (058681) 213
(5m W of Campbeltown on B843)
Magnificent seaside links of championship status. The 1st hole is the famous drive across the Atlantic. Sandy soil allows for play all year round. Large greens, easy walking, windy. Fishing.
18 holes, 6228yds, Par 70, SSS 70, Course record 66. Membership 850.

Visitors welcome Societies welcome (by letter)
Green fees £15 (£16 WE); £5 (9 hole course)
Facilities ⊗ by prior arrangement ⫼ by prior arrangement ♨ (ex Mon) ☕ (ex Mon) ♀ ⌂ ⊟ ϒ ☾ Kenneth Campbell
Hotel ★65% Seafield Hotel, Kilkerran Rd, CAMPBELTOWN ☎(0586) 54385 3⌐ Annexe:6⌐

Each golf course entry has a recommended hotel. For a wider choice of places to stay, consult *AA Hotels and Restaurants in Britain* or *AA-inspected Bed and Breakfast in Britain.*

MAUCHLINE
Map 6 D4

Ballochmyle ☎ (0290) 50469
Ballochmyle (1m SE on B705)
Parkland course. Squash, snooker.
18 holes, 5952yds, Par 70, SSS 69. Membership 840.

Visitors welcome Societies welcome (by letter)
Green fees £12.50 per day (£19 WE)
Facilities ⊗ ♨ ☕ (no catering Mon Oct-Mar) ♀ (ex Mon Oct-Mar) ⌂ ⊟
Hotel ★★61% Royal Hotel, 1 Glaisnock St, CUMNOCK ☎(0290) 20822 11rm(2⇐1⌐)

MAYBOLE
Map 6 D4

Maybole Municipal
Memorial Park
9 holes, 2635yds, Par 33, SSS 65, Course record 64. Membership 100.

Visitors welcome Societies welcome
Green fees Not confirmed
Hotel ★★★66% Malin Court, TURNBERRY ☎(0655) 31457 8⌐

MILNGAVIE
Map 6 D2

Clober ☎ 041-956 1685
Craigton Rd (NW side of town)
Parkland course. Testing 5th hole, par 3.
18 holes, 5068yds, Par 66, SSS 65, Course record 61. Membership 575.

Visitors welcome (before 1630) Societies welcome (☎)
Green fees £7 per round
Facilities ⊗ ⫼ ♨ ☕ ♀ ⌂ ⊟
Hotel ★★★59% Black Bull Thistle Hotel, Main St, MILNGAVIE ☎041-956 2291 27⇐⌐

Dougalston ☎ 041-956 5750
Strathblane Rd (NE side of town on A81)
Tree-lined with water features.
18 holes, 6683yds, Par 72, SSS 71.

Visitors welcome must contact in advance Societies welcome (☎ or letter)
Green fees £6 per round (£7 WE)
Facilities ⊗ ⫼ by prior arrangement ♨ ☕ ♀ ⌂
Hotel ★★★59% Black Bull Thistle Hotel, Main St, MILNGAVIE ☎041-956 2291 27⇐⌐

Hilton Park ☎ 041-956 4657
Stockiemuir Rd (3m NW on A809)
Courses set amidst magnificent scenery.
18 holes, 6003yds, Par 70, SSS 70. Membership 1200.

Visitors welcome (ex WE) must contact in advance Societies welcome (wkdays only)
Green fees £15 per day; £10 per round
Facilities ⊗ ⫼ ♨ ☕ ♀ ⌂ ⊟ ϒ ☾ W McCondichie
Hotel ★★★59% Black Bull Thistle Hotel, Main St, MILNGAVIE ☎041-956 2291 27⇐⌐

Milngavie ☎ 041-956 1619
Laigh Park (1.25m N)
Moorland course, hard walking, sometimes windy, good views. Testing 1st and 4th holes (par 4).
18 holes, 5818yds, Par 68, SSS 68. Membership 700.

Visitors welcome Member must accompany must contact in advance ✉ Societies welcome (☎)
Green fees Not confirmed
Facilities ⊗ by prior arrangement ⅷ by prior arrangement ⌊ ⯑ ⚲ (M & guests only) △
Hotel ★★★59% Black Bull Thistle Hotel, Main St, MILNGAVIE ☎041-956 2291 27⇨🏠

MOTHERWELL   Map 6 E3

Colville Park ☎ (0698) 63017
New Jerviston House, Jerviston Estate (1.25m NE on A723)
Parkland course. 1st 9 holes, tree-lined, 2nd 9, more exposed. Testing 10th hole par 3, 16th hole par 4.
18 holes, 6215yds, Par 71, SSS 70, Course record 64. Membership 750.

Visitors welcome (with M only ex parties) must contact in advance Societies welcome (wkdays only)
Green fees £12 per day (party booking)
Facilities ⊗ ⅷ ⌊ ⯑ ⚲ △ 🏠
Hotel ★★58% Silvertrees Hotel, Silverwells Crescent, BOTHWELL ☎(0698) 852311 7⇨ Annexe:19⇨🏠

MUIRHEAD   Map 6 E2

Crow Wood ☎ 041-779 2011
Garnkirk Estate (.5m W on A80)
Parkland course.
18 holes, 6209yds, Par 71, SSS 70. Membership 600.

Visitors welcome (with M only)
Green fees Not confirmed
Facilities ⚲ △ 🏠 ⚑
Hotel ★★64% Garfield House Hotel, Cumbernauld Rd, STEPPS ☎041-779 2111 27⇨🏠

NEW CUMNOCK   Map 6 E4

New Cumnock ☎ (0290) 20822
Lochhill (.75m N on A76)
Parkland course.
9 holes, 2365yds, Par 66, SSS 63.

Visitors welcome
Green fees Not confirmed
Hotel ★★61% Royal Hotel, 1 Glaisnock St, CUMNOCK ☎(0290) 20822 11rm(2⇨1🏠)

NEWTON MEARNS   Map 6 D3

Eastwood ☎ Loganswell (03555) 261
Muirshield (2.5m S on A77)
Moorland course.
18 holes, 5864yds, Par 68, SSS 68, Course record 62. Membership 911.

Visitors welcome (ex WE) must contact in advance Societies welcome (☎)
Green fees £15 per day ; £10 per round
Facilities ⊗ ⅷ ⌊ ⯑ ⚲ △ 🏠 ⌊ K McWade
Hotel ★★★67% Macdonald Thistle Hotel, Eastwood Toll, GIFFNOCK ☎041-638 2225 56⇨🏠

East Renfrewshire ☎ Loganswell (03555) 258
Pilmuir (3m SW on A77)
Undulating moorland course with loch ; prevailing SW wind.
18 holes, 6097yds, Par 70, SSS 70. Membership 500.

Visitors welcome must contact in advance Societies welcome
Green fees £20 per day ; £15 per round
Facilities ⊗ ⅷ ⌊ ⯑ ⚲ △ 🏠 ⌊
Hotel ★★★67% Macdonald Thistle Hotel, Eastwood Toll, GIFFNOCK ☎041-638 2225 56⇨🏠

Whitecraigs ☎ 041-639 4530
72 Ayr Rd (1.5m NE on A77)
Beautiful parkland course.
18 holes, 6230yds, Par 70, SSS 70. Membership 1150.

Visitors welcome Member must accompany ✉ Societies welcome (☎)
Green fees £15 per round
Facilities ⊗ △ 🏠 ⚑ ⌊ W Watson
Hotel ★★★67% Macdonald Thistle Hotel, Eastwood Toll, GIFFNOCK ☎041-638 2225 56⇨🏠

OBAN   Map 7 D8

Glencruitten
☎ (0631) 62868
Glencruitten Rd (NE side of town centre off A816)
There is plenty of space and considerable variety of hole on this downland course - popular with holidaymakers. In a beautiful, isolated situation, the course is hilly and testing, particularly the 1st and 12th, par 4's, and 10th and 15th, par 3's.

SCORE CARD: Medal Tees					
Hole	Yds	Par	Hole	Yds	Par
1	445	4	10	150	3
2	170	3	11	238	3
3	167	3	12	410	4
4	271	4	13	185	3
5	163	3	14	318	4
6	228	3	15	178	3
7	219	3	16	313	4
8	263	4	17	180	3
9	197	3	18	357	4
Out	2123	30	In	2329	31
			Totals	4452	61

18 holes, 4250yds, Par 61, SSS 63, Course record 55. Membership 620.

Visitors welcome (restricted Thu & Sat) Societies welcome (by letter)
Green fees £10 per day ; £8 per round (£9 WE)
Facilities ⊗ ⅷ by prior arrangement ⌊ ⯑ ⚲ △ 🏠
Hotel ★★★56% Caledonian Hotel, Station Square, OBAN ☎(0631) 63133 70⇨

To see a full range of AA guides and maps, visit your local AA Shop or any good bookshop.

PAISLEY
Map 6 D2

Barshaw ☎ 041-889 2908
Barshaw Park (1m E off A737)
Municipal parkland course.
18 holes, 5703yds, Par 68, SSS 67. Membership 77.

Visitors welcome
Green fees £3 per round
Facilities ⌂
Hotel ★★★58% Glynhill Hotel & Leisure Club, Paisley
Road, Renfrew, RENFREW ☎041-886 5555 125⇔↸

Paisley ☎ 041-884 3903
Braehead (S side of town off B774)
Moorland course, windy but with good views. Snooker.
18 holes, 6424yds, Par 71, SSS 71. Membership 700.

Visitors welcome (ex WE & PH) Member must
accompany must contact in advance ⊠ Societies
welcome (by letter)
Green fees £14 per day; £10 per round
Facilities ⊗ ⅏ ⅃ ⅊ (catering by prior arrangement)
⚲ (by arrangement) ⌂ 🏠 🏌 Grant Gilmour
Hotel ★★★58% Glynhill Hotel & Leisure Club, Paisley
Road, Renfrew, RENFREW ☎041-886 5555 125⇔↸

Ralston ☎ 041-882 1349
Strathmore Av, Ralston (2m E off A737)
Parkland course.
18 holes, 6071yds, Par 71, SSS 69. Membership 750.

Visitors welcome Member must accompany
Green fees Not confirmed
Facilities ⚲ ⌂ 🏠
Hotel ★★★58% Swallow Hotel, 517 Paisley Rd West,
GLASGOW ☎041-427 3146 119⇔↸

PORT GLASGOW
Map 6 D2

Port Glasgow ☎ (0475) 704181
Devol Rd (1m S)
A moorland course set on a hilltop overlooking the
Clyde, with magnificent views from Dunbarton to the
Cowal hills.
*18 holes, 5712yds, Par 68, SSS 68, Course record 63.
Membership 375.*

Visitors welcome (ex Sat) must contact in advance
Societies welcome (☎)
Green fees £12 per day; £8 per round
Facilities ⊗ ⅏ ⅃ ⅊ (catering on request) ⚲ ⌂
Hotel ★★★↝70% Gleddoch House Hotel, LANGBANK
☎(047554) 711 33⇔↸

PRESTWICK
Map 6 D4

Prestwick ☎ (0292) 77404
2 Links Rd (In town centre off A79)
Seaside links with natural hazards, fine views.
18 holes, 6544yds, Par 71, SSS 72. Membership 550.

Visitors welcome (ex WE & restricted Thu) must
contact in advance ⊠ Societies welcome (☎)

Green fees Not confirmed
Facilities ⊗ ⅏ by prior arrangement ⅃ ⅊ ⚲ ⌂
🏠 🏌 🏌 Frank C Remmic
Hotel ★★60% Parkstone Hotel, Esplanade,
PRESTWICK ☎(0292) 77286 15⇔↸

Prestwick St Cuthbert ☎ (0292) 77101
East Rd (.5m E of town centre off A77)
Parkland course with easy walking, natural hazards
and sometimes windy.
*18 holes, 6471yds, Par 71, SSS 71, Course record 66.
Membership 820.*

Visitors welcome (ex WE & BH) must contact in
advance Societies welcome (☎)
Green fees £12 per day; £7 per round
Facilities ⊗ (ex Thu) ⅏ by prior arrangement ⅃ ⅊
⌂
Hotel ★★60% St Nicholas Hotel, 41 Ayr Rd,
PRESTWICK ☎(0292) 79568 16rm(10↸)

Prestwick St Nicholas ☎ (0292) 70359 & 77608
Grangemuir Rd (S side of town off A79)
Seaside course with whins, heather and tight fairways.
It provides easy walking and has an unrestricted view
of the Firth of Clyde.
18 holes, 5926yds, Par 68, SSS 68. Membership 700.

Visitors welcome (ex WE & PH) must contact in
advance Societies welcome (☎)
Green fees Not confirmed
Facilities ⊗ ⅏ ⅃ ⅊ (no catering Mon) ⚲ ⌂ 🏌
🏌 Stewart Smith
Hotel ★★60% Parkstone Hotel, Esplanade, PRESTWICK
☎(0292) 77286 15⇔↸

RENFREW
Map 6 D2

Renfrew ☎ 041-886 6692
Blythswood Estate, Inchinnan Rd (.75m W off A8)
Tree-lined parkland course.
*18 holes, 6818yds, Par 72, SSS 73, Course record 67.
Membership 700.*

Visitors welcome Member must accompany must
contact in advance ⊠
Green fees Not confirmed
Facilities ⊗ ⅏ ⅃ ⅊ ⚲ ⌂ 🏠
Hotel ★★★64% Stakis Normandy Hotel, Inchinnan
Rd, Renfrew, RENFREW ☎041-886 4100 141⇔↸

SHOTTS
Map 6 F3

Shotts ☎ (0501) 20431
Blairhead (2m from M8 off Benhar Road)
Moorland course.
*18 holes, 5738yds, Par 70, SSS 70, Course record 63.
Membership 950.*

Visitors welcome (ex WE) must contact in advance
Societies welcome (by letter, wkdays only)
Green fees £12 per day (£15 WE)

Facilities ⊗ high tea ⛾ ☕ Y (all day) △ ⌂ ⚑ Gordon Graham
Hotel ★★★61% Popinjay Hotel, Lanark Rd, ROSEBANK ☎(055586) 441 40🛁🚿

SKELMORLIE Map 6 C2

Skelmorlie ☎ (0475) 520152
Beithglass (E side of village off A78)
Parkland/moorland course with magnificent views over Firth of Clyde. Fishing. Nature trails and steamer excursions. Designed by James Braid, the club celebrates its centenary in 1991.
13 holes, 5056yds, Par 64, SSS 65. Membership 355.

Visitors welcome (restricted Sat) must contact in advance Societies welcome (by letter to Sec.)
Green fees £8 per day; £5.50 per round (£11/£7.50 Sun)
Facilities ⊗ Ⅲ ⛾ ☕ Y (all day) △
Hotel ★★★⛼60% Manor Park Hotel, SKELMORLIE ☎(0475) 520832 7rm(5🛁1🚿)

SOUTHEND Map 6 A4

Dunaverty ☎ No telephone
(10m S of Campbeltown on B842)
Undulating, seaside course.
18 holes, 4597yds, SSS 63. Membership 250.

Visitors welcome Societies welcome (by letter)
Green fees Not confirmed
Facilities ⊗ by prior arrangement ☕ △
Hotel ★★63% Royal Hotel, Main St, CAMPBELTOWN ☎(0586) 52017 16rm(8🛁4🚿)

STEVENSTON Map 6 C3

Ardeer ☎ (0294) 64542
Greenhead (.5m N off A78)
Parkland course, with natural hazards. Snooker.
18 holes, 6630yds, Par 72, SSS 72, Course record 64. Membership 500.

Visitors welcome (ex Sat) Societies welcome (☎)
Green fees £10 per day; £6 per round (£14/£8 Sun)
Facilities ⊗ ⛾ ☕ Y △ ⌂
Hotel ★★★★63% Hospitality Inn, Annick Rd, Annickwater, IRVINE ☎(0294) 74272 128🛁🚿

STRATHAVEN Map 6 E3

Strathaven ☎ (0357) 20421
Overton Av, Glasgow Rd (NE side of town on A726)
Parkland course with panoramic views over town and Avon valley.
18 holes, 6226yds, Par 71, SSS 70, Course record 63. Membership 950.

Visitors welcome (wkdays only) must contact in advance Societies welcome (Mon only)
Green fees Not confirmed
Facilities ⊗ Ⅲ ⛾ ☕ Y △ ⌂ ⚑ M McCrorie
Hotel ★★★60% Stuart Hotel, 2 Cornwall Way, EAST KILBRIDE ☎(03552) 21161 39🛁🚿

TARBERT Map 6 B2

Tarbert ☎ (0880) 820565
(1m W on B8024)
Beautiful moorland course. Four fairways crossed by streams.
9 holes, 4460yds, Par 66, SSS 64, Course record 62. Membership 110.

Visitors welcome (ex competition days) Societies welcome (by letter)
Green fees £5 per day, £4 per round (9 holes)
Facilities Y (Sat & Sun) △
Hotel ★★★61% Stonefield Castle Hotel, TARBERT ☎(08802) 836 33rm(30🛁2🚿)

TIGHNABRUAICH Map 6 B2

Kyles of Bute ☎ (0700) 811601
(1.25m S off B8000)
Moorland course which is hilly and exposed to wind. Good views of the Kyles of Bute.
9 holes, 2389yds, Par 32, SSS 32. Membership 160.

Visitors welcome Societies welcome (3 weeks notice)
Green fees £5 per day
Facilities ☕ △
Hotel ★★77% Kilfinan Hotel, KILFINAN ☎(070082) 201 11🛁🚿

TROON   Map 6 D4

Royal Troon ☎ (0292) 311555
Craigend Rd (S side of town on B749)
Famous Championship Links. The current course record holder on the Old Course is Greg Norman with a 64 (1989).
18 holes, 6641yds, Par 71, SSS 73, Course record 64. Membership 800.

Visitors welcome (ex Wed, Fri, WE & PH) must contact in advance ✉ Societies welcome (by letter)
Green fees Not confirmed
Facilities ⊗ ⦀ ⮛ 🍺 ♀ △ 🏠 ⛳ ✆ B R Anderson
Hotel ★★★65% Marine Highland Hotel, TROON ☎(0292) 314444 72⇔🛏

See advertisement on page 271

Troon Municipal ☎ (0292) 312464
Harling Dr (100yds from railway station)
Three links courses.
Lochgreen Course 18 holes, 6840yds, Par 73, SSS 73, Course record 64. Darley 18 holes, 6327yds, Par 71, SSS 71, Course record 65. Fullerton 18 holes, 4784yds, Par 64, SSS 63. Membership 1600.

Visitors welcome must contact in advance Societies welcome (by letter)
Green fees Not confirmed
Facilities ⊗ ⦀ ⮛ 🍺 ♀ △ 🏠 ⛳ ✆ Gordon McKinley
Hotel ★★60% Ardneil Hotel, 51 Saint Meddans St, TROON ☎(0292) 311611 9rm(3⇔4🛏)

TURNBERRY   Map 6 C4

Turnberry See page 273

UDDINGSTON   Map 6 E3

Calderbraes ☎ (0698) 813425
57 Roundknowe Rd (1.5m NW off A74)
Parkland course with good view of Clyde Valley. Testing 4th hole (par 4) hard uphill.
9 holes, 5046yds, Par 66, SSS 67, Course record 65. Membership 230.

Visitors welcome (wkdays before 1700) Societies welcome
Green fees £8 per day (WE with M only)
Facilities ⊗ ⦀ ⮛ 🍺 ♀ △
Hotel ★★55% Redstones Hotel, 8-10 Glasgow Rd, UDDINGSTON ☎(0698) 813774 & 814843 18rm(16⇔🛏)

UPLAWMOOR   Map 6 D3

Caldwell ☎ (050585) 329
(.5m SW A736)
Parkland course.
18 holes, 6046yds, Par 71, SSS 69. Membership 600.

Visitors welcome (restricted WE & BH) Societies welcome (by letter)
Green fees £17 per day; £12 per round
Facilities ⊗ ⦀ ⮛ 🍺 ♀ △ 🏠 ✆ Keith Baxter
Hotel ★★55% Dalmeny Park Hotel, Lochlibo Rd, BARRHEAD ☎041-881 9211 18rm(3⇔10🛏)

WEST KILBRIDE   Map 6 C3

West Kilbride ☎ (0294) 833128
Fullerton Dr (W side of town off A78)
Seaside links course, fine view of Isle of Arran from every hole. Accommodation (self-catering).
18 holes, 6247yds, Par 71, SSS 70, Course record 63. Membership 960.

Visitors welcome (ex WE) ✉ Societies welcome (Tue & Thu ☎)
Green fees Not confirmed
Facilities ⊗ ⦀ by prior arrangement ⮛ 🍺 ♀ △ 🏠 ✆ Gregor Howie
Hotel ★★55% Elderslie Hotel, John St, Broomfields, LARGS ☎(0475) 686460 25rm(9⇔4🛏)

WISHAW   Map 6 E3

Wishaw ☎ (0698) 372869
55 Cleland Rd (NW side of town off A721)
Parkland course.
18 holes, 6051yds, Par 69, SSS 69, Course record 63. Membership 1000.

Visitors welcome (midwk before 1800, Sun after 1030) Societies welcome (apply by letter 4 wks prior)
Green fees £9 per day (mid week) (£15.50 Sun) no visitors Sat
Facilities ⊗ ⦀ ⮛ 🍺 ♀ △ 🏠 ✆ John Campbell
Hotel ★★★61% Popinjay Hotel, Lanark Rd, ROSEBANK ☎(055586) 441 40⇔🛏

TAYSIDE

ABERFELDY   Map 7 G7

Aberfeldy ☎ (0887) 20535
Taybridge Rd (N side of town centre)
Parkland course, situated by River Tay near the famous Wade Bridge and Black Watch Monument. Easy walking.
9 holes, 2733yds, Par 68, SSS 67. Membership 250.

Visitors welcome (booking advisable, essential WE Jun-Aug) Societies welcome
Green fees £10 per day; £7 per 18 holes
Facilities ⮛ 🍺 ♀ △
Hotel ★★61% Weem Hotel, Weem, ABERFELDY ☎(0887) 20381 14⇔🛏

ALYTH   Map 7 H7

Alyth ☎ (08283) 2268
Pitcrocknie (1m E on B954)
Windy, heathland course with easy walking.
18 holes, 6226yds, Par 70, SSS 70, Course record 66. Membership 850.

Visitors welcome must contact in advance Societies welcome (☎)
Green fees £16 per day; £12 per round (£20/£16 WE)

▶

SCORE CARD: Ailsa Course					
Hole	Yds	Par	Hole	Yds	Par
1	350	4	10	452	4
2	428	4	11	177	3
3	462	4	12	441	4
4	167	3	13	411	4
5	441	4	14	440	4
6	222	3	15	209	3
7	528	5	16	409	4
8	427	4	17	500	5
9	455	4	18	431	4
Out	3480	35	In	3470	35
			Totals	6950	70

TURNBERRY   Map6 C4

Turnberry ☎ (0655) 31000 (N side of village, on A719)

The hotel is sumptuous, the Ailsa and Arran courses beneath it are total magic. The air reaches down into your inner lung and of all places in Scotland, Turnberry has to be among the finest.

You are not obliged to stay at the superb hotel, and if you wish to fly in, then Prestwick Airport is only seventeen miles from the first tee.

What makes the place so desirable is the warmness of the welcome and, on occasions, local professional Bob Jamieson will tell you, this is literally so as the links is on the friendliest of gulf streams.

It was here that in the 1977 Open, Jack Nicklaus put up such a brave fight against Tom Watson. Then, a few years later, we had a wondrous victory from Greg Norman who loved the place so much that a few hours after the prize-giving he sat with his wife on the edge of the great links, drinking champagne, and watching the moon roll round the pure white lighthouse out by the ninth green.

Without any doubt, Turnberry is the stuff of dreams and you must go there if you possible can.

36 holes. Ailsa Course 18 holes, 6950 yds, Par 70, SSS 72. Arran Course 18 holes, 6249 yds, Par 69, SSS 70. Membership 347

Visitors   welcome. Must contact in advance ✉ . Societies welcome (by letter).

Green fees   £55; hotel residents £25

Facilities   ⊗ ♨ ▤ ⬛ ♀ (all day)   ⛳🏠🍴 R S Jamieson

WHERE TO STAY AND EAT NEARBY

HOTELS:

BARRHILL	★★★ ⊞ 77% Kilonan ☎ (046582) 360. 31 ⌣🍴 . ♀ French & Swiss cuisine.
GIRVAN	★★ 63% King's Arms, Dalrymple St ☎ (0465) 3322. 25 ⌣🍴 Scottish & French cuisine.
MAYBOLE	★★⊞ 79% Ladyburn ☎ Crosshill (06554) 585. 8rm (4⌣ 🍴). ♀ French cuisine.
TURNBERRY	★★★★ 63% Turnberry ☎ (0655) 31000. 115 ⌣🍴 . ♀ Scottish & French cuisine.
	★★★ 66% Malin Court ☎ (0655) 31457. 8 🍴

RESTAURANT:

ALLOWAY	✗ Burns Byre, Mount Oliphant ☎ (0292) 43644

Facilities ⊗ high tea ⋓ by prior arrangement 🛏 🍺 ⚲
△ 🗄 (Tom Melville
Hotel ★★🏨58% Lands of Loyal Hotel, Loyal Rd,
ALYTH ☎(08283) 3151 11⇨

ARBROATH
Map 7 J8

Arbroath ☎ (0241) 75837
Elliot (2m SW on A92)
Municipal seaside links course played upon by Arbroath
Artisan Golf Club.
18 holes, 5758yds, Par 68. Membership 800.

Visitors welcome Societies welcome (party 8 plus must
be booked)
Green fees Not confirmed
Facilities ⊗ high tea 🛏 🍺 ⚲ △ 🗄 ⚶ (Lindsay
Ewart
Hotel ★★58% Hotel Seaforth, Dundee Rd, ARBROATH
☎(0241) 72232 18⇨

Letham Grange ☎ (024189) 373
Colliston (4m N on A993)
A course of great variety including woodland and fine
parkland holes. Picturesque lakes. Accommodation.
*18 holes, 6789yds, Par 72, SSS 73, Course record 72.
Membership 620.*

Visitors welcome (restricted WE & Tue) must contact
in advance Societies welcome (☎)
Green fees £22.50 per day; £15 per round (£18 WE &
BH)
Facilities ⊗ ⋓ 🛏 🍺 ⚲ △ 🗄 ⚶ (David F G Scott
Hotel ★★★66% Letham Grange Hotel, Colliston,
ARBROATH ☎(024189) 373 19⇨

AUCHTERARDER
Map 6 F1

Auchterarder ☎ (0764) 62804
Orchil Rd (.75m SW on A824)
Parkland course with easy walking.
*18 holes, 5757yds, Par 69, SSS 68, Course record 65.
Membership 600.*

Visitors welcome (restricted on competition days) must
contact in advance Societies welcome (2 mths in
advance)
Green fees £11 per day (£17 WE); £8.50 per round (£12
WE)
Facilities △ 🗄 ⚶ (Keith Salmoni
Hotel ★★★★(red)The Gleneagles Hotel,
AUCHTERARDER ☎(0764) 62231 236⇨🐾

Gleneagles Hotel ☎ (0764) 63543
(2m SW of A823)
Famous moorland courses. Sumptuous hotel offering
unrivalled sports and leisure activities. Course record
holders are; Jose-Marie Olazabal (Kings Course) and
Craig Stadler (Queens Course). A new championship
course, designed by Jack Nicklaus, is currently under
construction and will be ready for play in 1992.
*Kings Course 18 holes, 6471yds, Par 70, SSS 71. Queens
Course 18 holes, 5965yds, Par 68, SSS 69.*

Visitors welcome (must be hotel resident) Member must
accompany must contact in advance Societies welcome
(must be resident in the hotel)
Green fees £30 per round
Facilities ⊗ ⋓ 🛏 🍺 (catering facilities Mar-Oct in
the Dormy House) ⚲ △ 🗄 ⚶ (Ian Marchbank
Hotel ★★★★★(red)The Gleneagles Hotel,
AUCHTERARDER ☎(0764) 62231 236⇨🐾

BARRY
Map 7 J8

Panmure ☎ (0241) 53120
Burnside Rd (S side of village off A930)
A nerve-testing, adventurous course set amongst
sandhills - its hazards belie the quiet nature of the
opening holes. Panmure has been used as a
qualifying course for the Open Championship.
18 holes, 6302yds, Par 70, SSS 70. Membership 500.

Visitors welcome (with M only Sat) Societies
welcome
Green fees Not confirmed
Facilities ⚲ △ 🗄
Hotel ★★59% Glencoe Hotel, Links Pde,
CARNOUSTIE ☎(0241) 53273 11rm(3⇨5🐾)

BLAIR ATHOLL
Map 7 G7

Blair Atholl ☎ (079681) 407
(.5m S off B8079)
Parkland course, river runs alongside 3 holes, easy
walking.
9 holes, 5710yds, Par 70, SSS 69. Membership 200.

Visitors welcome Societies welcome
Green fees Not confirmed
Facilities ⚲ △ ⚶
Hotel ★★60% Atholl Arms Hotel, BLAIR ATHOLL
☎(079681) 205 30⇨🐾

BLAIRGOWRIE
Map 7 H7

Blairgowrie ☎ (0250) 2622
Rosemount (2m S off A93)
Two 18-hole heathland courses, also a 9-hole course.
*Rosemount Course 18 holes, 6588yds, Par 72, SSS 72.
Lansdowne Course 18 holes, 6895yds, Par 72, SSS 73.
Membership 1200.*

Visitors welcome (no parties Wed, Fri & WE) must
contact in advance ✉ Societies welcome (by letter)
Green fees £30 per day; £20 per round (£25 per
round WE)
Facilities ⊗ ⋓ 🛏 🍺 ⚲ △ 🗄 ⚶ (Gordon
Kinnoch
Hotel ★★★🏨75% Kinloch House Hotel,
BLAIRGOWRIE ☎(025084) 237 21⇨🐾

Opening times of bar and catering facilities vary
from place to place – it is wise to check in
advance of your visit.

BRECHIN   Map 7 J7

Brechin ☎ (03562) 2383
Trinity (1m N on B966)
Parkland course, with easy walking and good views of
Strathmore Valley and Grampian Mountains. Squash.
18 holes, 5267yds, Par 65, SSS 66. Membership 650.

Visitors welcome (ex WE when competitions are being
held) Societies welcome (☎)
Green fees Not confirmed
Facilities ⊗ ⑪ (on request) ⓛ ⬛ ♀ △ 🏠 ⍟
⍟ Brian Mason
Hotel ★★56% Northern Hotel, Clerk St, BRECHIN
☎(03562) 2156 & 5505 17rm(4⇨11🏠)

CARNOUSTIE   Map 7 J8

Carnoustie Golf Links See page 276

COMRIE   Map 7 G8

Comrie ☎ (0764) 70544
(E side of village off A85)
Scenic highland course.
9 holes, 5250yds, Par 70, SSS 69. Membership 240.

Visitors welcome (restricted Mon & Tue eves) Societies
welcome (☎)
Green fees £6 per day (£7 WE & BH)
Facilities ⬛ △ ⍟
Hotel ★★64% Royal Hotel, Melville Square, COMRIE
☎(0764) 70200 9rm(8⇨)

CRIEFF   Map 7 G8

Crieff ☎ (0764) 2909
Perth Rd (.5m NE on A85)
This course is what you
might call 'up and down'
but the turf is beautiful and
the highland air fresh and
invigorating. There are
views from the course over
Strathearn. Of the two
courses the Ferntower is
the more challenging.
*Ferntower 18 holes, 6402yds,
Par 71, SSS 71, Course
record 67. Dornock 9 holes,
2386yds, Par 64, SSS 63. Membership 570.*

SCORE CARD: Ferntower Course (Medal Tees)					
Hole	Yds	Par	Hole	Yds	Par
1	163	3	10	414	4
2	380	4	11	379	4
3	418	4	12	467	4
4	124	3	13	191	3
5	532	5	14	353	4
6	482	5	15	377	4
7	454	4	16	412	4
8	303	4	17	139	3
9	511	5	18	303	4
Out	3367	37	In	3035	34
			Totals	6402	71

Visitors welcome must contact in advance ✉
Societies welcome (☎)
Green fees Ferntower £14 per round (£16 WE);
Dornock £9 per round (£10 WE)
Facilities ⊗ ⑪ by prior arrangement ⓛ ⬛ ♀ △
🏠 ⍟ ⍟ D Murchie & J M Stark
Hotel ★★67% Murray Park Hotel, Connaught Ter,
CRIEFF ☎(0764) 3731 13⇨

If you know of a golf course, not in this guide
already, which welcomes visitors, we would be
pleased to hear about it.

DUNDEE   Map 7 H8

Caird Park ☎ (0382) 453606
Mains Loan (1.5m N of city centre off A972)
Municipal parkland course.
18 holes, 6281yds, Par 72, SSS 70. Membership 400.

Visitors welcome
Green fees Not confirmed
Facilities ♀ 🏠 ⍟
Hotel ★★★59% Queens Hotel, 160 Nethergate,
DUNDEE ☎(0382) 22515 47⇨🏠

Camperdown ☎ (0382) 621145
Camperdown House, Camperdown Park (3m NW of city
centre off A923)
Parkland course. Testing 2nd hole. Other sporting
facilities available.
18 holes, 5999yds, Par 71, SSS 69. Membership 600.

Visitors welcome must contact in advance Societies
welcome (☎)
Green fees £7.50 per day/round
Facilities △ 🏠 ⍟
Hotel ★★★62% Angus Thistle Hotel, 10 Marketgait,
DUNDEE ☎(0382) 26874 58⇨🏠

Downfield ☎ (0382) 825595
Turnberry Av (N of city centre off A923)
A fine inland course of recent Championship rating
set in undulating woodland to the north of Dundee.
The Gelly burn provides a hazard for several holes.
Snooker.
18 holes, 6266yds, Par 70, SSS 70. Membership 776.

Visitors welcome (with member only WE) must
contact in advance Societies welcome (☎)
Green fees £24 per day; £16 per round
Facilities ⊗ ⑪ ⓛ ⬛ ♀ △ 🏠 ⍟ ⍟ Colin Waddell
Hotel ★★★62% Angus Thistle Hotel, 10
Marketgait, DUNDEE ☎(0382) 26874 58⇨🏠

DUNKELD   Map 7 G8

Dunkeld & Birnam ☎ (03502) 524
Fungarth (1m N of village on A923)
Interesting 9 hole heathland course with spectacular
views of surrounding countryside.
*9 holes, 5240yds, Par 68, SSS 66, Course record 64.
Membership 300.*

Visitors welcome must contact in advance Societies
welcome (☎)
Green fees Not confirmed
Facilities ⊗ ⓛ ⬛ ♀ △ 🏠 ⍟
Hotel ★★★★62% Stakis Dunkeld House Hotel,
DUNKELD ☎(03502) 771 92⇨

DUNNING   Map 7 G8

Dunning ☎ (076484) 312
Rollo Park (Off A9 NW)
Parkland course.
*9 holes, 4836yds, Par 66, SSS 64, Course record 63.
Membership 530.*

▶

SCORE CARD:					
Championship Course					
Hole	Yds	Par	Hole	Yds	Par
1	407	4	10	446	4
2	425	4	11	353	4
3	342	4	12	477	5
4	375	4	13	161	3
5	387	4	14	483	5
6	524	5	15	456	4
7	390	4	16	245	3
8	168	3	17	433	4
9	420	4	18	444	4
Out	3438	36	In	3498	36
			Totals	6936	72

CARNOUSTIE   Map7 J8

Carnoustie Golf Links ☎ (0241) 53789. Links Parade (SW side of town, off A930)

You love it, or hate it. But you respect it. Back in 1953 they came to see Ben Hogan play in the Open Championship. This little man from Texas had a magic about him, and the huge terrifying links, the dread of any short hitter, would certainly be a platform on which to examine the finest golfer of his day, and maybe of any day.

Carnoustie could be the graveyard for even the best players. If the wind blew, and it was chilly, some said it was hellish. Simply standing up to the buffeting was bad enough, but on those closing holes, across the Barry Burn (or into it) was a prospect which would gnaw at the mind, because it twists through the links like an angry serpent and has to be crossed no fewer than seven times.

Hogan came to this awesome place and not since 1860 had any golfer won the Open on his first attempt. Certainly he hadn't come for the money which, in those days, was a pittance. He had come to prove he was the best player in the world. That was pressure, but when he saw the 'Stone Age' course, dating back to the birth of the game, he was shocked because it lacked trees and colour, and looked drab.

All in all, the 7200 yard monster course came as a cultural shock to Mr Hogan. But the one Hogan beat for the 1953 Championship was, as they say, something else. 'Winning the British Open at Carnoustie gave me my greatest pleasure' he told the Fort Worth Star-Telegram. 'Certainly the other victories were pleasurable, but none gave me the feeling, the desire to perform, that gripped me in Scotland'.

Sadly, Hogan never returned and then the great links was taken from the Open Championship rota. Today there are hopes it may be re-instated.

36 holes. Championship Course 18 holes, 6936 yds, Par 72, SSS74, Course record 65. Burnside Course 18 holes, 6020 yds, Par 68. Membership 1200.

Visitors   welcome (restricted hours during week). Must contact in advance. Societies welcome (☎ or letter).

Green fees   £30 per round (Championship); £13 per round (Burnside).

Facilities   ⊗ �III ☎ ♀ ⅄

WHERE TO STAY AND EAT NEARBY

HOTELS:

ARBROATH   ★★★ 66% Letham Grange, Colliston ☎ Gowanbank (024189) 373. 19 ⌐ . ♡ International cuisine.

CARNOUSTIE   ★★ 59% Glencoe, Links Pde ☎ (0241) 53273. 11rm (3⌐ 5ſ   ). ♡ Scottish & French cuisine.

GLAMIS   ★★★⊯ 69% Castleton House ☎(030784) 340. 6⌐ſ . ♡ French cuisine.

LETHAM   ★★★⊯ 64% Fernie Castle ☎ (033781) 381. 16 ⌐ſ . ♡ French cuisine.

RESTAURANTS:

ARBROATH   ✗✗ Carriage Room, Meadow Bank, Montrose Rd ☎ (0241) 75755. ♡ Scottish & French cuisine.

INVERKEILOR ✗ Gordon's, Homewood House, Main St ☎ (02413) 364

Visitors welcome (Mon-Fri, Sat after 1600, Sun after 1300)
Green fees £5 per day/round
Facilities ⚑ △
Hotel ★★★58% Stakis City Mills Hotel, West Mill St, PERTH ☎(0738) 28281 78rm(76⇄)

EDZELL
Map 7 J7

Edzell ☎ (03564) 7283
(S side of village on B966)
This delightful course is situated in the foothills of the Scottish Highlands and provides good golf as well as conveying to everyone who plays there a feeling of peace and quiet. The village of Edzell is one of the most picturesque in Scotland.
18 holes, 6299yds, Par 70, SSS 71. Membership 850.

Visitors welcome (some restricted times) ✉
Societies welcome (☎)
Green fees £16.50 per day; £11 round (£21/£14 WE)
Facilities ⊗ ⅲ ⅃ ⚑ ♀ △ 🖻 ☗ Ⅽ A J Webster
Hotel ★★★58% Glenesk Hotel, High St, EDZELL ☎(03564) 319 25rm(22⇄ Ⅳ)

FORFAR
Map 7 H7

Forfar ☎ (0307) 62120
Cunninghill, Arbroath Rd (1m E on A932)
Moorland course with wooded, undulating fairways and fine views.
18 holes, 5522mtr, Par 69, SSS 69. Membership 850.

Visitors welcome Societies welcome (☎)
Green fees Not confirmed
Facilities ⊗ by prior arrangement ⅲ by prior arrangement ⅃ ⚑ ♀ △ 🖻 Ⅽ Peter McNiven
Hotel ★★★♨66% Idvies House Hotel, LETHAM ☎(030781) 787 9⇄ Ⅳ

GLENSHEE (SPITTAL OF)
Map 7 H7

Dalmunzie ☎ Glenshee (025085) 224
Dalmunzie Estate (2m NW of Spittal of Glenshee)
Grassy moorland course, highest in Britain, difficult walking. Testing 5th hole. Small but good greens. Accommodation, tennis, fishing and shooting.
9 holes, 2035yds, Par 30, SSS 30, Course record 32. Membership 51.

Visitors welcome (restricted Sun am) Societies welcome (☎)
Green fees £7 per day; £5 per round
Facilities ⊗ ⅲ ⚑ ♀ ☗
Hotel ★★♨64% Dalmunzie House Hotel, GLENSHEE ☎(025085) 224 17rm(15⇄ Ⅳ)

Each golf course entry has a recommended hotel. For a wider choice of places to stay, consult *AA Hotels and Restaurants in Britain* or *AA-inspected Bed and Breakfast in Britain*.

KENMORE
Map 7 G7

Taymouth Castle ☎ (08873) 228
(1m E on A827)
Parkland course set amidst beautiful mountain and loch scenery. Easy walking. Fishing.
18 holes, 6066yds, Par 69, SSS 69, Course record 63. Membership 200.

Visitors welcome must contact in advance Societies welcome (☎)
Green fees £17 per day; £11 round (£22/£15 WE)
Facilities ⊗ ⅃ ⚑ ♀ △ 🖻 ☗ Ⅽ Alex Marshall
Hotel ★★61% Fortingall Hotel, FORTINGALL ☎(08873) 367 9rm(6⇄ Ⅳ)

KINROSS
Map 6 F1

Green Hotel ☎ (0577) 63467
(NE side of town on B996)
Parkland course, with easy walking. Second course opening May 1991. Accommodation. Swimming pool, squash, fishing, sauna and solarium.
18 holes, 6223yds, Par 72 or 18 holes, 6392yds, Par 71. Membership 450.

Visitors welcome must contact in advance Societies welcome (☎)
Green fees £11-£15 (£15-£20 WE)
Facilities ⊗ ⅲ ⅃ ⚑ ♀ △ 🖻 ☗ Ⅽ Stuart Geraghty
Hotel ★★★62% Green Hotel, 2 The Muirs, KINROSS ☎(0577) 63467 40⇄ Ⅳ

Kinross Beeches Park ☎ (0577) 62237
(NE side of town on B996)
Parkland course on the banks of Loch Leven.
18 holes, 6124yds, Par 70, SSS 70. Membership 540.

Visitors welcome
Green fees Not confirmed
Facilities ♀ ⌂ 🏠 ⛳ 🥂
Hotel ★★★62% Green Hotel, 2 The Muirs, KINROSS
☎(0577) 63467 40⇔🐾

KIRRIEMUIR
Map 7 H7

Kirriemuir ☎ (0575) 72144
Northmuir (1m N off B955)
Parkland and heathland course with good view.
18 holes, 5553yds, Par 68, SSS 67, Course record 62.
Membership 600.

Visitors welcome (with M only WE) must contact in
advance Societies welcome (☎ (0575) 73317)
Green fees £12.50 per day; £7 per round after 1600
Facilities ⊗ ⛳ 🍴 🗑 ♀ (1100-2300) ⌂ 🏠 🥂 A Caira
Hotel ★★★⅟₂69% Castleton House Hotel, GLAMIS
☎(030784) 340 6⇔🐾

MILNATHORT
Map 6 F1

Milnathort ☎ Kinross (0577) 64069
South St (S side of town on A922)
Parkland course.
9 holes, 5969yds, Par 71, SSS 69, Course record 66.
Membership 400.

Visitors welcome (☎ for details)
Green fees Not confirmed
Facilities 🍴 by prior arrangement 🗑 ♀ ⌂
Hotel ★★★62% Green Hotel, 2 The Muirs, KINROSS
☎(0577) 63467 40⇔🐾

MONIFIETH
Map 7 J8

Monifieth ☎ (0382) 532678
8 Princes St (NE side of town on A930)
The chief of the two courses at Monifieth is the
Medal Course. It has been one of the qualifying
venues for the Open Championship on more than
one occasion. A seaside links, but divided from the
sand dunes by a railway which provides the
principal hazard for the first few holes. The 10th
hole is outstanding, the 17th is excellent and there is
a delightful finishing hole. The other course here is
the Ashludie, and both are played by four clubs who
share the links.
Medal Course 18 holes, 6657yds, Par 71, SSS 72.
Ashludie Course 18 holes, 5123yds, Par 68, SSS 66.
Membership 1500.

Visitors welcome (WE ☎ advisable) Societies
welcome (by letter)
Green fees Not confirmed
Facilities ⊗ ⛳ 🍴 🗑 ♀ ⌂ 🏠 ⛳ 🥂 Ian McLeod
Hotel ★★57% Carlogie House Hotel, Carlogie Rd,
CARNOUSTIE ☎(0241) 53185 11⇔🐾

MONTROSE
Map 7 J7

Montrose Links Trust
☎ (0674) 72932
Traill Dr (NE side of town
off A92)
The links at Montrose like
many others in Scotland
are on commonland and are
shared by three clubs. The
Medal course at Montrose is
typical of Scottish seaside
links, with narrow,
undulating fairways and
problems from the first hole
to the last.

SCORE CARD: Medal Tees					
Hole	Yds	Par	Hole	Yds	Par
1	393	4	10	382	4
2	390	4	11	440	4
3	156	3	12	153	3
4	363	4	13	323	4
5	288	4	14	416	4
6	478	5	15	524	5
7	372	4	16	234	3
8	331	4	17	415	4
9	444	4	18	349	4
Out	3215	36	In	3236	35
			Totals	6451	71

Medal Course 18 holes, 6451yds, Par 71, SSS 71,
Course record 63. Broomfield Course 18 holes,
4815yds, Par 66, SSS 63. Membership 920.

Visitors welcome (Medal-before 1400 Sat & 1000
Sun) must contact in advance Societies welcome (at
least 7 days notice ☎)
Green fees fr £7.50 per day; fr £5.50 per round (fr£8
WE)
Facilities ⊗ ⛳ 🍴 🗑 ♀ ⌂ 🏠 ⛳ 🥂 Kevin Stables
Hotel ★★★58% Park Hotel, 61 John St,
MONTROSE ☎(0674) 73415 59rm(48⇔5🐾)

MUTHILL
Map 7 G8

Muthill ☎ (076481) 523
Peat Rd (W side of village off A822)
Parkland course with fine views. Not too hilly with
tight course and narrow fairways.
9 holes, 4700yds, Par 66, SSS 63, Course record 64.
Membership 400.

Visitors welcome (restricted match nights)
Green fees £5 per day
Facilities ⌂
Hotel ★★67% Murray Park Hotel, Connaught Ter,
CRIEFF ☎(0764) 3731 13⇔

PERTH
Map 7 H8

Craigie Hill ☎ (0738) 24377
Cherrybank (1m SW of city centre off A952)
Slightly hilly, parkland course. Good views over Perth.
18 holes, 5379yds, Par 66, SSS 66, Course record 63.
Membership 610.

Visitors welcome (ex Sat) must contact in advance
Societies welcome (by letter)
Green fees £10 per day (£12 WE)
Facilities ⊗ (ex Tue) ⛳ (ex Mon & Tue, Sun high tea
only) 🍴 🗑 ♀ ⌂ 🏠 🥂 Frank Smith
Hotel ★★★58% Stakis City Mills Hotel, West Mill St,
PERTH ☎(0738) 28281 78rm(76⇔)

Opening times of bar and catering facilities vary
from place to place – it is wise to check in
advance of your visit.

King James VI ☎ (0738) 25170
Moncrieffe Island (SE side of city centre)
Parkland course, situated on island in the middle of
River Tay. Easy walking.
18 holes, 5661yds, Par 68, SSS 68, Course record 63.
Membership 600.

Visitors welcome (ex Sat) Societies welcome (ex Sat ☎)
Green fees £13.50 per day; £9 per round (£18 Sun)
Facilities ⊗ high tea 🍴 ⚑ ♟ 🛆 🏠 ⌜ Tony Coles
Hotel ★★★63% Queens Hotel, Leonard St, PERTH
☎(0738) 25471 50rm(40⇦9🐾)

Murrayshall Country House Hotel
☎ New Scone (0738) 51171
Murrayshall, Scone (E side of village off A94)
This course is laid out in 130 acres of parkland with
tree-lined fairways. Accommodation, tennis
(hardcourts) croquet and grass bowls.
18 holes, 6446yds, Par 73, SSS 71, Course record 68.
Membership 400.

Visitors welcome must contact in advance Societies
welcome (☎)
Green fees £30 per day; £20 per round (£40/£25 WE)
Facilities ⊗ ⫸ 🍴 ⚑ ♟ 🛆 🏠 ⌁ ⌜ Neil Macintosh
Hotel ★★★★78% Murrayshall Country House Hotel,
New Scone ☎(0738) 51171 19⇦🐾

Pitlochry ☎ (0796) 2792
Golf Course Rd (N side of town off A924)
A varied and interesting heathland course with fine
views and posing many problems. Its SSS permits
few errors in its achievement.
18 holes, 5811yds, Par 69, SSS 68, Course record 63.
Membership 300.

Visitors welcome Societies welcome (by letter)
Green fees £12 per day; £6 per round (£15/£9 WE)
Facilities ⊗ ⫸ by prior arrangement 🍴 ⚑ ♟ 🛆
🏠 ⌁ ⌜ James Wilson
Hotel ★★★★69% Pine Trees Hotel, Strathview
Ter, PITLOCHRY ☎(0796) 2121 19rm(18⇦🐾)

St Fillans ☎ (076485) 312
(E side of village off A85)
Fairly flat, beautiful parkland course. Fishing.
9 holes, 5580yds, Par 68, SSS 68, Course record 66.
Membership 400.

Visitors welcome (ex Sat am) Societies welcome (ex Jul/
Aug.£5 booking fee)
Green fees £7 per day (£8 WE & BH)
Facilities ⊗ ⚑ 🛆 🏠 ⌁
Hotel ★★★64% The Four Seasons Hotel, ST FILLANS
☎(076485) 333 12⇦🐾

For an explanation of the symbols and
abbreviations used, see page 33.

SCOTTISH ISLANDS

ARRAN, ISLE OF

Shiskine ☎ Shiskine (077086) 226
Shore Rd (W side of village off A841)
Seaside course. Other attractions include tennis courts
and bowling green.
12 holes, 2990yds, Par 42, SSS 42.

Visitors welcome (restricted Jul & Aug) Societies
welcome (by letter)
Green fees Not confirmed
Facilities ⊗ (Jun-Sep) ⚑ 🛆 🏠
Hotel ★★65% The Lagg Hotel, Kilmory, BRODICK
☎(077087) 255 15⇦🐾

Brodick ☎ (0770) 2349
(N side of village)
Short seaside course, very flat.
18 holes, 4405yds, Par 62, SSS 62, Course record 61.
Membership 550.

Visitors welcome Societies welcome (by letter)
Green fees £8 per day

BRIDGEND HOTEL ★★

The 'Golfing Centre' of Fife, Perthshire and Tayside

Family run Hotel by beautiful Loch Leven.
18 Bedrooms en suite — full facilities.

OPEN SEVEN DAYS PER WEEK

Location: 2 mins off M90 between
junctions 5 & 6. Perth 15 mins.
Edinburgh 30 mins. Glenagles 20 mins.
St Andrews 30 mins. Ladybank 20 mins.
Rosemount 45 mins.
We cater for GOLFING, SHOOTING
AND FISHING PARTIES.
(Hotel transport if required.)
For further information contact the Manager.

High Street, Kinross KY13 7EN
Tel: 0577 63413 Fax: 0577 64769

Facilities ⛳ ♀ ⛾ 🏠 🛠 ⚐ Peter McCalla
Hotel ★★★72% Auchrannie Country House Hotel,
BRODICK ☎(0770) 2234 & 2235 12⇨

CORRIE   Map 6 C3

Corrie
Sannox (2m N on A841)
A heathland course on the coast with mountain
scenery.
9 holes, 3896yds, Par 62, SSS 61. Membership 350.

Visitors welcome (restricted Sat when medal games)
Societies welcome
Green fees £3 per day/round (OAP's £1.50)
Facilities ⊗ ⏁ (Apr-Oct) ⛳ ⬛ 🏠 ⚐
Hotel ★★★72% Auchrannie Country House Hotel,
BRODICK ☎(0770) 2234 & 2235 12⇨

LAMLASH   Map 6 C4

Lamlash ☎ (07706) 296
Brodick Rd (.75m N on A841)
A hilly course with magnificent views of the mountains
and sea.
*18 holes, 4611yds, Par 64, SSS 63, Course record 62.
Membership 400.*

Visitors welcome Societies welcome
Green fees £6 per day
Facilities Tearoom 10am-8pm ♀ ⛾ 🏠 ⚐
Hotel ★57% Cameronia Hotel, WHITING BAY ☎(07707)
254 5🛏

LOCHRANZA   Map 6 B3

Lochranza ☎ (077083) 273
Parkland course.
9 holes, 1815yds, Par 29, SSS 40.

Visitors welcome
Green fees Not confirmed
Facilities ⛾ 🏠 ⚐
Hotel ★★65% The Lagg Hotel, Kilmory, BRODICK
☎(077087) 255 15⇨🛏

MACHRIE   Map 6 B4

Machrie Bay ☎ (077084) 267
Camus Ban (9m W of Brodick via String Rd)
Fairly flat seaside course. Designed at turn of century
by William Fernie. Tennis (hardcourt).
9 holes, 2143yds, Par 32. Membership 150.

Visitors welcome Societies welcome (☎)
Green fees £3 per day/round
Facilities ⬛ (May-Sep) ⛾
Hotel ★★65% The Lagg Hotel, Kilmory, BRODICK
☎(077087) 255 15⇨🛏

We make every effort to provide accurate information, but some details may change after we
go to print.

WHITING BAY   Map 6 C4

Whiting Bay ☎ (07707) 51607
(NW side of village off A841)
Heathland course.
18 holes, 4405yds, Par 63, SSS 63. Membership 290.

Visitors welcome
Green fees Not confirmed
Facilities ♀
Hotel ★★65% The Lagg Hotel, Kilmory, BRODICK
☎(077087) 255 15⇨🛏

BUTE, ISLE OF

KINGARTH   Map 6 C3

Kingarth ☎ Kilchattan Bay (070083) 648
Kingarth, Rothesay (1m W off A844)
Flat seaside course with good fenced greens.
*9 holes, 2497yds, Par 64, SSS 64, Course record 65.
Membership 120.*

Visitors welcome (restricted Sat)
Green fees £3 per day
Facilities ⛾
Hotel ★60% St Ebba Hotel, 37 Mountstuart Rd,
Craigmore, ROTHESAY ☎(0700) 2683 12rm(1⇨10🛏)

PORT BANNATYNE   Map 6 C2

Port Bannatyne ☎ (0700) 2009
Bannatyne Mains Rd (W side of village off A844)
Seaside hill course with panoramic views. Difficult hole:
4th (par 3).
13 holes, 4589yds, Par 67, SSS 63. Membership 200.

Visitors welcome Societies welcome (☎)
Green fees Not confirmed
Facilities ⛾
Hotel ★60% St Ebba Hotel, 37 Mountstuart Rd,
Craigmore, ROTHESAY ☎(0700) 2683 12rm(1⇨10🛏)

COLONSAY, ISLE OF

SCALASAIG   Map 6 A1

Colonsay ☎ Colonsay (09512) 316
(2m W on A870)
Traditional links course on natural machair (hard
wearing short grass) challenging, primitive. Colonsay
Hotel, 2 miles away, is the headquarters of the club,
offering accommodation and facilities.
18 holes, 4775yds, Par 72, SSS 72. Membership 120.

Visitors welcome Societies welcome (by letter)
Green fees Yearly family membership £5 no green fees
Facilities ⚐
Hotel ★71% Colonsay Hotel, SCALASAIG ☎(09512) 316
10rm(1⇨7🛏) Annexe:1rm

Opening times of bar and catering facilities vary
from place to place – it is wise to check in
advance of your visit.

ISLAY, ISLE OF

PORT ELLEN
Map 6 A3

Machrie Hotel ☎ (0496) 2310
Machrie (4m N off A846)
Seaside course playable all year, many blind holes.
Testing holes: 'Heather', par 4; 'Scotsman's Maiden',
par 4. Accommodation, fishing, riding stables, clay
pigeon shooting, snooker.
18 holes, 6226yds, Par 71, SSS 70, Course record 66.
Membership 30.

Visitors welcome (Club M details & h'cap cert required)
⊠ Societies welcome (☎)
Green fees Not confirmed
Facilities ⊗ ⅏ ⅃ ☊ ♀ 🖻 ⬩
Hotel ★★57% Lochside Hotel, 19 Shore St, BOWMORE
☎(049681) 244 & 266 7rm(2⊸)

LEWIS, ISLE OF

STORNOWAY
Map 7 C2

Stornoway ☎ (0851) 2240
Lady Lever Park (N side of town centre off A857)
Picturesque, tree-lined parkland course, fine views.
'Dardanelles' - most difficult par 5 in Europe.
18 holes, 5178yds, Par 68, SSS 66, Course record 62.
Membership 200.

Visitors welcome (ex Sun) Societies welcome (by letter)
Green fees £7.50 per day; £5 per round
Facilities ⊗ by prior arrangement ⅏ by prior
arrangement ☊ ⅃ by prior arrangement ♀ 🛆 🖻 ⬩
Hotel ★★★64% Caberfeidh Hotel, STORNOWAY
☎(0851) 2604 40⊸🟊

MULL, ISLE OF

CRAIGNURE
Map 7 D8

Craignure ☎ (06802) 370
Scallastle (1m N on A849)
A flat course, overlooking the sea.
9 holes, 2218mtrs, Par 64, SSS 64. Membership 63.

Visitors welcome Societies welcome (☎)
Green fees £5 per day
Facilities 🛆
Hotel ★★★58% Isle Of Mull Hotel, CRAIGNURE
☎(06802) 351 60⊸

TOBERMORY
Map 7 C7

Tobermory ☎ (0688) 2020
(.5m N off A848)
Hilly seaside course, no sand-bunkers, hard walking,
superb views over the Sound of Mull. Testing 3rd hole
(par 3).
9 holes, 4474yds, Par 64, SSS 64, Course record 70.
Membership 100.

Visitors welcome Societies welcome
Green fees £5 per day

Facilities 🛆 ⬩
Hotel ★56% Mishnish Hotel, Main St, TOBERMORY
☎(0688) 2009 12rm(7⊸3🟊)

ORKNEY

KIRKWALL
Map 7 K3

Orkney ☎ (0856) 2457
Grainbank (.5m W off A965)
Easy parkland course with few hazards, superb views
over Kirkwall and Islands.
18 holes, 5406yds, Par 70, SSS 68, Course record 65.
Membership 220.

Visitors welcome Societies welcome
Green fees £8 per day (£2 juniors)
Facilities ♀ (Apr-Sep) 🛆
Hotel ★★65% Ayre Hotel, Ayre Rd, KIRKWALL
☎(0856) 3001 32rm(4⊸6🟊)

STROMNESS
Map 7 J3

Stromness ☎ (0856) 850772
(S side of town centre off A965)
Testing parkland/seaside course with easy walking.
Beautiful holiday course with magnificent views of
Scapa Flow. Table tennis, bowling green and tennis
court.
18 holes, 4762yds, Par 65, SSS 64, Course record 62.
Membership 150.

Visitors welcome Societies welcome
Green fees £6 per round/day
Facilities ♀ (evenings only) 🛆 🖻 ⬩
Hotel ★★65% Ayre Hotel, Ayre Rd, KIRKWALL
☎(0856) 3001 32rm(4⊸6🟊)

WESTRAY
Map 7 K2

Westray ☎ (0856) 2197
(1m NW of Pierowall off B9066)
Interesting, picturesque seaside course, easy walking.
9 holes, 2405yds, Par 33.

Visitors welcome (ex Sun)
Green fees Not confirmed
Facilities ⬩
Hotel ★★65% Ayre Hotel, Ayre Rd, KIRKWALL
☎(0856) 3001 32rm(4⊸6🟊)

SHETLAND

LERWICK
Map 7 J2

Dale ☎ Gott (059584) 369
PO Box 18 (4m N on A970)
Challenging moorland course, hard walking. This is the
most notherly course in Britain. A burn runs the full
length of the course and provides a natural hazard.
Testing holes include the 3rd (par 4), 5th (par 4).
18 holes, 5776yds, Par 68, SSS 70, Course record 70.
Membership 343.

▶

Visitors welcome (restricted competition days)
Societies welcome
Green fees £5 per day
Facilities ♀ ⟆
Hotel ★★★58% Lerwick Hotel, South Rd, LERWICK
☎(0595) 2166 31⇌📶

SKYE, ISLE OF

SCONSER   Map 7 C5

Isle of Skye
(.5m E of village on A850)
Seaside course, often windy, splendid views.
9 holes, 4796yds, Par 66, SSS 63, Course record 62.
Membership 100.

Visitors welcome (ex Wed 1800-1830 & Sat 1000-1030)
Societies welcome
Green fees £6 per day
Facilities ⟆
Hotel ★★★59% Coolin Hills Hotel, PORTREE ☎(0478)
2003 17⇌📶 Annexe:9⇌📶

SOUTH UIST, ISLE OF

ASKERNISH   Map 7 A5

Askernish ☎ No telephone
Lochboisdale (5m NW of Lochboisdale off A865 via ferry)
Golfers play on machair, close to the Atlantic shore.
9 holes, 5312yds, Par 68, SSS 67. Membership 20.

Visitors welcome Societies welcome
Green fees Not confirmed
Facilities ⌐📶
Hotel ★★53% Lochboisdale Hotel, LOCHBOISDALE
☎(08784) 332 20rm(11⇌)

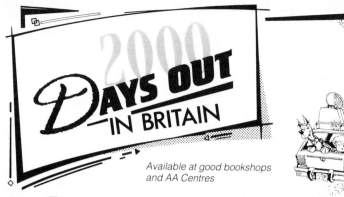

Index to Counties

Index to Courses

The first name is the name of the course or club; the second (*in italic*) is the name of the town under which the course or club appears in the gazetteer.

INDEX

INDEX

INDEX

290

Comments Please

We try to tailor our books to meet our readers' needs. Your comments would help us keep in touch with what you find useful and interesting. Listed below are a few suggested headings under which you may like to comment. However, if you have any other observations or ideas please mention these too.

1 Are there any courses that we do not list at present which you feel warrant inclusion?

_____

_____

_____

_____

2 Are there any courses included in the book that you feel do not warrant listing and why?

_____

_____

_____

_____

3 If you stayed at a hotel we recommended with the course entry, did you find it convenient for the course, and of the expected standard?

_____

_____

_____

_____

4 Would you find it helpful for the distance between the recommended hotel and course to be shown?

_____

_____

_____

5 Are there any further club facilities you would like to see mentioned?

_____

_____

_____

_____

_____

6 Are the course descriptions adequate or would you like to see more detail given?

_____

_____

_____

_____

7 Please indicate your usage of this guide

Usually linked to a business trip ☐

When holidaying ☐

General leisure ☐

8 How often do you play?

_____

9 Did you find the feature articles interesting?

Are there any further feature subjects which you would like to read about in the Guide?

_____

_____

_____

_____
_____
_____
_____

10 If you have any further improvements that you would like to see
incorporated in this book please list these below.

_____
_____
_____
_____
_____
_____

Name _____

Address _____

_____
_____
_____
_____

Signature _____

Date _____

The Editor
AA Guide to Golf Courses in Britain
The Automobile Association
Guidebooks Unit
Fanum House
Basingstoke
Hants
RG21 2EA

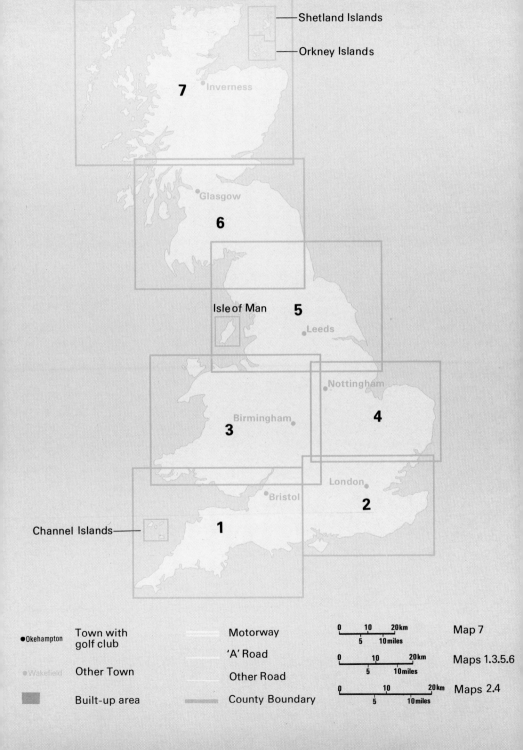

Shetland Islands

Orkney Islands

7 Inverness

6 Glasgow

Isle of Man

5 Leeds

Nottingham

3 Birmingham

4

London

Channel Islands

Bristol

2

1

●Okehampton   Town with golf club

Wakefield   Other Town

Built-up area

Motorway

'A' Road

Other Road

County Boundary

| 0 | 10 | 20km |
| | 5 | 10 miles |

Map 7

| 0 | 10 | 20km |
| | 5 | 10 miles |

Maps 1.3.5.6

| 0 | 10 | 20km |
| | 5 | 10 miles |

Maps 2.4

A120

A120

Bishop's Stortford

Frinton-on-Sea

ESSEX

Braintree

A120

4

Clacton-on-Sea

RDSHIRE

Ware

Tolleshunt D'Arcy

Harlow

A1060

Woodham
Walter

rickendon

Chelmsford

Maldon

Cheshunt

A414

A12

A414

Purleigh

Theydon Bois

A130

field

A127

Burnham-on-Crouch

Abridge

Stapleford
Abbotts

Brentwood

Chigwell

Chigwell
Row

Ingrave

Rochford

A127

Woodford
Green

Romford

Basildon

Benfleet

Ilford

Upminster

Thorpe Bay

LONDON

Leigh-on-
Sea

Southend
-on-Sea

South Ockendon

ONDON

Orsett

Barnehurst

Tilbury

A228

Bexleyheath

Dartford

Gravesend

Hoo

Sheerness

eckenham

Sidcup

Westgate-on-Sea

Bromley

Chislehurst

Herne Bay

Broadstairs

Orpington

Rochester

Gillingham

Whitstable

A299

Ramsgate

roydon

Downe

Chatham

Newington

Addington

West Kingsdown

Sittingbourne

Faversham

Canterbury

Sandwich

ley

Shoreham

A20

A228

M2

Biggin Hill

Addington

Maidstone

A252

Borough Green

M20

Bearsted

Barham

Deal

Woldingham

Sevenoaks

A20

A251

A260

Kingsdown

Limpsfield

KENT

Oxted

A256

Tandridge

Edenbridge

A229

Ashford

Dover

Cowden

Tonbridge

A27A

Southborough

M20

Folkestone

pthorne

Holtye

Tunbridge Wells

Hythe

instead

Forest Row

Lamberhurst

A262

Cranbrook

Tenterden

A259

Crowborough

Hawkhurst

Littlestone

A26

Ticehurst

A28

New Romney

aywards Heath

A272

A21

Uckfield

Rye

A22

A275

EAST SUSSEX

ENGLISH CHANNEL

Lewes

A271

Hastings

Bexhill

A259

A27

Newhaven

A259

Eastbourne

Seaford

F   G   H   J   K

2

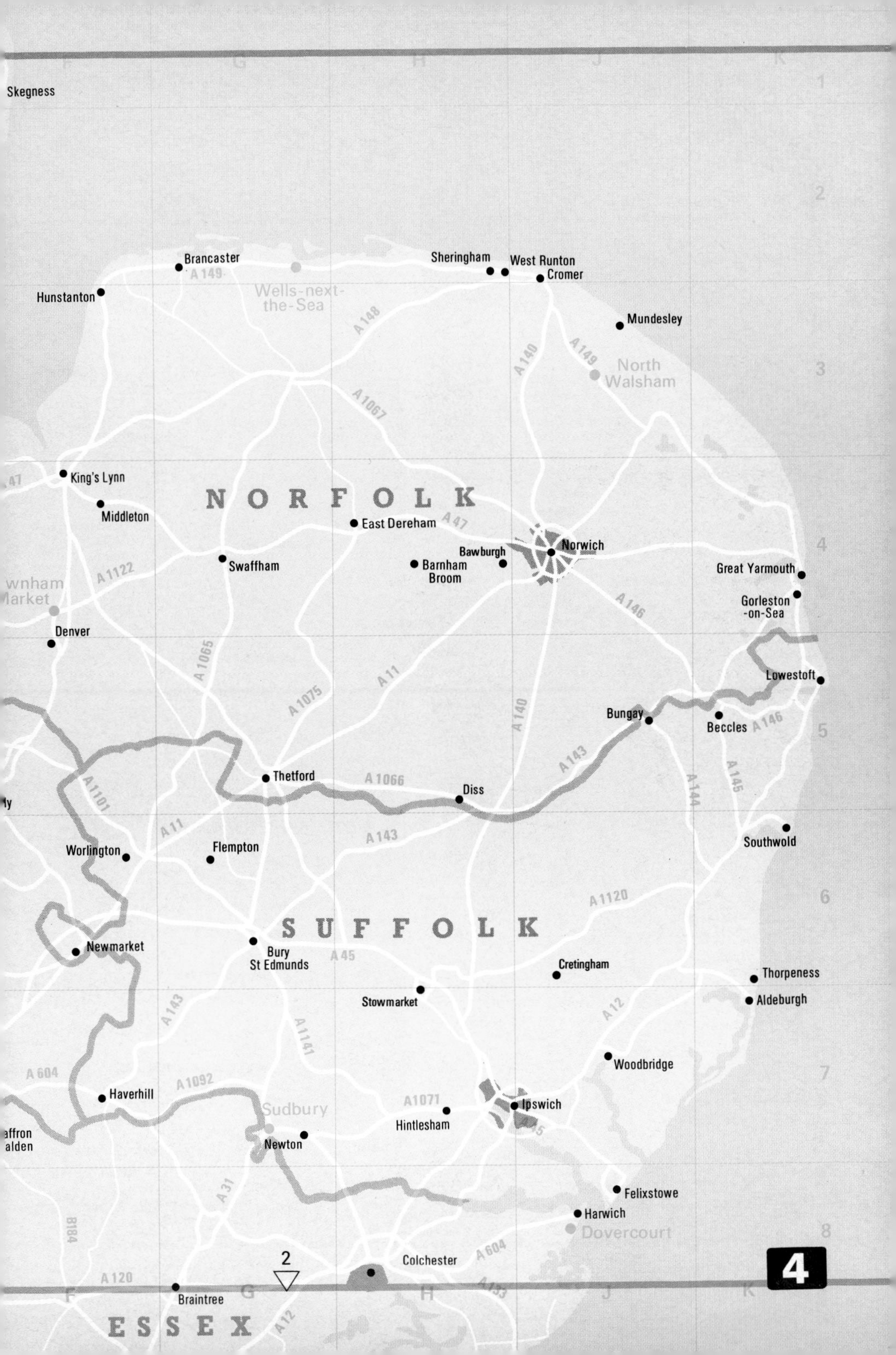

Skegness

Brancaster
A 149

Sheringham
West Runton
Cromer

Hunstanton

Wells-next-the-Sea

A 148

Mundesley

A 140
A 149
North Walsham

N O R F O L K

King's Lynn

A 47

Middleton

East Dereham

A 47

Norwich

Great Yarmouth

Swaffham

Bawburgh
Barnham Broom

Gorleston -on-Sea

wnham Market

A 1122

A 1067

A 146

Denver

A 1065

A 1075

A 11

A 140

Lowestoft

A 143

Bungay

Beccles
A 146

Thetford

A 1066

Diss

A 145

A 144

A 11

ly

A 1101

Worlington

Flempton

A 143

Southwold

A 1120

S U F F O L K

Newmarket

Bury St Edmunds

A 45

Cretingham

Thorpeness

A 143

Stowmarket

A 12

Aldeburgh

A 604

A 1141

Woodbridge

Haverhill

A 1092

Sudbury

A 1071

Hintlesham

Ipswich

affron alden

Newton

A 31

Felixstowe

B 184

Harwich

Dovercourt

A 120

Braintree

Colchester

A 604

E S S E X

A 12

2
▽

4

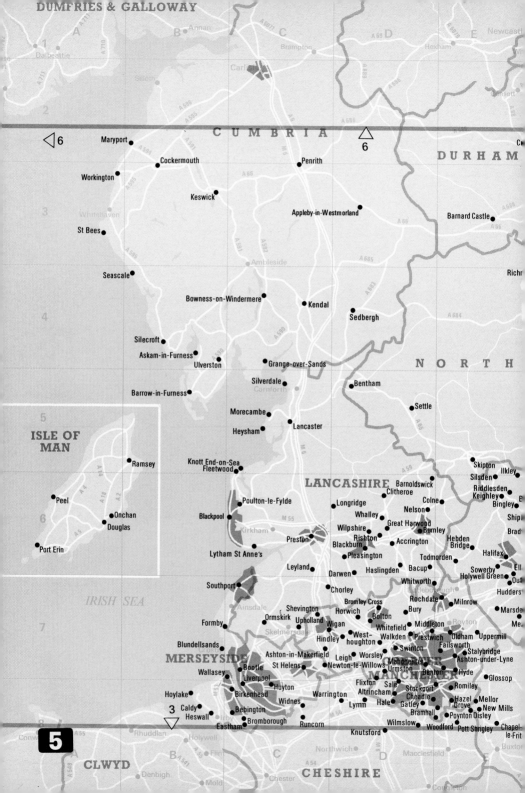

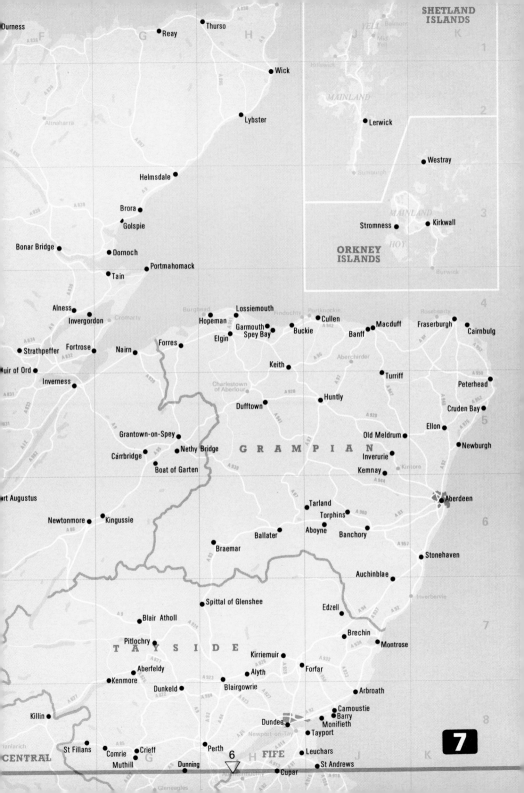

ACKNOWLEDGEMENTS

The Automobile Association wishes to thank the following library for its assistance:

Peter Dazeley Photo Library for:-

Picture of Johnny Miller *page 9*